T0367175

THE I TATTI
RENAISSANCE LIBRARY

James Hankins, General Editor

VERGIL
ON DISCOVERY

ITRL 6

POLYDORE VERGIL
✦ ✦ ✦
ON DISCOVERY

EDITED AND TRANSLATED BY

BRIAN P. COPENHAVER

THE I TATTI RENAISSANCE LIBRARY
HARVARD UNIVERSITY PRESS
CAMBRIDGE, MASSACHUSETTS
LONDON, ENGLAND
2002

Contents

❧❦❧

Introduction

※§※

Polydore Vergil (ca. 1470–1555) was an Italian scholar, priest and diplomat who spent most of his life in England. Born in Urbino, educated at Padua and (probably) Bologna, he published his first books in Italy just before the close of the fifteenth century and then moved to England in 1502. Having risen through the patronage of the court of Urbino, he entered the service of Adriano (later Cardinal) Castellesi as subcollector of the papal tax called Peter's Pence. His new life in England had its rocky moments, including loss of office and months of imprisonment in the Tower of London in 1515. Yet Polydore survived the shocks of the Reformation and Henry VIII's marriages. Except for a few trips to Basel and Italy, he stayed in England until 1553, two years before he died in Urbino, all the while holding church offices that required public assent to England's abrupt shifts of religious policy under Henry, Edward VI and Mary Tudor.

Despite its isolation, Urbino was a good place for a young humanist to learn his trade. While Polydore grew up there, Federico da Montefeltro, Urbino's ruler, was buying hundreds of manuscript volumes, many from the Florentine bookseller Vespasiano da Bisticci, to build a splendid collection of Latin, Greek and even a few Hebrew and Coptic texts for the elegant palace that still crowns this little cliff-top town. When he came to write a chapter on books for *On Discovery*, Polydore gratefully acknowledged the ducal library. One book that he read there was Niccolò Perotti's *Cornucopiae*, a huge commentary on the Latin epigrams of Martial that outgrew its genre to become a kind of accidental dictionary at a time when works of reference were still scarce. Another Urbino humanist, Lodovico Odassio, had prepared Perotti's work for the

press in 1489, propelling it quickly through several editions. One of those editions, published in 1496, was Polydore's first work.

In 1499, when Odassio was still in the service of Duke Guidobaldo da Montefeltro, Polydore dedicated *On Discovery* to him, having offered his second and previous book, *Proverbiorum libellus*, to the Duke himself in 1498. Whatever Polydore's debts to Odassio, these early works on proverbs and inventions surely owe even more to Perotti, whose name never appears in *On Discovery*. The ancients crowd the pages of Polydore's compulsively annotated history, while contemporaries (except Ermolao Barbaro and Platina) or even recent authorities are rarely visible. But comparison of *On Discovery* with the *Cornucopiae* shows that Perotti had more than broken the ground on proverbs and discoveries, topics on which Polydore nonetheless claims to be 'first among the Latins.'[1]

In his letter to Odassio, Polydore declares that one of his motives for writing on discovery is 'to see that no one is cheated of his glory since discovery is being first, before all others, while the honor of making a discovery draws many into such love of self that all . . . would wish to be founders if they could.' Controverted questions of priority are front and center in *On Discovery*, and such controversy was a theme of the author's life. Soon after his *Proverbs* appeared, Polydore was charged with having stolen the project. His first accuser, Lodovico Gorgerio, complained in obscurity, but around the same time (1500) Erasmus published one of the books that would make him famous, the *Adagia*, another collection of proverbs. Such ideas were in the air, as early editions of Perotti's *Cornucopiae* demonstrate: the index *de proverbiis* in the Aldine edition of 1513 lists 58 items; the index *de inventoribus* lists 115. Although Polydore claimed to have finished *On Discovery* in nine months, his editorial work on the *Cornucopiae* had given him a head start on both topics by several years.

Two decades after their competing collections of proverbs first appeared, Erasmus, Polydore and their supporters were still bick-

ering about who came first, though no great harm was done. In fact, some of the religious and devotional writing of Polydore's later career can be read as Erasmian. For his part, Erasmus helped Polydore make the connection with Johann Froben and other Basel printers that secured a larger European audience for his books after 1521. The best known of these is the *Anglica historia*, begun around 1506, first published in 1534 and revised by Polydore in 1546 and 1555. This humanist rewriting of English history — especially the Wars of the Roses and the first two Tudor reigns — passed through Edward Hall and Raphael Holinshed to Shakespeare's history plays and thence to its enduring place in Western cultural memory.

In this way, the influence of Polydore's *English History* became enormous and long-lasting, though its direct readership was never large since it was written in Latin and still lacks a complete and reliable English version. *On Discovery* was read, or perhaps consulted, much more widely. On the evidence of its publishing history, this third of Polydore's books was a foundational work of reference for early modern European readers. From its first printing in 1499 through the eighteenth century, *On Discovery* appeared in more than a hundred editions in eight languages, including Russian. Thirty Latin editions were printed in Polydore's lifetime. The first English translation was the severely abbreviated version published by Thomas Langley in 1546.

Polydore had no assurance of his book's success. He warned Odassio that 'spiteful persons may call my efforts rash because I alone have ventured to write on those who made discoveries *(de rerum inventoribus)*.' At first he divided his account of *inventores* and *inventiones* into sixty-seven chapters arranged in three books on the origins of the world, human society, religion and literacy, and on discoveries and inventions in the liberal arts and sciences; in political, civic, military and cultural institutions; and in arts, crafts, technology and commerce. Although religion is an issue in the

first three books of *On Discovery*, most of the discoveries discussed in them are not Christian: most are secular, in fact, and when Polydore finds (as he usually does) that their authors were neither Greek nor Roman, he most often gives credit to heroes of the Hebrew Bible. Eventually, however, he came to believe that these same questions of origins and inventions should be asked about Christian practices and institutions, which became the subject of five more books added to *On Discovery* in 1521. Thus, the first three books, edited and translated in this volume, were a prior and separate project, distinct from the last five in conception, execution and content.

As Polydore put his book together, he thought carefully about its construction, worrying about the order of presentation and transitions between topics. After book I opens with the origins of the divine, the natural and the human, the rest of its twenty-four chapters extend the concept of the seven liberal arts through the university curriculum and beyond, dealing not only with grammar, rhetoric and dialectic and with astronomy, geometry, arithmetic and music but also with history, poetry, magic and other discoveries in a broadly curricular context. Introducing book II, Polydore explains that 'I meant to include only the origin of the liberal disciplines in my first book and then to treat the invention of other things in the sequel, but the great scope of the topic caused me to go on longer than I wished' (*DIR* 2.1.1).

Polydore had covered theology and medicine in book I, but not law, the first topic of book II. There he dropped the curriculum as his principle of organization and turned to a framework that we would call institutional: law leads to politics and government and next to the calendar and time-keeping. But the art of government brings with it the art of war, whose tools are weapons, and one of them is the horse, demanding a chapter on horsemanship. Another series of transitions runs from public games as civic institutions back to truces and treaties as political institutions and then

to the celebration of triumphs in Rome where the victor was crowned with a wreath, whose use at banquets leads Polydore to condemn luxury (not for the first time) and then to append a chapter on perfumes. In the midst of all this he puts three chapters on books, libraries, printing, paper and the art of memory, subjects that might have come up in book I. Likewise, the last seven chapters of book II might have fit better with the technological material of book III since their topic is not institutional but material culture: metallurgy, coinage, jewelry, minerals, sculpture, painting and pottery.

If law (a favorite occupation of the Vergil family) was the fountainhead of book II, agriculture was the seedbed of book III. Having asked 'who first discovered agriculture, and how many advantages flow from it,' Polydore's next questions proceed predictably through viticulture, arboriculture, animal husbandry, hunting and textiles until the technology of urban and official architecture brings him to antiquity's most conspicuous buildings — labyrinths, pyramids and mausolea (3.10). The topic of tombs creates the occasion for one of several ethnographic digressions in *On Discovery*, this one on burial customs. Then the story returns, by way of the early Roman institution of asylum, to other monumental buildings, the theaters and public baths of Rome, and then moves on to carpentry, ship-building, navigation, trade and prostitution, the last two topics linked not only as types of commerce but also by moral censure from Polydore and his sources. Book III ends with a cursory and loosely organized chapter on new inventions, some discussed earlier in the book, though Polydore's story of discovery is mainly about the distant past.

The deepest past is one of origins, a topic connected with discovery and invention but separable from them. The world of nature originates from first principles or elements without discovery or invention, though humans later discover — but do not invent — those elements. The first chapters of book I show that Polydore

was aware of origins as a relevant area of inquiry, but he seems not to have regarded it as a separate problem or to have made the equally important distinction between discovery and invention. Many items in his history—tools, pipe-organs, water mills, warships, hexameter verse, the use of passwords by soldiers—are well within range of the English word 'invention,' meaning something (physical or not) made deliberately and originally to serve some purpose, as distinct from 'discovery,' meaning something found (rather than made) for the first time, whether deliberately or not. The distinction is important but fluid since discovery often leads to invention, as in Polydore's story of the god who discovered a dead tortoise with its sinews exposed and then invented the lyre (1.15.1).

The root sense of the Latin *invenire*, to come upon, is on the side of discovery, but the same verb also means to devise or invent. Polydore uses *invenire* and *inventor* along with *repertor, auctor* and other words to mean both finding and making, discovering and inventing. In the same way, when Langley turned *On Discovery* into English in 1546, he reduced one of Polydore's chapter titles—*De herbariae et medicamentariae atque melleae medicinae inventoribus*—to 'the inventours of herbs medicinable,' meaning those who *found* that certain plants could heal, without inventing anything. The distinction meant less to him and to Polydore not only because the key Latin word is ambiguous but also because the contemporary inventor as hero of artifice and innovation—Gutenberg and printing, Galileo and the telescope, Watt and the steam engine—was only then emerging in Europe's awareness. One of those who inspired Polydore in this regard (though not enough to earn a mention) was Giovanni Tortelli, whose *De orthographia* (ca. 1449), like Perotti's *Cornucopiae*, was a reference book that happily exceeded its aims. Under *Hippocrates*, this lexicon of Greek terms in Latin texts offers a concise history of medicine that Polydore reshaped into his chapters on medicine and pharmacy. Tortelli's entry on

horologium, an early and unusual appreciation of contemporary inventions, was also distilled into the chapter on *nova inventa* that concludes book III of *On Discovery*.

The few recent inventions that attracted Polydore's attention include printing, artillery, stirrups, the clock, the church organ and the navigational compass but not the discovery of the New World. They also include the beret and the 'leg-covering . . . that we call *caligae* [boots],' indicating that he had no clear taxonomy of novelties in mind (3.18.6,10). Being a bookish person, he was impressed most of all by the printed book, invented only a generation before he was born. Libraries like the one in Urbino are 'a great boon to mortals,' he writes,

> but . . . nothing in comparison with an achievement of our own day, a newly devised way of writing. In one day just one person can print the same number of letters that many people could hardly write in a whole year. Books in all the disciplines have poured out to us so profusely from this invention that no work can possibly remain wanting to anyone, however needy. (2.7.8)

Neither here nor elsewhere in *On Discovery* is the concept of progress explicit, but the unformed idea surely motivates this passage and others in the book. Polydore was even more alert to novelties that he found threatening. Speaking of ballistic weapons, he says that they were all 'invented to destroy human beings, especially the recent innovation called the bombard. Within mankind's memory, human ingenuity can have devised nothing more frightful than this.' The inventor of the cannon ought to have perished in the murderous thunder of his own making, suffering for his sins like Salmoneus and Perillus (2.11.5–6; 3.18.3–4).

That invention brings risks along with rewards became clearer as the development of new technologies accelerated after Polydore's day, but another source of his anxiety about discovery was distinctly ancient — Roman, to be precise — and hence less familiar

in our time. The basis of this idea is that whatever is older is better, just by reason of its age, than what is newer. Custom, tradition and familiarity trump innovation, invention and novelty. If the old ways are the best ways, originality, creativity and inventiveness are problematic, at best.

Polydore heard this anti-progressive note in Pliny's *Natural History*, the source that he cites more than any other on ancient discoveries. To account for inventions while preserving his conservative outlook, Pliny sometimes starts with nature as the source of something useful to humans, who find the natural object, imitate it and perhaps improve it but do not simply devise it anew. Sailors who landed on certain beaches in Phoenicia, for example, discovered glass when their campfires caused sand to fuse with various minerals native to the place (2.22.1). In such cases, 'nature seems to have given humans great plenty in the beginning,' and, as Cicero explains, the divine faculty of reason enables mankind to multiply such gifts:

> Yet, as Pliny presents it . . . , one cannot easily decide whether nature was a good mother to humanity or a hard step-mother because people when newborn had no immediate support or strength. Except what they got from day to day, they lacked clothing, shelter, fire and food, as well as the many other requirements of life that they themselves finally invented when driven by necessity, mistress of their affairs. Still, it must be admitted that we would be far better off if we were content with what nature has given us. (3.3.1)

What humans found in nature was hard, argues Pliny, and Polydore adds not only that inventions arose from this cruel necessity but that in some ways the harsh state of nature was better than a world made soft by human inventiveness. His topic at this point is wine, a product of culture that debased the natural state in which mankind first lived. Thinking of Noah's drunkenness, he main-

tains that people would be better off if they 'drank the water that nature first gave people . . . and not the wine whose effects were shameful even for its first inventor' (3.3.2).

Polydore's reading of Pliny reinforces his Christian abhorrence of luxury, enabling him to explain it as degeneration from a prior natural state. In the same way, the logic of his chapter on materials for building leads from mud to brick to the extravagance of marble, denounced by Pliny as a product of the greed that destroys nature: 'So great a taste for luxury once beguiled mortals that they nearly leveled the world in digging it up, hewing away the hills, opening headlands to the sea, tearing even the bowels of the earth into a thousand pieces' (3.8.3). The discovery of linen seems safer until Polydore explains that this cloth

> is especially good for making sails, which is why it deserves to be cursed as a danger to mankind . . . His was a reckless life full of iniquity who decided to sow a crop to catch wind and storm, says Pliny, for what springs from such a little seed carries the globe hither and yon, driving people to perish in the waters and find a grave in the belly of a sea monster, as if dying on land were not good enough. On account of this Pliny says it is hard to know what would be curse enough for this inventor. (3.6.1)

Invention here is not creative or ingenious but rash and overreaching. Pliny's perspective, passed on to Polydore, belongs to a culture for which the vice of excess is part and parcel of *curiositas*, seen not as a productive instinct but as pernicious.

'Will anyone deny that mankind gets its just deserts when convicted of madness and recklessness for not knowing how to keep safe within its own borders?' This is the question that opens Polydore's chapter on navigation, which cites Vergil, Horace and Propertius to prove that shipwreck, both moral and physical, awaits those whom greed tempts to forget their earthbound nature: 'God gave us the solid earth, an element well suited to sus-

tain us, but we venture into sky and sea, . . . blinded . . . by a fierce lust for wealth' (3.15.1). All commerce carries this burden of temerity; every traveling salesman is an Icarus. Yet 'trade is no small help to mortals,' Polydore admits — as he had to, given his stake in the commerce that linked his native Italy with England. 'Commerce was invented for the sake of survival,' he concedes, but he also insists that when Pliny acknowledged this necessity he was 'talking about . . . commerce . . . in the days of Troy . . . by bartering.' Polydore prefers this ancient and 'much nobler way' of exchanging goods to trade based on money and corrupted by the hunger for gold (3.16.1).

When inventions upset the moral order, reversion to a more primitive state is a proper remedy: this is the extreme form of a conservative reflex that runs through *On Discovery*. One way to account for change conservatively is to conceive of innovation as imitation, starting either with culture or with nature. In the latter case, as when the first builders made their houses by imitating the nests of swallows, the ground of mimesis is natural and organic (or less than organic, in other cases) rather than human. But culture too can be the basis for a conservative mimesis by restoration. At the end of a chapter on painting, after listing inventors recorded by Pliny and Quintilian, Polydore proudly declares that it was his townsman Raphael 'whose energy and genius have wholly restored *(restituit)* the art of painting to us today.' With all his *industria* and *ingenium*, what this great artist achieved was to recover and equal the ancients, not to surpass them (2.24.5).

In the same chapter on painting, however, Polydore repeats this remark by Quintilian: 'Examine all the arts, and you will find that none has stood still, remaining as it was when invented.' If no art stands still, if improvement is always possible, if nothing is 'so perfectly designed from the start that those who come after can add nothing useful,' Pliny's conservative position will be hard to sustain (2.11.3, 24.3). Perhaps because Quintilian's art was rhetoric,

which was so well developed in antiquity, he offers a brighter view of cultural change. He acknowledges the power of observation and the role of imitation, but he insists that imitation is not enough: 'If no one accomplished more than his predecessor, we would have no poetry beyond Livius Andronicus, no history beyond the *Pontifical Annals*; we would still be sailing on rafts.' Rafts become ships and ships carry commerce, which from Pliny's point of view is the route to moral ruin, but for Quintilian such earlier inventions should be enhanced by later ones (3.15.5).

Having absorbed the pessimism of Pliny's encyclopedia, Polydore found a countervailing optimism in Quintilian and other ancient authorities. From Diodorus Siculus, Vitruvius, and even from Vergil he learned the lesson of gradualism, that little by little, with forethought, cooperation and persistence, the first people struggled successfully to overcome a brutal nature and build a human society. Citing Vitruvius and Strabo, Polydore explains how the force of cold drove people to discover fire, organize communities, share their inventions with one another, and build the first structures that eventually produced the art of architecture:

> At first people were born in caves and forests like animals and spent their lives there feeding on what grows wild, but later . . . they discovered fire. Once they recognized that its warmth was good for keeping off the force of cold, they moved closer to it and many gathered into a single group, an assembly in which they easily managed whatever they wished because they shared a plan. Some built canopies out of foliage. Some dug caves beneath the hills . . . Others imitated swallows' nests, using clay and wattles to make dwellings that they could enter. Thus it happened that humans — who bragged about their new inventions, who showed them off to one another, whose talent was equal to its every aim — began constructing buildings, fabricating walls from forked uprights and wattles woven in clay, piling

dried clods of clay on top of one another and covering them with reeds or foliage to shield them from rain and heat, or erecting huts of sedge from the swamp. (3.7.1)

Although Polydore repeats Pliny's gloomy sermons and places them conspicuously in his book, his heart and his ambition pushed him in this other direction. After all, the huge task of exposing and settling so many disputed claims to priority implies that priority—and therefore discovery—is worthwhile. As he wrote to Odassio, 'discovery is being first, before all others,' and he himself was anxious to be 'first among the Latins.' As for other inventors, his final chapter proclaimed that great 'glory and reward are due those who by their own skill have at some time devised something useful, something in no wise irrelevant to the conduct of life or to the perfection of the spirit.' Discovery may be dangerous, but at the end of the day it is also glorious (3.18.1).

Labor omnia vincit: Polydore puts this phrase of Vergil's at the end of a condensed cultural history that starts with the biblical Genesis but then shifts to the story told by Protagoras and other Greeks since the fifth century BCE. On this account, best preserved by Diodorus Siculus, culture is the gradual and deliberate product of human effort:

God made two people in the beginning and from them descended the mass of the whole human race. And then, inasmuch as they had nothing, no help to sustain them, people led a hard life. But little by little, as Vergil says, they worked out various arts by thinking things through, for they came to understand a great deal when forced by necessity, and in a short time they discovered what else was helpful to human life. In this way arose the various arts because, as the same poet sings,
    Work—pitiless—always wins,
    And want, pushing when things go hard. (1.3.7)

This needful work has occurred in time, whose destructive power often thwarts Polydore's efforts to recover the relevant evidence.

But time has not dissolved all continuities. Polydore is particularly conscious of the survival of customs, sometimes into his own day, and this is one of the main sources of his ethnographic curiosity. Ever since Herodotus looked for Greek origins in Egypt, the ancients had often framed their inquiries into discovery in anthropological terms. If they could find no inventors at home, they looked abroad for them, and Polydore did the same, thus opening the question of alien customs as an appendix to his search for alien wisdom. 'Dionysius or Father Liber . . . was the first to hold a triumph,' he explains, and 'later the custom of holding triumph spread among most peoples' (2.16.1). Since the Creation, culture has accumulated diachronically, handed down from generation to generation, but it has also diffused synchronically from one people to another. Polydore's wish to tell a good story (Herodotus felt the same) also moved him to repeat the tales about strange peoples that he found in ancient and patristic sources; Jerome's polemic *Against Jovinian* was a favorite for this purpose. A lesser temptation than ethnography, but still prominent throughout *On Discovery*, was etymology, another type of obsession with origins.

Like any humanist, Polydore is quick to display his Greek, mainly in etymological conjectures, but his point of view is emphatically Roman. Geographically and culturally, despite his long sojourn in England, the center of his world is either Italy or sometimes Urbino when he brags about Raphael or Duke Federico's library or his uncles who prospered in the law (2.1.12). The origin of his historical coordinates, however, is ancient Rome, with which he feels his own world connected and continuous — certainly not distanced by any interruption of epochs, though he mentions a few inventors and inventions that we would call medieval. Polydore knows that he speaks as a Christian, as even Cicero and Vergil could not, but his 'we' is still a Roman 'we.' He also knows

that Greece captured her Roman conqueror culturally. But Greek cultural hegemony, manifest as discovery or invention, is his primary point of attack from a different angle. In outline his strategy is simple. Moses and the biblical patriarchs who preceded him lived before almost all the Greeks; therefore, many discoveries commonly attributed to the Greeks must be assigned instead to these ancient Hebrews. This is the main message of *On Discovery*. By discrediting the many Greek claims to priority, Polydore kills two birds with one stone. He diminishes Rome's debt to Greece, and what he subtracts from the Greeks he credits to the Jews as forerunners of Christianity.

Chronology, to which he frequently refers, is a critical part of Polydore's case. His chronology (see the Note on Chronology) comes from Eusebius, a Christian apologist who located almost all the major figures of Greek myth and history in post-Mosaic times. Although in principle he rejects the myths (*fabulae*) and sometimes dismisses their gods and heroes as unreal, Polydore makes no distinction in practice between mythic time and historical time. He questions discoveries attributed to Ceres, Heracles, or Mercury in the same way that he debates laws made by Solon or battles fought by Xerxes. At one moment he declares that only the one God is real and the rest are illusory; at another that evil demons were mistaken for gods; or again that the gods were really mortals falsely honored as divine by other mortals out of gratitude or admiration. He does not call this last theory by its name, euhemerism, but he is conscious of its ancient sources (1.1.5).

Indeed, Polydore's consciousness of all his sources is acute, not to say excessive. Anxious to show off his learning, he rarely lets more than a few sentences pass without naming an authority, almost always classical, patristic, or biblical. Although his Greek was good enough to make him alert to etymologies and able to criticize a line of verse, he wrote at the end of the Quattrocento, when most ancient Greek literature had already been recovered,

translated into Latin and printed. For Greek works he consistently depends on the Renaissance translators (Decembrio, Poggio, Trapezuntius, Traversari, Valla and others), and even his mistakes can be traced to incunabular printings of their texts (1.16.3). Despite the prominence of Eusebius, Herodotus, Strabo and many other Greek authors in *On Discovery*, Polydore used them in Latin versions, which made it easier to preserve a Roman point of view. More precisely, his perspective was that of the Latin classics of the late republic and early empire, the world of Cicero, Horace, Livy and Vergil. Not a Ciceronian in the narrow sense, he was nonetheless careful to advertise his allegiance to the princes of Latinity. For example, when he borrows passages of Cicero from the Christian apologist Lactantius (called the Christian Cicero), Polydore sometimes leaves the impression that he has gone to the *fons ipsissima* (1.1.3–5).

The evidence for Polydore's history of inventions comes from more than a hundred authors, very few of them contemporary or medieval. His ancient sources can be grouped in six categories: miscellanies and encyclopedias; history, geography, biography and doxography; poetry, mythography, literary criticism and commentary; rhetoric, grammar and lexicography; philosophical, scientific and technical literature; and biblical and patristic literature. In the first group, the *Saturnalia* of Macrobius was important, but nothing like Pliny's *Natural History*, far and away Polydore's leading source.

This Latin encyclopedia shaped the form and content of *On Discovery* even more than Perotti's (uncited) *Cornucopiae*, and its seventh book leads all the rest in citations. This description of the human animal, the first of Pliny's several books on zoology, ends with a staccato catalog of entries like the following:

Cinyras, son of Agriopa, invented tiles and copper-mining, both on the island of Cyprus, along with the tongs, hammer,

crowbar and anvil; wells were made by Danaus when he came into the part of Greece called Thirsty Argos; quarries by Cadmus at Thebes, or else in Phoenicia according to Theophrastus; walls by Thrason and, says Aristotle, towers by the Cyclopes or, according to Theophrastus, by the Tyrinthians. (2.19.3; 3.8.1; 3.9.3, 8–9)

This dense passage on tiles, tools, wells, quarries, walls and towers, characteristic of the whole section on inventors in book 7, shows Theophrastus disagreeing with his teacher Aristotle on discoveries in the field of building; the inventions listed here are a few of more than two hundred collected by Pliny.

Theophrastus and other Peripatetics wrote specialized works on discoveries (peri heurēmatōn), early entries in the genre later called heurematography. Another fourth-century author, Ephorus of Cyme, did the same, mainly to challenge what Herodotus had written in the previous century about Egypt and other Asian nations as sources of discoveries wrongly credited to Greeks. Herodotus focused on peoples rather than persons, probably because he found claims about individuals hard to verify. Even before Herodotus, Greek thinkers speculating on the origins of the world and man had to inquire about discovery in order to learn how humans had risen above other animals. Like Herodotus, the Sophists wanted to give a rational account of this success, to tell a story independent of theology and mythology and also supportive of their claims for custom and craft (nomos and technē) as against the power of nature (phusis). Clearly, this was an occasion to praise founders and inventors as heroes of culture.

But Hellas was a land of many regions and cities, each with its own heroes, who since the days of Homer and Hesiod had occupied a mythic landscape ruled by the gods on Olympus. So there was much to be sorted out in the Hellenic literature on discovery: human from heroic, heroic from divine, Argive from Athenian,

Doric from Ionian, and so on into the infinity of incompatible tales eventually compiled by the mythographers. But most mythography was written in the Hellenistic period or later, after Alexander's imposition of Greek culture on Asia had complicated the record of inventions even more. Jews, resisting Hellenization but seeing their kingdom wrecked in the Roman aftermath of Alexander's conquests, entered the ensuing debate armed with ancient scriptures to challenge the Greeks as latecomers, upstarts in the eons that reached back to Moses, Abraham and Adam. After Jerusalem fell to Rome and Rome became Christian, apologists for the new religion turned the arguments made by Josephus and other Jews to their own uses. Isidore of Seville and the medieval encyclopedists who copied him learned what little they knew about inventions from these patristic writers.

Thus the literature of discovery emerged over the course of a millennium, from before Herodotus until after Eusebius, in many genres of Greek and Latin writing. Pliny's book 7 preserves more of it than any other single text. Informed by Pliny and Perotti, Polydore read widely in other sources to assemble his book on inventors. Without knowing it, he reconstituted the ancient genre of heurematography in a post-medieval, Christian version.

After Pliny the authors that Polydore used most were historians and their cousins in geography, biography and doxography. Three Greek writers, Herodotus, Strabo and Diodorus Siculus, stand out in this group. All contribute heavily to the ethnography in *On Discovery*, though in this respect the selections made by Polydore fall short of the longer and fuller treatments of Egypt or Scythia by Herodotus. Likewise, though in shorter compass, Diodorus is more explicit and more persuasive than Polydore on cultural history as a phenomenon of development. Among historians of Rome, Polydore's favorites were Plutarch, Livy and Dionysius of Halicarnassus, two of whom wrote in Greek. From Livy's

Latin history, the books on the kings and the early republic were of primary interest.

Although Polydore's first words to Odassio in the preface to *On Discovery* dismiss the poets as 'having spent all their energies on mere fables,' he had to take them seriously because poetry was the main medium for myths of discovery. He names more than a dozen Latin poets and several Greeks, frequently decorating his prose with lines from Vergil, Ovid, Horace, Martial and others. Naturally, Vergil and Horace controlled his sense of Latin verse just as Cicero and Livy were the masters of his prose. As the Latin Homer, Vergil was also a primary avenue to Roman myths of origin—and to many Greek stories as well. But the most prolific mythographer among Latin poets was Ovid, whose *Metamorphoses*, *Fasti* and other works told hundreds of tales of heroes and gods famed, among other things, for discovery. Horace and other Roman poets refer constantly to this same range of myths, and Horace was also attractive for his moral serenity and mastery of form. Martial is a special case. Polydore knew him well because his poems are the subject of the hypertrophic commentary that became Perotti's *Cornucopiae*. Otherwise, this witty poet of the Silver Age would have remained beyond Polydore's horizon. His epigrams have even less room than Horace's lyrics for story-telling, and his social realism, focused on the moment and the occasion, can seem ephemeral and frivolous.

Myth, used since Hesiod and Aeschylus to teach lessons of high seriousness, has the advantage of moral and narrative weight, which explains why mythological poetry has so large a place in *On Discovery*. Mythography as such, apart from myths told by poets and other writers, appears hardly at all—perhaps a handful of uses of Hyginus behind one explicit reference. Deeper knowledge of mythography, no doubt, supports the vast learning of the *Cornucopiae* and hence, indirectly, Polydore as well. Except in this

sense, his primary access to explication of mythological verse came through writers of erudite miscellanies, especially Macrobius and Aulus Gellius, and through Servius, the great commentator on Vergil. Donatus and other literary critics were also useful to him. Between these genres and the related fields of rhetoric, grammar and lexicography no sharp line can be drawn. Quintilian is conspicuous not only for his authority on the literary topics of book 1 but also for his grasp of the roles of observation, imitation and invention in the transformation of culture. From Festus (or rather an early medieval epitome of his lexicon of classical Latin) Polydore took more mundane information about the meanings and etymologies of Latin words.

Even more than Quintilian, of course, it was Cicero who ruled rhetoric in the Renaissance, but Polydore read him mainly as a philosopher, almost always bypassing Plato and Aristotle for the derivative insights of this monarch of Latin prose and oratory. For philosophy as a technical field, he usually turned either to Cicero or to the doxography of Diogenes Laertius or to the Christian apologetics of Eusebius, Jerome, or Lactantius. Technical information from other experts — in agriculture, astrology, law, medicine, military science — was less important for his inquiry into discovery. Only the cultural insights transmitted by Vitruvius and the moral pronouncements of Cato were of broader use than the few excerpts that he took from Columella on farming or from Vegetius on war. Although law was a field of great personal value to him, his citations of Justinian are few.

References to biblical and patristic literature, by contrast, are frequent in *On Discovery*. Besides scripture itself, apologetics, chronology and theology all captured Polydore's attention, most often in the works of Eusebius, Jerome and Lactantius. Although he read Eusebius in defective translations, Jerome and Lactantius both wrote a stylish Latin that inspired the Christian humanism propagated by his colleague Erasmus. Among the Latin fathers

only Augustine, whom Polydore mentions just twice and peripher-
ally, surpassed Jerome in authority. Moreover, Jerome's attack on
Jovinian, defending Christian asceticism and celibacy, includes a
discussion of virginity and matrimony and hence of the marriage
customs that sparked ethnographic curiosity. Jerome also translated the *Chronology* of Eusebius, who expands much of the thinking behind this schematic work in the more discursive *Preparation
for the Gospel*. From these books Polydore learned that the giving of
the Mosaic law, the taking of Troy and the founding of the Olympic games were cardinal dates in a chronology that begins with
the expulsion of Adam from Paradise and continues through the
death of the emperor Valens. In this framework, where the Greeks
come late, the case against Greek priority is ironclad. In addition,
especially in the *Preparation*, Eusebius provides the particulars for a
critique of Greek theology and mythology, including the *topoi* of
origins, founders and inventors.

Clement of Alexandria also wanted to salvage cultural history
for Christians, but Polydore uses this Greek father only inciden-
tally. Lactantius, since he wrote in Latin, was a more accessible ad-
versary of pagan mythology and philosophy. Josephus, a Jewish
historian who wrote in Greek, played a critical role for Polydore as
he studied these Christian apologists and chronographers, since
their faith committed them (and him) to both parts of the Bible,
the Hebrew and the Greek. Like the Church fathers, Polydore
cites both Testaments often, but he reads sacred history through
Josephus, who retells and expands the biblical stories in the *Jewish
Antiquities* and attacks the competing Greek tales in *Against Apion*.
In this way, Josephus contributes no less than Eusebius to Polydore's account of inventions.

Reading his sources critically, Polydore is alert to their limita-
tions and thus to the constraints on his ability to write a complete
and credible history of discovery. He makes this point emphatically at the start of his chapter on new inventions, noting that

'though we have taken considerable pains to include . . . all discoverers, . . . yet because we use many things that are not at all
traceable . . . or that lack the expected tradition of authorship, the
evidence of discovery allowed us has diminished through time
which, as Varro says, destroys many things and distorts others.'
Time may be the great destroyer of evidence, but Polydore knew
even less about recent innovations than about older ones. 'The
greater surprise,' he notes, 'is that there are many new inventions
whose inventors are unrecorded and from whom we have no writings to tell us what names to give them' (3.18.1). The cause of his
surprise was his understanding of authorship and authority, both
expressed by the term *auctores*. For the high culture of the Renaissance, of which *On Discovery* is a typical (though unusually influential) product, there were no contemporary or recent voices on matters of secular culture that could speak with the *auctoritas* of the
ancients. The awe of antiquity felt by Polydore and other humanists drove their classicism in a vicious circle. If the only past worthy of serious inquiry is Greco-Roman and biblical — as implied
by Polydore's treatment of language, law, medicine, philosophy,
politics, and many other topics — the *auctores* must come from that
past, especially since the modern edifice of secondary scholarship
had only begun to be built in the Renaissance (by Polydore,
among others). But if all *auctores* are ancient, the more recent past
cannot be described with *auctoritas*. Obviously, the circle could be
broken; otherwise, Petrarch, Bruni, Valla, Poliziano, Erasmus and
many, many others could never have laid the foundations of modern history and philology, nor could Polydore have written the
English History.

Still, one failure of Polydore's sources was to have left many
titles to priority unrecorded or unresolved, and not only those
of later times. The name of the inventor of writing, for example,
'is forgotten, buried in antiquity, though it deserves the highest
honor' (1.6.1). Sometimes the ancients treated their ignorance of

such things for what it was—invincible—as when 'Celsus says . . . that the use of drugs to cure diseases is very old yet . . . does not propose an inventor' (1.21.4). But speculation came easier than silence. From the beginning, each city, region, or people had claimed inventions for itself, thus multiplying the number of candidates and sowing seeds of conflict among their advocates. The gods themselves had proliferated in this way, causing Cicero to catalog three Jupiters, four Vulcans, five Mercurys, and so on, each divine name a source of confusion on the discoveries attributed to them (1.6.2). Missing or muddled evidence limited Polydore's grasp of many topics nominally within reach of classical or biblical authority.

His chapter on weights and measures is a typical case. After summarizing what Diogenes, Eutropius, Gellius, Pliny and Strabo have to say, he defines the problem: 'those who write on this topic do not clearly agree among themselves.' His solution comes in two parts: first, 'different people discovered measures and weights in different places, as . . . Pythagoras first developed them for the Greeks'; next, 'the first of all mortals to establish them was Adam's son Cain, as one ought to believe' (1.19.1–2). The latter claim appeals to chronology in the context of biblical faith. The former is a secular historical inference. Polydore's premise leaves the authorities in conflict, but these two conclusions rescue them from mere discord. As Christians, he argues, we must acknowledge the patriarchs of Genesis, but as learned Christians we may also respect the heroes of Greece and Rome. His inquiries force him to confront the paradox of Renaissance classicism, which was that rescuing the remains of antiquity eroded confidence in what was rescued. A culture committed to mimesis and *auctoritas* found it hard to digest disputes among the many different sources of authority recovered by the humanists.

When he complains that inventions of one kind or another are too many to list, Polydore expresses exasperation at the intractable

scope of his topic, and if the ancients had left longer lists of discoveries, even more contention and confusion would have followed. 'Great disagreement among the better authors' is his typical diagnosis of the state of information on discoveries as he found it (1.6.2). His typical response is that 'the origin of this art remains in doubt, so it will be useful finally to clarify this issue' (1.14.5). His critical stance is usually positive, deferring to the authorities and applying an unspoken principle of charity to their disputes, but not always. Pagan ignorance of the plain Bible truth sometimes annoys him (1.5.7–8). Or a particular error — an internal lapse of consistency, for example — sometimes provokes him. 'Diodorus appears to contradict himself,' he notes at one point, and then complains that 'Diodorus was aiming at the truth in one place and telling stories in another, as he often does' (1.13.2).

Although Polydore worked out a consistent pattern of response to the defects of his sources, he did not turn it into an explicit critical method. Finding again and again that Greek and Roman *auctores* disagreed with one other and sometimes contradicted themselves, he points again and again to the Bible (through Josephus, Eusebius and others) as the incontestable record of Jewish priority. His secondary but very important response to differing pagan views is not simply to dismiss them as incompetent or malevolent but to explain them on the basis of temporal, spatial and cultural distance. Tubal was obviously the inventor of music, 'but reason requires that Amphion and the others were authors of this art at a later time' (1.14.4). Given Polydore's commitment to biblical priority, this additional concept of discoveries made by gentiles 'at later times in various places' implies that culture develops not just when one generation passes an invention on to the next or when a person or group transmits a discovery to contemporaries but also when the same novelty arises independently in different places at different times (1.17.5). All these outcomes are possible on Polydore's theory of discovery, but to call it a theory exaggerates

his methodological awareness. He never steps far back from his sources or the stories they tell to extract a theory of descent or diffusion or any other mode of cultural transmission. Nor when he occasionally applies tools of textual criticism to clarify his evidence does he treat these devices as principles of a method.

Had he done such things, he would have been far ahead of almost all his contemporaries as a pioneer of historical and philological theory. And in fact, he broke new ground—he truly was an inventor—in the practice of these disciplines as they were just entering the early modern phase of their development. When Jacob Burckhardt needed a phrase to sum up Polydore's age, he turned to Jules Michelet, who had seen 'the discovery of the world and of man' as the great work of the Renaissance. As author of the *English History*, Polydore has long been honored for his part in this work. In a different way, his book *On Discovery* earns the same honor.

Having begun my discovery of Polydore more than three decades ago, I have piled up more obligations than I can remember, above all to Kathleen, my patient and generous wife of these many years, and to Greg and Rebecca, Polydore's younger and livelier siblings. I owe many debts of learning to Michael Allen, Mortimer Chambers, William Gilbert, Jim Hankins, Andy Kelly, Jill Kraye, Charles Schmitt, Jennifer Snodgrass, Joe Trapp, Perkin Walker, Scott Waugh, Frances Yates and other friends, colleagues, students and teachers, and I owe debts of support to a number of institutions, including the American Council of Learned Societies, Western Washington University, Oakland University, UCR, UCLA and, most of all, the Warburg Institute of the University of London. I hope those who know the Warburg ideal will think of this book as aspiring to it, and with another aspiration I dedicate it to the next generation of Copenhavers, to Alexandra and Miranda.

Note

1. The prefatory letters mentioned in the Introduction are printed in this volume. Other references to *On Discovery* (*De inventoribus rerum*; abbreviated as *DIR*) are by book, chapter and paragraph number, indicating both the text and the notes. For persons mentioned in the Introduction, see the Index.

ON DISCOVERY

POLYDORI VERGILII URBINATIS AD LODOVICUM ODAXIUM PATAVINUM

Praefatio

1 Sum equidem nescius, Lodovice Odaxi, qua venia digni accipiantur illi qui longe a vero aberrantes, circa fabulas dumtaxat nervos prorsum omnes contenderint. In quorum sane numero quum poetae tum veteres philosophi maxime sunt. Verum illis quorum proprium est nugas sectari ignoscendum esse ducimus, his autem nequaquam.

2 Quippe qui quum veritatis (quae, sicuti praeclare Pindarus ait, magnum est virtutis principium) investigandae gratia talem scribendi materiam nacti essent ut eam suapte natura sese illis saepius offerentem facile depraehendere possent, adeo in obscuris versati sunt tenebris ut pro veritate magis magisque fingendi fabulas materiam praebuerint. Etenim hi—ut de initiis rerum, de mundi fabrica taceam—quum de Deo aut caeli motu dissererent physica quadam ratione, multo nempe maiorem quam foret deorum multitudinem reddiderunt. Qui induti specie humana fabulas poetis suppeditarunt, hominum autem vitam superstitione omni referserunt—veluti qui mox viros beneficiis excellentes in caelum (quemadmodum docuimus) fama ac voluntate tollere consueverint. Quae tametsi summae levitatis plena sunt, dicuntur tamen et stultissime creduntur.

3 Sed ipsi philosophi quum sapientiae laudem adepti sint eo quod pleno gressu veritatem sequi viderentur, nihil eos profecto, ut arbitror, tam devios egit quam veri Dei ignoratio. Ex quo haud dubie tot fabularum deliramenta manarunt, tunc potissime quum

POLYDORE VERGIL OF URBINO
TO LODOVICO ODASSIO
OF PADUA

Preface

For my part, Lodovico Odassio, I am loath to regard as deserving   1
any indulgence those who have spent all their energies on mere fables and have strayed far from the truth. Both the poets and the
ancient philosophers loom large in this group, to be sure. I find
that one should make allowance for the former, since poets are not
meant to be serious, but for the latter certainly not.

Although in searching for truth (virtue's main foundation, as   2
Pindar says so brilliantly) the philosophers had a topic that often
made it easy to find truth offering itself spontaneously for the taking, they lurked so long in dim shadows that instead of truth they
produced more and more material for spinning fables. The fact is
that by applying some sort of physical reasoning to God or the
motion of the heavens — not to speak of the origins or structure of
the world — they produced a multitude of gods, clearly many more
than there were. These gods in human guise supplied the poets
their fables, and they crammed human life full of every superstition — including those who soon started the custom of raising men
to heaven for their extraordinary services (as we have taught) on
the basis of reputation and good feeling. People repeat such notions and stupidly believe them even though they are the height of
foolishness.

Although these very philosophers won praise for wisdom be-   3
cause they seemed to be marching toward the truth, I believe that
nothing led them more astray than ignorance of the true God.
From this came all the delirium of the myths, without a doubt, es-

futilis esset hominum simplicitas. Nam nostro tempore, quo quidem impendio homines sapiunt, quis huiuscemodi deos colit quorum accipimus cupiditates, aegritudines, iracundias, bella, vulnera,
libidines? Quis Harpyias fuisse aut Chimaeram putat? Quaeve
anus tam excors inveniri potest quae illa quae quondam credeban-
tur apud inferos portenta extimescat? Quis tam hebetis ingenii est
ut metuat ne supra se caelum labet, sicut Galli Adriae vicini Magno olim Alexandro percontanti quidnam esset quod maxime per-
timescerent, sese formidare id tantum respondisse dicuntur? Ubi
gentium mensa Solis est quae divinitus epulas suppeditet, quam
Aethiopes se quondam habere iactabant?

4   Verissime igitur Marcus Tullius inquit diem opinionum co-
menta delere, naturae iudicia confirmare, quoniam — ut apud Gelium non minus scite quam eleganter legimus — solum tempus veritatis est parens. Quare hoc fabulis fidem habendi vitium magis
temporum quam hominum fuisse dixerim. At nobis qui longe
hercle foeliciore aetate geniti sumus propterea quod verum Deum
quotidie intuemur, contemplamur atque veneramur, nullisque amplius praestigiis daemonum ducimur, quid turpius magisve pudendum esse potest quam nugas terere et fonte veritatis omisso fabularum rivulos sectari, quum praesertim ita natura comparatum
constet ut nullus suavior animo cibus sit quam veri cognitio?

5   Ego itaque opus de rerum inventoribus orsus, partim ut nemo
sua laude, invenire enim primum praecipuum est, reique inventae
dignitas adeo multos trahit in amorem sui ut singuli si fieri possit
auctores se dici velint, fraudetur: partim ut qui imitari volent
sciant quos sequi debeant. Ne quid criminis subirem quam verissime potui omnia tradidi, maxime quum de origine deorum et eorum cultu, de rerum initiis, de hominis ortu prodidimus, quod
neutiquam facile fuit quando iam nugae cuncta oppleverant.

pecially at a time when people were weak and simple-minded. In our day, when people actually understand the cost, who worships such gods whom we know by their lusts, sorrows, rages, wars, wounds and appetites? Who thinks that Harpies existed or the Chimaera? What silly old woman can be found to take fright at the horrors once thought to dwell in the underworld? Who is so dull-witted that he fears the sky is about to fall upon him? They say that the Gauls living near the Adriatic replied that this was their only worry when Alexander the Great once asked what most terrified them. Where on earth is the Table of the Sun that carries the heavenly banquet? The Ethiopians used to brag that they once had it.

Cicero is quite right, then, to say that time wipes away figments 4 of imagination but confirms verdicts of nature because time alone begets truth — as we read in Gellius, who is no less learned than elegant. Accordingly, I should say that this vice of putting faith in myths had more to do with the times than the people. We have been born in an age far happier, surely, when we gaze every day upon the true God, contemplate him and worship him, and deceits of the demons no longer beguile us. Can anything shame or disgrace us more than to waste time on nonsense, to abandon the fount of truth and follow the streams of fable, especially since nature has plainly seen to it that the mind finds no food sweeter than knowing the truth?

Therefore, having undertaken a work on those who made dis- 5 coveries, I aim in part to see that no one is cheated of his glory since discovery is being first, before all others, while the honor of making a discovery draws many into such love of self that all of them would wish to be founders if they could; the other part of my purpose is to show those who want to imitate whom they ought to follow. In this I have tried to do no wrong and to report everything as accurately as possible, especially when dealing with the origin of the gods and their worship, the beginning of the

6   Caeterum sum ego itidem, fateor, in plerisque locis fabulas secutus, quibus etiam verum specie aliqua velatum subest, id tamen
nihilominus veritati inhaesimus quando hoc ratio ipsa exigere visa
est. Et quamquam Saturno, Iovi, Neptuno, Mercurio, Dionysio,
Apollini, Aesculapio, Cereri, Vulcano et aliis quos deos vocant
quaedam assignavimus, ea ipsa tamen illis tanquam mortalibus
non tanquam diis, licet ipse quoque deos nuncupaverim, attribui-
mus.

7   Haud me fugit insuper quosdam malivolentissimos fore qui industriam nostram fortasse temeritatem appellabunt quia ego solus
de rerum inventoribus scribere ausus sum, quod nemo ante me
praeter Plinium particulatim tentarat, qui in septimo *Naturalis historiae* de hac re strictim admodum meminit, et Marcum Antonium
Sabellicum, qui hexametro carmine ea fere ipsa itidem praestrin-
xit. Verum illi prorsus ignorabunt id multo esse praeclarius quo
difficilius extiterit. Quid enim laudis assecutus esset Caesar si facile fuisset Britannis bellum inferre? Aut Hannibal—quantum
gloriae sibi comparasset si pervias Alpes dum Italiam adiret citra
(ut dicitur) pulverem sudoremque ac non magna suorum caede fecisset? Propter quod nos etiam hoc opus, etsi arduum, magno
animo suscepimus maturavimusque.

8   In quo si quid desiderabitur, nemini mirum sit quando multa
non modo vetera sed novitia inventa sunt quorum, ut in calce operis perspicue demonstravimus, inventores in densissimis omnino
umbris latent. Non id tamen inficior (haud enim tantum mihi ar-
rogo quum sint hodie plures longe me doctiores) quin possit quispiam de hac re—veluti *De proverbiis*, quorum libellum proximo
anno Guido principi, Urbini Duci, inscripsimus—copiosius tradere. Verum quicunque hoc vel illud posthac ingredietur iter, quia

world and the origin of mankind, which was no easy task since all
this had already been obscured by nonsense.

Even so, I too have followed fables of this kind in many places, 6
I admit it. Beneath them also lies truth, veiled in one form or
another, and in following fables when reason itself seemed to
demand it, I have adhered to truth no less. While assigning certain discoveries to Saturn, Jupiter, Neptune, Mercury, Dionysius,
Apollo, Aesculapius, Ceres, Vulcan and others whom they call
gods, I have attributed these things to them as mortals, not as
gods, even though I myself have also called them gods.

Furthermore, it hardly surprises me that certain very spiteful 7
persons may call my efforts rash because I alone have ventured
to write on those who made discoveries. No one before me has attempted it case by case except Pliny, who gives a rather short summary of the subject in book 7 of the *Natural History*, and Marcantonio Sabellico, who squeezed almost the same content into
hexameter verse. My critics completely fail to realize that the
greater excellence comes from what is harder to do. What praise
would Caesar have won if making war on the Britons had been
easy? Or Hannibal—how much glory would he have gained for
himself had he crossed the Alps to invade Italy without dust and
sweat (as they say) and with no great slaughter of his own people?
In view of this, I also have taken up this work and finished it,
difficult though it was, with great enthusiasm.

If anything is wanting in it, no one should be surprised since 8
there are many discoveries, old and new alike, whose discoverers
lie completely hidden in the thickest shadows, as I have clearly
shown at the end of my work. Yet none of this causes me to deny
that someone may be able to give a fuller treatment of this subject—as in the case of my *Proverbs*, the book that I dedicated last
year to Prince Guido, Duke of Urbino—for I do not claim so
much for myself when there are many today far more learned than
I. But if anyone hereafter begins either of these journeys, perhaps

nos primi stadium currimus, is fortasse nostris vestigiis insistere non gravabitur.

9 Has autem, qualescunque sunt, lucubrationes tibi uni ex omnibus potissimum consecrare constitui: primum quod quum tu de me plurimum benemeritus sis, iure optimo tibi secunda ingenioli nostri foetura debetur; deinde quia tu uberrimus es ingeniorum fons, tuque commune utriusque linguae decus; postea quoniam tu in quo et naturae dotes et fortunae bona cumulatim congesta sunt, litteras amas, tu litteratos praesidio foves, tu opibus iuvas, tu studiorum studiosorum comercio delectaris; praeterea quod tu unica doctrinarum lux ita tuo splendore meas lucubratiunculas illustrabis ut a Sole reliquae stellae lumen habent; unde per te a doctis diligentur, complectentur atque legentur, ab invidis autem tuae inaccessae lucis fulgore nitentes minime conspici valebunt.

10 Cui postremo convenientius opus de rerum inventoribus dicari debuerat, in quo multarum rerum origo continentur quam tibi, qui ad unguem scriptorum omnium monumenta noris? Nam, uti divus Hieronymus inquit, illi tertium Vergilii *Aeneidos* librum lucidius intuentur qui a Troiade per Leucadem et Acroceraunia ad Siciliam et inde ad Hostia Tyberina navigaverint. Qui insuper Guido Urbini Duci nostro illustrissimo ab ineunte eius aetate a divo Federico, tamquam olim a Philippo Macedone Magno Alexandro Aristoteles, praeceptor datus es; qui quum te duce in utriusque linguae studiis mirum in modum ac plus quam dici possit perfectum fecerit, haud equidem immerito prae omnibus sibi charissimus es; apud quem, ut par est, summum dignitatis gradum habes; a quo denique tanti sis quanti certe fieri debes.

11 Nec quicquam tamen aliud mutavit in te huiuscemodi fortunae amplitudo nisi quod effecit ut innatam tibi humanitatem, facilitatem, liberalitatem (licet ea ipsa iugiter prae te feras) facilius modo omnes idemtidem conspiciant. Quid enim referam quam sis

he will not object to following my footsteps because I have run the course first.

These late-night studies of mine — such as they are — I have decided to dedicate to you alone, the best choice of all that I might make: first of all, since you have been so very kind to me, it is surely right that I owe you this second offspring of my small talent; next, you are a most plentiful fount of talents, pride of both languages alike; also, you are one upon whom both the gifts of nature and the goods of fortune have been heaped abundantly, as you love literature, as you cherish and protect the learned, as you aid and support them, as you delight in sharing scholarship with scholars. Moreover, because nothing outshines your light of learning, your brilliance will illuminate my little labors as the rest of the stars take light from the sun. Through you, then, the learned will esteem, embrace and read my work, but the envious can take little notice since it reflects the splendor of your unrivaled light. 9

To whom, then, if not to you, who know the works of all the authors to the last detail, might one have better dedicated a work on those who made discoveries, a work that contains the origin of many things? As St. Jerome says, those who have sailed from the Troad through Leucas and Acroceraunia to Sicily and thence to Ostia and the Tiber have a clearer view of the third book of Vergil's *Aeneid*. You, moreover, whom the divine Federico made the teacher of our most illustrious Duke Guido of Urbino at an early age, as Philip of Macedon once appointed Aristotle for Alexander the Great — you are the dearest person of all to him, and rightly so, since it was you who guided him to study both languages with wondrous and inexpressible perfection. It is just that you hold high rank in his following, and at last he has made you as great as you truly deserve. 10

Such great good fortune has changed nothing in you, however, except to make your native humanity, affability and generosity (traits that you constantly display, to be sure) easier somehow for 11

convictu comis, affatu blandus, aditu facilis, indulgens in tuos, liberalis in omnes? Quapropter non iniuria et Patavium quod te procreavit et Urbinum quod multis iam annis te fruitur, dum quodque Lodovicum Odaxium suum esse cupit, non secus inter se iam contendere incoeptant quam olim propter Homerum singularis alioqui doctrinae virum Athenas, Argos, Rhodum, Smyrnam, Salaminam, Colophonem et ius decertasse ferunt. Caeterum de te non opus est tamen ut plures certent quum totius Italiae (ut citra omnem assentationem vera profitear) communis aeque sis splendor.

12   Accipe igitur, Lodovice Odaxi, hilaro vultu hoc opus a Polydoro tuo Vergilio, idque ea frontis severitate perlegito qua huiusmodi scripta legere consuevisti. Nam si a te tuique similibus probabitur, verum quidem operaeprecium me fecisse putabo.

13   Vale. Urbini, Nonis Augusti, anno MCCCCXCIX.

all to keep in view. What can I say but that you are friendly in society, charming in conversation, easy to approach, indulgent to your own and generous to everyone? For these reasons, when every place wants Lodovico for its own, the Padua that bore you and the Urbino that now enjoys your company of many years are starting to argue among themselves, and justly so, the same as Athens, Argos, Rhodes, Smyrna, Salamis and Colophon also once fought it out in court, they say, because of Homer, another man of remarkable learning. For all that, there is no need for so many to fight over you since all Italy (to tell the truth, without flattery) shares equally in your brilliance.

So then, Lodovico Odassio, accept this work from your Polydore Vergil with a smile, and read it through with that sober look that you have always turned on such writings. For if you and your peers approve, I will think it truly worthwhile to have done my work. 12

Farewell. From Urbino, August 5, 1499. 13

POLYDORUS VERGILIUS URBINAS
IOANNI MATTHAEO VERGILIO
FRATRI SALUTEM DICIT

1   Reddam tibi frater studiorum meorum rationem quo plane intelli-
    gas me haud quaquam officii esse immemorem quod posteritati
    debetur. Porro ita natura comparatum est ut quemadmodum
    homo ac caeterae animantes suum genus perpetuis foetibus con-
    servare appetunt, sic nostri summates viri eruditissimi nihil prius
    semper habuerint quam bonarum artium modis omnibus semina-
    rium indesinenter facere quas per hunc modum quasi per manus
    traditas ad posteros propagarent, quibus illi suos subinde excole-
    rent animos ut sic quod natura in gignendis corporibus studium
    mortalibus invexerat hoc in nutriendis animis industria suppedi-
    taret. Hinc factum ut quocunque fere tempore fuerint qui oppido
    quam libenter voluerint scribendo aliquid exhaurire laboris, quo
    partim insequentibus prodessent, partim vero famae consulentes
    quo sibi immortalitatem prorogarent. Hoc officium denique est
    quod nepotibus impartiri debet, quo si quis fungi recusaverit me-
    rito ingratus habebitur.

2   Ego igitur quondam ut illud quoquo modo praestarem in ipso
    statim tirocinii nostri principio, proverbia ex omni veterum Lati-
    norum scriptorum genere passim sparsa quae celebriora essent
    complura collegi, in commentariolumque qui studiorum meorum
    anteludium foret redegi, dedicavique Guidoni duci nostro Urbi-
    nati, utriusque linguae principi ex aequo peritissimo, quem ille
    quamprimum in apertum proferri voluit. Placuit is sua praesertim
    novitate usque adeo, delectavitque usque adeo ut brevi mox terque
    quaterque (sicuti poeta ait) fuerit formis excusus.

3   Hac levi aura (fateor ingenue) evectus, tum maius aggressus
    opus de rerum inventoribus negocium suscepi, naviterque minus

POLYDORE VERGIL
GIVES GREETINGS TO HIS
BROTHER, GIAN MATTEO VERGIL

Brother, let me give you an account of my studies that will assure 1
you that I am not at all forgetful of the duty one owes posterity.
Nature has so arranged it that just as man and other living things
desire to preserve their kind by continuous breeding, so in turn
our most eminent men of learning have aways held nothing more
important than ceaselessly and variously to prepare a seedbed of
the liberal arts which, in this way, they might propagate and pass
on as if handing them down to those that follow. For their sake
they constantly cultivate their own minds so that industry might
supply that same zeal for nourishing minds which nature introduced to mortals for begetting bodies. Hence it happened that
with the greatest pleasure they took almost every occasion to finish
some task of writing, partly to benefit their successors, partly to
promote their fame and enlarge their immortality. This is the service that one should perform for descendants, and anyone that re-
fuses to provide it will rightly be thought to deserve no thanks.

Some time ago, then, to find a way to make good quickly on 2
this obligation, right at the start of my first campaign, I collected
from every type of ancient Latin writing many of the more famous
proverbs that were scattered in one place or another. These I arranged in a little commentary as prelude to my studies and dedicated it to our Guido, Duke of Urbino, a prince most expert in
both languages alike, and he wanted it published right away. He
took such special pleasure in its novelty, it delighted him so much,
that in short order it was printed three and four times over, as the
poet says.

Stirred by this pleasant breeze — I freely admit it — I next took 3
up a larger task on those who made discoveries, and in less than

mensibus novem confeci. Sic Polydorus ego primus apud Latinos utriusque rei argumentum attentavi, id quod in praefationibus unius et alterius operis affatim docuimus.

4   Veni post haec missu Alexandri sexti Romani pontificis in Britanniam, quae nunc Anglia est, ut quaesturam pontificiam apud Anglos gererem. Ubi ne bonum ocium tererem, rogatu Henrici eius appellationis septimi regis praestantissimi, res eius populi gestas scripsi, in historiae stilum redegi. Quod hercle opus duodecim annos sub literatoria incude laboratum, obstante fato, nondum absolvere licuit.

5   Interea tu (si recte recolis) in Ferrariense Academia medicam professus artem, et eius rei exercitio velut lucroso magis quam nobili non perinde oblectatus, statuisti per doctrinae studium te tollere humo, id quod vel ipse maxime probavi. Quapropter a Ferrariensibus principibus, utpote quibus tua tum latina tum graeca satis iam innotaverat eruditio, quam primum rogatus coepisti dialecticen publice profiteri, cum ecce tibi praeter spem a senatu Veneto, doctissimorum semper virorum altore, Patavium qui in ea urbe gymnasium temporum calamitate paucis ante annis desertum decreverat celebrius multo quam olim fuerat reddere accitus fuisti ut inibi philosophiam doceres.

6   Cum itaque Ferrariae non absque summo honore legeres, succisivis horis nostrum *De rerum inventoribus* opusculum denuo perlegisti, in quo, quia de initiis mysteriorum nostrae christianae religionis strictim admodum carptimque prodidissem, significasti mihi te opus illud mancum atque veluti appendicem — hoc est corpus (sic enim Marcus Tullius in *Hortensio* appellat) sine animo — iudicare, ac propterea rogasti ut ex proma cella divinarum literarum hoc immortalitatis quod desiderabatur mortali corpori restituerem copularemque. Quo cognito consilio, haud mora me negocio vo-

nine months of hard work I finished it. I, Polydore, first among the Latins, thus attempted both these subjects, as fully explained in the preface to each work.

After this I came to Britain — now England — on a mission 4 from the Roman Pontiff, Alexander vi, to manage the papal finances of the English. Not to waste this splendid opportunity, at the request of the most excellent King Henry, seventh of that name, I wrote down the deeds of his people and put them in the form of a history. This work, impeded by fate, I have not yet been able to finish, though I have certainly labored at writing it for twelve years.

Meanwhile, if you recall correctly, you taught medicine at the 5 University of Ferrara, but finding it more lucrative than ennobling you did not particularly enjoy your practice, and you decided to raise yourself from the ground by the pursuit of learning, which I very much approved. Therefore you began to offer a public course on dialectic as soon as you were asked by the princes of Ferrara, who were familiar with your mastery of Greek and Latin, and then — beyond all expectations — look what happened: the Venetian Senate, ever the patron of the most learned men, invited you to return to Padua to teach philosophy there because they had resolved to increase enrollment in that city's university, deserted only a few years before in a time of calamity.

And so, when you were studying at Ferrara and winning high- 6 est honors, for several hours in a row you re-read my little work *On Discovery*. As a result, you suggested to me that you found that work crippled and like an appendage — a body without a soul, as Cicero says in the *Hortensius* — because in it I dealt rather superficially and erratically with the origins of the mysteries of our religion. Therefore you asked that I draw on the storehouse of divine letters to restore the immortality that was missing and join it to the mortal body. Once I understood your advice, willingly and

lenter accinxi ut qui percupidus eram in sacris literis aliquid pariendi id quod iam diu parturieram.

7   Suscepi itaque huiusce argumenti pondus, sed longe profecto gravius quam putaram. Namque nos singula prospicienter (uti par erat) investigantes, ipsae saepenumero destituerunt divinae literae ita ut ad humanas crebro fuerit recurrendum. Dii boni, quam plurima instituta nostrae religionis sumpta translataque sunt ex ceremoniis ethnicorum, sicut suus quisque disseruit obiter locus! Sed quid de peregrinis loquimur, cum non parum multa a nostris heri (ut ita dicam) vel nudius tertius introducta forent de quorum initiis nihil non incertum extabat. Cuiusmodi erant ademptio connubii sacerdotalis, creatio illa solennis cardinalium, varii in religione ordines, sanctiones dierum quorundam festorum, excommunicatio—id est, dira illa in impios execratio—atque id genus complura.

8   Nos proinde hunc desudavimus laborem, et instituta omnia nostrae religionis aliarumve gentium complexi ac eorum primordia undecunque quaesita diligenter perscrutati, superioris aeditionis summae adglutinavimus sic ut pars haec pro gravitate rei multo maior accesserit.

9   Unde iam omnes quibus religio quae nos deo conciliat, indissolubilique nodo connectit, cordi est tuo rogatu facilius haurire queunt, a quo fonte et eius deinde rivulis (nam semper scitu gratum iucundumque fuit cuiusque rei nosse originem) manaverit tot ceremoniarum totve rituum flumen, quo demum cuncti mortales abluti hic placidam ac gaudialem agunt vitam, et alibi coelestem spe certa expectant. Cuius nos sospitator noster Christus participes facere dignetur.

10   Recognovimus insuper priorem aeditionem aliquot locis librariorum incuria (uti sit) depravatam, adiecimusque non inconcinniter quaepiam, ubi visa est materia sic poscere, quo legentibus fieret locupletior. Decurtavimus vero extra praefationem nihil ne quid in

without delay I girded myself for the task—I who badly wanted to bring to birth what I had long been gestating in sacred letters.

Thus I took up the burden of this topic, which was certainly far 7 heavier than I had thought. For as I looked into each problem with an eye to its future (as I should), I had to depend on human records where the sacred were often lacking. Heavens above, how many practices of our religion have been adopted and taken over from pagan ceremony, just as each locality has gone its own way! But why talk about alien customs when nothing certain has been found about a good many that we have introduced yesterday (so to speak) or the day before? Of this kind were the revocation of clerical marriage, the formal creation of cardinals, the various religious orders, certain holy days of obligation, excommunication—that dreadful curse against the impious—and many things of that sort.

Accordingly, I sweated over this task and, having summed up 8 all the practices of our religion and those of other peoples and having diligently researched their origins from all points of view, I added them on top of the previous text so that this part became the much larger in keeping with the weight of the subject.

Hence, because of what you asked, all can drink more easily 9 from this source who cherish the religion that makes us acceptable to God and binds us to him by a knot that cannot be untied. From its streams (since it was always deemed welcome and pleasant to know the origin of anything) has flowed a river of many rites and ceremonies, and all mortals who have washed in it lead a calm and joyous life here below, expecting in certain hope a celestial life elsewhere. In this life Christ our savior deigns to make us share.

I have also reviewed the earlier edition which was marred in a 10 number of places by the carelessness (so it goes) of publishers, and where appropriate I have added certain things when the material seemed to demand it in order to give readers more information. Apart from the preface, however, I have cut nothing out even if it

ea quoque redundaret quod lectorem ad novam foeturam deliban-
dam remoraretur properantem.

11   Iam habes, Iohannes Matthaee frater (etsi non parvo meo negocio) quod petiisti. Et quia id aetatis iam sumus ut spargamur canis
in dies singulos, cupimus propterea remissis laboribus iam rude
donari atque mature (ut aiunt) fieri senes quo diutius sim senex.
Tibi igitur negocium damus et iuvandi tuo labore studiosos et nomini familiae nostrae consulendi cui prope uni seculi nostri contigit ante sextum aetatis lustrum cum tanta morum probitate esse
philosopho, medico ac oratori perfecto.

12   Ex qua doctrinarum scintilla tota iam Italia lucem maximam
maturissime erupturam auguratur. Cave ne pariat tibi superbiam,
est enim Dei optimi maximi munus. Perge idcirco uti gnaviter facis. Habes enim (prout probe scis) Antonium Vergilium proavum
nostrum archetypon qui medicae etiam rei ac astrologiae peritissimus olim apud Gallos in Lutetia Parisiorum philosophiam docuit,
quam tu Patavii in praesenti publice profiteris. O nimium felix
propria haec si dona manerent! Non est infima utique laus duos ex
Vergiliana familia viros in duobus totius orbis praecipuis gymna-
siis haud longo temporis intervallo professores bonarum disciplinarum non absque nominis gloria publicitus extitisse.

13   Sed tu qui proavum iam iam longe relinquis, efficies (spero) ut
aliquando posteritas dicat fuisse olim Polydorum quendam qui illum Ioannem Matthaeum Vergilium a puero bonis moribus atque
disciplinis nutrierat.

14   Vale. Londini, nonis Decembris, anno MDXVII.

might be redundant and so delay a reader hurrying to get a first taste of the new vintage.

Now, Gian Matteo, my brother, you have what you wanted — 11 though for me it was no small effort. And since I am already at that time of life when grey sprinkles my hair day by day, I wish to stop working and be given my discharge now, aging early (as they say) in order to stay old longer. Therefore I charge you, who almost alone in our time have become an accomplished philosopher, physician and orator of great moral integrity before the age of thirty, to help the studious with your work and look after the name of our family.

From this spark of learning all Italy now predicts that the great- 12 est light will burst forth very soon. Beware lest it be a source of pride for you since it is a gift from God Almighty. Make your way diligently, then; for you have our ancestor Antonio Vergil as a model (as you well know), an expert in medicine as well as astrology, who once taught philosophy to the French in Paris as you now teach public courses in Padua. How very happy if these gifts remain your own! Surely it is no small basis for praise that in a short space of time two men of the Vergil family have been in the public eye as professors of higher learning, making our name glorious in the world's two leading universities.

But you, who have already gone far beyond your ancestor, will 13 see to it (I hope) that posterity may some day say that there was once a certain Polydore who had nurtured that Gian Matteo Vergil from his boyhood in good conduct and learning.

Farewell. From London, December 5, 1517. 14

POLYDORI VERGILII URBINATIS IN QUINQUE LIBROS DE INITIIS INSTITUTORUM REI CHRISTIANAE AD IOANNEM MATTHAEUM VERGILIUM FRATREM

Proemium

1 Christus Servator noster qui, quemadmodum ipse testatur, ad nos mortales venerat haud legis rescindendae sed atque adeo confirmandae causa, iam inde a principio omnia pura, nuda, aperta reddidit, quae antea Iudaei, umbram ipsius legis secuti, suffecerant, colorarant fucosaque fecerant, et denique quicquid isti laxarant ac quo minus pietatis plusque caerimoniarum introduxerant, ille astrinxit atque plus pietatis minusque caerimoniarum esse voluit. Quod Esaias fore praedixerat, inclamans: Quo mihi multitudinem victimarum vestrarum, dicit dominus? Caeterum deinceps sylva haec Iudaicarum caerimoniarum sic paulatim agrum dominicum occupavit, ut periculum sit ne aliquando ipse Dominus illud agricolis crimini det ab eisque quaerat. Quis enim quaesivit haec de manibus vestris?

2 Verum ut non parum multa a Iudaeis, ita non modica ab aliis gentibus instituta aut casu rationeve accepta tam in frequentem usum et consuetudinem venere ut pro nostris habeantur. Quod equidem fecit ut putarim me operaepretium facturum si origines eiusmodi rerum omnium quae ad religionem pertinerent proderem quo luculentius constaret quas Seruator, quas apostoli, quas deinde episcopi quasve alii introduxerint.

THE PREFACE TO FIVE BOOKS
BY POLYDORE VERGIL
ON THE BEGINNINGS OF
CHRISTIAN INSTITUTIONS,
TO HIS BROTHER,
GIAN MATTEO VERGIL

Proem

Christ our savior who, as he himself witnesses, came to us mortals 1
not at all to repeal the law but in fact greatly to strengthen it,
made everything clear, plain and unembellished right from the
start, while previously the Jews, who followed the shadow of that
same law, had colored over, varnished and misrepresented it, and
in the end whatever they had made lax, he made strict, where they
had brought in more ceremony with less piety, he wanted more piety and less ceremony. That this would happen Isaiah had predicted, crying out: What does your multitude of victims mean to
me, says the Lord? Moreover, this jungle of Jewish ceremonies
then took over the field of the Lord bit by bit, risking that at some
time the Lord himself might blame his farmers for it and ask
them: Who indeed required this at your hands?

But like no small number of Jewish practices, quite a few estab- 2
lished by other peoples were accepted either by chance or by plan
and came into such frequent use and custom that they were taken
for our own. This is what convinced me that it would be worthwhile to make known the origins of everything of this kind that
pertains to religion so that there would be better agreement on
what had been introduced by the Savior, what by the apostles,
what next by the bishops and what by others.

3   Et id, amantissime frater, tuo praesertim hortatu mihi officium
praestandum duxi, ut dum tu – qui graecis pariter atque latinis
literis es longe eruditissimus Patavii quo nuper a Senatu Veneto
philosophiae docendae causa accitus es – negociaris ne ipse ociarer.
Itaque omnes nostrae religionis ritus eorumque initia quinque libris explicui etsi nescio quam bene, tamen accurate, quos ad tres
illos *De rerum inventoribus* libellos ab hinc xviii annos a me et aetate et fortasse doctrina tyrone compositos adiunxi. Docuique Pa-
tres olim in bona illorum parte recipienda pie ac cum causa fecisse,
quippe qui, gentes etiam barbaras ad verae pietatis cultum ducere
aventes, arbitrati sunt humanitatis condimentis tractandas cum earum instituta haud prorsus horruerint nec sustulerint sed meliora
fecerint, quo ne ullum religioni periculum crearetur si vel minus
admisissent minusve mutassent, quemadmodum locis perappositis
commodum demonstravimus. Atque isto ipso labore, quem religionis causa non invitus suscepi, Deum Optimum Maximum nobis propitium reddidisse confido.

4   Vale. Nonis Decembris, Londini, mdxvii.

And at your special urging, most loving brother, I have made it   3
my duty to accomplish this so that I shall not be idle while you are
busy—you who are the most learned by far in Greek and Latin
letters alike and have been invited to Padua by the Venetian Senate to teach philosophy. Therefore in five books I have explained
accurately, if not very well, all the customs of our religion and
their beginnings, and I have added them to those three books *On
Discovery* that I wrote eighteen years ago as a beginner in years and
perhaps in learning. I have taught that the Fathers once assumed
piously and with reason that they ought to accept these beginnings
with good will. For in fact, wanting to lead even barbarian nations
to the habit of true piety, they thought that these nations should
be influenced by the delights of culture, since they did not just
shun or abolish their practices but improved them, so as to create
no risk to religion when they permitted less here or changed less
there, as I have taken the opportunity to show in the appropriate
places. And with this task of yours, which I have undertaken willingly in the cause of religion, I trust that I have won favor from
God almighty.

Farewell. From London, December 5, 1517.   4

IN POLYDORUM

Simon Grynaeus

Qui more et ritu argutae apis
Campos Thespiadum pervolat
Amicis passim floribus
Caute os impressus insidet
Succos miros, miras opes
Genere omni autorum convehit,
Divite mox alveario
Favos et mella dulcia
Subinde praebet omnibus,
POLYDORI non intelligo
Merito qui non summo sibi
Nomen venerandum vendicet.

ON POLYDORE

Simon Grynaeus

He that like the buzzing bee
Flies through fields of Thespiae
To press his face in friendly blooms
With care, and settle here and there,
And takes the sap with all its power
From each rich hive and every maker
To offer it to one and all,
Sweetest honeys, honeycombs —
He, I fail to understand,
Why in justice he would not
Claim first of all that honored name of
POLYDORE.

POLYDORI VERGILII URBINATIS
DE INVENTORIBUS RERUM
LIBER PRIMUS

: I :

De prima deorum origine et unde Deus dictus.

1 Cum terrestres olim daemones — hoc est, aerii sive inferni spiritus
quos sacri autores huius mundi principes appellant — per simulachra mortalibus hominibus dicata divinationes exercerent, et ma-
leficis artibus sese modo bonos daemones, modo deos coelestes ac
nunc heroum animas, nunc alios atque alios confingerent, tantum
errorum humanis pectoribus effuderunt ut brevi tempore bonae
partis hominum mentes a cultu veri Dei prorsum averterint. Nec
per tibi mirum videatur malos daemones suscipere personam deorum quandoquidem ipse Satanas, velut Paulus apostolus capite II
Epistolae posterioris ad Corinthios ait, transfiguratur in angelum
lucis, hoc est, Dei qui lux est. Quare apostoli, ut est apud Matthaeum evangelistam capite 14, cum in navi essent adversa tempestate in alto iactata et Iesus super mare ambulans ad eos iret turbati
sunt arbitrantes spectrum esse, et licet sit illis ipsis locutus, Petrus
tamen visum videre se animo ducens, haud prius Christum esse
credidit quam experimento cognovit qui eius iussu super aquam
itidem ambulavit, adeo fallacias daemonum usitato more factas ti-
mebant.

2 Ad rem redeo. Et quia spiritus erant tenues, sibi geniorum nomen assumebant. Nam genios singulis binos attribuit antiquitas
qui daemones quoque vocantur, nec hominibus modo, verumetiam
locis et aedibus, quorum alter nobis perniciem moliretur, alter pro-

BOOK I

: I :

On the origin of the gods and of the word 'God.'

Long ago when there were demons in the earth — aerial or infernal 1
spirits whom the sacred writers call the princes of this world —
they practiced divination with idols consecrated to mortal men.
Using evil arts, they would pretend that they were either good demons or heavenly gods or else souls of heroes or other beings of
that sort, and they flooded human hearts with so much error that
in no time they turned the minds of a good part of humanity completely away from the worship of the true God. You should not be
astonished that evil demons disguise themselves as gods since, as
the Apostle Paul says in 2 Corinthians 11, Satan himself takes the
form of an angel of light — of God, that is, who is light. And so,
according to the Evangelist Matthew, chapter 14, when the apostles
were in a boat tossed about on the deep with a storm beating
against them and Jesus came walking toward them on the water,
they were troubled, taking him for a ghost. Even though Christ
spoke to them, Peter supposed he was seeing a vision and did not
believe that it was Christ until he knew so through experience, after Christ commanded him to walk on the water in the same
way — all this because they were so wary of the tricks that demons
used to play.

To return to my topic, these demons took the name 'genius' be- 2
cause they were spirits of light substance. Antiquity attributed two
genii or demons to each thing, not only to persons but even to
places and buildings; one of them strove to do us evil, the other

27

desse studeret. De hoc bono custode non est quod ambigatur, quando teste Matthaeo capite 18 Christus docet nos in angelorum tutela esse, dicens: Dico enim vobis quod angeli eorum in coelis semper vident faciem patris mei. Hunc locum divus Hieronymus ita explanat: Magna dignitas animarum ut unaquaeque habeat ab ortu in custodiam sui angelum delegatum. Item hi daemones ostiatim domos occupabant facileque insinuabant se corporibus hominum et occulte in visceribus operti valetudinem corrumpebant, morbos citabant, animos somniis territabant, ac his malis cogebant mortales ad sua decurrere auxilia petereque suppliciter responsa quibus semper ambiguos dedita opera addebant exitus, ne suam patefacerent ignorantiam. Sed haec nocendi tela postremo illis adempta fuere, prout fusius explicabitur cum de nostrae Christianae religionis principio et institutis disseretur. Per haec igitur maleficia dii putabantur, ita ut alii alios (sicut inferius docebimus) et deos nuncuparent et summa religione colerent. Sic opinio de multitudine deorum, cum a simulacris ad invisibiles spiritus cogitatio raperet, uti vera usque eo crevit ut maior prope coelitum populus quam mortalium haberi coeperit.

3   Unde post innumerabiles philosophorum de diis undique sententiae confluxerunt, qui sese, abiectis omnibus publicis atque privatis actionibus quaerendae ac investigandae veritatis gratia, ad doctrinae studium contulerunt. Thales enim Milesius, qui primus (teste Marco Tullio in primo *De natura deorum* volumine) de talibus rebus quaesivit, aquam esse dixit a qua nata sint omnia, Deum autem esse mentem quae ex aqua cuncta formaverit. Pythagoras definivit Deum esse animum per naturam rerum omnem intentum et commeantem, ex quo omnia quae nascerentur animalia vitam capere. Cleanthes et Anaximines aerem Deum statuerunt. Vergilius in secundo *Georgicorum*:

tried to do good. About this good guardian there is no debate, for in Matthew 18 Christ teaches that we are in the care of the angels, saying: I tell you that their angels in heaven are always looking on the face of my father. St. Jerome explains this passage as follows: That each soul from the beginning should have an angel assigned to watch over it indicates that souls have great value. These demons also used to invade each and every house and quickly work themselves into people's bodies where they found secret hiding places in their entrails. Then they would ruin their health, bring on disease and fill their minds with terror in dreams, using these evil devices to force people to have recourse to their help and to beg humbly for answers which always contained conclusions meant to be ambiguous, so that they would not expose their ignorance. But finally these noxious weapons were taken from them, as will be explained more fully in discussing the foundation and institutions of our Christian religion. And so they were thought to be gods because of these evil deeds, and various beings (see below) named gods by various peoples were worshipped with the greatest reverence. Thus, when speculation carried people away from idols to invisible spirits, they accepted as true the notion that there were many gods, and the idea enjoyed such great success that the celestial population came almost to outnumber the mortal.

After this, innumerable philosophical teachings about the gods 3 poured in from everywhere. Having renounced all public and private business for the sake of seeking and investigating the truth, philosophers turned to the pursuit of learning. Thales of Miletus, who (according to Cicero in book 1 *On the Nature of the Gods*) first inquired about such things, said that it was water from which all things came forth but that God is the mind that formed all things from water. Pythagoras defined God as the spirit extended and moving to and fro through the whole of nature, from which all living things that come to be take life. Cleanthes and Anaximenes concluded that God is air, as Vergil writes in the second *Georgic*:

Tum pater omnipotens foecundis imbribus aether
Coniugis in gremium laetae descendit, et omnes
Magnus alit magno commistus corpore foetus.

Anaxagoras Deum esse censuit infinitam mentem quae per seip-
sam moveretur. Antisthenes dixit multos esse quidem deos popu-
lares, unum tamen naturalem summae totius artificem. Chrysippus naturalem vim divina ratione praeditam interdum divinam
necessitatem Deum vocat. At Zeno divinam naturalemque legem.
Xenocrates vero octo deos esse putavit.

4   Quidam autem deos esse aut sibi minime constare dixerunt aut
prorsus sustulerunt. Nam Protagoras sese negavit omnino de diis
quid liqueret scire, id est, an aliqua esset divinitas necne, propter
quod Athenienses eum suis finibus exterminarunt. Diagoras vero
Atheos item Cyrenaicus Theodorus nullum esse omnino Deum
existimarunt. Epicurus Deum quidem esse dixit sed nihil cuiquam
tribuentem, nihil gratificantem, nihil curantem. Lucretius:

Non bene pro meritis capitur nec tangitur ira.

Item Vergilius in Damone:

Nec curare Deum credis mortalia quenquam.

Quare non temere Cicero in extremo primo libro *De natura deorum*
ait: Si talis est Deus ut nulla gratia, nulla hominum charitate te-
neatur, valeat, etc. Quo fit ut nihil ab Epicuro absurdius dici potuerit. Si is enim talis est ut ait, non utique Deus appellandus est
sed immane monstrum. Quapropter ex animis hominum radicitus
religionem extraxit.

5   Anaximandri autem, sicut testis est Marcus Tullius, opinio est
nativos esse deos, longis intervallis orientes occidentesque. De

Then in fertile showers mighty Father Sky
Falls in the lap of his fruitful wife
And in her great body the great one breeds
All the infant crops.

Anaxagoras believed that God is infinite mind moved of itself. Antisthenes said that though the gods of the people are many, there is one natural maker of everything as a whole. Chrysippus calls God natural force endowed with divine reason, sometimes divine necessity. But Zeno calls him divine and natural law. Xenocrates thought that there are really eight gods.

But certain thinkers either have said that the existence of the gods is unclear to them or have denied it altogether. Protagoras said that he knew nothing at all certain about the gods — whether there is any divinity or not, in other words, and because of this the Athenians banished him from their territory. Diagoras the atheist as well as Theodorus of Cyrene thought that there is no God at all. Epicurus said that God does indeed exist but that he gives nothing, pleases no one, cares for nothing, as Lucretius writes: 4

not won by virtuous service nor touched by wrath.

And Vergil in his poem on Damon:

nor believe that God's concern is mortal men.

And so it is significant that toward the end of book I *On the Nature of the Gods* Cicero says: If God is such that he is touched by no kindness, no affection for humanity, then good riddance to him, and so on. Thus, Epicurus could have said nothing more absurd. If God is as he says, he is by no means to be called God, but a vicious monster. Thus has he ripped religion by the roots from the human soul.

It was Anaximander's opinion, according to Cicero, that the gods come to be by birth, appearing and disappearing at long in- 5

huiusmodi igitur deorum origine eatenus nobis edisserendum est quoad ad ipsam veritatem veniamus. Aegyptii apud se deorum genus primum extitisse gloriantur, utpote qui—sicut infra ostendemus—primi omnium, teste Diodoro Siculo libro suarum *Historiarum* primo, geniti. Duos esse deos et eos aeternos arbitrati sunt, Solem et Lunam, et illum quidem Osirim, hanc Isim certa nominis ratione appellarunt. Verum Lactantius in primo *Divinarum institutionum* volumine Saturnum omnium deorum parentem vocat quod, autore Ennio in *Sacra historia*, ex Ope Iovem, Iunonem, Neptunum, Plutonem, et Glaucam filios suscepisset, qui cum de mortalibus plurimum essent bene meriti dii habiti sunt.

6   Sed multi denique sunt deorum ortus cum singuli populi, ut Perseus Zenonis auditor ait, eos a quibus magna utilitas ad vitae cultum esset inventa—vel gentis et urbis conditores, vel foeminas castitate insignes, seu viros fortissimos—etsi mortali genitos in numero deorum habuerint, ut Aegyptii Isim, Mauri Iubam, Afri Neptunum, Macedones Gabyrum, Persae Mithram, Rhodii et Massagetae Solem, Poeni Uranum, Latini Faunum, Sabini Sabum, Romani Quirinum, Athenae Minervam, Samos Iunonem, Paphos Venerem, Delphos Apollinem, Lemnos Vulcanum, Naxos Liberum, Cretenses Iovem, Armenii Anaitidem, Babylonii et Assyrii Belum, Berecyntes Rheam, et alii alios denique ex hominibus. Et quod dictu post homines natos valde pudendum ac importunissimum est, ex animalibus deos fecerint sibique constituerint.

7   Hinc Graeci, teste Herodoto in primo, non temere sentiebant deos ex hominibus esse ortos. Quare esset admodum difficile deorum originem definire, cum dii ipsi praesertim vanissimi, nullumque eorum genus non mortale fuerit, quandoquidem illi fugas, mortes et vulnera perpessi sunt. Quanto igitur rectius est eo ocu-

tervals. We must explain enough about the origin of these gods so that we can get to the real truth. The Egyptians boast that the race of gods first appeared among them, for they were the first who came to be, according to Diodorus Siculus in the first book of his *Histories* — as we shall show below. They thought that there are two gods, the Sun and the Moon, who are eternal; they called the Sun Osiris and the Moon Isis according to a reliable interpretation of the name. But Lactantius, citing the *Sacred History* of Ennius in the first book of his *Divine Institutes*, calls Saturn the parent of all the gods because he begot Jupiter, Juno, Neptune, Pluto and Glauce as children from Ops, and they were held to be gods because they were great benefactors of mortals.

In short, the gods have many origins because, as Perseus the 6 disciple of Zeno says, each people included among the gods those who discovered something of great usefulness for the improvement of life — either founders of a people or a city, or women famous for chastity, or men of great courage — even though they were born mortal. The Egyptians did so with Isis, the Moors with Juba, the Africans with Neptune, the Macedonians with Gabyrus, the Persians Mithras, the Rhodians and Massagetes Sol, the Carthaginians Uranus, the Latins Faunus, the Sabines Sabus, the Romans Quirinus, Athens Minerva, Samos Juno, Paphos Venus, Delphi Apollo, Lemnos Vulcan, Naxos Liber, the Cretans Jupiter, the Armenians Anaitis, the Babylonians and Assyrians Bel, the Berecynthians Rhea, and others accordingly with other humans. And though it was the most shameful and indecent thing in mankind's history, they made gods of animals and set them up for themselves.

Hence it was not unreasonable that the Greeks, according to 7 Herodotus in book 1, thought that the gods came from men. But as a result it is rather difficult to establish the origin of the gods, since clearly these gods themselves are completely illusory, nor was there any immortal race of gods, seeing that they endured exile,

los et orationem tendere ubi veri Dei sedes est, quem pura, integra, incorrupta et mente et voce venerari debemus.

8   Quamquam de Deo loqui et vera dicere, ut sapientes aiunt, periculosum est: id quoniam oculi intueri nequeunt cum siquidem accessu lucis et fulgore aspectus mortalis, qui nobis divino munere tributus est, prorsus amittitur, neque animo neque ulla mentis acie concipi potest, ut probe admodum Simonides poeta sapientissimus docuit. Nanque cum ab eo, autore Marco Tullio, tyrannus Hiero quaesisset quid aut qualis esset deus, deliberandi causa sibi unum diem postulavit. Cum idem ex eo postridie quaereret, biduum petivit. Cum saepius duplicaret numerum dierum, admiransque Hiero quaereret cur ita faceret. Quia quanto, inquit, diutius considero, tanto mihi res videtur obscurior. Id quod si fecissent philosophi—qui more andabatarum in tenebris versantes tot deliramenta commenti sunt—profecto deum creatorem suum tam impiis sententiis non offendissent. Satius enim prope est vera ignorare quam falsa docere.

9   Semper itaque Deus est unus, qui, teste Macrobio, vices temporum nesciens in uno semper quod adest consistit aevo. Et rerum omnium principium nominatur, qui apud Esaiam ait: Ego sum Deus, ante me non fuit alius, et post me non erit. Cuius, ut Cicero libro *Tusculanarum* primo inquit, nulla est origo, dicente Mose: In principio creavit Deus coelum et terram. Et divus Hieronymus epistola quarta ad Damasum scribens, ait: una est Dei sola natura quae vera est; ad id enim quod subsistit non habet aliunde, sed suum est. Deinde et subdit: Deus solus, qui aeternus est, hoc est, qui exordium non habet, essentiae vere nomen tenet, etc. De quo Vergilius, tametsi longe fuit a veritate, natura tamen ducente, ita libro sexto *Aeneidos* cecinisse videtur:

death and injury. How much better, then, to turn one's eyes and prayers to the place where the true God resides, whom we ought to worship with pure, whole and uncorrupted mind and voice.

And yet to talk about God and speak the truth is, as wise men 8 say, a dangerous business: eyes cannot look on him since mortal sight, given us as a divine gift, utterly vanishes in a flood of light and brilliance, nor can mind or any acuteness of intellect comprehend him, as Simonides, wisest of poets, taught so well. For according to Cicero, when Hiero the tyrant asked Simonides about God's substance or essence, he asked one day to reflect on the question. When the next day brought the same question, he requested two days. And when he kept doubling the number of days, Hiero was puzzled and asked why he did it. The longer I think about it, he said, the more obscure it seems to me. If the philosophers had done this — they who have whirled about in the shadows like blindfolded gladiators and invented so much nonsense — surely they would not have offended God their creator with so many impious teachings. It is almost better to be ignorant of the truth than to teach lies.

God is always one, then. As Macrobius says, he does not experience the changes of time but always goes on existing in the one present time. He is called the beginning of all things, and according to Isaiah, he said: I am God; before me was no other, and after me no one will be. Of him there is no origin, according to Cicero in book 1 of the *Tusculans*, and as Moses says: In the beginning God created heaven and earth. St. Jerome, writing his fourth letter to Damasus, says: There is only one nature in God that is real, for that which subsists takes nothing from outside it, but is itself alone. And then he says: Only God, who is eternal, who has no beginning, in other words, truly possesses the name of essence, and so on. Vergil seems to have been singing about this in the sixth book of the *Aeneid*; as far as he was from the truth, he had nature as his guide:

Principio coelum ac terras camposque liquentes,
Lucentemque globum lunae, titaniaque astra
Spiritus intus alit, totamque infusa per artus
Mens agitat molem, et magno se corpore miscet.

Et Ovidius in primo *Metamorphoseos*:

Ille opifex rerum mundi melioris origo.

Atque reliqua.

10   Et Plato quoque, qui omnium sapientissimus iudicatur, unum
Deum nominat et ab eo hunc mundum esse factum confirmat,
quem, licet nobis ut poetis invocandi mos non sit, hoc tamen de
primis rerum inventoribus opus orsis prosperos successus praestet
omnibus oramus precibus. Quando Deum dictum putant quod
omnia dat commoda hominibus, licet alii nominatum Deum velint
ex verbo graeco θεός quod Deum significat sive quod ei nihil de-
sit, vel ἀπὸ τοῦ θεάομαι quod est video, speculor, aut ἀπὸ τοῦ
δέος, quod dicitur timor. Utrunque divus Ambrosius probat scribens: Deus dicitur quod spectet omnia et timeatur a cunctis.

: II :

De initiis rerum.

1   Etsi nostri operis exordium esse videbatur ut primum de rerum
initiis dissererem, deinde vero ut deorum originem traderem qui
ab iisdem principiis, ut ostendimus, ortum habent, veri tamen Dei
religio me movit fecitque ut ab eo qui ante omnia est hoc opus in-
choare maluerim. Hoc igitur loco aliquanto rationabilius philoso-

From the beginning, sky and land and flowing flats,
Moon's shining globe and the Titan stars
Were fed by spirit inwardly, and mind spread through their
    limbs,
Stirring the whole mass and joining with its great body.

And Ovid in *Metamorphoses* 1 writes:

The maker of all and start of a better world.

And so on.

Plato also, reckoned the wisest of them all, names one being   10
God and confirms that this world was made by him. Though the
custom of invocation belongs to the poets, not to us, we beg him
with all our prayers to grant good success to this work that we
have begun on those who first discovered things. For some think
he is called God because he gives all good things to men, though
others suppose he is named God from the Greek word *theos* which
means God or that which lacks nothing, or from *theaomai*, which
is I see, I observe, or from *deos*, which means fear. St. Ambrose ap-
proves both theories, writing: God is so called because he sees everything and all fear him.

: II :

On the first principles of things.

Though it might seem fitting to open our work with the first prin-   1
ciples of things and then to treat the origin of the gods who, as we
have shown, have their beginning in these same original principles,
yet reverence for the true God, who is before all things, has moved
and compelled me to start this work instead with him. In this

phorum de rerum primordiis sententias, donec ad veritatem me
sensim insinuavero percurremus.

2   Thales itaque Milesius unus ex septem sapientibus aquam (sicut supra demonstravimus) dixit esse initium rerum Deumque
esse eam mentem quae ex aqua cuncta gigneret. Contra Hippasus
Metapontinus et Heraclitus Ephesius, qui propter obscuritatem
scripturae, teste divo Hieronymo *Contra Iovinianum*, a Graecis
σκοτεινός, id est, tenebricosus est appellatus, omnia igne pro-
creari censuerunt. Empedocles vero ex quatuor elementis. Hinc
Lucretius:

> Ex imbri, terra atque anima nascuntur et igne.

Anaximines principium aera opinatur. Metrodorus Chius sempi-
ternum esse universum dicit. Epicurus autem, qui ex Democriti
fontibus suos hortos irrigavit, ponit duo principia, corpus et inane,
omne enim quod est aut continet aut continetur. Corpus vult esse
atomos, id est quasdam minutissimas partes quae τομήν, id est
sectionem, non recipiant. Unde atomi dictae sunt quas Lucretius
his corporibus minutiores dixit quae infusis per fenestram solari-
bus radiis videmus. Inane vero dicit spacium in quo sunt atomi.
Ex his principiis quatuor—ignem, aerem, aquam, terram—vult
creari, et ex illis caetera. Ex quo Maro in Sileno ait:

> Nanque canebat uti magnum per inane coacta
> Semina terrarumque animaeque marisque fuissent
> Et liquidi simul ignis ut his exordia primis
> Omnia et ipse tener mundi concreverit orbis.

3   De philosophorum sententiis haec dicta sint; ea nunc quae sacris continentur literis prodamus ne rationis aut veritatis expertes
esse videamur. Deus igitur ab initio, uti Moses testatur et ex eo Io-

chapter, then, let us proceed a little more methodically through the opinions of the philosophers on the basic principles of things until eventually we reach the truth.

Thales of Miletus, one of the seven wise men, said that water 2 was the first principle of things (as we showed above) and that God was the mind that brought forth all things from water. Hippasus of Metapontum, on the other hand, proposed that everything was begotten from fire, as did Heraclitus of Ephesus, whom the Greeks called *skoteinos* or dark because of the obscurity of his writing, according to St. Jerome *Against Jovinian*. But Empedocles suggested four elements. Hence Lucretius writes:

They are born from rain, earth, wind and fire.

Anaximenes supposes that air is the original principle. Metrodorus of Chios says that the universe is everlasting. But Epicurus, who watered his gardens from the springs of Democritus, establishes two original principles, body and the void, for everything that exists either contains or is contained. He maintains that body is composed of atoms, those tiniest parts that cannot undergo *tomē* or 'cutting.' Whence those things are called atoms that Lucretius said were tinier than the objects we see in the sun's rays pouring through a window. But the space in which the atoms are he calls the void. He maintains that from these first principles are made the four — fire, air, water and earth — and from these four the rest. And thus in his poem on Silenus Vergil says:

For he sang how the seeds alike of earth and air
And sea and flowing fire had congealed through the great void,
And the young sphere of the world itself solidified
And all things had their beginning from these, the first.

Having described the opinions of the philosophers, let us set 3 forth what sacred literature contains lest we seem wanting in truth or reason. As Moses declares and, following him, Josephus plainly

sephus in primo *Antiquitatum Iudaicarum* plenissime edocet, ex nihilo cuncta fecit. Ioannes quoque Evangelista: Omnia per ipsum facta sunt. Id quod Lactantius Firmianus libro *Divinarum institutionum* 2 perspicue demonstrat scribens: Nemo quaerat ex quibus ista materiis tam magna, tam mirifica opera Deus fecerit, omnia enim fecit ex nihilo. Et alibi: Deus autem facit ex eo quod non est. Et in libro *De ira Dei:* Unus est igitur, inquit, princeps et origo rerum, Deus. Et divus Hieronymus: Quis dubitat Deum omnium creatorem? Idem Plato in *Timaeo* sensit et docuit.

4   Atque tale rerum denique omnium verum principium fuit, unde geniti homines multa quae ad usum vitae pertinent deinde adinvenerunt, de quibus cum ego scripturus sim, operaeprecium me fecisse duco primum rerum originem prodidisse, ut intelligatur unde materia orta sit ex qua homines, qui ex eo quod est faciunt, aliquid effinxerint.

: III :

De primo hominum ortu et linguarum varietatis origine;
an Romanis lingua una eademque
Latina communis fuerit necne;
atque ibidem de prima gentium divisione.

1   Prima hominum origo, ut testis est Diodorus, apud praestantissimos viros qui de natura rerum tradiderunt duplex fertur. Quidam enim ingenitum mundum et incorruptibilem et genus hominum sine ullo ortus principio ab aeterno fuisse opinati sunt. Cuius sententiae, teste Censorino, fuerunt Pythagoras Samius, Archytas

teaches in the first book of *Jewish Antiquities*, God made all things from the beginning out of nothing. Also John the Evangelist: All things were made through him. Lactantius Firmianus demonstrates this clearly in book 2 of the *Divine Institutes*, writing: Let no one ask from what materials God made these works, so great and so wondrous, for he made them all from nothing. And elsewhere: But God makes from what is not. And in his book *On the Wrath of God*: Thus, he says, there is one author and origin of things, God. And St. Jerome: Who doubts that God is the creator of all things? Plato perceived the same thing and taught it in his *Timaeus*.

Such, then, was the true original principle of all things. Humans, once they were begotten, eventually devised many things useful for life from this original material. Since I am about to describe these things, I think it was worthwhile for me to have made known the original source of them all, so that one might understand whence came the matter out of which people, who make things from what exists, were to fashion whatever they made.

4

: III :

On the origin of humans and on the source of variety in
languages; whether or not one and the same Latin tongue
was common to the Romans; and also on the original
division of nations.

Diodorus tells us that the foremost authorities on the nature of things viewed the origin of man in two ways. Some held that a world without generation or corruption and a human race with no point of origin had existed from eternity. Pythagoras of Samos, Archytas of Tarentum, Plato the Athenian, Xenocrates and Aris-

1

Tarentinus, Plato Atheniensis, Xenocrates, Aristoteles Stagirites, multique alii Peripatetici idem senserunt, dicentes omnium quae in sempiterno isto mundo fuerunt et futura sunt principium fuisse nullum, sed orbem esse quendam generantium nascentiumque in quo uniuscuiusque geniti initium simul et finis esse videatur.

2   Quidam vero mundum genitum et corruptibilem arbitrati sunt et homines ortus initium tempore esse consecutos. Quapropter Aegyptii apud se a principio primos homines genitos esse ferunt, cum propter soli felicitatem aerisque temperiem tum propter Nilum, qui multa ob limi ubertatem generet et suapte natura nutriat. Nam eodem Diodoro autore, in Thebaidis agro mures gignuntur qua ex re multum stupent homines cum priorem quorundam partem pectore tenus animatam moveri in limo videant, posteriore nondum inchoata sed informi.

3   Verum Psammeticho regnum adepto cum incessisset cupiditas dignoscendi qui revera primi hominum extitissent, ex eo tempore didicerunt Phrygas primos fuisse, se vero secundos. Psammetichus enim, veluti libro secundo testatur Herodotus, cum haud aliter deprehendere posset, duos pueros paulo ante natos inter pecora educandos pastori tradidit, iubens neminem coram eis vocem edere ne alicuius sermonem perdiscerent, ut qualis esset prima vox quae erumperet intelligeretur. Pueri itaque biennio post passa ianua intus enim a capris nutriebantur, ambo porrectis pastori manibus βεκòς, id est, *becus* clamitarunt, quo quidem verbo Phryges constet panem appellare. Tali igitur modo Phrygas primos omnium natos compertum est. Caeterum magna diu inter Aegyptios et Scythas, autore Iustino libro secundo, de generis antiquitate

totle the Stagirite had this view, according to Censorinus, and many other Peripatetics thought the same, saying that of everything that was and will be in this everlasting world there was no beginning, but that of things being born and giving birth there is a certain cycle in which the beginning and end of everything begotten seem to exist simultaneously.

Others considered the world generated and corruptible, however, and thought that people had their beginning in time. Accordingly, the Egyptians reason that the first men were originally begotten among them, as much because of the fertility of the soil and the moderation of the weather as because of the Nile, which brings forth many things from the richness of its mud and nourishes them from its own substance. According to the same Diodorus, the land of the Thebaid produces mice that amaze those who see them moving in the mud, living animals in the front part as far as the breast while the rear part is shapeless and still unformed.

After Psammetichus took over the kingdom and conceived the desire to discover who had really been the first people, from that time they taught that the Phrygians had been first, they themselves second. Since Psammetichus had no other way to find out, as Herodotus says in his second book, he handed over two newborn boys to a shepherd to be raised among his flocks, commanding that no one utter a sound in their presence lest they learn anyone's speech; in this way one might observe what sort of sound would first escape their lips. Two years passed until one day the shepherd opened the door where his goats were suckling the boys, and both held out their hands to him and bawled out *bekos* or *becus*, the word the Phrygians are known to use for bread. By such means it was discovered that the Phrygians came to be before any other people. On the other hand, according to Justinus in his second book, there was long and great contention between the Egyp-

contentio fuit, in quo certamine superatis Aegyptiis Scythae antiquiores visi sunt.

4   Aethiopes itidem ferunt primos hominum omnium creatos esse, et eius rei coniecturam faciunt quod non aliunde homines in eam regionem accesserint sed in ipsa geniti merito indigites omnium consensu appellentur, de quibus Diodorus libro quarto ita disserit: Et equidem simile veri est eos qui sub meridiem habitant primos e terra fuisse homines genitos, nam solis calore terram quae humida est arefaciente atque omnibus vitam dante, decens fuit locum soli propinquiorem primo naturam animantium tulisse.

5   Hinc Anaximander Milesius ex aqua terraque calefactis homines exortos esse tradit. Empedocles fere idem confirmat, ait enim membra singula ex terra quasi praegnante passim edita, deinde coisse et effecisse solidi hominis materiam igni simul et humori permistam. Democritus Abderites ex aqua limoque primum homines creatos esse dicit. Zeno autem Citiaeus principium humano generi ex novo mundo constitutum putavit primosque homines ex solo adminiculo divini ignis, id est, Dei providentia genitos. Poetae vero fingunt homines primum aut Promethei molli luto esse formatos aut Deucalionis Pyrrhaeque ex duris lapidibus natos. Vergilius:

> quo tempore primum
> Deucalion vacuum lapides iactavit in orbem
> Unde homines nati durum genus.

Verum ne huiusmodi ineptias referendo probare videamur, ea quae sacris continentur literis ac longe veriora sunt aperiamus.

6   Primus igitur hominum ortus apud Iudaeos fuit. Deus enim— divum pater atque hominum rex, ut poeta ait—perfecto mundo (auctore Iosepho in primo *Antiquitatum* volumine ut etiam in veteri

tians and Scythians about antiquity of race; when the Egyptians lost this argument, the Scythians were seen to be the older.

Likewise they say that the Ethiopians were the first of all peo-   4
ple created, and they draw this conclusion from the fact that people did not enter their region from elsewhere but emerged in that very place and by common consent deserve to be called indigenous. Diodorus speaks thus of them in book [3]: Surely it is probable that those who dwell beneath the southern sun were the first people begotten from the earth, for with the heat of the sun drying out the damp soil and giving life to all things, it was proper that a place nearer the sun should have first brought forth the substance of living things.

Hence Anaximander of Miletus teaches that people arose from   5
warm water and earth. Empedocles asserts almost the same thing, for he says that each limb was produced separately out of the earth as if it were pregnant; then they joined together and formed the fabric of a whole person, with fire and water mixed together. Democritus of Abdera says that people were originally created from water and mud. Zeno of Citium, however, thought that the human species arose from a new world and that the first people were begotten by the help of the divine fire alone, by the providence of God, in other words. The poets imagine that the first people were either formed of the soft mud of Prometheus or born of the hard stones of Deucalion and Pyrrha, as Vergil writes:

> from the first times when
> Deucalion threw stones into a vacant world
> And from them were born humans — that hardy race.

But by rehearsing such trifles we may seem to approve them, so let us disclose what sacred literature contains since it is truer by far.

Accordingly, the first origin of mankind was among the Jews,   6
for God — father of gods and king of men, as the poet says — made Adam, the first human of all, from the mud after he had finished

45

est instrumento) Adam primum omnium ex limo hominem fecit, dicente etiam Ovidio:

Natus homo est, sive hunc divino semine fecit
Ille opifex rerum, etc.

Et divo Hieronymo epistola 49: Fabricatur homo de limo. Et alibi: Deus nos ad imaginem sui tales condidit. Quare Lactantius in 6 scienter hominem Dei simulacrum appellat. Item *De opificio Dei:* Vas est, inquit, quodam modo fictile quo animus, id est homo ipse verus, continetur, et quidem non a Prometheo fictum, ut poetae loquuntur, sed a summo illo rerum conditore et artifice Deo. Et Cicero hoc idem tradidit, quamvis expers coelestium literarum, in primo *De legibus* sic scribens: Hoc animal providum, sagax, multiplex, acutum, memor, plenum rationis et consilii quem vocamus hominem praeclara quadam conditione generatum esse a summo Deo, solus enim est ex tot animantium generibus atque naturis particeps rationis et cogitationis cum caetera sint omnia expertia.

7   Adam itaque primus a Deo creatus postquam illius mandatum fregit (uti divo Hieronymo placet) ducta in matrimonium Eva totius futuri generis autor fuit. Idem Hieronymus: Duos homines ab exordio fecit Deus ex quibus totius humani generis sylva descendit. Ita deinceps homines tanquam omnis rei expertes nulloque subsidio fulti duram agebant vitam, sed paulatim, quemadmodum Vergilius ait, varias meditando extuderunt artes, nam multarum rerum notitia percepta necessitate compulsi, brevi tempore caeteras vitae hominum commoditates adinvenerunt. Tunc igitur variae venere artes, quando, sicut idem poeta canit:

labor omnia vincit
Improbus et duris urgens in rebus egestas.

with the world, according to Josephus in the first book of the *Antiquities* and the Old Testament as well. Even Ovid says that:

> Man was born: either made from the divine seed
> of the maker of things [etc.]

In letter [59] St. Jerome also writes: Man is fashioned from mud. And elsewhere: God made such creatures as us in his own image. This is why Lactantius in book 6 wisely calls man a likeness of God. In *The Workmanship of God* he also says: The soul, the true person, is contained in a kind of earthen vessel, and in fact it was not made by Prometheus, as the poets say, but by God himself, the greatest workman and maker of things. And Cicero, though he was without heavenly learning, taught the same thing, writing in his first book *On the Laws*: This animal that we call human — prudent, shrewd, versatile, acute, strong of memory, full of reason and counsel — was produced by almighty God in an excellent state, for he alone of so many living kinds and species shares in reason and thought while all the others lack them.

And so Adam was the first human created by God. After he 7 broke God's commandment (as St. Jerome explains it), he took Eve in matrimony and became the founder of the whole species to come. Jerome also writes: God made two people in the beginning and from them descended the mass of the whole human race. And then, inasmuch as they had nothing, no help to sustain them, people led a hard life. But little by little, as Vergil says, they worked out various arts by thinking things through, for they came to understand a great deal when forced by necessity, and in a short time they discovered what else was helpful to human life. In this way arose the various arts because, as the same poet sings,

> Work — pitiless — always wins,
> And want, pushing when things go hard.

8   Caeterum cum Deus, ut docuimus, hominem fecerit illique in
ore linguam incluserit quae sola animi interpres vocem motibus
variis in verba distinguit, non immerito quispiam mirabitur unde
tanta homini sermonis varietas innata sit, ut quot orbis regiones
sunt totidem hominum linguae sint. Cuius rei originem non prae-
tereundam putavi. Cum enim Nemroth filius Cham, filii Noe,
post diluvium homines a Dei timore aquarum vim formidantes
avocare conaretur, spem suam in propria virtute ponendam ratus,
turrim (velut alibi apposite dicemus) altissimam aedificandam sua-
debat quam aquae superare non possent. Iis itaque iam incoepto
opere ita insanientibus, Deus linguam divisit, ut per multas abso-
nasque voces intellectu inter se carerent. Haec igitur tot linguarum
quibus etiam nunc homines utuntur varietatis origo est, autor Iosephus in primo *Antiquitatum*.

9   At hic non abs re videtur esse ut aliquid dicatur de antiqua inter doctos controversia, quaerentes utrum Romani generatim latine loquuti sint an duplicem habuerint linguam, quemadmodum
nos et Graeci ac aliae gentes ad hodiernum diem habemus, qui alteram vulgarem et vernaculam, alteram latinam et atticam appellamus. Et ne in re meo iudicio perspicua laboremus, eam ex Cicerone teste locupletissimo planam faciemus. Is enim in libro tertio
De oratore ait certam fuisse Romani generis urbisque propriam vocem, idque probat exemplo Laeliae mulieris, quae ita loqueretur ut
qui eam audiret sibi Plautum aut Nevium audire videretur. Sed ut
ne quispiam putaret Laeliam alteram linguam didicisse, id est latinam, alteram domi ab ineunte aetate patrio sermone imbibisse,
paulo inferius inquit: Nemo enim unquam est oratorem quod latine loqueretur admiratus; si aliter irridebant. Item *De perfecto oratore*: In versu quidem theatra tota exclamant si fuerit una syllaba
aut brevior aut longior. Et libro I *Tusculanarum*: Frequens enim

Now since God made man, as we have shown, and put in his   8
mouth a tongue which, as sole interpreter of his mind, separated
sound into words by moving in various ways, one may rightly
wonder how so much variety has grown up in human speech, giving people as many tongues as the globe has regions. It seemed to
me that the origin of this state of affairs should not be overlooked.
When Nemroth, son of Ham, the son of Noah, undertook after
the deluge to turn people who dreaded the power of the waters
away from the fear of God, he meant that they should rest their
hopes on their own strength, and he persuaded them to build a
tower (described elsewhere in a suitable place) so lofty that the waters could not rise above it. Then, when they were already madly
involved in the work they had started, God divided language, so
that they could not understand one another because their tongues
were many and discordant. This, then, is the origin of the variety
of the many languages that people use even now, according to
Josephus in book 1 of the *Antiquities*.

It will not seem beside the point to say something here about   9
an old scholarly controversy — whether the Romans in their several
groups all spoke Latin or divided their language like our speech
and that of the Greeks and other peoples down to this day, calling
the one tongue vulgar or vernacular, the other Latin or Attic. Not
to bother with my opinion in a clear case, let us settle the issue
with a most trustworthy witness, Cicero, who says in the third
book *On the Orator* that the Roman people and city had their own
particular speech. He proves it with the example of the woman
Laelia, who spoke so that one who heard her seemed to be listen-
ing to Plautus or Naevius. Lest anyone think that Laelia had
learned one language, Latin, and drunk in another from an early
age with her family's conversation at home, he says a little further
on: Indeed, no one has ever admired an orator for speaking good
Latin; anything else and they would laugh at him. Also in *The Perfect Orator*: Whole theaters cry out in verse if a single syllable is too

49

consessus theatri, in quo sunt mulierculae et pueri, movetur audiens tam grande carmen. Haec ille. Ex quo satis patet unam
linguam et eam quidem Latinam omnibus communem fuisse,
quando pueri et mulierculae latine sciebant.

10   Verum ille erat literarum peritus qui verborum delectum habere
ac eum recto aurium iudicio ponderare scivisset, id quod sine literis fieri non poterat, nam omnes Romanos latine locutos non item
literas scisse ex eiusdem quoque testimonio liquet, qui in *Bruto* Titum Pomponium Atticum ita loquentem facit: Vides elocutionem
emendatam latinam cuius penes quos laus adhuc fuit non fuit rationis aut scientiae sed quasi bonae consuetudinis. Et subiicit: Titum Flaminium, qui cum Quinto Metello consul fuit, pueri vidimus; existimabatur bene latine sed literas nesciebat. Est igitur
quisquam qui, si ista consideraverit a principe latinitatis dicta,
possit suspicari perinde Romanis non unam fuisse linguam ac nobis est? Nanque ut apud Romanos illi minus pure et ornate loque-
bantur qui extra urbem vixissent, ita apud Latinos partim barba-
ries a feris populis qui Italiam aliquando occuparant profecta,
partim vetustas sermonem domesticum iampridem infuscaverat.

11   Ad prima redeo. Idem Iosephus inde quoque factum prodit ut
post eiusmodi linguarum discrimen ex Noe pronepotibus et ex iis
qui ab illis orti sunt, inter se quamprimum divisi, alii alias terrarum oras velut in colonias profecti occuparint, atque ita secutum
ut non solum gentes populique quorum conditores fuissent ab eorum sint nominibus appellati sed pleraeque etiam urbes inde no-
minatae. Caeterum Graeci postea barbaram vocem abhorrentes
aut illa ex integro, ut idem ait, immutarunt aut magna ex parte in-
versa ut a prisca voce multum discreparent effecerunt. Probat tamen adhuc quaedam durare quae veteri opinioni consentiant, id
est, in Phoenicia Tyrum, Tharsum in Cilicia, Cappadoces, Paphla-
gonas, Pamphylios, Phryges, Palaestinos, Cilices, Sabaeos, Syros,

long or too short. And in book 1 of the *Tusculans:* Hearing so grand a poem, the crowded audience in the theater becomes excited, boys and mere women among them. This is what Cicero says, making it clear enough that that was one language common to all—Latin—if even boys and women knew it well.

But one who was trained in letters knew how to choose his words and had a good ear for judging them, which an unlettered person could not do, for not all Romans who spoke Latin were lettered. This is clear from what Cicero has Titus Pomponius Atticus say in the *Brutus:* The perfect Latin diction so much esteemed in them came, you see, not from method or learning but as if from good habit. And then he adds: As boys we knew Titus Flaminius, who was consul with Quintus Metellus; his Latin was considered good, but he was unlettered. Is there anyone, then, after reflecting on these statements by the prince of Latinity, who could believe that the Romans did not have the same language that we know? For indeed, just as those Romans who lived outside the city spoke less purely and elegantly, so among the Latin races barbarism came partly from the savage peoples who once occupied Italy, partly because time had long since obscured the native speech.

Now back to my main topic. The same Josephus next reports that after this division of tongues some of Noah's grandsons and their descendants, having separated from one another as soon as possible, set off in colonies to occupy different regions of the earth. Thus it followed not only that the races and peoples of which they were founders were called by their names but also that many cities were named in this way. But afterwards the Greeks, who abhorred barbarian speech, either changed these names completely, as Josephus says, or greatly altered them to sound much unlike their originals. He proves, however, that some still remain and conform to ancient usage: Tyre in Phoenicia, Tarsus in Cilicia, the Cappadocians, the Paphlagonians, the Pamphylians, Phrygians, Palestin-

et ad meridiem Aegyptios, Libes et Mauros. Adiicit etiam Medos, Armenios, et Iberas, quae sane nomina sint ab ipsarum gentium conditoribus qui iidem et Hebraei fuerunt et ab Noe prognati.

12 Eusebius etiam docet idem, ita *Chronicorum libro* scribens: Filii Noe Sem, Cham et Iaphet. Filii Sem Elam, unde Elamitae; Assur, unde Assyrii; Arphaxad, unde Arabi; Lud, unde Lydi; Aram, unde Syrii; Aramei autem Syriace dicuntur filii Aram. Filii Cham Chus, unde Aethiopes; Mestre, unde Aegyptii; Furfur, unde Aethiopum gens; Chanaam, Chananei. Filii autem Chus Saba, unde Sabaei dicti; Evilat, gens Evilea. Filius Iaphet Gomer, filius Gomer Asconez, unde gentes Gothicae. Haec ille. Sicut item aequum est credere ab illis alias nationes profectas quae deinde orbem ipsum multitudine oppleverint.

: IV :

De origine coniugii et vario apud gentes usu; et qui in propatulo pecudum more coirent; ac quis liceret ante virum novam inire nuptam; et ibidem de divortii initio ac qui in matrimonio veterum ritus.

1 Deus simul atque mundo caeterisque rebus summam manum imposuerat, ut Moses tradit, postremo hominem finxit propter quem haud dubie ipsum mundum, sicut Marcus Tullius in 2 *De natura deorum* probe docet, cunctaque animalia fecerat. Utrunque etiam testatur Ovidius in primo *Metamorphoseon* dicens:

ians, Cilicians, Sabaeans, Syrians, and to the south, the Egyptians, Lybians and Moors. He also adds the Medes, Armenians and Iberians, who surely were named after the founders of those nations who were the same as the Hebrews and descendants of Noah.

Eusebius teaches this too, writing as follows in his *Book of* 12 *Chronicles:* the sons of Noah were Sem, Cham, and Japhet. The sons of Sem were Elam, from whom came the Elamites; Assur, whence the Assyrians; Arphaxad, whence the Arabians; Lud, the Lydians; Aram, the Syrians, called in Syriac Aramaeans or sons of Aram. The sons of Cham were Chus, whence the Ethiopians; Mestre, whence the Egyptians; Furfur, whence a tribe of Ethiopians; Chanaan, whence the Canaanites. And the sons of Chus were Saba, after whom the Sabaeans were named, and Evilat, whence the Evilean race. Gomer was the son of Japhet, Asconez the son of Gomer, from whom came the Gothic races. This is what Eusebius says. And it is reasonable to believe that the rest of the nations whose numbers later filled the globe also came from these people.

: IV :

On the origin of marriage and its various ethnic forms; on those who copulate in the open like cattle; who was allowed to take the bride before the husband; and also on the origin of divorce and on ancient marriage customs.

As soon as God had given the world and other creatures the final 1 touch, as Moses relates, at last he fashioned man for whose sake, certainly, he had made the world and all living things, as Cicero properly teaches in book 2 *On the Nature of the Gods.* Ovid also vouches for both these facts in the first book of the *Metamorphoses,* saying:

Sanctius his animal mentisque capacius altae
Deerat adhuc et quod dominari in caetera posset,
Natus homo est.

Et Cicero in primo libro *De legibus* ait: Nunc quoniam hominem, quod principium reliquarum rerum esse voluit, generavit et ornavit Deus. Et Iosephus: Deus hominem omnium dominum fecit. Plinius quoque: Principium iure tribuetur homini, cuius causa videtur cuncta alia genuisse natura. Etenim, uti eleganter idem Cicero inquit, quis coelum suspicit nisi homo? Quis solem, quis astra, quis opera Dei miratur nisi homo? Terrenorum item commodorum in quo est dominatus nisi in homine? Nam nos terram colimus, ex ea fructum capimus, nos navigamus mare, nos pisces, nos volatilia, nos quadrupedes in potestate habemus. Cuncta igitur propter hominem Deus fecit cum usui hominum omnia cesserint.

2   Proinde ad propagandum humanum genus ut una non interiret aetate necessum erat et foeminam formare et eam deinde viro ne more ferarum degerent sacris quibusdam conubii vinculis adiungere. Quare Deus (quae finxerint fabulae postea subiiciam) Adam, autore Iosepho in primo *Antiquitatum,* quem primum fecerat hominem antequam — sicut quidam volunt — peccaret, confestim Evam ad ipsius hominis exemplar confictam matrimonio copulavit ut duo inter se permisti sexus propagare sobolem possent et omnem terram multitudine opplere. Divus autem Hieronymus in epistola ad Eustochium de virginitate servanda id a Deo factum tradit postquam Adam et Eva eius mandatum sunt transgressi, sic scribens: Eva in paradiso virgo fuit; post pelliceas tunicas initium sumpsit nuptiarum. Item in libro *Contra Iovinianum:* ac inquit de Adam quidem et Eva illud dicendum, quod in paradiso ante offensam virgines fuerint, post peccatum et extra paradisum statim nuptiae. Atque haec vera coniugii origo.

Still missing was a beast that could think high thoughts
And strive to rule the rest. So man was made.

And in the first book *On the Laws* Cicero says: Now, seeing that he had begotten man and equipped him, he wished him to have precedence over all other things. And Josephus: God made man the lord of all. Also Pliny: Precedence is rightly granted man, for whose sake nature seems to have produced all else. And truly, as Cicero neatly puts it, who but man looks up at heaven? Who wonders at the sun, the stars, the works of God but man? And in whom but man is there dominion over the good things of the earth? For we till its soil, take its fruit, sail its waters, and have in our power fish, flying things and four-footed beasts. So God made all things for man's sake since all are for man to use.

Accordingly it was necessary to fashion woman so that the human race might be propagated and not die out in one generation and, lest they live like beasts, to join her to man in certain sacred bonds of marriage. Later I will add what the myths say of this, but here I will tell what Josephus writes in the first book of the *Antiquities*. God made Adam the first man and then — as some suppose — before Adam sinned he fashioned Eve in the form of this very man and brought the two together in matrimony so that they might beget children in sexual union and fill the whole earth with their number. But St. Jerome in his letter to Eustochium on the preservation of virginity teaches that God did this after Adam and Eve had broken his commandment, writing thus: In paradise Eve was a virgin; she entered into the state of marriage after she put on garments made of skins. Also in his book *Against Jovinian* he says: This should be said about Adam and Eve, that in paradise before they sinned they were virgins, but outside and after the sin, marital relations began right away. And this is the true origin of marriage.

3   Caeterum antiquitas autore Trogo tradidit Cecropem, Atheniensium regem ante Deucalionis tempora, matrimonium constituisse, propter quod hunc bifrontem prodidere.

4   Verumenimvero haud unum omnes matrimonii foedus faciebant nec uno modo servabant; porro Numidae, Mauri, Aegyptii,
Indi, Hebraei, Persae, Garamantes, Parthi, Taxili, Nasamones et
Thraces atque omnes pene barbari singuli pro opibus quisque
quam plurimas uxores, alii denas, alii plures habebant. Scythae,
Agathyrsi, Scoti Britanniae populi, Attici promiscuas uxores et liberos ex Platonis republica communes habere et more pecudum
lascive coire. Massagetae singuli singulas ducebant uxores sed
communiter utebantur, uti apud Britannos etiam, teste Caesare,
fieri consuevit. Apud Arabes qui Felicem incolunt Arabiam consuetudo erat ut una omnibus consanguineis uxor esset. Ex iis
enim, teste Strabone libro 16 *Geographiae*, qui primus ingrediebatur
posito pro foribus baculo (nam baculum ex more quisque gerebat)
cum ea coibat, ipsa tamen cum natu grandiore noctes agebat.
Quapropter omnes omnium erant fratres. Adulter apud eos capitis
damnabatur qui ex eo deprehendebatur quod alius generis esset.

5   Hoc memoria dignum aliquando accidit. Erat enim cuiusdam
regis filia, mira quidem pulchritudine, cui quindecim erant fratres
qui eius omnes aeque amore flagrabant, propterea alius sub alium
continenter ad eam ingrediebatur. Illa autem assiduo coitu iam de-
fessa, rem huiusmodi commenta est: Fecit enim surculos non
utique fratrum surculis absimiles, ac statim ut quispiam exibat,
surculum aliquem similem ante ianuam ponebat, quo fratres qui
deinceps sequebantur, surculum pro foribus fixum cernentes, eo-

According to Trogus the ancients taught otherwise—that Cecrops, king of the Athenians before the time of Deucalion, established matrimony, because of which they said that he had two faces. 3

In truth, not everyone made just one marriage contract, nor did all keep it in just the same way. No, the Numidians, Moors, Egyptians, Indians, Hebrews, Persians, Garamantes, Parthians, Taxili, Nasamones, Thracians and almost all the barbarians each took as many wives as they could afford, some ten apiece, others more. The Scythians, the Agathyrsi, the British people called Scots and the Athenians had their wives promiscuously and their children in common, as in Plato's republic, and they commingled wantonly like cattle. Each of the Massagetes took his own wife, but they enjoyed them communally, as was also the custom among the Britons, according to Caesar. Among the Arabs who dwell in Arabia Felix it was the custom to have one wife for all the kindred. According to Strabo, in book 16 of the *Geography*, the one who first entered left his staff (by custom they all carried one) outside the woman's door while copulating with her, even though she spent her nights with the one who was senior. Thus, all of them were each other's brothers. They condemned an adulterer to death if he was found to be of another clan. 4

The following notable incident once occurred. One of their kings had a daughter of wondrous beauty, and she had fifteen brothers, all of them alike passionately in love with her, so they would come to her continually, one after the other. Presently, when the unremitting sex wore her out, she devised the following solution for her problem: She prepared some sticks resembling those her brothers carried, and as soon as one of them left, she put a stick like his in front of her door, so that the brothers who came after him, seeing a stick planted in front of the door, would be stopped and not go in, thinking that one of them was inside. But one day when they were all together in the marketplace, one of 5

rumque aliquem intus esse arbitrantes ab ingressu arcerentur. Verum cum aliquando omnes in foro essent, unus ad fores accessit, et cum baculum vidisset suspicatus adulterum intus esse; sciebat enim se omnes fratres in foro reliquisse. Currens ad patrem, sororem stupri accusavit, sed cognita re eam falso criminari convictus est.

6   Babylonii et Assyrii uxores ex publica auctione emebant, quod hodie apud Arabes ac Saracenos servatur. Cantabri uxoribus dotes dabant. Alii cum sanguine coniunctis coibant, praesertim cum matribus et sororibus, quas etiam in matrimonium ducebant, ut Anthropophagi, Athenienses, Medi, Magi et Aethiopum quidam atque Arabes. Apud Nasamones et Augylas Libyae populos moris erat cum quis primum duxisset uxorem, ut sponsa prima nocte cum singulis convivis coiret Veneris gratia, post perpetuo castitatem servaret. Adyrmachidae, Poenorum populi qui ad Aegyptum pertinent, teste Herodoto libro 4, soliti erant virgines nupturas regi exhibere, qui quam vellet primus vitiaret.

7   Fuit idem mos apud Scotos ut novam nuptam dominus loci ante virum comprimeret. Quod nempe institutum post homines Christianos natos turpissimum, Malcolmus tertius, eorum rex princeps optimus, sustulit circiter annum salutis humanae MXC, constituitque ut nubentes pudicitiae redimendae causa locorum dominis numum aureum penderent, id quod hodie etiam servatur. Lydorum filiae eatenus vulgato corpore quaestum faciebant quoad sibi dotem comparassent, deinde nubebant. Alii demum sine coniugibus degere, ut quidam Thraces qui *ctistae*, id est, creatores vocantur, et Esseni, tertium apud Iudaeos philosophorum genus. Ex his autem in propatulo pecudum more concumbebant — Indi, Massagetae, Nasamones et Anthropophagi.

8   Sane hinc videre licet quam turpiter isti omnes libidini frena laxarent. Sed quid mirum est gentes huiusmodi quae lumine carebant, hoc est, Deum ignorabant, libidine flagrantes in omne nefas

them went up to her doorway, and when he saw the staff he assumed there was an adulterer inside for he knew that he had left all his brothers in the marketplace. Running to his father, he accused his sister of whoring, but when the case was investigated he was convicted of bringing false charges against her.

The Babylonians and Assyrians bought their wives at public 6 auction, as the Arabs and Saracens still do today. The Cantabrians gave dowries to their wives. Others had sex with blood relatives, particularly their mothers and sisters, and even married them: examples are the Man-eaters, Medes, Magi, also some Ethiopians and the Arabs. Among the Nasamones and Augylans, peoples of Libya, it was the custom that when one of them took a wife, the bride should spend the first night with each of the wedding guests as a tribute to Venus, and afterward she preserved her chastity forever. The Adyrmachidae, a Punic people who live near Egypt, according to Herodotus in book 4, used to show their king the girls they were about to marry, and he first would deflower the one he wanted.

The Scots had the same custom: the lord of the manor would 7 lie with the new bride before her husband. Because this practice was obviously the most disgraceful thing in Christian memory, King Malcolm III, their greatest leader, did away with it around the year 1090, and he established that those marrying should pay a gold coin to their local lords as the price of virtue, as they still do today. The daughters of the Lydians put their bodies on the market until they raised a dowry, and then they married. Finally, others lived without wives, as did certain Thracians, called *ctistae* or creators, and the Essenes, the third group of philosophers among the Jews. But some lay together in the open like cattle — Indians, Massagetes, Nasamones and Man-eaters.

They all gave free rein to lust, disgracefully, as one can plainly 8 see. But is it any wonder that such people, lacking the light and not knowing God, burned with lust and fell madly into every

ruisse, nulloque discrimine omne facinus factu dictuve pudendum ac foedum edidisse? Nos igitur multo profecto iis feliciores sumus, quibus ipse Deus, teste Hieronymo *Contra Iovinianum* et ad Eustochium de virginitate servanda, illud magnum matrimonii foedus constituit, quod nunc homines Christiana religione imbuti, una duntaxat uxore contenti, longe mehercle sanctius servant atque venerantur quam olim Hebraei, qui tametsi primi a Deo id acceperunt, uxorum tamen multitudine (plures enim ut diximus habebant) foede turpificabant. Id tamen qua ratione apud illos factum aliquando fuerit docebimus in 5 huius operis volumine cum de re Christiana agetur, ibidemque declarabitur quotus olim ac nunc propinquitatis gradus sit nubentibus interdictus.

9 Sed domum revertamur. Romanorum quoque inviolatum prorsus matrimonium fuisset si divortium non habuisset. Quod licet in causa esset quamobrem matronae constantius pudicitiam tuerentur, id tamen non tam facile religio sancta concedit. Primus enim Spurius Carvilius, Dionysio Halicarnasseo libro secundo et Plutarcho in *Vita* Romuli autoribus, anno urbis conditae DXXIII Marco Pomponio II Gaio Papyrio consulibus, cum uxore sterilitatis causa divortium fecit. Hinc sane cognoscere licet iam inde ab initio apud Romanos foedus matrimonii sanctissimum fuisse quando tandiu inviolatum permansit. Et Spurius Carvilius qui quanquam coram censoribus iuratus se matrimonium liberorum tantum causa colere, illud violarat postea ob id facinus semper a populo male audivit.

10 Quod ex Mosis decretis tralatitium esse constat qui primus divortii autor fuit, ut extat in Deuteronomio capite 24, Moses enim videns, autore Hieronymo, Iudaeorum alios avaritia, alios molestia domestica, alios libidine commotos suas uxores iniuria et aliquando morte afficere, quo sibi integrum foret novas ducere uxores

wickedness or that they indiscriminately committed every crime, every deed shameful to do and loathsome to describe? We are indeed much more fortunate than they: According to Jerome's *Against Jovinian* and his letter to Eustochium on preserving virginity, since God himself has established that great covenant of matrimony for us, men instructed in the Christian religion, content with one wife only, now preserve and honor this contract far more solemnly, I daresay, than the Hebrews used to do. Even though they were the first to receive the contract from God, they carried on scandalously with a multitude of wives (for they took several, as we have said). The reason why they sometimes did so we will discuss in book 5 of this volume when we deal with Christian affairs, and in the same place we will show how many degrees of relationship are forbidden in marriage, now and in the past.

But let us turn homeward. Roman matrimony would also have 9 been entirely inviolable if there had been no divorce in it. Though divorce makes married women more constant in defending their virtue, holy religion does not on that account allow it so easily. The first to divorce his wife, for reason of sterility, was Spurius Carvilius, in the consulate of Marcus Pomponius (for the second time) and Gaius Papirius, AUC 523, according to Dionysius of Halicarnassus in book 2 and Plutarch in the *Life* of Romulus. Hence, one can surely agree that the bond of matrimony was most sacred among the Romans from the very beginning since it remained inviolate for so long a time. As for Spurius Carvilius, though he swore before the Censors that he wanted marriage only for the sake of children, after he had violated it the people thought poorly of him because he had committed such villainy.

The identity of the first author of divorce has clearly been 10 handed down in the laws of Moses, as one can see in Deuteronomy, chapter 24. For according to Jerome, when Moses saw that the Jews hurt their wives and sometimes killed them when driven by greed or lust or trouble at home, after which they would be free

aut ditiores, pulchriores iunioresve, ut domesticae quieti consuleret facultatem illis dedit divortii faciendi cum prioribus uxoribus. Sed voluit ut vir daret uxori ita reiectae libellum divortii, in quo, teste Iosepho libro *Iudaicae antiquitatis* 4, in hanc ferme sententiam inscriptum esset: promitto me non repetiturum te; quo sic mulier posset cuivis rursum nubere. Nec de ea re aliter est lege sancitum ne fieret contra illud quod Deus copulavit, homo non separet. Ac ita permissu Mosis non iussu divortium primum apud Iudaeos factum constat.

11   Testatur utrunque Christus apud Matthaeum caput 19: Quod Deus copulavit, homo non separet. Et subiicit: Moses ad duritiam cordis vestri permisit vobis repudiare uxores vestras, caeterum ab initio non fuit sic. Ad duritiam dixit quod saevitiam exercuerint in uxores, quas nimis ferum ac durum sit non diligere. Istuc exin divortium minime respuendum Christus sanxit si stupri tantum causa factum esset. Atque haec de divortii Iudaeorum Romanorumque primordio dicere habui. Sed differebant tamen quod apud Hebraeos non erat mutuum divortii ius, sed soli marito fas erat ab uxore discedere. Contra apud Romanos utrique licebat id facere.

12   Sed age, iam dicamus qui in matrimonio fuerint veterum ritus, quique adhuc durent. Apud Romanos, teste Festo, patrimi et matrimi pueri tres (id est, qui patrem et matrem haberent) nubentem ducebant, unus qui facem ex alba spina praeferret (nam noctu, ut ait Plutarchus in *Problematis*, nubebant), duo qui sponsam tenerent. Et ea fax vel Cereris honore praeferebatur ut quemadmodum Ceres mortales alit quae terrae mater ac cunctarum frugum creatrix habetur, ita nova nupta materfamilias post facta filios nutriret. Quod cum alibi hodie tum praecipue in Anglia servatur ut duo pueri velut paranymphi, id est, auspices qui olim pro nuptiis cele-

to marry new wives — wealthier, fairer, younger — he made it possible for them to divorce their first wives for the sake of domestic peace. But he determined that a man should give the wife he rejected a bill of divorce, which, according to Josephus in the fourth book of *Jewish Antiquities*, would be worded to this effect: I promise that I will not seek after you again. And so the woman could remarry whom she would. No other law has been established in this matter to contradict the rule that what God has joined together no man may put asunder. And so it is clear that it was by permission of Moses, not by his command, that divorce first appeared among the Jews.

In Matthew 19, Christ bears witness to both these facts: what 11 God has joined together let no man put asunder. And he goes on: Moses permitted you to put away your wives because of your hardness of heart, but it was not so from the beginning. 'Hardness' he said because they were brutal to their wives, whom it is harsh and cruel not to cherish. On this question Christ next ordained that divorce was not to be rejected if it was done only because of lewdness. And this is what I have to say about the origin of divorce among the Jews and Romans. There was this difference, however, that among the Hebrews there was no mutual right of divorce; it was legal only for the husband to leave his wife. Among the Romans, on the other hand, it was permitted to both.

But now let us move on to discuss the matrimonial customs of 12 the ancients, which survive even now. Among the Romans, according to Festus, three boys called *patrimi et matrimi* (having a mother and father, that is) brought the bride in, one of them walked ahead carrying a torch of hawthorn (for they married at night, as Plutarch says in the *Problems*), while the other two held the bride. They carried the torch in honor of Ceres, so that the new bride would care for her sons after she became mother of a family, as Ceres cares for mortals and is considered earth-mother and begetter of all growing things. Where this custom is honored

brandis auspicia capiebant, nubentem ad templum ubi ei et marito
sacerdos benedicat et inde domum duo viri deducant, et tertius
loco facis vasculum aureum vel argenteum praeferat. Spicea item
corona sponsa redimita caput praesertim ruri ducitur vel manu ge-
rit ipsam coronam, seu dum ingreditur domum boni ominis causa
super eius caput iacitur triticum, quasi inde consecutura sit foecunditas.

13 Interim autem Talassii nomen saepe invocabatur velut virginita-
tis assertoris quod ei in raptu Sabinarum virgo obtigisset aut quod
matresfamilias sic operum et lanificii admonerentur per Talassii
vocem qui dicitur calathus ad id aptus. Inde factum quoque est,
autore Plutarcho et Plinio, ut sponsae colum lana comptam cum
fuso secum ferrent, quod in Venetia regione Italiae adhuc durat.
Dabantur praeterea ante viri congressum ignis et aqua attingenda
quod iis elementis purgatio fieret (sicut alio loco dicetur) per hoc
significando castam ac puram futuram. Item sponsae introductae
potio factitia porrigebatur degustanda. Ovidius in *Fastis*:

Nec pigeat tritum niveo cum lacte papaver
  Sumere et expressis mella liquata favis.
Cum primum cupido Venus est deducta marito
  Hoc bibit, ex illo tempore nupta fuit.

Pro his omnibus nunc Romae mel tantum degustandum tradunt.
Sic sponsa apud Anglos postquam benedixerit sacerdos in templo
incipit bibere, sponso et reliquis astantibus idem mox facientibus.

14 Tum supra caput hastam de gladiatoris corpore eductam ponebant, tanquam promptum violati thori supplicium, vel quod ma-

elsewhere today, particularly in England, two boys act as bridesmen, as the attendants who once took the auspices for those celebrating the marriage. They lead the bride to church where a priest blesses her and the groom, and then two men lead them home while a third goes in front carrying a little vessel of gold or silver instead of a torch. It is a special custom in the countryside to weave a wreath of wheat leaves for the bride's head or for her to carry such a wreath in her hand. And when she enters the house, they throw wheat on her head for good luck, as if it would bring fertility.

To proclaim maidenhood, they kept calling out the name Talassius because during the rape of the Sabine women that person had acquired a maiden or else, since the word Talassius refers to a handbasket suitable for such work, they used it as a reminder of maternal duties and wool-working. According to Plutarch and Pliny, brides would also carry with them a distaff full of wool and a spindle, which remains the custom in Italy in the Veneto. Moreover, before they lay with their husbands they give them fire and water to touch because these elements are purgative (as will be explained in another place), signifying that the bride should be chaste and pure. Also, they make up a potion and give it to the new bride to drink, as Ovid tells us in the *Fasti*:

> Take the seed of poppy ground with snowy milk—
> Don't be shy—honey-water pressed from combs and strained.
> When they first brought Venus to her lusting mate,
> That's what she drank and then was truly wed.

Instead of all this, in Rome they now say that she should drink only honey. In England also the bride takes a drink after the priest has given his blessing in church, and then the groom and other members of the party do the same.

Then they used to hold a spear drawn from the body of a gladiator over her head—quick punishment, as it were, for a marriage

tronae Iunonis Curetis in tutela sint, quae ita appellabatur a ferenda hasta quae Sabinorum lingua *curis* dicitur, vel quod nuptiali
iure nubens viri imperio subiiciatur, quia hasta armorum et imperii summa est. Germani hunc morem nunc retinent cum primis.
Fuerat insuper tam Graecis quam Romanis virginibus consuetudo
fascia genitalia succingere usque ad diem matrimonii, quod Homerus in *Odyssea* de Tyro virgine a Neptuno compressa testatur. Et
Catullus:

Quod zonam solvit diu ligatam.

Nova praeterea nupta cinniligio praecingebatur, id vir in lecto sol-
vebat, factum ex lana ovis, ut cum illa in domum sublata sic vir
vinctus cinctusque esset. Item Romae, autore Festo, nubentes solebant asses tris ferre, atque unum quem in manu tenerent tanquam
virum ementes marito dare, alterum quem in pede haberent in
foco larium familiarium ponere, quod hodie nonnullis in Italiae locis servatur; tertium in sacciperio (ita Nonius Marcellus appellat
hoc marsupii genus) in compito vicinali resonare certo tempore solere.

15   Sed longe alia erat coemptio quae fiebat cum convenirent in
manum, quam Boetius *Super topicis Ciceronis* refert his caeremoniis
consuevisse peragi: sese enim in coemendo invicem interroga-
bant—vir ita an sibi mulier materfamilias esse vellet, illa respondebat velle; item mulier interrogabat an vir sibi paterfamilias esse vellet, ille respondebat velle. Ita mulier viri conveniebat in manum.
Quo facto inter se iunctis dextris osculabantur, ac postremo vir
sponsae digitum annulo aureo ornabat, quasi eam sibi devinciens
tali insigni pignore. Utrunque testatur Tertullianus libro *De virgini-*

dishonored. This was either because wives are in the care of Juno Curetis, who got that name for carrying a spear called *curis* in the Sabine language, or because by right of marriage the bride becomes subject to her husband's authority, the spear being supreme in force and authority. The Germans especially preserve this custom now. It was also a practice for both Greek and Roman maidens to wrap their genitals with a band until the wedding day, as Homer shows in the *Odyssey*, speaking of the maiden Tyro when Neptune lay with her. Catullus also writes:

It loosed her girdle, too long tied up.

A new bride, moreover, wore a little girdle made of sheep's wool tied about her, and her husband would remove it in bed. When she had been carried into the house, her husband was thus enclosed and encircled. According to Festus new brides in Rome also used to carry three pennies: one they kept in the hand to give to the groom, as if buying a husband; another they carried in the shoe to place at the altar of the household gods, a custom kept today in some places in Italy; the third they put in a *sacciperium* (as Nonius Marcellus calls this kind of purse) to let it ring out in a local crossroads at the right moment.

But marriage by purchase, which brought the woman under the husband's power, was a much different matter. As Boethius reports in his commentary on Cicero's *Topics*, they used to perform it with the following ceremonies: In the purchase they asked each other these questions — the man, whether the woman wished to be the mother of his family, and she answered yes; then the woman asked whether the man wanted to be the father of her family, and he answered yes. Thus the woman agreed to come under the man's power. With this done and their right hands joined, they kissed, and finally the man put a golden ring on his wife's finger, as if binding her to himself with so distinctive a token. Tertullian testifies to both these things in his book on the *Veiling of Virgins*

15

bus velandis et in *Apologetico* capite 6. De hac coemptione rei uxoriae meminit Vergilius in illo versiculo:

Teque sibi generum Tethys emat omnibus undis.

Sponsa rursus domus coniugalis postes ungebat adipe suillo quod sic ab ea mala depulsum iri ducerent, unde ab 'ungendo' uxor dicta, quasi unxor. Item non permittebatur transcendere limen sed transportabatur, perinde quasi coacta pudicitiam amitteret. Ac non parum multa superstitionis plena alia alibi servabantur quae ociosum omnino duximus commemorare.

: V :

De religionis origine; et qui colendorum deorum primi autores fuerint et Deo vero sacrificaverint.

1 Non dubium est quin homines, qui antea agrestem vitam sine ullo rectore vivebant, primos suos reges laudibus ac novis honoribus usque eo ad coelum ferre coeperint ut etiam, daemonum praestigiis adducti veluti docuimus, deos appellarent sive ob miraculum virtutis, sive (ut solet) ad adulationem praesentis fortunae, sive ob beneficia in se collata. Ita cum ipsi reges chari essent, magnum sui posteris desiderium relinquebant, ex quo homines eorum simulacra fingebant ut ex imaginum contemplatione voluptatem caperent. Inde et honores illis habere tanquam diis coeperunt, virtutis praesertim acuendae causa, nam libentius reipublicae periculum optimus quisque adibat sciens virorum fortium memoriam honore deorum immortalium consecratum iri. Hac igitur ratione, ut divus

and in chapter 6 of the *Apology*. Vergil is thinking of this purchase of bride-right in this verse:

And Tethys trades her waves to make you her son-in-law.

Also, the wife smears the door-posts of her bridal home with pork-fat because they suppose this will drive evil away from it, and so the wife is called *uxor* from *unguendum* or smearing because she smears. In addition, she was forbidden to walk across the threshold and was carried across, as if she were being forced to give up her virginity. And they observed quite a few other superstitious customs which we have thought it useless to recount here.

: V :

On the origin of religion; and who were the first to worship the gods and to offer sacrifice to the true God.

There is no doubt that humans, who in earlier times led an uncivi- 1 lized and ungoverned life, began praising their first kings and giving them new honors until they made celestial beings of them. Prompted by the illusions of the demons that we have described, they even called them gods. They did this either because of the astonishing excellence of these leaders or (as usual) to flatter what fate had given them or because of benefits conferred on them. Since these kings were beloved, they left their survivors with a great feeling of bereavement, who therefore fashioned images of them so that people might take pleasure from looking at their likenesses. Next they began to honor them as if they were gods, mainly in order to excite excellence, for a person of merit would more willingly run a risk for the public good if he knew that honor befitting the immortal gods would hallow the memory of the

docet Cyprianus in libello *De idolis*, paulatim vana religio esse coepit cum primi parentes eo ritu suos liberos, et illi suos, ac deinde omnes posteros imbuerent.

2   Quare Iovis temporibus, autore Lactantio, libro secundo, capite undecimo, primo templa constitui et novi deorum cultus esse coeperunt, vel paulo ante. Quippe fieri potest, sicut idem ait, ut vel ante vel adhuc puero Iove, Melissus Iovis nutritor (a quo, ut infra dicemus, colendorum Deorum ritus effluxit) colere instituerit alumni sui matrem, et aviam Tellurem et patrem Saturnum. Sed ut ad unguem origo constet, faciamus initium huius rei fuisse tempore Beli, patris Nini, qui anno ab orbe condito circiter ter millesimo CLXXX apud Assyrios primus regnavit. Hunc Belum sibi deum nominatum Babylonii et Assyrii colebant. Idcirco errant qui deorum cultus ab exordio rerum fuisse contendunt.

3   Veri autem Dei religio non equidem aliunde manavit nisi ab ipso Deo. Etenim Deus, teste Lactantio in libro *De ira Dei*, religionis causa nos fecit, ut sibi nos statim geniti iustos et debitos honores haberemus, ipsum solum veneraremur, ipsum sequeremur, in ipso denique acquiesceremus, uti est in Deuteronomii capite sexto, ita iubente Domino: Deum tuum adorabis, et illum solum coles. Ex quo hoc vinculo pietatis obstricti et religati Deo sumus unde, ut eidem placet, religio nomen accepit. At Cicero in secundo *De natura deorum*, a relegendo fluxisse opinatur, scribens: qui autem omnia quae ad cultum deorum pertinerent diligenter tractarent, et tanquam relegerent, hi dicti sunt religiosi ex relegendo, etc.

4   Sed ad deorum cultores revertamur, de quibus magna apud autores est quaestio. Nam primi omnium Aegyptii, autore Herodoto libro secundo et Strabone libro *Geographiae* decimo septimo, diis et

brave. For this reason, as St. Cyprian teaches in his treatise *On Idols*, religion gradually became false as parents first trained their children in this practice, they their children, and then all posterity.

Thus, according to Lactantius, book 2, chapter 11, temples were 2 first constructed and new ways of worshipping the gods began in Jupiter's time or a little before. The same author says that it could have happened either while Jupiter was still a boy or earlier when Melissus (from whom rites of divine worship became known, as we shall explain below) brought Jupiter up and began the worship of his foster son's mother, of his grandmother Tellus and of his father Saturn. But in order to establish its origin precisely, let us put the beginning of this custom in the time of Belus, the father of Ninus, who first reigned over the Assyrians about 3180 years after the creation of world. The Babylonians and Assyrians called this Belus their god and worshipped him. Those who maintain that the gods have been worshipped since the beginning are therefore mistaken.

But in any case, the religion of the true God had no other ori- 3 gin than from God himself. In fact, according to Lactantius in his book *On the Wrath of God*, religion was the cause of God's making us, so that once begotten we would render him just and due honor, worship him alone, obey him, and at last find our rest in him, as in Deuteronomy 6, where the Lord commands: You shall adore your God, and him alone shall worship. And so we are bound and linked to God by this chain of piety whence, Lactantius says, religion took its name. But Cicero, in book 2 *On the Nature of the Gods*, claims that it came from *relegere*, to go over, writing: But those who carefully practiced and, as it were, went over everything having to do with the worship of the gods were called religious from *relegere*, and so on.

Let us return to the worshipers of the gods, about whom there 4 is great dispute among the authorities. According to Herodotus in book 2 and Strabo in book 17 of the *Geography*, the Egyptians first

aras et simulacra et delubra statuere, sacrificiaque curarunt ritusque eos deinde peregrinis commonstrarunt. Quidam vero volunt Mercurium primum instituisse quibus sacris dii colerentur, at alii Mennam regem, autor Diodorus libro primo. Sed idem in quarto Aethiopes primos Deos coluisse autumat, ita scribens: asserunt autem deorum apud eos cultum primitus adinventum, sacra insuper, pompas, celebritates aliaque quibus diis honores impenduntur ab eis fuisse reperta. Qua ex re ipsorum in deos pietate religioneque inter omnes vulgata, videntur Aethiopum sacra diis admodum grata esse. Huius rei testimonium afferunt antiquissimi fere ac celeberrimi apud Graecos poetarum, qui in sua *Iliade* Iovem reliquosque una deos introducit in Aethiopiam, tum ad sacra quae eis de more fierent, tum ad odorum suavitatem commigrantes. Aethiopes etiam dicuntur suae erga deos pietatis praemium tulisse, quod nunquam ab externis regibus subacti sint, semper enim liberi permanserunt.

5   Verum Lactantius libro *Institutionum* primo tradit Melissum Cretensium regem primum diis sacrificasse ac ritus novos sacrorumque pompas introduxisse. Huius Amalthea et Melissa filiae fuerunt, quae Iovem puerum caprino lacte ac melle nutrierant, quam ob rem poetae tradiderunt advolasse apes atque os pueri melle complesse.

6   Alii praeterea alia id genus sacra apud gentes adinvenerunt, veluti Faunus in Latio qui, eodem Lactantio autore, Saturno avo sacra constituit. Quidam scribunt ante Faunum imperasse Ianum ac deorum cultum demonstrasse. Apud Romanos Numa Pompilius novae religionis autor fuit, sicut Orpheus sacra Liberi patris primus in Graeciam introduxit, quae orgia vocabantur, quo nomine (teste Servio super 4 *Aeneidos*) olim apud Graecos omnia sacra dicebantur, quemadmodum apud Latinos caerimoniae. Item initiandi morem atque alia mysteria intulit, Diodorus et Lactantius autores, at Eusebius non plane hoc sentit, in 10 de *Evangelica prae-*

of all set up altars and statues and shrines for the gods, offered them sacrifices and then fully explained these practices to travelers. But some think that Mercury first established rites to worship the gods, and others think it was King Mennas, according to Diodorus in book 1. Yet in book [3] the same author asserts that it was the Ethiopians who first worshipped the gods, writing thus: They claim that they first devised divine worship, also that they invented the rites, processions, gatherings and other activities that pay honor to the gods. Their piety and reverence for the gods is known everywhere, so the rites of the Ethiopians are considered particularly pleasing to the gods. As witness to this fact, they call on the most famous and nearly the oldest of the Greek poets, who in his *Iliad* brings Jupiter and the other gods together into Ethiopia; they traveled there partly because of the rites customarily performed for them, partly because of the sweetness of the smells. The Ethiopians are also said to have gained from their devotion to the gods, for they have always remained free, never conquered by foreign kings.

But Lactantius in book 1 of the *Institutes* teaches that Melissus, 5 king of the Cretans, first made sacrifice to the gods and introduced new practices and processions of sacrifices. His daughters were Amalthea and Melissa, who reared the boy Jupiter on goat's milk and honey, which is why the poets said that bees flew into the boy's mouth and filled it with honey.

Other pagans also devised other rites of this sort. Lactantius 6 says that Faunus set up rites in Latium for his grandfather Saturn. Some write that Janus had ruled before Faunus and showed how to worship the gods. Among the Romans Numa Pompilius was the founder of a new religion, just as Orpheus first introduced the rites of Father Liber into Greece; they were called *orgia*, the name the Greeks once gave to all rites (according to Servius on book four of the *Aeneid*), just as the Latins called them ceremonies. He also started the custom of initiation and other mysteries, according

paratione sic scribens: Primus enim omnium ex Phoenicia Cadmus Agenoris filius mysteria et solennitates deorum Graeciae tradidit simulacrorum consecrationes etiam et hymnos, deinde ex Thracia Orpheus.

7   Herodotus vero libro secundo Graecos omnino religionem deorum — partim ab Aegyptiis, partim a Pelasgis — accepisse affirmat, et Athenienses ante omnes quando in Graecia Dodonaeum oraculum omnium vetustissimum conditum erat. Sed apud Graecos, sicut idem ait, Hesiodus et Homerus deorum opifices in primis extiterunt. Cum Herodoto consentit Eusebius, qui in praefatione in *Chronicon* suum ita dicit: Cecrops Diphyes primus omnium Iovem appellavit, simulacra reperit, aram statuit, victimas immolavit, nequaquam istiusmodi rebus in Graecia usquam visis, siquidem Cecrops primus Atticae rex fuit et aequalis Mosis. Item orgia Thracibus, teste eodem Eusebio, Aetio adinvenit. Ac talis fuit apud gentes religionis origo.

8   Deo autem omnipotenti quem nos Christiani colimus, cuius nutu omnia geruntur, Cain et Abel Adam filii, autore Iosepho in primo *Antiquitatum*, primi sacrificarunt. Enos vero primus, ut testatur Hieronymus *Contra Iovinianum* et Eusebius, invocavit nomen Domini. Et sic deinceps eorum posteri nullis sacris initiati sacrificium fecere quoad Deus sacerdotium constituit, quod primo, teste Iosepho in 3 *Antiquitatum*, Aaron Mosis fratri detulit. Ex quo solenne apud Hebraeos fuit ut nemo divinum pontificatum gereret nisi Aaron genere ortus foret. Iis enim sacerdotibus tantum rem divinam facere licebat, sicuti nunc apud nos sacerdotes illi duntaxat illud idem factitant qui per episcopos sacris initiantur. Sed

to Diodorus and Lactantius, but Eusebius plainly does not think so, writing in book 10 of the *Preparation for the Gospel* that Cadmus, son of Agenor, first of all brought the mysteries and rituals of the gods along with hymns and the consecration of statues from Phoenicia to Greece, and later Orpheus brought them from Thrace.

In book 2 Herodotus indeed affirms that the Greeks got all 7 their religion elsewhere—some from the Egyptians, some from the Pelasgians—and the Athenians were first since the oracle of Dodona was the oldest founded in Greece. But among the Greeks, as the same writer says, Homer and Hesiod stood out as the foremost fabricators of gods. Eusebius agrees with Herodotus, as he explains in the preface to his *Chronicle:* Double-formed Cecrops first of all called upon Jupiter, invented statues, set up an altar and immolated victims, none of which had ever before been seen in Greece, since Cecrops in fact was the first king of Attica and a contemporary of Moses. Also, according to the same Eusebius, Aetion introduced orgiastic rites to the Thracians. Such was the origin of religion among the pagans.

It was the sons of Adam, however, Cain and Abel, who first 8 made sacrifice to the omnipotent God whom we Christians worship and whose nod rules all things, according to Josephus in book one of the *Antiquities.* But as Jerome *Against Jovinian* and Eusebius testify, Enos first called on the name of the Lord. Then their descendants made sacrifice without initiation in any rites until God established the priesthood, which he first conferred upon Aaron, the brother of Moses, according to Josephus in book three of the *Antiquities.* After this it was the rule among the Hebrews that no one but a descendant of Aaron's line should exercise the divine office of priest. Only these priests were permitted to perform divine ritual, just as we now allow the same role only for those whom bishops initiate as priests in the sacred rites. The fourth

de verae religionis ac sacerdotii initio in quarto operis huius volumine diffusius tradetur.

: VI :

Quis primus literas invenerit vel in Latium attulerit, et de earum numero aucto, varietate, vi atque sono.

1 Quoniam solo literarum usu memoriae fulcitur aeternitas ab omnique oblivionis iniuria res memoria dignae vindicantur, has ante omnia esse tractandas ducimus, cum earum inventio plane demonstret valde admirabilem fuisse vim iuxta ingenii atque memoriae in eo homine qui primus sonos vocis qui infiniti videbantur paucis eiusmodi literarum notis terminaverit, cuius nomen antiquitate obrutum non proditur, tametsi honore maximo dignatur.

2 Mercurium itaque literas in Aegypto omnium primum reperisse testatur Diodorus libro primo. Cicero libro *De natura deorum* tertio hunc quintum Mercurium fuisse tradit qui literas Aegyptiis dederit. At idem Diodorus paulo inferius (de primo enim earum inventore magnum apud idoneos autores certamen esse video) Aegyptiis literarum inventionem attribuere videtur, ita scribens: Asserunt Aegyptii literas, astrorum cursus, geometriam, artesque plurimas ab se fuisse inventas. Nonnulli has in Aegypto invenisse quendam nomine Menona affirmant. Sed apud eos quod non est silentio praetereundum animalium effigies loco literarum erant, quippe quae sensus mentis, sicut docebimus cum de obeliscis meminerimus, repraesentabant.

3 Plinius autem libro *Naturalis historiae* 7 circa finem ait se literas semper arbitratum esse Assyrias fuisse. Alii apud Syros repertas volunt. Cadmum vero, idem autor est, a Phoenicia primum in

book of this work will treat the beginning of true religion and the
priesthood more extensively.

: VI :

*Who first invented letters or brought them into Latium, and
on their increased number, their variety, use and sound.*

Since only the use of letters makes memory endure and protects 1
things worthy of memory from all damage of forgetfulness, we
conclude that we should treat letters before anything else. Their
invention plainly shows how very admirable was the force of genius and memory alike in that person who first confined the seem-
ingly infinite sounds of the voice in a few written signs of this
kind. That name is forgotten, buried in antiquity, though it deserves the highest honor.

Diodorus testifies in book 1 that Mercury first of all invented 2
letters in Egypt. In book 3 *On the Nature of the Gods* Cicero reports
that it was this fifth Mercury who gave letters to the Egyptians.
But Diodorus a little further on also seems to attribute the invention of letters (about their inventor I note great disagreement
among the relevant authors) to the Egyptians, writing thus: The
Egyptians claim that they discovered letters, the motions of the
stars, geometry, and most of the arts. Some maintain that a man
named Menon invented them in Egypt. But one must not fail to
mention that instead of letters they used pictures of animals which
in fact represented mental notions, as we shall explain when we
deal with obelisks.

Pliny, however, toward the end of book 7 of the *Natural His-* 3
tory, says that he had always thought that letters were Assyrian,
while others claim that the Syrians discovered them. But Pliny

Graeciam attulisse sexdecim numero, A B C D E G I L M N O P R S T V; quibus Troiano bello Palamedem adiecisse quatuor hac figura, Θ Ξ Φ Υ; totidem post eum Simonidem melicum, Ψ Z H Ω, quarum vis in nostris recognoscitur. Aristoteles decem et octo priscas fuisse commemorat, A B Γ Δ E Z I K Λ M N O Π P Σ T Υ Φ, et duas ab Epicharmo, non a Palamede additas, hoc est, Θ et P, vel Ψ, ut Hermolaus prodit.

4   Quidam vero aut non Cadmum literas in Graeciam sed Phoenices qui cum eo venerant aut omnino non primo Cadmum sed multis post seculis advexisse contendunt. Nam Herodotus Halicarnasseus, historiarum pater ut aiunt Graeci, libro quinto de Phoenicibus ita loquitur: Phoenices isti qui cum Cadmo advenerunt, quorum Gephyraei fuere, dum hanc regionem incolunt, cum alias multas doctrinas in Graeciam introduxere tum vero literas quae apud Graecos, ut mihi videtur, antea non fuerant, et primae illae quidem extiterunt e quibus omnes Phoenices utuntur. Affirmat itidem Diodorus libro sexto: Nam qui dicunt Phoenices a Musis perceptas literas tradidisse postmodum Graecis; hi sunt qui cum Cadmo in Europam navigarunt. Ex quo a Graecis literae Phoeniceae appellatae sunt. Hinc Lucanus:

Phoenices primi, famae si credimus, ausi
Mansuram rudibus vocem signare figuris.

At omnino Cadmum non primum ad Graecos literas portasse sed longo post tempore Diodorus perspicue demonstrat, qui ait: Cum Actinus Solis filius in Aegyptum transiens astrologiam Aegyptios docuisset, demum Graecia diluvio oppressa; plurimos homines periisse, literarumque monimenta deleta fuisse, et eam ob causam post multa secula existimatum esse Cadmum, Agenoris filium,

also says that Cadmus first brought sixteen of them into Greece from Phoenicia, A B C D E G I L M N O P R S T V; that to these Palamades added four shaped like this, Θ Ξ Φ Υ, at the time of the Trojan War; and that after him Simonides the lyric poet added the same number, Ψ Z H Ω, whose uses are recognized in our letters. Aristotle mentions that there were originally eighteen letters, A B Γ Δ E Z I K Λ M N O Π P Σ T Υ Φ, and that not Palamades but Epicharmus added two more, namely Θ and P or Ψ, as Ermolao presents it.

Some argue, however, either that it was not Cadmus but his 4 Phoenician companions who brought letters into Greece or else that Cadmus was just not the first to bring them in but did so many centuries later. Herodotus of Halicarnassus, whom the Greeks call the father of history, speaks thus of the Phoenicians in book 5: When the Phoenicians who came with Cadmus, among whom were the Gephyraei, settled this region, they introduced many different kinds of learning into Greece but especially letters which I believe the Greeks lacked before then, and indeed the earliest letters developed from those that all the Phoenicians use. Diodorus claims the same in book [5]: They say that the Phoenicians learned about letters from the Muses and afterward taught them to the Greeks; it was they who sailed to Europe with Cadmus. For this reason letters are called Phoenician by the Greeks. Hence Lucan writes:

> Phoenicians, if we believe the story, first ventured
> To set sound fixed in crude characters.

Yet Diodorus clearly shows that Cadmus was by no means the first to bring letters to the Greeks but did so much later, for he says: After Actinus, the son of the Sun, had gone over into Egypt and taught the Egyptians astrology, then Greece was devastated by a flood; most men perished, literary records were destroyed, and so after many centuries it came to be thought that Cadmus, son of

primum literas in Graeciam adduxisse; atque ideo Graecos quadam communi ignorantia ductos literarum inventionem illi acceptam retulisse.

5   Caeterum Iosephus in primo *Antiquitatis contra Appionem* Graecos omnino ante Homeri aetatem literis caruisse affirmat, cum inquit: Postea multa quaestio atque contentio facta est utrum literis
usi sint, et magis veritas obtinuit eo quod usus recentium literarum illis fuisset incognitus. Constat autem quoniam apud Graecos
nulla invenitur absolute conscriptio poemate Homeri vetustior, et
hunc etiam post bella Troiana fuisse manifestum est. Atqui Cicero
in *Bruto* secus tradit, aiens: Nec dubitari debet quin fuerint ante
Homerum poetae, quod ex eis carminibus intelligi potest quae
apud illum et in Phaeacum et in procorum epulis canuntur. Item
Eusebius in 10 *De evangelica praeparatione* ostendit scripsisse apud
Graecos ante Homerum, Linum, Philamonem, Thamyram, Amphionem, Orpheum, Musaeum, Demodotum, Epimenidem, Aristaeum et plerosque alios. Alii, teste Diodoro in 4, asserunt Aethiopes literas primum reperisse, ab iisque Aegyptios eorum
colonos exin illas accepisse, et ab his deinde reliquos.

6   Verum Eupolemus, ut Eusebius opinatur, proculdubio veram literarum originem reddit, affirmans Mosen (qui teste eodem Eusebio *De temporibus* et in 10 *De praeparatione evangelica* longe ante Cadmum fuit) literas Iudaeis primum tradidisse et a Iudaeis Phoenices
accepisse, Graecos vero postremos a Phoenicibus. Idem etiam Eusebius libro 8 et 10 pulcherrime probat. Cui opinioni congruit illud
quod ex Plinio ante retulimus, apud Syros literas repertas esse
quando Syri ipsi quoque, teste Eusebio, Hebraei sunt, atque adeo
Iudaea Syria est, ita Plinio libro 5 dicente: Syria quondam terra-

Agenor, first introduced letters to Greece; thus, misled by their general ignorance, the Greeks traced to him the tradition of the invention of letters.

Josephus, on the other hand, claims that before Homer's time 5 the Greeks lacked letters altogether; in the first part of the *Antiquities against Apion* he says: Afterward arose great doubt and contention whether they had the use of letters, and the truth was that the use of letters of the modern kind was unknown to them. It is clear, however, that no well-attested work of literature older than the poetry of Homer is found among the Greeks, and it is also obvious that Homer came after the Trojan War. And yet in the *Brutus* Cicero teaches otherwise, saying: One should not doubt that there were poets before Homer, as one can learn from the songs that he says were sung at the banquets of the Phaecaeans and the suitors. Also in book 10 of the *Preparation for the Gospel*, Eusebius shows that Linus, Philamon, Thamyras, Amphion, Orpheus, Musaeus, Demodotus, Epimenides, Aristaeus and many, many others wrote in Greece before Homer. Others, according to Diodorus in book [3], claim that the Ethiopians first discovered letters, and that the Egyptians, who were their colonists, then took them from the Ethiopians, and finally other peoples from the Egyptians.

Eusebius believes that Eupolemus actually relates the true ori- 6 gin of letters when he affirms that Moses (who lived long before Cadmus, according to the same Eusebius in his *Chronicle* and in book 10 of the *Preparation for the Gospel*) first taught letters to the Jews, that the Phoenicians got them from the Jews and finally that the Greeks got them from the Phoenicians. Eusebius also gives an outstanding proof of the same thing in books 8 and 10. This finding matches what we reported above from Pliny, that letters were discovered in Syria since the Syrians, according to Eusebius, are the same as the Hebrews, and to that extent Syria is Judaea, as Pliny says in book 5: Syria was once the greatest of lands and was

rum maxima et pluribus distincta nominibus: nanque Palaestina vocabatur qua contingit Arabas, et Iudaea, et Coele, dein Phoenice, etc.

7   Sed reperimus ante diluvium Noe apud eos omnino usum fuisse literarum, Iosephus enim in 1 *Antiquitatum* tradit liberos Seth, Adam filii. in duabus columnis, uti cum de astrologia tractabitur subtilius dicemus, disciplinam rerum coelestium a se primo inventam conscripsisse. Quo apparet iam tum literas fuisse quas fieri potuit vi aquarum deletas, Mosen dein adinvenisse — quamvis ex his columnis alteram, id est lapideam, Iosephus usque ad aetatem suam in Syria durasse affirmet. Quapropter rectius mea quidem sententia Philo primam literarum inventionem Abraham assignat, qui Mose antiquior est, nisi hoc sit potius filiis Seth attribuendum, qui ipsum Abraham multis annis praecesserant.

8   Hebraeorum autem literae, ut idem Eusebius ait, numero vigintiduae sunt, quotidem nostrae latinae; quae, si divo Hieronymo credimus, novae sunt et ab Esdra inventae. Ille enim in *Praefatione* in libros Regum ita scribit: Certumque est Esdram, scribam legisque doctorem, post captam Hierosolymam et instaurationem templi sub Zorobabel alias literas reperisse quibus nunc utimur, cum ad illud usque tempus iidem Samaritanorum et Hebraeorum characteres fuerint, etc.

9   Graecas vero veteres literas fuisse easdem pene quae nunc latinae sunt indicio est Delphica tabula aenea, quae Romae in Palatio, Minervae dicata, in bibliotheca conspiciebatur Plinii (ut ipse testatur) temporibus. In Latium eas, teste Plinio et Solino, intulere Pelasgi. Quidam volunt Nicostratam, Evandri Arcadis matrem, Latinis primum dedisse. Dionysius in primo ait ipsos Arcades primos attulisse in Italiam qui post Pelasgos venerant. Livius

known by many names; the part nearest the Arabians, for example, was called Palestine, Judaea, Hollow-Syria, then Phoenicia, and so on.

That they definitely had the use of letters before Noah's flood   7
we learn from the first book of *Antiquities*. There Josephus teaches that the children of Seth, Adam's son, wrote down on two pillars the knowledge of the heavens that they first discovered, as we shall explain more precisely when we deal with astrology. Thus it is obvious that even in those days there were letters that the force of the waters could have obliterated, and then Moses discovered them later — though Josephus confirms that one of these pillars, the one made of stone, still survived in Syria in his day. And so I believe Philo is right to assign the original invention of letters to Abraham, who is older than Moses, unless one should attribute it to the sons of Seth, who preceded Abraham by many years.

The letters of the Hebrews, as Eusebius also says, are twenty-   8
two in number, the same as our Latin letters. If we believe St. Jerome, they are a replacement invented by Esdra, for in his *Preface* to the Books of Kings Jerome writes: It is certain that after the capture of Jerusalem and the restoration of the temple under Zorobabel, Esdra, a teacher of the Law and a scribe, invented the other letters that we now use, though until that time the Hebrews and the Samaritans used the same symbols, and so on.

That the ancient Greek letters were almost the same as the   9
present Latin letters is evident from a bronze tablet of Delphi, dedicated to Minerva, which was seen in Pliny's time at Rome in the library on the Palatine, as he himself says. The Pelasgians brought these letters into Latium, according to Pliny and Solinus. Some suppose that Nicostrata, the mother of Evander the Arcadian, first gave them to the Latins. Dionysius says in book 1 that it was the Arcadians, coming after the Pelasgians, who first brought them into Italy. Livy calls Evander their inventor, writing thus in book 1 *From the Foundation of the City*: Evander, having fled the

Evandrum autorem vocat, libro *Ab urbe condita* primo ita scribens: Evander tum ea profugus ex Peloponneso autoritate magis quam imperio regebat loca, venerabilis vir miraculo literarum, rei novae inter rudes artium homines. Sentit idem Cornelius Tacitus, qui tradit aborigines ab Evandro Arcade didicisse literas.

10 Quod autem Plinius in septimo Epigenis autoritate probare conatur aeternum literarum esse usum, qui, veluti ex Iosephi testimonio probavimus omnino antiquissimus est. Non id plane sentit Herodotus, qui, ut supra demonstratum est, nullas literas ante Phoenices in Graecia fuisse autumat. Neque Eupolemus aut Eusebius, qui Mosi primam literarum inventionem, sicut ostendimus, assignant. Neque demum Diodorus, qui in primo inquit: Qui primi fuerint in orbe reges nequaquam compertum habemus, cum nulli historici eos tradant, fieri quippe non potest literas aeque ac primos reges vetustas extitisse. Haec ille.

11 Sero etiam in Latium venere, quod testatur Livius ita scribens in fronte libri 6 *Ab urbe condita*: Tum quod parvae et rarae per eadem tempora literae fuere — una custodia fidelis memoriae rerum gestarum. Quapropter idem libro nono ait Romanos deinde pueros non modo Graecis sed Hetruscis quoque literis erudiri solitos, ex quo scire licet Hetruscos etiam suas olim habuisse literas, quas — ut nostra denique caetera omnia — ita tempus consumpsit ut nunc ne nota quidem illarum cognita extet. Has autem literas, Cornelius Tacitus libro *Augustae historiae* 11 autor est, Demaratum Corinthium Hetruscos primum docuisse. Phrygibus quoque proprias fuisse literas testatur Cicero *De natura deorum*, sic scribens: Alter Hercules traditur Nilo natus Aegyptius, quem aiunt Phrygias literas conscripsisse.

12 Atqui cum Graeci ita suarum literarum numerum paulatim auxissent, sicut supra demonstravimus, Latini quoque idem studentes postea literas sex ad suas priscas sexdecim addiderunt, F K

Peloponnesus, then ruled these places more by leadership than by power. He was a man revered for the miracle of letters, a thing wonderful to people unskilled in the arts. Cornelius Tacitus, who teaches that the aborigines learned letters from Evander the Arcadian, thinks the same.

But in book 7 Pliny tries to show on the authority of Epigenes   10
that the use of letters is immeasurably old, and from the testimony of Josephus we have proved that it is by all accounts very ancient. Plainly, Herodotus does not think so; as shown above, he holds that there were no letters in Greece before the Phoenicians. Nor do Eupolemus and Eusebius agree; as we have indicated, they assign the first invention of letters to Moses. Neither, finally, does Diodorus agree, who says in book 1: Who were the first kings in the world we have by no means ascertained, since no historians record them, for in fact letters and the first kings cannot be equally ancient. Thus Diodorus.

Letters also came late into Latium, as Livy shows when he   11
writes as follows in the first part of book 6 *From the Foundation of the City*: Writing—the only faithful guardian of the memory of events—was in those times rare and unimportant. The same author says in book 9 that because of this Roman boys used to be instructed not only in Greek but also in Etruscan letters. One can see from this that the Etruscans also once had their letters, which time destroyed—as it will ours and all others—so that now not even a trace of their letters remains known. In book 11 of his *Imperial History*, however, Cornelius Tacitus tells us that Demaratus of Corinth first taught these letters to the Etruscans. The Phrygians also had their own letters, as Cicero testifies, writing thus on *The Nature of the Gods*: Another Hercules, they say, was born of the Nile, an Egyptian, and wrote in Phrygian letters.

But since the Greeks gradually increased the number of their   12
letters, as we showed above, the Latins, anxious to do the same, later added six letters to their original sixteen, F K Q X Y Z

Q X Y Z et H; haec tamen non est litera sed tantum aspirationis nota. F digammon ab Aeolibus acceperunt quod, teste Prisciano, apud antiquissimos Latinorum eandem vim atque apud ipsos Aeoles habuit. Eum enim prope sonum quem nunc habet F significabat P cum aspiratione, quo nos in verbis Graecis utimur ut Orpheus. Deinde Claudius Caesar, prout Tacitus prodit, F loco V consonantis recipiendum constituit, ut fulgus pro vulgus, fixit pro vixit. Quintilianus: Nec inutiliter, inquit, Claudius Aeolicam illam ad hos usus F literam adiecerat. Ita Germanum vulgus latine loquendo etiamnum pronunciat. Postremo in latinis vocibus pro P et H poni F coeptum est, ut fama, facio. K etiam litera a Graecis accepta, in nullis verbis apud nos boni autores utendum putant. Q adiecta est quod pinguiorem sonum edere visa est quam C. X de Graecis quaesivimus, qua tamen carere potuimus, ut ait Quintilianus, nam pro ea C et S vel G et S utebamur, ut apecs et gregs pro apex et grex. Y et Z ex Graeco similiter fonte manarunt, et id quidem ut istarum literarum usus in Graecis foret duntaxat verbis.

: VII :

De origine grammaticae et quantum valeat.

1 Consentaneum videtur ut, prodita literarum origine, antequam ad alia explicanda aggrediar de grammatices origine disseram, utpote quae pluris est quam omnium liberalium artium scientia, quia reliquarum unicum est fundamentum. Nomenque a literis accepit; nam γράμμα graece litera dicitur. Grammatica ipsa apud nos, teste Fabio, literatura nuncupatur et grammatici literatores aut literati, quamvis nonnulli, autore Tranquillo *De grammatica*, literatores vocent mediocriter doctos sicut Graeci grammatistas. Est au-

and H, though this last is only a breathing, not a letter. They took the F or *digamma* from the Aeolians because, according to Priscian, it had the same use for the earliest Latins as for the Aeolians themselves. P with a breathing actually signified almost the same sound now given to F; we use it in Greek words like *Orpheus.* Finally, as Tacitus presents it, Claudius Caesar used F to replace the consonant V, as *fulgus* for *vulgus, fixit* for *vixit.* Quintilian says it was not useless that Claudius applied that Aeolian letter F to these purposes. Even now the German people pronounce it this way when speaking Latin. Later, F came to be used for P plus H in Latin words, as in *fama, facio.* The letter K was also borrowed from the Greeks, though our better authors think there are no words requiring its use. Q was added because it seemed to pro‑ duce a sound fatter than C. X we borrowed from the Greeks, though we could have done without it, as Quintilian says, since in its place we used to put C plus S or G plus S, as *apecs* and *gregs* for *apex* and *grex.* Y and Z came likewise from a Greek source, and that only inasmuch as these letters may occur in Greek words.

: VII :

On the origin and value of grammar.

Having made known the origin of letters and before going on to explain other matters, it seems appropriate that I should discuss the origin of grammar, seeing that it is more important to know grammar than all the other liberal arts, of which it is the unique foundation. Besides, grammar takes its name from letters; for let‑ ter in Greek is *gramma.* According to Quintilian, we call grammar itself *literatura* and grammarians *literatores* or *literati* although some, according to Suetonius *On Grammar,* use *literatores* for those who

tem grammatica ars quae in emendate loquendo scribendoque
consistit ut literae suas custodiant voces et velut depositum red-
dant legentibus. Et autore Quintiliano libro primo in duas partes
dividitur, in recte loquendi scientiam et poetarum enarrationem.
Cicero *De oratore:* In grammaticis poetarum pertractio, historiarum cognitio, verborum interpretatio et pronunciandi quidam sonus.

2   Eius autem initium, ut testis est Suetonius in libro *De grammatica,* tale ferme fuit quale habuit rhetorice; ex observatione enim
eorum quae in loquendo apta aut inepta erant, homines ea ipsa ad
imitandum vitandumque notantes hanc artem fecerunt veluti ora-
toriam, nam grammatici pariter ac oratoris scientia est quomodo
loqui deceat, ut ex Cicerone colligere licet cum libro 3 *De oratore*
ait: Atque ut latine loquamur, non solum videndum est ut et verba
efferamus ea quae nemo iure reprehendat et ea sic et casibus et
temporibus et genere et numero conservemus ut ne quid perturba-
tum ac discrepans aut praeposterum sit, sed etiam vocis sonus est
ipse moderandus. Ista omnia grammatica sola docet.

3   Hanc autem, ut Laertius libro 10 ait, Hermippus autor est Epi-
curum primum docuisse, cuius vim Plato primus speculatus est.
Romae vero, autore Suetonio, olim ne in usu quidem nedum in
ullo honore fuit. Inde in urbem eius studium intulit Crates Mallotes missus ad Senatum ab Attalo rege inter secundum et tertium
bellum Punicum, sub ipsam Ennii mortem.

4   Caeterum haec omnium artium praeclarissima est; praebet enim
iter ad caeteras capessendas. Fabius: Nec ad ullius rei summam
nisi praecedentibus initiis perveniri potest. Et alibi: Quo minus,
inquit, sunt ferendi qui hanc artem ut tenuem ac ieiunam cavillan-
tur, quae nisi oratoris futuri fundamenta fideliter iecerit, quicquid

have little learning, as the Greeks use *grammatistae*. But there is an art of grammar, which consists in writing and speaking correctly so that letters preserve their sounds and pay a sort of deposit to those who read them. According to Quintilian in book 1, grammar is divided into two parts, the science of right speaking and the explication of the poets. Cicero *On the Orator* says: In grammar one studies the poets, acquires information, interprets words and pronounces certain sounds.

Its beginning was almost the same as that of rhetoric, as 2 Suetonius is our witness in his book *On Grammar*; it came from observing what was suitable or unsuitable for speaking. Noting what they should imitate and what they should avoid, people built up this art as they did oratory, for the grammarian's knowledge as well as the orator's tells how one should speak, as one can gather from Cicero when in book 3 *On the Orator* he says: In order to speak good Latin, not only must we take care to utter words that no one can rightly criticize, keeping them in cases, tenses, gender and number so that nothing is confused or out of agreement or in wrong order, but we must also control the sound of the voice. All this only grammar teaches.

On the authority of Hermippus, Diogenes Laertius says that 3 Epicurus first taught grammar, whose importance Plato was the first to explore. But at Rome there was a time when it was not even used, according to Suetonius, much less held in honor. And then Crates of Mallos brought the study of grammar into the city when King Attalus sent him to the Senate, between the second and third Punic Wars, just before Ennius died.

Moreover, grammar is the most excellent of all the arts, for it 4 provides a way of approaching the others, as Quintilian says: One cannot get to the depths of any subject except through the introductory matter that goes before. And elsewhere: Those people are intolerable, he says, who jeer at this art as trivial and barren, for unless grammar lays firm foundations for the future orator, what-

superstruxeris corruet. Necessaria pueris, iucunda senibus; dulcis
secretorum comes et quae vel sola omni studiorum genere plus habet operis quam ostentationis. Haec ille.

5   Illud praeterea quamobrem magnifieri debeat facile docet quia
ex huiusmodi artis negligentia in poetis, oratoribus, historicis, in
arte medicinae, in iure civili caeterisque disciplinis quotidie sexcenti errores existunt, ineptissimaeque interpretationes, id quod
non accideret si grammaticam primum discerent qui aliquando essent sese ad scribendum daturi, illive non ignorarent grammatici
partes esse ut cunctas fere calleat artes, quando apud antiquos soli
grammatici omnium scriptorum censores et iudices fuere, qui idcirco critici ἀπὸ τοῦ κρίνω appellati sunt. Igitur cum quis pingue
quiddam Latine sonare incipit, non debet ad opus aliquod scribendum aggredi prius quam grammaticam didicerit.

6   In hac autem olim praecelluerunt Didymus, quem Macrobius
omnibus grammaticis praeponit; Antonius Enipho, cuius scholam
M. Tullius post forensia negocia frequentabat; Nigidius Figulus;
Marcus ille Varro omnium doctissimus; Marcus Valerius Probus;
Palaemon ille arrogantissimus; multique deinde alii. Apud Grae-
cos Aristarchus, Aristoteles, Theodotes.

: VIII :

De poeticae artis origine et eius praestantia, ibique locus
Ciceronis in Catone emendatus.

1   Poetica ars multis mehercle de causis reliquas antecedit disciplinas
vel quia homines nullam pene artem assequi possunt nisi in illam
diu incubuerint vel quod scientias fere — ut Strabo in primo *Geo-*
graphiae adversus Eratosthenem pulchre demonstrat — in se conti-

ever you build on top will collapse. To the young it is a necessity, to the old a delight; it is a sweet sharer of secrets, and alone of all studies more deed than show. This is what Quintilian says.

Besides, one quickly learns why grammar should be held in 5 great esteem when every day in poetry, oratory, history, medicine, civil law, and other disciplines hundreds of mistakes arise from the neglect of this art. Such gross misunderstandings would not occur if people who ever intend to take up writing would first learn grammar and not forget that the grammarian's job is to understand almost all the arts. Among the ancients, grammarians alone were judges and examiners of all writers, wherefore they were called critics from *krinō*. Therefore, when someone's Latin begins to sound clumsy, he should not work any further at his writing until he learns grammar.

In the past these excelled in grammar: Didymus, whom Macro- 6 bius puts ahead of all grammarians; Antonius Enipho, whose school Cicero visited after he became an advocate; Nigidius Figulus; Marcus Varro himself, the most learned of all; Marcus Valerius Probus; Palaemon, that most arrogant fellow; and many others after them. Among the Greeks were Aristarchus, Aristotle and Theodotes.

: VIII :

On the origin and excellence of the art of poetry, and here we emend a passage of Cicero's Cato.

There are many reasons, God knows, why the art of poetry comes 1 before the rest of the disciplines, either because people can grasp almost no other art without devoting long study to it or because it contains nearly all the forms of knowledge — as Strabo nicely

net omnes, vel demum quod ex omnibus artibus quae ab humani ingenii excellentia proficiscuntur sola poetica divino furore percipitur.

2   Nam poetae furore afflati res omni admiratione et stupore dignas canunt, sine quo, teste Cicerone in primo *De divinatione*, Democritus negabat magnos esse poetas, quippe qui, ut idem quoque Democritus et Plato aiebant, non arte sed natura constant, tuncque veri vates sunt cum insaniunt. Horatius in *Poetica arte*:

> Ingenium misera quia fortunatius arte
> Credit et excludit sanos Helicone poetas
> Democritus.

Et alibi:

> Natura fieret laudabile carmen an arte
> Quaesitum est.

Non fiunt igitur poetae, sed nascuntur, unde in *Bucolicis* Vergilius:

> Pastores, hedera nascentem ornate poetam.

Quare Ovidius in 3 *De arte amandi* dicit:

> Est deus in nobis, sunt et commercia coeli.

Et Maro divinum vocat poetam

> Tale tuum carmen nobis divine poeta, [etc.]

cum vatem esse Dei munus sit.

3   Sed Cicero *Pro Archia poeta* multo luculentissime illud quo fiat pacto docet, dicens: Atqui sic a summis hominibus eruditissimisque accepimus caeterarum rerum studia et doctrina et praecep-

proves against Eratosthenes in the first book of the *Geography* — or finally because poetry, alone of all the arts that proceed from the perfection of human genius, comes in a divine frenzy.

For what the poets sing when in a frenzy and inspired is altogether stunning and deserves amazement. Democritus denied that poets were great without this frenzy, according to Cicero in book 1 *On Divination*. In fact, as Plato and Democritus both said, they rely not upon art but nature, and they are true poets just in the moment of their madness, as Horace writes in the *Art of Poetry*: 2

> Better talent, thought Democritus,
> Than the pain of craftsmanship,
> And banned poets from Helicon if they were sane.

And again:

> What wins a poem praise — nature or art?
> That's the question.

Poets are not made, then, but born, and so Vergil says in the *Bucolics*:

> Shepherds, dress with ivy your poet aborning.

And Ovid in the third book of the *Art of Love*:

> The god is in us; we get messages from heaven.

And Vergil calls the poet divinely inspired:

> Your song, godlike poet, was to us as, [etc.]

because being a poet is a gift from God.

But in his oration *For Archias the Poet* Cicero offers by far the most brilliant explanation, saying: From the greatest and most learned people, nonetheless, we take it that learning other things depends on doctrine and precept and technique, while the poet gets power from something natural; the forces of the mind waken 3

tis et arte constare, poetam natura ipsa valere et mentis viribus ex-
citari et quasi divino quodam spiritu afflari. Quare suo iure noster
ille Ennius sanctos appellat poetas quod quasi deorum aliquo
dono atque munere commendati nobis esse videantur.

4   Origo autem huius artis admodum vetusta est et, teste Eusebio
in libro II *De praeparatione evangelica*, apud antiquissimos Hebraeorum, qui multo ante Graecorum poetas fuere, primum floruit.
Nam Moses, magnus Hebraeorum imperator, cum ex Aegypto eos
in patriam reduceret, statim atque Mare Rubrum divinitus ceden-
tibus aquis transgressus est, divino numine afflatus, autore Iosepho
in 2 *De antiquitatibus Iudaeorum*, hexametrum carmen quo Deo gratias ageret edidit. Deinde David, ille divinus Dei vates, vario metro
hymnos composuit. Idem Iosephus libro 7 *Antiquitatum:* Expeditus
itaque David a praeliis et periculis cum pace iam altissima fruere-
tur, cantica in Deum hymnosque vario metro composuit, alios quidem trimetros, alios quidem quinquemetros. Haec ille.

5   Divus quoque Hieronymus in *Praefatione in Chronicon Eusebii*,
longe scienter id demonstrat, scribens: Denique quid Psalterio ca-
norius, quod in morem nostri Flacci et Graeci Pindari, nunc
iambo currit, nunc alcaico personat, nunc sapphico tumet, nunc
semipede ingreditur. Quid Deuteronomii et Esaiae cantico pul-
chrius? Quid Solomone gravius? Quid perfectius Iob? Quae omnia hexametris et pentametris versibus apud suos composita decurrunt. Non immerito igitur huius artis initium Hebraeis
acceptum referre debemus, veluti reliquarum propemodum disciplinarum.

6   Oracula quoque aliorum vatum versibus edita sunt, quod Horatius in *Poetica* testatur:

    dictae per carmina sortes.

the poet, and a kind of divine spirit breathes into him. Our Ennius is right, then, when he calls the poets holy, for it seems they have been entrusted to us by some kind of gift or endowment from the gods.

The origin of this art is very old and, according to Eusebius in 4 book II of the *Preparation for the Gospel*, it flourished first among the most ancient of the Hebrews, who lived long before there were any Greek poets. For when Moses, the great commander of the Hebrews, led them out of Egypt straight through the Red Sea with the waters miraculously retreating and he crossed back into his native land, a divine power inspired him to utter a poem in hexameters giving thanks to God, according to Josephus in book 2 of the *Jewish Antiquities*. David, God's divine poet, later composed hymns in various meters, as Josephus says in book 7 of the *Antiquities*: Thus, freed of his battles and dangers and enjoying the deepest peace, David composed songs and hymns to God in various meters, some in trimeter, others in pentameter. This is what Josephus says.

In his *Preface to the Chronicle of Eusebius*, St. Jerome also dem- 5 onstrates this very expertly, writing: Finally, what could be more melodious than the Psalter? Like our Horace and Pindar the Greek, it runs along now in iambs, rings now in alcaics, now swells with sapphics, now takes up the half-measure. What is more beautiful than the singing of Deuteronomy and Isaiah? What more dignified than Solomon? What more perfect than Job? In their originals these all flow along in well-constructed pentameter and hexameter verse. So it is reasonable enough that we should credit the beginning of this art to the Hebrews, as we do almost all the rest of the disciplines.

Other poets also produced oracles in verse, as Horace tells it in 6 the *Art of Poetry*:

Oracles spoken in song.

Verum Orpheus, autore Porphyrione, primum poeticam illustravit, deinde Homerus et Hesiodus. Nos autem serius illam accepimus, nam Livius Andronicus, ut Marcus Tullius in primo *Tusculanarum* et Fabius Quintilianus in 10 prodiderunt, fabulam primus dedit, Appio Claudio, Caeci filio, Marco Tuditano consulibus anno ante natum Ennium, qui fuit annus ab urbe condita quingentesimus tertiusdecimus. Caeterum ex ratione temporis inita a Livio ac testimonio eiusdem Ciceronis in *Catone* cum Livii Andronici meminit, satis constat Marci Sempronii Tuditani id temporis collegam fuisse Gaium Claudium Centonem, licet exemplaria in *Catone* perperam habeant pro Centone Cethego, non Appium Claudium. Ac sic ratio temporis (cuius rei causa hoc loco Consulum mentio facta est) conveniet si ita legas: sin minus non item. Antea enim, velut idem Marcus Cicero ait, nullus honos erat poeticae artis. Quinetiam usque adeo probro habebatur ut si quis, quemadmodum Gellius ex Catone, libro *Noctium atticarum* undecimo, capite secundo, testatur, eam rem studeret grassator vocaretur.

: IX :

De origine metri et metrorum plura
esse genera.

1 Quanquam nonnullis fortasse haud iniuria accusandus videbor quod antea de poeticae artis initiis scripserim quam metri originem traderem ex quo illa constat, nec eo tamen quispiam mihi succenseat, rei enim dignitas in causa fuit cur id fecerim, non valde indecens ratus de metro statim tractare.

Orpheus, according to Porphyrio, was actually the first to make poetry famous, then Homer and Hesiod. We learned it later, however. In the consulship of Appius Claudius, son of Caecus, and Marcus Tuditanus, the year before Ennius was born, AUC 513, Livius Andronicus was the first to put on a play. This is what Cicero in book 1 of the *Tusculans* and Fabius Quintilian in book 10 have reported. On the other hand, from the chronology worked out by Livy and also from Cicero's testimony in the *Cato* when he speaks of Livius Andronicus, it is clear enough that the colleague of Marcus Sempronius Tuditanus at that time was Gaius Claudius Cento, not Appius Claudius, although copies of the *Cato* have *Cethegus* wrongly for *Cento*. The chronology (which is the reason for mentioning the consuls in this passage) works out if you read it this way; otherwise, not. Before this, as Cicero says, there was really no respect for the art of poetry. Citing a work of Cato's, Gellius tells us in book 11, chapter 2, of the *Attic Nights* that it was considered so disgraceful that anyone who pursued it was called a vagrant.

: IX :

On the origin of meter, and that there are several kinds of meter.

Though some may justly reproach me for having written about the   1 beginnings of the art of poetry before treating the origin of meter, which is the basis of that art, still, no one should be angry with me on that account since I did so out of concern for due order, thinking it not too unbecoming to treat meter immediately after poetry.

2   Metri itaque origo a Deo Optimo Maximo est, qui hunc terrarum orbem et omnia ab eo contenta certa ratione, quasi metro, disposuit, harmoniam enim, uti Pythagoras docuit, in coelestibus terrenisque rebus nemo hercle esse dubitat. Nam quo pacto mundus consisteret nisi certa ratione et numeris praefinitis ageretur? Omnia quoque instrumenta quibus utimur mensura quadam, id est, metro fiunt. Quod si hoc in caeteris rebus accidit, quanto magis in oratione, quae cunctas complectitur?

3   Diodorus etiam, tametsi fabulas sequitur, cum de Musarum officio libro sexto loquitur, metri inventionem Iovi, hoc est, Deo immortali assignat. Musis, inquit, a patre concessa est literarum inventio et carminum quae poesis appellatur ratio. Atque metrum a Deo initium habuit, quo apud mortales eius vates (quos commemoravimus) divini spiritus pleni primum usi sunt.

4   Sed metrorum plura sunt genera quae, autore Servio, vel a rebus quae describuntur nomina accepere, ut heroicum quod hexametrum. Licet Moses, uti dictum est, primus usurpaverit, tamen quia Homerus et caeteri qui deinceps secuti sunt heroum res gestas hoc carmine scriptitarunt heroicum nominatum est, quo etiam ante Homeri aetatem Apollinis Pythii oracula reddi consueverant propter quod, ut opinor, Plinius in 7 ait: Versum heroicum Pythio oraculo debemus. Ipsa insuper oracula soluta etiam oratione, teste Strabone libro nono *Geographiae*, referebantur, id quod affirmat Cicero in secundo *De divinatione*, dicens: Praeterea Pyrrhi temporibus iam Apollo versus facere desierat.

5   Vel ab inventoribus ut asclepiadaeum, vel a pedibus ut iambicum quod Archilochus primus invenit. Horatius in *Poetica*:

Archilochum proprio rabies armavit iambo.

The origin of meter, then, is from God Almighty, who set out   2
the globe of the earth and all it contains in fixed order, as if by meter, for surely no one doubts that there is harmony in heaven and
earth, as Pythagoras taught. How could the world endure if it
were not moved according to fixed order and determined quantities? All the instruments we use are also made according to a certain measure or meter. But if this is the case in other matters, how
much more so in language, which comprehends them all?

When he speaks about the role of the Muses in his [fifth] book,   3
Diodorus assigns the invention of meter to Jupiter, to immortal
God, in other words, even though he follows the myths. The invention of letters and the ordering of songs called poetry, he says,
were granted the Muses by their father. And so meter had its beginning from God. Among mortals the first to use it were God's
poets (whom we have mentioned) when they were full of the divine spirit.

Of meter there are several kinds. According to Servius, they   4
sometimes took their names from what they described, as with the
heroic hexameter. Although Moses first used the hexameter, as I
have said, it was still called heroic because Homer and later authors wrote about the deeds of heroes in this verse. Even before
Homer's time the oracles of the Pythian Apollo used to be delivered in hexameters, because of which, I believe, Pliny in book 7
says: We owe heroic verse to the Pythian oracle. They gave the
same oracles in prose as well, according to Strabo in book 9 of the
Geography, and Cicero affirms this in the second book *On Divination*, saying: Moreover, Apollo had stopped making verses already
by the time of Pyrrhus.

Other meters like the asclepiadic were named after their inven-   5
tors, or after their feet like the iambic that Archilochus first invented, as Horace writes in the *Art of Poetry*:

Rage armed Archilochus with his trusty iambic.

Vel a numero pedum ut hexametrum et pentametrum, quae et ele-
giaca dicuntur, quorum repertor, ut aiunt, ignoratur. Horatius:

> Quis tamen exiguos elegos emiserit autor
> Grammatici certant, et adhuc sub iudice lis est.

Bucolicum carmen, autore Diodoro in 5, Daphnis Mercurii filius
excogitavit, et sic alii alia metra adinvenerunt quae nos in praesentia studio brevitatis omittimus, metri tantum originem prodidisse
contenti.

: X :

De tragoediae atque comoediae initiis.

1 Initium tragoediae et comoediae, teste Donato, a rebus divinis est
factum quibus antiqui pro fructibus vota solventes operam dabant.
Nam olim incensis altaribus et admoto hirco, id genus carminis
quod sacer chorus reddebat Libero Patri tragoedia dicebatur. Autoribus enim tragicis hircus praemium cantus proponebatur. Horatius:

> Carmine qui tragico vilem certabat ob hircum.

Qui Libero Patri immolabatur quia, ut ait Varro, noxium est vitibus animal.

2 Unde tragoedia ἀπὸ τοῦ τράγου, hoc est, ab hirco nominata
est, vel ut quibusdam placet quod hirco donabatur eius carminis
poeta; vel quod uter ex hircina pelle vini plenus pro praemio erat;
vel a faece, quia ante usum personarum ab Aeschylo repertum

Or else they named them after the number of their feet like the hexameter and pentameter. Together the two are called elegiac, and the inventor is unknown, they say. Horace again:

Who discharged those short little distichs?
It's still a debate, the grammarians feuding.

Daphnis, Mercury's son, devised bucolic verse, according to Diodorus in book [4]. Others likewise came upon other kinds of meter which in our concern for brevity we omit here, satisfied just to have made known its origin.

: X :

On the beginnings of tragedy and comedy.

The beginning of tragedy and comedy, according to Donatus, lay   1
in the religious customs of the ancients, when they fulfilled vows in return for crops. For in those days when fires burned at the altars and they led a goat to sacrifice, the sacred chorus offered to Father Liber the kind of song called a tragedy. In fact, they presented a goat to the writers of tragedy as a prize for their poetry, as Horace writes:

With tragic verse they fought for a worthless goat.

They sacrificed this animal to Father Liber because, as Varro says, it does harm to the vine.

Thus, the name tragedy comes from *tragos*, which means goat.   2
But some say it was so called because they gave the poet a goat for his poem; or because the prize was a goatskin bag full of wine; or else it was named after the dregs of wine because, before Aeschylus invented the use of masks, mimes used to smear their faces

mimi peruncti ora olei faecibus fabulas agebant. Horatius in *Poetica*:

> Ignotum tragicae genus invenisse camoenae
> Dicitur et plaustris vexisse poemata Thespis,
> Quae canerent agerentque peruncti faecibus ora.
> Post hunc personae pallaeque repertor honestae
> Aeschylus.

Tragoedias, autore Fabio in 10, primus in lucem protulit Aeschylus, sed longe clarius illustrarunt Sophocles atque Euripides. Apud nos, autore Donato, Livius Andronicus tragoediam primus invenit, in qua floruit Accius, Pacuvius, Ovidius et Seneca.

3   At vero nondum coactis in urbem Atheniensibus cum, ut testatur Varro, iuventus Attica circum vicos, villas, pagos et compita festum carmen solenniter quaestus gratia cantaret, orta est comoedia ἀπὸ τοῦ κωμάζειν quod est lascive agere vel κώμου, hoc est, a comessatione seu κώμης qui vicus est et ᾠδής, cantus. Quam tamen apud Graecos, uti Donatus sentit, dubium est quis invenerit primus, apud quos, sicut infra dicemus, duplex erat, antiqua et nova. Praecipui autem eius autores fuerunt Aristophanes, Eupolis et Cratinus. Apud Latinos eam primus omnium, ut Livius *Ab urbe condita* et Donatus testantur, reperit Livius Andronicus.

4   In tragoedia autem heroes, duces, reges introducuntur, et est sermo grandiloquus. Ovidius:

> Omne genus scripti gravitate tragoedia vincit.

In comoedia vero amores fere et virginum raptus. Tristitia tragoediae peculiaris est, propter quod Euripides, petente Archelao rege ut de se tragoediam scriberet, abnuit et precatus est ne accide-

with the dregs of wine in oil and act out stories, as Horace writes in the *Art of Poetry*:

> The tragic type of verse was still unknown, they say,
> When Thespis put his plays on wagons,
> His singers and actors smeared with lees of wine,
> Before Aeschylus invented the mask
> And attractive costumes.

It was Aeschylus who first made tragedy famous, according to Quintilian in book 10, but Sophocles and Euripides added much more to its renown. According to Donatus, the first of our people to devise a tragedy was Livius Andronicus; Accius, Pacuvius, Ovid and Seneca were accomplished tragedians.

But even before the Athenians gathered together in a city, as 3 Varro tells us, in village, manor, hamlet and crossroads, the young people of Attica sang traditional, festive songs to turn a profit; thus arose comedy from *kōmazein*, to frolic, or from *kōmos*, revel, or from *kōmē*, village, plus *ōdē*, song. Who first devised comedy among the Greeks is undecided, so Donatus believes. As we shall explain below, the Greeks had comedy of two kinds, old and new. The foremost comic authors were Aristophanes, Eupolis and Cratinus. Among the Latins, Livius Andronicus first composed comedy, as Livy in *From the Foundation of the City* and Donatus testify.

Tragedy introduces kings, generals and heroes, and its language 4 is lofty, as Ovid writes:

> For serious matters, tragedy beats any type of writing.

In comedy, on the other hand, everything is love-affairs and maidens abducted. Sorrow is the specialty of tragedy. For this reason, when King Archelaus asked Euripides to write a tragedy about him, he refused and prayed that nothing worthy of tragedy would

ret Archelao aliquid tragoedia dignum quoniam semper infelices
exitus habet, contra comoedia felices.

: XI :

De origine satyrae novaeque comoediae.

1 Satyrarum genera duo esse manifestum est, alterum antiquius tam
a Graecis quam a Latinis usurpatum quod sola carminum varietate
constabat, comoediae pene par nisi plus habuisset lasciviae. Huius
satyrae scriptores fuerunt Demetrius ex Tharso poeta satyricus, ut
autor est Laertius, et Menippus servus, sicut Apuleius et Gellius
ostendunt, cuius libros Marcus Varro in satyris imitatus eas latine
Menippeas appellavit. Alterum satyrarum genus recentius maledi-
cum et ad carpenda hominum vitia compositum, quod soli Latini
excogitaverunt. Teste Fabio Quintiliano, satyra quidem tota nostra
est, quae, autore Donato, hinc exordium sumpsit.

2 Nam cum in veteri comoedia per priscos poetas non penitus
ficta argumenta sed res gestae a civibus palam, tum eorum crebro
qui gessissent nomine decantarentur, quod tunc nequaquam moribus hominum obfuit cum pro se quisque caveret culpa aut domes-
tico probro ne spectaculo caeteris esset. Et inde ipsi poetae abuti
licentius stylo, et passim ex libidine laedere coepissent plures bonos. Id propter, ne quispiam hominum vitia amplius nominatim
carperet, lege sanxerunt. Ex huius igitur hoc pacto veteris comoediae interitu, satyra — quam nostri condiderunt — initium habuit.

3 Tunc autem poetae novam comoediam invenerunt quae generatim ad omnes homines qui mediocribus agunt fortunis pertineret,

happen to Archelaus since tragedies always have unhappy endings, while comedies end happily.

: XI :

On the origin of satire and new comedy.

There are two kinds of satire, obviously. The older type, used as 1 much by Greeks as by Latins, consisted merely of a variety of poems; it was almost like comedy except that it was more risqué. Writers of this kind of satire were the satiric poet, Demetrius of Tarsus, according to Diogenes Laertius, and, as Apuleius and Gellius point out, Menippus the slave, whose books Marcus Varro imitated in his *Satires* and called them in Latin Menippean. The other, more recent kind of satire is scurrilous and meant to snipe at human vice; only the Latins developed it. In fact, Quintilian says that satire is entirely ours, and according to Donatus its origin was the following.

In old comedy the ancient poets used subjects that were not 2 completely fictional, things that people did in public, and they regularly named the names of those who had done the deeds. At the time this was anything but harmful to civic morals since everyone feared being a spectacle before the others because of mischief or scandal at home. But then these same poets grew bolder in abusing the pen, and in their willfulness they began to strike indiscriminately at many upstanding citizens. Because of this they passed a law against them, to prevent them attacking anyone by name for his vices again. And so when old comedy collapsed in this way, satire — which we established — got its start.

But then the poets invented new comedy, which applied gen- 3 erally to all people of average means; it was less bitter, and for

et minus amaritudinis et eadem opera multum delectationis spec-
tatoribus afferret. Cuius Menander et Philemon autores fuere, qui
omnem prioris comoediae acerbitatem mitigarunt. Ab illis nostri
poetae Latini—Caecilius, Naevius, Licinius, Plautus, Terentius
atque alii antiquissimi comici—modum componendae comoediae
iucundae pariter ac gratae sumpserunt. Verum ii, si Quintiliano
credimus, vix levem Graecorum umbram consecuti sunt, quod
sermo Romanus non videatur posse recipere illam dicendi venerem, solis Atticis in hoc genere linguae concessam.

4   Satyra vero a satyris, ut Donato placet, qui illoti semper et pe-
tulantes dii sunt, nomen traxit; vel a satyra cibi genere, quod, autore Festo, ex variis rebus conditum erat. In hac satyra, teste Quintiliano in 10, primus insignem laudem adeptus est Lucillius; sed
eiusdem iudicio, purus magis ac tersior fuit Horatius. Persius
iuxta, quamvis uno libro, multum gloriae promeruit. Sed in primis
Iuvenalis lepidus fuit, de quo Quintilianum cum in 10 dixit, sunt
clari hodie quoque et qui olim nominabuntur, intellexisse ferunt.

: XII :

Quis primus historiam condiderit et de eius utilitate;
aut solutam orationem invenerit
deque texendae ipsius historiae regula.

1   Historia, quae tanto caeteris scriptis antecellit quanto plura exempla rerum complectitur diuturnitas temporis quam hominis aetas,
ad vitae institutionem utilissima censenda est quod, ut Cicero *De*
oratore praeclare ait, sola sit testis temporum, lux veritatis, vita memoriae et magistra vitae. Multarum enim rerum exemplis privatos

that reason it gave the audience more pleasure. Its authors were Menander and Philemon, who softened all the harshness of earlier comedy. Our Latin poets—Caecilius, Naevius, Licinius, Plautus, Terence and the other ancient comedians—adopted from them a way of composing comedy that was enjoyable and popular. If we believe Quintilian, however, they were scarcely a pale shadow of the Greeks because Roman speech seems incapable of that beauty of language attributed only to the Attic in discourse of this sort.

Donatus thinks that we took the word 'satire' from the satyrs, 4 gods who are always filthy and randy; or else it comes from *satura*, a dish made of a mixture of things, according to Festus. Lucillius was the first to attain outstanding fame in this kind of satire, according to Quintilian in book 10; in Quintilian's judgment, however, Horace was purer and cleaner. Persius likewise earned great glory with only one book. But Juvenal was especially witty. They say that Quintilian had him in mind when in book 10 he said: Today there are also distinguished writers who one day will be famous.

: XII :

Who first wrote history and on its utility;
who invented prose,
and on a rule for composing history.

History surpasses other types of writing by as much as the whole 1 span of time includes more notable events than the life of a man. Thus, history must be judged the most useful preparation for life because, as Cicero *On the Orator* says very clearly, she alone is the witness of ages, the light of truth, the life of memory and the mistress of life. With examples of many events, history makes ordi-

viros imperio dignos reddit, imperatores ob immortalem gloriam ad praeclara facinora impellit, milites propter laudem, quae eos qui vitam egregie profuderint comitatur, promptiores efficit ad pericula pro patria adeunda, improbos infamiae metu a vitiis deterret.

2   Hanc, ut Plinius libro 7 ait, Cadmus Milesius omnium primus condidit, sed Iosephus in primo *Antiquitatis* volumine rectius omnino sentiens, eum apud Graecos duntaxat primum historias scripsisse tradit: Nam Graeci cum, ut idem inquit, heri et nudiustertius fuerint, veri similius est antiquissimos Hebraeorum, qui sacros libros scripserant (Cadmus enim Milesius, ut apud Eusebium colligimus in 10 *De praeparatione evangelica,* longe post Mosen fuit), historias primo condidisse, vel Aegyptiorum aut Babyloniorum sacerdotes, sicut ipse Iosephus in primo *Contra Appionem* sentire videtur, aiens: Quoniam vero apud Aegyptios et Babylonios ex longissimis olim temporibus circa conscriptiones diligentia fuit, quando sacerdotibus erat iniunctum et circa eas ipsi philosophabantur. Et deinde infert: De nostris vero progenitoribus quia eandem quam praedicti habuerunt in conscriptionibus diligentiam desino dicere, etiam potiorem, pontificibus et prophetis hoc imperantes. Ex quo Eusebius (verissime, ut mea fert opinio) hoc potius Mosi assignare videtur, in 11 *De praeparatione evangelica* dicens: Unde sapientissimus ille Moses qui primus cuiusque hominis vetustissimi vitas Hebraeorum conscripsit, civilem atque in actione positum vivendi modum narratione historica docuit.

3   Verum nec illud profecto probabile videtur quod idem Plinius in septimo et Apuleius in *Floridis* tradit — Pherecydem Syrum primum solutam orationem condere instituisse tempore Cyri regis — nanque quis non videt hoc potius esse illis tribuendum qui primi historias scripserint? Quae uti luce clarius est soluta oratione

nary people fit for command, urging commanders to act nobly for the sake of immortal glory and soldiers for the sake of fame. She stands by those who valiantly give their lives and makes them the readier to meet danger on behalf of the fatherland; the dishonorable she frightens from their faults with the fear of infamy.

In book 7 Pliny says that Cadmus of Miletus was the first to compose history, but Josephus, reasoning much more accurately in the first book of the *Antiquities,* teaches that he was merely the first Greek who wrote history. For since the Greeks lived yesterday or the day before, as he says, it is more likely that the most ancient of the Hebrews, who wrote the sacred scriptures, were the first to compose histories — indeed, as we gather from Eusebius in book 10 of the *Preparation for the Gospel,* Cadmus of Miletus came long after Moses. Or else it was the priests of the Egyptians or Babylonians, as Josephus himself seems to believe in the first book *Against Apion,* stating: Since the Egyptians and Babylonians took pains with their writings from the most ancient times, they assigned this duty to their priests, who thought carefully about them. Then he adds: I do not neglect to say of our ancestors that they had the same concern for their writings as the aforesaid, even a stronger concern, commanding their priests and prophets to look after them. Thus (quite correctly, in my opinion) Eusebius seems to assign this to Moses instead, writing in book 11 of the *Preparation for the Gospel:* Whence Moses, that wisest of men and first of all the ancients to record the lives of the Hebrews, described their political and practical way of life in historical narrative.

Thus, what Pliny again in book 7 and Apuleius in the *Florida* teach — that Pherecydes of Syros first invented prose composition in the time of King Cyrus — does not really seem likely, for who does not see that this should be attributed instead to those who first wrote histories? That history was written in prose is as clear

conscribuntur. Quando etiam Pherecydes (ut de Aegyptiorum et Babyloniorum sacerdotibus sileam, qui et ipsi longe ante Graecos historias scriptitarunt) multo post Mosen fuit, quem ex testimonio Eusebii primum omnium historiam condidisse diximus. Pherecydes enim Syrus, autore Eusebio *De praeparatione evangelica* volumine 10, circiter primae Olympiadis tempora floruit. A Mose autem, quemadmodum ex eodem collegimus, ad Ioathan Iudaeorum principem, cuius temporibus Olympiades coeperunt, interfuerunt anni DCC et circiter LXXXVIII. At Strabo in primo *Geographiae* non solum Pherecydi sed Cadmo ac Hecataeo pariter assignat, qui et ipsi Mose uti liquido constat posteriores fuerunt.

4   Ex philosophis autem, Laertio Diogene autore, historias primus composuit Xenophon, de quo Quintilianus cum de historicis loquitur ait: Xenophon non excidit mihi, sed inter philosophos reddendus est. In ea apud Graecos floruit Thucydides, Herodotus, Theopompus. Apud nos Titus Livius, Crispus Sallustius et plerique alii. A principio Romani, veluti Fabius testatur, pro historiis annales pontificum habebant, in quos res gestae per annum referebantur.

5   De historiae initio haec dicere habui, nunc de componendae regula aliquid subiiciendum duximus. Prima est lex historico data, teste Cicerone *De oratore*, ne quid falsi dicere audeat, deinde ne quid veri non audeat; ne qua suspicio gratiae sit in scribendo, ne qua simultatis. Ipsa autem historiae aedificatio posita est in rebus et verbis. Rerum enim ratio tam temporis ordinem quam locorum

as day. Pherecydes (if I may pass over the priests of the Babylonians and Egyptians, who themselves also wrote histories long before the Greeks) also came long after Moses, whom we have described as the first historian of all, on the testimony of Eusebius. Pherecydes of Syros lived around the time of the first Olympiad, according to Eusebius in book 10 of the *Preparation for the Gospel*. Yet from the same source we have learned that about 788 years passed between Moses and Joathan, the prince of the Jews in whose time the Olympiads began. But Strabo in book 1 of the *Geography* assigns it not only to Pherecydes but to Cadmus and Hecataeus as well, who obviously were also later than Moses.

It was Xenophon, according to Diogenes Laertius, who was the 4 first of the philosophers to compose history. When he speaks about the historians, Quintilian says of him: I have not forgotten about Xenophon, but he is to be treated among the philosophers. Thucydides, Herodotus, and Theopompus were famous historians among the Greeks. Ours were Livy, Sallust and many others. From the start the Romans had the annals of the priests for histories, as Quintilian shows; into them they entered events year by year.

Having said this much about the origin of history, I believe that 5 I ought to add something now about a rule for composing it. The first law given the historian, according to Cicero *On the Orator*, is that one should never dare say anything false, the second that one should always dare tell the truth; there should be no hint of favoritism in what the historian writes and none of feuding. The edifice of history is built on events and words. An account of events demands chronology as much as geography, and also the customs, lives, plans, purposes, speeches, deeds, misfortunes and fates of

descriptionem poscit, item hominum mores, vitas, consilia, causas, dicta, facta, casus et exitus. Verborum vero ratio orationis genus desiderat lene, fusum ac pura illustrique brevitate ornatum.

: XIII :

De origine rhetorices et quibus rebus eius ratio contineatur.

1 Non dubium est quin geniti protinus homines ab ipsa rerum natura, hoc est, a Deo a quo primum creati sunt, sermonem acceperint. Qui mox, ut Fabius ait, sicut in medicina cum viderent alia salubria, alia insalubria ex observatione eorum effecerunt artem, ita cum in dicendo alia utilia, alia inutilia deprehenderent rhetoricen constituerunt.

2 Cuius, ut Diodorus in primo et poetae volunt, Mercurius autor fuit. Flaccus Horatius in *Carmine:*

Mercuri facunde nepos Atlantis
Qui feros cultus hominum recentum
Voce formasti, [etc.]

Quamvis in sexto idem Diodorus sibi repugnare videatur, dicens: Unde interpretis nomen assumpsit, non quod nominum aut orationis, ut quidam tradunt, fuerit inventor, sed quia diligentius quam caeteri mandata referebat. Nisi intelligatur, ut sui moris est, alibi fabulas, alibi veritatem esse secutus.

3 Verum Aristoteles primum Empedoclem artis inventorem fuisse ait, et Quintilianus idem fere sentit in tertio, sic scribens: Nam primus post eos quos poetae tradiderunt movisse aliqua circa

mankind. But the right choice of words demands the sort of language that is smooth, fluent and marked by a clear and distinct brevity.

: XIII :

On the origin of rhetoric and how its parts are organized.

There is no doubt that as soon as people came to be, they received   1
speech from nature—from God, in other words, by whom they were first created. Later on, as Quintilian says, just as they constructed an art of medicine by observing that some things were healthful and others unhealthful, in the same way, having recognized what was workable and unworkable in speaking, they established rhetoric.

Its founder, as Diodorus in book 1 and the poets suppose, was   2
Mercury. In one of his *Odes*, Horace calls him:

Mercury, eloquent heir of Atlas,
Who shaped with speech
The wild ways of primitive people.

And yet in book [5] Diodorus appears to contradict himself, saying: Hence he seems to have taken the title interpreter not, as some claim, because he was the inventor of names or of speech but because he reported more carefully than others what had been entrusted to him. Or perhaps Diodorus was aiming at the truth in one place and telling stories in another, as he often does.

Aristotle says that Empedocles was the first inventor of the   3
art, and in book three Quintilian expresses almost the same opinion, writing: Now after those whom the poets have recorded, Empedocles is said to be the first who tried anything in rhetoric.

rhetoricen Empedocles dicitur. Hanc autore Suetonio *De claris oratoribus* constat nonnunquam Romae prohibitam esse exerceri, sed cum paulatim deinde ipsa utilis et honesta apparuisset, adeo multi eam praesidii causa et gloriae expetivere, ut nonnulli ex infima fortuna in ordinem senatorium atque ad summos honores aspirarint. Artis autem huius scriptores antiquissimi fuerunt Corax et Thysias Siculi, quos Gorgias Leontinus eiusdem insulae insecutus est. Sed inter caeteros, apud Graecos longe princeps fuit ille Demosthenes, sicut apud nos Marcus Tullius Cicero lux doctrinarum fulgentissima ac Romanae eloquentiae fons uberrimus.

4   De initio rhetorices hactenus, sed et eius vis atque facultas dicatur. Ea, autore Cicerone *De oratore*, in quinque dividitur partes: ut orator debeat primum reperire quae dicat; deinde inventa ordine dispensare; tum ea denique ornare oratione; post memoriae mandare; et ad extremum cum dignitate aeque ut venustate agere. Et agendo illud, teste Quintiliano, praestare ut delectet, doceat, moveat. Bonus enim orator delectat audientium animos cum apte dicit, nam quod decet fere prodest atque delectat. Deinde docet cum exponit negocium quod in controversiam venit et quales sint personae inter quas illud sit. Postremo movet cum iudicum affectus excitat ad favendum miserendumve aut tristes solvit digna risu tempestive interponendo, si id opus esse perspicit. Atque iis rebus et verbis omnis ferme rhetorices ratio continetur.

5   Quod autem Graeci oratores causarum ῥητόρας, id est, rhetores vocent, nos tamen ita distinguimus ut orator sit qui causas agit, rhetor qui rhetoricen profitetur, declamator vero qui sive alios docendi sive se exercendi gratia fictam causam orat.

According to Suetonius *On Famous Orators*, it is known that the practice of rhetoric was sometimes forbidden in Rome. But then after it eventually proved useful and respectable, many sought it for fame and self-defense, and quite a few persons of the meanest circumstances aspired to senatorial rank and the highest honors. The most ancient writers in this art were the Sicilians Corax and Thysias; Gorgias of Leontini from the same island followed them. Of the others, Demosthenes was by far the best of the Greek rhetoricians, just as Cicero was our brightest light of learning and the richest source of Roman eloquence.

Having said this much about the beginning of rhetoric, I   4
should also describe its nature and content. According to Cicero *On the Orator*, it is divided into five parts: first, the orator needs to discover what to say; then he must put what he has found in order; next he must embellish these things with eloquence; then commit them to memory; and finally make his delivery with as much dignity as elegance. And in his delivery, according to Quintilian, he should amuse, teach and provoke. For the good orator gives his audience intellectual pleasure when he speaks properly, since what is correct is usually helpful and amusing. Next he teaches by explaining the issues in the case and the personalities involved. Finally he provokes when he rouses the emotions of his judges to support or sympathy or eases their sad feelings by injecting some timely humor, if he sees the need for it. Almost the whole organization of rhetoric is contained in these words and actions.

The Greeks call the orators who speak in law-suits *rhētores* or   5
rhetoricians, but we distinguish between the orator who argues cases, the rhetorician who professes rhetoric, and the set-speaker who gives speeches about fictional cases in order to practice or to teach others.

: XIV :

Quis primus musicam repererit, et quantum ea valeat ad tolerandos humanae vitae labores.

1   Musicen antiquissimam esse poetae clarissimi testimonio sunt, nam Orpheus et Linus, ambo diis geniti, musici insignes fuerunt, cum alter eorum rudes atque agrestes hominum animos demulceret, cantusque suavitate non feras modo sed saxa etiam, ut fabulae tradunt, sylvasque duceret. Horatius in *Poetica arte*:

> Sylvestres homines sacer interpresque deorum
> Caedibus et victu foedo deterruit Orpheus,
> Dictus ob hoc lenire tigres rapidosque leones.

Vergilius in *Ecloga* quarta:

> Non me carminibus vincet, nec Thracius Orpheus,
> Nec Linus, huic mater quamvis atque huic pater adsit,
> Orphei Calliopeia Lino formosus Apollo.

2   Apud quoque eosdem autores inter regalia convivia laudes deorum atque heroum ad citharam canuntur, ut Iopas ille Vergilianus canit errantem lunam, solisque labores. Musices autem repertor, teste Plinio libro 7, Amphion ex Antiopa Iovis filius fuisse dicitur, propter quod poeta in *Bucolicis* ait:

> Canto quae solitus, si quando armenta vocabat,
> Amphion Dircaeus in Actaeo Aracyntho.

Ipse quoque saxa movisse fertur. Horatius in *Poetica*:

: XIV :

Who first discovered music, and how much power it has to make the hardships of human life bearable.

The testimony of the best poets is that music is very old, for Orpheus and Linus, both god-begotten, were excellent musicians; the former soothed the crude and rustic spirits of humans, and the sweetness of his singing charmed not only wild beasts, as the myths tell it, but even rocks and plants. Horace writes in the *Art of Poetry*:

> Orpheus, when we lived in the woods,
> Spoke for the gods,
> And made men give up their jungle gore,
> This tamer of tigers and ravening lions.

Also Vergil in the fourth *Eclogue*:

> He will not subdue me in singing, not Thracian Orpheus,
> Though Calliope his mother help him,
> Nor Linus and splendid Apollo his father.

The same authors tell us that they sing the praises of gods and heroes to the lyre at royal banquets, as Vergil's Iopas sings the wandering moon and the labors of the sun. But according to Pliny in book 7 they say the inventor of music was Amphion, son of Antiope and Jupiter, wherefore the poet says in the *Bucolics*:

> I sing as Dirke's Amphion would sing,
> Calling cattle to Arakynth in Attica.

They claim that he also moved rocks. Horace in the *Art of Poetry*:

Dictus et Amphion Thebanae conditor urbis
Saxa movere sono testudinis.

Et Statius in primo *Thebaidos:*

   penitusque sequar quo carmine muris
Iusserit Amphion Tyrios accedere montes.

3   Sed Graeci, teste Eusebio *De praeparatione evangelica* libro 2, musicae harmoniae inventionem Dionysio attribuunt; ipse vero in 10
eiusdem operis Zethum et Amphionem fratres, qui Cadmi temporibus fuerunt, musicae repertores vocat. At Solinus huius artis
studium ex Creta manasse sentit, qui inquit: Studium musicum
inde coeptum cum Idaei Dactyli modulos crepitu ac tinnitu aeris
deprehensos in versificum ordinem transtulissent. Polybius tamen
in 4 hoc Arcadum maioribus assignat, quippe qui huius rei semper
studiosi fuerint. Vocum harmonias Mercurium adinvenisse Diodorus est autor in primo; ἁρμονίαν Graeci vocant quam nos dis-
similium concordiam appellamus.

4   Verum Amphionem et caeteros posthac huius rei autores fuisse
ratio poscit, cum Tubal Hebraeum, Lamech filium, qui multis aetatibus praecesserat omnes illos qui musicae inventores produntur,
Iosephus in primo *Antiquitatum* dicat musicam studiose coluisse et
psalterio citharaque cecinisse. Haec hactenus.

5   Sed artis origo nihilominus in dubio versari videtur: igitur ex-
pedit ut quaestio eiusmodi tandem aliquando plana fiat. Itaque
natura iam inde a principio mortalibus musicam velut muneri
dedisse videtur quando id ad tolerandos humanae vitae labores
plurimum valet. Siquidem homo statim natus cum in cunabulis
vagire incipit, continuo nutriculae cantitantis voce sopitus dormi-
tat. (Quippe infantes statim plorant quod crurum brachiorumque

They say that Amphion, who founded Thebes,
Struck his lyre and moved the stones.

And Statius in the first book of the *Thebaid*:

I'll tell it all: how Amphion summoned boulders
With a lyric to lay his walls at Thebes.

But the Greeks attribute the invention of musical harmony to   3
Dionysius, according to Eusebius in book 2 of the *Preparation for
the Gospel*, though in book 10 of the same work he names the
brothers Zethus and Amphion, who lived in the time of Cadmus,
as inventors of music. Solinus thinks that interest in this art came
from Crete, for he says: Musical study began from the time when
the Dactyls of Ida translated into poetic order the measures perceived in the sounding and ringing of bronze. In book 4, however,
Polybius assigns this to the ancestors of the Arcadians, who indeed were always very interested in music. The first book of
Diodorus is our authority that Mercury devised the harmonies of
sound; the Greeks call *harmonia* what we call the joining together
of the dissimilar.

But reason requires that Amphion and the others were authors   4
of this art at a later time, since in the first book of *Antiquities*
Josephus says that the Hebrew Tubal, son of Lamech, who by
many ages preceded all others deemed inventors of music, worked
zealously at it, playing on the lyre and the harp. So much for inventors.

For all that, it seems that the origin of this art remains in   5
doubt, so it will be useful finally to clarify the issue. Nature seems
to have given mortals the boon of music from the beginning
because it has such power to make the hardships of human life
bearable. In fact, as soon as the new-born begins to cry in the cra-
dle, it goes to sleep if lulled by the voice of a nurse steadily singing. (Actually, infants wail right from the start because they are

recte producendorum causa fasciis colligantur, ac ita a supplicio miseram vitam vivere incipiunt.) Deinde in omnibus ferme operibus modulatio aliqua rudis hominum defatigationem semper consolatur. Vergilius:

Hinc alta sub rupe canet frondator ad auras.

Sic remiges incitantur. Sic arator, auriga, mulio, longo inter laborem viamque sibilo reficitur. Quid quod non modo ii, verumetiam eorum sarcinaria iumenta eo cantu simul labore levantur? Nam assiduo usu compertum est mulos valde delectari tintinabulorum sonitu, quapropter muliones multiiugia tintinabula ad illorum colla suspendere solent, quo facilius sarcinarum labores perferant.

6   Eandem vim in caetera similiter animalia musicam habere inter omnes constat. Ita equi in bello tubarum clangore arrecti stare loco nesciunt ac iamiam in certamen ruere ardent. Ita leones stridore ferri maxime territantur. Sed quaeso unde ille avium concentus quo omnis ager suo tempore resonat? Ecquis docuit lusciniam varios canendi modos? Haec enim avicula sonum aedit perfecta musicae scientia modulatum: qui nunc continuo spiritu trahitur in longum, nunc variatur inflexo, nunc distinguitur conciso, copulatur intorto, promittitur, revocatur, infuscatur ex inopinato; interdum et secum ipsa murmurat—plenus, gravis, acutus, creber, extentus. Et breviter, audire licet omnia tam parvulis in faucibus concini quae tot exquisitis tibiarum tormentis, ut ait Plinius, ars hominum excogitavit. Huius harmoniae natura magistra est; quae vel ab initio alias animantes quibus ad sonum quempiam vox apta est musicam docuit, quemadmodum ostendimus. Atque haec vera artis origo.

7   Caeterum musicam quam Aegyptii, ut Diodorus testis est, tanquam virorum effoeminatricem prohibebant iuvenes perdiscere, et

120

wrapped in bindings to straighten their legs and arms, and thus they begin their wretched lives in torment). Thereafter, in almost all mankind's labors, there is always some crude melody to relieve weariness. Vergil writes:

Under the tall cliff the leaf-stripper sings to the wind.

In this way, oarsmen are urged on. In this way, a long whistle relieves the plowman, the charioteer and the muledriver in the midst of their working and journeying. How is it that when singing accompanies their labor, not only these men but even their pack-animals feel relief? For regular experience shows that mules take great delight in the sound of bells, which is why muledrivers usually hang sets of bells on the necks of their animals so that they may better stand the work of carrying.

Everyone agrees that music has the same power over other animals. Thus, when the blaring of trumpets rouses horses in battle, they cannot stand still and are eager to rush straight into the fray. The clanging of iron terrifies lions in the same way. But I wonder where that symphony of birds comes from that resounds through every field in its season? And who teaches the nightingale its many songs? For this little bird emits a sound tempered by a perfect knowledge of music: now it is long and drawn-out in one breath, now the breathing varies, now it splits into segments, then twists and rejoins, swells, diminishes, and darkens unexpectedly; sometimes she murmurs to herself—deep, low, treble, staccato, prolonged. To be brief, says Pliny, from these little throats one can hear as much as human skill has extracted from any pipes by torturing them so often and so exquisitely. Nature is mistress of this harmony; from the very beginning she taught music to other living things whose voices were capable of any sound at all, just as we have shown. And this is the true origin of this art. 6

The Egyptians forbade their young men to learn music, so Diodorus tells us, as if it would make women of them, and 7

Ephorus, autore Polybio in prooemio suarum *Historiarum*, ad delu-
dendos ac fallendos homines inventam tradidit, magno olim precio
aestimatam testatur Fabius qui dicit Socratem iam senem institui
lyra non erubuisse, et Cicero qui libro *Tusculanarum* primo ait The-
mistoclem quod in epulis recusasset lyram esse habitum indoctio-
rem, et Salii apud Romanos qui per urbem versus canebant, sed in
primis David, ille magnus vates, qui divino carmine Dei mysteria
canit—illud quoque Graecorum adagium, indoctos a Musis atque
Gratiis abesse, quod in nostris *Proverbiis* explanavi.

8   Tria praeterea genera sunt ex quibus musica constet: unum genus est quod instrumentis agitur, de quo infra dicetur; alterum
quod fingit carmina, ex quo ut poesis pars sit musices necesse est;
tertium quod instrumentorum opus carmenque diiudicat. Ex quo
recte ait Cicero *De oratore*, libro I, musicam versari in numeris, et
vocibus et modis.

: XV :

*Qui primum instrumenta diversi generis invenerint et ea in
Latium attulerint; ac quod sit organum; et de antiquissimo
tibiarum usu in praeliis.*

I   Mercurius Maiae filius lyram omnium primus ex testudine fecisse
dicitur. Tradunt enim cum aliquando Nilus suum egressus alveum
totam inundasset Aegyptum, et postea intra suos limites regressus
esset varias animantes in campis relictas inter easque remansisse
testudinem. Et hanc cum ille invenisset, consumpta iam carne sed

Ephorus taught that it was invented for deluding and deceiving men, according to Polybius in the proem to his *Histories*. Yet Quintilian shows that it was once so highly valued that Socrates was not embarrassed to be taught the lyre when he was already an old man, and in the first book of the *Tusculans* Cicero says that Themistocles was considered uncultured because he declined the lyre at banquets. And then there were the Roman *Salii*, who went through the city singing verses. But above all remember David, that great prophet, who sings God's mysteries in sacred poetry. The Greeks also had a saying, 'Ignore the Muses and forget the Graces,' which I have explained in my *Proverbs*.

Music, moreover, is of three kinds: the first kind, which is 8 played on instruments, will be treated below; the second composes songs, and so it is that poetry must be part of music; the third kind distinguishes instrumental art from song. Thus Cicero is right to say in book 1 *On the Orator* that music consists of rhythm, sound and mode.

: XV :

Who first invented instruments of various kinds and brought them into Latium; what an organ is; and on the oldest use of flutes in battle.

They say that Mercury, son of Maia, first made the lyre out of a 1 tortoise shell. The story goes that when the Nile sometimes rose out of its bed and flooded all Egypt, leaving many living things stranded on the flats as it later returned to its channels, one animal left there was the tortoise. When Mercury found it, the flesh had been eaten away but the sinews remained; striking them, he

superstitibus nervis, et percussione sonum excitasset ad exemplum illius lyram composuisse. Horatius in primo *Carminum:*

> Te canam magni Iovis et deorum
> Nuntium, curvaeque lyrae parentem.

Cui ex nervis trium chordarum instar trium anni temporum, autore Diodoro Siculo, tres instituit voces, acutam, gravem, et mediam—acutam ab aestate, gravem ab hyeme, mediam a vere sumens; qua, teste Servio super quarto *Aeneidos,* donavit Apollinem, accepto ab eo caduceo, de quo Vergilius:

> Tum virgam capit, hac animas ille evocat
> Orco Pallentes, alias sub tristia Tartara mittit.

Quidam eam non Apollini sed Orpheo primum tradidisse ferunt, alii vero ab Apolline post Orpheo concessam volunt.

2   Ad eam qui decantandos faciebant versus lyrici poetae nuncupati sunt. Reperio insuper (ut nihil quod attinet ad hanc rem omittatur) septem in ea chordas appositas iuxta numerum septem Atlantidum quod Maia Mercurii mater ex illarum numero fuisset, deinde superadditas duas ut repraesentaretur unum nomen Musarum. Haec autem tantae suavitatis fuisse perhibetur ut arbores, saxa, feras, veluti supra dictum est, traxisse Orpheus dicatur.

3   Mercurius praeterea, teste Plinio libro septimo, monaulum, id est, simplicem tibiam invenit. Primus autem tibias, autore Diodoro et Eusebio, Marsias adinvenit; Plinius vero geminas illum reperisse tradit. Alii hoc Apollini assignant, sicut lyrae et fistulae inventionem. Nam simulacrum eius quod erat in Delo habuisse dicitur in dextera quidem arcum, in laeva Gratias, quae singulae singula musicae instrumenta manibus gerebant, una lyram, altera tibias, quae autem media erat fistulam tenebat. Obliquae tibiae Midas in Phrygia autor fuit. Tibiae primo ex gruum tibiis, unde

produced a sound, and this became the model for the lyre that he put together. Horace in the first book of *Odes*:

> You, messenger to great Jove and all the gods,
> Maker of the curved lyre, you I sing.

With its sinews, according to Diodorus Siculus, he made strings of three tones, treble, bass and middle, following three seasons of the year—treble for summer, bass for winter and middle for spring; according to Servius on the fourth book of the *Aeneid*, he presented it to Apollo, from whom he received the caduceus, of which Vergil says:

> He takes the wand and raises fading souls from Orcus,
> Dismissing others to the gloom of Tartarus.

Some say he gave it first not to Apollo but to Orpheus, but others think that Apollo turned it over to Orpheus afterward.

2 Those poets who made verses to be sung to it were called lyric poets. I find, moreover (not to omit anything pertaining to this subject), that seven strings were put on it after the number of the seven daughters of Atlas because Maia, Mercury's mother, was one of them. Two more were added later, so that it represented only the fame of the Muses. This lyre is said to have been of such sweetness that Orpheus could attract trees, rocks and beasts, as mentioned above.

3 According to Pliny in book 7, Mercury also invented the *monaulos*, the pipe with a single tube. But according to Diodorus and Eusebius it was Marsyas who first devised pipes, and Pliny says he invented the double pipes. Others assign this to Apollo, as they do the discovery of the lyre and the syrinx. In fact, they say that his statue in Delos had a bow in its right hand and the Graces in its left, each of whom in turn carried a musical instrument in her hands, one a lyre, another the pipes, while the one in the middle held a syrinx. Midas in Phrygia was the originator of the slanted

nomen habent, tum ex arundinibus factae sunt, cum quibus voce canere Troezenius Dardanus instituit. Lydios modulos Amphion excogitavit, Dorios Thamyras Thrax, Phrygios Marsias Phryx, plures alios Terpander.

4   Fistulam, ut Plinius et Servius aiunt, Pan deus rusticus invenit. Nam cum Syringam Arcadiae nympham, autore Ovidio in primo *Metamorphoseon*, ardenter amaret, et illa fugiens ad Ladonem fluvium pervenisset et fluvio impedita non amplius fugere posset, implorato aliarum Nympharum auxilio in palustres cannas mutata est, quas cum Pan excidisset ex iis ad amoris solatium primus sibi fistulam confecit. Maro in Corydone:

> Pan primus calamos cera coniungere plures
> Instituit.

Sunt tamen qui hoc Apollini attribuant.

5   Venarum pulsum in musices pedes Herophilus primus discrevit per aetatis gradus. Fistulam vero quam Graeci *syringa* vocant, teste Eusebio in 2 *De praeparatione evangelica*, Cybele invenit. Citharae, ut Plinio placet, repertor fuit Amphion, ut aliis Orpheus, ut aliis Linus, ut vero Diodoro Apollo, qui libro quinto inquit: Apollo primum cithara simplici usus est, Marsias vero tibiis. Sentit idem Higinius. Septem chordas addidit Terpander. Vergilius in sexto:

> Obloquitur numeris septem discrimina vocum.

Octavam apposuit Simonides, nonam Timotheus. Cithara sine voce primus cecinit Thamyras, cum cantu Amphion, ut alii Linus. Haec ex Plinio.

6   At cithara tamen longe ante, uti superiore capite ostendimus, Tubal Hebraeus usus est, quam omnino ab ea dissimilem fuisse quam illi invenerunt quos commemoravimus testatur divus Hiero-

pipes. Pipes were first made from the shinbones of cranes, whence their name, and later from reeds. Dardanus of Troezen began the custom of singing to their accompaniment. Amphion developed the Lydian modes, Thamyras the Thracian composed the Dorian, Marsyas from Phrygia the Phrygian and Terpander several others.

Pan, god of the countryside, invented the syrinx, so Pliny and 4 Servius claim. In the first book of the *Metamorphoses*, Ovid says that though Pan burned with love for Syrinx, a nymph of Arcadia, she ran away to the river Ladon; there, when the river stopped her from fleeing further, she cried out for help to the other nymphs and was changed into marsh-reeds, which Pan cut to make the first syrinx as consolation for his love. Vergil in his poem on Corydon writes:

Pan showed how to put reeds together with wax.

There are those, however, who attribute this to Apollo.

Herophilus first analyzed the pulse in the veins by age-level, us- 5 ing musical measures. According to Eusebius in book 2 of the *Preparation for the Gospel*, however, Cybele invented the reed-pipe that the Greeks call a *syrinx*. Pliny is convinced that Amphion was the discoverer of the lyre; others say Orpheus, others Linus, but in book [3] Diodorus opts for Apollo, saying: Apollo first used the lyre without accompaniment, but Marsyas used pipes. Hyginus thinks the same. Terpander added seven strings, as Vergil writes in book 6:

He plays with seven intervals of sound.

Simonides put the eighth in, Timotheus the ninth. Thamyras first played the lyre without vocal accompaniment, and Amphion added the singing; others say Linus did it. All this Pliny tells us.

But as we have shown in the previous chapter, Tubal the He- 6 brew used the lyre much earlier. In his letter to Dardanus on mu- sical instruments, Jerome (or whoever the author is, since there is

nymus in epistola de instrumentis musicis ad Dardanum (aut quisquis illius autor est, quia de ea re ambigitur), scribens citharam apud Hebraeos vigintiquatuor chordas habuisse factam ad formam Δ literae.

7   David etiam ille magnus Dei vates varia instrumenta invenit, teste Iosepho in septimo *Antiquitatum* qui ait: Diversaque faciens organa, docuit ut Levitae secundum ea Deo hymnos edicerent per sabbatorum dies aliasque solennitates. Organorum autem species huiusmodi est canora, cithara quidem decem chordis coaptata, et haec cum plectro percutitur. Nabla vero, duodecim sonos habens, digitis tangitur, et reliqua.

8   Hinc perspicere licet istiuscemodi organa a David confecta diversa fuisse a nostris, quorum nunc usus in templis est perquam frequens, quando illa plectro pulsabantur, nostra vero inflantur follibus, unde multis meatibus quasi cicutis imparibus vox erumpit concentumque efficit. Quanquam Iosephus hoc loco dicens diversaque faciens organa videtur organum pro instrumento quocunque musico ponere. Idipsum sentit Augustinus, qui instrumenta musicorum cuncta speciatim excellentiora etiam organa vocat. At autor nostri organi tam concinni non proditur, cum magna eius nominis iactura, sicut in extremo tertio libro dicetur.

9   Sambucam item musicum instrumentum, autore Clemente, Troglodytae (Africae, ut Solino placet, populi) invenerunt. Tubam aeneam teste Plinio Piseus Tyrrhenus reperit, quod Diodorus libro sexto non Piseo tantum, sed Tyrrhenis omnibus tribuit, ita scribens: Tyrrheni, pedestri quoque exercitu praevalidi, tubam primam adinvenerunt, bello admodum utilem. (Non eo tamen inficias Diodorum in Plinii sententiam ire, quandoquidem iure a Graecis dicitur victus Hector quamvis a solo Achille interemptus fuerit.) Sentit idem Vergilius in octavo *Aeneidos*, dicens:

doubt about it) testifies that this lyre was altogether different from the one invented by those whom we have mentioned, writing that the Hebrew lyre had twenty-four strings and was made in the shape of the letter Δ.

David, that great poet of God, also invented various instruments, according to Josephus, who says in book 7 of the *Antiquities*: Making various instruments, he instructed the Levites to compose divine hymns arranged for them and to use them on Sabbath days and other festivals. One instrument of this kind was the *canora*, a lyre fitted with ten strings and struck with a plectrum, though the *nabla*, which had twelve tones, was plucked with the fingers, and so on.

Hence it seems clear that the various instruments of this sort constructed by David were different from our organs now widely used in churches. His were struck with a plectrum, while ours are blown with a bellows to produce sound from many openings in pipe-like affairs of different sizes and thus make a harmony. Although in this passage Josephus says 'making *organa* of various kinds,' he seems to use 'organ' for any musical instrument whatever. Augustine does the same, and he too calls the whole class of better musical instruments organs. The originator of our very harmonious organ is not known, though the loss of that name is a great one, as will be explained in the last part of book 3.

According to Clement, the Troglodytes (whom Solinus calls an African people) invented another musical instrument—the *sambuca*. Pliny says that Pisaeus the Tyrrhenian first made a bronze trumpet, which Diodorus in book [5] attributes not so much to Pisaeus as to all the Tyrrhenians, writing thus: The Tyrrhenians, working hard to form their infantry as well, devised the first trumpet, so useful in war. (One should not deny that Diodorus supports Pliny, however, for it is correct to say that Hector was defeated by the Greeks, though he was killed by Achilles alone.) Vergil thinks the same in the eighth book of the *Aeneid*, saying:

Tyrrhenusque tubae mugire per aethera clangor.

10   Verum Acron super hoc Horatianum in *Poetica arte*,

    post hos, insignis Homerus
Dircaeusque mares animos in martia bella
Versibus exacuit,

tradit Dircaeum poetam primum tubam comperisse, quoniam is, ut Porphyrio dicit, primus tubae modulos dedit hac de causa: Nam cum Lacedaemonii, autore Iustino libro 3, bellum adversus Messenios gererent diuque extraherent dubium Martis eventum, responsum acceperunt ab Apolline, si vellent vincere Atheniensi duce uterentur. A quibus rogati Athenienses contumeliae causa ipsis Dircaeum quendam, claudum, luscum, omnique ex parte corporis deformem dederunt. Usi sunt auxilio eius Lacedaemonii, quibus ille cantum monstravit tubarum quarum inaudito territi sono Messenii fugam fecerunt, adeptique sunt victoriam Lacones. (Sed in codicibus Iustini invenio Tyrtaeum per t et t in antepenultima, ut in alterutris mendum sit.) Quidam etiam tubae autorem volunt Maletum sive Maleum dictum.

11   Verum quid multa, cum tubae inventor fuerit Moses, ille divinus Hebraeorum dux, dicente Iosepho in tertio *Antiquitatum*: Adinvenit autem modum tubae ex argento factae quae est huiusmodi; longitudinem habens pene cubiti, est autem angusta fistula calamo capacior, praebens latitudinem quae conveniat ori ad susceptionem spiritus, et classico sono vicina quae Hebraica lingua vocatur 'asosra.' Haec ille. Sed haud scio unde de primis tubae inventoribus tanta dissensio inter scriptores orta sit nisi intelligamus

Across the sky a noise of Tuscan trumpets groans.

But Acro, writing on the following passage from Horace's *Art of* 10
Poetry,

> After them,
> Dircaeus and Homer spread their fame, driving
> Virile minds to war with martial verses,

teaches that the poet Dircaeus first learned how to make a trumpet, since, as Porphyrio says, he first gave the trumpet its melodies
for the following reason: When the Lacedaemonians were waging
war against the Messenians and were long in doubt about the
outcome of the conflict, according to Justinus in book 3, they
interpreted an oracle from Apollo to mean that if they wished
to win, they should employ an Athenian general. When they were
asked, the Athenians contemptuously gave them a certain Dircaeus, lame, one-eyed, and deformed in every part of his body.
The Lacedaemonians took his help, and he showed them the
trumpet-calls that put the Messenians to flight, terrified by the
strange new noise, so the Laconians won their victory. (But in the
texts of Justinus I find 'Tyrtaeus' beginning with a 't' and with 't' in
the antepenult, so that it should be emended in both places.)
Some think that a person called Maletus or Maleus was the inventor of the trumpet.

Yet why go on? The inventor of the trumpet was Moses, that 11
divine leader of the Hebrews, as Josephus explains in book 3 of the
Antiquities: He invented a kind of trumpet made of silver in the
following way; it is almost a cubit in length, but its tube is narrow,
somewhat wider than a reed-pipe, large enough for the mouth to
breath into; called *asosra* in Hebrew, it sounds like a war-trumpet.
This is what Josephus says, but I find it hard to understand why
the authors came to disagree so much about the first inventors of

alios aliud tubarum genus — sunt enim plura genera — et alibi invenisse.

12   In Latium instrumenta musica, teste Dionysio Halicarnassaeo, Arcades primi omnium attulerunt, cum antea fistulis pastoralibus tantum uterentur. Placet insuper antiquum usum tibiarum in praeliis ponere. Thucydides itaque autor gravissimus tradit Lacedaemonios tibiarum modulis in praeliis esse usos: Etenim cum paratae essent classes et instructae acies coeptumque iri in hostem, tibicines inter exercitum positi canere inceptabant, non voluptatis causa sed ut aequali modulatoque sensim ingressu convenientes pugnam capesserent. Cuius rei Polybius libro quarto, et Fabius in primo, Gellius itidem in primo, et Plutarchus in *Vita* Lycurgi meminit. Hunc morem additis tympanis etiam nunc noster peditatus servat.

13   Alyattes quoque Lydorum rex, autore Herodoto libro primo, in bello adversus Milesios fistulatores et fidicines concinentes habuit. Sicuti memoriae proditum est, Cretenses praelia ingredi solitos praecinente ac praemoderante cithara gressus, autor Gellius. At Parthos consuevisse tympanorum sonitu pugnam inire, testatur Plutarchus in *Vita Crassi* et Appianus Alexandrinus in *Libro parthico*. Reliqui fere omnes, ut hodie fit, tubis in praelio utebantur. Unde Vergilius de Miseno tubicine inquit:

> quo non praestantior alter
> Aere ciere viros, Martemque accendere cantu.

the trumpet unless we take it that various people invented various kinds of trumpet in various places—for there are several kinds.

The Arcadians first of all brought musical instruments into 12 Latium, according to Dionysius of Halicarnassus, since formerly they used only shepherd's pipes there. I think it right, moreover, to locate the oldest use of pipes in battle. Thucydides, a most important authority, accordingly teaches that the Lacedaemonians used the melodies of pipes in battle: When they had drawn up their ranks, prepared the line and set off against the enemy, pipers placed among the troops began playing, not to give pleasure but in order to join battle marching in unison at an equal and measured pace. Polybius in book 4, Quintilian in book 1, Gellius also in book 1, and Plutarch in his *Life* of Lycurgus all make note of this. Even now our infantry keep this custom and add drums as well.

Alyattes, king of the Lydians, also had pipers and harpers 13 playing together in his war against the Milesians, according to Herodotus in book 1, and the Cretans, so we are told, used to begin their battles with a lyre playing in front of them and setting a cadence; Gellius is our source for this. But it was the custom of the Parthians to enter battle at the sound of drums, according to Plutarch in his *Life of Crassus* and Appian of Alexandria in the *Book of Parthia*. Almost all others used trumpets in battle, as we do today. Whence Vergil says of Misenus the trumpeter:

No one better to rouse troops with the trumpet
And play the brass to light the blaze of Mars.

: XVI :

De origine philosophiae et de duobus eius principiis; et quis
primus invenerit ethicen et dialecticen ac dialogos introduxerit.

1 Philosophiam, quam Cicero in *Officiorum* libris studium sapientiae vocat et in *Tusculanis* virtutis indagatricem atque vitiorum expultricem, a barbaris ad Graecos fluxisse plerique volunt. Nam apud Persas primum Magos eorum sapientes claruisse dicunt. Apud Babylonios et Assyrios Chaldaeos; apud Indos Gymnosophistas, quorum sectae princeps, teste Hieronymo *Contra Iovinianum*, Budda nuncupabatur; apud Britannos et Celtas sive Gallos Druides; apud Phoenices Ochum; apud Thraces Zamolsim et Orpheum; apud Libycos Atlantem; quos omnes, autore Laertio, pro sapientibus habuerunt. Aegyptii vero Nili filium Vulcanum fuisse dicunt eumque philosophiae aperuisse principia. Sed idem Laertius a Graecis philosophiam manasse affirmat quoniam apud eos Musaeum et Linum primos fuisse sapientes ferunt.

2 Verum teste Eusebio primum philosophia, sicuti reliquae fere omnes disciplinae, ab Hebraeis originem duxit. Ex quo philosophos Graecorum, qui Porphyrionis testimonio amplius mille annis post Mosen fuere, Eusebius in II *De praeparatione evangelica* philosophiam a Iudaeis accepisse plenissime demonstrat, quando nec ipsius nomen philosophiae apud eos primum fuit, sed deinde. Nam Pythagoras omnium primus, Lactantio autore in tertio, philosophiam, id est, amorem sapientiae, et se philosophum, id est, amatorem sapientiae, nominavit, dicens solum Deum sapientem esse; antea enim *sophia*, hoc est sapientia, dicta est quae nunc philosophia vocatur, et qui hanc profitebantur *sophi*, id est, sapientes vocitati sunt.

: XVI :

On the origin of philosophy and of its two sources; who first invented ethics and dialectic and introduced dialogues.

Philosophy, which Cicero's *On Duties* calls devotion to wisdom and   1
his *Tusculans* explorer of virtue and expeller of vices, is generally
supposed to have come to the Greeks from the barbarians. For
they say that the Magi were the first famous wise men among
the Persians. Among the Babylonians and Assyrians it was the
Chaldaeans; among the Indians the Gymnosophists, the founder
of whose school was named Buddha, according to Jerome *Against
Jovinian*; among the Britons and Celts or Gauls it was the Druids;
among the Phoenicians Ochus; among the Thracians Zamolsis
and Orpheus; among the Lybians Atlas; all these, according to
Laertius, were considered wise men. The Egyptians, however, say
that Vulcan was the son of the Nile and that he revealed the elements of philosophy. But Laertius also declares that philosophy
came from the Greeks since they say that their Musaeus and Linus
were the first wise men.

According to Eusebius, philosophy actually originated with the   2
Hebrews, as did almost all the other disciplines. Citing Porphyry,
who says that the philosophers of the Greeks came more than a
thousand years after Moses, Eusebius demonstrates most abundantly in book II of the *Preparation for the Gospel* that they took
their philosophy from the Jews, since at first they did not even
have a name for philosophy, only afterward. For according to
Lactantius in book 3, Pythagoras was the first of all to use the
term philosophy or love of wisdom and to call himself philosopher
or lover of wisdom, saying that God alone is wise; what is now
called philosophy was formerly called *sophia* or wisdom, and those
who professed it were called *sophoi* or wise men.

3   Philosophiae autem duo fuere principia: Alterum quod ab Anaximandro Ionicum est appellatum eo quod Thales Milesius fuerit ex Ionia, et hic Anaximandrum instituerit; alterum vero ex Pythagora Italicum est dictum, quoniam eius autor Pythagoras valde multum in Italia philosophiae operam dedit. Eusebius in 10 *De praeparatione evangelica* tertium addit, id est, Cleaticum, cuius Xenophanes Colophonius autor dicitur.

4   Dividunt insuper philosophiam, autore Cicerone *De oratore*, in tres partes: In naturae obscuritatem, in disserendi subtilitatem, in vitam atque mores; et primam physicam, alteram dialecticam, tertiam ethicam Graeci vocant. Quam etiam divisionem Plato, ut ait Eusebius, ab Hebraeis sumpsit, sicuti singula ipsius philosophiae praecepta. Physicae proprium est de mundo et de his quae sunt in eo disserere, quam ex Ionia Athenas Archelaus primus importavit. Ethicae vero de vita moribusque tractare, quam Socrates comperit. Cicero libro quinto *Tusculanarum*: Socrates autem primus philosophiam devocavit e coelo, et in urbibus collocavit, et in domos etiam introduxit, et coegit de vita et moribus rebusque bonis et malis quaerere. Dialectica autem ambarum partium affert rationes, quae a Zenone Eleate initium sumpsit. Quamvis secundum alios in quinque partes dividatur: in physicam, metaphysicam, ethicam, mathematicam et logicam.

5   Verum nos iam fines nostros egressi sumus, non enim res definire et de singulis planum facere, sed de earum initiis docere nostri tantummodo est muneris; proinde ad institutum opus redeamus. Dialogos, uti apud Laertium discimus, Plato omnium primus introduxit — vel potius maxime omnium illustravit, nam Aristoteles libro *De poetis* primo illud scribendi genus inventum tradit ab Alexameno Scyreo Teiove.

There were two sources of philosophy, however: Anaximander 3
called one Ionian because Thales of Miletus was from Ionia and
Thales was Anaximander's teacher; the other was called Italian after Pythagoras, who founded it and did a great deal of work on
philosophy in Italy. In book 10 of the *Preparation for the Gospel*,
Eusebius adds a third, the Cleatic, of which Xenophanes of Colophon is called the author.

In addition, they divide philosophy into three parts, according 4
to Cicero *On the Orator*: The obscurity of nature, the subtlety of
discourse and then life and morals; the first the Greeks call physics, the second dialectic and the third ethics. Plato also took this
division from the Hebrews, as Eusebius says, as he did each of the
precepts of this philosophy. Physics treats of the world and what it
contains; Archelaus first brought it to Athens from Ionia. But ethics, which Socrates revealed, deals with life and morals. Cicero in
the fifth book of the *Tusculans* writes that Socrates first called philosophy down from heaven, established it in cities, even introduced it into homes, and compelled it to inquire about life and
morals, good and evil. Dialectic, which contributes to the methods
of both the other parts, originated with Zeno of Elea. Others,
however, divide philosophy into five parts: physics, metaphysics,
ethics, mathematics and logic.

But we have overstepped our limits, for it is not our business to 5
define and clarify every topic, only to give information about origins; so let us return to our appointed task. We learn from Diogenes Laertius that Plato first of all introduced dialogues — or rather
wrote better dialogues than anyone else, for Aristotle in the first
book *On Poets* teaches that Alexamenus of Styra or Teos invented
writing of this type.

: XVII :

Qui primi astrologiam adinvenerint aut quorundam
syderum cursus deprehenderint, et sphaeram
ventorumque rationem atque quot illi sint, et observationes
syderum in navigando reppererint.

1 Terra potissimum ex syderum temperatione fructus fert uberiores, ut nos in eo proverbio demonstravimus, annus fructificat non tellus. Hominumque natura, si Iulii Firmici (ut ita dicam) somniis credimus, maxime syderibus subiecta est. Ait enim: Qui habebit horoscopum in quarta parte Mercurii erit ratiocinator; qui in Equo auriga; qui in septima parte Arietis gibber aut gibberosus. Et alibi: Luna, inquit, candidos, Saturnus nigros, Mars rubicundos gignit.

2 Et hoc ab Aegyptiis profectum dixerim, nam Herodotus de hac religione ita scribit: Alia insuper sunt ab Aegyptiis excogitata— quis mensis diesve cuius deorum sit, et quo quis die genitus qualia sortietur, et quam mortem obibit et qualis existet. Chaldaei vero, teste Diodoro libro tertio, dicebant planetas plurimum conferre ad bona vel mala consequenda. Unde Hermione apud Ovidium ita conqueritur:

Quae mea coelestes iniuria fecit iniquos?
Quodque mihi miserae sydus obesse querar?

Hinc igitur ab hominibus ex observatione coelesti inventa est astrologia, in qua coeli conversio, ortus, obitus, motusque syderum arte quadam conclusus est.

: XVII :

*Who first devised astrology or recognized the cycles
of certain heavenly bodies, invented the astronomical sphere,
discovered the pattern and number of the winds,
and began to observe the stars in navigation.*

The earth bears fruit in good plenty chiefly by reason of the mod-   1
erating influence of the heavenly bodies, as we showed in explaining the proverb, 'The year brings fruit, not the land.' Human nature is also quite subject to them, if we believe the fantasies (so I
call them) of Julius Firmicus, for he states: Whoever has a horo-
scope in the fourth part of Mercury will be an accountant; a horo-
scope in the Horse makes a charioteer; in the seventh part of the
Ram, a crookback or hunchback. Elsewhere he claims: The Moon
brings forth white complexions, Saturn black and Mars ruddy.

I would say that this came straight from the Egyptians, for this   2
is how Herodotus writes about their religion: The Egyptians
worked out other things besides—what month or day to dedicate to each god, what would befall the people born on each day,
what death they would die and how they would live. But the
Chaldaeans, according to Diodorus in book [2], said that the planets contribute greatly to good or evil events. Which is why, according to Ovid, Hermione laments as she does:

What have I done to make the heavens hate me?
To what star should I make my sad complaint?

For such reasons, then, people observed the heavens and devised
astrology, in which the revolution of the heavens and the rising,
setting and motions of the heavenly bodies become topics in a sort
of art.

3   Hanc Aegyptii, ut autor est Diodorus, a se primum repertam asserunt, alii vero a Mercurio. Sed idem libro quinto Actinum Solis filium ad eos astrologiae notitiam traduxisse docet, id quod Clemens primum Chaldaeis, dein ipsis Aegyptiis assignat. At Iosephus in primo *Antiquitatum* perspicue demonstrat Abraham primum Aegyptiis astrologiam inventam a suis maioribus, ut infra dicemus, tradidisse cum in Aegyptum ille aufugerat, et ab his eam inde simulque Chaldaeis, qui huius quoque disciplinae autores feruntur ob iugem operam quam observandis syderibus impendebant, ad Graecos fluxisse tradit, in primo *Contra Appionem* dicens: Sed eos etiam qui de coelestibus et divinis primitus apud Graecos philosophati—id est, Pherecydem Syrum et Pythagoram et Thaletem—omnes concorditer confitentur Aegyptiorum et Chaldaeorum fuisse discipulos.

4   Caeterum Plinius libro septimo Atlantem Libyae filium astrologiam invenisse dicit, quapropter poetae tradiderunt hunc sustinere coelum humeris. Vergilius in sexto:

> ubi coelifer Atlas
> Axem humero torquet stellis ardentibus aptum.

Sed idem Plinius libro 6 Iovi Belo hoc adscribit, dicens: Durat adhuc ibi Iovis Beli templum; inventor hic fuit syderalis scientiae. Et in 5 libro aliter, scribens: Ipsa gens Phoenicum in gloria magna literarum inventionis et syderum. Alii volunt Assyrios reperisse, quibus tamen Servius super sexta *Ecloga bucolicorum* ait Prometheum prius astrologiam indicasse.

5   Verumenimvero horum quos prodidimus postea alios alibi huius rei autores fuisse ducimus, quando a primordio statim orbis liberi Seth (Adam, primi hominis, filii), teste Iosepho autore sane

The Egyptians say that they discovered astrology themselves, 3
Diodorus tells us, though others say it was Mercury. But in book 5
Diodorus claims that Actinus, the son of the Sun, first brought
them knowledge of astrology, which Clement assigns originally to
the Chaldaeans and later to the Egyptians. Yet in the first book of
the *Antiquities*, Josephus clearly demonstrates that Abraham, when
he had fled into Egypt, first taught the Egyptians astrology, which
had been invented by his ancestors, as we shall explain below. The
Chaldaeans are also considered the authors of this discipline because of the continuous attention they paid to observing the stars,
as Josephus says in the first book *Against Apion*, where he maintains that it came from the Chaldaeans and Egyptians to the
Greeks: Those also among the Greeks who first philosophized
about heavenly and divine matters—Pherecydes of Syros, Pythagoras and Thales, that is—are by common consent called disciples
of the Egyptians and Chaldaeans.

Pliny, on the other hand, says in book 7 that Atlas, son of 4
Libya, invented astrology, wherefore the poets have taught that he
holds up heaven on his shoulders, as Vergil does in book 6:

Where Atlas holds the heavens on his shoulders
And twists the axis joined to blazing stars.

Yet Pliny also ascribes this to Jupiter Belus in book 6, saying: The
temple of Jupiter Belus still stands there; he was the inventor of
the science of the stars. Pliny has something different in book 5,
where he writes: Discoveries in letters and in the heavens earned
great glory for these Phoenician people. Others think that the
Assyrians discovered it, though Servius, commenting on the sixth
Eclogue, says that Prometheus had made astrology known to them
earlier.

But we conclude that those we have mentioned were actually 5
originators of astrology at later times in various places, since the
children of Seth (son of the first man, Adam) first invented the

gravissimo in primo *Antiquitatum*, disciplinam rerum coelestium primum invenerunt; qui, ut ne dilaberentur quae reperissent, neve antequam venirent ad cognitionem deperirent cum praedixisset Adam rerum omnium futurum interitum, duas columnas fecerunt, ex quibus una ex lateribus constructa erat, altera ex lapidibus, ut si lateritia ab imbribus destrueretur, lapidea permanens integram scripturam legentibus praeberet. His igitur in columnis ea quae ad observationem syderum pertinerent inscripserunt. Proinde ab Hebraeis ad Aegyptios et Chaldaeos et deinde ad reliquos astrologiam manasse credere par est. Ac tale fuit astrologiae artis nempe ad sanarum mentium delyrationem duntaxat excogitatae initium.

6   Defectus solis et lunae primus Romani generis, teste Plinio libro 2, Sulpitius Gallus, apud Graecos Thales Milesius deprehendit. Lunae cursum, ut idem ait, Endymion. Sed defectum lunae Plutarchus Anaxagoram primum monstrasse dicit, in *Vita* Niciae dicens: Primus autem qui lunaris luminis atque umbrae causam deprehenderit ac literis mandare ausus sit Anaxagoras fuit. Etenim quod is antea ignotus esset ex eo probat, quod cum Nicias male gestis rebus Siciliam deserere decrevisset et noctu forte luna defecisset, omnes milites propter rei ignorationem—quanquam paulo ante Anaxagoras claruerat—turbati malum aliquod sibi portendi arbitrati sunt.

7   Veneris syderis naturam Pythagoras Samius investigavit. Quod idem esse quem luciferum vocamus quia ante matutinum tempus oritur et vesperum quia post solis occasum refulget Parmenides primus animadvertisse dicitur, autor Laertius in nono. Sphaerae, teste Cicerone libro *Tusculanarum* primo, Archimedes Syracusanus repertor fuit, quod Diogenes Musaeo adscribit, Plinius vero in 7

science of heavenly phenomena immediately after the origin of the world, according to a most important authority indeed—Josephus, in the first book of the *Antiquities*. Lest their discoveries be lost, lest they be destroyed before they were understood, they set up two columns, one built of brick, the other of stone, after Adam had predicted the coming destruction of all things. Should the brick column be destroyed by the rains, the one made of stone would remain and provide a complete account for those who might read it. They inscribed on these columns matters pertaining to the observation of the heavenly bodies. And so it is reasonable to believe that astrology came from the Hebrews to the Egyptians and Chaldaeans, and from them to other peoples. Such was the beginning of the art of astrology, which doubtless was devised simply to befuddle sound minds.

The first of the Roman people to observe eclipses of the Sun 6 and Moon was Sulpitius Gallus, according to Pliny in book 2. Thales of Miletus was the first of the Greeks to do so. First to observe the Moon's cycle was Endymion, says Pliny. But Plutarch says that Anaxagoras first taught about the eclipse of the Moon, writing in the *Life* of Nicias: Anaxagoras was the first who understood the cause of light and shadow on the Moon and dared to set it down in writing. And indeed he shows that this was previously unknown because, when Nicias decided to abandon Sicily after events had taken a bad turn, one night an eclipse happened to occur, and all the soldiers were disturbed since they were ignorant of the phenomenon and thought it to portend something evil—even though Anaxagoras had explained it shortly before.

Pythagoras of Samos investigated the nature of Venus as a 7 heavenly body. Parmenides, they say, first noticed that the object we call Lucifer because it rises before dawn is the same as the Evening Star that shines after sunset, and our source is Laertius in book 9. Archimedes of Syracuse invented an astronomical sphere, according to Cicero in book 1 of the *Tusculans*. Diogenes ascribes it

Anaximandro vel potius (ut est in secundo volumine, capite octavo) Atlanti.

8   Ventorum rationem Aeolus reperisse fertur, quod ideo proditum esse duco quia, autore Strabone libro sexto et Plinio in tertio, ex fumo insularum prope Siciliam in quibus ipse Aeolus regnavit, incolae quinam flaturi essent venti triduo praedicebant, unde etiam Aeolo ventos parere existimatum est.

9   Ventos autem nonnullis placuit esse quatuor: Ab oriente aequinoctiali Solanum, a meridie Austrum, ab occidente aequinoctiali Favonium, a septentrione Septentrionem, ut unaquaeque coeli regio suum haberet ventum, sunt enim totidem regiones — ortus, occasus, meridies, septentrio. Ortus et occasus mobilia atque varia, meridies vero septentrioque statu perpetuo permanent. Sed qui diligentius rem hanc pertractarunt tradiderunt ventos esse numero octo, reliquosque quatuor posuerunt, Eurum, Africum, Chorum sive Caurum, Aquilonem, et id in primis Andronicus Cyrrhestes. Is Athenis, teste Vitruvio, locavit turrim et in singulis lateribus imagines ipsorum ventorum exculptas contra cuiusque flatus, supraque metam marmoream posuit ac in ea Tritonem aereum dextera manu virgam porrigentem, quem ita fabricatus est ut vento circumageretur staretque semper contra venti flatum, virga interim ad eius venti imaginem versa.

10   Est itaque Eurus ab oriente hyberno collocatus inter Solanum et Austrum; inter Austrum et Favonium ab occidente hyberno Africus: inter Favonium et Septentrionem Chorus: inter Septentrionem et Solanum Aquilo, a vehementi aquilae volatu dictus, (graece Boreas vocatur ἀπὸ τοῦ βοᾶν, quod est clamare, quia sonoro flatu est). Igitur orientales venti tres sunt, id est, ut ab hyberno orientali incipiamus, Eurus, Solanus (quem quidam Vulturnum nuncupant), et Aquilo; ac totidem occidentales, Africus, Favonius, Chorus. Atque ita Eurus flat adversus Africum, Solanus

to Musaeus, but in book 7 Pliny assigns it to Anaximander, or (in book 2, chapter [6]) to Atlas instead.

They say that Aeolus discovered the pattern of the winds — for 8 the following reason, I suppose. According to Strabo in book 6 and Pliny in book 3, the natives could tell three days in advance what winds were going to blow from the smoke of the islands near Sicily that Aeolus ruled, and so it was thought that even the winds obeyed Aeolus.

Some say there are four winds: Solanus blows from the quarter 9 where the sun rises at equinox, Auster from the South, Favonius from the quarter where the sun sets at equinox, Septentrio from the North, so that each region of the heavens has its wind; for the number of regions is the same — East, West, South and North. East and West are variable and movable, but South and North remain always in the same place. Those who have examined the question more closely, however, especially Andronicus of Cyrrhus, have taught that the winds are eight in number, and to the others they add four, Eurus, Africus, Chorus or Caurus and Aquilo. According to Vitruvius, Andronicus put up a tower in Athens with images of these winds carved on its sides so that each faced into one breeze; on top he set a marble pillar and upon it a bronze Triton holding out a staff in his right hand, constructed so that it would move about in the wind and always face toward the wind that was blowing, with the rod pointing at the image of that wind.

And so Eurus blows from the winter sunrise between Solanus 10 and Auster; from the winter sunset between Auster and Favonius blows Africus; between Favonius and Septentrio blows Chorus; between Septentrio and Solanus Aquilo, so called from the powerful flight of the eagle. (In Greek it is called *Boreas,* from *boan,* to cry out, because its blowing is noisy.) There are three east winds, then, beginning with the one that blows from the winter sunrise, Eurus, Solanus (which some call Vulturnus), and Aquilo; and the same number of West winds, Africus, Favonius, and Chorus.

adversus Favonium, Aquilo contra Chorum. Verum Favonius clarus et saluberrimus est, quem nos a fovendo nominamus quod genitalem habeat spiritum. A Graecis Zephyrus vocatur, quasi ζωὴν φέρων, hoc est vitam afferens. Quemadmodum Auster nebulosus et pestifer praesertim Romae, qui a Graecis Notus dicitur quibus νοτίς humor est.

11   Per hunc modum Andronicus Cyrrhestes ostendit unde certi ventorum flatus spirarent, quem nunc ubique gentium servant, positis in summitate locorum pinnis aeneis per quas ventorum flatus indicentur. At quoniam ventus nihil aliud est nisi aeris fluctus, et idem fluctus pro locorum natura alius alibi concitatur, idcirco factum est ut incolae in suis quisque regionibus nomina aliquot ventis dederint eosque suos proprios habuerint, ut Scyron Atheniensium, ut Circius Narbonensis provinciae, ut Iapyx Apuliae ventus est, et alii aliarum regionum.

12   Observationes autem syderum in navigando Phoenices adinvenisse, autor est Plinius in 7 *Naturalis historiae*.

: XVIII :

Qui primi geometriam et arithmeticam invenerint.

1   Nilus totius orbis fluviorum celeberrimus a solstitio aestivo usque ad autumnale aequinoctium, ut Herodotus libro 2 et Diodorus in 1 testatur, immensa aquarum mole quotannis totam Aegyptum exundat, ex cuius incremento Aegyptii vim aut penuriam futurarum frugum praevident. Aegyptus enim cum Nilus in 12 cubitos excrescit famem sentit; in 13 etiamnum esurit; 14 cubiti hilaritatem afferunt, 15 securitatem, 16 delitias, quod iustum fertur esse incre-

Eurus thus blows opposite Africus, Solanus opposite Favonius, Aquilo opposite Chorus. Now Favonius is clear and very healthful, and we name it after the word for nurturing because its breath brings birth. The Greeks call it *Zephyr*, as if it were *zōēn pherōn* or life-bearing. Auster, in turn, is cloudy and noxious, especially in Rome; the Greeks call it *Notus* because *notis* is their word for moisture.

With his device Andronicus of Cyrrhus showed the directions from which the fixed winds blow, and now people use it everywhere, setting bronze arrows atop various places to indicate the directions of the winds. But since wind is nothing more than a disturbance of the air and the nature of the location causes a similar disturbance to behave differently in different places, for that reason it happened that in various regions the natives gave various names to the winds, so that each had its own, as Sciron is a wind in Athens, Circius in Provence, Iapyx in Apulia, and others in other regions.

The Phoenicians developed observations of the stars for navigation, according to Pliny in book 7 of the *Natural History*.

: XVIII :

Who first invented geometry and arithmetic.

In all the world the most famous river is the Nile. Each year from the summer solstice to the autumnal equinox, as Herodotus shows in book 2 and Diodorus in book 1, it floods all of Egypt with an immense quantity of water. In its rise the Egyptians foresee either abundance or scarcity for the crops to come. For when the Nile rises twelve cubits, Egypt knows famine; with thirteen cubits she still goes hungry; fourteen cubits bring cheer, fifteen security and

mentum. Maximum autem aetate Claudii principis fuit cubitorum 18, sicut minimum Pharsalico bello veluti caedem magni Pompeii prodigio quodam aversante, autores Plinius libro 5 et Strabo 17. Cum huiusmodi itaque Nili inundationes limites agrorum confunderent, nunc minuendo, alias immutando, nonnunquam delendo signa quaedam quibus proprium ab alieno discerneretur, iterum atque iterum metiri eam terram oportebat, propter quod Strabo 17 *Geographiae* et Herodotus 2 aiunt nonnullos prodidisse geometriam ab Aegyptiis primo inventam esse, quemadmodum arithmeticam, id est, numeralem scientiam a Phoenicibus propter mercaturas.

2   Sed Iosephus utrunque Hebraeis attribuere videtur, in 1 *Antiquitatum* sic scribens: Illi nanque cum essent religiosi cum et eis pabula ad maius tempus existerent praeparata, tot annorum circulis rite vivebant; deinde propter virtutes quas iugiter perscrutabantur, id est, astrologiam et geometriam, Deus eis amplius vivendi spatium condonavit. Et deinde, cum de Abraham mentionem facit, subiicit: Arithmeticam eis quoque contulit et quae de astrologia sunt ipse quoque contradidit, nam ante adventum Abraham in Aegyptum haec Aegyptii penitus ignorabant.

3   Artem postea, ut Marcus Tullius autor est, Pythagoras multum amplificasse dicitur. Geometria, teste eodem Cicerone *De oratore*, versatur in lineamentis, in formis, in intervallis, in magnitudinibus quae ita sub se continet geographiam quae situm orbis pingit. In qua floruit Strabo tempore Tiberii Caesaris et Ptolemaeus Traiani et Antonini imperatorum principatu. Apud nos Plinius absolutissime de hac re tractavit, et Solinus in *Collectaneis*.

sixteen exultation. This is said to be the regular level of the rise, but the highest was eighteen cubits in the time of the Emperor Claudius, and the lowest came with the battle of Pharsalus as if by some prodigy to show horror at the killing of Pompey the Great, according to Pliny in book 5 and Strabo in book 17. Thus, since these Nile floods muddled the borders of the fields, reducing their sizes, changing their shapes, sometimes destroying the markers that distinguished one property from another, it was necessary to measure the land over and over again. For this reason some have claimed that the Egyptians first discovered geometry, just as the Phoenicians invented arithmetic, the science of numbers, for commercial purposes, according to Strabo in book 17 of the *Geography* and Herodotus in book 2.

But Josephus seems to attribute both discoveries to the Hebrews, writing thus in book 1 of the *Antiquities:* Because they were religious and because they had foods that gave them longer lives, living so many years was normal for them; God also granted them a longer period of life because of the important things that they continually investigated, such as astrology and geometry. And later, when Josephus makes mention of Abraham, he suggests that Abraham also brought arithmetic to them, as well as giving them the facts about astrology, for the Egyptians were entirely ignorant of these things until Abraham came into Egypt.

Pythagoras is supposed to have added a great deal to the art afterward, as Cicero tells us. In his work *On the Orator* he also says that geometry has to do with lines, shapes, distances and sizes; thus, it includes geography, which depicts the regions of the globe. Strabo was a famous geographer in the time of Tiberius Caesar, as Ptolemy was in the principate of the emperors Trajan and Antoninus. For us Latins, Pliny produced the most complete treatment of geography, and we also have Solinus in his *Collected Writings*.

: XIX :

Quis primus reppererit pondera et mensuras ac numeros,
et de vario apud gentes numerandorum annorum modo.

1 Videtur omnino locus exigere ut antequam hinc digrediamur quis
pondera et mensuras ac numeros reppererit indicemus, cum praesertim geometriae atque arithmeticae partes sint scriptoresque de
hac re non plane inter se consentiant. Eutropius itaque statim in
principio 1 libri Sidonium mensuras et pondera eo tempore invenisse tradit quo apud Albanos Procas, apud Iudaeos Aza, apud
Hierosolymos Hieroboam regnavit. Alii secundum Mercurium
ex Creta, Iovis filium, comperisse volunt. At Plinius libro 7 in primis hoc Phidoni Argivo vel, ut Gellio placet, Palamedi assignat.
Strabo autem libro 5 Phaedonem Elidensem reperisse affirmat.

2 Ex quo ita intelligendum puto ut alii aliis primum mensuras et
pondera invenerint, velut Diogenes Laertius libro 9 affirmat Pythagoram primum adinvenisse Graecis. Et Iosephus 1 *Antiquitatum*
dicit Cain Adam filium mortalium omnium, ut credere convenit,
primum haec constituisse. Numerorum autem repertorem sunt
qui dicant Samium Pythagoram; alii non hunc sed alium Pythagoram Rhegynum sculptorem; alii vero Mercurium. Livius dicit numerum putari inventum Minervae.

3 Modus numerandi annos apud Graecos per Olympiades fuit,
qui autem per notas suarum literarum numerum notabant. Apud
Romanos primum per lustrum, quod quinto quoque anno claude-
batur (de quo fusius libro proximo capite 4 dicemus); deinde per
clavos—qui idcirco annales vocabantur—aut per consules id fie-

: XIX :

Who first devised weights and measures and numbers,
and on the various methods of counting years that people use.

Before we move on from here, context certainly seems to require   1
that we show who devised weights and measures and numbers, especially since they are parts of geometry and arithmetic and because those who write on this topic do not clearly agree among
themselves. Right at the beginning of book 1, Eutropius teaches
that a Sidonian invented measures and weights at the time when
Procas ruled in Alba, Aza in Judaea, and Jeroboam in Jerusalem.
Others think that the second Mercury from Crete, the son of Jupiter, discovered them. But Pliny in book 7 assigns this first of all to
Phidon of Argos or else, as Gellius would prefer, to Palamedes. In
book [8], however, Strabo affirms that the discoverer was Phaedon
of Elis.

Hence, I think it must be understood that different people dis-   2
covered measures and weights in different places, as Diogenes
Laertius confirms in book 9 that Pythagoras first developed them
for the Greeks. And Josephus in book 1 of the *Antiquities* states
that the first of all mortals to establish them was Adam's son Cain,
as one ought to believe. Yet there are those who say that Pythagoras of Samos was the inventor of numbers; others say it was not
him but another Pythagoras, a sculptor from Rhegium; others say
it was Mercury. Livy says that number is considered an invention
of Minerva.

In Greece the way of counting years was by olympiads, but they   3
used the letters of their alphabet as numerals. At first the Romans
used the lustration, which was completed every fifth year (we will
describe this in more detail in chapter four of the next book); later
it was done with nails — called annual for this reason — or by con-

bat. Clavi enim in pariete aedis Iovis, ea parte qua erat templum Minervae, in singulos annos figebantur ut per eos numerus annorum colligeretur. Sane lex, priscis literis ac verbis scripta, erat ut qui praetor maximus esset Idibus Septembris clavum pangeret, nam quia rarae per ea tempora literae erant, notae numeri annorum clavi fuere. Minervae autem templo ea lex dicata erat quod numerus eius deae inventum sit. Volsinii quoque clavos numerorum indices habuere fixos in templo Nortiae, Hetruscae deae. Postea consules id officium fecere, et postremo solenne clavi figendi ad dictatores translatum est. At more intermisso cum post longum tempus pestilentia laboraretur, et seniorum memoria repetitum foret aliquando eum morbum sedatum fuisse ob clavum a dictatore fixum, eius rei causa Lucius Manlius dictator dictus est, qui Titum Pinnarium magistrum equitum dixit.

4   Bella scilicet placatio, vel potius puerorum certamen qui ita solent ludere! Ecquid religionis cultusve in eo pangendo clavo esse potuit, qui parietem templi magis aperiebat quam claudebat? Sed ea erat illius temporis calamitas, cum nondum ad Romanos pervenisset Dei optimi maximi cognitio. Nos similiter his septem literis, C D I L M V X, numerum notamus, vel aliis notis, 1 2 3 4 5 6 7 8 9, satis omnibus cognitis ut nihil sit quod reliquas ponamus earumve rationem explicemus.

suls. Each year they drove nails into that part of the wall of the temple of Jupiter where the sanctuary of Minerva was so that they could reckon the number of years from them. In fact, there was a law, written in ancient letters and words, that whoever was chief praetor should drive a nail on the Ides of September, for since writing was uncommon in those days, the nails marked the number of years. This law specified the sanctuary of Minerva because number was the invention of that goddess. The Volsinians also had nails fixed as counters in the sanctuary of Nortia, an Etruscan goddess. Later the consuls did this job, and finally the rite of driving the nail passed to the dictators. But the custom had long been neglected when the city was struck by a pestilence, and it was learned from the memory of the elders that such a sickness had once been relieved when the dictator drove a nail. For this reason they named Lucius Manlius dictator, and he made Titus Pinnarius master of the horse.

A charming means of propitiation, to be sure, or rather a pastime for boys given to such games! What religion or piety could there be in this nail-driving that broke open the wall of the sanctuary rather than closing it up? But this was the misfortune of that age, when knowledge of the best and greatest God had not yet reached the Romans. Like them, we use these seven letters, C D I L M V X, to write numbers, or else we use these other signs, 1 2 3 4 5 6 7 8 9, which everyone knows so well that we need say nothing more about them nor explain how they work.

: XX :

Quis primus medicinam invenerit, et in quot ea divisa sit partes, ac apud quos olim non fuerit medicorum usus.

1 Medicina, quae suis divinis (ut ita dicam) remediis haud dubie mortalibus inter tot morborum undique erumpentium genera versantibus magno ubique praesidio praestoque est, diis primum inventores suos — nec mehercule iniuria — assignavit et coelo dicavit, ipsaque ab oraculis deorum multifariam petita est.

2 Hanc enim, teste Diodoro, volunt Mercurium apud Aegyptios primum invenisse; secundum vero veteres, Apis Aegyptiorum rex reperit; quod alii, autore Plinio libro 7, Arabo Apollinis et Babylonis filio tribuunt, alii vero ipsi Apollini. Unde ad Daphnen virginem apud Ovidium libro primo *Metamorphoseos* dicit:

Inventum medicina meum est, opiferque per orbem
Dicor.

Et Oenone apud eundem:

Ipse repertor opis vaccas pavisse Pheraeas
Fertur.

Macrobius in 1 *Saturnalium* huius rei veram reddens rationem, de Apolline ait: Hinc est quod eidem attribuitur medendi potestas, quia temperatus solis calor morborum omnium fuga est. Clemens autem Aegyptiis omnino adscribit, eius vero amplificationem Aesculapio primo Apollinis filio. Meruit et in ea arte laudem tertius Aesculapius, Arsippi et Arsinoae filius, qui praeter caetera primus,

: XX :

Who first discovered medicine; into how many parts it is divided; and who once made no use of physicians.

With its divine remedies (if I may call them so) medicine is 1 doubtless a great and ready defense everywhere for mortals subject to the many kinds of disease that break out all around them. At first — meaning no offense, to be sure — medicine counted her discoverers among the gods and raised them to heaven, and people in many places have looked for medicine from the oracles of the gods.

According to Diodorus, they maintain that Mercury actually 2 invented it among the Egyptians; but the ancients say that Apis, king of the Egyptians, discovered it; while others, according to Pliny in book 7, attribute it to Arabus, son of Apollo and Babylon, and still others to Apollo himself. Hence, in the first book of Ovid's *Metamorphoses*, Apollo says to the maiden Daphne:

Medicine is my discovery, and helper is what the world
Calls me.

And Ovid's Oenone says:

The first healer himself tended cattle for Admetus,
They say.

Macrobius gives a true account of this in book one of the *Saturnalia*, where he says of Apollo: So it is that the power of healing is attributed to him, because the temperate heat of the Sun drives out every disease. Clement, however, gives all credit to the Egyptians, though he ascribes the improvement of medicine to the first Aesculapius, Apollo's son. The third Aesculapius, son of Arsippus and Arsinoe, also earned praise in this art because before any oth-

teste Cicerone *De natura deorum*, dentis evulsionem ac purgationem alvi invenisse fertur.

3   Hanc tamen quisquis primitus invenerit, hoc quippe pacto excogitasse fertur: Nam cum homines (ut Fabio Quintiliano placet, sicut antea diximus) ex observatione rerum ea quae salubria aut insalubria visa sunt probe notassent, huiuscemodi artem corpora curandi gratia confecerunt. Atqui Cornelius Celsus inventionem artis scienter ponit libro I, scribens: Saepe causa apparet—utputa lippitudinis, vulneris—neque ex his patet medicina. Quod si scientiam non subiicit evidens causa, multo minus ea potest subiicere quae in dubio est. Cum igitur illa incerta incomprehensibilisque sit, a certis potius et exploratis petendum est praesidium, id est, ab his quae in ipsis curationibus experientia docuit, sicut in caeteris omnibus artibus.

4   Nam ne agricolam quidem aut gubernatorem disputatione sed usu fieri liquet. Ac istae cogitationes nihil ad medicinam pertinent, cum de his rebus qui diversa senserunt non ab obscuris causis neque a naturalibus actionibus sed ab experimentis, prout cuique responderant in perducendo homines in eandem sanitatem, medendi vias traxerint. Notarunt enim aegrorum qui sine medicis erant alios propter aviditatem primis diebus cibum protinus sumpsisse, alios propter fastidium abstinuisse, et levatum magis morbum eorum qui abstinuissent; itemque alios in ipsa febre aliquid edisse, alios paulo ante eam, alios post remissionem eius, et optime iis cessisse qui post finem febris id fecissent. Eadem ratione alios inter principia statim usos esse cibo pleniore, alios exiguo, et graviores eos factos qui se implevissent. Haec similiaque cum quotidie inciderent, diligentes homines talia animadvertentes ad extre-

ers he invented tooth-pulling and purging the bowels, as Cicero
tells us in *The Nature of the Gods*.

In any event, whoever originally discovered medicine, the story 3
is that they thought it out in the following way: When people had
made observations and duly noted what seemed good for health
and what seemed bad (this is Quintilian's view, as we have said before), they developed an art of just this kind in order to care
for their bodies. And in his first book Cornelius Celsus makes a
well-informed proposal on the invention of the art, writing: There
is often a clear cause—of inflamed eyes, for example, or of a
wound—and no treatment follows from these causes. Now if a
manifest cause does not lead to understanding, much less can
something doubtful suggest an answer. So when the cause is uncertain and unintelligible, one should seek help instead from what
is certain and tested, from what experience has taught in the
course of treatment, in other words, just as in all the other arts.

Clearly, what makes even a farmer or a pilot is experience, not 4
disputation. Such deliberations have nothing to do with medicine:
Those who hold different beliefs on these questions have found
the paths of healing not in hidden causes or physiology but in experience, insofar as each got good results in bringing people to the
same state of heath. They noted, for instance, that some of the
sick who had no physicians took food right away in the first days
of their illness because they were hungry, while others had no appetite and did not eat, and that those who had abstained found
more relief from their complaints. They also noted that some of
the sick would eat something even during a fever, others shortly
before, and others after the fever lifted, and that those who had
eaten afterwards got the best results. Likewise they saw that some
took a good deal of food at the beginning while others ate lightly,
and that those who filled themselves became more ill. As these
and similar things happened day after day, careful people who
were alert to them finally understood what would be of use to the

mum perceperunt quae aegrotantibus utilia forent. Sic medicinam ortam inter omnes constat. Haec ille.

5   Postea medicina in tres divisa est partes, ut una esset quae victu, altera quae medicamentis, tertia quae manu mederetur. Primam διαιτητικὴν secundam φαρμακευτικὴν tertiam χειρουρ-γικὴν Graeci appellant. Ita morbi aut victu aut medicamentis purgantur manuve curantur. Huius autem partis, id est, chirurgiae inventor dicitur primus Aesculapius, quem Graeci tradunt primum obligavisse vulnus.

6   Sed medicina cum nulla artium, ut Plinius ait, inconstantior sit et saepius mutetur — quia nulla est fructuosior — longo tempore in nocte densissima delituit quam omnino perditam (teste eodem Plinio libro *Naturalis historiae* 29) Hippocrates, genitus in insula Co Aesculapio dicata, in lucem revocavit. Nam cum fuisset mos (ut ait Strabo in 8 *Geographiae*) liberatos morbis inscribere in templo eius Dei qui auxiliatus esset quo postea similitudo proficeret, exscripsisse ea traditur et ita ex his hanc artem excerpsisse, qui, teste Plinio libro 26, primus medendi praecepta longe post hominum memoriam clarissime condidit.

7   Romam constat primum ex medicis venisse Peloponnensem Archagathum, Lysaniae filium, Lucio Aemilio Paulo Marco Livio consulibus anno urbis DXXXV, eique ius quiritium datum et tabernam in compito Acilio emptam. Is primo vulnerarius, inde ob secandi urendique saevitiam carnifex appellatus fuit. Et cum alii accurrerent Graeculi medici idemque facerent, omnes simul cum sua medicina in taedium venerunt. Quare a Marco Catone Censorio reprobati urbe et Italia pulsi sunt, de quibus ipse Cato ad filium in hunc modum scripsit: Dicam de istis alio loco, Marce fili, quid

sick. Everyone recognizes that this is how medicine came to be.
Celsus tells us this.

Later, medicine was divided into three parts: one healed with 5
diet; another with drugs, a third with the hand. The Greeks call
the first *diaitētikē*, the second *pharmakeutikē*, the third *cheirourgikē*,
whereby diseases are either purged with diet or drugs or cured
with the hand. Of this last part, which is surgery, the first Aesculapius is called the inventor, and the Greeks claim that he was the
first to bind up a wound.

But since none of the arts, as Pliny says, is more inconstant or 6
changes more often — because none is more profitable — medicine
lay hidden for a long time in night so dense that it was entirely
lost (again see Pliny, book 29 of the *Natural History*), and then
Hippocrates, born on the island of Cos, sacred to Aesculapius, restored it to the light. For it was the custom (says Strabo in book 8
of the *Geography*) for those freed from illness to make an inscription in the temple of the god who had helped them because a record might be useful later. They say that Hippocrates copied these
out and from them gathered his art — he who was far and away
the first in human memory to give a completely clear account of
the precepts of healing, according to Pliny in book 26.

It is agreed that the first of the physicians who came to Rome 7
was Archagathus, son of Lysanias, from the Peloponnese, in the
consulate of Lucius Aemilius Paulus and Marcus Livius, 535 AUC.
Citizen rights were given him, and a shop purchased in the
Acilian crossroads. He was at first a wound-specialist and eventually came to be called 'torturer' because of his ferocity in cutting
and cauterizing. And when other Greekling physicians hurried
over and did the same, all of them along with their art of medicine fell into disrepute. For this reason they were condemned by
Marcus Cato the Censor and driven from the city and from Italy.
Cato wrote to his son about them as follows: I will tell you elsewhere, Marcus my son, what I have discovered in Athens about

Athenis exquisitum habeam et quod bonum sit illorum literas as-
picere—non perdiscere. Vincam nequissimum et indocile genus illorum, et hoc puta vatem dixisse. Quandocunque ista gens suas literas dabit, omnia corrumpet, tunc etiam magis si medicos suos
huc mittet. Iurarunt inter se barbaros necare omnes medicina, sed
hoc ipsum mercede faciunt ut fides his sit et facile disperdant. Nos
quoque dictitant barbaros et spurios nosque magis quam alios opi-
cos appellatione foedant.

8   Plinius etiam de huiusmodi carnificibus (sunt enim et medici
peritissimi, unicum profecto adversus tot morborum genera hominibus subsidium) in fronte 29 libri ait: Nec dubium est omnes is-
tos famam novitate aliqua aucupantes animas statim nostras nego-
ciari. Hinc illae circa aegros miserae sententiarum concertationes,
nullo idem censente ne videatur assertio alterius. Hinc illa infelicis
monumenti inscriptio: turba se medicorum perisse. Et paulo inferius subdit: Nulla praeterea lex quae puniat inscitiam capitalem,
nullum exemplum vindictae, discunt periculis nostris et experi-
menta per mortes agunt, medicoque tantum hominem occidisse
summa impunitas est, etc.

9   Atqui sapienter Babylonii factitabant, qui, teste Herodoto libro
1 et Strabone in 16 *Geographiae*, medicis non utebantur sed aegrotos
in forum efferebant ut viri qui eos adirent consulerent hortaren-
turque ad ea quae ipsi faciendo effugissent similem morbum aut
alium novissent effugisse, nec fas erat quempiam aegrotum silentio
praeterire. Idem factitabant Bastetani, homines montani qui id
Hispaniae latus incolunt quod ad aquilonem spectat, et Aegyptii.
Ex quo Strabo libro 3 *Geographiae* cum de Lusitanis meminit, Bastetani, inquit, aegrotos vetusto ritu Aegyptiorum in plateis depo-

these people and that it may be good to glance at their writings — not to make a study of them. I will confound the lot of them, worthless and impervious to learning, and you may think me a prophet for having said so. Whenever this breed publishes anything, everything goes to ruin. So much the worse if they send their physicians here. They have sworn among themselves to kill all barbarians with medicine, but they do it for pay in order to gain our confidence and destroy us easily. They also keep calling us barbarians and bastards, and they defame us more than others by naming us Oscan yokels.

Pliny too speaks about torturers of this sort in the beginning of book 29 (obviously there are highly skilled physicians as well who are a special protection for humanity against so many kinds of disease): There is no doubt that they all do a steady trade in our lives, making a grab for fame with some new gimmick. So they surround the sick and argue their wretched theories, none of them agreeing on anything lest it seem another's pronouncement. Hence that inscription on the unhappy monument: A gang of physicians killed him. And a little further on he adds: Moreover, there is no law to punish capital ignorance, no precedent for vengeance; they learn at our peril and do deadly experiments; only a physician can kill a man with total impunity, and so on. 8

The Babylonians had a wise custom, however. According to Herodotus in book 1 and Strabo in book 16 of the *Geography*, they made no use of physicians but carried their sick out into the marketplace so that people who came upon them might advise them and urge them to do what they themselves had done to escape a similar illness or what they knew another had done to escape, and they were not allowed to pass by a sick person in silence. The Bastetani, mountain-dwellers who live in the northern part of Spain, had the same custom, as did the Egyptians, and thus when Strabo speaks of the Lusitanians in book 3 of the *Geography*, he says that the Bastetani follow an ancient practice of the Egyptians 9

nunt ut qui eo morbi genere tentati sunt commonefacere eos va-
leant. Quanquam non eundem semper ritum Aegyptiis fuisse
Herodotus docet libro 2 ita scribens: Iam vero medicina apud eos
hunc in modum distributa est, ut singulorum morborum singuli
sint medici non plurium. Itaque omnia referta sunt medicis: Alii
enim sunt oculis curandis constituti, alii capiti, alii dentibus, alii
alvi partibus, alii morbis occultis.

10   In medicina vero deinde quamplurimi floruerunt, et in iis: Cassius Calpitanus, Aruncius Rubrius, Antonius Musa (Augusto
Caesari charissimus), Galenus tempore Antonini Pii, et non longe
post Avicenna.

: XXI :

*De herbariae et medicamentariae atque melleae medicinae
inventoribus, et quae homines ab animalibus remedia
didicerint.*

1   Non dubium est quin natura herbas aut salutis aut voluptatis gratia, ut multis constat exemplis, genuerit. Nam Xanthus historiarum autor, teste Plinio libro 25, tradit occisum draconis catulum
revocatum ad vitam a parente herba quam *balin* vocant. Picus itidem avis adactum eius cavernis cuneum admota quadam herba
exilire cogit. Quinimo Indorum quidam, ait Herodotus libro 2,
herba tantum victitant. Appianus etiam Alexandrinus scribit Parthos ab Antonio fugatos cum fame premerentur in quandam herbam incidisse, quam qui comederent nihil aliarum rerum reminis-

by putting their sick out in the streets so that those who have been attacked by the same disease can advise them. And yet Herodotus teaches in book 2 that this was not always the Egyptian practice, writing thus: Now they organized medicine in this way, so that each physician treated one illness and no more. As a result, the whole place was full of physicians: Some were appointed to treat the eyes, some the head, some the teeth, others the parts of the stomach, and others hidden diseases.

But since that time many have become famous in medicine, among them: Cassius Calpitanus, Aruncius Rubrius, Antonius Musa (the favorite of Augustus Caesar), Galen in the time of Antoninus Pius, and Avicenna not long afterward.

: XXI :

On the inventors of herbal and pharmaceutical medicine and of medicine made from honey, and what remedies people have learned from animals.

Nature doubtless brought forth plants for the sake of health or pleasure, as many examples show. Xanthus the historian, for instance, teaches that the parent of a young serpent that had been killed used a plant called *balis* to bring it back to life, according to Pliny in book 25. Likewise, the woodpecker is a bird that uses a particular plant to force a wedge driven into its hole to spring out again. And there are certain Indians who actually live on plants alone, as Herodotus says in book [3]. Appian of Alexandria also writes that when hunger gripped the Parthians fleeing from Antony, they happened upon a certain plant, and those who ate it neither remembered nor understood anything else but to keep digging up stones as if they were about to build something of great

cerentur aut intelligerent nisi quod lapides continue effoderent quasi quidpiam magni operis facturi, et sic debacchati bilem demum evomentes interirent. Quid demum plura? Nihil non herbarum vi effici posset si plurimarum vires non ignorarentur.

2   Haec itaque, teste Plinio, erat antiqua medicina cuius, idem testis in 7, repertor fuit Chiron Centaurorum iustissimus, Saturni ex Phyllira filius, qui et medicamentariam medicinam ad vulnera aut ulcera et huiusmodi curanda invenit, quam tamen alii Apollini assignant. Ex quo ipse apud Ovidium dicit:

herbarum subiecta potentia nobis.

Alii vero Aesculapio eius filio, quem Ovidius in 2 *Metamorphoseos* dicit medicinam hanc a Chirone didicisse, cum illi nutriendum Apollo pater tradidisset. Alii demum Samothracum filiis, teste Eusebio, adscribunt.

3   Verum Chironem ideo fortasse dixerunt hanc primum comperisse quia (ut Plinius ait libro 25 capite 4) herbam centauream reperit, qua (sicut idem testatur) curatus dicitur a vulnere pedis inflicto ex lapsu improviso sagittae Herculis ex suis manibus illitae veneno Hydrae. Nam Chiron cum attrectaret arma Herculis, quem receperat hospitio, sagitta in eius pedem decidit. Ovidius in 5 *Fastorum*:

Dumque senex tractat squalentia tela venenis,
      Excidit et laevo fixa sagitta pede.

Ovidius tamen eum ex hoc vulnere perisse sentit, ita scribens:

Nona dies aderat cum tu, iustissime Chiron,
      Bis septem stellis corpore cinctus eras.

importance, and thus they raved on, vomiting bile until they died. What more to add? There is nothing the power of plants could not do if people were not unaware of the powers that so many of them have.

And this in ancient times was medicine, according to Pliny, 2 who tells us in book 7 that its discoverer was Chiron, the most righteous of Centaurs, Saturn's son from Phyllira. He invented pharmaceutical medicine for treating wounds or sores and ailments of that kind, though others ascribe this to Apollo, who says, according to Ovid:

the power of plants is ours.

Others claim it was Aesculapius, his son, and in book 2 of the *Metamorphoses* Ovid says that he learned this kind of medicine from Chiron, since his father Apollo sent him to the Centaur to be educated. Still others, according to Eusebius, assign it to the sons of the Samothracians.

Perhaps they said that Chiron discovered it because (as Pliny 3 mentions in book 25, chapter 4) he found the plant centaury, which was thought (see Pliny) to have cured a wound inflicted on his foot when one of Hercules' arrows, smeared with the Hydra's venom, dropped accidentally from his hands. For when Chiron began handling the arms of Hercules, whom he had received as a guest, an arrow fell and struck his foot, as Ovid says in book 5 of the *Festivals*:

The shafts the old one handled were sticky with venom;
One arrow slipped and stuck in his left foot.

Ovid believes that he died from the wound, however, writing:

Nine days passed and then, Chiron, most just,
Were you girded round with two times seven stars.

4   At medicamentorum quibus morbi curantur usum Celsus in
principio libri quinti dicit antiquissimum esse; autorem tamen non
ponit sed tradit Asclepiadem medicum peritissimum magna ex
parte eum usum sustulisse quod omnia medicamina et mali succi
sint et stomachum laedant. Et definit omnes medicinae partes ita
innexas esse ut separari nequeant; ac ideo medicinam quae victu
curat aliquando adhibere medicamentum; et eam quae medicami-
nibus purgat adhibere rationem victus; atque hoc pacto sanitatem
aut conservari amissamve recuperari.

5   Ad herbas revertor. Et sic alii alias herbas invenerunt, ut Mercurius moly, Achilles achilleam, Aesculapius panacem, complu-
resque alias, quod admodum longum esset minimeque necessarium persequi, cum praesertim Plinius illud ipsum disertissime
prodat. Medicinam vero ex melle, teste Plinio, Sol Oceani filius invenit.

6   Animalia praeterea quaedam—mirum quam multa a bestiis
homo didicerit—nonnullas herbas atque remedia commonstrarunt quae homini postea usui forent. Nam dictamum herbam ad
extrahendas sagittas utilem cervi hominibus monstravere, percussi
eo telo pastuque eius herbae eiecto, id quod Cicero in secundo *De
natura deorum* feris capris adscribit. Iidem cervi percussi a *phalan-
gio*, quod est aranei genus aut aliquod simile, cancros edendo sibi
medentur. Chelidoniam visui saluberrimam hirundines docuere
vexatis pullorum oculis illa medentes, id quod Cornelius Celsus libro sexto naturae eius avis non herbae assignat, ita scribens: Si ex-
trinsecus ictus oculum laedat ut sanguis in eo suffundatur, nihil
commodius est quam sanguine vel columbae vel palumbi vel hirundinis inungere. Neque id sine causa fit, cum horum acies ex-
trinsecus laesa interposito tempore in antiquum statum redeat, ce-
leberrimeque hirundinis. Unde etiam locus fabulae factus est per

Celsus says in the beginning of his fifth book that the use of 4
drugs to cure diseases is very old, yet he does not propose an inventor; he reports instead that Asclepiades, a most expert physician, mostly stopped using them because all drugs are harmful po-
tions and injure the stomach. And Celsus defines all the parts of
medicine as so interconnected that they cannot be separated; one
treatment that cures with diet sometimes uses drugs; another that
purges with drugs sometimes uses a system of diet; and in this
way either health is preserved or lost health is restored.

Let me return to the subject of plants, of which various kinds 5
were discovered by various figures, as Mercury discovered moly,
Achilles achillea, Aesculapius panacea; many others found other
plants, but it would be a long and needless task to describe them,
especially since Pliny treats them so clearly. According to Pliny it
was Sol the son of Ocean who invented medicine from honey.

Certain animals, moreover, pointed out a number of herbs 6
and remedies that people eventually found useful — amazing how
many things man has learned from the beasts! Dittany, for one, is
a plant useful for drawing out arrows; deer revealed this to humans when they were struck with such a weapon and forced it out
by eating this plant, which Cicero ascribes to wild goats in the second book *On the Nature of the Gods*. The same deer heal themselves
by eating crabs when bitten by a *phalangium*, which is a kind of spider or something of that sort. Swallows taught us that celandine is
very good for the vision by healing the injured eyes of their chicks
with it, though in book 6 Cornelius Celsus assigns this to the nature of the bird, not the plant, writing thus: If a blow from outside
injures the eye so that it fills with blood, nothing works better
than to apply the blood of a dove, a wood-pigeon or a swallow.
Nor does this happen without a cause, since when something external damages the sight of these birds — most notably the swallow — vision returns to its former state after some time passes.
And this gave rise to the story that the parents use a plant to

parentes id herba restitui quod per se sanescit. Testudo *cunilae*, quam bubulam vocant, pastu vires contra serpentes refovet. Hedera apri in morbis sibi medentur.

7   Ab hippopotamo, id est, ab equo quasi fluviatili — est enim animal in Nilo — medici mittere in morbis sanguinem quod phlebotomare vocant didicerunt. Assidua nanque is satietate gravedinosus factus, exit in littus recentes harundinum caesuras perspeculaturus, atque ubi acutissimum videt stipitem, imprimens corpus venam quandam in crure vulnerat, atque ita profluvio sanguinis morbidum corpus exonerat, plagam vero rursus limo obducit. Simile quiddam et avis in eadem Aegypto monstravit quae vocatur ibis, ciconiae fere similis et ipsa quoque serpentum pernicies. Haec rostri aduncitate per eam partem se perluit qua reddi ciborum onera consuevere. Hinc clysteris usum medici primum didicerunt. Mustela in anguium venatu ruta sibi salutem quaerit; ciconia origano.

8   De herbis autem primus omnium quos memoria novit Orpheus accuratissime scripsit, post eum Musaeus (etsi per idem temporis ambo fuisse dicuntur) necnon et Dioscorides. Apud nos primum Marcus Cato, deinde Pompeius Leneus, Magni Pompeii libertus, qui exemplaria Mithridatis regis *De vi herbarum*, iussu Magni Pompeii, omnia regia praeda potiti in nostrum sermonem transtulit. Quo primum tempore Plinius se animadvertisse ait hanc scientiam ad Romanos pervenisse.

restore what really heals on its own. The tortoise refreshes its strength against snakes by feeding on *cunila*, which they call ox-plant. Sick boars cure themselves with ivy.

Physicians learned to use phlebotomy or bloodletting in diseases from the hippopotamus, a sort of river-horse — an animal that actually lives in the Nile. When its continual gluttony makes it catch cold, it comes out onto shore and looks about for fresh cuts in the reeds, and when it finds the sharpest plant, it presses its body down and wounds a certain vein in its leg. By shedding blood in this way it relieves its unhealthy body, but then it covers over the area again with mud. Also from Egypt is the bird called the ibis, resembling a stork and likewise dangerous to snakes, and it has shown us something similiar. With the curve of its beak it cleanses itself in the place where the wastes of food are usually let out. Thus physicians first learned the use of the enema. When it hunts snakes, the weasel tries to protect itself with rue; the stork uses marjoram.

Orpheus wrote very accurately about plants before anyone known to memory, and after him Musaeus (though they say that both lived at the same time) as well as Dioscorides. Among us Marcus Cato was first and then Pompeius Lenaeus, freedman of Pompey the Great, who translated into our language transcripts of the work of King Mithridates *On the Power of Plants*. This was at the command of Pompey the Great, who acquired them all as royal booty. It was at this time, says Pliny, that he could tell that knowledge of this sort had first come to Rome.

: XXII :

Quis primus magicam artem invenerit et a quibus celebrata; et quis modum effugandi daemones aut incantationes ediderit quibus morbi sedarentur.

1 Exigit locus ut de origine magicae artis prius dicatur quam libri finem faciamus quandoquidem natam primum a medicina nemo dubitat. Haec itaque a Zoroastre in Perside, autore Plinio libro 30 ut inter autores convenit, ortum habuisse fertur. Iustinus in principio suae *Epitomes* hunc Zoroastrem qui magicam artem reperit Bactrianorum regem fuisse dicit, qui teste Eusebio *De temporibus* et in 10 *De praeparatione evangelica* plus DCCC fere annis ante Troiana tempora fuit, quo etiam tempore Abraham et Ninus fuerunt, cum ageretur annus ab orbe condito ter millesimus ac CLXXXV. At annos deinde post DCCC et circiter XV Troia a Graecis capta est, qui fuit annus orbis conditi quater millesimus.

2 Lactantius autem et Eusebius malos daemones hanc simul cum caeteris improbis artibus invenisse tradunt, quam omnium artium fraudulentissimam Plinius esse asserit miraturque quo modo multis seculis in toto terrarum orbe valuerit. Atque id ob eam causam evenisse putat, quod sola artium treis alias imperiosissimas humanae mentis complexa in se unam redegerit. Quippe a medicina primo, ut dictum est, manavit, ac specie salutari irrepsit sanctior quam medicina. Ita desyderatissimis promissis addidit vires religionis, ad quam maxime alligantur hominum mentes. Post haec miscuit mathematicas artes, nullo non avido de se futura sciendi atque ea e coelo verissime peti credente. Ita possessis hominum sensibus triplici vinculo, eo usque adolevit ut in magna humana-

: XXII :

*Who first discovered the art of magic and who practiced it;
who made known a way of driving out demons or using
incantations to check diseases.*

Since no one doubts that magic first grew out of medicine, context   1
demands that something be said about the origin of the magical
art before we put an end to this book. They say that magic had its
origin in Persia from Zoroaster, as Pliny in book 30 and other authorities agree. In the beginning of his *Epitome*, Justin writes that
this Zoroaster who discovered the magical art was king of the
Bactrians. According to the *Chronicle of Eusebius* and book 10 of his
Preparation for the Gospel, he lived a little more than eight hundred
years before the time of Troy, at the time when Abraham and
Ninus also lived, 3185 years after the creation of the world. The
Greeks captured Troy about 815 years later, in the four-thousandth
year since the creation of the world.

But Lactantius and Eusebius claim that evil demons invented   2
magic along with the other evil arts. Pliny says that it is the falsest
of all the arts and wonders at the influence it had over the whole
globe for so many centuries. He thinks the reason was that,
alone of all the arts, it included the three others that most held
sway over the human mind and subjected them to itself alone. In
fact, magic grew out of medicine, as noted above, and under the
pretext of bringing health insinuated itself as holier than medicine.
To these great expectations it added the powers of religion, to
which human minds are very much attached. Then it put the astrological arts in the mix since all were anxious to know their future and thought they could find it out most accurately from the
heavens. With human feelings thus bound by this triple chain,
magic grew until it prevailed among the greater part of human-

rum gentium parte plurimum valuerit, magnamque vim, uti poetae testimonio sunt, semper habuerit.

3 Nam Vergilius in Damone de Circe ait:

Carminibus Circe socios mutavit Ulyssis.

Et quemadmodum fruges alio pellicerentur idem:

Atque satas alio vidi traducere messes.

Quinetiam elementa quoque concuti et menses hominum turbari, et sine ullo veneni haustu sola carminis violentia homines interimi putarunt. Maro:

Carmina vel coelo possunt deducere lunam.

Item:

Frigidus in pratis cantando rumpitur anguis.

Et Ovidius de sine titulo:

Carmine laesa Ceres sterilem vanescit in herbam,
Deficiunt laesi carmine fontis aquae.

Lucanus:

Mens, hausti nulla sanie polluta veneni,
Incantata perit.

4 Huius autem veneficii, quamvis per totum orbem terrarum pervaserit, Lucano in sexto *Pharsaliae* et Apuleio *De magia* libris 1 et 2 et Plinio in 30 autoribus, Thessaliam in primis infamia flagrasse constat, quod Thessalis nihil antiquius foret quam maleficam artem curiose perdiscere et alios vicinos populos edocere. Extabant etiam aetate Plinii, ut ipse testis est, eius vestigia apud Italicas gentes in 12 tabulis. Circe etiam, Circeum montem habitans iuxta

kind, and it has always had great power, as the poets are our witnesses.

In his poem on Damon, Vergil says of Circe: 3

Circe chanted to change the friends of Ulysses.

And he tells us that the crops of the earth are moved about in the same way:

I've seen him whisk away the harvest wheat.

Yes, they thought that magic shook even the elements and disturbed human minds, and that the force of poetry alone killed people without the drinking of a potion. Vergil:

Poems can even call the moon down from heaven.

And again:

Cold in the meadow, the snake falls to pieces enchanted.

And Ovid in an untitled poem:

Wheat withers, water dries up
When magic songs hurt Ceres.

Lucan:

He swallows no vile potion,
But the mind dies enchanted.

Though this infamous sorcery spread through all the earth,   4
Thessaly in particular was ablaze with it, according to Lucan in
book 6 of the *Pharsalia*, Apuleius in books 1 and 2 *On magic* and
Pliny in book 30: In Thessaly no custom was more venerable than
carefully learning the evil art and teaching it to other neighboring
peoples. Also in Pliny's time, as he says himself, traces remained in
the Twelve Tables of its use by Italian tribes. And Circe, dwell-

Caietam, ex ea arte mirandos ostendit eventus. Ac tale est magiae inventum.

5   De hac quis scripserit non plane compertum habemus. Plinius libro 30 dicit Hostanem de ea primum commentatum esse, atque Pythagoram, Empedoclem, Democritum et Platonem ad hanc discendam navigasse, hanc reversos praedicasse et in arcanis habuisse—sed praesertim Democritum, unde magiam Democrito, medicinam eadem aetate Hippocrate illustrante, floruisse approbat, circiter ccc urbis annum. Idem Plinius (in hac parte longe post homines natos haud modestissimus): Est et alia, inquit, magices factio a Mose etiamnum et Iochobel Iudaeis pendens.

6   Fuit autem Iochobel ipsius Mosis mater. Caeterum ex Plinii ore piaculum illud idcirco, ut arbitror, temere prodiit, quoniam cum Deus signa quaedam edidisset quibus Hebraicus populus facile crederet Mosen sibi ab ipso ducem esse constitutum, rex Pharao (sic enim Aegyptii patria lingua, teste Iosepho in 8 *Antiquitatum*, regem nominant) haec tanquam vana deridens iussit Aegyptiorum sacerdotes eadem facere, qui statim virgas in draconem verterunt. At Moses ut humanis divina multo maiora esse demonstraret virgam in terram proiecit quae in colubrum versa Aegyptiorum virgas in draconem translatas repente voravit, autor Iosephus in 2 *De Iudaeorum antiquitatibus* et Eusebius libro 9 *De praeparatione evangelica.* Cum Moses igitur haec et plura alia divinitus ageret, homines qui magis falsis quam veris inhaerent magica arte fieri putabant.

7   Modum autem effugandi daemones quibus saepe corpora humana vexantur et incantationes quibus morbi sedari solent Solomon rex primus docuit, dicente Iosepho in 8 *Antiquitatum*. Praestitit autem Deus etiam ei ut contra daemones artem ad utilitatem hominum edisceret; et incantationes instituit quibus aegritudines

ing on the promontory of Circeii near Gaeta, showed wondrous effects from this art. Such was the discovery of magic.

Precisely who wrote about magic we have not learned. Pliny 5 says in book 30 that Hostanes was the first to compose a book about it, also that Pythagoras, Empedocles, Democritus and Plato went abroad to learn about it, taught it when they returned and treated it as one of their secrets — especially Democritus. Pliny is satisfied that magic prospered with Democritus at the same time that Hippocrates was shedding light on the art of medicine, around 300 AUC. Pliny also says (and on this topic he is scarcely the most temperate of mortal men) that there was yet another magical sect that came from the Jews, Moses and Iochobel.

Now Iochobel was the mother of Moses himself, but I believe 6 that this wicked notion came rashly from Pliny's lips, for this reason: That when God produced certain signs to make it easy for the Hebrew people to believe that he had made Moses their leader, Pharaoh the king (this was how the Egyptians said 'king' in their native language, according to Josephus in book 8 of the *Antiquities*) mocked the signs as false and commanded the Egyptian priests to produce them also, and then they promptly changed their staves into snakes. But Moses, in order to show that divine deeds are far greater than human, threw his rod to the ground where it turned into a serpent that quickly swallowed the staves changed into snakes. Josephus tells the story in book 2 of the *Jewish Antiquities* and Eusebius in book 9 of the *Preparation for the Gospel*. Thus, although Moses did this and many other deeds by divine power, people who stick closer to falsehood than truth thought they were done by the art of magic.

King Solomon first taught how to drive out the demons that 7 often afflict human bodies as well as the incantations that may check disease, says Josephus in book 8 of the *Antiquities*: And God also provided that Solomon should learn the art for mankind's benefit against the demons; he devised incantations that often alle-

soleant mitigari; modum etiam coniurationum quibus obstricti daemones ne denuo redeant effugantur invenit. Et quonam pacto huiusmodi daemones expellerentur perspicue demonstrat: Vidi etenim, inquit, quendam Eleazarum de gente nostra, praesente Vespasiano et eius filiis et tribunis alioque simul exercitu, curantem eos qui a daemonibus vexabantur. Modus autem medicinae fuit huiusmodi: Intulit naribus eius qui a daemone vexabatur annulum habentem subter signaculum radicem a Solomone monstratam; deinde daemonem per nares odorantis abstraxit, et repente cecidit homo; postea coniuravit eum, iuramentum obiiciens Solomonis ne ad eum denuo remearet, id est, cantica quae ille composuit super eum dicenda volens, etc.

8   Hodie etiam sacerdotes nostri, uti videmus, sacris quibusdam verbis daemones ex humanis corporibus exire cogunt, et quibus benedicunt aegrotis ii ut plurimum belle habent. Quam sane potestatem Christus servator noster apostolis dedit cum apud Marcum evangelistam dixit: Ite in mundum universum et praedicate evangelium omni creaturae. Qui crediderit et baptizatus fuerit salvus erit; qui vero non crediderit condemnabitur. Signa autem eos qui crediderint haec sequentur. Per nomen meum daemonia eiicient; linguis loquentur novis; et si quid mortiferum biberint, non nocebit eis. Super aegrotos manus imponent, et bene habebunt. Haec autem mihi hoc loco potissimum commemorare placuit quo legentes facile intelligerent divina verba longe quam daemones aut artem magicam vim maiorem habere.

viate disease; and he also invented a way of conjuring that drives the demons out and binds them not to return again. How demons were thus expelled Josephus clearly demonstrates: In the presence of Vespasian, his sons, the tribunes and the rest of the army besides, he says, I have actually seen one of our people, a certain Eleazar, curing those who were afflicted by demons, and the method of treatment was as follows: He held a ring up to the nose of the person afflicted by a demon, and under its seal the ring had a root indicated by Solomon; he then drew the demon out through the nostrils of the person smelling it, who suddenly fell down; then he conjured the demon, reproaching him with Solomon's oath not to come back to the person, directing that a chant which Solomon composed be said over the person, and so on.

Even today we see that our priests use certain sacred words to 8 force demons to leave human bodies, and they bless the sick with them to improve their health. Christ our savior gave this power to the apostles, of course, when he said, according to Mark the Evangelist: Go into the whole world and preach the Gospel to every creature. Whoever believes and is baptized will be saved, but he who does not believe will be condemned. And these signs will attend those who believe. In my name they will cast out demons; they will speak in strange tongues; and if they drink anything deadly, it will not harm them. They will lay hands upon the sick, and they will be well. It is especially important that I note these things here so that the reader may readily understand that the words of God have far greater power than demons or the art of magic.

: XXIII :

De origine necromantiae, pyromantiae, aeromantiae,
hydromantiae, geomantiae et chiromantiae.

1   Magi (qui Persica lingua sapientes appellantur) apud Persas potissimum, teste Laertio, deorum cultui vacabant, precando illis vota
et sacrificia faciebant, de eorum substantia—id est, vi ac natura—
et genealogia disserebant, vitam in primis frugaliter viventes. Sed
usque eo aucta est eorum vanitas ut non solum observatione syderum futura praedicere, verum artibus quibusdam veritatis umbras
habentibus et rerum ac verborum maleficiis et scire se omnia et facere posse profiterentur. Ab his igitur sex magices artis species
fluxerunt: Necromantia, pyromantia, aeromantia, hydromantia,
geomantia atque chiromantia, quamvis Marcus Varro libro 7 *Divi-*
narum rerum illas priores quatuor tantum assignaverit.

2   Est autem necromantia divinatio per cadavera, ut mortuus apud
Lucanum in 6 suscitatus eventum belli Pharsalici Sexto Pompeio
praedixit. Pyromantiam vocant qua per ignem divinatur, dum in-
spicimus quid fulgur, quid fulmen quidve ignea vis significet, ut
Tanaquil, Tarquinii Prisci regis uxor (teste Livio *Ab urbe condita* et
Dionysio in 4), videns flammam lambere Servii Tullii caput, illum
Romanorum regem fore praedixit. Aeromantia divinatio per aerem—utputa per avium volatum, gustum, cantum ac ventorum
grandinumque insuetas procellas, ut ferrum (sicut ait Plinius libro
2) quo in Lucanis pluit significavit Marci Crassi in Parthis interitum, veluti quoque lapides quibus (autore Livio in 1 *De secundo*

: XXIII :

On the origin of necromancy, pyromancy, aeromancy,
hydromancy, geomancy and chiromancy.

Among the Persians the Magi (which means 'wise men' in the Per- 1
sian tongue) devoted themselves above all to worshipping the
gods, according to Laertius. At first they led simpler lives than
anyone else, making offerings and sacrifices to the gods when they
prayed to them and disputing about their substance — their power
and nature, in other words — and their ancestry. But they grew
so enormously vain that they claimed the ability not only to predict the future from observing the stars but also to know and do
all things through evil spells of deed and word by certain arts
that contain shadows of truth. Six varieties of the magical art
have come down from them: Necromancy, pyromancy, aeromancy,
hydromancy, geomancy and chiromancy, though Marcus Varro
lists only the four earlier types in book 7 of his *Theology*.

Necromancy is divination done with corpses, as in Lucan's sixth 2
book when a man raised from the dead predicted the outcome of
the battle of Pharsalus for Sextus Pompey. Divination with fire
they call pyromancy, as when we interpret the meaning of a flash
of lightning, a thunderbolt or a fiery force: Tanaquil, wife of King
Tarquinius Priscus (according to Livy's *History from the Foundation
of the City* and book 4 of Dionysius), seeing a flame licking the
head of Servius Tullius, predicted that he would be king of the
Romans. Divination from the air is aeromancy — through the flying, feeding and singing of birds, for example, and through unusual storms of wind and hail, as when the iron that rained on
Lucania (so Pliny says in book 2) signified that Marcus Crassus
would be killed in Parthia, or when the similar reports (according

bello punico) in Piceno pluisse nunciatum fuit strages illas indicarunt quas Annibal Italiae intulit.

3   Hydromantia ex aqua, quemadmodum Varro prodidit puerum vidisse in aqua effigiem Mercurii quae CL versibus omnem Mithridatici belli pronunciavit eventum. Geomantia divinatio per terrarum hiatus. Chiromantia divinatio per linearum manuum inspectionem. Iuvenalis *Satyra* sexta:

> frontemque manumque
> Praebebit vati.

Quae omnia superstitiosa sunt atque omnino ridicula, nam illis qui ea exercent egestas semper imperat, qui, ut Marcus Tullius libro I *De divinatione* prope finem ait, sibi semitam non sapiunt, aliis monstrant viam, quibus divitias pollicentur, ab iis drachmas ipsi petunt. Hos igitur tanquam maleficae superstitionis homines omnia corrumpentes, omnia inquinantes, ac propterea dignos qui male semper audiant, declinemus; ac potius insectemur ut vera sanctaque religione imbutos decet.

: XXIV :

De duobus divinandi generibus; et de origine aruspicinae artis et sortium Praenestinarum; et quis somniorum interpretationem docuerit.

1   Duo sunt, autore Cicerone *De divinatione* volumine I, divinandi genera quorum unum naturae est, alterum artis. Est autem natura in iis qui non ratione aut coniectura observatis ac notatis signis, sed concitatione quadam animi aut soluto liberoque motu futura praesentiunt. Quod et somniantibus saepe contingit et nonnunquam vaticinantibus per furorem, ut accidisse legimus Sibyllae Erythraeae et sacerdotibus nonnullis. Cuius generis oracula etiam

to Livy's first book *On the Second Punic War*) of stones raining on Picenum proclaimed the havoc that Hannibal wreaked on Italy.

Hydromancy is done with water, as when Varro reported that a   3
boy saw an image of Mercury in water that predicted the entire outcome of the Mithridatic War in 150 verses. Geomancy is divination done through openings in the earth. Divination by examining lines in the hand is chiromancy. Juvenal in *Satire* 6:

Hand and head she'll offer the seer.

All these are superstitious and completely ridiculous, for poverty always rules those who engage in such things, as Cicero says near the end of book 1 *On Divination*: They lose the path and show others the road; they promise riches to those whom they beg for pennies. Therefore let us shun them as people of wicked superstition who corrupt and defile everything and thus deserve the evil reputation they always bear. Better for us to pursue them with our words as befits those inspired with true and holy religion.

: XXIV :

On the two kinds of divination; on the origin of the art of the haruspex and the lots of Praeneste; and who taught the interpretation of dreams.

There are two ways of divining, according to Cicero in book 1 *On*   1
divination, one natural, the other artificial. Divination is natural in those who foresee things to come, not by any calculation or interpretation of signs observed and noted, but by a kind of excitement in the mind or by free and unfettered inspiration. This happens often to people dreaming and sometimes to those in prophetic frenzy, as with the Erythraean Sibyl and certain priests of whom

habenda erant qualia fuerunt oracula Apollinis aut Ammonis aut reliquorum in quibus homines crebro illudebantur, veluti quae arte daemonum humanaque fraude reddebantur. Verum prophetae, qui divino spiritu non furore lymphatico afflati erant, nunquam fallebant.

2   Ars vero in iis est qui novas res coniectura persequuntur et veteres observatione didicerunt, quae apud priscos habuit aruspicinam, auguria, astrologiam et sortes.

3   Aruspicina, teste Marco Tullio libro 1 *De divinatione*, apud Hetruscos, ut illi futiliter praedicabant, primum ortum habuit, nam, ut idem in 2 *De divinatione* ait, aranti cuidam in agro Tarquiniensi et sulcum altius imprimenti subito e terra extitit quidam qui Tages appellatus, facie quidem puerili sed senili prudentia, a quo universa Hetruria aruspicinam edocta est, quae ab ara et inspiciendo sibi nomen vindicavit.

4   Sed Plinius libro 7 aruspicii inventionem cuidam Delpho tribuit, sicut ignispicii Amphiarao. Haec autem continet in se exta, fulgura et ostenta. Mactata enim hostia ad aram eaque aperta, quomodo cor, hepar et reliqua exta sese haberent inspiciebant ex eorumque habitu atque colore futura coniectabant, ut quo die primum in sella aurea sedit Caesar in bove quem immolavit cor non apparuit, Cicero et Appianus Alexandrinus libro 2 *De bellis civilibus* autores, ex quo futuram infelicitatem praedixerunt aruspices. Ostenta autem sunt quae praeter naturam evenientia futurum aliquid significant, ut cum in exercitu Xerxis, autore Herodoto libro *Historiarum* 7, in Europam traiecto equa bellicosissimum animal leporem timidissimam feram peperit, quod fertur portendisse tantum exercitum fugam moliturum. Haec vero, ut Cicero inquit,

we read. Also included in this type were the oracles of Apollo or Ammon or others who have tricked people so often, just like those produced by demonic contrivance or human fraud. But the prophets never deceived, for they were filled with the spirit of God and not panic frenzy.

Divination is artificial in those who seek new knowledge 2 through interpretation after they have learned the old by observation. In this the ancients included the art of the *haruspex*, augury, astrology and lots.

According to Cicero in book 1 *On Divination*, the art of the 3 *haruspex* had its origins among the Etruscans, whose predictions were worthless. Cicero says in book 2 *On Divination* that a figure called Tages suddenly appeared out of the earth to a man who was plowing in the region of Tarquinii and cut his furrow to an unusual depth. Tages had a boy's face but an old man's wisdom, and from him all Etruria learned the art of the *haruspex*, which takes its name from *altar* and *inspecting*.

But Pliny in book 7 attributes the invention of this art to a cer- 4 tain Delphus, just as he assigns divination by fire to Amphiaraus. It includes the inspection of entrails, lightning and portents. After they sacrificed a victim at the altar and opened it up, they examined the situation of the heart, liver and other entrails and interpreted the future from their condition and appearance. Hence, when no heart was found in the ox that Caesar sacrificed on the day that he first sat on a golden throne, the *haruspices* predicted misfortune to come, according to Cicero and Appian of Alexandria in book 2 of the *Civil Wars*. Portents are unnatural happenings that signify something in the future, as in the story Herodotus tells in book 7 of his *Histories*: When the army of Xerxes had crossed over into Europe, a mare, the most warlike of animals, gave birth to a hare, a very timid beast, which was taken to presage a rout for this great army. These things are called por-

quia ostendunt, portendunt, monstrant, praedicunt, ostenta, portenta, monstra, prodigia dicuntur.

5   Tertia pars aruspicinae in fulmine et in fulgure et tonitru consistit. Vergilius:

De coelo tactas memini praedicere quercus.

Haec omnia sub aruspicina sunt, nam idem Cicero ait: Sed quoniam de extis et de fulguribus satis est disputatum, ostenta restant ut tota aruspicina sit pertractata. Atque haec est aruspicina quam qui exercent tum aruspices, tum extispices nuncupantur.

6   In secunda autem parte eius divinationis, quae est artis, auspicia sive auguria ponuntur. Auspicia—quae ab avibus inspiciendis sicut auguria ab avium gustu vel garritu dicuntur—Tiresiam Thebanum invenisse Plinius in 7 autor est. Auguria vero, idem testis, ex avibus Caras a quo Caria dicta est, reperit, ex caeteris vero animalibus adiecit Orpheus. Verum huiuscemodi augurandi artem quidam a Chaldaeis ad Graecos (apud quos Amphiaraus, Mopsus, Chalcas, summi augures fuerunt), a Graecis ad Hetruscos, ab Hetruscis ad Latinos venisse volunt.

7   In avibus autem tria erant divinandi genera: aliae enim aves volatu ut praepetes (quarum volatum Phryges, teste Clemente, primi observaverunt); aliae cantu ut oscines; aliae gustu futura praedicebant. Tertium genus ex tripudio solistimo futura indicabat. Porro solistima tripudia dicebantur auguria quae fiebant quoties offa quae pullis dabatur aliquo modo cadebat in solum, ac ita a solo solistimum vocamus.

8   Sed haec augurandi ars quanti facienda sit Mossolamus Iudaeus, vir equidem sapientissimus, perspicue demonstravit. Is enim, sicut Iosephus in 1 *Antiquitatis contra Appionem* ex Hecataeo tradit, cum in bello esset et vates quidam dum iter facerent statim

tents, presages, revelations and prodigies, as Cicero says, because they portend, presage, reveal and predict.

The third part of the art of the *haruspex* depends upon thun- 5 derbolts, flashes of lightning and thunder. Vergil:

Oaks touched by heaven foretold this, I recall.

These are all included in the art of the *haruspex*, as Cicero says, once again: Since there has been enough argument about entrails and lightning, we are left with portents to complete our treatment of the art of the *haruspex*. And this is that art whose practitioners are sometimes called *haruspices*, sometimes *extispices*.

Auspices or auguries are included in the second or artificial part 6 of divination. The term auspices comes from *bird* and *inspecting*, just as augury comes from the *feeding* or *chattering* of birds. Pliny says in book 7 that Tiresias of Thebes invented it, but he also testifies that Caras, after whom Caria was named, discovered augury from birds and that Orpheus added augury from other animals. But some say that the technique for this sort of augury came from the Chaldaeans to the Greeks (whose greatest augurs were Amphiaraus, Mopsus and Chalcas), from the Greeks to the Etruscans and from the Etruscans to the people of Latium.

And there were three ways of divining with birds: some birds, 7 the straight-flyers, predicted the future by their flying (Clement tells us that the Phrygians first observed their flights); others, the song-birds, did so by singing; and others by eating. The third kind told the future in the *tripudium solistimum*, so called because in these auguries pieces of feed fell on the ground in some way when they were fed to the chickens, and so the term *solistimus* came from *soil*.

But Mossolamus the Jew, a very wise man indeed, clearly 8 showed how much is to be made of this art of augury. Citing Hecataeus in book 1 of his *Antiquities against Apion*, Josephus reports that when Mossolamus was at war and a certain soothsayer

iussisset omnes eatenus consistere quoad ex ave quae in proximo
erat augurium ageret, tacitus sumpto raptim arcu ac emissis sagittis avem interemit. Ac vati et nonnullis aliis id iniquo animo feren-
tibus, Quid furitis, inquit, mali daemones? Haec enim avis, suae
ipsius salutis nesciens, nostri itineris eventum nobis potuit praedicere? Si enim praescire futura potuisset, in hunc locum nequaquam venisset, metuens ne sagittis a Mossolamo Iudaeo peteretur.

9   Caeterum haec quantum olim apud omnes fere gentes autorita-
tis haberet multis in locis testatur Cicero *De divinatione*, praesertim
in primo scribens: Quis rex unquam fuit, quis populus, qui non
uteretur praedictione divina, neque solum in pace sed in bello, et
reliqua? Sed Romani in primis usi sunt, eodem dicente: Omitto
nostros, qui nihil in bello sine extis agunt, nihil sine auspiciis domi
habent. Haec ille. Apud eos insuper, ut Livius, Dionysius et Fenestella testimonio sunt, summa religione augurum collegium colebatur, quorum ius in Romana republica Cicero in secundo *De legibus* maximum et praestantissimum appellat. Quid quod augur, ut
ait Plutarchus in *Problematis*, ob nullum maleficium sacerdotio pri-
vabatur? Quia non honoris et magistratus sed scientiae et artis nomen est augur.

10   Divinabant etiam per sortes, quas in Latio Numerius Suffusius,
teste Marco Tullio in secundo *De divinatione*, primus invenit apud
Praenestinos, sculptas in robore literarum priscarum notis, quae
fortunae monitu pueri manu miscebantur atque ducebantur, de
quibus etiam Tranquillus in Tiberio meminit. Somniorum inter-
pretationem, autore Plinio in septimo, Amphictyon primus docuit, quod Trogus Ioseph Iacob filio attribuit, quem omnino

suddenly commanded everyone to halt in the middle of a march until he could perform an augury with a bird that was nearby, he quickly and quietly took up his bow and killed the bird by shooting arrows at it. The soothsayer and some others took this badly, but Mossolamus said to them: Why are you angry, you devils? Could this bird, ignorant of its own welfare, predict the outcome of our journey for us? If he had actually foreseen the future, he would never have come to this place at all, fearing to be shot by the arrows of Mossolamus the Jew.

On the other hand, many passages of Cicero's *On Divination* 9 witness the great authority that these practices once had among almost all peoples, particularly book 1, where he writes: Was there ever king or people who did not use divine foreknowledge, not only in peace but in war, and so on? But the Romans especially made use of it, as the same author says: I leave aside our own people, who do nothing in war without the entrails, nothing at home without the auspices. So much from Cicero. In addition, Livy, Dionysius and Fenestella give evidence that the Romans treated the college of augurs with the greatest reverence; in his second book *On the Laws* Cicero calls its authority the highest and most distinguished in the Roman Republic. Why is it, asks Plutarch in his *Questions*, that an augur was never deprived of his priesthood for any offense? Because an augur's title was not one of honor and office but of knowledge and technique.

They also used lots for divination. Numerius Suffusius first in- 10 vented them in Latium among the Praenestines, carving them on oak in ancient writing, according to Cicero in the second book *On Divination*. They were mixed and drawn by the hand of a boy and taken as a prognostic of fate. Suetonius also mentions lots in his *Life of Tiberius*. According to Pliny's seventh book, Amphictyon first taught the interpretation of dreams, but Trogus attributes it to Jacob's son, Joseph, whose absolute expertise in the interpreta-

peritissime somnia esse interpretatum Iosephus in secundo *Antiquitatum* itidem affirmat. Clemens vero Telmessinis assignat.

11   Sed haec omnia fallaciis inventa sunt, aut ad superstitionem aut ad errorem vel ad quaestum, quando homines qui haec profitentur tantum abest ut ulla in parte prodesse queant ut etiam maxime noceant: Nam, sicut Phavorinus, teste Gellio libro *Noctium atticarum* decimoquarto, dicebat: Si dicunt prospera et fallunt, miser fies, frustra expectando; sin adversa dicunt et mentiuntur, miser fies, frustra timendo. Si vero non prospera respondent, iam inde ex animo miser fies antequam fato fias; sin felicia ventura omnino promittunt, expectatio spei te adeo suspensum fatigabit ut omnem futurum gaudii fructum spes ipsa tibi ademerit.

12   Praeterea ecquid iuvat aut quid affert ad cavendum scire aliquid futurum, cum id certe futurum sit cum tamen nullo modo praenosci possit? Vergilius:

Nescia mens hominum fati sortisque futurae.

Quapropter Moses ille sapientissimus istiusmodi pestiferas artes populo suo vetuit, mandans ac dicens: Non augurabimini nec observabitis somnia; non declinetis ad magos nec ab ariolis aliquid sciscitemini. Et per illud primum divinae legis praeceptum— unum verum Deum colito—iuxta prohibuit easdem, imo Deus ipse. Quae omnia et servator noster Christus procul nobis esse voluit, cum dixit: Serva mandata. Sed haec alibi, cum de re christiana agetur.

LIBRI PRIMI FINIS.

tion of dreams Josephus affirms in book 2 of the *Antiquities*. Clement assigns it to the Telmessians, however.

But all these things have been devised as tricks, either for superstition or deception or profit, seeing that the people who profess them have so little success in anything and do very great harm besides. Thus, according to Gellius in book 14 of the *Attic Nights*, Favorinus used to say: If they say you'll prosper and they're wrong, you're miserable, hoping in vain; but if they say you'll do badly, and they're lying, you're miserable, fearing for nothing. If they're right to answer that you won't prosper, then you'll feel miserable before fate makes you so; yet if they promise nothing but happiness to come, you'll be so worn out with expectation and anxiety that hope itself will have taken away all the delight to come of your joy. 11

Besides, what help is it to know that something will be? Or why should it make you wary? Surely it will come to be though it can in no way be foreseen. Vergil: 12

Mortal mind that knows not fate nor future.

On this account, Moses, wisest of men, forbade his people these pestilential arts, commanding and saying: You shall make no auguries nor shall you pay attention to dreams nor go off to magicians nor seek to know anything from soothsayers. And through the first precept of divine law—you shall honor the one true God—he prohibited nearly the same things, or rather God himself did. Christ our savior also wished us to stay far away from all these things when he said: Keep the commandments. But I will deal with these matters elsewhere, when my topic is Christianity.

END OF BOOK I.

POLYDORI VERGILII URBINATIS DE INVENTORIBUS RERUM LIBER II

: I :

De iuris ac legum origine et qui primi mortalibus leges dederint et quae causa a principio dandi fuerit.

1 Quanquam disciplinarum liberalium originem primo tantum libro complecti, deinde autem in reliquis aliarum rerum inventionem tradere statueram, rei tamen magnitudo fecit ut multo sane quam volebam longior essem. In hoc itaque secundo libro de iuris primum atque legis origine commode dicam.

2   Ius, ut Paulo iurisconsulto placet, uno modo bonum semper dicitur. Lege vero nihil aptius est ad conditionem humanae naturae, dummodo (ut Cicero vult in 3 *De legibus)* pro imperio capiatur. Sine ea enim nec domus ulla, nec civitas, nec gens, nec hominum universum genus stare, nec rerum natura omnis, nec ipse mundus potest, nam et haec Deo paret, et huic obediunt maria terraeque, et hominum vita iussis supremae legis obtemperat. Est itidem lex, ut Chrysippus definit, divinarum humanarumque rerum notitia, item recti iussio, pravique depulsio, donum dei, dogma hominum sapientium, de qua mox dicemus.

3   Ius autem, quamvis plurimis modis dicatur, Ulpianus dividit in naturale, gentium et civile. Naturale appellat quod non solum humani generis proprium est sed omnium quae in terra, quae in mari coeloque nascuntur. Nam in nonnullis animalibus videmus maris et foeminae coniunctionem, liberorum procreationem educationemque quodam iure naturae quod, teste Marco Tullio in 1 *De legibus* in natura positum est et ab ea — hoc est, a Deo — initium

BOOK II

*On the origin of justice and laws and who first gave laws to
mortals and why they were originally given.*

I meant to include only the origin of the liberal disciplines in my 1
first book and then to treat the invention of other things in the sequel, but the great scope of the topic caused me to go on much
longer than I wished. Hence it will be best to start this second
book with the origin of right and law.

In one sense, the right is said to be what is always fair, as Paul 2
the jurist agrees. Truly, nothing suits the human condition better
than law, provided (as Cicero says in book 3 *On the Laws*) that law
is taken to mean government. Without it no household, no city,
no people can endure — not the whole human race, nor all of nature, nor the world itself; for nature submits to God, earth and sea
obey nature, and human life complies with the decrees of the highest law. Law, as Chrysippus defines it and of which we shall soon
speak, is also the knowledge of divine and human matters, likewise
the imperative to virtue, the rejection of vice, the gift of God and
the teaching of the wise.

Although one may speak of law in many ways, Ulpian divides it 3
into natural, national and civil law. He calls that law natural which
belongs not only to the human race but to everything that lives in
earth, sea and sky. Indeed, in some animals we see a joining of
male and female and a begetting and rearing of offspring according
to a kind of law of nature which, according to Cicero in his first
book *On the Laws*, has been established in nature and takes its be-

habet. Ius gentium, quo solum homines utuntur. Civile, ut Romanorum, Spartanorum, Atheniensium, quod legibus, interpretatione duodecim tabularum, plebiscitis, senatus consultis, decretis principum et autoritate prudentum constat.

4   Principis vero legis non scriptae sed in natura positae, ex qua homines deinde leges condiderunt, quae origo sit et quid ipsa sit Cicero in 2 *De legibus* facile declarat, cuius ideo verba ponam. Hanc igitur, inquit, video sapientissimorum fuisse sententiam legem neque hominum ingeniis excogitatam nec scitum aliquod esse populorum, sed aeternum quiddam quod universum mundum regeret imperandi prohibendique sapientia. Ita principem legem illam et ultimam mentem esse dicebant omnia ratione aut cogentis aut vetantis Dei. Ex quo illa lex, quam dii humano generi dederunt, recte est laudata; est enim ratio mensque sapientis, ad iubendum et ad detrahendum idonea. Et infra subdit: orta est autem simul cum mente divina. Quamobrem lex vera atque princeps, apta ad iubendum et ad vetandum, ratio est recta summi Iovis. Deinde suggerit, ita concludens: Est ergo lex iustorum iniustorumque distinctio, ad illam antiquissimam et rerum omnium principem expressa naturam, ad quam leges hominum diriguntur quae supplicio improbos afficiunt et defendunt et tuentur bonos.

5   Huiuscemodi ergo legum originem hoc loco prodendam censeo. Has itaque leges mortalibus omnium prima dedit Ceres. Ovidius in 5 *Metamorphoseon:*

Prima dedit leges, Cereris sunt omnia munus.

Diodorus itidem libro 6 ait: nam praeter ab ea repertum frumentum, leges dedit quibus iuste pieque homines vivere assuescerent, ex quo et legiferam dixerunt. Herodotus etiam in 6 inquit: Cum in agrum Ephesium ingressi essent, sub noctem ad urbem contende-

ginning from nature — from God, in other words. Next comes the
law of nations, used only by humans. Then civil law, as in Rome,
Sparta and Athens, which consists of statutes, exposition of the
Twelve Tables, resolutions of the people, recommendations of the
Senate, decrees of sovereigns and juridical opinion.

The words that follow are from book 2 *On the Laws*, where   4
Cicero has no trouble showing the origin and character of the primary, unwritten law established in nature, from which humans
constructed their laws later. I note, says he, the view of the greatest sages: that law was not contrived out of human ingenuity nor
was it a popular resolution of some sort; rather, it is something
eternal that governs the whole cosmos through its wisdom in commanding and forbidding. This law, they say, is the primal and ulti-
mate plan of God, whose reason either compels all things or for-
bids them. Hence, this law that the gods gave to humankind is
rightly to be praised, for it is the reason and intelligence of a wise
being, and it is well suited to issuing orders and prohibitions. Further on he adds: Law and the divine intelligence arose together.
Therefore, the true and primal law, fit for commanding and forbidding, is the right reason of mighty Jupiter. And in conclusion
he says: Law is the distinction between just and unjust, modeled
on nature, the first and most ancient of things, upon which are
based the human laws that afflict the wicked with punishment
while they defend and protect the good.

The origin of such laws I mean to set forth here. Ceres first of   5
all gave them to mortals. Ovid in *Metamorphoses* 5:

She first gave laws; all things are Ceres' gift.

Diodorus says the same in book [5]: Besides the grain that she
discovered, she gave the laws whereby people have grown used to
living in justice and duty, because of which they called her lawbringer. And in book 6 Herodotus says: After they had entered

bant, cum illic a mulieribus sacra legiferae Cereris fierent. Et Vergilius in quarto *Aeneidos,*

> mactant lectas de more bidentes
> Legiferae Cereri.

6   Idem sentit Plinius libro 7. Caeterum ut alii volunt Rhadamanthus primus edidit. Postea alii aliis primo leges tulerunt. Draco enim primus dedit Atheniensibus, deinde Solon; Aegyptiis quintus Mercurius aut Aethiopes, quorum ipsi Aegyptii coloni dicuntur. Minos Cretensibus, Lycurgus Lacedaemoniis, Turiis Charundas, Phoroneus Argivis, Romulus Romanis, Italis Pythagoras (uti Dionysio placet) Arcades, ipsis vero Arcadibus Apollo quartus.

7   Sed ne veri Dei erga nos divini muneris immemores videamur, ipsi primum hanc recte beateque vivendi normam, sicuti caetera omnia, acceptam referre debemus. Quod nec Ciceronem etiam tam prope, ut monstratum est, duce natura ad verum accedentem latuisset si ullam veri Dei unquam cognitionem habuisset.

8   Deus enim, autore Iosepho libro 3 *Antiquitatum,* leges quas deinde hominibus constitutas volebat primo Mosi tradidit, qui deinde primus legislatorum omnium quos commemoravimus, quippe quibus teste Eusebio longe aetate superior fuit, eas Hebraeis dedit. Testis idem Iosephus *Contra Appionem:* Dico igitur nostrum legislatorem quemlibet qui memorantur legislatorum antiquitate praecedere; Lycurgus enim et Solon et Zaleucus Locrensis, et omnes qui apud Graecos mirabiles sunt novelli atque recentes quantum ad illum comparati esse noscuntur, quando nec ipsum nomen legis fuisse olim apud Graecos agnoscitur, testis Homerus est qui nusquam in opere suo hoc usus est nomine. Et

the region of Ephesus, they marched on the city by night, when the women were performing the rites of Ceres the lawbringer there. Vergil in the fourth book of the *Aeneid*:

> Custom was to kill chosen victims
> For Ceres, giver of law.

Pliny expresses the same opinion in book 7, while some hold 6 the contrary view that Rhadamanthus first made laws known, and then others first brought them to other peoples. Draco first gave them to the Athenians, and Solon came later; for the Egyptians it was the fifth Mercury or else the Ethiopians, whose colonists the Egyptians themselves are said to be. Minos gave law to the Cretans, Lycurgus to the Lacedaemonians, Charundas to Thurii, Phoroneus to the Argives, Romulus to the Romans, Pythagoras or (as Dionysius thinks) the Arcadians to the Italians, and the fourth Apollo to the Arcadians.

But lest we seem to forget the true God's divine generosity to 7 us, it is to him first that we ought to trace our acquisition of this rule for living rightly and happily, as of all other things. If Cicero ever had any notion of the true God, this would not have escaped him; as we have seen, he actually came quite near the truth with nature as his guide.

According to Josephus in book 3 of the *Antiquities*, God first 8 gave Moses the laws that he wanted to establish among humans, and then Moses — first of all the lawgivers we have mentioned and far more ancient than any of them, according to Eusebius — gave them to the Hebrews. In *Against Apion* the same Josephus testifies: I tell you, then, that our lawgiver excels in age any other lawgiver mentioned, for in comparison to him Lycurgus, Solon, Zaleucus the Locrian and all whom the Greeks admired are known to be newcomers just arrived, seeing that the very term 'law' was once unknown among the Greeks, as evidenced by Homer, whose works never use the word. And a little further on Josephus adds:

paulo inferius addit: Nam cum sit tempus infinitum, si quis eum comparet aliorum legislatorum aetatibus, hunc ultra omnes inveniet. Eusebius quoque in 10 *De praeparatione evangelica* Mosen multo ante Cererem quae fertur prima, ut diximus, leges edidisse fuisse testatur. A Deo igitur, quem Cicero Iovem vocitat, lex originem habet, et eam mortalium omnium primus Moses Hebraeis constituit quae caeteris deinceps hominibus condendarum legum haud dubie exemplar fuit. Ac talis iuris atque legum origo.

9 Verum hoc loco illud disputandum videtur, quid fuerit quamobrem lex ista scripta non perinde ut altera bona postremo lata sit: Quae, ut apostolus Paulus ait, iram operatur et sexcentis poenis mortales obligat. Contra illa prior lex, quae non scribitur sed nascitur ac profluvio quodam naturae fonte in humanum ingenium a primo fluit, sine fraude, sine dolo est; particeps iustitiae, expers iniquitatis. Quapropter e re nostra minus fuisse videtur ut altera introducta sit quae nobis malo est.

10 Proinde operaeprecium est de origine istius legis subtilius tractare, et quia divus Ambrosius *Epistola* 71 ad Irenaeum illud plane facit, eum ideo ita dicentem attendamus: Certum est, inquit, non fuisse legem necessariam quae per Mosen data est; nam si naturalem legem quam Deus creator infudit singulorum pectoribus homines servare potuissent, non fuisset opus ea lege quae innodavit magis quam soluit humani generis infirmitatem. Solvit eam naturae legem Adam, qui voluit sibi arrogare quod non acceperat ut esset sicut eius creator, qui ita per inobedientiam contraxit offensam, nam si non rupisset imperium, praerogativam naturae atque ingenitae sibi innocentiae haeredibus propriis reseruasset. Ergo quia lex violata est, ideo praescriptum novae legis necessarium fuit ut vel partem haberet qui totum amiserat. Simul quia causa deiectionis superbia fuit, debuit ea lex dari quae eum Deo subiectum redderet; nam sine ista lege peccatum nesciebatur, et minor erat culpa ubi erat culpae ignorantia. Unde Dominus ait: Si non venis-

Although immeasurable time has passed, anyone who compares his age to that of other lawgivers will find him far beyond them all. Eusebius in book 10 of the *Preparation for the Gospel* also shows that Moses came long before Ceres; as we have said, she is thought to have been the first to publish laws. So law has its origin from God, whom Cicero calls Jupiter. Moses, before any other mortal, established law for the Hebrews, and this doubtless was the model for laws eventually set up among other peoples. Such is the origin of justice and laws.

But this seems the right place to discuss the reason why this 9 written law was not in the end treated like another benefit: As the Apostle Paul says, it brings anger and makes people liable to a thousand penalties. That earlier law, by contrast, is not written but inborn, flowing from its original source into the human spirit by a kind of natural effusion; it is harmless and guileless, partaking in justice and free of iniquity. Hence it seems to have done us no good to introduce the other kind which is bad for us.

This makes it worthwhile to treat the origin of this later law 10 more precisely, and since St. Ambrose explains it in *Letter* [73] to Irenaeus, let us hear what he says: It is certain, he explains, that the law given through Moses was not necessary, for if people had been able to keep that natural law which God the creator poured into each person's heart, there would have been no need of this other law that knotted up the weakness of the human race rather than undoing it. Adam undid the law of nature, wishing to take what had not been given him so that he would be like his creator; in disobeying he caused offense, for if he had not broken the commandment, he would preserved for his heirs the prerogative of nature and of his inborn innocence. But since the law was violated, it was necessary to prescribe a new law so that the one who had lost the whole might keep at least a part. At the same time, because pride caused Adam's fall, it was fitting to establish a law that would make him subject to God, for without such a law he would

sem et locutus fuissem eis, peccatum non haberent; nunc autem excusationem non habent. Lata est ergo lex primum ut excusatio tolleretur cum praescriptum ante non esset quod pro se quisque caveret; deinde ut omnes subiicerentur Deo. Sed dices: Lex auxit peccatum; coepit mihi obesse scire. Verum dicis; est tamen quod consolari potest tuam solicitudinem, quia si per legem abundavit peccatum per eandem abundavit et gratia per Iesum Christum, sicut testificatus est Ioannes, dicens: ecce agnus dei, ecce qui tollit peccatum mundi.

11   Habes igitur legem non necessariam fuisse si illam naturae legem servare potuissemus, sed quia non servavimus, idcirco ista lex per Mosen data facta est necessaria, ut doceret me obedientiam et transgressionis Adam solveret laqueum qui totam astrinxit haereditatem, etc.

12   Caeterum extra tripartitam illam iuris divisionem quam Ulpianus fecit, habemus in nostra religione ius pontificium in quo multi cum memoria nostra excellunt tum antea claruerunt, qui olim non sine honoris praefatione nominabuntur, et in primis Theseus Pinnius avunculus meus quem nemo aut nimis valde unquam aut nimis saepe laudaverit. Fuit enim vir pontificii pariter atque civilis iuris peritissimus; qui in praeclarissimis Italiae civitatibus maximis honoribus functus, ubique summae iustitiae virtutisque omnis se specimen praestitit. A quo profecto haud longe abest Petrus Matthaeus eius frater, iurisconsultissimorum consultissimus.

have been ignorant of sin, and guilt was less where guilt was ignored. Wherefore the Lord said: If I had not come and spoken to them, they would have no sin, but now they have no excuse. Thus, the law was given in the first instance to take away the excuse, since before it had not been determined that each person was responsible for himself; the second reason was to make everyone subject to God. But you say: The law has increased sin; knowledge has come to harm me. What you say is true; still, it should ease your worry that grace abounds in the same law where sin abounds — through Jesus Christ, as John has testified, saying: Behold the lamb of God, behold him who takes away the sin of the world.

You understand, then, that the law would not have been necessary if we had been able to keep nature's law, but because we have not kept it, the law given through Moses was made necessary, to teach me obedience and to loose the snare of Adam's transgression which has held all posterity, and so on. 11

Beyond the tripartite division of law that Ulpian made, we have in our religion another law, pontifical, in which many are eminent in our day and many also were renowned in the past. By your leave, I will mention them here, especially Teseo Pinnio, my uncle, whom no one ever praised too much or too often. Indeed, he was a great expert in pontifical and civil law alike; he held high office in the most famous cities all over Italy, proving himself an example of the loftiest justice and of every virtue. Very near him is his brother, Piero Matteo, a most judicious jurist. 12

: II :

Qui regiam vel popularem civitatem principio instituerint
tyrannidemque exercuerint et diadema vel servitium
invenerint, et quis Areopagitarum magistratum constituerit
aut suffragia invenerit.

1   Quoniam de legis origine, sine qua nulla respublica consistere potest, proximo capite huius voluminis docuimus, porro res ipsa postulat ut priusquam hinc digrediar, quale apud gentes regimen civitatis principio fuerit demonstremus. Est igitur apud mortales,
teste Platone libro *De regno*, trifariam divisa reipublicae administratio: una enim vocatur monarchia, id est, unius imperium; altera
aristocratia, hoc est, optimatum regimen; tertia vero democratia,
id est, popularis principatus. Quarum quae praeferenda sit non facile dixerim. Rex enim cui pro libidine omnia licet impune agere,
ac ob id nihil interdum potius est quam quod in rem suam esse videt, raro bene imperat. Plebs etiam, cui proprium est nihil intelligere, aliquanto peius. Pauci vero, id est, optimates, cum princeps
esse pro se quisque optet nec satis concordes regnant. Quare Dio-
cletianus, autore Vopisco, dicere solitus erat nihil esse difficilius
quam bene imperare. Optime tamen unus, optime populus, optime pauci imperant, si boni sunt.

2   Ex quo alii aliam constituerunt civitatem. Aegyptii primi omnium, teste Plinio libro 7, regium principatum habuerunt, ut qui,
veluti ait Herodotus, nullo temporis momento poterant sine rege
vivere. Apud quos primus quod memoriae proditum sit mortalium
Menes regnavit, autores Herodotus libro 2 et Diodorus in 1. Caeterum nemo, teste Platone in libro *De regno*, rex creabatur nisi qui
sacerdotio praeditus foret. At si ita usu veniret ut unus aliquis pro-

: II :

Who originally established a royal or a popular state;
who practiced tyranny and invented the diadem and slavery;
and who set up the office of the Areopagites and
invented ballots.

Because we taught about the origin of law, without which no com-　1
monwealth can stand, in the preceding chapter of this book, the
subject demands that before moving on we show next how people
originally governed their states. According to Plato in his book *On
Government*, then, the regulation of the commonwealth is divided
into three kinds: one is called monarchy or rule by a single person;
another is aristocracy, government by the noblest; and democracy
or popular leadership is the third. Which of these is to be preferred is hard to say. For if a king can always act willfully and
without restraint so that nothing seems more important than personal advantage, he rarely rules well. The people are even a bit
worse for it is in their nature to understand nothing. But the few,
the nobility, rule without enough harmony because each wants
to pursue his own interest. For this reason, writes Vopiscus,
Diocletian used to say that nothing is more difficult than to rule
well. And yet the one rules best, the people rule best, the few rule
best if they are good.

Hence, various peoples established states of various kinds. The　2
Egyptians were the first to have royal leadership, according to
Pliny in book 7, so that they were never able to live without a
king, as Herodotus says. The first human known to memory who
ruled over them was Menes, according to Herodotus in book 2
and Diodorus in book 1. Moreover, as Plato testifies in his book
On Government, no one was made king unless he held priestly

phanus regnum per vim adipisceretur, is postea sacris initiari coge-
batur quo esset rex et sacerdos.

3   Diadema autem, quod regium est insigne, Liberum patrem
adinvenisse autor est Plinius in 7, cuius nimirum rei Diodorus veram rationem reddere videtur, aiens: Mitra vero caput ei ligatur
propter dolores qui fumante vino caput aggrediuntur. Popularem
civitatem Attici, ut Plinius in 7 tradit, primi instituerunt, sed iidem reges etiam habuere, quorum primus fuit Cecrops Diphyes,
aequalis Mosis.

4   Nam autore Iustino libro 1, ab initio quaeque civitas et gens rerum publicarum imperium penes reges habebat, quos ad fastigium
huius maiestatis non ambitio popularis sed spectata inter bonos
moderatio provehebat. Ex quo, teste Aemilio Probo in *Vita Agesi-
lai*, apud Lacedaemonios reges erant qui nomine magis quam imperio reges appellarentur. Et primus rex fuit Eurysteus, Argis II,
Archestratus III, Lobotes IIII, Doristus V, Agesilaus VI, Archelaus
VII, Telechus VIII, Alcamenes IX et ultimus. Ninus autem, testis
est idem Iustinus, rex Assyriorum primus omnium veterem gentium morem nova imperii cupiditate mutavit, atque idem primus
omnium, sicut ait Eusebius in 10 *De praeparatione evangelica*, totius
Asiae, excepta India, imperio potitus est.

5   Verum quod Attici popularem civitatem primum constituerunt,
uti Plinius prodidit, nemo est qui ambigat hoc a vero valde esse
alienum. Hebraei enim, a quibus Iosephus in 1 *Antiquitatum* caeteras nationes originem traxisse pulcherrime probat, uti superius ostendimus, multis ante seculis quam aut Attici imperarent aut
Athenae conditae forent, regnarunt, quorum respublica, eodem Iosepho autore libro 20 *Antiquitatum*, primo quidem sub populari
potestate diu permansit. Ab his proinde democratiam primum

office. So it was customary that if some unsanctified person took the kingship by force, he was then required to be initiated in the rites that would make him king and priest.

Pliny in book 7 is our authority that Father Liber devised the 3 diadem, which is the badge of royalty. Diodorus doubtless gives the real reason, saying: a band is tied around his head because of the headache that comes from vaporous wine. The Athenians, as Pliny reports in book 7, first founded a popular state, but they also had kings, of whom the first was Cecrops Diphyes, a contemporary of Moses.

According to Justinus in book 1, every city and people in the be- 4 ginning kept power over the commonwealth in the control of kings; it was the moderation respected among gentlemen, not currying favor with the people, that carried them to the heights of majesty. Hence, according to Aemilius Probus in his *Life of Agesilaus*, the Lacedaemonians had kings who were called kings by title rather than by their power. Their first king was Eurysteus, Argis the second, Archestratus third, Lobotes fourth, Doristus fifth, Agesilaus sixth, Archelaus seventh, Telechus eighth, Alcamenes ninth and last. But the same Justinus testifies that Ninus, king of the Assyrians, first changed the ancient ways of all peoples with his new lust for power, and he was also the first to seize control of all Asia, except for India, as Eusebius says in book 10 of the *Preparation for the Gospel*.

But to claim with Pliny that the Athenians first established a 5 popular state is far from true — as no one doubts. We showed above how Josephus makes an excellent case in book 1 of the *Antiquities* that the other nations originated from the Hebrews, who ruled for many centuries before the Athenians governed or Athens was founded. Josephus also writes in book 20 of the *Antiquities* that at first their government remained under popular control for some time. Thus it is more accurate to believe that democracy

manasse rectius est credere quam ab Atticis, qui posteriores fuerunt.

6   Aristocratiam, id est, optimatum imperium quale Romani post exactos reges diu habuerunt, qui primi constituerint non facile tradiderim — si illud non sit assignandum Thebaeis, qui (teste Eusebio) temporibus Nini regis Aegyptiis imperabant, quorum dominatus δυναστεία dicebatur, hoc est, potestas quod qui potentiores nobilioresque essent, iis reipublicae administrandae imperium daretur. Et hoc circiter annum ab orbe condito ter millesimum et CLXXXV, quo Abraham natus est.

7   Post Theseum tyrannum, primus fuit Phalaris Agrigenti, ait Plinius in 7, propter quod innuere videtur Theseum primum omnium fuisse tyrannum, secundum vero Phalaridem. Sed Nemroth ex stirpe Noe ortus non multo post diluvium, Babylone tyrannus fuisse perhibetur. Ita ait Iosephus in primo *Antiquitatum*: Nemroth quoque filius Chusi permanens apud Babylonios tyrannidem exercuit, sicut a me primo etiam declaratum est — haec ille. Tyrannum olim vocabant bonum dominum ac (teste Trogo) fortem. Vergilius:

Pars mihi pacis erit dextram tetigisse tyranni.

Postea haec vox ad eos translata est qui vi quadam ac libidine dominantur, quorum lex est, Hoc volo, sic iubeo, sit pro ratione voluntas quando omnia potentia et voluntate metiuntur.

8   Servitium, teste Plinio, Lacedaemonii invenere, quandoquidem Cleomenes Lacedaemonius, teste Macrobio libro I *Saturnalium*, ex servis manumissis bellatorum novem millia conscripsit qui, quoniam in bello non necabantur sed vivi servabantur, servi appellati sunt. Hi sub corona postea vendebantur. Cato: Ut populus sua opera potius ob rem bene gestam coronatus supplicatum eat quam re male gesta coronatus veneat.

arose first from them rather than from the Athenians, who came later.

I would not venture to say who first established an aristocracy, a 6 government of nobles such as the Romans had for a long time after the kings had been driven out, unless it should be assigned to the Thebans, who (according to Eusebius) ruled over the Egyptians in the time of King Ninus. Their lordship was called *dynasteia* or power because authority to run the commonwealth was given to those who were more powerful and nobler. And this was around the year 3185 after the creation of the world, when Abraham was born.

Pliny says in book 7 that Phalaris of Agrigentum came first af- 7 ter the tyrant Theseus, which seems to suggest that Theseus was the first tyrant of all and Phalaris the second. But Nemroth, born of the stock of Noah not long after the flood, is said to have been tyrant in Babylon. This is what Josephus claims in the first book of the *Antiquities*: Nemroth, son of Chus, remained among the Babylonians and practiced tyranny, just as I said before — this from Josephus. Tyrant is what they used to call a lord who was good and (according to Justinus) strong. Vergil:

Peace, for my part, is to give the tyrant my hand.

Later the term was transferred to those who rule by a kind of force and willfulness, whose law says: I want it, I demand it, let will replace reason since power and will cover everything.

The Lacedaemonians invented slavery, according to Pliny. Ma- 8 crobius testifies in book 1 of the *Saturnalia* that Cleomenes the Lacedaemonian drafted nine thousand warriors from manumitted slaves; they were called servants because they were not killed in battle but had their lives preserved. Later they were sold under the crown. Cato: Let the people crown their own efforts and be thankful for a good deed rather than be crowned and sold for a bad one.

9   Reperio tamen antequam Lacedaemonii, teste Iosepho *Contra Appionem*, rerum potirentur apud Hebraeos multos fuisse servos, et eius servitutis originem profectam a Chanaan, filio Cham, qui fuit unus ex filiis Noe—is enim treis genuit, Sem, Cham, et Iaphet. Quippe Cham cum videret patrem Noe forte ebrium humi parum honeste iacentem, vituperavit eum apud fratres. Quare permotus senex Chanaan, nepotem ex filio Cham, servitute mulctavit, re tum nova ac gravissima, uti in libro Genesis capite 9 est.

10   Sed hic dices: Ecquid fuit quamobrem Chanaan ob patris peccatum in servitutem datus fuerit cum iuxta proverbium filius non debeat plecti ob patris culpam? Non equidem de nihilo dubitas: id etenim factum tradunt ut poena Chanaan filio illata dolori esset patri Cham quando ita solent parentes angi filiorum cruciatu. Nam cum Deus Noe pariter atque eius filiis antea benedixisset, senex postea non est ausus in filium, etsi impium, quicquam statuere; idcirco nepotem punivit quo eius pater filii vicem dolens sic delicti poenas daret.

11   Ac tale servitutis initium cum inciperent homines iam molliter vivere. Forma autem manumittendi servi talis apud antiquos fuit: Dominus caput aliudve membrum servi tenens aiebat, Hunc hominem liberum esse volo, atque his dictis eum de manu emittebat.

12   Areopagitarum autem magistratum Plutarchus a Solone constitutum affirmat quod de Areopagitis a Dracone nulla unquam mentio facta sit. In eo primum Athenis capitis iudicium actum est, autor Plinius libro 7. Areopagus vero latine dicitur curia sive pagus Martis. Causa nominis ex iudicio est quo Mars, qui graece ἄρης vocatur, cum homicidii reus fieret iudicantibus duodecim diis in eo pago, ut scribit Augustinus in 18 *De civitate dei*, sex sententiis absolutus est; ubi enim pares sunt sententiae, absolutio

But I find that before the Lacedaemonians came to power there 9
were many slaves in Hebrew times, according to Josephus *Against Apion*, and this slavery started with Chanaan, son of Cham, one of the sons of Noah, who begot three sons — Sem, Cham and Japhet. For when Cham happened to see his father Noah very drunk and lying indecently on the ground, he reviled him in front of his brothers. This provoked the old man to punish Chanaan, his grandson by Cham, with slavery, which was then something new and very grievous, as chapter 9 of the book of Genesis says.

But here you will ask: Why should Chanaan have been sent 10
into slavery for the sin of his father since the son should not be punished for the father's offence, according to the proverb? The question is not unreasonable: They say it was done so that the penalty imposed on Chanaan, the son, would hurt the father, Cham, because the pain of their children usually distresses the parents. Since God had already blessed Noah and his sons equally, from then on the old man dared not take any action against his son, undutiful though he was; therefore, he punished his grandson so that the father would pay the price of his wrongdoing by suffering on account of the son.

Such was the beginning of slavery when people were already 11
starting to live a life of ease. But the ancients used this procedure to free a slave: Holding the slave's head or another part of his body, the master said, 'I want this man to be liberated,' and with these words he freed him from his power.

Because Draco never mentioned the Areopagites, Plutarch 12
affirms that Solon established their office. It was there that the first capital judgment was made in Athens, according to Pliny in book 7. In Latin Areopagus means the court or district of Mars. The name comes from the court that acquitted Mars (in Greek *Arēs*) of an accusation of murder by six votes of the twelve divine judges sitting in that district, as Augustine writes in book 18 of the *City of God*, for when the votes are equal, acquittal is preferred to a

damnationi praeponitur. Fuit inde Areopagitarum magistratus, uti dictum est, institutus, quorum summa erat autoritas. Ii erant iudices qui de capitalibus causis pronunciabant tanta gravitate tantaque integritate ut noctu non interdiu causas cognoscerent, quo non dicentes sed duntaxat quae dicerentur spectarent secumque ponderarent. Suffragia quibus in deliberando iudicandoque utimur Palamedes primus omnium reperit.

: III :

De triplici regiminis genere romanae civitatis; et de origine insignium regum; et ex qua arbore fierent magistratuum virgae; atque quis primus censum instituerit, et de senatorio atque equestri censu; vel carcerem edificaverit; et ibidem quid esset lustrum conditum; ac de initio tributi imponendi.

1 Ego mediusfidius semper illam Plinii sententiam, posteris laxitas mundi et rerum amplitudo damno fuit, tanquam omnium verissimam plurimi feci. Etenim ne a primordio orbis repetam cum homines, rerum fere omnium egentes, probe degebant, quot nobis florentissimae civitates exemplo sunt? Quae paucis minimisque contentae, dum in illis paupertati parsimoniaeque honos fuit, indies magis imperio, moribus bonisque artibus excelluerunt. At contra ubi divitiae, ubi sacrae pecuniae fames, ubi voluptas immigravit, tunc ire coeperunt praecipites, tunc sensim dominandi libido desyderium per luxum perdendi omnia invexit.

verdict of guilt. From that time the office of the Areopagites was established, as has been said, and their authority was supreme. They were judges who pronounced on capital cases so gravely and righteously that they met at night rather than by day in order to investigate and deliberate among themselves only about what was said to them, not about the people who said it. Palamedes first of all invented the ballots that we use in taking counsel and judging.

: III :

On three ways of ruling the Roman state; on the origin of royal trappings; from what tree the rods of the magistrates were made; who first established a census, and on the senatorial and equestrian census; who built the jail; why the lustration was made; and on the origin of the imposition of tribute.

As God is my witness, I have always honored this statement of   1
Pliny's as absolutely true: that the great space of the world and the great plenty of things in it have been hurtful to posterity. And truly, without going back to the beginning of the world when people lived as they should, in need of almost everything, how many states at the peak of prosperity are an example to us? As long as they held poverty and thrift in honor, content with few things and little, they distinguished themselves day after day in government, conduct and the useful arts. But when wealth, when luxury, when hunger for cursed riches came in, then they became rash, then gradually the lust for mastery brought on longing as they indulged themselves by squandering everything.

2   Quod Lycurgus, legumlator sapientissimus prospiciens animo, nummum omnem aureum et argenteum, teste Plutarcho, irritum fecit, ferreoque solum utendum imperavit. Cuius sanctionem ut primum Lacedaemonii excessere, ex maximis longe minimi sunt effecti.

3   Sed ut de caeteris sileam, hoc potissimum Romanae civitati accidit. Ea enim ubi Publicolas, Aemilios, Fabritios, Curios, Scipiones, Scauros, paupertatis continentiaeque amantissimos imperatores sibi deligebat, incredibile memoratu est quam brevi cresceret quantumque cum ipsa praeclare ageretur. Contra ubi senator censu legebatur, iudex fiebat censu, magistratum ducemque nil magis exornabat quam census, captatio in quaestu fertilissimo ac sola gaudia in possidendo erant, adeo declinare de statu suo coepit ut nunquam in aliquo postea consistere potuerit.

4   Nanque omne regiminis genus perpessa est. Primum enim monarchiam, hoc est, regium imperium, habuit, nam Romulus, autore Floro, eius conditor a Marte genitus et Rhea Silvia, primum imperium tenuit. Post quem sex deinde reges secuti sunt sub quibus, teste Livio in primo *Ab urbe condita*, CCXLIIII annos monarchia duravit. Exin pulso Tarquinio Superbo, qui regum ultimus fuit, mutata civitatis forma, secuta est aristocratia, id est, optimatum principatus. Nam pro regibus duo consules, ut Livius in secundo et Dionysius in quarto testatur, creati sunt: Lucius Iunius Brutus, qui libertatis uindex extiterat, et Lucius Tarquinius Collatinus, qui consules dicti a consulendo, hoc est, providendo. Apud eos summa totius imperii erat. Ii exercitum ductabant, et ab eorum magistratu — qui annuus erat, uti alibi dicemus — numerus annorum notabatur.

5   Post annum deinde duodecimum, vel, ut non nemo vult, octavum quam exacti sunt reges, quod Livius et Fenestella non satis

Lycurgus, that most clever and sagacious lawmaker, made all 2 gold and silver coins worthless, according to Plutarch, and commanded that only iron was to be used. As soon as the Lacedaemonians violated his ordinance, they were reduced from a great people to a petty one.

If I may pass over the others, this was the special misfortune of 3 the Roman state. For when she chose leaders for herself so devoted to poverty and moderation — Publicolae, Aemilii, Fabricii, Curii, Scipiones, Scauri — it is amazing to recall how quickly and how much she grew while things went well with her. But when a senator was appointed because of wealth, when a judge was named because of wealth, when nothing distinguished the magistrate and the general more than wealth, when legacy-hunting was the most fruitful occupation and the only joys were in ownership, then she began to decline so much from her position that never after could she remain steadfast in anything.

In fact, Rome endured every kind of rule. First she had a mon- 4 archy, a royal government, that is; her founder Romulus, begotten of Mars and Rhea Sylvia, was the first to hold power, according to Florus. After him followed six kings under whom the monarchy lasted for 244 years, according to Livy in the first book *From the Foundation of the City*. Then, when Tarquin the Proud, last of the kings, was driven out and the form of the state was changed, there followed an aristocracy, and noblemen were supreme. In place of the kings two consuls were created, as Livy testifies in his second book and Dionysius in his fourth: they were Lucius Junius Brutus, famous as liberty's avenger, and Lucius Tarquinius Collatinus, and they were called consuls because they gave counsel or made plans. Theirs was the totality of all power. They led the army, and the number of years was reckoned from their term of office — which, as we shall explain elsewhere, was annual.

Twelve years after the expulsion of the kings — or, as some 5 would have it, eight, because Livy and Fenestella say the evidence

constare aiunt, cum 40 Latinorum urbes, concitante Octavio Manilio, Tarquinii genero, coniurassent in Romanos, Titus Largius primus dictator creatus fuit, autor Livius in 2 *Ab urbe condita.* Quod institutum Dionysius libro quinto *Antiquitatum* putat Romanos a Graecis sumpsisse, apud quos *esymnetae* tanquam dictatores Romae creabantur. At Licinius ab Albanis accepisse tradit. Carthaginenses etiam, autore Trogo, dictatorem habebant. Hic autem summus fuit in urbe magistratus, quippe qui habebatur in summo periculo ultimum remedium. In sex tantum menses, uti Fenestella ait, durabat.

6   Nam eo designato praeter tribunatum omnes magistratus, teste Polybio volumine suarum *Historiarum* 3 et Plutarcho in *Vita Fabii Maximi,* autoritatem suam amittebant. Et ideo dictator dicebatur quod is imperaret, quia, sicut idem in *Vita Marcelli* testatur, iussa magistratuum edicta Romani vocabant. Item dictator non poterat nisi a consule dici neque alio tempore nisi oriente nocte et silentio, ut Livius libro *Ab urbe condita* 8 tradit. Attamen, teste eodem libro 4, cum aliquando Veientes castra Romana cepissent, Aulus Cornelius Cossus tribunus militum Mamercum Aemilium dictatorem dixit quod augures consulti urgente necessitate eam religionem exemissent.

7   Post annum deinceps CCC alterum quam condita Roma erat, velut Livius in 3 prodit, iterum mutata est forma civitatis — ab consulibus ad decemviros, quemadmodum ab regibus ante ad consules venerat; qui, uti quibusdam placet, tertio anno depositi sunt libidine Appii Claudii, qui Virginiam cuius stuprandae amore deflagrabat in servitutem asserere voluit. Qui cum pro libidine omnia agerent, officium suo commodo metientes, ac quod ex ipsorum usu, non e republica esset in primis facientes — et eos ob id nonnulli senatores, uti inquit Fenestella, decem Tarquinios appellarent — videtur tunc Romae magis monarchia quam aristocratia

is unclear—when at the instigation of Tarquin's son-in-law, Octavius Manilius, forty towns of the Latins conspired against the Romans, Titus Largius was made the first dictator, according to Livy in book 2 *From the Foundation of the City*. In the fifth book of the *Antiquities* Dionysius concludes that the Romans borrowed this institution from the Greeks, who appointed *esymnetae* as the Romans appointed dictators. But Licinius claims that they took it from the Albans, and according to Justinus the Carthaginians also had a dictator. At any rate, it was the highest office in the city since it was considered the final remedy in times of greatest danger. It lasted only six months, as Fenestella says.

According to Polybius in volume 3 of his *Histories* and Plutarch   6
in his *Life of Fabius Maximus*, all offices except the tribunate lost their authority once a dictator was chosen. Hence, he was called a dictator because he was in command and because the Romans called the orders of magistrates edicts, as the same Plutarch says in his *Life of Marcellus*. Also, a dictator could be named only by a consul and at no time but at nightfall and in silence, as Livy reports in book 8 *From the Foundation of the City*. And yet, according to the same author in book 4, when the Veii once captured a Roman camp, the military tribune Aulus Cornelius Cossus named Mamercus Aemilus dictator because the augurs had waived the restriction when they were consulted in this pressing necessity.

Then, 302 years after Rome was founded, as Livy tells it in   7
book 3, the form of the state was changed again—from consuls to decemvirs, just as it had already gone from kings to consuls; some say they were deposed three years later because of the lust of Appius Claudius, who wanted to declare Virginia a slave because he was burning with the desire to dishonor her. Since everything they did was out of lust, measuring duty by their own comfort, and since they acted mainly for their own benefit and not for the commonwealth—because of which some Senators called them the Ten Tarquins, says Fenestella—it seems that Rome was then more

fuisse. Hoc pacto exactis decemviris, ad prioris formam regiminis reditum est.

8 At dein anno CCCX conditae urbis, pro consulibus primum tribuni militum creati sunt: Aulus Sempronius Atratinus, Lucius Attilius Longus, et Titus Caecilius Siculus. Democratia autem, id est, popularis principatus, sensim irrepsit, plebe paulatim per seditiones adipiscente nobilitatis magistratus. Primum enim, Gaio Canuleio autore, plebeii connubia promiscua cum patritiis habere coeperunt; deinde, cum tribuni plebis quotidie magis magisque instarent, a patritiis tandem concessum est ut ex plebe tribuni quoque militum consulari potestate fierent, et ita Publius Licinius Calvus primus creatus est anno urbis conditae CCCLV. Deinde plebs consulatum assecuta est; et Lucius Sextius Lateranus de plebe primus consul factus anno urbis conditae CCCLXXXIX. Novissime obtinuit et dictaturam, summum in urbe decus; primusque ex plebe Gaius Martius Rutilius dictator dictus fuit, anno ab urbe condita CCCXCIX. Haec ex Livio libris 4 et 5 et 6 et 7 *Ab urbe condita* et Plutarcho in *Vita Camilli.*

9 Eo denique pacto reipublicae administratio ex optimatibus ad popularem principatum venerat, ex quo novissime iterum in monarchiam, id est, ad unius imperium, forma civitatis redacta est; quae a Sylla et Mario, teste Appiano in primo *De bellis civilibus,* coepit, fracta omni senatus potestate. Eam postea Caesares adauxerunt, sub quibus primum ipsa Roma toto pacato orbe floruit, inde insequentium Caesarum inertia contabuit atque ad interitum devenit. Habuit igitur Romana civitas primum monarchiam, id est, regium imperium; subinde aristocratiam et democratiam, hoc est, consulum, dictatorum, decemvirum et tribunorum consularium regimen; at novissime rursus monarchiam, id

monarchy than aristocracy. With the decemvirs thus expelled, the state returned to its earlier form of rule.

Next, 310 years after the foundation of the city, military tri- 8 bunes having the authority of consuls were first created: Aulus Sempronius Atratinus, Lucius Attilius Longus and Titus Caecilius Siculus. But democracy or leadership by the people gradually crept in as the people little by little acquired the offices of the nobility through political strife. Led by Gaius Canuleius, the people first began to make a common practice of intermarriage with patricians; then, as pressure from the tribunes of the people mounted day by day, the patricians finally conceded that military tribunes with consular power should be appointed from the people as well, and Publius Licinius Calvus was the first thus created in 355 AUC. Finally, the people attained the consulate; in the year 389 AUC Lucius Sextius Lateranus became the first consul appointed from the people. Last of all they achieved the dictatorship as well, the city's highest office; the first of the people named dictator was Gaius Martius Rutilius in the year 399 AUC. This comes from Livy, books 4 through 7 *From the Foundation of the City* and from Plutarch's *Life of Camillus*.

In this way, then, the administration of of the commonwealth 9 passed from the nobles to the leadership of the people until ultimately the form of the state returned again to monarchy, to government by one person, in other words; according to Appian in the first book *On the Civil Wars*, this started with Sulla and Marius when the Senate's power was completely broken. Later on the Caesars built the monarchy up: Rome at first flourished under them, and the whole world was at peace, but then with the idleness of the later Caesars it wasted away and fell into ruin. And so the Roman state had a monarchy or a royal government at first; then she had aristocracy and democracy, which was the rule of consuls, dictators, decemvirs and consular tribunes; and finally she

est, tum dictatorum cum Caesarum tyrannidem saevissimam, pertulit, unde eius virium labes facta est.

10 Romanorum autem regum insignia—hoc est, fasces cum securibus, corona aurea, sella eburnea, trabeae curules, falerae, annuli, paludamenta, praetexta, togae pictae tunicaeque palmatae et omnia denique decora quibus imperii dignitas eminebat—ex XII Tusciae populis, autore Dionysio in tertio, et Floro, et Strabone in 5 *Geographiae*, quos Tarquinius Priscus subegit, originem habuere; quibus Tarquinius, ut Dionysio placet, simul atque id senatus permisit primus usus est. Quare miror Macrobium in 1 *Saturnalium* scribere Tullium Hostilium, tertium Romanorum regem, debellatis Hetruscis, primum sellam curulem, lictores, togam pictam atque praetextam instituisse Romae haberi.

11 Verum Romulus ex more XII Hetruriae populorum, qui singuli, Livio et Dionysio autoribus, singulos regi statim creato lictores dabant, antea XII lictores sumpsit, cuius sententiae esse haud Livium poenitet. Alii a numero avium quae augurio regnum portenderant eum secutum numerum autumant. Hi magistratibus ministrabant fascesque virgarum alligatos cum securibus gestabant. Eiusmodi autem virgas ex betulla arbore fieri consuevisse Plinius libro 16, capite 18, *Naturalis historiae* innuere videtur, sic scribens: gaudet frigidis sorbus et magis etiam betulla; gallica haec arbor mirabili candore atque tenuitate terribilis magistratuum virgis.

12 Censum primus omnium Servius Tullus rex instituit, rem, veluti Livius ait, saluberrimam tanto futuro imperio. Ex quo belli pacisque munia non viritim, ut ante, sed pro possessione pecuniarum cives obirent. Quorum classes, id est, ordines quinque descripsit. Prima itaque classis fuit ex iis qui centum millium aeris aut maiorem censum haberent; quos in octoginta centurias divisit, in quadragenas seniorum ac totidem iuniorum, seniores ad urbis cus-

endured monarchy again, the very cruel tyranny of dictators and
Caesars both, who caused her power to collapse.

The trappings of the Roman kings—fasces with axes, golden 10
wreath, ivory chair, robes of state, breastplates, rings, military
cloaks, ornaments, embroidered togas and tunics, and all the other
decorations that displayed the ruler's distinction—originated from
the twelve peoples of Etruria whom Tarquinius Priscus subdued,
according to Dionysius in book 3, Florus and Strabo in book 5 of
the *Geography*; Dionysius thinks that Tarquinius was the first to
use them, as soon as the Senate gave permission. Hence I am surprised when Macrobius in book 1 of the *Saturnalia* writes that
Tullius Hostilius, third king of the Romans, first started the use
of the curule chair, lictors, and embroidered and bordered togas in
Rome after he had brought the Etruscans under control.

Actually, according to Livy and Dionysius, Romulus took the 11
twelve lictors at an earlier time from a custom of the twelve peoples of Etruria, who each presented a lictor to the king as soon as
he was appointed, and it is helpful that Livy holds this opinion.
Others claim that the number comes from the number of birds in
the augury that predicted his reign. The lictors attended the magistrates and carried bundles of rods bound with axes. Pliny, in
chapter 18 of book 16 of the *Natural History*, seems to suggest that
it was customary to make such rods from the birch-tree: the ser-
vice-tree likes cold places, he writes, and the birch likes them even
better; this tree of Gaul, wonderfully white and slim, is fearful because of the rods that magistrates use.

King Servius Tullius first of all instituted the census, a very 12
sound action, as Livy says, for a government with so great a future. On this basis citizens would perform the duties of war and
peace not one by one, as before, but in keeping with their possession of wealth. Servius Tullius described five classes or orders of
citizens. The first class was of those whose registered assets were
valued at 100,000 *asses* or more; these he divided into eighty cen-

todiam ut praesto essent, iuniores ut foris bella gererent, arma his imperata galea, clypeus, ocreae, lorica, tela in hostem hasta et gladius. Secunda classis intra centum usque ad quinque et septuaginta millium censum instituta; et ex his senioribus iunioribusque viginti conscriptae sunt centuriae, armaque imperata praeter loricam omnia eadem. Tertiae classis in quinquaginta millium censum esse voluit, totidem centuriae sunt conscriptae. In quarta classe census quinque et viginti millium, totidem centuriae factae. Quinta classis undecim millibus censebatur.

13   Sed iam rationem ineamus qua nobis constet quanti unaquaeque classis aestimata sit. Illud enim primum scire licet centum aera (nam aes nummulus erat) non pluris fuisse uno nostro ducato sive coronato aureo nummo, ac ita mille aera valuisse decem aureos. Primae igitur classis census aestimatus est mille aureis, secundae septingentis et quinquaginta, tertiae quingentis, quartae ducentis et quinquaginta, quintae vero centum et decem. At maximus Servio Tullo rege census, teste Plinio libro 33, fuit assium centum et decem millia, ex quibus summa fit mille et centum aureorum. Et haec, ut ait idem Plinius, prima classis, adeo id temporis Romanorum opes exiguae fuerant; quae posthac immensae extitere quando, autore Tranquillo, census senatorius fuit duodecies centena millia sestertium nummum. Quam quidem summam ut recte putemus, notare oportet singula sestertia valuisse vicenos quinos aureos, sic ut centum sestertia summam facerent duorum millium et quingentorum aureorum. Qua ratione colligimus censum senatorium fuisse ad numerum triginta millium aureorum et equestrem duodecim millium et quingentorum, hoc est, constitisse ex quingentis sestertiis. Atque talis origo et forma fuit census Romani qui, ut Eutropius ait, adhuc per orbem terrarum incognitus erat. Sed illud verius Mosi assignandum est, qui, ut infra demonstrabitur, primus populum recensuit.

turies, forty of elders and the same number of youths, so that the elders would be ready to guard the city and the youths to wage war abroad, requiring them to have a helmet, round shield, greaves and cuirass as armor, and a lance and sword as offensive weapons. He set up the second class with assets between 100,000 and 75,000; from these were enrolled twenty centuries of elders and youths, with all the same arms required except the cuirass. The third class should have 50,000 in assets, he decided, and should enroll the same number of centuries. The fourth class had assets of 25,000, making the same number of centuries. The fifth class was valued at 11,000.

But now let us reckon the evidence for estimating the wealth of 13 each class. To begin, we may note that a hundred *asses* (an *aes* was a small coin) were not worth more than one of our ducats or gold crowns, and thus a thousand *asses* were worth ten gold pieces. Therefore, the assets of the first class were valued at 1,000 gold pieces, the second at 750, the third at 500, the fourth 250 and the fifth 110. But when Servius Tullius was king, according to Pliny in book 33, the highest census was 110,000, which makes 1,100 gold pieces. And this, as Pliny says, was in the first class, so scanty were the resources of the Romans at that time; later they became huge when the senatorial census was 1,200 *sestertia*, according to Suetonius. In fact, to determine this amount correctly, it should be recognized that each *sestertium* was worth twenty-five gold pieces, so that a hundred *sestertia* would make 2,500 gold pieces. From this calculation we conclude that the senatorial census was at the level of 30,000 gold-pieces and the equestrian at 12,500—that the equestrian total was 500 *sestertia*, in other words. Such was the form and origin of the Roman census which—so Eutropius says—was as yet unknown throughout the world. But it is more accurate to assign it to Moses, who first counted the people, as we shall point out below.

14   Atqui census agi dicitur cum hominum facultates recensen-
tur — unde tributi imponendi ratio inita est — vel cum numerus civium putatur. Utrunque testatur Livius in vita ipsius Servii Tulli.
Et cum in censendo finis erat factus, lustrum conditum appellabatur quod tum Servius exercitum omnem sue, ove taurisque tribus
lustravit, hoc est, purgavit. Idque lustrum quinto quoque anno
Romae condebatur, cum censores numero duo creabantur, qui
censum agerent. Is postea magistratus annuus factus, eique morum civitatis cura est tradita. Item cum vectigalia et tributa solve-
bantur, tum fiebat sacrificium civitatis purgandae causa. Ex quo
perinde Romani annos etiam per lustrum numerabant atque
Graeci per Olympiades. Caeterum cum ita quinto quoque anno
lustrum condi diceretur, sunt qui putent illud fuisse spatium quatuor annorum, argumentantes annum quo sequens lustrum incipiebat dici quintum, qui esset primus sequentis lustri. Quae sane
ratio, si vera sit, similiter indicat Olympiada fuisse spatium quatuor tantum annorum, quemadmodum infra suo loco demonstrabitur.

15   Census autem agendi et tributi ex censu imperandi pariter
atque conferendi initium factum est apud Hebraeos cum de ea re
Deus mandatum Mosi dederit, ita in Exodo capite 30 loquens:
Quando tuleris summam filiorum Israel iuxta numerum, dabunt
singuli precium pro animabus suis domino, et non erit plaga in eis
cum fuerint recensiti. Hoc autem dabit omnis qui transit ad nomen dimidium sicli iuxta mensuram templi. Qui habetur in numero a viginti annis et supra dabit precium. Ita tributum impera-
tum est in singula capita eorum qui viginti annis maiores essent —
quique arma ferre possent.

16   Siclus nummus argenteus Hebraicus, quem Graeci staterem dicunt, teste Iosepho libro 3 *Antiquitatum*. Pondere erat drachmarum
Atticarum quatuor, drachma vero ex senis obolis Atticis constat,
atque sic tetradrachmus siclus valebat quaternos et vicenos Atticos
obolos, Hebraicos vero vicenos. Sed quia dicitur iuxta mensuram

In any case, a census is said to be taken when the number of citizens is reckoned or when the people's resources are counted, providing a way to impose tribute. Livy gives evidence of both in his life of the aforementioned Servius Tullius. When the census-taking was finished, it was called closing the lustration, because that was when Servius lustrated or purified the whole army with a pig, a sheep and three bulls. They performed this lustration at Rome every fifth year, creating two censors to take the census. Later they made it an annual office with jurisdiction over public morals. They made the same sacrifice to purify the city when taxes and tributes were paid. Hence, the Romans counted their years by lustrations just as the Greeks did by olympiads. Although the lustration was said to be performed every fifth year, there are those who think it was a period of four years, arguing that the year in which the next lustration began was called the fifth, even though it was the first year of the next lustration. If this reasoning is correct, it surely indicates that the olympiad was a period of four years only, as we shall point out in the proper place below.

But taking the census as well as assigning and collecting tribute through the census began with the Hebrews when God gave Moses a commandment on this topic, speaking thus in Exodus 30: When you give an accounting of the children of Israel by number, each will pay the Lord a ransom for his soul, so that when they are registered there will be no plague among them. Every one who goes over to enroll will give half a shekel according to the measure of the temple. Whoever is counted as twenty years old or more will pay the ransom. Thus was tribute required for each person older than twenty — for anyone who could bear arms.

The shekel was a silver coin of the Hebrews; the Greeks call it a stater, according to Josephus in book 3 of the *Antiquities*. It was of the weight of four Attic drachmas, but a drachma was six Attic obols, so the shekel of four drachmas was worth twenty-four Attic obols, but twenty of the Hebrew. Since it says 'according to the

templi, iam satis liquet sacerdotes ponderis mensuraeque genus habuisse aliud ab eo quod vulgus usurparit. Atqui drachma eiusdem est ponderis ac Romanus argenteus denarius—quem Matthaeus evangelista capite 22 numisma census vocat, cuius nota Caesaris effigies erat, et capite 20 appellat denarium diurnum quod tantum valeret quantum mercedis in die dari solet operis—extant etiamnum istiusmodi denarii Caesarum figura signati qui pari sunt pondere atque nummi quos grossos nuncupant, ita scire licet drachmam Atticam a nostris grossum vocitari et siclum quatuor valere grossos.

17   Carcerem quo custodiae continentur ad terrorem, teste Livio *Ab urbe condita*, Ancus primus aedificavit, quod Eutropius Tarquinio Superbo assignat, item vincula, fustes, compedes, catenas et huiusmodi supplicia quibus homines afficiuntur. Atque haec omnia a Romanis Romae primum inventa, nam alibi isthaec tormentorum genera ad cruciandos homines longe ante in usu fuisse, ex Iosepho et Herodoto satis patet. Unde cum instrumenta sola sint quibus tyranni in primis ad suam tuendam dominationem utantur, eorum inventionem recte Nemroth primo tyranno assignemus licet.

: IV :

Qui primi constituerint annum et quam varium; et qui invenerint hunc annum quo utimur vel menses atque eos diviserint in Nonas, Idus, Calendas: ac quis excogitarit numerum aureum.

1   Etsi de prima anni observatione statim post traditam astrologiae originem dicendum erat, ad quam potissimum huiusmodi ratio pertinet, non possunt tamen omnia uno loco explicari, hic proinde de anno tractabimus.

measure of the temple,' the priests quite clearly had some set of weights and measures different from those that the common people used. But since the drachma is of the same weight as the Roman silver *denarius* (which Matthew the Evangelist in chapter 22 calls tribute money, marked with the likeness of Caesar, and in chapter 20 the daily coin because it was worth a day's wage) and since even today there exist *denarii* of this sort stamped with a picture of the Caesars and equal in weight to the coins we call groats, it follows clearly that we should call the Attic drachma a groat and that a shekel would be worth four groats.

Ancus first built a jail to hold prisoners and to inspire fear, according to Livy's *From the Foundation of the City*, but Eutropius assigns it to Tarquin the Proud, along with chains, cudgels, shackles, fetters and punishments of this sort used to torment people. The Romans invented these first for Rome, but such instruments of torture had long been in use elsewhere, as one can see clearly from Josephus and Herodotus. Thus we may rightly assign their invention to Nemroth, the first tyrant, since these are the only devices of which tyrants make special use as the means of protecting their dominion.

17

: IV :

Who first established the year and how it varied; who invented the year and months that we use and divided them into Nones, Ides and Kalends; and who devised the Golden Number.

Although I should have described the first way of reckoning the year immediately after treating the origin of astrology, to which a calculation of this kind is especially pertinent, not everything can be explained in the same place, so now I will deal with the year.

1

2   Hunc Aegyptios primo instituisse Herodotus libro *Historiarum* 2 prodit, ita scribens: quae autem humanarum rerum sunt, haec ita referebant, inter se constare omnium hominum primos Aegyptios annum comperisse, distinguentes eum in 12 temporum menses, idque comperisse ex astris, eo scientius—ut mihi videtur— hoc agentes quam Graeci, quod Graeci quidem tertio quoque anno intercalarem mensem introducunt temporis gratia; Aegyptii vero tricenis diebus quibus 12 menses taxant, adiiciunt huic numero quotannis quinos dies, unde eis ratio circuli temporum constat eodem redeuntis. Herodotus hactenus. Clemens itidem comprobat. Huiusmodi tamen inventionem Diodorus Thebaeis assignat libro 1. Sed non ideo inficior Diodorum Herodoto suffragari, quoniam Thebaei iuxta Aegypti populi sunt, a Thebis, urbe in Aegypto, nominati, velut Thebani a Thebis in Boeotia—quod apud idoneos autores observatum est. Quinetiam, ut ait Herodotus in praenotato libro, olim Thebae Aegyptus vocabatur.

3   At Servius super 5 *Aeneidos* dicit Eudoxum primum annum deprehendisse, post quem Hipparchum, et ultimo, ut infra dicemus, Caesarem. Laertius autem Thaleti Milesio ascribere videtur in primo cum inquit: Anni tempora illorumque vicissitudines priorem invenisse ferunt, eumque in CCCLXV dies divisisse. Sed hoc illi censeo apud Graecos duntaxat esse attribuendum. Verum reperimus apud Iosephum in 1 et in 4 *Antiquitatum* Hebraeos ante diluvium Noe annum XII mensibus constitutum habuisse, qui, eodem teste in 1 *Antiquitatum,* annum primi etiam in Aegypto instituerant.

4   Est insuper operaeprecium quam varia fuerit anni ratio apud priscos demonstrare. Arcades enim, ut Plutarchus in *Vita Numae* et Macrobius in 1 *Saturnalium* meminerunt, tribus duntaxat mensibus annum suum complebant, Cares et Acarnanes sex; Aegyptii

The Egyptians developed it first, as Herodotus discloses in 2 book 2 of the *Histories*, writing thus: They represent human history in this way, agreeing among themselves that the Egyptians were the first people of all who learned about the year and divided it into twelve months. They learned this from the stars and did so more expertly than the Greeks—it seems to me—for the Greeks actually introduce an intercalary month every third year to regulate the seasons, while the Egyptians set the twelve months at thirty days each and add five days to this number every year to make the calculation of the cycle of seasons agree on each recurrence. Herodotus says this, and Clement agrees with him. But in book 1 Diodorus assigns a discovery of this sort to the Thebaeans. Yet on that account I do not deny that Diodorus supports Herodotus, for the Thebaeans are just as much a people of Egypt and take their name from Thebes, a city in Egypt, as the Thebans do from the Thebes in Boeotia—a usage observed by the best authors. In the book mentioned above, in fact, Herodotus says that Egypt was once called Thebes.

Commenting on book 5 of the *Aeneid*, Servius says that Eudoxus first grasped the meaning of the year, after him Hipparchus, and last of all Caesar, as we shall explain below. But Laertius in his first book seems to ascribe it to Thales of Miletus when he says: They claim that he first discovered the seasons of the year and their changes and divided it into 365 days. However, I believe that this should be attributed to him only for the Greeks. Indeed, we find in books 1 and 4 of the *Antiquities* of Josephus that the Hebrews had established a year of twelve months before Noah's flood and, again in book 1, that they had also first instituted the year in Egypt.

To show how various were the ancient methods of keeping the 4 year is also worthwhile. As Plutarch notes in his *Life of Numa* and Macrobius in book 1 of the *Saturnalia*, the Arcadians filled out the year with just three months, the Carians and the Acarnanians

primis temporibus, teste Solino, quatuor, sed antea, ut Censorino placet, duobus tantum. At Macrobius in I *Saturnalium* ait anni certum modum apud solos Aegyptios semper fuisse, ut etiam ex Herodoti autoritate liquido constat.

5   Erat praeterea annus triginta dierum, id est, lunaris, autor Servius super 3 *Aeneidos*. Habebant et annum magnum quem volebant confici omnibus planetis in eundem recurrentibus locum, qui secundum Ciceronem continet duodecim millia noningentos quinquagintaquatuor solares annos. At Iosephus in I *Antiquitatum*, capite 8, dicit annum magnum DC annorum spatio impleri. Sed de hoc, uti Censorinus demonstrat, inter autores non plane convenit. Reliqui Graeci CCCLIIII diebus annum proprium computabant.

6   In hac varietate Romani quoque ab initio, prout Macrobius dicit, autore Romulo annum X mensibus constitutum habuerunt, a Martio incipientes qui conficiebatur diebus CCC et IIII. Romulus enim primum mensem Martium a patre suo Marte; alterum Aprilem quasi aphrilem a spuma, quae graece ἀφρὸς vocatur, unde Venus mater Aeneae nata est; tertium Maium a maioribus; quartum Iunium a iunioribus nominavit. Ovidius:

> Hinc sua maiores tribuere vocabula Maio,
>   Iunius a iuvenum nomine dictus adest.

Sic ante populum in maiores et minores diviserat. Reliquos sex a numero Quintilem, Sextilem, Septembrem, Octobrem, Novembrem et Decembrem appellavit. Verum postremo Quintilis a Iulii Caesaris nomine Iulius et Sextilis Augusti honore Augustus est nominatus.

7   Sed iste annus cum neque solis cursui neque lunae rationibus congrueret, Numa Pompilius inde ad lunae cursum redegit additis 50 diebus. Quibus postea sex alios dies adiecit, retractos ex illis sex mensibus qui triginta dies habebant, id est, de singulis singulos,

with six; the Egyptians used four in early times, claims Solinus, but Censorinus believes that previously they had only two. And Macrobius says in book 1 of the *Saturnalia* that only the Egyptians have always had a fixed measure for the year, which is also quite clear from the evidence that Herodotus gives.

In addition, there was a lunar year of 300 days, for which our   5
authority is the commentary of Servius on book 3 of the *Aeneid.* They also had a Great Year which they considered complete when all the planets came around again to the same place, and according to Cicero it contains 12,954 solar years. But in chapter 8 of book 1 of the *Antiquities,* Josephus says that the Great Year is completed in the space of 600 years. On this question there is no clear agreement among the authorities, as Censorinus shows. The rest of the Greeks counted 354 days in their year.

Given such diversity, as Macrobius says, at first the Romans   6
under Romulus also established a year of ten months; it began with March and had 304 days. Romulus called the first month March after his father, Mars; the second April, like *aphril* from *aphros,* the Greek word for the foam from which Venus, mother of Aeneas, was born; the third May from the *maiores* or elders; and the fourth June from the *iuniores* or youths. Ovid writes:

> The old men gave May their own name;
> June was called after the young.

Thus it was before he had divided the people into older and younger groups. The six months remaining he named numerically: the Fifth, Sixth, Seventh, Eighth, Ninth and Tenth months. Later on the Fifth was named July after Julius Caesar and the Sixth August in honor of Augustus.

But since this year would fit neither the sun's cycle nor the   7
phases of the moon, Numa Pompilius next brought it into agreement with the moon's cycle by adding fifty days to it. Then he added six more days, taking one each from the six months that

eosque sex et quinquaginta dies pari ratione partitus est in menses duos. Et alterum quem primum posuit nuncupavit Januarium a Jano, qui Latinorum primus rex fuerat, tanquam bicipitis dei mensem, ut qui transacti anni finem respiceret ac principium futuri prospiceret. Nam Ianus cum vir esset aeque prudens atque solers, dictus est habere geminam faciem, ut una quae ante, altera quae post tergum forent intueretur, id quod ad vigilantem civitatis custodem attinet.

8   Alterum vero Februarium vocavit deoque Februo dedicavit, qui creditur praeesse lustrationibus, quia tum extremo anni mense populus februabatur, hoc est, purgabatur. Postea Numa—religionem secutus quod numero Deus, quemadmodum poeta ait, impare gaudet—dedit singulis mensibus Ianuario, Aprili, Iunio, Sextili, Septembri, Novembri et Decembri undetricenos dies, Martio vero, Maio, Quintili et Octobri singulos et tricenos. Februarius suos octo et viginti dies retinuit. Ita annus conficiebatur diebus CCCLV.

9   Romani deinde Graecorum more intercalarem mensem constituerunt, ut qui praeessent fastis libris quibus totius anni res populi explicabantur intercalarent: id est, vocarent populum ut quando lege agi liceret scirent. Sed cum ita usu veniret ut per eam varietatem anni saepe nundinae caderent aut in primum anni diem in nonasve, quibus nefas erat conventus haberi, permissum est ut sacerdotes quando vellent suo arbitratu vocarent. At cum illi commodi gratia publicanorumque ex usu minus suo tempore vocarent, tum demum Caesar pontifex maximus addidit anno dies decem horasque sex, quorum dierum binos ad singulos menses Ianuarium, Sextilem et Decembrem adiunxit, in Aprilem autem Iunium, Septembrem et Novembrem singulos distribuit. Sic Caius Iulius Caesar, autore Suetonio et Appiano Alexandrino et Plinio, primus

had thirty days and dividing these fifty-six days into two months of equal size. He called the one he put in first place January for Janus, who had been the first king of the Latins, as if it were the month of a two-headed god, looking back on the end of the past year and forward to the beginning of the next. Since Janus was a man as prudent as he was shrewd, he was said to have a double face, one looking forward, the other backward, in order to watch carefully over the city.

Numa called the second month February and dedicated it to 8 the god Februus, believed to be the patron of lustrations, since in those days the people underwent purification or februation in the last month of the year. Believing with the Poet that God delights in an odd number, Numa then gave twenty-nine days each to the months of January, April and June and to the Sixth, Seventh, Ninth and Tenth months, but to March, May and the Fifth and Eighth months he gave thirty-one days. February kept its twenty-eight days. And so the year was made up of 355 days.

The Romans next established an intercalary month in the man- 9 ner of the Greeks so that those who kept the registers that set forth the whole year's public business might intercalate: that is, make an announcement to the people so that they would know when legal affairs could be transacted. When it turned out that the irregular year often caused market-days to fall either on the first day of the year or on the Nones, times when all meetings were forbidden, the priests were allowed to announce them when they wished and at their discretion. But since these priests would make their announcements not on their own schedule but to suit the tax-farmers and make a profit, Caesar as Pontifex Maximus finally added ten days and six hours to the year, attaching two each to January and the Sixth and Tenth months, but allotting one each to April, June and the Seventh and Ninth months. Thus, according to Suetonius and Appian of Alexandria and Pliny, it was Caius Julius Caesar who first of all adjusted the year to the cycle of the

omnium annum ad cursum solis accommodavit ut ccclxv dierum esset. Et intercalario mense sublato, unus dies quarto quoque anno intercalaretur, quod bissextum vocant. Causa autem nominis est quia duobus continuis diebus bis dicimus 6 Calendas Martias, duos dies pro uno computantes.

10 Menses vero, hoc est, lunae cursus qui, uti Cicero in 2 *De natura deorum* ait, quia mensa spatia conficiunt menses nominantur, Thebaeos, id est, ipsos Aegyptios (sunt enim, ut diximus, iidem) omnium primos instituisse Diodorus affirmat. Quod tamen magis Hebraeis, qui haud dubie primi annum constituerant, tribuendum esse videtur. Atque annus menses habet xii, quorum quatuor — Aprilis, Iunius, September et November — ex triginta constant diebus, at plus uno septem — Ianuarius, Martius, Maius, Iulius, Augustus, October et December. Minimus vero Februarius octo et viginti suis contentus est diebus. Item hebdomadas duas et quinquaginta et diem unum — dies vero ccclxv ac horas sex, uti dictum est.

11 Praeterea cum apud priscos Romanos, pontifices, prout supra demonstravimus, ita intercalarent, factum est ut mensis eiusmodi rei causa divisus sit in Calendas, Nonas et Idus. Primusque dies Calendae dictae sint, ἀπὸ τοῦ καλῶ, voco, etenim minor pontifex observabat quando nova primum appareret luna, qua visa id protinus sacrificulo regi nunciabat. Tum facto ut moris erat sacrificio, pontifex incipiebat eos vocare qui in agris essent quo scirent feriarum pariter causas atque quid eo mense agi liceret. Ita calata, hoc est, vocata in Capitolium plebe, pronunciabat quot dies a Calendis ad Nonas superessent. Unde Nonae ipsae dictae quia semper dies novem a nonis ad initium Iduum intersunt. Idus autem circiter medium mensem ponebant, idque verbum ab Hetruscis sumpserant quorum lingua *iduare* dividere est.

sun so that it had 365 days. With the intercalary month gone, one day — called the Second Sixth — was intercalated in every fourth year. The reason for this name is that we call two days in a row the sixth day before the Kalends of March, counting two days instead of one.

The months or cycles of the moon are called *menses* because 10 they provide measured intervals, as Cicero says in book 2 *On the Nature of the Gods*, and Diodorus affirms that the first to establish them were the Thebaeans — the Egyptians, in other words, for they are the same, as we have said. Yet it seems that this should be attributed instead to the Hebrews, who beyond any doubt first set up the year. The year has twelve months, of which four — April, June, September and November — have thirty days, while seven have one more — January, March, May, July, August, October and December. February, the shortest, consists of twenty-eight days. There are fifty-two weeks and one day in a year — actually 365 days and six hours, as noted.

When the priests of the ancient Romans intercalated, as shown 11 above, they did so to divide a month of this sort into Kalends, Nones and Ides for the conduct of public business. Kalends — from *kalō*, I call — was the name of the first day, for when a lesser priest observed the first appearance of the new moon he immediately announced his sighting to the priest in charge of sacrifices. Then, after the customary sacrifice, the priest began his announcement to those who were in the fields so that they would know the occasions for festivals and what things could be done during the month. After the people were convoked or called together in this way into the Capitolium, the priest proclaimed the number of days between Kalends and Nones. The Nones took their name from the fact that it was always nine days from the Nones to the start of the Ides. They placed the Ides around the middle of the month, taking the term from the Etruscans in whose tongue *iduare* means to divide.

12 Igitur sic computabant verbi gratia: ultimum diem Decembris antecedentis mensis notabant pridie Calendas Ianuarias; penultimum tertio Calendas; atque sic alios suo ordine, sursum versum numerando usque ad Idus. Nam mensibus quatuor — Martio, Maio, Iulio et Octobri — singulis senas dederunt Nonas, reliquis quaternas, sicut singulis quoque mensibus Idus octonas.

13 Verum modus istiusmodi dierum mensis numerum ineundi iam vulgatior est quam ut a nobis sit rursum demonstrandus. Qui profectus est ab illa pontificum intercalatione quae duravit usque ad annum urbis conditae CCCCL; cum Publio Sulpitio Averrione, Publio Sempronio Sopho Longo consulibus, Caius Flavius scriba aedilis curulis invitis patribus civile ius repositum in penetralibus pontificum evulgavit; fastosque circa forum in albo proposuit ut quando lege agi posset sciretur. Testis Livius *Ab urbe condita* in extremo 9 libro.

14 Postea fuit alius modus quem aureum numerum ob excellens rei artificium appellant, excogitatus a divo (ut fertur) Bernardo vel ab ipso Iulio Caesare, sicut libro *Divinorum officiorum* 8 extat, ad inveniendum diem coniunctionis lunae per singulos menses. Quo quidem numero nostri deinceps usi sunt ad notandos quoque dies festos in singulos annos quos mutabiles vocant, quemadmodum est Pascha, Pentecoste nonnullique alii, eo quod non semper in eosdem mensium dies cadant. Fuit sane inventum suo dignum autore, cuius usus et ratio ita omnibus nota est ut non sit quod hoc loco quicquam de aureo numero doceatur.

Their computations worked in this way, then: They counted 12 the last day of December from the following month, making it the day before the Kalends of January; the next to last day they called the third before the Kalends, and so on, counting backwards until the Ides. To four months — March, May, July and October — the gave six Nones each, to the others four, just as they gave eight Ides to each month.

But this way of counting the days of the month is already so 13 well-known that we need not explain it again. It began with that intercalation by the priests that lasted until 450 AUC; then, in the consulate of Publius Sulpicius Averrio and Publius Sempronius Sophus Longus, the scribe Caius Flavius, who was curule aedile, ignored the wishes of the Senate and published the civil law that had been kept in the sanctuaries of the priests; he also displayed the public registers about the forum on white tablets so that one might know when legal business could be done. For this Livy is our witness at the end of book 9 of his history *From the Foundation of the City*.

Later on, another method for discovering the date of the 14 moon's place in each month was devised by St. Bernard (so they say) or by Julius Caesar himself, as is clear from book 8 of the *Divine Offices*; it was called the Golden Number because it was a device of eminent ingenuity. Eventually our people also used this number for calculating the feast days in each year — such as Easter, Pentecost and some others — which are called movable because they do not always fall on the same days of the month. This invention was certainly worthy of its author, but its method and use are so well known to all that we need teach nothing about the Golden Number here.

: V :

Quis horas primus constituerit aut horologia diversi generis invenerit.

1   Horae quibus numero 24 dies noxque conficitur teste Macrobio
ab Apolline, id est, sole qui Horus Aegyptiaca lingua vocatur nomen acceperunt. Quatuor itidem tempora—hoc est, ver, aestas,
autumnus et hyems—quibus annuus orbis impletur horae dicuntur. Quae initio duodecim constitutae sunt, eiusque rei talis fuisse
origo memoratur. Quodam tempore Hermes Trismegistus cum in
Aegypto sacrum quoddam animal Serapi dicatum in tota die duodecies urinam facere pari semper temporis intervallo observasset,
per XII horas diem dividi debere coniecit. Exinde hic horarum numerus longo tempore custoditus, postea in XXIIII horas divisus est
dies.

2   Horologium autem solarium, in quo umbilici solis, quem gno-
monem vocant, umbra horas ostendit, Anaximenes Milesius Lace-
daemone, teste Plinio libro 2, capite 78, primus invenit. Ipsumque
ἀπὸ τῆς σκιᾶς, hoc est, ab umbra sciotericon appellavit.

3   Romae multo serius contigit; in XII enim tabulis, ut autor est
Plinius in 7, ortus tantum et occasus solis nominabatur. Post aliquot annos adiectus fuit et meridies. Accensus consulis, id est,
praeco, eum pronunciabat cum e curia inter rostra et graecostasin
solem prospiciebat; a columna vero aenea ad carcerem inclinato sy-
dere, supremam horam pronunciabat. Sed hoc serenis tantum diebus usque ad primum Punicum bellum. At Marcus Varro primum
horologium solarium in publico secundum rostra in columna statutum fuisse tradit bello primo Punico a Marco Valerio Messala
consule, Catina in Sicilia capta. Postea Scipio Nasica primus
Romae duntaxat, ut opinor, aqua horas divisit aeque noctium

: V :

Who first established hours or invented timepieces of various kinds.

The twenty-four hours that make up day and night took their   1
name from Apollo or the Sun, according to Macrobius, for in the
Egyptian tongue Apollo is called Horus. The four seasons that fill
out the year's cycle—Spring, Summer, Autumn and Winter—are
also called hours. At first they were set at twelve, and they say the
origin of this fact was as follows: Hermes Trismegistus in Egypt
had once observed that a certain sacred animal consecrated to
Serapis made urine twelve times a day and always at equal intervals; from this he concluded that the day should be divided into
twelve hours. For a long time afterward they kept this number of
hours, but eventually the day was divided into twenty-four hours.

According to Pliny in book 2, chapter 78, Anaximenes of   2
Miletus first invented the solar timepiece in Lacedaemon; called a
gnomon, it shows the hours of sunlight with the shadow of a pin.
Anaximines named it *sciotericon* from *skia*, which means shadow.

At Rome this happened much later: the Twelve Tables, as Pliny   3
says in book 7, mention only sunrise and sunset. Noon was added
some years after. The herald, the consul's attendant, announced
noon when he caught sight of the sun from the Senate House between the Rostra and the Greek Station; he announced the last
hour when the sun had sunk from the Bronze Column to the jail.
This was only on clear days, however, until the First Punic War.
Marcus Varro reports that the Consul Marcus Valerius Messala
set up the first public solar timepiece on a column near the Rostra
during the First Punic War after the capture of Catania in Sicily.
Later, in the year 595 AUC, Scipio Nasica used water to tell the
hours apart by day and by night as well, and he set up this time-

atque dierum, idque horologium sub tecto dicavit anno urbis
DXCV.

4   Caeterum horologium, teste Vitruvio libro 9 *De architectura*, ex
aqua Ctesibius Alexandrinus primus repperit. Utriusque meminit
Cicero libro *De natura deorum* 2. Quid igitur, inquit, convenit cum
solarium vel descriptum aut ex aqua contempleris intelligere decla-
rari horas arte non casu? Et alibi in extremo 2 *Tusculanarum* libro:
Cras ergo ad clepsydram—ita vas vocant e quo guttatim effunde-
batur aqua ad horas notandas.

5   Inventum est deinde divini quodam ingenii acumine horologium quod nunc frequens cernitur, e metallis, rotis dentatis atque
ponderibus, partim umbilicis horas indicantibus, partim testanti-
bus tintinabulis. Quinetiam eodem artificio planetarum omnium
ac solis et lunae cursus adeo facile repraesentantur ut coelum ipsum prope conspici videatur. Est etiam aliud horologii genus ad
pyxidis formam excogitatum. Item e tenuissimis harenis Aegyptiis;
quorum tamen autores, uti in calce operis dicemus, in aperto non
sunt. Sic denique quotidie aliquid admiratione dignum hominum
industria invenit, velut pyxidem illam qua nautae navigationem peritissime moderantur. Et multa demum sunt quibus prisca aetas
caruit de quibus nos suis locis meminerimus.

6   Illud adiiciam: ut alibi horologia a sole occidente usque ad solem iterum occidentem perpetuo cursu vigintiquatuor horas desi-
gnant, sic nunc totus fere occidens horologia habet quae bis in die
duodenas horas indicant ita ut semper duodecima hora in media
nocte et in meridie notetur. Quod profecto quo aptius quadrat,
hoc commodius fit ne quempiam, cum velit scire quota sit hora,
tot simul numerare oporteat.

piece in a roofed building—but this was something original only at Rome, I believe.

Otherwise, it was Ctesibius of Alexandria who first discovered 4 the water-clock, according to Vitruvius in book 9 *On Architecture*. Cicero mentions both kinds of clock in book 2 *On the Nature of the Gods*. Why then, he asks, when you look at a sundial or a water-clock, is it easily understood that art, not chance, tells the hours? And elsewhere, at the end of book 2 of the *Tusculans*: Tomorrow, then, we'll use the clepsydra—which is what they call the vessel from which water flows drop by drop to mark the hours.

Later still, some spark of divine genius invented the time-piece 5 that one often sees nowadays, made of metals, toothed wheels and weights, some pointing to the hours with pins, some announcing them with bells. In fact, the same device also represents the courses of the sun and moon and all the planets so easily that one seems to view the planets themselves close-up. There is another kind of time-piece constructed in the form of a little box; another uses the finest Egyptian sands. But the inventors of these have not been discovered, as we shall explain at the end of this work. In this way, human industry invents something admirable every day, such as the little box that sailors use so cleverly to guide their navigation. And indeed there are many discoveries unknown to antiquity that we shall mention in their places.

Let me add this: While elsewhere timepieces show the twenty- 6 four hours in a continuous series from one sunset to the next, almost all the West now has timepieces that indicate the twelve hours twice a day, noting the twelfth hour on each occurrence of midnight and noon. Because this arrangement is clearly more efficient, it is better not to count all the hours together when one wants to know what time it is.

: VI :

Quomodo ab initio alii aliter dies observarint ac
noctes diviserint.

1 Diem alii aliter observabant quod ab Aegyptiis fluxisse volunt quos, ut inter nonnullos autores convenit, primos omnium annum et menses constituisse ferunt. Ii itaque a media nocte ad mediam totum id spatium unius diei nomine appellavere. Romani quoque eodem modo diem observabant quod, ut Plutarchus in *Problematibus* ait, ortus solis initium agendi, nox vero consilii et praeparationis faciat. Quippe apud illos cuiquam etiam diei horae aliquid actionum tribuebatur. Martialis:

> Prima salutantes atque altera continet hora.
> Exercet raucos tertia causidicos.
> In quintam varios extendit Roma labores.
> Sexta quies lassis, septima finis erit.
> Sufficit in nonam nitidis octava palaestris.
> Imperat extructos frangere nona toros, [etc.]

Babylonii inter duos solis exortus omne id tempus diem vocabant; Athenienses inter duos occasus. Umbri a meridie in meridiem unum diem putabant, vulgus omne a luce ad tenebras: autores Varro, Plinius in 2, Gellius et Macrobius.

2 Nos porro more Atheniensium a sole occaso ad solem iterum occidentem omne id medium tempus unum diem esse dicimus, sicut transalpini omnes Umbrorum ritu a meridie in meridiem diem suum terminant—prout eorum horologia, quae superiori capite posuimus, indicant. Vel eadem ratione, a media nocte ad mediam

: VI :

How various people originally arranged the days in various ways and how they divided the nights.

The day that various peoples arranged in various ways was   1
thought to have come down from the Egyptians, who, as some authorities agree, first of all established the year and the months.
The whole interval from midnight to midnight they called one day.
The Romans also arranged the day in the same way because, as
Plutarch says in the *Roman Questions*, sunrise begins the time for
action, but night is for counsel and planning. Indeed, they assigned some activity to every hour of the day, as Martial writes:

> Greeters gather in the first hour and the second,
> But the third keeps screaming shysters busy.
> Rome stays on the job up to the fifth.
> The sixth hour brings rest to the weary,
> And at the seventh it's quits,
> Leaving time in the eighth
> For the sleek to work out until the ninth
> Calls them to crush the cushioned couch.

The Babylonians called the day the whole time between two ris-
ings of the sun; the Athenians put it between two settings. The
Umbrians reckoned the day from noon to noon, but all common
people count from dawn to dusk. See Varro, Pliny in book 2,
Gellius and Macrobius.

Like the Athenians, we say that one day is all the time between   2
one sunset and the next, just as all transalpine peoples define their
day from noon to noon in the Umbrian manner—and their timepieces work accordingly, as we have stated in the previous chapter.
One can say that they arrange their day on the same plan as the

noctem, veteri Romanorum instituto illorum dies dici potest confici. Nox vero, sicut Vegetius tradit, in quatuor dividebatur vigilias quae singulae, teste Hieronymo *Super psalmos,* trinarum horarum spatio supputabantur.

: VII :

Qui primi libros ediderint, et de prima bibliotheca; et a quo aut ubi usus imprimendarum literarum primo inventus.

1 Cum in dies magis magisque hominum ingenia sola librorum copia vigeant, et ad capessendas disciplinarum liberalium artes facilius omnes alliciantur, ipsaque literarum studia mirum in modum ubique gentium floreant, peccare hercle me ducerem si tale inventum silentio praeterirem. Cuius nos etiam, quantum exiguum tulerit ingenium, augendi gratia hunc nempe laborem suscepimus, praesertim cum huiusmodi scriptorum libri, uti divus Hieronymus ad Marcellam ait, ingeniorum effigies et vera et aeterna monimenta sint. Quapropter Agesilaus, autore Plutarcho, cum bene multi vellent eius corporis simulacrum gratis effingere, nunquam id fieri passus est, animi tantum monimenta posteris relinquere studens: illud enim sculptorum, hoc suum; illud divitum, hoc bonorum opus esse ducebat.

2 Omnium igitur primus Anaxagoras, teste Laertio volumine 2, librum ab se scriptum edidit. Gellius vero libro 6 scribit Pisistratum tyrannum omnium primum libros publice legendos praebuisse. Sed profecto quis non videt perperam Graecos, hominum genus in sui laudem effusissimum, hanc sibi gloriam vindicare? Qui, ut Iosephus *Contra Appionem* perspicue demonstrat, recentis-

old Roman system, from midnight to midnight. But night is divided into four watches, as Vegetius reports, each of them reckoned as three hours long, according to Jerome's *Tractates on the Psalms*.

: VII :

Who first published books; on the first library; and where and by whom the practice of printing letters was first invented.

Since the abundance of books alone makes human talent grow 1 stronger and stronger every day, since books attract people to engage more readily in all the liberal arts, and since these literary studies are flourishing wondrously among peoples everywhere, it would surely be wrong of me to pass by such a discovery in silence. Clearly, I too have taken up the present work to promote literature, as much as a meager talent permits, especially since books of this kind are the portraits, the true and eternal monuments of their authors' talents, as St. Jerome writes to Marcella. For this reason, says Plutarch, Agesilaus would never allow a likeness of his person to be fashioned, though many wished to make one out of gratitude, for he was determined to leave posterity only the monuments of his spirit: the one would be the sculptor's memorial, the other his own; and he thought of the one as the achievement of rich men, the other as that of the virtuous.

Anaxagoras was the first to publish a book written by himself, 2 according to Laertius in book 2. But in book 6 Gellius writes that the tyrant Pisistratus first of all provided books for the public to read. But truly, who does not see that the Greeks — in their own praise the most effusive of people — claim this honor for themselves wrongly? They are very recent arrivals, as Josephus *Against*

simi sunt. Ex quo haud dubie multo ante Graecos antiquissimi Hebraeorum — qui sacram historiam scripserunt — et Aegyptiorum sacerdotes vel Chaldaei libros ediderunt. Atque ita Anaxagoram et Pisistratum apud Graecos tantum primos foras dandos libros curasse credere par est.

3   Deinde autem, ut idem Gellius testatur, ipsi Athenienses numerum librorum studiosius accuratiusque auxerunt. Verum omnem illam postea librorum copiam Xerxes Athenarum potitus abstulit asportavitque in Persas. Eos porro libros universos multis post tempestatibus Seleucus, Macedoniae rex qui Nicanor appellatus est, referendos Athenas curavit. Ingens postea numerus librorum in Aegypto a Ptolemaeis regibus confectus est, ad millia ferme voluminum DCC, sed ea omnia priore bello Alexandrino incensa sunt.

4   Caeterum Strabo libro 13 *Geographiae* scribit Aristotelem omnium primum bibliothecam instituisse; ait enim: E Scepsi fuere philosophi Socratici, Erastus et Coriscus et Nereus, Corisci filius, qui Aristotelem et Theophrastum audivit et successor fuit bibliothecae Theophrasti in qua Aristotelica inerat. Nam Aristoteles et bibliothecam et scholam reliquit Theophrasto; et primus omnium quos scimus libros congregavit, et Aegypti reges bibliothecae ordinem docuit. Theophrastus vero eam tradidit Neleo; Neleus eam Scepsim detulit ac posteris tradidit. Haec ille.

5   Fuit et Pergami bibliotheca praeclarissima, autor Plinius libro 35 statim in principio, ubi inquit: an priores coeperint Alexandriae et Pergami reges, qui bibliothecas magno certamine instituere, non facile dixerim.

6   Romae bibliothecam Asinium Pollionem primum fecisse, testatur idem in praenotato libro, scribens: Non est praetereundum et novitium inventum, siquidem non solum ex auro argentove aut

Apion clearly proves, leaving no doubt that the most ancient of the Hebrews — who wrote the sacred story — and the priests of the Egyptians or the Chaldaeans published books long before the Greeks. The correct view, then, is that Anaxagoras and Pisistratus were the first people who saw to the publishing of books only as far as the Greeks are concerned.

But later, as Gellius again is our witness, the Athenians were   3
more zealous and more attentive in increasing the number of books. Then, after Xerxes had become master of Athens, he carried away all that great store of books and took it to Persia. Seleucus, the king of Macedonia who was called Nicanor, took care that after many years this entire lot of books was restored at last to Athens. The Ptolemaic kings in Egypt later collected a huge number of books, almost 700,000 volumes, but all these were burned in the first war with Alexandria.

Strabo nonetheless writes in book 13 of the *Geography* that Aris-   4
totle first of all established a library, for he says: From Scepsis came the Socratic philosophers, Erastus and Coriscus and Neleus, the son of Coriscus, who studied under Aristotle and Theophrastus and was heir to Theophrastus in the library that included Aristotle's collection. For Aristotle left both library and school to Theophrastus; he was the first of all whom we know who collected books, and he taught the method of arranging a library to the kings of Egypt. Theophrastus passed the library on to Neleus; Neleus brought it to Scepsis and passed it on to posterity. This much from Strabo.

There was also a very famous library in Pergamum, according   5
to Pliny in the very beginning of book 35, where he says: I cannot easily tell whether the kings of Alexandria and Pergamum, who were great rivals in founding libraries, began this practice earlier.

Asinius Pollio was the first to build a library at Rome, as Pliny   6
again writes in the aforementioned book, where he says: Here is an innovation not to be omitted, when statues not only of gold or

certe ex aere in bibliothecis dicantur illi quorum immortales animae iisdem locis ibi loquuntur, quinimo etiam quae non sunt finguntur pariuntque desideria non traditi vultus, sicut in Homero evenit quo maius, ut equidem arbitror, nullum est felicitatis specimen quam semper omnes scire cupere qualis fuerit aliquis. Asinii Pollionis hoc Romae inventum, qui primus bibliothecam dicando ingenia hominum rem publicam fecit.

7   Sunt etiam plures hodie in Italia bibliothecae, sed illa in primis omnium iudicio longe celeberrima quam divus Federicus Feltrius dux Urbini condidit, quam postea Guido princeps eius filius, omnis doctrinae decus ac doctissimorum hominum praesidium, cum auro et argento tum librorum copia adauxit ornavitque.

8   Fuit illud igitur omnino magnum mortalibus munus, sed nequaquam conferendum cum hoc quod nostro tempore adepti sumus, reperto novo scribendi genere. Tantum enim uno die ab uno homine literarum imprimitur quantum vix toto anno a pluribus scribi posset. Ex quo adeo disciplinarum omnium magna librorum copia ad nos manavit ut nullum amplius superfuturum sit opus quod ab homine quamvis egeno desiderari possit. Illud insuper adde, quod autores quoque plurimos, tam Graecos quam Latinos, ab omni prorsus interitus periculo vindicavit.

9   Quare tantae rei autor non est sua laude fraudandus, praesertim ut posteritas sciat cui divinum beneficium acceptum referre debeat. Itaque Ioannes Cuthenbergus, natione Theutonicus equestri vir dignitate (ut ab eius civibus accepimus), primus omnium in oppido Germaniae quam Moguntiam vocant hanc imprimendarum literarum artem excogitavit, primumque ibi ea exerceri coepit. Non minore industria reperto ab eodem, prout ferunt, autore novo atramenti genere quo nunc literarum impressores tantum utuntur. Decimosexto deinde anno, qui fuit salutis humanae MCCCCLVIII, quidam nomine Conradus, homo itidem Germanus, Romam

silver or at least of bronze are set up in the libraries, portraying those whose immortal spirits speak in those same places, but likenesses are imagined even of the non-existent, and faces engender longing though we have no record of them. This happens in the case of Homer, and I think there is no greater sign of success than that the world always wants to know what some such person was like. At Rome this was the invention of Asinius Pollio, who first made human talent a public good by setting up a library.

There are also many libraries today in Italy, but the divine 7 Federico da Montefeltro, Duke of Urbino, founded the one that all people judge by far the most famous. Prince Guido his son, the ornament of all learning and mainstay of the greatest scholars, enlarged it with an abundance of books and embellished it with gold and silver.

This discovery was a great boon to mortals, to be sure, but it is 8 nothing in comparison with an achievement of our own day, a newly devised way of writing. In one day just one person can print the same number of letters that many people could hardly write in a whole year. Books in all the disciplines have poured out to us so profusely from this invention that no work can possibly remain wanting to anyone, however needy. Note too that this invention has freed most authors, Greek as well as Latin, from any threat of destruction.

The inventor of so great a thing should not be cheated of his 9 glory; posterity ought to know to whom it should credit the divine favor it has received. And so it was Johann Gutenberg, a Teuton by nation and a man of knightly rank (as we gather from his compatriots), who first of all worked out this technique of printing letters in a German town called Mainz, where he first began to work at it. With no less diligence, the same inventor developed the new kind of ink that printers now use exclusively. Sixteen years later, in the year of grace 1458, one Conrad, likewise a German, first brought printing into Italy, to Rome. Then the Frenchman Nicho-

primo in Italiam attulit, quam dein Nicolaus Ienson Gallicus primus mirum in modum illustravit, quae passim hac tempestate per totum fere terrarum orbem floret. De qua plura loquendi labore supersedeo, eius inventorem ac simul unde ad nos delata fuerit prodidisse haud me parum fecisse ratus, cum ea omnibus longe notissima sit. Quae propterea ut ab initio non minore quaestu quam hominum admiratione vulgari coepit, sic paulatim, velut auguror, futura est vilior.

: VIII :

De primo usu scribendi apud priscos; etiam per notas;
et quando primum inventa
charta vel membrana.

1   Ante usum chartarum, quo maxime humanitas vitae constat et memoria, palmarum foliis, teste Plinio in 13 *Naturalis historiae*, primo scriptitatum est; Vergilius in sexto:

    foliis tantum ne nomina manda.

Deinde quarundam arborum libris, postea publica monimenta plumbeis voluminibus, inde et privata linteis conficere coeperunt, deinde ceris. Nam pugillarium usum ante Troiana tempora fuisse testatur Homerus. Papyrum autem post Alexandri Magni victoriam; condita in Aegypto Alexandria, Marcus Varro autor est, ante chartarum usum ab eo rege inventam esse quae fiebat ex frutice qui nascitur in paludibus Aegypti.

2   Verum contra Varronem, qui chartarum usum non nisi condita in Aegypto Alexandria fuisse scribit, Plinius Cassii Heminae annalium scriptoris autoritatem adducit. Ille enim tradit Cnaium Te-

las Jenson first made it extremely famous, and during this period it flourished far and wide over almost all the world. I forgo the effort of giving many details about printing, its inventor and how it was passed on to us. Nor do I think that I have done too little to make this known since these matters are quite familiar to everyone. Therefore, though printing made its start to no less profit than the general amazement of humanity, I predict that the future will gradually hold it cheaper.

: VIII :

On the first use of writing among the ancients; also on writing with special signs; and when paper or parchment was first invented.

Before people used paper, on which human culture and the writ- 1
ten record of life greatly depend, they wrote on palm-leaves, according to Pliny in book 13 of the *Natural History;* in book 6 Vergil writes:

> only don't put the names on leaves.

Next they began to write on the bark of certain trees; then they put public records on lead rolls; and later private records on linen and finally on wax. In fact, Homer testifies to the use of writing tablets before the time of Troy. But papyrus came after the victory of Alexander the Great; Alexandria was founded in Egypt, according to Varro, before that king discovered that they were using paper made from a plant that grows in the swamps of Egypt.

Against Varro, however, who writes that there would have been 2
no use of paper had Alexandria not been founded in Egypt, Pliny adduces the authority of Cassius Hemina, the annalist. For Cas-

rentium scribam, agrum suum in Ianiculo repastinantem, offendisse arcam in qua Numa Rex situs fuerat, et in eadem libros eius repertos, qui e charta erant. Nam Magnus Alexander amplius trecentis annis post Numam fuit, qui Alexandriam, autore Livio libro 8, eo anno in Aegypto posuit qui fuit urbis conditae CCCCXXVIII, Lucio Papyrio Mugillano sive Cursore, Caio Paetilio Galbo consulibus. Caeterum Livius in decimo *De bello Macedonico* a Cassio dissentit, scribens duas arcas lapideas octonos ferme pedes longas (non unam) repertas a fossoribus in agro Lucii Paetilii scribae (non Cnaii Terentii) et in altera earum sepultum fuisse Numam, in altera vero eos libros inventos de quibus loquimur. Idem etiam Lactantius affirmat, et Plutarchus in *Vita Numae*.

3   Postea vero id genus chartae inventum est quo nunc passim utimur, cuius autor haud palam est. Haec autem fit ex linteolis contritis; nihilominus tamen papyri nomen a frutice sumptum, veluti chartae ab urbe Tyri, retinet. Membranas a tectu membrorum nominatas, est enim proprie ipsum corium. Varro scribit per aemulationem circa bibliothecas Ptolemaei et Eumenis regum Pergami inventas fuisse, unde vulgo pergamenae vocantur.

4   Verum ego affirmarem membranas multo ante quam tradit Varro esse repertas. In iisque primum scriptitatum quando sacros Hebraeorum libros (Hebraei enim, ut ostendimus, primi rerum gestarum monimenta condiderunt) e membrana fuisse testatur Iosephus. Nam cum in 12 *Antiquitatum* tradit, quemadmodum Eleazar — princeps sacerdotum, per LXXII interpretes — sacros libros ad Ptolemaeum Philadelphum miserit ut in Graecum sermonem verterentur, sic inquit: cum vero ostenderent tenuitatem membranae vel incomprehensibilem eorum compaginem, rex miratus est. Herodotus etiam in quinto testis est prisca consuetudine in pellibus caprinis et ovillis esse scriptitatum.

sius reports that the scribe Gnaeus Terentius was trenching his field on the Janiculum when he came across the coffin in which King Numa had been laid: his books were discovered in the same coffin, and they were of paper. Now Alexander the Great, according to Livy in book 8, founded Alexandria in Egypt during the consulate of Lucius Papirius Mugillanus (or Cursor) and Gaius Petillius Galbus, in the year 428 AUC, more than three hundred years after Numa. Besides, in his tenth book *On the Macedonian War*, Livy disagrees with Cassius, writing that there were two stone coffins (not one) almost eight feet long discovered by ditch-diggers in the field of Lucius Petillius the scribe (not Gnaeus Terentius) and that Numa was buried in one of them, while the books that we have mentioned were found in the other. Lactantius affirms this, as does Plutarch in his *Life of Numa*.

Later on, the kind of paper was discovered which is now used 3
everywhere and whose inventor is entirely unknown. It is made from ground linen rags; yet it keeps the name paper, taken from the papyrus plant, like the papers from the city of Tyre. *Parchment* is named after the covering of the body's *parts*, for it is actually the hide itself. Varro writes that it was invented at Pergamum because of the rivalry over libraries between kings Ptolemy and Eumenes, whence it is commonly called pergamene.

But I maintain that parchment was discovered far earlier than 4
Varro reports. Josephus testifies that it was first used for writing when the sacred books of the Hebrews were made of it (for the Hebrews, as we have shown, were the first to set down records of past deeds). In book 12 of the *Antiquities*, when Josephus shows how Eleazar — chief-priest and translator for the Seventy-two — sent the sacred books to Ptolemy Philadelphus for rendering into Greek, he says this: When they showed how thin the parchment was and the wonderful way it was put together, the king was amazed. Herodotus in his fifth book also witnesses to the ancient custom of writing on sheepskin and goatskin.

5   Sunt praeterea plura chartarum genera: ut hieratica, antiquitus sacris tantum voluminibus dicata; amphitheatrica, a loco dicta; bibula et emporetica, inutilis scribendo et involucris duntaxat chartarum atque mercium usum praebens, propterea ἀπὸ τῶν ἐμπόρων, id est, a mercatoribus nominata.

6   Usus autem scribendi per notas pervetustus est quando Tiro, Ciceronis libertus, autore Eusebio, ipsas notas primus reperisse fertur. Et eiusmodi scripta furtiva dicuntur quae artificio quodam fiunt ne legi possint ab alio nisi ab eo ad quem scribuntur. Gellius: Res quasdam occultas nunciare regi furtivo scripto volebat. Est et Caesar, teste Suetonio, usus. Hodie vero ita frequens est modus iste scribendi ut nullus videlicet sit, neque princeps neque civis, quin suas habeat notas, vulgo zipheras nuncupatas.

: IX :

Quis primus memoriae artem monstraverit, aut qui eiusdem gloriam adepti sint.

1   Proximum est ut de memoria dicatur qua, ut Fabius ait, omnis disciplina constat, quae et necessarium maxime est vitae bonum et unicus eloquentiae thesaurus. Huius ars, Plinio in septimo et Quintiliano in undecimo autoribus, a Simonide melico primum inventa est, qua in re multum valuit. Nam cum aliquando in Thessalia, teste Cicerone *De oratore*, epularetur apud Scopam nobilem virum et nunciatum esset ei ut prodiret ad duos iuvenes ante ianuam stantes, contigit ut hoc interim spatio conclave corruerit, ac ea ruina adeo convivae omnes contriti fuerint ut non possent internosci a suis qui humare eos vellent. Tum dicitur Simonides, ex eo quod meminisset quo eorum loco quisque cubuisset, demonstrator

Moreover, paper is of several kinds: *hieratic,* reserved in ancient 5
times for sacred volumes only; *amphitheatric,* named after the place;
absorbent and *mercantile,* no good for writing and useful only for
wrapping papers and packages, which is why it is named after
emporoi or merchants.

The use of special signs for writing is very old, since Tiro, 6
Cicero's freedman, is said to have devised them first, according to
Eusebius. Scripts of this kind are called secret because the technique of putting them together makes them unreadable by anyone
but the person addressed. As in Gellius: He wanted to relate certain private matters to the king in a secret script. Caesar also used
them, according to Suetonius. But today this way of writing is so
common that no one, sovereign or subject, is without his special
signs, called ciphers in the vernacular.

: IX :

Who first demonstrated the art of memory, or who
got the credit for it.

The next topic to discuss is memory: as Quintilian says, every dis- 1
cipline depends on memory, an indispensable resource in life and a
unique treasury of eloquence. According to Pliny in his seventh
and Quintilian in his eleventh book, the lyric poet Simonides invented the art of memory, and he was very good at it. Once in
Thessaly, according to Cicero *On the Orator,* when Simonides was
dining with a nobleman named Scopas and was told to go greet
two young men standing outside the door, at that very moment it
happened that the room caved in and all the guests were so completely crushed in the collapse that the relatives who came to bury
them could not tell them apart. They say that Simonides then

uniuscuiusque sepeliendi fuisse. Ac ita videtur memoria valde iuvari signatis animo sedibus aut mutato annulo qui nos moneat cur
id fecerimus, quod ipse Fabius late prosequitur.

2   Memoria autem plurimis praecipua fuit, ut Plinius et Solinus
autores sunt: Cyrus enim rex Persarum omnibus in exercitu suo
militibus nomina reddidit. Cineas, Pyrrhi regis legatus, postero
die quam Romam advenerat utriusque ordinis viros nominatim
appellavit. Mithridati regi duae et viginti linguae (tot enim natio-
nibus imperavit) traduntur notae fuisse. Caesarem vero scribere et
legere simul dictare et audire solitum accepimus. Idem etiam, teste
Spartiano, Hadrianus imperator facere consuevit.

: X :

*A quo primum militaris ars inventa et utrum literis praestet;
item in exercitu ordines et tesserae et vigiliae et de primo
pugnandi modo.*

1   Nunc venio ad disciplinam militarem, praecipuum imperatorum
decus, qua sola multi quidem mortales aeternam sibi gloriam com-
pararunt, unde tanto literis praeferenda videtur quanto facta dictis
praestant. Quanquam illud non facile Cicero concedendum iudi-
cat, quando, ut ipse *Pro Marco Marcello* ait, bellicas laudes solent
quidam extenuare verbis, easque detrahere ducibus communicare
cum multis ne propriae sint imperatorum. Certe in armis militum
virtus, locorum opportunitas, auxilia sociorum, classes, commea-
tus multum iuvant; maximam vero partem quasi suo iure Fortuna
sibi vendicat, et quicquid prospere gestum est id pene omne ducit

identified every one for burial from his memory of the places where each had reclined. Thus it seems that we can greatly improve memory by marking out locations in the mind or by turning a ring around to remind ourselves why we did so; this is a subject that Quintilian pursues at great length.

But Pliny and Solinus give evidence that many people excelled 2 at memory. King Cyrus of Persia produced the names of all the solidiers in his army, for example. Cineas, the ambassador of king Pyrrhus, called the roll of both orders name by name on the day after he had arrived in Rome. King Mithridates knew twenty-two languages, so they claim, the same number as the nations in his empire. Caesar, so we are told, used to read, write, dictate and listen all at once. The emperor Hadrian did the same, according to Spartianus.

: X :

By whom military science was first invented and whether it is more important than literature; also on the organization of the army, passwords, guard-duty and the way battles were first fought.

Now I come to military science, special pride of generals, whereby 1 alone mortals earn themselves eternal glory, whence it would seem more important than literature by as much as deeds excel words. And yet Cicero thinks one should not grant this so quickly since, as he says in his *Defense of Marcus Marcellus*, some are inclined to belittle martial honors in their speech, robbing the commanders to share glory among the troops lest it become the property of generals. Certainly, much help in war comes from the valor of soldiers, the fitness of the field, the aid of allies, fleets and supplies; but in the main Fortune has the right to claim success, as it were, and

suum. At gloriae quam tu recte scienterque scribendo adeptus fueris socium habebis neminem.

2   Ad artem redeo. Sed haec in rudi seculo admodum turpis fuit utpote quae ferino more, ut infra ostendemus, exercebatur. Huius, sicut Ciceroni libro *De natura deorum* 3 placet, inventrix Pallas fuit, ex quo Bellona dicta est. Papinius:

> regit atra iugales
> Sanguinea Bellona manu.

Ut vero Diodoro, ipse Mars morem bellandi reperit. Martialis,

> Belliger invictis quod Mars tibi saevit in armis.

Sed reperimus apud Iosephum, in 1 *Antiquitatum* volumine, Tubalcain, qui ante diluvium Noe fuit, fortitudine cunctis excellentem res bellicas fortiter exercuisse. Quamobrem apparet militarem artem esse antiquissimam, proinde eius autorem neutiquam prodi facile posse suspicor.

3   Veteres autem ante usum armorum, pugnis, unde pugna nomen habet, calcibus ac morsu certabant. Et haec prima pugnae origo fuit. Lucretius:

> Arma antiqua manus, ungues, dentesque fuerunt.

Exin lapidibus fustibusque pugnari coeptum, testis Herodotus libro quarto, cum de quibusdam populis loquitur qui haud procul a Tritone Libyae fluvio habitabant. Ait enim horum virgines anniversario Minervae festo in honorem ipsius deae inter se bifariam divisae praeliantur lapidibus fustibusque. Affirmat idem Diodorus libro primo scribens: Eodem modo clava et leonis pellis antiquo Herculi conveniunt, quo tempore nondum arma adinventa sed fustibus homines iniurias propulsabant ac ferarum pellibus tegebant pro armis corpora. Plinius vero in septimo dicit Afros contra

whatever is well done she makes her own. For writing well and wisely, however, you will have no ally in the glory that you get.

Let me return to this science. In uncivilized times war was 2 quite disreputable because it was waged in a savage way, as we shall explain below. In book 3 *On the Nature of the Gods*, Cicero maintains that its inventor was Pallas, who was called Bellona for that reason. As Statius writes:

Black Bellona guides the team with bloody hand.

But Diodorus says that Mars himself began the practice of making war, as in Martial:

With arms invincible Mars gives his rage for you.

Yet in Josephus, book 1 of the *Antiquities*, we find that Tubalcain, living before Noah's flood, made war courageously and surpassed all others in bravery. Since it seems that military science is very ancient, I suspect that its inventor cannot easily be found.

Before the ancients learned the use of weapons, they fought by 3 biting, kicking and battering with their fists, from which comes the word 'battle.' And this was the first origin of battle, as Lucretius writes:

Hands, nails and teeth were weapons in the old days.

Then they started fighting with sticks and stones, according to Herodotus in book 4, where he speaks about certain people who lived near the river Triton in Libya. He says that during a yearly feast of Minerva their young women split into two groups and fought in honor of the goddess with sticks and stones. Writing in book 1, Diodorus makes the same point: The club and the lion's skin are likewise attributes of the ancient Hercules, in whose time arms were still undiscovered and men fended off injuries with sticks and covered their bodies with the skins of beasts instead of

Aegyptios primos praelium fecisse fustibus, quos vocant phalangas.

4   Verum paulatim haec disciplina tanti fieri coepit ut nulla maiore cura, studio ac ordine apud omnes prope gentes constaret, repertis exercitus ordinibus, signi dationibus, tesseris et vigiliis a Palamede bello Troiano, et sub idem tempus speculari significatione a Sinone, autor Plinius, qui libro quinto et Phoenicibus bellicarum artium inventionem assignat — sed apud Syros credo. De his satis; sed iam ad ipsa arma transeamus.

: XI :

De primo armorum et aeneorum tormentorum usu.

1   Ferunt, autore Diodoro libro 6, Martem primum fabricatis armis milites armasse, cui ob id primus armorum usus (appellatur enim belli deus) attribuitur, quod etiam Vergilius sensisse videtur cum in principio suae *Aeneidos* dixit:

> at nunc horrentia Martis.
> Arma virumque cano.

Caeterum arma, quae pro omnibus bellicis instrumentis autores usurpant, alii alia invenerunt.

2   Galeam enim, gladium, hastam, Lacedaemonii, ut testis est Plinius in 7, invenerunt. Herodotus tamen libro 4 putat scutum et galeam ab Aegyptiis Graecis esse traditam. Loricam Midias Messenius, clypeos Proteus et Acrisius inter se belligerantes repererunt, sive Chalcus Athamantis filius. Ocreas et cristas Cares, lanceas Aetolos, iaculum cum amento ferunt invenisse Aetolum

armor. But Pliny says in book 7 that Africans fighting against Egyptians first did battle with sticks, which they call staves.

Little by little this skill became so important that almost all na- 4 tions gave it more care, study and organization than any other, once Palamedes had worked out the order of the army, the giving of watchwords, passwords and guard-duty during the Trojan War. Around the same time, Sinon invented signaling with mirrors, according to Pliny, who also attributes the invention of the arts of war to the Phoenicians in his fifth book—though I believe it was the Syrians. Enough about this, however; now let us move on to the weapons themselves.

: XI :

On the first use of weapons and of bronze cannon.

According to Diodorus in book [5], they say that Mars first 1 equipped soldiers with manufactured weapons, which is why they attribute the first use of weapons to him and call him the god of war. Vergil also seems to have believed this, writing at the start of the *Aeneid*:

> but now the terrors of Mars.
> Arms and a man I sing.

Others invented the various kinds of arms, the term that the authorities use to describe all the tools of war.

The Spartans, so Pliny testifies in book 7, invented the helmet, 2 sword and spear. Yet in book 4 Herodotus thinks that the long shield and the helmet came to the Greeks from the Egyptians. Midias of Messene made the breastplate, Proteus and Acrisius the round shield when they were making war on each other, or else it was Chalcus, son of Athamas. They say the Carians invented

Martis filium. Falcem, secundum Clementem, Thraces; hastas velitares et pilum Tyrrhenus. Usus autem velitum, autore Valerio
Maximo libro secundo, eo bello primum repertus est quo Capuam
Fulvius Flaccus imperator obsedit. Securim Pantesilea Amazonum
regina reperit, venabula Piseus. Arcum autem et sagittas Scythes
Iovis filius; sagittas, ut aliis placet, Perseus Persei filius primum invenit. Haec ex Plinio. At Diodorus Apollini assignat, in 6 scribens: Arcus insuper sagittandique fuisse repertorem Apollinem ferunt.

3   Verum Artapanus, cuius testimonium Eusebius *De praeparatione
evangelica* libro 9 citat, Mosen omnium primum bellica instrumenta invenisse tradit; qui adhuc iuvenis in Aegypto, teste Iosepho in 2 *Antiquitatum*, primam gloriose expeditionem in Aethiopes
apparauerit. Nec eo tamen caeteri quos memoravimus minus laudis merentur, quando non unius generis arma ubique usurpantur,
sed alia alibi. Nihil quoque ab initio tam perfectum excogitatur cui
non aliquid ab insequentibus commode addi possit.

4   In tormentis Cretenses scorpionem, catapultam Syri, Phoenices
balistam et fundam, ut testatur Plinius, invenerunt. Vegetius vero
libro 1 *De re militari* fundarum usum dicit incolas insularum in
mari Hispano quas Baleares vocamus comperisse, unde Strabo libro tertio *Geographiae* illos optimos funditores esse vocitatos affirmat. Idem Vergilius sentit in primo *Georgicon*:

Stupea torquentur Balearis verbera fundae.

Artem bellicarum machinarum, teste Plutarcho in *Vita Marci Marcelli*, Eudoxus et Architas inchoarunt. Machinam ad ferenda gra-

greaves and crests, the Aetolians lances, Aetolus the thonged javelin—he was the son of Mars. The Thracians developed the scimitar, says Clement. Tyrrhenus first fashioned spears for skirmishing
and the heavy javelin. But skirmishers were first used during the
war in which Fulvius Flaccus commanded the siege of Capua,
according to Valerius Maximus in his second book. Panthesilea,
queen of the Amazons, invented the axe, Piseus hunting-spears.
Scythes, the son of Jupiter, devised the bow and arrows, though
others believe that Perseus, son of Perseus, first invented arrows.
This we learn from Pliny. But Diodorus Siculus assigns them to
Apollo, writing in book 6: They say that Apollo was the inventor
of the bow and of archery as well.

And yet Artapanus, whose testimony Eusebius cites in book 9   3
of the *Preparation for the Gospel*, reports that Moses first of all invented instruments of war; while still a youth in Egypt, according
to Josephus in book 2 of the *Antiquities*, he fitted out the first expedition against the Ethiopians with splendid equipment. Still, the
others whom we have mentioned deserve no less praise, since people do not use weapons of the same kind everywhere, but different
types appear in different places. Nor is anything so perfectly designed from the start that those who come after can add nothing
useful.

To turn to ballistic devices, the Cretans invented the scorpion,   4
the Syrians the catapult, the Phoenicians the stone-thrower and
sling, as Pliny is our witness. But Vegetius in book 1 of his *Military
Science* says that the inhabitants of the islands in the Spanish Sea
that we call the Balearics learned how to use slings, and so Strabo
in book 3 of the *Geography* maintains that they are known as the
best slingers. Vergil notices this in the first *Georgic*:

With hempen thongs they twirl a Balearic sling.

Eudoxus and Archytas originated the art of war-machines, according to Plutarch in his *Life of Marcus Marcellus*. Vitruvius says that

viora onera primus, teste Vitruvio, extruxit Ctesiphon, qua usus
est ad deportandas ex lapidicinis columnas Ephesum ad Dianae
fanum. Equum autem, qui aries dicitur, in muralibus machinis,
autore Plinio in 7, Epeus ad Troiam invenit; Vitruvio vero, libro 10
De architectura, Carthaginenses ad Gades oppugnandas. Testudines
Artemon Clazomenius invenit.

5   Et haec omnia ad hominum perniciem inventa sunt, et illud novitium inventum in primis quod bombardam vocant, quo post hominum memoriam nihil terribilius ab humano ingenio excogitari
potuit, cuius inventorem fuisse tradunt hominem Germanum admodum ignobilem cui casu in mentem venit tale quid efficere. Fertur enim homo, ad exitium humanum natus, servasse aliquando
domi in mortario pulverem sulphureum cuiusdam medicinae fa-
ciendae causa; illudque texisse lapide ac inde contigisse ut dum
ignem ex silice prope excuteret, scintilla intro ceciderit, subitoque
flamma eruperit atque lapidem in altum tulerit. Et ille eius rei casu
doctus, postea facta ferrea fistula et pulvere confecto machinam reperisse. Ac eius usum Venetis in illo bello primum ostendisse
quod ad fossam Clodiam est cum Genuensibus gestum, qui fuit
annus salutis humanae MCCCLXXX.

6   Is itaque tam mortiferae machinae repertor pro mercede, opinor, accepit ut nomen eius perpetuo occultaretur ne omni tempore
a cunctis mortalibus male audiret, dignus scilicet qui prior ipse
vice Salmonei fulmine flagrasset. Salmoneus enim Aeoli filius cum
vellet Iovem in fulminibus iaciendis aemulari, ab eo de coelo tactus
ad inferos detruditur, quando haec fulmini odore, luce, sonitu, im-
petu simillima est. Magna enim vi ignis collecti emissis repente aut
ferreis aut lapideis pilis, quicquid obvium offendit quassat, dissi-
pat, frangit, contundit adeo ut nullus sane sit locus, quamvis natura munitus, quin facile expugnetur. Ex quo iam usu venit ut in
ea hoc tempore omnis ferme vis peditum, omnis equestris splen-

Ctesiphon first constructed a machine for carrying heavy loads and used it to transport columns from the quarries to the temple of Diana at Ephesus. Of the devices used against walls, according to Pliny in book 7, Epeus at Troy invented the horse, also called the battering-ram, but in book 10 *On Architecture* Vitruvius says that it was the Carthaginians who developed it for their assault on Gades. Artemon the Clazomenian invented the tortoise-shelter.

All these things were invented to destroy human beings, espe- 5 cially the recent innovation called the bombard. Within mankind's memory, human ingenuity can have devised nothing more frightful than this. The story goes that its inventor was a base-born German fellow who realized by accident how to construct such a thing. They say that this person, born for the ruination of humanity, used to keep some sulfurous powder at home in a mortar for the purpose of making a certain medicine; after he covered the mortar with a stone, a spark fell inside when he happened to strike fire near it from a flint, and suddenly flame shot forth and lifted the stone up high. Learning from this chance event, he then invented his device by making an iron tube and loading it with the powder. He first showed how to use it when the Venetians waged war against the Genoans at the Inlet of Chioggia, which was in the year of grace 1380.

And so, the author of such a deadly device got his reward, I 6 suppose, when his name was hidden forever so that he would not be disgraced eternally with all mankind, though he deserved instead, like Salmoneus, to be the first die in its blast. For when Salmoneus, son of Aeolus, wished to contend with Jupiter in casting thunderbolts, the god struck him and cast him down from heaven to the nether regions. Now in smell, light, sound and violence this weapon is very much like a thunderbolt. When iron or stone missiles suddenly shoot forth with the great power of compressed fire, they shatter, demolish, fracture and crush whatever they strike, so that no place is hard to conquer, however well

dor, omnis denique bellica virtus indecore consistat, iaceat, obtor-
peat. Haec bombarda vocatur, a bombo, id est, sonitu qui βόμβος graece dicitur; quidam alii tormentum aeneum malunt nun-
cupare.

7   Eius tametsi modo plura fiunt genera quae varie vulgo nominantur. Et unum illud minimum, quo nunc pedites utuntur, qui
factitio nomine sclopus vocitatur; sclopus enim est sonus ille qui
ex buccarum inflatione erumpit. Persius:

    Nec sclopo tumidas intendis rumpere buccas.

Sed vel alio nomine appellatur arcusbusius, a foramine, opinor,
quo ignis in puluerem fistula contentum immittitur. Nam Itali bu-
sium vulgo foramen dicunt, et arcus quod instar arcus pugnanti-
bus sit. Quippe hodie huiusmodi tormenti usus in primo statim
pugnae loco est, quem olim sagittariis dabant cum a missilibus
praeliari inciperent.

8   Sed iam hinc oratio nostra ad equum bellicosissimum animal
sese, non extra utique propositum, transferat.

: XII :

Quis primus equitandi artem aut usum equos domandi
vel eorum ungulas ferreis soleis muniendi
ac ornamenta invenerit; et bigas atque quadrigas iunxerit
et vehiculum cum quatuor rotis repererit;
et qui ex equo pugnare primum instituerint.

1   Equo, qui magno mortalibus cum in rebus bellicis tum in itineri-
bus faciundis et usui et adiumento est, primum omnium vehi Bel-
lerophontem Glauci regis filium docuisse, Plinius in 7 est autor,

fortified by nature. Using this weapon means that today almost all the might of infantry, all the splendor of cavalry, in short all martial valor lies shamefully inert, immobilized and paralyzed in the face of it. It is named bombard from its booming, the sound called *bombos* in Greek, though some prefer to call it a bronze cannon.

At present, however, this weapon has many forms whose names 7 vary in the common speech. The smallest of them, now used by infantry, is called by the artificial term *sclopus*; this is the sound that comes from blowing air out of the cheeks, as Persius writes:

Nor puff your cheeks and make them pop.

Another term for this weapon is arquebus, from the hole through which the fire goes into the powder contained in the pipe, I imagine. For in the Italian vernacular *buco* means hole, and *arcus* is like the bow used for fighting. Indeed, cannon of this sort are currently deployed in the first stage of battle, where archers used to be stationed to launch the attack with their missiles.

Now, and not by chance, our discussion moves on to the horse, 8 the most warlike of beasts.

: XII :

Who first invented the art of horsemanship or the practice of taming horses or protecting their hooves with iron shoes and making trappings for them; who harnessed them in teams of two and four and invented a vehicle with four wheels; and who first began to fight from horseback.

The horse is of great use and a great help to humans both in mili- 1 tary affairs and for purposes of travel. When Bellerophon, son of King Glaucus, went to fight the Chimaera, he mounted the

qui Pegasum alatum equum cum in Chimaeram iret ascendit. Horatius in *Carmine:*

> et exemplum grave praebet ales
> Pegasus terrenum equitem gravatus
> > Bellerophontem.

Sed Diodorus libro 6 scribit Neptunum equos primum domuisse artemque equitandi ab illo traditam. Alii volunt equum hominibus antea ignotum primum edidisse, quod asserit Lucanus, dicens:

> Primus ab aequorea percussis cuspide saxis
> Thessalicus sonipes bellis feralibus omen
> Exilit.

Et Vergilius:

> Tuque o cui prima frementem
> Fudit equum magno tellus percussa tridenti,
> Neptune.

2   Frenos autem et ephippia Peletronii, qui Thessaliae populi sunt, primi invenerunt; iidem, ut quibusdam placet, domandorum equorum usum primi docuere, testificante utrunque Vergilio in tertio *Georgicon:*

> Frena Peletronii Lapithae gyrosque dedere
> Impositi dorso, atque equitem docuere sub armis
> Insultare solo, et gressus glomerare superbos.

Plinius libro septimo idem affirmat. Hos quoque primos equorum ungulas munire ferreis soleis coepisse ferunt. Numidae, ut vel hoc subiungam, teste Appiano in libro *De rebus Lybicis,* equo nudo, id est, sine ephippiis in bello utebantur.

3   Bigas primum Phrygum natio iunxit, ut Probus et Plinius autores sunt. Quadrigis vero Erichthonius primus est usus. Nam cum Vulcanus, autore Ovidio in secundo *Metamorphoseon* et Servio su-

winged horse Pegasus and first showed how to ride this animal, as Pliny tells us in book 7. In his *Ode* Horace writes:

> Down to earth winged Pegasus threw
> Bellerophon the horseman,
> Who learned a heavy lesson.

But Diodorus writes in book 6 that Neptune first tamed horses and handed down the art of riding. Others hold that people knew nothing of the horse before he showed it to them, as Lucan maintains, saying:

> When the sea-trident struck rock, out pranced the first steed
> And warned of deadly wars in Thessaly.

And Vergil:

> With your great trident, Neptune, you touched
> The earth and first let loose a whinnying horse.

The Peletronians, a Thessalian people, first invented bridles 2
and saddle-cloths; some believe they were also the first to teach how to tame horses. Vergil gives evidence on both points in the third *Georgic*:

> Mounted on horseback, the Peletronian Lapiths
> Gave us the bridle and the training ring
> And showed armed cavalry how to jump the turf
> Or move their mounts in short, proud steps.

Pliny confirms this in book 7. They say the Peletronians were also the first to begin protecting the hooves of horses with iron shoes. The Numidians, if I may add this besides, rode bareback in war, without blankets, according to Appian in his book *On Africa*.

Probus and Pliny tell us that the people of Phrygia first har- 3
nessed horses in teams of two. But Erichthonius first used four-horse teams. According to Ovid in the second book of the *Meta-*

per tertio *Georgicon*, impetrato a Iove Minervae coniugio et illa re-
luctante, semen libidinis proiecisset in terram, inde natus est puer
draconteis pedibus qui appellatus est Erichthonius, quasi de terra
et lite procreatus, nam ἔρις est lis et χθών terra. Is ad tegendam
pedum foeditatem, iunctis equis primus omnium usus est curru.
Maro:

> Primus Erichthonius currus et quatuor ausus
> Iungere equos rapidisque rotis insistere victor.

Affirmat itidem Plinius. Eusebius tamen hoc illi apud Graecos
tantum adscribit, dicens: Erichthonius primus quadrigas iunxit in
Graecia; erant enim antea apud alias nationes. Id autem fuit Danao regnante Argis.

4   At Arcades istuc inventum Minervae assignant, et id credo
apud se tantum. De qua Cicero *De natura deorum* ita scribit: Minerva quarta Iove nata et Coriphe Oceani filia, quam Arcades Co-
riam nominant et quadrigarum inventricem ferunt. Vehiculum
quatuor rotarum, ut testis est Plinius, Phryges invenerunt.

5   Pugnare ex equo, sicut idem ait, Thessali docuere qui Centauri
dicti sunt, habitantes secundum Pelium montem. Hinc de Cen-
tauris fabula orta apud poetas quod semihomines et semiequi essent, quamvis non me praetereat quandam fabellam super hac re a
Servio narrari in 3 *Georgicon* quae veluti nugae respuenda videtur.
Vera sunt igitur extra omnem controversiam, uti etiam Lactantius
inquit, quae loquuntur poetae, sed figmento aliquo specieque ve-
lata, sicut de Aeolo rege ventorum supra demonstravimus. Sed
nonnulli tradunt Centauros primos equitare—non ex equo pugnare—esse ausos. Diodorus in quinto: Centauros nonnulli volunt
in Pelio a nymphis nutritos, postea equos subagitasse, exque eis

morphoses and the *Commentary* of Servius on the third *Georgic*, when Vulcan got Jupiter's permission to make love to Minerva and she remained unwilling, he sowed the seed of his passion into the earth, whence came a boy with reptile feet called Erichthonius, as if begotten from earth and discord, for *eris* means discord and *chthōn* means earth. To hide his hideous feet, he first of all used a chariot and harnessed horses, as Vergil writes:

> Erichthonius first dared yoke a team of four
> And stand victorious above the spinning wheels.

Pliny confirms this also. Yet Eusebius ascribes it to Erichthonius only for the Greeks, saying: Erichthonius first harnessed four-horse teams in Greece; other peoples already had them, of course. Danaus was reigning in Argos at that time.

The Arcadians assign this discovery to Minerva, but just for 4 their region, I believe. Cicero *On the Nature of the Gods* writes as follows about the goddess: The fourth Minerva was born of Jupiter and Coryphe, daughter of Oceanus; the Arcadians call her Coria and make her the inventor of the four-horse team. The Phrygians, so Pliny tells us, invented a four-wheeled vehicle.

He also says that the Thessalians who were called Centaurs and 5 lived alongside Mount Pelion showed how to fight from horse-back. Thus arose the tale told by poets that the Centaurs were half-man and half-horse, though it does not escape me that Servius in his *Commentary* on the third *Georgic* tells a story about this that looks as if one should reject it as nonsense. Some things that the poets say, as even Lactantius declares, are true beyond dispute though veiled somehow beneath fictions and figures, as we have shown above about Aeolus, king of the winds. But some claim that the Centaurs first ventured to ride—not fight on horse-back—as Diodorus says in book [4]: Some hold that the Centaurs were raised by nymphs on Pelion, that later they had sex with horses, and that the Hippocentaurs were born from them.

Hippocentauros natos. Creditum quod primi equitare ausi sint, ex eoque natam fabulam veluti equi essent hominisque natura. Haec ille hactenus.

6   Et ista omnia ex iumentis commoda apud alias gentes paulatim inventa non defuisse illis primis mortalibus credere convenit quando satis constat Hebraeos, Assyrios, Arabes, Aegyptios, equis, mulis et aliis iumentis a principio usos, quae aut dorso ferunt vel armis currum trahunt.

7   Sed de quorundam ludorum et saltationum origine iam disseramus quando haec rei bellicae quoque augendae gratia instituta sunt. Sed opus est ut modus adsit ne, sicut Cicero in *Officiis* ait, voluptate elati in aliquam turpitudinem iuvenes dilabantur.

: XIII :

Quis primus instituerit apud Graecos Olympicum certamen et alios id genus ludos et Pyrrhicam saltationem atque palaestram; et a quibus inuentus ludus pilae, aleae, tesserarum, furunculorum, talorum, par-impar et micare; ac quid sit tessera vel talus.

1   Quatuor ludorum genera apud Graecos praecipua fuisse comperio, quorum primi et longe celeberrimi Olympici appellati sunt ab omnibus fere poetis decantati quoniam in Olympo monte apud Pisam et Elidem, oppida Arcadiae, Iovi dedicati Pelopis honore celebrabantur. Quos, teste Diodoro libro 5 et Plinio in 7 et Plutarcho in *Vita Thesei*, Herculem Iovis et Alcmenae filium quidam constituisse, ibique primum decertasse et palmam consecutum tradunt. Sed Eusebius in 10 *De praeparatione evangelica* dicit in Olympico

Once people believed that it was they who first ventured to ride, the story arose that by nature they were horse and human both. This much from Diodorus.

The correct view is that all these uses of beasts of burden which 6 various peoples gradually discovered were not lacking among the first humans since it is clear enough that Hebrews, Assyrians, Arabs and Egyptians used horses, mules and other beasts of burden from the beginning, either to bear things on their backs or to draw the chariot in war.

But now let us examine the origin of certain games and dances 7 since these too were established to improve the waging of war. But one must set some limit to this topic lest, as Cicero *On Duties* says, pleasure sweep the young away into one vile habit or another.

: XIII :

Who among the Greeks first established the Olympic Games and other contests of that kind as well as the Pyrrhic dance and wrestling; who invented games of ball, gambling, dice, bandits, knuckle-bones, odds and evens and flashing; and what the die and the knuckle-bone are.

I find that the Greeks had games mainly of four kinds. First and 1 most famous by far were those called Olympic because, as almost all the poets repeat, they were held on Mt. Olympus near Pisa and Elis, towns in Arcadia, where they were dedicated to Jupiter in honor of Pelops. According to Diodorus in book 5, Pliny in book 7 and Plutarch in his *Life of Theseus*, some say it was Hercules, son of Jupiter and Alcmene, who began them and first competed there and won a victory. But in book 10 of the *Preparation for*

stadio Corylum Argivum primum victorem fuisse declaratum. Alii autem, ut idem Diodorus in 6 et Strabo in 8 *Geographiae* autores sunt, Herculem unum ex Idaeis Dactylis hoc certamen invenisse asserunt. Verum idem Strabo in praenotato libro ab Epeis compertum affirmat. Et inferius ait ab Iphito Olympicum agonem institutum constare. Fuit is Praxonidis sive Haemonis filius. Sed Solinus hoc illustrius declarat, statim in principio sui operis ita scribens: Quippe certamen Olympicum, quod Hercules in honorem atavi materni Pelopis ediderat, intermissum Iphitus filius instauravit, post excidium Troiae anno quadringentesimo octavo.

2   Herodotus libro 8 scribit Olympicum certamen gymnicum atque equestre fuisse praemiumque propositum oleaginam coronam qua donabantur victores. Quapropter Tritantechines Artabani filius, eo tempore quo Xerxes bellum in Graecia gerebat, ut idem testis est, audiens praemium Graecis coronam esse non pecuniam, generosam illam meritoque laudandam sententiam dixit: Pape, Mardoni (is enim Xerxi persuasit ut in Graecos bellum moveret) in quos viros induxisti nos ad pugnandum qui non pecuniarum certamen agitant sed virtutis? Celebrabantur autem hi ludi quinto quoque anno, sic ut quatuor anni interessent a primo olympiados anno ad initium et primum annum sequentis, si vera est ratio eorum qui de olympiadis aeque ut de lustri spatio ita putant. Idque tempus olympiadem appellabant, ac deinceps apud Graecos tempora per olympiades numerata sunt veluti apud Romanos per consules quorum magistratus annuus erat. Martialis:

Bis iam pene mihi consul trigesimus instat.

3   Alteri erant Pythii. Nam cum Apollo Pythonem serpentem, qui a Iunone immissus Latonam matrem persecutus fuerat, sagittis

the Gospel, Eusebius says that Corylus of Argos was first declared victor in the Olympic stadium. And yet others, according to Diodorus again in book 6 and Strabo in book 8 of the *Geography*, assert that one of the Dactyls of Ida named Hercules invented this contest, though Strabo, also in the book mentioned above, maintains that it was the Epeians who learned how to do it. And a little further on Strabo says that Iphitus clearly established the competition at Olympia. He was the son of Praxonides or else of Haemon. Solinus gives a fuller account of this in the very beginning of his work: The Olympic Games, which Hercules set up in honor of his mother's ancestor, Pelops, were evidently renewed by his son Iphitus of Elis after a lapse, in the year 408 after the fall of Troy.

Herodotus writes in book 8 that the Olympic Games were   2
equestrian as well as gymnastic and that the prize offered the victors was a wreath of olive-leaves. And so when Xerxes was waging war on Greece, as Herodotus tells it, Tritantechines, son of Artabanus, hearing that the Greeks used a wreath rather than money for a prize, uttered that noble and praiseworthy thought: Astounding, Mardonius! (He was the one who persuaded Xerxes to go to war against the Greeks.) Who are these amazing people you have convinced us to fight, who hold their contests not for gain but for glory? They celebrated the games every fifth year so that four years passed between the first year of one olympiad and the beginning of the first year of the next, if those who reckon the olympiad and the lustration as equal intervals calculate correctly. They called that space of time an olympiad, and the Greeks numbered their eras by successive olympiads just as the Romans did by the annual office of the consuls. So Martial writes:

Two times thirty — almost that many consuls.

There were also Pythian Games. After Apollo's arrows de-   3
stroyed the Python, the serpent that Juno had loosed to pursue his

confecisset, ne huius victoriae memoriam ulla temporis diuturnitas obliteraret, ipse a Pythone Pythius dictus, ludos Pythios constituit; Ovidius in primo *Metamorphoseon,*

> Neve operis famam posset delere vetustas,
> Instituit sacros celebri certamine ludos,
> Pythia perdomitae serpentis nomine dictos.
> Hic iuvenum quicunque manu pedibusve rotave
> Vicerat, esculeae capiebat frondis honorem.
> Nondum laurus erat, longoque decentia crine,
> Tempora cingebat de qualibet arbore Phoebus.

4   Tertii Isthmii, ab Isthmo parte Achaiae nominati, et a Theseo inventi, dicente Plutarcho in eius *Vita*: Gloriari etiam quandoque est solitus ob illum (de Hercule loquitur) Iovi Olympia, ob se vero Neptuno Isthmia a Graecis celebrari. Isti ludi, teste eodem Plutarcho, ut quidam volunt in honorem in primis celebrabantur Scyronis, ut alii Sinnis, ut alii Palaemonis, quem Latini Portunum vocant. Ovidius in 6 *Fastorum,*

> Quem nos Portunum sua lingua Palaemona dicet.

Hic, autore eodem Ovidio in 4 *Metamorphoseon,* ex Melicerta homine precibus Veneris deus marinus effectus est. Verum Plutarchus alios illi dicatos fuisse ludos sentire videtur, in eadem Thesei *Vita* aiens: Quod ibidem in Melicertae honorem constitutum est noctu agebatur, initiandi magis quam spectaculi aut celebritatis speciem prae se ferens. Haec ille.

5   In iis autem ludis victoribus pinea corona dabatur, de quibus etiam Strabo libro 8 *Geographiae* meminit, dicens: In Isthmo Neptuni quem Isthmium vocant templum eminet picearum arborum luco circunclusum, ubi ludos Isthmios decertantes Corinthii cele-

mother Latona, the god called Pythian after the Python founded the Pythian Games lest any passage of time erase the memory of this victory, as Ovid writes in book 1 of the *Metamorphoses*:

> Lest time delete his deed, he set up sacred games
> For the swift struggle and called them Pythian
> After the now-dead dragon's name.
> Here any of the lads who won by hand or wheel
> Or foot would take the honor of the oak-crown –
> Not yet the laurel, long before Phoebus used
> That or any tree to wreath his graceful locks.

Third were the Isthmian Games, named after Isthmus, a part   4
of Achaia, and founded by Theseus, as Plutarch tells it in his *Life*: He also boasted that someday while the Greeks hold the Olympian Games in Jupiter's honor because of *him* (meaning Hercules), they would hold the Isthmian Games in honor of Neptune because of Theseus. Some suppose that these same games were originally celebrated in honor of Scyron, as again Plutarch says, though others claim it was Sinnis and others Palaemon, whom the Latins call Portumnus. In book 6 of the *Fasti* Ovid writes:

> In his own tongue our Portumnus will be called Palaemon.

And according to book 4 of Ovid's *Metamorphoses*, Palaemon was a man named Melicerta, changed into a sea-god at the behest of Venus. But Plutarch seems to think that other games were dedicated to him, as he says in the aforementioned *Life* of Theseus: Games established in the same place in honor of Melicerta occurred at night, giving the appearance of a rite of initiation rather than a feast or a show. This much from Plutarch.

A wreath of pine was given the victors in these games. Strabo   5
mentions this too in book 8 of the *Geography*, saying: In Isthmus, where contestants from Corinth used to hold the Isthmian Games, stands a temple of Neptune called Isthmian, surrounded

brare soliti sunt. Et Solinus itidem affirmat, scribens huiusmodi spectaculum per Cypselum (qui, teste Herodoto in 1, Periandri Corinthiorum regis pater fuit) intermissum, Corinthios Olympiade XLIX solennitati pristinae reddidisse.

6   Quarti Nemeaei a Nemea sylva vocitati, quos Argivi, autore Strabone libro 8 *Geographiae* et Polybio libro suarum *Historiarum* 2, celebrare consueverunt ob Herculis memoriam qui Nemeaeum leonem interfecisset. Vergilius:

Compressit Nemeae primum virtute leonem.

7   Pyrrhicam saltationem pro iuvenibus ad militarem artem exercendis Pyrrhus, autore Plinio libro 7, in Creta primus invenit. Solinus vero scribit a Pyrrhico repertam fuisse, dicens: Pyrrhico repertore equestres turmas Creta prima docuit lascivas vertigines implicare, ex qua disciplina bellicae rei usus convaluit. Verum Strabo cuidam Cureti assignans secus videtur sentire (nisi fortasse Pyrrhicus unus ex Curetibus fuerit) in 10 cum de Creta loquitur: Quos principio Curetem illis ostendisse ferunt, deinde instruxisse ut saltationem quam Pyrrhicam appellaverit saltarent. Et alibi idem asserere videtur, scribens Curetes primo armiferam saltationem introduxisse, quando Dionysius Halicarnasseus in 7 aperte demonstrat Pyrrhicen saltationem esse armatam et ab ipsis etiam Curetibus aut a Pallade institutam. Plinius tamen in 7 manifestissime ostendit armatam saltationem aliam esse ab ea quam Pyrrhicam vocant et illam a Curetibus hanc a Pyrrho inventam et utranque in Creta.

8   Tranquillus autem dicit ludum ipsum quem vulgo Pyrrhicen appellant Troiam vocari, et eius originem expressit in libro *De puerorum lusibus*. Quis igitur mentis compos in tanta super huiusce rei

by a grove of pitch-pines. Solinus also confirms this, writing that after this sort of show had been discontinued by Cypselus (father of Periander, king of the Corinthians, according to Herodotus in book 1), the Corinthians restored the original performance in the forty-ninth olympiad.

The fourth set of games was called Nemean, after the forest of 6 Nemea. According to Strabo in book 8 of the *Geography* and Polybius in book 2 of his *Histories*, it was an Argive custom to hold these games in memory of Hercules, who had slain the Nemean lion, as Vergil writes:

He first overpowered the lion of Nemea.

Pyrrhus in Crete first invented the Pyrrhic dance to give young 7 men practice in the military art, according to Pliny in book 7, but Solinus writes that it was discovered by Pyrrhicus, saying: With the discovery of Pyrrhicus, Crete was first to teach elaborate twistings and turnings to her troops of cavalry, and this training improved their skill at waging war. Dealing with Crete in book 10, Strabo seems to feel otherwise, assigning it to one of the Curetes (unless perhaps Pyrrhicus was one of them): They say that a Curete had originally shown them these things, and then he taught them to perform the dance that he called Pyrrhic. Elsewhere Strabo seems to make the same point, writing that the Curetes first introduced dancing under arms, while Dionysius of Halicarnassus clearly shows in book 7 that the Pyrrhic was an armed dance and also that it was the Curetes themselves or else Pallas who established it. And yet in book 7 Pliny very plainly claims that the armed dance is something other than the Pyrrhic and that both were invented in Crete, the former by the Curetes, the latter by Pyrrhus.

But Suetonius shows that the very game called Pyrrhic is 8 named Troy, and he described its origin in his book *On Children's Games*. With so much disagreement among those who have writ-

origine scriptorum dissensione pro certo quicquam auderet affirmare? De hac saltatione insuper Apuleius in 10 *De asino aureo* abunde meminit. Troiae vero spectaculum ludicrum quale foret Maro in 5 disertissime tradit, ubi a Troianis ostendit nomen habere illo versu,

> Troiaque nunc pueri Troianum dicitur agmen.

De quo etiam Suetonius in *Caesare* meminit. Festus lusum equestrem puerorum vocat.

9   Gymnicos ludos, id est, in quibus nudi et peruncti se exercebant Lycaon, teste Plinio, primus invenit. Funebres Acastus, ut idem ait, in Iolcho, post eum Theseus in Isthmo. Palaestram, ut Diodorus est testis, Mercurius instituit. Horatius in *Carmine*,

> Mercuri facunde nepos Atlantis,
> Qui feros cultus hominum recentum
> Voce formasti catus et decorae
>   More palaestrae.

10   Aleae vero tesserarumque ludum et pilae caeteraque lusoria animi recreandi gratia inventa—praeterquam talaria—Lydi, populi Asiae, teste Herodoto libro 1, omnium primi excogitaverunt. Quare miror Plinium ab Herodoto discrepare, qui in 7 scribit Pythum quendam lusoriam pilam reperisse—nisi fortasse alter eorum de alia pila (sunt enim plura pilarum genera) intellexerit. Atqui Lydos eiusmodi aleatorias artes non tam voluptatis quam compendii gratia excogitasse idem Herodotus tradit. Nam cum gravitate annonae patria premeretur, sic famem consolari solebant altero quidem die cibum sumentes altero ludis operam dantes.

ten on this origin of this thing, what person in his right mind would dare to claim anything certain about it? In book 10 of the *Golden Ass*, moreover, Apuleius has much to say of this dance. Vergil gives an eloquent account of the playful spectacle of Troy in book 5, where he shows that it took its name from the Trojans in this verse:

The boys they call Troy now and their troop Trojan.

Suetonius also mentions it in his *Life of Caesar*. Festus calls it a boy's equestrian game.

Lycaon, according to Pliny, first invented gymnastic games, 9 those in which they exercised naked and oiled. He also says that Acastus invented funeral games in Iolchus and that Theseus did it after him in Isthmus. Mercury, as Diodorus is our witness, invented wrestling. An *Ode* by Horace speaks of

Eloquent Mercury, grandson of Atlas,
Who took the wild ways of early man
And shaped them with clever talk
And elegant exercise.

According to Herodotus in book 1, the Lydians, an Asian peo- 10 ple, first of all devised a gambling game or dice or ball as well as other amusements (except for checkers) invented to refresh the spirit. Thus I am surprised that Pliny disagrees with Herodotus and writes in book 7 that a certain Pythus invented the game of ball—unless one of them had in mind some other sort of ball, perhaps, since there are several kinds. In any case, Herodotus also reports that the Lydians devised these techniques of gaming for reasons of economy rather than pleasure. For when the high price of grain squeezed their country, their practice was to ease their hunger by eating food on one day and spending the next on games.

11   Est vel aliud ludi genus quo calculis in tabula lusoria, id est, fritillis et alveolis luditur. Inventum olim circiter annum orbis conditi ter millesimum DCXXXV a quodam viro sapiente nomine Xerxe qui, ita tyranni saevitiam coercere metu ac eum documento monere volens, ostendit maiestatem sine viribus hominumque adminiculis parum admodum valere atque tutam esse, quando per istiusmodi ludum satis patebat regem facile oppressum iri nisi invigilaret a suisque defenderetur. Vocant hodie hosce calculos seu scrupos furunculosve quibus praeliando ludimus (est enim certamen instar praelii) schacos, a scandendo forsitan dictos, quod calculi cum moventur in alteram adversariam partem scandere videantur. Ludus omnibus notus est, quare satis de eo habeo dictum cum monstraverim originem.

12   Caeterum de tesseris ac talis apposite aliquid disputemus cum haec ludicra sint tam notissima quam eorum nomen multis adhuc non planissimum factum videatur. Sane tesseram dicimus quod ex omni parte quadrata sit; quae octo habet angulos et sex latera punctis notata, qua in tabula lusoria plurimum luditur. Vulgus tesseram vocitat talum sive per diminutionem taxillum, qui nunc nusquam fere gentium in usu est, tantum abest ut ille quid sit talus intelligat. Porro talus est ossis genus quod in articulis pedum duntaxat posteriorum eminens, concava in vertebra suffraginum, quae eadem sunt in posterioribus animalium pedibus atque genua in prioribus. Ligatur solidis nervis, forma pene quadratum, et parte altera concavum, altera aliquantulum curvum, estque animalibus bisulcis, hoc est, bobus, ovibus, capris, damis et reliquis, praeterea nullis aliis solidas ungulas aut digitos habentibus.

13   Hoc genere ossiculi veteres ludebant sic. Latus quod unicum numerum notabat canis aut canicula appellabatur. Si quis iactando

Another sort of game played with counters on a board—with 11
pieces to move and gaming-boards, that is—deserves mention. A
certain wise man named Xerxes invented it long ago, around the
year 3635 after the beginning of the world. Wishing to check a tyrant's aggression by frightening him with a warning lesson, Xerxes
showed that royalty is by no means strong or safe without the
strength and support of subjects, using a game of this sort to make
it obvious that a king would easily be overwhelmed unless he kept
watch and had subjects to protect him. These counters or stones
or bandits that we use to play at battle (for the game is like a battle) they call *scacchi*, perhaps from the term 'to rise up,' because
when the counters are moved they seem to rise up against an opponent on the other side. Everyone knows this game; having
shown its origin, I have said enough about it.

But let us give due attention to dice and knuckle-bones, names 12
that still seem unclear to many even though the games are quite
well known. We call the die a cube, of course, because it is square
in every part; it has eight corners and six sides marked with dots,
and generally it is used with a playing board. Knuckle-bone or its
diminutive is the common term for this cube, but nowadays people use the knuckle-bone almost nowhere and have little sense of
what the word means. It is a type of bone that occurs only in the
joints of the hind feet, in the hollow joints of the hock, which in
the hind feet of animals are the same as the knees in the forefeet.
Joined by firm ligaments, it is almost square in shape, hollow on
one side and slightly curved on the other; it is found in animals
with cloven hooves—oxen, sheep, goats, deer and others—and
except for these in no other animals that have whole hooves or
digits.

The ancients used to play with this type of little bone in the 13
following way. The side that signified a single number was called
dog or bitch. Anyone who threw and turned up a bitch had to pay

caniculam vertisset, is nummum unum deponebat vel quantum inter ludentes convenisset. Unde Persius,

> damnosa canicula quantum
> Raderet.

Contra in altero latere Venus sive Cous dicebatur, septenarium numerum significans. Is qui eum numerum iactando talos reddidisset sex lucrabatur et quicquid etiam ex iactu caniculae depositum esset. Duo alia latera Chius et senio nominabantur, et ille ternarium hic quaternarium significabat. Quippe in talis neque binarius neque quinarius erat numerus. Igitur qui Chium iactabat tris nummos, qui senionem quatuor lucrabatur, qui propterea dexter nuncupabatur. Persius:

> quid dexter senio ferret,
> Scire erat in voto.

Si enim pluribus positis talis eadem foret facies, pro uno accipiebatur quia diversitas numerum augebat.

14   Fuit et alius ludendi modus per vulturios ac Herculem basilicum. Plautus:

> talos poscit sibi in manum,
> Provocat me ad aleam, iacit vulturios quatuor.
> Talos arripio, Herculem iacto basilicum.

Ita apud nos sexcenti sunt modi ludendi ad aleam, est enim alea omnis ferme ludus qui in varietate fortunae consistit, ut sunt tesserae cum primis et chartae lusoriae. Cum quibus qui se valde delectant maxime omnium semper egent.

15   Sed talorum usus haud penitus obsolevit. Vidi ego in Flandria mulieres talis ludentes, quae multos habebant vario colore pictos vel ex ebore factos, quemadmodum veteres praeter naturales talos ex alia materia factis usos esse memoriae proditum est. De origine vero ludi non habeo quicquam certi tradere. Ratio ipsius ludi,

one coin or else as much as the players agreed among themselves, whence Persius writes:

The bitch bit me that deep.

On the other side it was called Venus or Coan, meaning the number seven. Whoever made this number in throwing the knuckle-bones won six coins plus whatever had been lost in the throw of the bitch. The other two sides were named Chian and six; they represented throws for three and four respectively. There was no number two or five in knuckle-bones. Thus, whoever threw the Chian won three coins, six four coins, wherefore six was called lucky, as in Persius:

Hope to know what lucky six would bring.

If the same face appeared when playing several knuckle-bones, it was counted as one because a different throw would increase the number.

Another way of playing was to throw vultures and royal Hercu- 14 les, as Plautus writes:

He asks to hold the bones, challenges me to play;
He rolls four vultures; I snatch the bones
And roll a royal Hercules

Thus we have hundreds of ways of playing to gamble. Gambling is what we call almost any game that depends on a change of luck, like dice especially and playing cards. People who play a great deal with them are always those most in need.

And yet the use of knuckle-bones is not entirely a thing of the 15 past. In Flanders I have seen women playing with knuckle-bones, many of them painted in different colors or made of ivory, just as the ancients are said to have used knuckle-bones made from artificial material as well as natural ones. On the origin of the game I have nothing certain to report. The method of play, as set forth

quam supra posuimus, videtur significare Romanum esse inventum: fuit tamen celebris et apud Graecos, siquidem Euripides talorum numerum usque ad quadraginta auxisse fertur. Talus Graecis ἀστράγαλος dicitur.

16   Alia quoque fuerunt apud antiquos ludorum genera quibus etiam nunc utimur autoribus tamen minime proditis — ut illud par-impar ludere, cum quis nummos manu occultat petitque ab altero par ne an impar eorum numerus sit. Suetonius de Augusto: Scripsit ad filiam, Misi tibi denarios ducentos quinquaginta, quos singulis convivis dederam si vellent inter se post coenam vel talis vel par-impar ludere.

17   Item aliud digitis sortiri, quod fit cum duo clausis manibus vocando certum numerum subinde digitos porrigunt. Verbi causa, ego tres digitos explico, tu totidem; ipse quatuor nomino, tu vero sex, ita tu qui numerum vocando divinasti iam vicisti. Et quia digiti ita explicati subito apparent, idcirco per metaphoram micare dicitur. Varro: Micandum erit cum Graeco utrum ego illius numerum, an ille meum sequatur. Italis ludus notus est, vulgoque *mor* appellatur, quasi μωρῶν, id est, stultorum ludus, quod digitorum iactatio signum sit levitatis. Ideo virum gravem micare non decet.

: XIV :

De quorundam ludorum origine apud Latinos.

1   Lupercal quod, autore Dionysio, spelunca erat sub monte Palatino ab Evandro sacrata Pani deo Arcadiae, qui Lycaeus dicitur, ex eo dictum nonnulli autumant quia ibi per caprum luebatur, hoc est, sacrificabatur, tametsi Plutarchus in *Vita Romuli* proprium eius

above, suggests that it was a Roman invention; yet it was also well known among the Greeks, seeing that Euripides is said to have increased the number of knuckle-bones to forty. In Greek the knuckle-bone is called *astragalos*.

The ancients also had other kinds of games that we still use to- 16 day though their inventors remain unknown — playing odds and evens, for example, where a person hides coins in his hand and asks someone else if their number is odd or even. In his life of Augustus, Suetonius mentions this. Augustus wrote to his daughter: I have sent you 250 *denarii*, the sum I would have given each of my guests had they wished to play each other at knuckle-bones or odds and evens after dinner.

Guessing the fingers is another game, played by calling out a 17 number with both hands closed and then suddenly extending the fingers. When I hear the word, I put out three fingers, you the same number; I call four, you call six, and you win because your call guessed the number. And since the extended fingers appear so suddenly, the game is called flash by a figure of speech, as Varro says: With a Greek one flashes to see whether I get his number or he gets mine. This game is known in Italy where the people call it *mor*, as if it were a game for *mōroi* or fools because shaking one's fingers about is a sign of silliness. A serious person does not flash.

: XIV :

On the origin of certain games among the Latins.

The Lupercal, according to Dionysius, was a cave beneath the Pal- 1 atine hill which Evander consecrated to the Arcadian god Pan, called Lycaean. Some think the place got its name because they sacrificed or made atonement there with a goat, though Plutarch

celebritatis fuisse inquit ut Luperci canem immolarent. Alii scribunt a lupa quae ibi Romulum et Remum nutrierit aut quod hic locus, quod verisimilius est, Pani Lycaeo consecratus esset—λύκος enim latine lupus dicitur—aut quod Pan lupos arceat. Unde Lupercalia ludicra, quae teste Plutarcho expiationis causa fiebant, Lycaea dicta a Pane Lycaeo, numine Arcadico quem, autore Livio *Ab urbe condita*, Romani Inuum vocabant. Et idem putabatur esse Faunus vel, ut Fenestella tradit, Sylvanus.

2   Sacrificabatur autem Lycaeo mense Februario in hunc ferme modum: Iuvenes nudi Lycaeum Pana venerantes per luxum atque lasciviam currebant ferentes scuticas ex caprinis pellibus factas, unde Festus tradit crepos, id est, lupercos a Romanis dictos a crepitu pellicularum quem faciebant verberantes. Mulieres ultro se ad verbera offerebant, arbitrantes eam rem ad foecunditatem conducere. Iuvenalis:

Nec prodest agili palmas praebere luperco.

Hoc autem ludicrum Evander ex Arcadia primus in Latium intulit. Ovidius:

Transtulit Evander sylvestria numina secum.

Testantur idem Vergilius in 8, Livius, Dionysius et Fenestella. Quod vero nudi currebant, Trogus et Ovidius libro 2 *Fastorum* ex imitatione habitus ipsius dei cui haec sacra fiebant hunc morem fluxisse tradunt, sed Fenestella et Servius alias etiam huius rei rationes reddunt quas, Ovidio late prosequente, ego in medium proferre supersedeo. In iis autem ludis, quod non longe ab re est, Marcus Antonius nudus et perunctus, autore Appiano in 2 *De bellis civilibus*, Caesaris capiti diadema intulit.

says in his *Life of Romulus* that the special mark of its fame was that the Luperci offered up a dog. Others write that the name comes from the she-wolf that nursed Romulus and Remus there or, more likely, because the site was sacred to the Lycaean Pan — for *lukos* is *lupus* in Latin — or because Pan keeps wolves away. Hence, the games of the Lupercalia, whose purpose according to Plutarch was purification, were called Lycaean after the Lycaean Pan, the Arcadian deity whom the Romans named Inuus, as Livy says in *From the Foundation of the City*. Pan was thought to be the same as Faunus or, as Fenestella reports, Sylvanus.

In the month of February they made sacrifice to the Lycaean 2 god in this way: Young men honoring the Lycaean Pan with lewdness and debauchery ran about naked carrying whips made of goat-hide, whence Festus relates that the Romans called them Crepi or Luperci from the cracking of the hides made by those who were doing the scourging. Women willingly offered themselves to be flogged because they believed it brought fertility, whence Juvenal writes:

No good to offer a hand to a nimble Lupercus.

It was Evander who first imported this game to Latium from Arcadia, as Ovid writes:

Evander brought the forest gods along with him.

In book 8 Vergil also is a witness, along with Livy, Dionysius and Fenestella. As for their running about naked, Justinus and Ovid in book 2 of the *Fasti* report that this custom arose from imitating the dress of the god for whom the rites were held. While generally in line with Ovid, Fenestella and Servius offer other reasons which I forbear mentioning. It is not much out of the way to note that Mark Antony, naked and oiled for these festivities, put a diadem on Caesar's head, according to Appian in book 2 of the *Civil Wars*.

3   Erant deinde circenses, sic enim appellabantur quasi circum enses. Nam teste Servio super 3 *Georgicon*, cum rudis vetustas nondum loca huiuscemodi ludis apta aedificasset, inter enses et flu-
mina eos celebrabat ut ab utraque parte esset ignavis praesens
periculum. Exin Circus, id est, locus muris septus ab ipsis circen-
sibus denominatur in quo ludi fiebant, aedificatus est, de quo Livius *Ab urbe condita* ait: Tum primum Circo qui nunc Maximus dicitur designatus est locus. Disponebatur autem circus in formam
spatii oblongi. Et in summitate circi carceres erant unde equi curribus vincti ad cursum movebantur, et cum ad summum devenissent
revolvebantur donec ad priorem metam devenirent. Exercebantur
etiam pugiles in medio loco muneribus collocatis. Vergilius in 5
Aeneidos:

Munera principio ante oculos circoque locabant.

4   Solennes deinde mansere huiusmodi ludi Romani, et magni varieque appellati. Erant insuper Saturnalia quorum dies laetitiae
pleni erant, et mense Decembris magnifice apparateque celebrabantur. Hinc Martialis in *Xeniis* dicit:

Postulat ecce novos ebria bruma sales.

In quibus, ut idem testis est, amici inter se munera mittebant, et
quae primo mittebantur xenia quasi hospitalia, hoc est, ad hospites
missa vocabantur, ξένος enim Graece hospes appellatur. Quae
vero remittebantur apophoreta quod ἀποφέρειν significat referre.
Haec autem sacra Ianus, autore Macrobio, Saturno qui cum una
concors regnavit primus instituit. Quidam a Pelasgis, alii ab Athe-

Later came games in the Circus, named as if they were played   3
around the swords. For according to the commentary of Servius
on the third *Georgic*, before primitive people had built places suitable for these games, they held them in spaces bordered by swords
and streams so that cowards would find danger on both sides. Afterward they built the Circus, the place in which games were held,
and it was surrounded by walls and named after the games around
the swords. Livy has this to say about it in *From the Foundation of
the City*: At that time they first set aside the place for the Circus
now called Maximus. They laid out the Circus in the shape of an
oblong area. At the top of the circle were starting-traps from
which horses harnessed to chariots were driven for the race, and
when they came to the end of the track they were turned around
until they reached the first turning-post. Boxers also fought in the
middle of the grounds where prizes were set up, as Vergil writes in
book 5 of the *Aeneid*:

First they put prizes in the center for all to see.

In later times, Roman festivals of this sort — important ones   4
with a variety of names — were still observed. There were also the
festive days of the Saturnalia, celebrated in the month of December with pomp and plenty. Hence, in the *Xenia* Martial says:

Look, drunken winter demands fresh wit.

During the Saturnalia, as Martial testifies, friends sent presents to
one another, and those sent first were called *xenia* or guest-pres-
ents because they were sent to guests, for the Greek word *xenos*
means guest. But those sent in return were called *apophoreta* because *apopherein* means to repay. According to Macrobius, Janus
first established these rites for Saturn when they ruled together in
harmony, and yet, as Macrobius also says, some hold that they
originated with the Pelasgians, while others say it was the Athenians. And since all things were held in common under Saturn, it

niensibus, ut idem dicit, ortum habuisse volunt. Et quoniam sub Saturno omnia communia erant, hinc, teste Iustino in 43 suae *Epitomes*, cautum erat ut Saturnalibus, exaequato omnium iure, passim in conviviis servi cum dominis recumberent.

5   Erant et ludi gladiatorii, quos divus Cyprianus ad Donatum execratur: Paratur, inquit, gladiatorius ludus ut libidinem crudelium luminum sanguis oblectet. Homo occiditur in hominis voluptatem, et quis possit occidere, peritia est, usus est, ars est; scelus non tantum geritur, sed docetur, etc. De eorum autem origine et causa, Iulius Capitolinus in *Vita* Maximini et Balbini principum haec commemorat: Multi dicunt apud veteres hanc devotionem contra hostes factam ut civium sanguine litato specie pugnarum se Nemesis, id est, vis quaedam fortunae, satiaret. Alii hoc literis tradunt quod verisimilius credo, ituros ad bellum Romanos debuisse pugnas videre et vulnera et ferrum et nudas inter se cohortes, ne dimicantes in bello armatos hostes timerent aut vulnera et sanguinem perhorrescerent. Hinc mos tractus videtur ut imperatores ad bellum proficiscentes munus darent gladiatorium.

6   Habebant praeterea plura ludorum genera quae Campus Martius, uti in *Officialibus* libris Cicero ait, iuvenibus exercitationis bellicae causa suppeditabat. Quae nos hic studio brevitatis omittimus, alibi reliqua dicturi, libro 4, capite ultimo, cum eos exponemus ritus qui hodie apud nos quoque servantur et ludos qui religionis causa in primis fiebant.

was stipulated that during the Saturnalia, when everyone's rights were equal, servants might recline at table side by side with their masters, as Justinus testifies in the forty-third chapter of his *Epitome*.

They also had gladiatorial games, which St. Cyprian condemns   5 when writing to Donatus. Gladiatorial games are designed, he says, for blood to slake the lust of merciless eyes. One man dies for another's pleasure, and if one of them can kill, it's skill, experience, technique; not only do they put crime on like a play, they give instruction in it, and so on. In his *Life* of Maximinus and Balbinus, Julius Capitolinus says a few words about the cause and origin of these games: Many claim that the ancients performed rituals against the enemy so that the blood of citizens, offered under the appearance of combat, might appease Nemesis, the power of fortune. I find more probable what other writers report, that when the Romans were about to go to war they needed to see fighting, wounds, weapons and troops struggling naked, lest when battle began they would fear the armed enemy or shudder at wounds and blood. So it seems the custom grew up that emperors setting off for war should present gladiatorial shows.

They had several kinds of games besides which, as Cicero says   6 *On Duties*, were available as military exercise to young men in the Campus Martius. We omit these here for the sake of brevity, but later, in the last chapter of book 4, we will describe others when we deal with customs that we still observe today, including games originally established for religious reasons.

: XV :

*Quis primus invenerit inducias et foedera, et de eorundem
vario faciendorum ritu, ac quot essent genera.*

1   Inducias primus omnium, autore Plinio libro 7, invenit Lycaon.
Sunt autem induciae (non est enim hoc silentio praetereundum)
pactum quoddam et cessatio pugnae manente tamen bello, uti testis est Gellius in 1 *Noctium Atticarum*, paucorum dierum. Hoc est
ut usque ad certum diem non pugnetur nihilque incommodi detur, sed ex eo die postea uti iam omnia belli iure agantur. Quinetiam horarum quoque atque annorum induciae sunt. Gellius enim
in praenotato libro tradit in primo *Annalium* Quadrigarii scriptum
esse Gaium Pontium Samnitem a dictatore Romano sex horarum
inducias postulasse. Livius vero *Ab urbe condita* libro 1: Induciae, inquit, Veientibus in 40 annos datae. Et in 7: Caeriti populo in centum annos.

2   Foedera idem Plinius est autor Theseum primum comperisse,
sed Diodorus libro 6 Mercurio assignat, ita scribens: Tribuunt
praeterea Mercurio praeconia, dissidia ac foedera quae in bellis
fiunt. Haec ille.

3   Verum ego puto Theseum apud Graecos duntaxat foederis autorem fuisse, quando ex Iosepho *De antiquitatibus iudaeorum* facile
deprehendimus, cum antea tum Cecropis temporibus, post quem
teste Eusebio in 10 *De praeparatione evangelica* omnia apud Graecos
memoratu digna narrantur, foederis paciscendi morem apud Assyrios et Aegyptios nonnullosque alios fuisse, sed praesertim apud
Hebraeos. Nam Iacob, qui multo ante Cecropem fuit, apud eundem Iosephum legimus cum Laban socero foedus fecisse. Deinde

: XV :

Who first invented truces and treaties, on various ways of making them, and how many kinds there were.

Lycaon, according to Pliny in book 7, first established truces. But   1
we should go no farther without saying that a truce is a kind of
agreement, a suspension of combat for a few days while war still
goes on, as Gellius testifies in book 1 of the *Attic Nights*. The agreement, in other words, is that there shall be no fighting nor any
trouble until a certain day, but that from that day forward everything proceeds once again according to the rules of war. Actually,
there are also truces that last for hours or for years. In the book
just mentioned, Gellius reports that Quadrigarius wrote in the
first volume of his *Annals* that Gaius Pontius the Samnite asked
the Roman dictator for a truce of six hours. And Livy in book 1
From the Foundation of the City says that the Veientes were given a
truce of forty years; he also reports a truce of a hundred years for
the people of Caere in book 7.

Pliny, once again, is our source for the claim that Theseus first   2
learned about treaties, but in book [5] Diodorus assigns this to
Mercury, writing thus: Moreover, they attribute proclamations,
interruptions and treaties made in war to Mercury. So says
Diodorus.

But I think that Theseus invented the treaty only for the   3
Greeks, since we have had no trouble discovering from the *Antiquities of the Jews* by Josephus that the custom of negotiating treaties
existed among the Assyrians, Egyptians and others, particularly
the Hebrews, in the days of Cecrops and before; according to
Eusebius in book 10 of the *Preparation for the Gospel*, everything
worth remembering about the Greeks came after the time of
Cecrops. Again in Josephus, we read that Jacob, who lived long be-

Mosen — qui, autore Eusebio, Cecropis tempore fuit — ultro certum foedus obtulisse quibusdam regibus cum sibi per deserta loca
tutum iter peteret. Exin etiam Iesum Mosis successorem cum Ga-
baonitis foedus percussisse constat. Quapropter huius rei certum
autorem, temporis longinquitate obliteratum, nequaquam in lucem
proferri posse duco.

4   Foederum autem tria olim fuisse genera reperio. Unum cum
bello victis dabantur leges a victore, ipsiusque ius et arbitrium erat
ex iis quae dedita fuissent habere quae vellet et mulctare. Alterum
cum bello pares aequo foedere in pacem et amicitiam veniebant,
tunc enim fas erat repeti res reddique ac componi eas per quas
possessio turbata foret. Tertium cum qui hostes nunquam fuerint
ad amicitiam sociali foedere inter se iungendam coibant, tum ii
neque dare neque accipere leges debebant, id quod aut victoris aut
victi esse constat.

5   Foedus praeterea alio alibi ici consuevit modo. Apud Romanos
enim, teste Livio *Ab urbe condita* volumine primo, fecialis sacerdos
ex iussu regis sumpta ex arce graminis herba pura (ut in nostris
Proverbiis docuimus) feriebat porcum silice, dicens: Sic a Iove feria-
tur is qui sanctum hoc fregerit foedus, ut ego hunc porcum ferio,
etc. At Polybius libro 3 cum de primo foedere inter Romanos
et Carthaginenses icto meminit, alium ritum fuisse demonstrat,
ait enim: Simul atque de foedere inter partes convenerat, fecialis
sumpto in manibus lapide dicebat: Si sine dolo malo hoc foedus
facio, dii mihi cuncta felicia praestent; sin aliter aut ago aut cogito,
caeteris salvis solus ego peream, ut hic lapis e manibus meis deci-
det. Et mox lapidem deiiciebat.

fore Cecrops, made a treaty with Laban, his father-in-law. Moses voluntarily offered a secure treaty to certain kings while seeking safe passage for himself through the wilderness — and Moses lived in the time of Cecrops, according to Eusebius. We also know that Joshua, the successor of Moses, later struck a treaty with the Gabaonites. I conclude therefore that nothing can shed light on the author of this device because the passage of time has eliminated all certainty about him.

But I find that there used to be three kinds of treaty. In the 4 first, a conqueror would make rules for those conquered in war, and it was his right and prerogative to exact what he wanted from the goods surrendered and keep it. In the second, parties well matched in war would find peace and friendship through a treaty between equals, adjusting by give and take those cases where property had been disturbed. In the third type, those who had never been enemies would join each other in friendship through a treaty of alliance, and in this case there was no thought of dictating terms or accepting them since that would imply a victor and a vanquished.

Moreover, there were different ways of concluding treaties in 5 other times. In Rome, as Livy says in the first book *From the Foundation of the City*, the fetial priest took a fresh blade of grass from the citadel at the king's command and then (as we have shown in our *Proverbs*) he struck down a pig with flint, saying: Thus, as I strike this pig, let Jupiter strike down the one who would break this sacred treaty, and so on. But when Polybius in his third book mentions the first treaty made between Rome and Carthage, he describes a different ceremony, for he says: As soon as the two sides had agreed on a treaty, the fetial priest took a stone in his hand and said: If I make this treaty without willful fraud, may the gods give me all good fortune; but if I think or do otherwise, let me perish alone while the others live, as this stone falls from my hands. And then he threw the stone down.

6   Arabes autem quoties foedus faciebant cum aliis, quidam medius inter utrunque stans acuto lapide feriebat volam iuxta maiores digitos ipsorum qui foedus agebant; deinde sumpto flocco ex utriusque vestimento inungebat eo sanguine septem lapides in medio positos, inter ungendum invocans Dionysium et Uraniam. Hoc acto, idem qui fuerat sequester foederis inter amicos contrahendi vadabatur pro hospite aut forte pro cive, si cum cive res agebatur. Quod foedus et ipsi qui amicitiam contrahebant servare iustum censere.

7   Scythae vero hoc quippe modo sanciebant: Infuso in grandem calicem fictilem vino commiscebant eorum sanguinem qui ferirent foedus, percutientes cultello aut incidentes gladio aliquantulum corporis, deinde in calice tingebant sagittas, securim, iaculum. Haec simul atque fecerant, sese multis verbis devovere, postea vinum epotare—non modo ii qui foedus faciebant sed etiam comites illi qui erant maximae dignitatis.

8   Sic ferme apud Romanos iusiurandum inter factiosos confirmabatur, testificante Sallustio, qui scribit Catilinam humani corporis sanguinem vino permistum in pateris circuntulisse sociis coniurationis, et eos singillatim degustasse quo inter se magis fidi forent. Atqui hodie illud idem fit inter eos, qui ad aliquod insigne scelus faciendum conspirant. Item Barcaei pactionem in hanc formulam conflabant. Feriebant enim foedus super occultam fossam, et quoad humus ea ita se haberet tandiu foedus in ea regione ratum fore sentiebant: autor Herodotus libro 3, 4 et 5.

9   Et sic alii alio pacto denique faciebant, id quod si persequi vellem, essem profecto longior aequo simulque parum utiliter excluderer tempore.

Whenever the Arabs made a treaty with other peoples, they 6
had someone stand between those making the treaty and strike the
palms of their hands next to the middle finger with a sharp stone;
then this person took a bit of wool from the garment of either
party and used it to smear blood on seven stones set between
them, calling on Dionysius and Urania while doing so. After this
was done, the person who had mediated the treaty between the
friends would pledge his word if one of them was a foreigner — or
even for a countryman, should there be some question about him.
And those who had made the bargain of friendship resolved to
preserve this treaty fully.

The Scythians, on the other hand, ratified their treaties in this 7
way: In a large clay cup they mixed wine with the blood of those
who made the treaty, cutting them with a small knife or nicking
the body slightly with a sword, and then in the cup they dipped
arrows, an ax and a javelin. As soon as they had done this, they
swore lengthy vows and then drank the wine — not only those who
had made the treaty but also their most honored companions.

Conspirators in Rome confirmed their oaths in nearly the same 8
way, as Sallust testifies, writing that Catiline passed bowls of wine
mixed with blood from a human body among the partners in his
plot, who drank it one after another to bind themselves closer together. Those who conspire to commit some great crime do the
same today. Likewise, the Barcaei used the following procedure to
put a bargain together: They struck a treaty above a hidden
trench, regarding the treaty as good in that region for as long as
the ground remained in place, according to Herodotus in books 3,
4 and 5.

In short, various peoples had various ways of making treaties, 9
and if I meant to describe them all, I would surely take longer
than I ought and slow my progress for little purpose.

: XVI :

A quo mos triumphandi fluxerit, et quis primus apud Romanos triumphum aut ovationem duxerit, ac quis triumphare aut ovare liceret; et de ritu uspiam ponendi trophaei.

1 Dionysium, hoc est, Liberum Patrem, primum omnium, multarum gentium spoliis onustum, triumphasse, Diodorus libris *Historiarum* 5 et 6 et Plinius in 7 atque Solinus tradunt. Deinde apud plerosque populos usus triumphandi increbruit. Nam Carthaginensium imperatores rebus bene gestis triumphum ducere solebant, dicente Iustino libro suae *Epitomes* 19: Hasdrubal graviter vulneratus, imperio Hamilcari fratri tradito, interiit, cuius mortem tum luctus civitatis tum et dictaturae II et triumphi quatuor insignem fecere.

2 Verum apud Romanos praecipuus triumpho honor fuit. Romulus enim primus omnium, teste Dionysio, devicto Acrone Ceninensium rege, lauro coronatus et quatuor vectus equis, urbem ingressus est spoliaque hostilia Iovi Feretrio consecravit. Caeterum Livius de corona laurea et curru in hac pompa non meminit neque Plutarchus in *Vita Romuli*. Eutropius vero primum triumphum Tarquinio Prisco tribuit, devictis Sabinis.

3 Sed deinceps pompa triumphi insolens atque sumptuosissima omnem priscae mediocritatis formam exuit modumque excessit: nam triumphantes vehebantur equis albis, quibus primus omnium, teste Livio *Ab urbe condita* libro 5 et Plutarcho, Camillus usus est, eiusque triumphus ea de causa clarior fuit quam gratior, et curru inaurato. Corona, ut testis est Gellius, aurea redimitus, et

: XVI :

From whom came the custom of holding triumphs; who among the Romans first made a triumph or an ovation; to whom a triumph or an ovation was permitted; and on the practice of setting up a trophy at some spot.

Dionysius or Father Liber, laden with the spoils of many nations, was the first to hold a triumph, according to Diodorus in books [3] and [4] of his *Histories*, Pliny in book 7 and Solinus. Later the custom of holding triumph spread among most peoples. Carthaginian generals, for example, used to mark noble exploits with a triumph, as in the following passage from book 19 of the *Epitome* of Justinus: Hasdrubal died after he had been gravely wounded and command had been transferred to his brother Hamilcar, but the mourning of the city, eleven dictatorships and four triumphs made his death glorious. 1

For the Romans a triumph was a special honor. Romulus, wreathed with laurel and driving four horses, first entered the city to dedicate enemy spoils to Jupiter the Striker after he had beaten Acron, king of the Caeninenses — so says Dionysius. Yet neither Livy nor Plutarch in his *Life of Romulus* mentions the laurel wreath and chariot in this procession. And Eutropius attributes the first triumph to Tarquinius Priscus, after the conquest of the Sabines. 2

But eventually the triumphal procession became excessive, extravagant and too lavish, losing all trace of its original moderation: the triumphant generals, for example, were conveyed in a gilded chariot by white horses, which Camillus, according to Plutarch and Livy in book 5 *From the Foundation of the City*, was the first to use, for which reason his triumph was more famous than pleasing. 3

devictus hostis oneratus colla catenis currum sequebatur praeeunte Senatu, et sic in Capitolium ascendebant ad templum Iovis Optimi Maximi ubi mactato tauro albo, deinde domum redibant.

4   Erat praeterea minor triumphus, quae ovatio appellabatur — vel quia, ut Plutarchus sentit in *Vita Marcelli*, ovis mactabatur, vel quia, sicut Festo placet, redeuntes ex pugna victores milites laetabundi ingeminabant *o* literam. Ovandi autem ac non triumphandi, autore Gellio libro 5, causa erat cum aut bella non rite indicta neque cum iusto hoste gesta erant aut hostium nomen humile, ut servorum, aut deditione repente facta si incruenta victoria obvenisset, minusve quinque millia hostium una acie cecidissent, ita enim lege exceptum erat. Et ne prior lex ex cupiditate laureae antiquaretur, ei altera suppetias tulit, quae imperatoribus poenam minabatur qui aut hostium occisorum aut amissorum civium falsum numerum literis Senatui ausi essent referre, autor Valerius Maximus libro 2.

5   Non fiebat insuper ius omnibus triumphandi, licet res triumpho dignas gessissent. Quod quatenus Livius volumine 1 *De bello Macedonico* plenissime declarat, eius ideo verba ponam. Ait enim: Per idem tempus Lucius Cornelius Lentulus proconsul ex Hispania rediit, qui cum in Senatu res ab se per multos annos fortiter feliciterque gestas exposuisset postulassetque ut triumphanti sibi invehi liceret in urbem, res triumpho dignas esse censebat Senatus, sed exemplum a maioribus non accepisse ut qui neque dictator neque consul neque praetor res gessisset triumpharet. Et infra suggerit: Et senatusconsulto Lucius Lentulus ovans urbem est ingressus.

6   Ovantes vero, teste Plinio libro 15, myrto coronabantur quia haec arbuscula, ut Plutarchus ait, vim maxime bellumque perosa

The general was crowned with a golden wreath, Gellius tells us, and the defeated enemy with chains loaded about their necks followed the chariot as the Senate led; thus they marched up the Capitoline to the temple of Jupiter Optimus Maximus and sacrificed a white bull, and then they returned home.

There was a lesser triumph besides, called an ovation—either 4 because they sacrificed a sheep, as Plutarch thinks in his *Life of Marcellus*, or because soldiers returning victorious from battle kept exulting and repeating the sound 'o,' as Festus believes. The reason for giving an ovation rather than a triumph, according to Gellius in book 5, was either that war had not been declared correctly or that it had not been fought with a proper enemy or that the enemy was of low repute, as with slaves, or that in the case of a bloodless victory surrender had come suddenly, or that less than five thousand enemy had fallen in one battle, for this is what the law required. So that lust for the laurel would not annul this first law, a second law supporting it threatened generals with punishment if they dared send the Senate a false report of enemy killed or citizens lost, according to Valerius Maximus in book 2.

Moreover, not everyone had the right to a triumph, even those 5 who had done deeds deserving one. Since Livy gives a very full account of this in his first book *On the Macedonian War*, I will record what he says: At the same time, the proconsul Lucius Cornelius Lentulus returned from Spain, and having given an account in the Senate of his brave and successful exploits over many years, he asked to be allowed to enter the city in triumph. The Senate judged his deeds worthy of a triumph but decided that their forefathers had left no precedent allowing a triumph for someone who had not acted as dictator or consul or praetor. And further on he adds: By decree of the Senate Lucius Lentulus entered the city with an ovation.

Those honored with an ovation, according to Pliny in book 15, 6 were crowned with myrtle because this shrub especially abhors

est. Et equo vecti ibant militibus deinde comitantibus in Capitolium, ubi ex ove sacrificabant sicut triumphantes ex tauro. At Lacedaemonii (ut hoc quoque commodum subnectam), autore Plutarcho in *Vita Marcelli*, contrario Romanorum more, cum bellum dolo malo confecissent, taurum mactabant, sin armis, rem gessissent gallum.

7   Sed ad rem redeamus. Sabinus Massurius, teste Gellio, pedibus ingredi ovantes dicit, sequentibus eos non militibus sed universo Senatu. Primus autem omnium, autore Plinio libro 15, Posthumius Tubertus ovans ingressus est urbem.

8   Fuit item, teste Cicerone libro posteriore *De inventione*, usus Graecis, cum inter se bellum gessissent, ut hi qui vicissent trophaeum aliquod in finibus statuerent, victoriae modo in praesentia declarandae causa, non ut in perpetuum belli memoria maneret. Quare cum Thebani aliquando Lacedaemonios bello superavissent et aeneum trophaeum posuissent, apud commune Graeciae concilium accusati sunt quod contra quam ritus esset aeternum inimicitiarum monumentum statuissent.

9   Sed consuetudo vetus fuit ut eo loci ubi hostes devicti fuissent arborum ramos inciderent et in truncis suspenderent spolia hostibus detracta—aut in montibus idem facerent. Sic Aeneas de Mezentii exuviis trophaeum posuit. Vergilius libro 11:

> Ingentem quercum decisis undique ramis
> Constituit tumulo, fulgentiaque induit arma,
> Mezenti ducis exuvias, tibi magne trophaeum
> Bellipotens aptat rorantes sanguine cristas,
> Telaque trunca viri.

Caeterum cum de coronis facta sit mentio, non alienum erit earum originem subiicere.

violence and war, as Plutarch says. They came in on horseback and went to the Capitol escorted by their troops, where they offered a sheep, just as those in triumph sacrificed a bull. Unlike the Romans, the Lacedaimonians (if I might add this now) offered a bull when they won a war by low trickery but sacrificed a cock if they won by force of arms, according to Plutarch in his *Life of Marcellus.*

But let me return to my topic. Sabinus Massurius, according to 7 Gellius, says that those making an ovation came in on foot, followed not by their troops but by the whole Senate. The first to enter the city with an ovation, according to Pliny in book 15, was Posthumius Tubertus.

According to Cicero in the latter part of *On Invention*, when the 8 Greeks made war on one another the winner by custom set up a trophy of some sort at the border, but only to declare victory, not to remain forever as a memorial of the war. Hence, when the Thebans once beat the Lacedaemonians in war and set up a bronze trophy, a general council of Greece accused them of violating custom and erecting an eternal monument to the hostilities.

But it was an ancient custom to cut branches from the trees in 9 the place where the enemy had been conquered and to hang spoils taken from them in the trunks — or to do the same on hilltops. In this way Aeneas set up a trophy with the arms stripped from Mezentius, as Vergil writes in book 11:

A lofty oak tree, branches lopped all round,
He set on a barrow to hold the gleaming armor,
Leavings of Lord Mezentius — your trophy,
Mighty war-god — trimmed with blood-wet crests,
The warrior's weapons broken.

Otherwise, since wreaths have been mentioned, it will not be out of place to deal with their origin next.

: XVII :

Qui primi coronas invenerint et de variis earum generibus; et a quibus cives coronandi consuetudo manaverit; et de usu coronarum in conviviis (inibique locus Vergilii enodatus); ac unde mos ut coronati supplicarent Deo, epularenturque in funere faciundo ac spectarent ludos.

1 Coronarum repertorem, teste Plinio libro 16, ferunt Liberum Patrem fuisse, qui primus omnium imposuisset capiti suo coronam ex hedera. Postea deorum honori sacrificantes sumpserunt, victimis simul coronatis. Reperimus tamen longe antiquiorem coronarum usum, nam Moses (qui multis seculis, ut testis est Eusebius in 10 *De evangelica praeparatione*, praecessit Liberum Patrem) multas aureas coronas fecit, de quibus Iosephus plene meminit in 3 *Antiquitatum* cum de sacerdotum indumentis loquitur et in 8 scribens: Corona vero in qua *Deum* Moses inscripserat una fuit quae ad hunc usque diem permansit.

2 Principio ex arborum ramis fieri coronas in ludis et sacris certaminibus mos fuit, postea varia florum mistura componi coeperunt. Has Glycera primum adinvenit, ut ait Plinius libro 35, capite 11, cum de Sycionio pictore meminit. Amavit in iuventa Glyceram municipem suam, inventricem coronarum; certandoque imitatione eius ad numerosissimam florum varietatem perduxit artem illam. Verum idem libro 21 utrisque hoc potius assignare videtur, scribens: Postea variari coeptum mistura versicolori florumque invicem odores coloresque accendere Sicyonii ex ingenio Pausiae pic-

: XVII :

Who first invented wreaths and on their various kinds; on the origin of the custom of civic coronation; on the use of wreaths at banquets (clarifying a passage of Vergil); and whence comes the custom of wearing wreaths when praying to God, banqueting at funerals and watching games.

They say that the inventor of wreaths was Father Liber, who first   1
of all put an ivy wreath on his own head, according to Pliny in
book 16. Later those who made sacrifices put them on to honor
the gods, and their victims also wore wreaths. But we have discovered a use of wreaths far more ancient, for Moses (who preceded
Father Liber by many centuries, as Eusebius testifies in book 10 of
the *Preparation for the Gospel*) made many golden wreaths, which
Josephus describes fully in book 3 of the *Antiquities* when he speaks
of the vestments of the priests, and in book 8, writing: But the
crown on which Moses had written *God* was unique and has survived to this day.

   In the beginning it was customary to make wreaths from the   2
boughs of trees for games and sacred contests, and then they began to make them by combining various flowers. The first to devise them was Glycera, as Pliny says in book 35, chapter 11, when
he mentions the painter from Sicyon. As a young man the painter
loved Glycera, a woman of his town who invented wreaths; by
imitating her and striving for the widest variety of flowers, he improved the technique. But in book 21 Pliny seems to assign it instead to both of them, writing: Later on they introduced varia-
tions by mixing different colors, and they intensified the play of
odors and colors in the flowers, using the technique of the painter,

toris atque Glycerae coronariae, dilectae admodum illi cum opera eius pictura imitaretur.

3   Paulo post subiere quae vocantur Aegyptiae sive hybernae—tunc cum terra horret—factae e bracteis ligneis sive eburneis variis coloribus infectis. Venerunt deinde e lamina aenea tenui, inaurata aut argentata, quae propter gracilitatem corollae dicuntur. Crassus autem Dives, autore Plinio libro 21, primus suis ludis coronam aureis argenteisque foliis dedit, et alii alias, obliteratis tamen eorum nominibus.

4   Hinc denique multiiuges coronae manarunt, erant enim militares coronae, id est: triumphalis, qua donabantur imperatores; muralis, quam imperator dabat illi qui primus muros subiisset; castrensis, qua eum donabat imperator qui primus in hostium castra pugnans introisset; navalis, qua donari assolebat is qui primus in hostium navem transilivisset. Et hae ex auro fiebant, sed triumphalis primitus ex lauro fuerat.

5   Oleagina, qua (uti antea diximus) victores in Olympico stadio donabantur; myrtea, quo ovantes coronabantur; obsidionalis, quam Plinius in 22 cunctis coronis praeponit. Hanc autem illi qui liberati erant obsidione dabant ei duci qui liberasset, et ea graminea erat—ex eo gramine quod ibi natum fuerat ubi obsidebantur. Erat praeterea civica corona proculdubio celeberrima, quam civis civi a quo servatus fuisset in praelio testem vitae salutisque perceptae dabat. Ea fiebat ex fronde querna quoniam quercus primum mortalibus victum praebuisset vel quia, sicut Plutarcho placet, Iovi, in cuius tutela sunt civitates, sacra quercus est, vel aliis de causis quas ipse in *Vita Coriolani* affatim exponit. De hac Plinius libro 16 meminit, appellans eam militum virtutis insigne clarissimum. Ex quo non temere Antoninus Pius, teste Capitolino, Scipionis auream illam (ut ita dixerim) sententiam frequenter usurpa-

Pausias of Sicyon, and of Glycera, the wreath-maker, whom he greatly admired since he imitated her works in painting.

A bit later appeared those wreaths called Egyptian or winter 3 wreaths — for the season when the earth shivers — made of wood or ivory veneers tinted in various colors. Then came those made of thin bronze leaf, gilded or silvered, called garlands because they were so light. But it was Crassus the Rich, according to Pliny in book 21, who first awarded a wreath made of silver and gold leaves at his games, and then others added other touches, but their names have been forgotten.

From these came a great variety of wreaths — military wreaths, 4 for example: the triumphal, awarded to commanders; the mural, which the commander awarded to the first man to climb a wall; the camp wreath, which the commander gave to the first man to fight his way into the enemy camp; and the naval wreath, which used to be given to the first man to leap across to an enemy ship. These were made of gold, but the triumphal wreath had originally been of laurel.

The wreath awarded to victors in the Olympic stadium (as ex- 5 plained before) was of the olive tree. A myrtle wreath was awarded in an ovation. But the siege wreath is the one that Pliny rates above all others in book 22. The besieged gave it to the general who had freed them, and it was made of grass — from the grass that grew in the place of the siege. The civic wreath, of course, was also quite important: a man whose life another had saved in battle gave it to his benefactor in recognition of being alive and safe. It was made of oak-leaves because the oak first provided food for mankind or, as Plutarch would have it, because the oak is sacred to Jupiter, patron of cities, or for other reasons that Plutarch sets forth at length in his *Life of Coriolanus*. Pliny mentions this wreath in book 16, calling it the most distinguished badge of military valor. Thus according to Capitolinus, it was not without reason that Antoninus Pius often used that golden saying (as I call it)

bat, dictitans malle se unum civem servare quam mille hostes occidere.

6   Hanc autem consuetudinem cives coronis donandi, autore Valerio Maximo libro 2, Athenienses primi omnium introduxerunt, hoc honore uberrimo virtutis alimento primum Periclem decorantes. Erant insuper coronae gemmatae, vallares, rostratae et spicea, quam Plinius libro 18 tradit primam apud Romanos fuisse coronam. At coronas ex cinnamomo, idem autor est in 12, interrasili auro inclusas primus omnium in templis Capitolii atque Pacis dicavit Imperator Vespasianus.

7   Sic demum eo coronarum luxuria processit ut Graeci in conviviis symposiisque (ita enim Graece compotationes vocantur) coronis uterentur, infunderentque in pateris hilaritatis gratia. Cuius rei, ut in tertio huius operis volumine dicemus, Iones autores extiterunt.

8   At illud Cleopatrae exemplum occurrit. Nam apparatu belli Actiaci, gratificationem ipsius reginae Antonio timente nec nisi praegustatos cibos sumente cum eo lusit extremis coronae floribus venenatis. Sane procedente hilaritate invitavit Antonium ut coronas biberent. Ecquis scilicet istas timeret insidias? Ergo coniecta in scyphum corona Antonio incipienti haurire, opposita manu: En ego sum, inquit, illa, chare Antoni, quam tu nova praegustantium diligentia caves, adeo mihi si, possem sine te vivere, occasio et ratio nocendi adest. Inde eductum e custodia vinctum bibere iussit; qui sumpto potu illico occidit, autore Plinio libro *Naturalis historiae* 21.

9   Artaxerxem etiam Persarum regem, in potatione corona esse usum a Plutarcho in *Vita Pelopidae* accipimus. Ad hunc igitur bibendi morem dixerim poetam allusisse in 1 *Aeneidos*, illo versu:

of Scipio, always insisting that he would rather save one citizen than kill a thousand enemies.

Before any others, the Athenians introduced this custom of 6 presenting wreaths to citizens, according to Valerius Maximus in book 2, when they first honored Pericles with this decoration as rich nourishment for excellence. There were also jeweled wreaths, rampart wreaths, beaked wreaths and the wheat wreath, which in book 18 Pliny says was the first that the Romans had. In the temples of the Capitoline Jupiter and of Peace, the emperor Vespasian first dedicated wreaths of cinnamon enclosed in embossed gold, according to the same author in book 12.

So the profusion of wreaths continued until at last the Greeks 7 used them at banquets and symposia (as the called their drinking parties in Greek), serving them in drinking bowls for amusement. The Ionians, as we shall explain in the third book of this work, were the authors of this custom.

But the famous story about Cleopatra comes to mind. Making 8 ready for the battle of Actium, Anthony feared the queen's kindness and would take no food unless it had been tasted beforehand, so she toyed with him by poisoning the tips of the flowers in his wreath. In the midst of their carousing she invited Anthony to drink the wreaths with her. Now who would fear such a trap? So with the wreath in the cup and Anthony about to drink, she raised her hand and said: I am she, Anthony dear, against whom you are guarding with your new attentiveness to tasting, so much do I have means and method to harm you could I but live without you. Then she had a bound captive led out and ordered him to drink; he emptied the cup and died on the spot, as Pliny tells it in book 21 of the *Natural History*.

We gather from Plutarch's *Life of Pelopidas* that Artaxerxes, king 9 of Persia, also used the wreath at drinking-parties. I would say, then, that this is the drinking-custom to which the poet alluded in the first book of the *Aeneid*, in this verse:

Crateras magnos statuunt, et vina coronant.

Et in 7 eiusdem operis:

Crateras laeti statuunt, et vina coronant.

10   Item moris fuit olim Italorum ut coronati supplicarent Deo pro
se suisque. Sic, teste Cicerone libris *Tusculanarum* I et *Ad Atticum* 8,
Neapolitani coronati ac municipia vota fecerunt pro Pompeio ae-
grotante. Sic Graeci epulabantur dum funus facerent, idem Cicero
autor qui libro *De legibus* 2, cum de ordine exequiarum apud Graecos meminit, ita scribit: Sequebantur epulae quas inirent propinqui coronati. Sic Romani coronati ludos Romanos ac Apollinares,
autore Livio libris extremo x decadis I et v decadis III, spectabant.

11   Sicque hodie, cum alibi tum apud Anglos, statis solennibusque
diebus sacerdotes coronati in supplicationibus publicis incedunt—
et praesertim Londini sacerdotes Paulini, mense Iunio die divo ipsi
Paulo apostolo sacro, qui simul omnia eius diei sacra coronati curant faciuntque. Sed iam ad unguentum transeamus, quod haudquaquam minus quam coronae ad luxum pertinet.

: XVIII :

*De antiquissimo usu unguentorum et quando primum ea
cognita Romanis.*

1   Quis primus unguenta invenerit non traditur. Iliacis temporibus
non erant, ait Plinius, cui Iosephus in 2 *Antiquitatum* minus assen-
tiri videtur, scribens: Iacob (qui teste Eusebio multis tempestati-

They set down great goblets and crown the wine.

And in book 7 of the same work:

They set the goblets down and crown the wine in joy.

Likewise, it used to be customary for the Italians to wear   10
wreaths when praying to God for themselves and their own. Thus,
according to Cicero in book 1 of the *Tusculans* and book 8 of the
Letters to Atticus, the Neapolitans wore wreaths and offered the
prayers of the town for Pompey when he was ill. And the Greeks
held banquets at their funerals, as again Cicero tells us in book 2
On the Laws when he mentions the order of funeral rites among
the Greeks, writing: There followed banquets to which the kin
came wearing wreaths. The Romans wore wreaths when they
watched the Roman games and the games of Apollo, according to
Livy at the end of book 10 of the first decade and book 5 of the
third decade.

And so today, both in England and elsewhere, priests wear   11
wreaths for occasions of public prayer on appointed feast days —
especially the priests of St. Paul in London, who in June, on the
feast of the holy apostle Paul, perform the rites of that day together while wearing wreaths. But now let us move on to perfumes, which no less than wreaths have to do with luxury.

: XVIII :

*On the oldest use of perfumes and when they first became
known to the Romans.*

Who first invented perfumes is not recorded. There were none in   1
the age of Troy, says Pliny, but in book 2 of the *Antiquities* Josephus
seems not to agree, writing: Jacob (who lived ages before the Tro-

bus ante Troianum bellum fuit) misisse in Aegyptum ad Ioseph filium suum, id temporis apud Pharaonem annonae praefectum, inter caetera munera unguentum. Et in 3 eiusdem operis, cum de purgatione tabernaculi et sacerdotum sermonem habet quam Moses instituit, qui fuit ante CCCL annos quam Troia excisa est, ait: Purificavit autem et tabernaculum et sacerdotes hoc modo: sumpsit myrrhae electae siclos quingentos et totidem ireos, cinnamomi et calami (est autem et haec species suavis odoris) priorem mensuram, et medietatem horum iussit contusam misceri; oleique olivarum pondus mensurae provinciae quae dicitur *bin* duas choas Atticas capiens; quibus permistis et coactis facta est arte unguentariorum unctio suavissima, et reliqua. Ex quo cum huiusmodi Hebraeorum antiquissimos unguento usos constet, eos huius rei autores fuisse haud credere absurdum fortasse fuerit. Nos tamen hanc rem in medio relinquimus.

2   Sed Plinius in 13 et Solinus prodiderunt primum castris Darii regis expugnatis in reliquo eius apparatu Alexandrum cepisse scrinium unguentorum; posteaque voluptatem eius a nostris quoque inter laudatissima atque etiam honestissima vitae bona admissam esse. Verum apud Persas etiam ante Darium unguenta fuisse testatur Herodotus libro 3, scribens Cambysem, Cyri filium, misisse legatos cum maximis donis ad Aethiopum Macrobiorum regem— inter quae unguenti alabastrum fuisse—regem vero cum ab Ichthyophagis (hi enim missi fuerant) rationem confecturae huiusmodi unguenti didicisset, id penitus aspernatum esse. Quando autem primum ad Romanos unguentum pervenerit haud propalam est. Certum est, teste Plinio in 13, Antiocho rege Asiaque devictis urbis anno DLXV, Publium Licinium Crassum et Lucium Iulium Caesarem censores edixisse ne quis venderet unguenta exotica, id est, externa et aliunde asportata.

jan War, according to Eusebius) sent perfume with other gifts into Egypt with his son Joseph, who at that time was Pharaoh's master of the harvest. And in book 3 of the same work, when he speaks of the cleansing of the tabernacle and priests that Moses ordained 350 years before the fall of Troy, he says: He purified the tabernacle and the priests in this way. He took five hundred shekels of choice myrrh, the same amount of iris, the former measure of cinnamon and calamus (another sweet-smelling species), and of this he ordered half to be ground and mixed. Then he took a quantity of olive oil known locally as a *bin*, equal to two Attic *choes*. When these were mixed and compounded, the perfumer's art produced a very sweet ointment from them, and so on. Since it is clear from this that the most ancient of the Hebrews used perfumes of this kind, perhaps it would not be unreasonable to suppose that they were its inventors. We leave this question undecided, however.

Pliny in book 13 and Solinus reported that when Alexander first   2 stormed the camp of King Darius, he captured a case of perfumes among the remains of Darius' gear, and that after this our people recognized the enjoyment of perfumes as among the most commendable and even respectable pleasures of life. But Herodotus testifies in book 3 that the Persians had perfumes even before Darius, writing that Cambyses, son of Cyrus, sent ambassadors loaded with gifts — among them a jar of perfume — to the king of the Long-lived Ethiopians. But when the king learned the method of making this kind of perfume from the Fish-eaters (it was they who had been sent), he would have nothing to do with it. When perfume first came to the Romans is unknown. According to Pliny in book 13, however, it is clear that after King Antiochus and Asia had been defeated in AUC 565, the censors Publius Licinius Crassus and Lucius Julius Caesar issued an edict against the sale of exotic perfumes — those from abroad, in other words, imported from another country.

: XIX :

Qui primi invenerint aurum, argentum, ferrum, plumbum, aes, fabriliaque instrumenta et ignem primo, dein e silice aut lignis, et folles atque lucernae usum.

1   Ex metallis quibus nunc humanae constant opes, aurum pretiosissimum est, cuius habendi tanta mortales libido iam inde ab initio invasit ut in eo effodiendo iamiam ad inferos propemodum penetraverint. Ovidius in 1 *Metamorphoseon*:

> sed itum est in viscera terrae,
> Quasque recondiderat Stygiisque admoverat umbris
> Effodiuntur opes irritamenta malorum.
> Iamque nocens ferrum, ferroque nocentius aurum
> Prodierat.

Unde de hominibus intente fodientibus illud Phalerii dictum — Plutonem brevi ad superos adductum iri — Strabo in 3 *Geographiae* commemorat. Quare Diogenes, teste Laertio, rogatus cur palleret aurum, admodum scite respondit: Quia multos, inquit, habet insidiatores.

2   Hoc, autore Plinio libro 7, Cadmus Phoenix ad Pangaeum montem primus invenit, ut aliis placet Thoas et Eaclis in Panchaia, aut Sol Oceani filius. Argentum vero Mercurius quintus, unde vivum argentum vulgo Mercurium appellant; vel Erichthonius Atheniensis aut Ceacus. Ad Pangaeum autem Thraciae montem haec metalla ideo (ut mea quidem fert opinio) primum inventa traduntur quoniam ibi, teste Herodoto libro 7, aurum et argentum maxime abundat.

3   Ferrum Idaei Dactyli in Creta adinvenerunt. Plumbum ex insulis contra Celtiberiam sitis, quas Strabo libro 2 Cassiterides appel-

: XIX :

*Who first discovered gold, silver, iron, lead, copper, tools for
metal-working and fire, then fire-making from flint or wood,
the bellows and the use of the lamp.*

Of the metals that now make up mankind's wealth, gold is the   1
most precious. From the start, people have been so much gripped
by the passion to possess it that now they have almost penetrated
the underworld to dig it up, as Ovid writes in book 1 of the *Metamorphoses:*

> into the bowels of the earth they went,
> And brought up what he had hidden in Stygian shade,
> Dug out the wealth, enticing to evil.
> Out came the hurtful iron and gold more
> hurtful still.

Along these lines, Strabo recalls in book 3 of the *Geography* what
Phalerius said about why people dug for it so vigorously: so that
Pluto would soon be raised to the surface. Asked why gold is pale,
Diogenes gave a clever answer, according to Laertius: Because so
many lie in wait for it, he replied.

Cadmus the Phoenician first discovered it at Mt. Pangaeus, ac-   2
cording to Pliny in book 7, or else it was Thoas and Eaclis in
Panchaia, or Sol the son of Ocean, so others say. But the fifth
Mercury discovered silver, which is why quicksilver is commonly
called mercury; or else it was Erichthonius of Athens or Ceacus.
In my opinion, they say that these metals were first found at Mt.
Pangaeus in Thrace because gold and silver abound there, accord-
ing to Herodotus in book 7.

The Dactyls of Ida discovered iron in Crete. Midacritus first   3
brought lead from the islands off Celtiberia that Strabo calls the

lat, Midacritus primus asportavit. Aes in Cypro insula Cynira, Agriopae filius, reperit, item forcipem, marculum, vectem, incudem, ex Plinio libro 7 et 34, a quo Solinus discrepat, ita scribens cum de Creta loquitur: Calthis eadem habita est apud priscos, ut Calidemus autor est, aere ibi primum reperto. Sicuti nec de ferro Clemens assentitur, tradens Selmentem et Damnameneum Iudaeos in Cypro invenisse. Aerariam fabricam alii Chalybas, alii Cyclopes invenisse volunt, qui ferrariam primo exercuerint, autor Plinius. Atqui aeris usum Pannonios monstrasse Clemens tradit. Aes conflare Aristoteles ait Lydum Scytham docuisse; Theophrastus Delam Phrygem putat. Strabo vero libro 14 *Geographiae* dicit Telchines populos ferrum et aes omnium primos esse fabricatos, utpote qui harpen, id est, ensem falcatum Saturno fecerint. Compactionem ferri Glaucus Chius, teste Herodoto in 1, excogitavit. Auri conflaturam ipse Cadmus, ut ait Plinius, invenit.

4   Caeterum haec fere omnia Diodorus cum Idaeis Dactylis tum Vulcano assignare videtur, ita libro 6 scribens: Idaei Dactyli traduntur ignis usum ac aeris ferrique naturam quoque modo fabricentur in loco quem Berecyntum dicunt invenisse. Et alibi: Vulcanum, inquit, ferri, aeris, argenti, auri, omniumque quae igne fabricantur artem invenisse ferunt.

5   Verum huiusmodi metallorum usus in ipso primordio prope orbis apud Hebraeos, qui mortalium omnium primi geniti sunt, ex Iosepho *De antiquitatibus Iudaeorum* in plerisque locis fuisse deprehendimus; qui volumine 1 ferrariam artem Tubalchain Lamech filio assignat, sicut Clemens temperiem ferri Delae Iudaeo attribuit, quamvis Hesiodus Delam ex Scythia fuisse affirmet. Quare eorum qui huiusmodi rerum autores produntur alios alibi primos haec metalla, etsi diu ante reperta, monstrasse par est credere.

Cassiterides in book 2. Cynira, son of Agriopa, discovered copper on the island of Cyprus, as well as the tongs, hammer, crow-bar and anvil according to Pliny in books 7 and 34. Solinus disputes this when he speaks as follows about Crete: The same island was known as Calthis to the ancients, according to Callidemus, because copper was first found there. Clement also disagrees about iron, reporting that the Jews Selmens and Damnameneus discovered it in Cyprus. Some say the Chalybes invented the working of bronze. Others claim it was the Cyclopes; they were the first to work with iron, according to Pliny. But Clement reports that the Pannonians showed how to use copper. Aristotle says that the Lydian Scythes taught how to melt copper, but Theophrastus thinks it was Delas the Phrygian. Yet in book 14 of the *Geography* Strabo says that the first people of all to work iron and copper were the Telchines, since it was they who made his scimitar or sickle-shaped sword for Saturn. Glaucus of Chios learned how to weld iron, according to Herodotus in book 1. Cadmus himself, says Pliny, discovered the melting of gold.

Diodorus, on the other hand, seems to assign almost all of this 4 to the Dactyls of Ida and to Vulcan, writing in book [5]: They say that in a place called Berecynthus the Dactyls of Ida discovered the use of fire, the nature of copper and iron and also how to work them. Elsewhere he writes: They report that Vulcan invented the art of working iron, copper, silver, gold and all metals treated with fire.

From many passages in the *Antiquities of the Jews* by Josephus, 5 however, we have learned that the Hebrews, first-born of all mortals, had the use of these metals almost at the beginning of the world. In book 1 Josephus assigns the blacksmith's art to Tubalcain, son of Lamech, just as Clement attributes the tempering of iron to Delas the Jew, though Hesiod claims that Delas was from Scythia. Thus, it is reasonable to believe that those considered inventors of these things were the first to teach about metals in one place or another, though they had long since been discovered.

6   Ignem, teste Diodoro libro 1, quidam sacerdotes affirmant Vulcanum reperisse et eo beneficio ducem ab Aegyptiis constitutum.
Vitruvius in 2 *De architectura* dicit arbores ab initio ventis agitatas
inter se terentes ramos hunc primum excitavisse inde vero homines
ligna adiicientes conservasse. Alii hoc Idaeis Dactylis adscribunt,
sed rectius profecto factitarent si Deo coeli et terrae ac cuiusque
rei quae coeli ipsius ambitu continetur creatori—ut decet—hoc
etiam humanae vitae adversus vim frigoris praesidium acceptum
referrent. Ignem e silice Pyrodes Cilicis filius invenit, at eundem
servare in ferula Prometheus docuit, autor Plinius in 7.

7   Hic magis meo iudicio admiratione dignum occurrit exploratorum in castris pastorumque inventum: qui cum ad excutiendum
ignem non eis semper lapidis occasio esset, ignem ex diversis arboribus concipere didicerunt, dicente Plinio in 16: calidae morus,
laurus, hedera et omnes quibus igniaria fiunt, exploratorum hoc
usus in castris pastorumque reperit. Teritur igitur lignum ligno,
ignemque concipit attritu—excipiente materia aridi fomitis fungi
vel foliorum facillime conceptum. Sed nihil hedera praestantius
quae teratur lauro laurumque terat.

8   Folles vero, id est instrumentum quo attrahitur ventus atque
emittitur ad ignem excitandum, Anacharsis Scytha, teste Strabone
libro 2 *Geographiae*, reperit. Lucernae usum Aegyptii invenerunt,
autor Clemens.

Certain priests claim that Vulcan discovered fire, according to 6
Diodorus, and that in return for this favor the Egyptians made
him a leader. Vitruvius says in book 2 *On Architecture* that fire was
first kindled in trees moved about by the winds so that their
branches rubbed together, and people then added pieces of wood
to keep the fire going. Others ascribe this to the Dactyls of Ida.
But surely they would do better — as decent people should — to
credit the God of heaven and earth, creator of everything contained in the circuit of that heaven, with their having this defense
of human life against the force of cold. Pyrodes, son of Cilix, discovered how to make fire with flint, and Prometheus showed how
to keep it in a stalk of fennel.

What scouts and shepherds have found in the field strikes me 7
as more remarkable in this regard: Since a stone was not always
handy when they needed to strike a fire, they learned how to get it
from various trees, as Pliny explains in book 16: Of a hot nature
are blackberry, bay, ivy and all those woods from which fire-sticks
are made, as shown by what scouts and shepherds do in the field.
When wood rubs against wood, friction makes fire — catching very
quickly when some dry fungus or leaves are added as kindling. But
nothing works better than ivy rubbed with bay and bay with ivy.

Anacharsis the Scythian, according to Strabo in book 2 of the 8
Geography, invented the bellows, an implement for drawing wind in
and forcing it out to kindle fire. The Egyptians discovered the use
of the lamp, according to Clement.

: XX :

*A quibus primum numus aureus inventus, aut quis argentum
et aes signaverit, atque speculum argenteum fecerit.*

1 Utinam aurum—sacra fames, ut poeta dixit—posset e vita hominum penitus tolli, ab optimis quibusque conviciis proscissum, id
quod Crates ille Thebanus ita esse faciendum exemplo docuit.
Qui, teste Divo Hieronymo *Contra Iovinianum* (quamvis Laertius
aliter tradat), proiecto in mare non parvo auri pondere: Abite, inquit, pessum malae cupiditates; ego vos mergam, ne ipse mergar a
vobis. Quod haud mehercule temere fecit; aurum enim etiam bonos, nedum pravos, transversos plerumque agit. Quanto igitur
cum rebus humanis felicius ageretur si res ipsae inter se permuta-
rentur, sicut Troianis temporibus Homerus tradit esse factitatum.

2 Quamvis usum pecuniarum ex quocunque essent metalli genere
antiquissimum constet, quia apud Iosephum legimus, Cain Adam
primi hominis filium anxie in cumulandas pecunias incubuisse.
Pessimum itaque vitae scelus fecit qui primus ex auro denarium signavit, quod Plinius libro 33 penitus latere dicit autore incerto. Verum Herodotus, gravis utique autor, in 1 *Historiarum* volumine
scribit Lydos primos omnium nummum aureum et argenteum ad
utendum percussisse. Quod Plinius fortasse minus silentio
praeterisset nisi ibi, ut opinor, tantum de Romano nummo locutus
esset. Romae autem, ut idem Plinius ait, nummus aureus percus-
sus est anno urbis DCXXXXVII, qui coepit deinceps ubique gentium
cudi et communis esse. Et ille in primis qui quod Romae cudere-
tur ducatus est dictus a Romano ducatu, qui magistratus a Lon-
gino fuerat primum constitutus, quem Iustinus Imperator Narseti
Italiae praefecto successorem dederat.

: XX :

*Who first invented the gold coin, who stamped coins in silver
and bronze and who made the silver mirror.*

Would that gold — the cursed craving of which the Poet spoke —   1
could be removed completely from human life, for all decent people have reviled it, as taught by the example of Crates the Theban.
According to St. Jerome *Against Jovinian* (though Laertius gives a
different version), Crates threw a great weight of gold into the sea
and said: Sink, evil desires; I will drown you and not be drowned
by you. What he did was right, surely, for gold usually leads even
good people astray, let alone the wicked. How much happier human life would be, then, if it was goods that were exchanged, as
Homer says they used to be in the days of Troy.

Still, the use of money made from various kinds of metal is   2
clearly very ancient, for in Josephus we read that Cain, son of
Adam, the first man, sought avidly and anxiously to heap up his
money. The person who first coined a golden denarius committed
the worst crime in the world; according to Pliny in book 33, it
remains entirely unsolved and the perpetrator unknown. But
Herodotus, obviously an important authority, writes in book 1 of
the *Histories* that the Lydians were the first to strike silver and gold
coinage for their use. That Pliny would have failed to mention this
is not likely unless, as I believe, he was speaking only of Roman
money in this passage. A gold coin was struck at Rome in AUC
647, says Pliny; then all the nations began striking them and they
became common. The one originally struck at Rome was called a
ducat from the Roman *ducatus*, which had first been established as
an office by Longinus, whom the Emperor Justin made exarch of
Italy in succession to Narses.

3   Argentum primus omnium, autore Strabone libro 8 *Geographiae*, signari docuit Phaedon. At Ephorus, ut idem autor est,
scriptis prodidit primo in Aegina a Phidone signari coeptum argentum. Ex quo, ut videre videor, huiusmodi scriptores primum
ab Herodoto (qui, sicut ostendimus, Lydis hoc assignat) deinde
inter se dissentiunt, nisi in alterutro mendum sit in dictione Phidone, unius mutatione literae. Romae signatum anno ab urbe
condita CCCCLXXXIIII, autor Plinius. Livius itidem *Ab urbe condita*
testatur sero esse signatum argentum. Eutropius vero in 2 suarum
Historiarum dicit nummum argenteum primum in orbe esse signatum anno urbis Romae circiter CCCCLXXXIII, primi autem Punici
belli 6. Nota argenti, velut Plinius ait, fuere bigae atque quadrigae.

4   Aes Ianus primus signavit, Macrobius libro *Saturnalium* 1: Hic
igitur Ianus cum Saturnum classe pervectum excepisset hospitio et
ab eo edoctus peritiam ruris, ferum illum et rudem ante fruges co-
gnitas victum in melius redegisset, regni eum societate muneravit.
Cum primus quoque aera signaret, servavit et in hoc Saturni reve-
rentiam ut (quoniam ille navi fuerat advectus) ex una quidem
parte sui capitis effigies, ex altera vero navis exprimeretur quo Saturni memoriam etiam in posteros propagaret. Ovidius quoque
testatur in primo *Fastorum* scribens:

> Multa quidem didici, sed cur navalis in aere
>   Altera signata est, altera forma biceps?

Et deinde infert:

> At bona posteritas puppim formavit in aere,
>   Hospitis adventum testificata dei.

Phaedon first of all taught how to coin silver, according to 3
Strabo in book 8 of the *Geography*, but from Ephorus the same
source records that Phidon first began the coining of silver in
Aegina. So it seems to me that these authorities disagree not only
with Herodotus (who assigns it to the Lydians, as we have shown)
but also with each other, unless in one of the passages 'Phidon' is a
bad reading, with one letter out of place. Pliny tells us that silver
was coined at Rome in AUC 484, and Livy likewise testifies that it
happened late in *From the Foundation of the City*. But in book 2 of
the *Histories* Eutropius says that the world's first silver coin was
struck around AUC 483, in the sixth year of the first Punic War.
The picture on the silver, says Pliny, was horses pulling a chariot,
either a pair or a team of four.

Janus first coined in bronze, as Macrobius writes in book 1 of 4
the *Saturnalia*: After Saturn had arrived by ship, Janus received
him here as a guest. Having learned the skills of farming from Saturn to improve the crude, rough diet that people had before they
knew how to grow crops, Janus rewarded him with partnership in
his kingdom. When Janus also became the first to coin bronze, in
this too he continued to honor Saturn by marking one side of the
coin with a likeness of his own head, the other with a ship (since
Saturn had arrived by ship) in order to prolong Saturn's memory
as well for posterity. Ovid also gives evidence of this in the first
book of the *Fasti*, writing:

> Much have I learned,
> But why stamp a ship on one side,
> A two-faced form on the other?

And then he concludes:

> Grateful posterity shaped a ship in copper
> To prove the god had come as a guest.

5   Quapropter miror hoc a Plinio Servio regi Romanorum assignari, libro 33 ita scribente: Servius rex primus signavit aes; antea rudi usos Romae Timaeus tradit. Signatum est nota pecudum, unde et pecunia appellata. Cum praesertim ipse etiam inferius de primo aeris signo meminerit, dicens: Nota aeris fuit, ex altera parte Ianus geminus, ex altera rostrum navis. Sed Plinius ut arbitror forsitan intellexit Servium (sicuti credere par est) aes signasse vel primum apud Romanos duntaxat vel primum (ut idem in principio libri 18, capite 3, dicit) ovium boumque effigie, nam Ianus multo ante conditam urbem, teste Macrobio, in Latio regnavit. Eutropius autem secus etiam sentit, in 1 scribens Saturnum nummos aereos Latinis primum instituisse. Sed utcunque res se habeat, Saturni tempore vel paulo post institutum signandi aeris coepisse iam liquido liquet.

6   Speculum argenteum, autore Plinio in 33, Praxiteles primus fecit Magni Pompeii aetate. Inventa sunt item specula ex ferro, plumbo, crystallo, vitro mistisque materiis in quibus effigiem nostram contemplamur ab Aesculapio primo, Apollinis filio, autor Marcus Tullius libro *De natura deorum* 3.

: XXI :

De origine annulorum, ac primo gemmarum usu et cur
digitus sinistrae manus minimo proximus annulo coronari
consueverit.

1   Cum Prometheus, ut poetae tradunt, coelestem ignem furatus esset, ferunt Iovem illum in monte Scythiae Caucaso ferrea catena vinxisse aquilamque addidisse quae iecore eius assidue renascente perpetuo pasceretur. Martialis:

I am surprised, then, that Pliny assigns this to the Roman king 5
Servius. In book 33 he writes: King Servius was the first to coin
bronze; Timaeus reports that before his time they used the unfinished metal at Rome. It was stamped with a picture of a herd-ani-
mal, so it was called money. He writes this even though a few lines
later he mentions the coining of bronze again and says: There was
a picture on the bronze, on one side two-faced Janus, on the other
the prow of a ship. But I believe Pliny thought that Servius was either the first to coin bronze only among the Romans (which is
credible enough) or the first to use a likeness of sheep and cattle
(as he says in the beginning of book 18, chapter 3), for Janus
reigned in Latium long before the founding of the city, according
to Macrobius. Eutropius has yet another view, writing in book 1
that Saturn established bronze coinage among the Latins. In any
case, it is perfectly clear by now that the coining of bronze began
in Saturn's time or a little later.

In the days of Pompey the Great, Praxiteles first made a mirror 6
of silver, according to Pliny in book 33. In addition, the iron, lead,
crystal, glass and composite mirrors in which we see images of
ourselves were invented by the first Aesculapius, son of Apollo, according to Cicero in book 3 *On the Nature of the Gods*.

: XXI :

*On the origin of rings, on the first use of jewels and why they
used to put a ring around the finger nearest the little finger of
the left hand.*

When Prometheus stole fire from heaven, the poets say that Jupi- 1
ter bound him down with an iron chain on a mountain of Scythia
in the Caucusus and sent an eagle to feed relentlessly on his liver
while it kept growing back. Martial:

Qualiter in Scythica religatus rupe Prometheus
   Assiduam nimio pectore pavit avem.

Post haec Prometheum ut sibi Iovem conciliaret hac arte usum
fuisse: Iupiter amore Thetidis conspecta eius pulchritudine forte
exarserat, quod sentientes Parcae, quarum providentia non fallitur,
cecinerunt quicunque Thetidi connubio iunctus esset, eius filium
patris gloriam longe superaturum. Hoc cum forte intellexisset Prometheus, Iovi renunciasse dicitur, qui veritus talionem—id est, ne
quod ipse Saturno patri fecisset a filio pateretur—omnem de The-
tide cogitationem deposuit. Et ne erga Prometheum parum gratus
videretur, vinculis eum liberavit. Et ut liberationis eius perpetua
memoria foret, facto ex utraque re—hoc est, saxo ad quod alliga-
tus fuerat et ferro ex quo catena constabat—annulo digitum eius
sinistrae manus minimo proximum cinxit.

2   Quae prima annuli et gemmae inventio fuit, quod Plinius libro
37 probe nimirum sentiens fabulosum appellat, dicens: Fabulae
primordium a rupe Caucasea tradunt, Promethei vinculorum interpretatione fatali; primumque saxi fragmentum inclusum ferro
ac digito circundatum, hoc fuisse annulum et hoc gemmam. Quis
tamen invenerit annulum ipse in 33 ait omnino ignorari.

3   Constat veteres, ut idem autor est, ferreo annulo esse usos, et,
ut 3 *Bello Punico* Appianus ait, omnes praeter tribunos usurpasse.
Ac longo certe tempore ne Senatum quidem Romanum habuisse
aureos manifestum est, tam sero inventi sunt. Qui in eodem libro
inquit: Nec Iliacis temporibus ullos fuisse annulos video. Nusquam certe Homerus dicit cum et codicillos missitatos epistola-

324

As Prometheus, chained to a cliff in Scythia,
Fed the relentless bird his generous breast.

To make his peace with Jupiter, Prometheus later used this device:
By chance, Jupiter had seen the beautiful Thetis and fell passionately in love with her. When the Fates learned of this — their fore-
sight never fails — they prophesied that the son of him who joined
her in marriage would far surpass his father in fame. They say that
when Prometheus happened to learn of this, he made it known to
Jupiter, who put aside all thought of Thetis because he feared retaliation — in other words, that he might suffer from his son what
he himself had done to his father Saturn. Wishing not to seem
ungrateful to Prometheus, Jupiter freed him from his chains. And
to perpetuate the memory of his liberation, he encircled the finger
nearest the little finger of his left hand with a ring made of two
objects — the rock to which he had been bound and the iron of
which the chain was made.

This was the first invention of a ring with a jewel, but in book   2
37 Pliny understands the story well enough and calls it a myth,
saying: The myths tell us that it came from a cliff in the Caucasus,
a risky interpretation of the chains of Prometheus; a piece of the
rock was first set in iron and put round his finger, the one making
a ring, the other a jewel. He says in book 33, however, that the real
inventor of the ring is altogether unknown.

According to the same source, we know that the ancients used   3
iron rings, and, as Appian says in book 3 of the *Punic War*, everyone beyond the rank of tribune made use of them. At any rate,
since gold rings were invented so late, it is clear that not even the
Roman Senate had them. Pliny in the same book says: I observe
that there were no rings in the time of Troy. Certainly, Homer nowhere speaks of them even though he gives evidence of little notes
sent about like letters and of clothes tightly packed along with ves-

rum gratia indicet et conditas arte vestes ac vasa aurea argenteaque, et ea colligata nodi non annuli nota. Haec ille.

4   At in Genesis libro, capite 38, patet Plinium non investigasse annulorum vetustatem. Ibi enim legimus Iudam filium Iacob rem habuisse cum Thamar nuru sua, et id fecisse imprudentem, quod mulier mutato vestitu personam dissimulaverit; ac illi promisisse munus fideique servandae pignus dedisse annulum et armillas.

5   Item Iosephus cum in 3 *Antiquitatum* de vestibus sacerdotum meminit quas Moses constituerat (qui, ut saepius ex testimonio Eusebii ostendimus, fuit ante CCCL et eo amplius annos quam est gestum bellum Troianum) annulis etiam in vestibus aliisque operibus veteres Hebraeos Iliacis temporibus esse usos sic scribens testatur: Ad haec autem, inquit, tertio induitur indumento quod dicitur Ephot. Fit enim hoc modo ut sit textus eius magnitudine cubiti de cunctis coloribus auroque variatis, amplectens omnem pectoris locum. Et infra: Unitur Ephot cum rationali annulis aureis per circulos singulos sub aequalitate commissis per vittam hyacinthinam quae immittitur pro ligaturis et consertionibus alterutris annulorum. Et deinde subiungit: Cum ergo per se illi quos diximus annuli sint infirmi nec possint pondus lapidum sustinere, alii duo maiores, et reliqua. Et cum de mensa loquitur, quam idem Moses fecerat, ait: Et per singulos eius pedes superiore labio erant annuli per quos vectes deaurati mittebantur. Idem testimonio est iam id temporis gemmas coepisse esse preciosas ac celebres, cum dicat Ephot (quod nos superhumerale vocamus, prout infra dicetur cum de nostrorum sacerdotum indumentis sermo fiet) habuisse in utroque humero duos lapides onyches (vel, ut alii volunt, smaragdos) et rationale duodecim fuisse ornatum lapillis. Hinc igitur — hoc est, ab Hebraeis — si antea non fuerit annulorum

sels of gold and silver, all of them tied together and sealed with a knot rather than a ring. This much from Pliny.

But from Genesis 38 it appears that Pliny did not realize how 4 old rings are. There we read that Jacob's son, Judah, had relations with his daughter-in-law, Thamar, and did so unawares, for the woman had changed clothing and disguised herself; he promised her a reward, giving her a ring and bracelets as a pledge that he would keep his word.

In book 3 of the *Antiquities*, speaking of the priestly vestments 5 ordained by Moses (who lived 350 years or more before the Trojan War was fought, as we have often shown from the testimony of Eusebius), Josephus testifies that the ancient Hebrews in Trojan times used rings even in their clothing and other handiwork, writing as follows: On top of these came a third garment called an ephot, he says. They make it a cubit in size and of a multicolored weave with gold worked into it, enclosing the whole area of the breast. And further on: The ephot is joined to the breastplate by gold rings connected to each of an equal number of circles with a hyacinth-colored band put through the rings to tie them together and bind them. And then he adds: Since the rings we mentioned were too weak to support the weight of the stones by themselves, two larger ones, . . . and so on. And when he describes the table, which Moses also made, he says: For each of the feet there were rings on the upper lip through which gilded poles were passed. There is evidence in the same author that jewels had already come to be valued and honored in those days, for he says that on each shoulder the ephot (which we call the superhumeral, as will be explained below in discussing the garments of our priests) had two onyx stones (or emeralds, as others would have it) and that the breastplate was decorated with twelve precious stones. Thus, we may believe that the use of rings and jewels came from this source, if not from an earlier—from the Hebrews, that is—though the

gemmarumque usum fluxisse credamus licet, eorum tamen veluti multarum quoque rerum obliteratis certis autoribus.

6   Macrobius autem libro *Saturnalium* 7 inquit: Veteres non ornatus sed signandi causa annulum secum circumferebant. Unde nec plus habere quam unum licebat, nec cuiquam nisi libero. Et imprimebatur sculptura materiae annuli, sive ex ferro sive ex auro foret. Postea usus luxuriantis aetatis signacula preciosis gemmis coepit insculpere, et haec certatim omnis imitatio lacessivit ut homines aliquanto studiosius lapides pretiosos requirerent. Hinc factum est ut annulus in digito qui minimo proximus est sinistrae manus gestaretur ne pretiosi lapides — est enim haec manus ociosior — frangerentur. Vel ideo ille digitus, ut idem Macrobius ait, annulo coronatur quia ab eo nervus quidam ad cor pertinet. Deinde, teste Plinio libro 33, gemmas violari nefas putarunt, ac ne quis annulis amplius signaret solidas gemmas addiderunt. Annuli insuper, ut hoc quoque ponam, apud Romanos distinxerunt alterum ordinem — id est, equestrem, cuius ipsi annuli notae erant — a plebe, ut semel coeperunt esse celebres, sicut tunica ab annulis Senatum tantum.

: XXII :

De origine vitri et electri, et quis primus invenerit
minium, et myrrhina in urbem asportaverit
et de crystallo.

1   Quoniam Plinius libro *Naturalis historiae* 36 de vitri origine eleganter scribit, eius ideo verba ponam, quae sunt: Pars est Syriae quae Phoenice vocatur finitima Iudaeae, intra montis Carmeli radices

exact inventors of them, as of so many other things, have been erased from memory.

In book 7 of the *Saturnalia*, however, Macrobius says that the rings that the ancients carried round with them were signets, not ornaments. No one was allowed more than one ring, therefore, and only a free man could wear one. In the metal of the ring, be it iron or gold, a design was engraved. Next an extravagant age began the practice of carving seals in precious jewels, and every imitation of the fashion was a further enticement, so that people went looking for precious stones all the more eagerly. Then, in order not to break the precious stones, it was decided that the ring should be worn on the finger nearest the little finger of the left hand — for this hand does less work. Or else, as Macrobius also says, they put a ring around that finger because a certain nerve leads from there to the heart. Later, according to Pliny in book 33, when they thought it criminal to do harm to jewels, they put solid jewels in rings so that no one would use them for sealing. Let me note as well that in Rome, once rings became common, they also distinguished another order — the equestrian, whose badge was the ring — from the people, just as the tunic made the Senate distinct from those who only had rings.

6

: XXII :

On the origin of glass and amber; who first discovered vermilion; who brought agate vases into the city; and on crystal.

Since Pliny gives so fine a description of glass in book 36 of the *Natural History*, I will set down his words here, as follows: A region of Syria called Phoenicia borders Judaea. There in the foothills of

1

paludem habens quae vocatur Candeboea; ex ea creditur nasci Belus amnis, quinque milium passuum spatio in mare profluens, iuxta Ptolemaidem: lentus hic currit, insalubris potu sed caerimoniis sacer, limosus, vado profundus, non nisi refuso mari harenas fatetur. Fluctibus enim volutatae nitescunt detritis sordibus. Nunc et a marino creduntur astringi morsu, non prius utiles. Quingentorum est passuum non amplius litoris spatium, idque tantum multa per secula gignendo fuit vitro. Fama est appulsa nave mercatorum nitri cum sparsi per litus epulas pararent, nec esset cortinis attollendis lapidum occasio, glebas nitri e nave subdidisse quibus accensis permista harena litoris translucentes nobilis liquoris fluxisse rivos. Et hanc fuisse originem vitri.

2   De hoc amne Iosephus etiam in 2 *De bello Iudaico* stadiis ait duobus a Ptolemaide Belus amnis distat, iuxta quem sepulchrum Memnonis est. Et vitrea in rotunda valle harena quam venti ex circumiectis iugis convehunt inexhausta seculis vi, sed ante omnia mirabili natura mutandi alia quoque in vitrum quae attigerit metalla.

3   Electrum, teste Diodoro libro 6, primo in Basilia insula inventum est, quae Scythiae supra Galatiam opposita in Oceano est; in quam, ut idem ait, tempestas electrum plurimum eiicit nulla alia in parte orbis repertum. Nec me praeterit fabulas ex lachrymis sororum Phaethontis fieri tradere. Sed de electro, id est, succino variae sunt scriptorum opiniones, quas Plinius libro *Naturalis historiae* ultimo late exequitur.

4   Minium quod in argentariis quoque reperitur inventum est, ut autor est Plinius in 33, a Callia Atheniense, initio sperante aurum posse excoqui harena rubente in metallis argenti. Id quod in Ephe-

Mt. Carmel is a swamp called Candebia, from which the river Belus is believed to rise and flow five miles to the sea, near Ptolemais. Deep, muddy, sluggish, unfit to drink but ritually sacred, it moves along showing no sign of sand except when the sea recedes. For when the waves roll the grains around and rub the dirt away, they become shiny. And at this point the corrosive action of the sea is thought to compact them, before which they are useless. The extent of the beach is no more than half a mile, and in just that much space was glass produced for many centuries. The story goes that when a merchantman bearing natron beached here and the crew scattered along the shore to make their meals, there were no stones on which to rest their kettles. So they used lumps of natron from the ship instead, and when the sands of the shore mixed with the heated lumps of natron, shining streams of a strange, new liquid flowed forth. This was the origin of glass.

Josephus also speaks of this river in book 2 of the *Jewish War*. 2 The river Belus lies two stadia from Ptolemais, he says, and near it is the tomb of Memnon. In its rounded valley occurs a glassy sand that the winds carry there from surrounding ridges; over the centuries its supply has remained unexhausted—and, more important, its strange power to change other minerals that it touches into glass.

Amber, according to Diodorus Siculus in book [5], was first 3 discovered on the island of Basileia, which is opposite Scythia in the Ocean north of Galatia; there, as Diodorus says, storms cast ashore an abundance of amber, found nowhere else in the world. I will not fail to mention the tale that it comes from the tears of Phaeton's sisters. But on the topic of amber or resin the views of the authorities differ; Pliny treats them fully in the final book of the *Natural History*.

The cinnabar also found in silver mines was discovered, accord- 4 ing to Pliny in book 33, by Callias of Athens, who hoped at first that he could melt gold out of the reddish sand of silver mines.

siorum agris Vitruvio libro 7 *Architecturae* repertum placet. At minium priscis Romanis sacrum fuisse constat, quare Iovis simulacri faciem diebus festis minio illini solitam—triumphantiumque corpora, ac sic Camillum triumphasse, idem Plinius testatur. Myrrhina quae, teste Plinio Oriens mittit (est enim humor sub terra calore densatus) Pompeius Magnus primo in triumpho quem de piratis duxit in urbem invexit.

5   De crystallo cum in plerisque locis reperiatur nullo huius rei ab initio inventore prodito, non habeo quicquam dicere, nisi quod Plinius libro ultimo *Naturalis historiae* prodit crystallum gigni gelu vehementiore concreto, nec aliubi certe reperiri nisi ubi maxime hybernae nives rigent, et glaciem denique esse. Quod Solinus falsum esse probat. Nam si ita foret, inquit, nec Alabanda Asiae nec Cyprus insula hanc materiam procrearent quibus regionibus citatissimus calor est. Verum hoc significantius a Diodoro in 3 declaratur, sic scribente: Crystallus enim lapis ex aqua oritur pura congelata, non quidem a frigore sed divi caloris vi qua duritiem servet variosque suscipiat colores.

Vitruvius says in book 7 *On Architecture* that it was discovered in the region of Ephesus. Vermilion was sacred to the ancient Romans, as is well known, for on feast-days they used to rub vermilion on the face of Jupiter's statue—also on the bodies of those holding triumph, as Camillus did in his triumph, so Pliny likewise testifies. It was the East, says Pliny, that sent us the agate vases (formed of a liquid thickened by heat beneath the earth) that Pompey the Great first brought to the city in the triumph held for his victory over the pirates.

Since crystal is found in many places and no one is known to be 5 its original inventor, I have nothing to say about it, except that Pliny in the last book of the *Natural History* reports that especially hard freezing produces crystal; that it is definitely not found in any place except where the winter snows become very hard; and, finally, that it is made of ice. Solinus proves this false. If it were true, he says, neither Alabanda in Asia nor the isle of Cyprus would produce this substance since the heat in these places is quite intense. Diodorus explains this more clearly in book [2], writing: The mineral crystal comes from the hardening of pure water—not from cold, however, but from the power of a sacred warmth whereby it preserves its hardness and takes on various colors.

: XXIII :

De origine simulacrorum et qui primi statuas posuerint;
et Graecos contrario Romanorum more eas non velare;
et de usu incendendi thus cereosque ad ipsas statuas, et qui
primi thus vendere coeperint; item quaedam memoratu
digna de imagine Magni Alexandri.

1 Ut posset eorum memoria retineri qui vel morte subtracti vel absentia separati essent, idcirco ab hominibus, ut nemo sane ambigit, fingendarum similitudinum ratio inventa est. Quo fit ut cum Deus ubique praesens sit, nihil a principio post homines natos stultius visum sit quam eius simulacrum fingere. Quam ob rem Moses, vir sanctus et innocens ac sapientissimus, autore Iosepho in 1 *Contra Appionem* et in 17 *Antiquitatum*, suis legibus prohibuit omnino simulacrum fieri aut in templo poni. Ex quo cum Caius princeps Petronium legatum in Syriam misisset eique mandasset ut omni ope modisque omnibus curaret suum simulacrum in templo Hierosolymis erigendum, Iudaei, ne patrias leges frangerent, adeo resistere coeperunt ut iamiam ad arma ventum esset nisi, ut idem testis est libro 18 *Antiquitatum*, Agrippa Iudaeorum rex a Caio impetrasset ne huiusmodi statua in templo poneretur.

2 Apud Seres etiam, sicut tradit Eusebius libro *De praeparatione evangelica* 6, lege exceptum erat ne simulacra colerentur. In Romanorum quoque templis Clemens ait ex decreto Numae, Mosaica dogmata penitus aemulati, annis C atque LXX ab urbe condita nullam imaginem neque fictam neque pictam esse conspectam. Asserit idem et Plutarchus in *Vita Numae*. Persae itidem, teste Herodoto libro 1 et Strabone 15 *Geographiae*, statuas non extruebant.

: XXIII :

On the origin of effigies and who first set up statues; that the Greeks, contrary to the practice of the Romans, did not drape them; on the custom of burning incense and candles before these statues; who first began the selling of incense; and certain memorable facts about the image of Alexander the Great.

No one doubts that people first devised a way of making like- 1 nesses in order to preserve the memory of those removed by death or separated by absence. But since God is everywhere present, nothing in the course of human history seems more foolish than representing God by an effigy. This was why the laws of Moses, who was holy and innocent and very wise, absolutely forbade making an effigy or erecting one in the Temple, according to Josephus in book 1 *Against Apion* and book 17 of the *Antiquities*. And so when the Emperor Caius sent Petronius as legate to Syria and ordered him to use all ways and means to see that his effigy was set up in the Temple in Jerusalem, the Jews, to avoid breaking the laws of their fathers, began a resistance that would have led eventually to war (our source is the same, book 18 of the *Antiquities*) had not Agrippa, king of the Jews, obtained permission from Caius not to put such a statue in the Temple.

According to Eusebius in book 6 of the *Preparation for the Gospel*, 2 the law of the Chinese also specified that effigies were not to be worshipped. And Clement says that no image, painted or carved, was to be seen in the temples of the Romans for 170 years after the founding of the city; this was by a decree of Numa, who copied directly from the teachings of Moses. Plutarch makes the same point in his *Life of Numa*. The Persians likewise made no statues, according to Herodotus in book 1 and Strabo in book 15 of the *Ge-*

Verum ut ne nostri peccasse videantur qui postremo colendarum imaginum institutum admiserunt alibi causam ponemus.

3   Sed unde simulacra fingendi usus profectus sit non facile inter autores convenit. Macrobius enim ab Hercule autumat, qui libro *Saturnalium* 1 Epicadus — inquit — refert Herculem, occiso Geryone, cum victor per Italiam armenta duxisset, Ponte qui nunc Sublicius dicitur, ad tempus instructo, hominum simulacra pro numero sociorum quos casu peregrinationis amisisset in fluvium demisisse ut aqua secunda in mare devecta pro corporibus demortuorum veluti patriis sedibus redderentur. Et inde usum talia simulacra fingendi inter sacra mansisse. Verum deinde sibi magis placere ait hunc morem a Pelasgis fluxisse.

4   Sane illi, teste Dionysio Halicarnasseo in 1 *Annalium Romanorum*, postquam diu errabundi in Latium venerant in lacu Cutuliensi enatam insulam deprehenderunt, decima praedae secundum responsum Apollini consecrata erectisque Diti sacello et Saturno ara, illum humanis capitibus hunc virorum victimis placare se existimabant propter oraculum in quo erat — Et capita inferno et patri transmittite lumen — Saturni sacra Saturnalia nominantes. Post haec Herculem ferunt cum Geryonis pecore per Italiam reventem suasisse illorum posteris ut faustis sacrificiis infausta mutarent, offerentes Diti non hominum capita sed oscilla, id est, parva ora ad humanam figuram formata, et Saturni aras non mactatis viris sed accensis cereis excolentes. Inde fuit consuetudo ut et cerei Saturnalibus mitterentur et sigilla, hoc est, oscilla arte fictili fingerentur.

5   Alii, autore Diodoro libro 4, dicunt Aethiopes simulacrorum usum primum invenisse et ab eis dein Aegyptios accepisse. Sed

ography. Elsewhere we shall show why it should not be seen as sinful that our people later allowed the practice of honoring statues.

The origin of the custom of making effigies is not a settled   3
question among the authorities. Macrobius maintains that it came
from Hercules, for in book 1 of the *Saturnalia* he cites the report of
Epicadus on Hercules' exploits after he killed Geryon: After the
victor had led his herds through Italy, he threw effigies of men into
the river from the structure now called the pile-bridge, which had
been built for the occasion; they were equal in number to the companions lost as casualties in his wanderings, and the water flowing
down to the sea would return them to their native lands — replacing the bodies of the dead, as it were. Since then the practice of
making such effigies has survived as a religious rite. But then
Macrobius says that he believes this custom came down from the
Pelasgians instead.

These Pelasgians, according to Dionysius of Halicarnassus in   4
book 1 of the *Roman Annals,* came into Latium after wandering for
a long time and saw an island that had emerged in Lake Cutulia.
Obeying an oracle, they consecrated a tenth of their booty to
Apollo and set up a shrine for Dis and an altar for Saturn, thinking to appease the former with human heads and the latter with
human sacrifices because of what was in the oracle — Yield up
heads to the underworld and light to the father. This they called
the Saturnalia, the rites of Saturn. Some say that Hercules, returning later through Italy with Geryon's cattle, convinced their
descendants to change these baleful sacrifices for better, to offer
Dis not human heads but little masks or figurines shaped like the
face of a man, and to deck Saturn's altars with burning candles instead of slaughtered men. From this came the custom of sending
candles for the Saturnalia and of making little earthenware figures
or masks.

Others, according to Diodorus in book [3], say that the Ethio-   5
pians first discovered the use of effigies and that the Egyptians

Lactantius Firmianus a Prometheo manasse huiusmodi usum tradit libro *Divinarum institutionum* 2 cum inquit: Verum quia poetas dixeram non omnino mentiri solere sed figuris involvere et obscurare quae dicant, non dico esse mentitos, sed primum omnium Prometheum simulacrum hominis formasse de pingui et molli luto ab eoque natam esse primo artem statuas et simulacra fingendi. Haec ille.

6   Reperimus tamen longe ante Prometheum, qui teste Eusebio post Ogygium diluvium in Attica fuit, simulacrorum usum fuisse. Nam Rachel, teste Iosepho in 1 *Antiquitatum,* cum Iacob eius vir e Mesopotamia a Laban socero aufugisset, simulacra deorum furata est. Eusebius etiam ex testimonio Plutarchi in 3 *De evangelica praeparatione* simulacrorum fictionem esse antiquissimam comprobat.

7   Sic ut si eorum originem accurate exquiramus, facile invenerimus Deum ipsum primum demonstrasse modum fingendarum similitudinum, qui ut sui intelligentiam rudes rerum coelestium homines a principio doceret, sibi humana membra assumpsit ut quasi oculis occurreret qualis esset. Ait enim (ut est in Genesis libro, capite 18): Clamor Sodomorum et Gomorrhae multiplicatus est, et peccatum eorum aggravatum est nimis. Descendam et videbo utrum clamorem qui venit ad me opere compleverint. Idem Exodo capite 7: Immittam manum meam super Aegyptum. Descendere hic et videre ac immittere manum est habentis pedes, oculos et manum. Quin et propheta, ut planius personam Dei nobis ostendat, dat ei aures et faciem, Psalmo 16 canens: Auribus percipe orationem meam. Et Psalmo 50: Averte faciem tuam a peccatis meis. At Esaias integrum dat corpus cum capite 6 inquit: Vidi dominum sedentem super solium.

8   Formulam igitur fingendae similitudinis Dei, quo eius memoriam facilius animo complecteremur, ipse Deus nobis praemonstravit. Proinde homo, qui suopte ingenio paratus est ad imitan-

later took it over from them. But in book 2 of the *Divine Institutes*, Lactantius Firmianus teaches that this custom came down from Prometheus: Since I have said that the poets are not complete and habitual liars, he writes, but that they obscure the tales they tell and wrap them in figures, I do not claim that they have lied but that Prometheus first of all formed the effigy of a man in thick, soft clay, from which event the art of making statues and effigies first arose. This much from Lactantius.

But we have found that effigies were used long before Prome-   6
theus, who lived in Attica after the flood of Ogygus, according to Eusebius. For according to Josephus in book 1 of the *Antiquities*, when Rachel's husband Jacob fled from Mesopotamia and from Laban, his father-in-law, she stole the effigies of his gods. Citing Plutarch, Eusebius also proves in book 3 of the *Preparation for the Gospel* that the making of effigies is very old.

Thus, if we look carefully into their origin, we shall soon find   7
that God himself first showed how to make likenesses. In order to teach primitive people from the start to understand heavenly matters, God took on human features so that something of what he is like might meet the eye. For he says (as it appears in the book of Genesis, chapter 18): The noise of Sodom and Gomorrah has increased, and their sin has grown too heavy. I will go down and see what the reason is for all the noise that has come to me. The same in Exodus, chapter 7: I will direct my hand against Egypt. Here, 'go down' and 'see' and 'direct the hand' imply having feet, eyes and a hand. In order to show us the person of God more clearly, the prophet actually gives him ears and a face, singing in Psalm [17]: Hear my prayer with your ears. And in Psalm [51]: Turn your face from my sins. Isaiah even gives him a whole body when in chapter 6 he says: I saw the Lord sitting on a throne.

Therefore God himself has given us reason to represent him   8
with a likeness so that we can get a better mental grasp and remember him. And this is why people, having the native ability to

dum si quid sit quod ad ipsius disciplinam, contemplationem delectationemque attineat, Dei memoriae retinendae gratia quam prudentissime ab initio ipsius Dei simulacrum sibi finxit, ut qui intelligebat oportere se eum (quemadmodum Christus apud Marcum testatur) diligere ex toto corde suo, et ex tota intelligentia, et ex tota anima et ex totis viribus. Idcirco putavit se diligentius facturum officium si ob oculos exemplar continenter haberet. Atque istaec vera simulacrorum origo.

9   Sed caetera prosequamur. Romae, teste Plinio in 34, simulacrum ex aere factum Cereris primum constat ex peculio Spurii Cassii, quem regnum affectantem pater ipsius interemerat. Postea a diis ad homines statuae transierunt, et id quidem cum excellentium virorum memoriae perpetuandae tum virtutis imitandae causa, quod Sallustius in initio sui *Iugurthini* plene testificatur, scribens: Nam saepe audivi Quintum Maximum, Publium Scipionem praeterea civitatis nostrae praeclaros viros solitos ita dicere: Cum maiorum imagines intuerentur, vehementissime sibi animum ad virtutem accendi, scilicet non ceram illam neque figuram tantam vim in sese habere sed memoria rerum gestarum eam flammam egregiis viris in pectore crescere neque prius sedari quam virtus eorum famam atque gloriam adaequaverit. Quare Athenienses primi statuas publice posuisse Harmodio et Aristogitoni tyrannicidis dicuntur — id quod haud prorsus Plinius se scire affirmat.

10   Statuam auream et solidam primus omnium Gorgias Leontinus Delphis in templo sibi posuit LXX circiter olympiade. Quamvis, ut idem ait, statua ex auro solida (quam Graeci *holosphyraton* vocant) omnium prima in templo Anaitidis posita dicatur. Argenteam quidam primam fuisse volunt quam sibi fecit Pharnaces, quam Magnus Pompeius in triumphis transtulit, autor Plinius. In Italia, teste Valerio Maximo libro 2, Manius Attilius Glabrio primus sta-

copy whatever helps them learn, observe and enjoy, very wisely made themselves effigies of God from the first and as a way of keeping God's memory, for they understood (as Christ is our witness in Mark) that one should love God with his whole heart, whole mind, whole soul and strength. And they thought they could do their duty better with a likeness constantly before their eyes. This is the true origin of effigies.

But we should move on to other topics. A Ceres funded from 9 the estate of Spurius Cassius, killed by his own father when he sought the throne, was the first bronze statue made in Rome: this is well known, according to Pliny in book 34. Statues of the gods then became statues of humans, to preserve the memory of outstanding men and to imitate their virtues. Sallust gives abundant witness to this in the beginning of his book *Jugurthan War*, writing: I have often heard what Quintus Maximus, Publius Scipio and other distinguished men of our city used to say: that gazing on the likenesses of their ancestors was the strongest spark for a valorous spirit, not that the wax or its shape had so much power over them but that in the hearts of the best men the memory of great deeds fuels a fire which is not damped until their valor wins its equal share of fame and glory. This is why the Athenians are said to have set up their first public statues for the tyrannicides, Harmodius and Aristogeiton — something of which Pliny does not claim to be entirely sure.

Gorgias of Leontini was the first to set up a solid statue of gold 10 for himself, in the temple of Delphi around olympiad 70, though Pliny also mentions that the very first solid statue of beaten gold (the Greeks call them *whole-hammered*) is said to have been set up in the temple of Anaitis. Some say that the first silver statue was the one Pharnaces had made of himself; Pompey the Great imported it for his triumphs, according to Pliny. In Italy, according to Valerius Maximus in book 2, Manius Attilius Glabrio set up the

tuam equestrem auream patri suo posuit. Fiebant etiam ex aere, ebure, ligno et marmore.

11   Romanis antiquitus, quod non est praetereundum, statuas velare, contra Graecis nudas ponere mos fuit. Illi item solebant ad eas thus et cereos incendere, testis Cicero qui libro 3 *Officiorum* de statuis Caio Mario a multitudine positis ita scribit: Omnibus vicis statuae factae sunt, et ad eas thus et cerei. Quem morem nos retinemus, id quod non fuerat olim, autore Plinio libro 13, ubi inquit: Iliacis temporibus thure non supplicabatur. Thus autem in Arabia nascitur, cuius alio vecti mercaturam primi Arabum Minaei, velut idem scribit, fecerunt.

12   In hac statuaria arte plurimi olim floruerunt, quos Plinius in 34 luculenter explicat. Ante omnes tamen Phidiam Atheniensem magnis ad coelum fert laudibus, de quo Fabius itidem libro 12 meminit.

13   Occurrit hic memorandum uti Romae Macrianorum familia solenne semper habuit ut Alexandrum Magnum — viri in auro et argento, mulieres in reticulis et annulis — exculptum gestarent quod, sicut Iulius Capitolinus in vita triginta tyrannorum testatur, diceretur iuvari in omni actu suo qui Alexandrum sculptum aut auro aut argento gestaret. Quare, ut opinor, Augustus Caesar in signandis epistolis Magni etiam Alexandri imagine diu usus est, autor Tranquillus.

first gold equestrian statue for his father. Statues were also made of bronze, ivory, wood and marble.

It should not be omitted that in ancient times the Roman prac- 11 tice was to set up their statues draped, while the Greeks left theirs nude. The Romans also used to burn incense and candles before their statues, as Cicero testifies in book 3 *On Duties*, writing as follows of the statues that the mob set up for Caius Marius: They made statues for every neighborhood, and they brought incense and candles to them. This is a custom that we keep, but once it was not so, according to Pliny, who says in book 13 that in the days of Troy they did not use incense when praying. Incense comes from Arabia, and the first to carry it abroad and sell it were the Arab Minaei, as Pliny also writes.

Many once won fame in this art of sculpture; Pliny gives a 12 splendid account of them in book 34. But the one that he most praises to the skies is Phidias of Athens, and Quintilian also mentions Phidias in book 12.

Here it seems proper to note a practice always kept by the fam- 13 ily of the Macriani in Rome. They wore a carved figure of Alexander the Great — the men in gold and silver, the women in hair-nets and rings — because, as Julius Capitolinus says in his life of the Thirty Tyrants, whoever wore Alexander's likeness carved in gold or silver was said to be helped in his every deed. I believe this is why Augustus Caesar also used a likeness of Alexander for a long time in sealing his letters, according to Suetonius.

: XXIV :

De origine picturae et quis primus colores invenerit aut penicillo pinxerit.

1   Proximum est ut post statuariam artem de picturae initiis primum dicatur, quando illa effigies rerum lignis, ebure, metallis, ut dictum est, fingit, haec imagines colorum varietate aut lineamentis quibusdam similitudines reddens facit.

2   Picturam itaque, teste Plinio libro 7, Gyges Lydius omnium primus invenit in Aegypto, in Graecia vero Pyrrhus Daedali cognatus, ut Aristoteli placet, ut Theophrasto Polygnotus Atheniensis. Quod haudquaquam idem Plinius libro 35, capite 9, approbare videtur, sic scribens: Sicut Polygnotus Thasius, qui primus mulieres lucida veste pinxit, capita earum mitris versicoloribus operuit, plurimumque picturae primus contulit, siquidem instituit os adaperire dentes ostendere, vultum ab antiquo rigore variare. Incerta igitur de picturae initiis quaestio est, nam et Aegyptii, eodem Plinio teste, ante sex milia annorum apud se inventam quam in Graeciam transiret affirmant. Graeci autem alii apud Sicyonios, alii apud Corinthios repertam dicunt.

3   Omnes ab umbra hominis lineis circunducta, quod Fabius aperte testatur in 10, dicens: Non esset pictura nisi quae lineas modo extremas umbrae quam corpora in sole fecissent circunscriberet. Ac si omnia percenseas, nulla sit ars qualis inventa est nec intra initium stetit. Quintilianus hactenus.

4   Talis itaque prima fuit pictura. Altera singulis coloribus postea operosior inventa est duratque talis etiamnum. Linearis, ut Plinius in 35 tradit, a Philocle Aegyptio vel a Cleanthe Corinthio inventa

: XXIV :

On the origin of painting; who invented colors; and who first used the brush.

Next after the art of sculpture, something should first be said 1
about the origins of painting, seeing that the one shapes copies of
things in wood, ivory and metal, as we have explained, while the
other makes pictures by rendering likenesses with a mixture of
colors or a variety of lines.

Gyges the Lydian was the first to invent painting in Egypt, ac- 2
cording to Pliny in book 7, but in Greece it was Pyrrhus, a relative
of Daedalus, as Aristotle tells it, though Theophrastus says it was
Polygnotus, an Athenian. Pliny does not agree at all, writing in
chapter 9 of book 35 as follows: Polygnotus of Thasos, who first
painted women in transparent garments and covered their heads
with multicolored headbands, first achieved great things in painting, since it was he who began opening the mouths of his subjects
to show their teeth, thus moving away from the earlier stiffness of
expression. The question of painting's origin thus remains unset-
tled, for the Egyptians also claim (again, see Pliny) that they invented painting six thousand years before it came to Greece. But
some Greeks claim that the Sicyonians discovered it, while others
say it was the Corinthians.

All agree it was done by tracing the outline of someone's 3
shadow, a fact to which Quintilian clearly testifies in book 10, writing: There would be no art of painting but the drawing of lines
around the edges of shadows made by bodies standing in the sun.
Examine all the arts, and you will find that none has stood still,
remaining as it was when invented. This much from Quintilian.

Such was the original art of painting. Another type, much more 4
elaborate in its use of a various colors, was discovered later and

est. Primi eam Ardices Corinthius et Telephanes Sicyonius exercuerunt, sine ullo etiam colore. Cleophantus Corinthius colores
invenit. Idem autor. Penicillo gloriam primus Apollodorus Atheniensis contulit. In hac illustres fuerunt Timagoras Chalcidensis
Pythis, deinde Polygnotus, Aglaophon, alii quoque post hos, de
quibus Plinius et Fabius Quintilianus in 12 affatim scribunt, quos
studio brevitatis omitto, cum praesertim tale minime sit instituti
operis munus.

5   Non silebo tamen de cive meo, qui nobis sua industria et ingenio picturam velut de integro in praesentia restituit, atque illos qui
in ea olim maxime claruere naviter vel arte refert vel peritia aequat,
adeo proprios ducit de coloribus vultus. Is est Raphael, cognomine
Sanctus, unde eius quoque metiri posses et mores et vitam.

: XXV :

*De primis plastices inventoribus, et quis rotam
figulariam repererit.*

1   Convenit picturae contexere plasticen—hoc est, figulinam artem—quae ex terra similitudines itidem fingit. Hanc, ut Plinius in
7 ait, Choroebus Atheniensis invenit, sed idem libro 35 Dibutadi
hoc assignat, dicens: Dibutades Sicyonius figulus primus invenit
Corinthi, filiae opera, quae capta amore iuvenis, illo abeunte per-
egre umbram ex facie eius ad lucernam in pariete lineis circun-
scripsit, quibus pater eius impressa argilla typum fecit, et cum

still exists in the same form. Line-drawing, as Pliny notes in book 35, was invented either by Philocles the Egyptian or by Cleanthes of Corinth. First to practice this art were Ardices of Corinth and Telephanes of Sicyon, neither of them yet using color. The Corinthian Cleophantus invented colors. We learn this from the same author. Apollodorus of Athens was the first to make the paintbrush glorious. At the Pythian festival Timagoras of Chalcis won fame for it, as Polygnotus and Aglaophon did later, and others followed them. Pliny and Quintilian have plenty to say about them that we omit in our zeal for brevity, especially since it is not our task in the present work.

But I will not be silent about my townsman, whose energy and 5 genius have wholly restored the art of painting to us today, whose skill so much recalls those who once excelled in this art, whose knowledge equals theirs, so well does he draw real faces out of his colors. I mean Raphael, called Sanzio, whose life and conduct you can measure by his name.

: XXV :

On the first inventors of ceramics, and who devised the potter's wheel.

To connect ceramics — the potter's art — with painting is proper 1 since ceramics also makes images out of earth. Pliny says in book 7 that Choroebus of Athens invented it, but he assigns it to Dibutades in book 35, saying: a Sicyonian potter named Dibutades invented it in Corinth, thanks to his daughter. She had fallen in love with a young man who was leaving home, so she traced the shadow cast by his face in lamplight on a wall. Then her father

caeteris fictilibus induratum igni proposuit, eumque servatum in nymphaeo donec Corinthum Mummius everteret tradunt.

2   Sunt qui in Samo primos omnium plasticen invenisse Rhoecum et Theodorum prodant, Demaratumque Corinthium profugum — qui Tarquinium Priscum populi terrarum principis regem in Hetruria genuit — comitatos fictores Euchiram et Eugrammum, et ab iis Italiae deinde traditam plasticen. E proplastice, id est, forma quae ad fingenda alia opera adhibetur, effigiem formare primus invenit Lysistratus Sicyonius, frater Lysippi. Idem hominis figuram gypso e facie ipsa primus omnium expressit. Sic res usque eo crevit ut nulla signa statuaeve sine argilla fierent, quo apparet antiquiorem hanc fuisse scientiam quam fundendi aeris. Haec ex Plinio. Hinc insuper plurima vasorum fictilium genera reperta sunt, quae modo humanae vitae usui sunt.

3   Rotam figulariam, autore Ephoro ut ait Strabo libro 7 *Geographiae* et Laertio libro 1 et Plinio in 7, Anacharsis Scythes philosophus primus invenit, in quo tamen ipse Strabo Ephorum arguit: Haec, inquit, ipsa autem loquor aperte, haud ignarus quod hic ipse non omnia verissime proferat, et illud praecipue de Anacharside. Nam quomodo rota ipsa ex eius inventione est quam Homerus antiquior illo noverit? *Ceu figulus cui dextra rotam quatit ocyus aptam*, et reliqua. Hyperbios Corinthius, ut alii volunt, invenit. Diodorus vero libro 5 dicit Talum Daedali sororis filium reperisse. Figuli autem, teste Plinio, laudatissimi fuere Dimophilus et Gorgasus.

LIBRI SECUNDI FINIS.

pressed clay into the tracing and made a relief, putting it with other clay objects in the fire to harden. They say it was preserved in the Nymphaeum until Mummius destroyed Corinth.

There are those who would claim that Rhoecus and Theodorus 2 first invented ceramics in Samos, that when Demaratus fled Corinth — the one who in Etruria begot Tarquinius Priscus, king of the chief nation of the earth — the potters Euchiras and Eugrammus were among his companions, and that ceramics came to Italy with them. Lysistratus of Sicyon, brother of Lysippus, first formed a likeness from a mold, which is a form used for shaping other pieces. He was also the first to take a person's likeness in plaster directly from the face. Such work progressed until no figure or statue was made without clay, whence it is clear that this craft is older than the casting of bronze. Pliny tells us these things. Moreover, a great variety of clay vessels was invented in this way, and their only purpose was to be useful for human living.

Pliny in book 7, Laertius in book 1 and Strabo in book 7 on 3 the authority of Ephorus tell us that the Scythian philosopher Anacharsis first invented the potter's wheel, yet in saying this Strabo himself criticizes Ephorus. I tell you this frankly, he says, knowing as I do that Ephorus does not always report things with the greatest accuracy, particularly this remark about Anacharsis. For how can this wheel be his invention when Homer knew of it and came long before him? . . . *as the potter's hand strikes the wheel made to run faster,* and so on. Others believe that Hyperbios of Corinth invented it. But in book [4] Diodorus says that it was Talus, son of the sister of Daedalus. Dimophilus and Gorgasus, according to Pliny, were potters of the highest reputation.

END OF BOOK II.

POLYDORI VERGILII URBINATIS
DE INVENTORIBUS RERUM
LIBER TERTIUS

: I :

*A quibus primum inventa agricultura, et quot ea
redundet bonis.*

1 Non sum equidem nescius quosdam fore qui vehementer dimira-
buntur nos postremo fere loco de inventoribus agriculturae aliquid
tradere distulisse, cum praesertim, uti Cicero in *Officialibus* libris
inquit, omnium rerum ex quibus aliquid exquiritur nihil sit agricultura melius, nil uberius, nihil dulcius, nihil homine libero dignius. Verum nec eo mihi succenseant quatenus hoc ipsum consulto vel, ut verius dicam, ex industria fecimus ut longo legentes
itinere defatigati novum tandem pastum sive, ut ita dixerim, nectar
offenderent quo vires recreare et veluti diutinam famem explere
possent. De huiusce igitur rei initiis hic commode dicemus — postquam demonstravero quantis eam laudibus iure ac merito praestantissimi autores efferant utpote quae multis abundat bonis.

2 Columella itaque in I *De re rustica* conquerens sui temporis mol-
litiem ait: At mehercule vera illa proles Romuli, assiduis venationi-
bus nec minus agrestibus operibus exercitata, firmissimis praeva-
luit corporibus ac militiam belli, cum res postulavit, facile sustinuit
durata pacis laboribus, semperque rusticam plebem urbanae prae-
posuit. Cato itidem *De agricultura* inquit: Fortissimi viri et milites
strenuissimi ex agricolis gignuntur, minimeque male cogitantes. Ex
quo, teste Cicerone *De senectute,* in agris senatores erant, ut Lucius
Quintius Cincinnatus qui dum agrum arabat renunciatus est dic-

BOOK III

: I :

*Who first discovered agriculture, and how many advantages
flow from it.*

I am by no means unaware that delaying any discussion of the in-   1
ventors of agriculture almost to the last will strike some as very
strange, especially since of all gainful pursuits none is better, none
more fruitful, none more pleasant, none worthier of a free person
than agriculture, as Cicero says in his books *On Duties*. But this
delay should annoy no one, for it was by choice or, more precisely, by design, so that my readers, wearied by their long journey,
might at last find some fresh nourishment—nectar to renew their
strength, so to speak—and satisfy their lasting hunger. I shall
speak of the origins of this practice here; then, in due course, I
shall show how much the foremost authors glorified it, as they
were right to do since its blessings are so abundant.

Columella, bewailing the softness of his age in book 1 *On Coun-*   2
try Life, says: The true stock of Romulus had strong and very powerful bodies, heaven knows, trained by constant hunting as well as
field work, and when the need arose they did their wartime service
easily because the labors of peace had hardened them, and they always preferred country folk to city people. Cato *On Agriculture* says
the same thing: From farmers come the strongest men and the
keenest soldiers, who never show malice. This is why senators
kept to their fields, according to Cicero *On Old Age*: Lucius Quintius Cincinnatus was called to be dictator while he was plowing a

tator, ut Curius et caeteri senes. Quare qui eos accersebant viatores nominati sunt.

3   Quid quod etiam, teste Plinio libro 18, agrum male colere censorium probrum iudicabatur? Atque, ut inquit Cato, quem virum bonum colonum dixissent amplissime laudasse existimabant? Et id sane quia (quemadmodum Cicero *Pro Roscio Amerino* docet) rustica vita parsimoniae, diligentiae, iustitiae magistra est, at urbana non item quam luxuries facile inficit. Ex luxuria necesse est existat avaritia, ex avaritia erumpat audacia, inde omnia maleficia gignantur.

4   Sed ne putes hoc tantum in romana republica contigisse, de cultura agri praecipere principale etiam, ut Plinius dicit, fuit apud exteros siquidem et reges fecere—Hiero, Philometor, Attalus, Archelaus. Unde non iniuria Xenophonti, quemadmodum testis est Marcus Tullius in *Catone*, nihil tam regale videbatur quam studium agri colendi. De laudibus hactenus!

5   Agriculturam primum omnium, teste Diodoro in 1, Osirim, qui et Dionysius dicitur, reperisse ferunt. Affirmat item Tibullus, ita scribens:

> Primus aratra manu solerti fecit Osiris,
>   Et teneram ferro sollicitavit humum.
> Primus inexpertae commisit semina terrae,
>   Pomaque non notis legit ab arboribus.

Sed hoc, ut opinor, apud Aegyptios tantummodo, sicut Triptolemus primus in Graecia et Asia, teste Iustino in 2, invenit, de quo Ovidius in 4 *Fastorum*:

> Iste quidem mortalis erit, sed primus arabit
>   Et seret et culta praemia tollet humo.

Et in Latio Saturnus, ut suo loco dicemus.

field, as were Curius and other elders as well. Those who fetched them were called travelers for this reason.

But why, according to Pliny in book 18, was it considered a misdeed within the jurisdiction of the censors to run a farm badly? Why did they think it the highest compliment to call a man a good farmer, as Cato says? Doubtless (as Cicero tells us in his *Defense of Roscius of Ameria*) because the country life teaches how to be just, thrifty and frugal, unlike life in the city, which luxury quickly corrupts. Inevitably, greed soon emerges from luxury, and from greed erupts impudence, thus begetting every wickedness.

Do not suppose, however, that such things happened only in the Roman state. Setting rules for agriculture was also a matter of the first importance for foreigners, as Pliny says, since even kings did it—Hiero, Philometor, Attalus, Archelaus. Thus it was fitting that Xenophon found nothing so kingly as an interest in agriculture, as Cicero is our witness in his *Cato*. But enough of praising!

According to Diodorus in book 1, they say that the first to discover agriculture was Osiris, also called Dionysius. Tibullus makes the same point, writing:

> The first plows Osiris built with expert hand
> And used iron to stir the tender soil,
> First trusted seeds to land untried,
> And gathered fruit from trees he did not know.

But this discovery was only for the Egyptians, I believe. Likewise, Triptolemus was first in Greece and Asia, according to Justinus in book 2 and book 4 of Ovid's *Fasti*:

> Mortal man he'll be, but first to plow and sow
> And turn a profit from the dirt.

And in Latium it was Saturn, as we shall explain in the proper place.

6   Sed omnium primam Cererem quae, uti Ciceroni libro 2 *De natura deorum* placet, a gerendis frugibus quasi Geres nominata est, mortales agriculturam docuisse testatur Vergilius in primo *Georgicorum*, sic scribens:

> Prima Ceres ferro mortales vertere terram
> Instituit.

Testatur et Ovidius libro 5 *Metamorphoseon:*

> Prima Ceres unco glebam dimovit aratro,
> Prima dedit fruges alimentaque mitia terris.

7   Verum haec haud scio quantum fide digna sint quando illud verius esse duco quod Iosephus in 1 *Antiquitatum* tradit. Dicit enim Cain Adam filium omnium primum comperisse terram colere primumque terrae terminos posuisse. Atque hoc agriculturae initium haud dubie fuit. Quapropter, ut dubium non est, ex illis quos commemoravimus deinceps agriculturam alios aliis primos monstrasse credere par est. Sed iam ad alia quae pertinent ad cultum agrorum transeamus.

: II :

*Quis primus mortalibus fruges et eas molendi aut
stercorandorum agrorum vel pinsendi frumenti usum
monstraverit; et boves aratro iunxerit aut ferramenta rustica
invenerit vel cribra diversi generis.*

1   Rerum naturam primum homines glandibus aluisse Plinius in prooemio 16 libri autor est. Item et Naso testatur in 1 *Metamorphoseon* dicens:

But of all these Ceres was first. Cicero's opinion in book 2 *On   6
the Nature of the Gods* is that her name was like Geres because she
gets the crops, and Vergil testifies in his first *Georgic* that she
taught agriculture to mortals:

Ceres first taught humankind to turn the earth
with iron.

As does Ovid in book 5 of the *Metamorphoses*:

Ceres was first to break the clods with crooked
plow, first gave fruits and sweet foods from earth.

I am not sure how far to trust these statements, however, for I   7
regard what Josephus reports in book 1 of the *Antiquities* as more
truthful. He says that Cain, Adam's son, first learned how to till
the earth and first set boundaries on it. This undoubtedly was the
beginning of agriculture. Therefore, since the matter is beyond
question, a fair conclusion is that those mentioned above were inventors of agriculture in various places after the original discovery.
But now let us move on to other topics pertaining to agriculture.

: II :

*Who first showed mortals the fruits of the earth, how to mill
them, how to manure the fields and how to grind the grain;
who first yoked oxen to a plow or invented farming tools or
sieves of various kinds.*

Nature first fed people on acorns, as Pliny tells us in the proem to   1
book 16, and Ovid makes the same claim in book 1 of the *Metamorphoses*:

Contentique cibis nullo cogente creatis,
Arbuteos foetus montanaque fraga legebant,
Cornaque et in duris haerentia mora rubetis,
Et quae deciderant patula Iovis arbore glandes.

Deinde inventum est frumentum. Vergilius in 1 *Georgicorum*:

cum iam glandes atque arbuta sacrae
Deficerent sylvae, et victum Dodona negaret.
Mox et frumentis labor additus.

Quod, ut Plinius libro 7 dicit, Ceres cum antea, velut dictum est, homines glande vescerentur invenit. Eadem et molere et conficere docuit in Attica, Italia et Sicilia ob id dea iudicata. Idem quoque Maro affirmat et Diodorus, volumine 6 scribens Cererem primam invenisse usum frumenti, quod forte inter alias herbas nasceretur ignotum caeteris, docuisseque homines servandi ac serendi modum. Sed eidem in Sicilia tantum placet esse inventum quoniam iis in locis agreste triticum oriretur.

2 Strabo etiam libro 15, cum de Indiae foecundidate loquitur dicit in Musicani regione frumentum sua sponte nasci tritico persimile. Atqui idem Diodorus in 1 huius frugis inventionem Isidi tribuit. Nec eo tamen ut opinor a priore sententia discrepat quandoquidem ipse paulo superius Isidem dicit eandem esse quam Cererem nuncupant. Huic deae Ovidius non modo frumenti sed omnium frugum usum assignat:

Prima dedit fruges alimentaque mitia terris.

3 Verum Iustinus libro suae *Epitomes* 2 scribit sub Erichtheo Athenarum rege frumenti sationem apud Eleusin a Triptolemo repertam, cui scilicet, teste Diodoro libro 6, a Cerere mandatum fuit ut id ab ea ante inventum homines doceret. Sed idem Iustinus

Happy with what grew wild, none working for it,
They picked strawberries and mountain fruit,
Cherries and the riches of rough brambles,
And acorns that fell from Jupiter's spreading oak.

And then they discovered grain, as Vergil writes in the first *Georgic*:

When acorns and berries ran short in the sacred forest,
And Dodona denied them a way to find their food,
Soon they had to work harder to grow the grain.

Pliny says in book 7 that Ceres invented this since humans used to feed on the acorn, as has been explained. She also taught how to mill and prepare the grain, for which Attica, Italy and Sicily judged her a goddess. Vergil also confirms this as does Diodorus, writing in book [5] that Ceres first invented the use of grain, which grew scattered among other plants and remained unknown to humans, and she taught people how to preserve and sow it. But Diodorus believes it was discovered only in Sicily because wheat comes up wild there.

Describing the fertility of India in book 15, Strabo also says that 2 a grain very similar to wheat grows on its own in the region of Musicanus. In book 1, however, the same Diodorus attributes the discovery of grain to Isis. Nonetheless, I do not believe that this contradicts his earlier statement because, just before this, he says that Isis is the same as the goddess named Ceres. To her Ovid assigns not only the use of grain but all the fruits of the earth:

She first gave fruits of the field and a ripe harvest.

In book 2 of his *Epitome*, however, Justinus writes that Trip- 3 tolemus invented the sowing of grain at Eleusis when Erichtheus was king of Athens. Ceres directed Triptolemus to teach people what she had already discovered, according to Diodorus in book

inibi diversum sentiens hoc potius Atheniensibus adscribere videtur, dicens: Primi lanificii et olei et vini usum docuere, arare
quoque et serere frumenta glande vescentibus monstraverunt. Cui
Aristoteles consentit, aiebat enim Athenienses (sic eos reprehen-
debat) frumenta et leges invenisse, verum eos frumentis quidem
uti, non item legibus. Quod Diodorus probe declarat in 6, scribens Cererem post Siculos usum frumenti primos Athenienses
docuisse, quo fieri potest ut secundum Cererem et Siculos ipsi
primi hoc aliis ostenderint.

4   In Latio autem, teste Macrobio, Saturnus omnium primus docuit, de quo Eutropius ipse inquit: Saturnus adhuc rudes populos
domos aedificare, terras colere, plantare vineas docuit, atque humanis moribus vivere, cum antea semiferi glandium tantummodo
alimentis vitam sustentarent.

5   Usum autem stercorandorum agrorum, teste Servio super 9 *Ae-*
neidos, Pitumnus invenit, unde et Sterquilinus dictus est. (Pilumnus vero eius frater pinsendi frumenti, propter quod a pistoribus
colebatur. Pistores autem sive pisores a veteribus vocabantur qui
tam in pistrino farinam pinsebant quam ii qui panem faciebant co-
quebantque. Hos Romani tarde publice habuerunt, Plinius libro
18, capite II: Pistores Romae non fuerunt ad Persicum usque bellum, anno urbis conditae super DLXXX.) Ad rem revenio. Quamvis
Plinius in 17 hunc stercorandi usum iam Homeri aetate fuisse, et
Augeam regem in Graecia excogitasse, divulgasse vero in Italia
Herculem tradat.

6   Boves ad aratrum Diodorus libro 4 et 5 ait Dionysium secundum ex Iove et Proserpina genitum (vel, ut alii sentiunt, ex Cerere) primum iunxisse, cum terra prius manibus hominum colere-
tur. Plinio vero libro 7 teste, aratrum Briges Atheniensis invenit,

[5]. But in the same passage Justinus expresses his doubts and seems to ascribe it instead to the Athenians, saying: They first taught spinning and the use of wine and oil, and they also showed those who lived on acorns how to plow and to raise grain. Aristotle agrees, for in rebuking the Athenians he used to say that they discovered both grain and law but that they had less use for law than for grain. Diodorus gives a clear account of this in book [5], writing that Ceres taught the Athenians the use of grain immediately after the Sicilians, so it is possible that after Ceres and the Sicilians they were the first to show it to others.

But in Latium, says Macrobius, the first to teach about this was Saturn, of whom Eutropius says: Saturn taught the still savage people to build houses, till the soil, plant vines and behave like human beings, since until then they had led a half-bestial life, sustaining themselves with acorns as their only food.   4

According to Servius on book 9 of the *Aeneid*, Pitumnus invented the practice of manuring the fields, whence he was called Sterquilinus. (But his brother Pilumnus discovered how to crush the grain, because of which the millers honored him. Those who ground flour in a mill as well as those who made and cooked bread were called grinders or pounders by the ancients. Public bakers came late to Rome, for in book 18, chapter 11, Pliny says there were no bakers in Rome up to the time of the war against Perseus, after the year 580 AUC.) To return to my topic, however, Pliny suggests in book 17 that the practice of manuring already existed in Homer's time, that King Augeas devised the practice in Greece but that Hercules made it known in Italy.   5

The second Dionysius, born of Jupiter and Proserpina (or Ceres, as others believe), first yoked oxen to a plow, according to Diodorus in books [3 and 4]. Until then, people worked the earth by hand. But according to Pliny in book 7, Briges the Athenian in-   6

ut alii tradunt, Triptolemus, de quo poeta in I *Georgicorum* intellexit cum dixit:

> uncique puer monstrator aratri.

Quo in loco Servius: Alii, inquit, Triptolemum, alii Osirim, quod verius est, nam Triptolemus frumenta divisit. Tacuit autem de nomine quia non unus in orbe aratri monstrator fuit sed diversi in diversis locis. Ex quo Trogus prodidit Habidem Hispaniae regem barbarum populum primo docuisse boves aratro domare frumentaque sulco serere. De Osire, ut ostendimus, sentit etiam Tibullus.

7   Caeterum omnia ferramenta rustica quibus terra vertitur simul, ut puto, cum aratro Cererem comperisse Vergilius proculdubio hoc versu demonstrat:

> Prima Ceres ferro mortales vertere terram
> Instituit.

Quod vel Servius approbat, dicens: Ceres prima omne genus agriculturae hominibus indicavit, nam quamvis vel Osirim vel Triptolemum aratrum invenisse dicant, illa tamen omnem agriculturam docuit; quia ferrum dicendo omnia agriculturae ferramenta expressit.

8   Verum aut illi quos commemoravimus novissimi vel alii alibi haec commonstrarunt, nam ut Eusebii atque Lactantii testimonio constat ante multas tempestates quam esset Ceres, Dionysius, Saturnus, Triptolemus frumenti usus apud mortales erat—praesertim apud Hebraeos et Aegyptios, uti ex Iosepho cognoscere licet. Ille enim in secundo ubi—ne altius repetam—tradit quemadmodum Iudaea caritate annonae laborante Iacob ad emendum frumentum filios in Aegyptum miserit. Ex quo cum Hebraei, ut superiore capite indicavimus, primi omnium terram coluerint, porro extra omnem controversiam credibile est ab eis tum agrorum cul-

vented the plow, though some claim it was Triptolemus, whom the poet had in mind when he wrote in the first *Georgic*:

The boy showed how to use the crooked plow.

Servius comments on this passage as follows: Some say that Vergil means Triptolemus, others Osiris, which is the more accurate since Triptolemus divided the grains. He mentioned no name, however, because there was no single inventor of the plow for the whole world but various inventors in various places. This is why Trogus reported that Habis, king of Spain, first taught his barbarous people to break oxen for the plow and to sow grain in a furrow. And Tibullus also believes this about Osiris, as we have shown.

In any case, it was Ceres who brought knowledge of the plow 7 along with all the other tools that farmers use to turn the earth, so I think, as Vergil clearly proves in this verse:

Ceres first taught people to turn the dirt with iron.

Servius actually confirms this when he says: Ceres was the first to reveal every variety of agriculture to humans, for even though they say that Osiris or Triptolemus invented the plow, it was she who taught agriculture as a whole; when he said 'iron,' Vergil meant all the tools of agriculture.

But the inventors whom we have mentioned pointed out these 8 discoveries only recently or else in particular places, for it is clear from the testimony of Eusebius and Lactantius that people had the use of grain ages before Ceres, Dionysius, Saturn or Triptolemus — especially among the Hebrews and Egyptians, as one can ascertain from Josephus. In his second book — not to trace it back farther — he notes how Jacob sent his sons to Egypt to buy grain when Judaea was struggling under a scarcity of food. Thus, since we have shown in the previous chapter that the Hebrews were the first to cultivate the land, it is incontrovertibly certain

turam, tum fruges ac molendi usum, tum et ferramenta rustica ad posteros manasse, et hos ea ipsa—nulla enim ars, ut Fabius ait, intra initium suum stetit—deinde adauxisse.

9   Cribrorum genera, teste Plinio libro 18, e setis equorum Gallia invenit. Hispania ex lino excussoria ad excutiendam farinam et pollinaria ad purgandum pollinem, id est, crassiusculum pulverem. Aegyptus vero ex papyro iuncoque postea ex pellibus suillis Italia.

: III :

Quis primus vites et alias arbores plantaverit earumque
insitionem docuerit et usum vini repererit
et vino aquam miscuerit; deque novo vitandae
ebrietatis modo et qui caupones primi vel quis oleam
et usum olei et mel adinvenerit; vel ex hordeo
potum fecerit atque lac coagulaverit.

1   Etsi abunde videtur natura homini suppeditasse cum eum principio talem procreaverit ut ipse ex omnibus animantibus unus ratione, sicut ait Cicero, ad Deum quamproxime accedere posset, tamen cum statim genitus nullo foret subsidio fultus (carebat enim indumentis, aedibus, igne, cibo praeterquam in diem quaesito multis denique rebus vitae necessariis quas deinde urgente necessitate, quae rerum magistra est, ipse invenit) non facile est, ut Plinius in initio 7 libri perhibet, aestimare natura homini melior parens an tristior noverca fuerit. Fatendum est tamen si nos his quae illa nobis tradidit contenti essemus, longe melius res sese habituras.

that from them posterity received agriculture, the raising of crops, the practice of milling them and the tools of farming, and that the Hebrews later improved these techniques—for no art has stood still, as Quintilian says, remaining as it was when invented.

Gaul devised the type of sieve made from the bristles of horses, 9 according to Pliny in book 18. Spain invented linen bolting-sieves for separating flour and fining-sieves for cleaning the fine flour, which is a rather dense powder. Egypt made sieves from papyrus and rushes, and Italy later from pigskins.

: III :

Who first planted grape-vines and other trees, showed how to graft them, discovered the use of wine and mixed it with water; on a strange method of avoiding drunkenness and the first tavern-keepers; who discovered the olive-tree and the use of oil and honey; and who made a drink from barley and learned to curdle milk.

Nature seems to have given humans great plenty in the beginning 1 since they alone of all living things have been created with the power to approach God by reason, as Cicero says. Yet, as Pliny presents it in the beginning of book 7, one cannot easily decide whether nature was a good mother to humanity or a hard step-mother, because people when newborn had no immediate support or strength. Except what they got from day to day, they lacked clothing, shelter, fire and food, as well as the many other requirements of life that they themselves finally invented when driven by necessity, mistress of their affairs. Still, it must be admitted that we would be far better off if we were content with what nature has given us.

2   Nam ut de caeteris sileam, ecquis modo fieret temulentus—
quod foedissimum est vitae dehonestamentum sexcentorumque vitiorum origo—si aquam primum a natura potum homini datum, non vinum potaremus cuius vim, ut infra dicemus, eius etiam primus inventor turpiter perpessus est? Quare divus Hieronymus *Ad Eustochium de virginitate servanda* inquit: Sponsa Christi vinum fugiat pro veneno; haec adversus adolescentiam prima arma sunt daemonum. Non sic avaritia quatit, inflat superbia, delectat ambitio. Facile aliis caremus vitiis; hic hostis nobis inclusus est. Et infra subdit: Vinum voluptatis incendium est, unde proximus a Libero patre intemperantiae gradus ad inconcessam Venerem esse consuevit. Propter quod matronae Romanae vino se abstinebant.

3   Quod tamen haud obesset si esset, ut par est, modus in rebus, nam autore Plinio non est quicquam aliud vino modice sumpto utilius. Quinetiam Persae existimabant fomitem esse quendam et incitamentum ingenii virtutisque si mens et corpus hominis vino flagraret, qui, teste Strabone libro 15 *Geographiae*, de rebus maximis inter vinum consultabant, quas ipsi firmiores putare quam quae in sobrietate fuissent deliberatae. Caeterum Plato vinum magis senibus utile esse ducebat, qui illud in dialogo 2 *De legibus* non facile utendum concedit iuvenibus, item militibus in castris, servis, magistratibus, gubernatoribus, iudicibus, consiliariis et liberis operam daturis quia partus gigni debet ex moderato puroque semine, quod vino refertus quasi rabie concitatus serere minus potest, unde filii saepe fatui et amentes procreantur.

4   Sed iam ipsum vini inventorem indicemus. Vites et vini usum atque caeterarum arborum fructus Dionysium invenisse Diodorus libro 4 autor est, ubi dicit Dionysium orbem cum exercitu perambulantem et vitem plantare et ex racemis vinum torculari, ex quo ipsum Lenaeum appellant, educere monstrasse. Et alibi vinum repperisse et arborum fructus testatur, quanquam idem alibi dicit

Leaving other questions unasked, let us only inquire how there 2
could be any drunkenness—life's vilest blemish and source of a
thousand vices—if we drank the water that nature first gave people to drink and not the wine whose effects were shameful even
for its first inventor, as we shall explain below. In his *Letter to
Eustochium on the Preservation of Virginity*, St. Jerome says: Let the
bride of Christ shun wine as if it were poison; it is the chief
weapon of the demons against youth. Greed does not excite one
so, nor pride puff up nor flattery entice. We may easily avoid the
other vices, but this is an enemy within. And then he adds: Wine
lights the flame of lust, so from Father Liber to the forbidden delights of Venus was often a near and reckless step. This is why
married women in Rome abstained from wine.

Yet wine would be harmless if our behavior were temperate, as 3
it should be, for nothing is better than wine taken in moderation,
according to Pliny. The Persians actually believed that wine glow-
ing in a person's mind and body is kindling and fuel for genius and
excellence. According to Strabo in book 15 of the *Geography*, they
used to discuss the gravest problems while drinking, deeming such
decisions more reliable than those debated when they were sober.
Plato considered wine more beneficial for the old, however. In his
second dialogue *On the Laws* he allows its sparing use by the
young, by soldiers in the field, slaves, magistrates, pilots, judges,
counselors and those about to beget children. Offspring should be
conceived from pure and well-tempered seed, but a man full of
wine, excited and half-crazed, is less able to produce seed, so the
children he fathers are often fools or idiots.

Now we will identify the actual inventor of wine. It was Diony- 4
sius who discovered grape-vines and the use of wine and the fruits
of other trees, writes Diodorus in book [3], where he says that
Dionysius and his troop marched through the world and gave lessons in planting the vine and pressing wine from bunches of
grapes, which is why they call him Lenaeus. Elsewhere he testifies

vites ab eo non esse satas, verum terram cum caeteris plantis sponte sua tulisse. Item Vergilius hunc vitium ac reliquarum arborum inventorem fuisse asserere videtur, cum de vitibus et aliis arboribus scripturus statim in principio 2 libri *Georgicorum* dixit:

Nunc te Bacche canam.

5 Caeterum Capella *De nuptiis Mercurii* tradit eum apud Graecos tantum primum vini usum edocuisse, sicuti Saturnum apud Latinos Servius in 8 *Aeneidos* et Eutropius testimonio sunt. Alii Icarium Penelopes patrem apud Athenienses id reperisse tradunt eumque post dedisse poenas a colonis ebriis interemptum. Propertius in fine libri *Elegiarum* 2:

Icare, Cecropiis merito iugulate colonis, [etc.]

At Athenaeus ait apud Aetnam montem Siciliae vitem inventam quod cum Oresteus Deucalionis filius eo regnatum venisset, eius canis ramum forte evellit, quem ille defodi iusserat, et inde vitium germina nata, quae a nomine canis oenon appellavit. Unde apud veteres Graecos vitis οἴνη vocabatur et οἶνος vinum dicitur. Idem in Aegypto apud Plinthinam civitatem vinum primo repertum tradit.

6 Ad Gallos primum ferunt vinum detulisse Aruntem Tyrrhenum. Is vir nobilissimus a Lucumone alumno suo domo pulsus ad Gallos confugit, eisque dulcedine vini allectis facile persuasit ut sibi auxilio in Italiam venirent, qui illuc facto agmine concurrentes, postea pulsis Tyrrhenis, ea terra potiti sunt, autor Plutarchus in *Vita Camilli*.

7 Quidam autem ex arboribus alimenta hominibus a Seculo Venti filio reperta volunt, autor Eusebius in 1 *De praeparatione evangelica*. Culturas earum vel aliarum arborum, teste Plinio in 7, Eu-

that Dionysius discovered wine and the fruits of trees, though in another place he says that he did not plant the vines: the earth produced them spontaneously along with other plants. Vergil likewise seems to maintain that this god discovered vines and other trees; just at the beginning of book 2 of the *Georgics*, before writing of vines and other trees, he said:

Now, Bacchus, I sing of you.

In *The Marriage of Mercury*, however, Capella reports that Bacchus was the first to give such instruction only among the Greeks, as Saturn was first among the Latins, according to Eutropius and Servius on book 8 of the *Aeneid*. Others report that Icarius, Penelope's father, discovered it in Athens and that he later paid a price for it when drunken peasants killed him, as Propertius writes at the end of his second book of *Elegies*: 5

Icarus, justly slain by Attic peasants.

But Athenaeus says that the vine was discovered in Sicily near Mount Aetna, for when Deucalion's son Oresteus came to the throne there, it happened that his dog rooted out a stick. He ordered it buried, vine-shoots sprang up from it, and he named them *oenos* after his dog. Thus, the ancient Greeks called the vine *oinē* and wine *oinos*. The same author reports that wine was first discovered in Egypt near the city of Plinthine.

They say that Aruns the Tyrrhenian first brought wine to the Gauls. Aruns was a great nobleman driven from home by Lucumon, his foster-son. He took refuge with the Gauls and easily persuaded them to come to his aid in Italy by charming them with the sweet taste of wine. They formed an army, marched there to fight, drove out the Tyrrhenians and then took possession of the land, according to Plutarch in his *Life of Camillus*. 6

Some believe that food from trees was discovered for mankind by Aeon, son of Wind, according to Eusebius in book 1 of *The* 7

molphus Atheniensis docuit, quamvis verisimilius sit id Dionysium priorem praestitisse mortalibus qui eas, ut ferunt, arbores
plantavit. Inserenti autem arbores modum primus docuit Saturnus, testis Macrobius libro *Saturnalium* primo ita scribens: Huic
deo insitiones surculorum pomorumque eductiones et omnium
eiusmodi fertilium arborum tribuunt disciplinas. Insitionum vero,
ut Columella libro suo de arboribus tradit, tria sunt genera: aut
enim fissam in arborem surculi inseruntur, aut inter lignum et cor-
ticem ponuntur, aut gemma alterius arboris sed aestivo duntaxat
tempore in cortice alterius intercluditur.

8   Sed haec apud posteros inventa, cum satis constet Noe statim
atque egressus est ex arca, terram studiose coluisse atque vineam
primum omnium sua manu sevisse. Unde arguuntur qui autorem
vini Liberum putant. Qua ex vinea cum primum fructum cepisset,
laetus factus bibit usque ad ebrietatem iacuitque nudus, id quod
Iosephus in I *Antiquitatum* tradit. Cauponam, id est tabernam vina-
riam, primi aperuerunt Lydi populi Asiae, ut ait Herodotus, quo
credo suis ludis locum idoneum haberent, nam, quemadmodum
supra demonstravimus, varia ludorum genera invenerant; quippe
tale opus in cauponis maxime semper fervet.

9   Vino aquam admisceri Staphilus Sitheni filius, ut prodit Plinius in 7, instituit, cuius rei Diodorus luculenter in 5 cum de Dionysio loquitur rationem reddit: Aiunt cum purum in coenis vinum
detur, omnes deum sospitem optare bibenti; cum vero post coenam aqua mistum sumitur, Iovem vocare servatorem. Nam puri
vini potus ad insaniam redigit, aqua vero mistus voluptatem laeti-
tiamque affert et prohibet insaniam. Unde in conviviis aquam
vino admiscendi mos fluxit, medicamentum utique praecipuum ad

Preparation for the Gospel. Eumolphus the Athenian taught the cultivation of vines and other trees, according to Pliny in book 7, though it is more likely that Dionysius first showed them to mortals since it was he who planted trees, so they say. But Saturn first taught a technique for grafting trees, according to Macrobius, who has this to say in book 1 of the *Saturnalia*: To this god they attribute the grafting of branches, the raising of fruit-trees and whatever is known about all the productive trees of this sort. There are three kinds of grafts, as Columella notes in his book on trees: Either grafts are implanted in a tree which has been split, or they are put between the wood and the bark, or else the bud of one tree is set in the bark of another—though this last method is used only in summer-time.

Now these were inventions of later generations, for it is well known that as soon as Noah emerged from the ark he eagerly cultivated the earth and was the first to plant a vine with his own hand. This refutes those who think that Liber was the inventor of wine. The first time Noah took the fruit of this vine, he enjoyed it so much that he drank till he was drunk and lay down naked, as Josephus tells it in book 1 of the *Antiquities*. The Lydians, a people of Asia, were the first to open a tavern or a public house for selling wine, so Herodotus says, and I believe their motive was to have a place good for playing games because they had invented a number of them, as we have shown above, and taverns are always full of such wild behavior.

Pliny writes in book 7 that Staphilus, son of Sithenus, began the practice of mixing wine with water, a custom of which Diodorus renders an excellent account in book [4] when he speaks of Dionysius: They say that when wine is served at table unmixed, the prayer they say is 'may the god keep us'; but when they drink it mixed with water after the meal, they call on 'the savior Jupiter.' Drinking straight wine drives one mad, but wine mixed with water brings joy and pleasure and averts madness. Thus arose the

ebrietatem vitandam. Sed aliud ponit Plinius libro 30, capite 14, scribens: Hirundinis rostri cinis cum myrrha tritus et in vino quod bibetur inspersus securos praestabit a temulentia. Invenit hoc Horus Assyriorum rex.

10   Potum ex hordeo, ut idem ait, Dionysius, id est Liber pater, primus confecit, quem, teste Eusebio in 2 *De evangelica praeparatione*, cervisiam vocant, secundum Diodorum zythum dicunt, paulum a vini sapore differentem. Olim in primis fuit communis Aegyptiorum potus, autores Herodotus et Strabo. Quod Dionysius potionis genus eos potissimum conficere docuit quorum regio vites non ferret. Quapropter hodie Angli, Scoti, Hyberni, item Galli Germanique, omnes Oceani occidentalis septentrionalisque accolae eo utuntur potu qui advectitii tantum vini copiam habent. Sed Germani dum cervisiam faciunt, admiscent frugibus herbam lupum, quam vulgo lupulum vocant; haec enim reddit potum salubriorem.

11   Quanquam Dioscorides non valde potionem probat, ita libro 2 scribens: ex hordeo potus fit qui ζῦθος nominatur; is urinam cit, renes et nervos tentat, membranis (praesertim cerebrum vestientibus) officit, inflationem parit, vitiosum succum creat, elephantiasin gignit. Qui eo potus genere perluitur agilis et ad opus obeundum expeditus evadit. Haec ille. Sed eam vim zythus in eos minus habere videtur qui a pueritia eo sunt usi.

12   Oleam autem Minerva Athenis invenit. Vergilius:

> oleaeque Minerva
> Inventrix.

In hunc sane modum. Cum enim Neptunus atque Minerva, teste Servio, de Athenarum nomine contenderent, placuit diis ut eius nomine appellaretur urbs qui munus melius mortalibus attulisset.

custom of adding water to wine at banquets, surely an excellent prescription for avoiding drunkenness. But Pliny gives a different remedy, writing in chapter 14 of book 30: The ashes of a sparrow's beak ground up with myrrh and sprinkled on your wine before you drink will keep you safe from inebriation. Horus, king of the Assyrians, discovered this.

Pliny also says that Dionysius or Father Liber was the first to 10 prepare a drink from barley. According to Eusebius in book 2 of the *Preparation for the Gospel*, they call it *cervisia*, but Diodorus says its name is *zythus*, not much different from wine in flavor. It was once the most common drink of the Egyptians, according to Herodotus and Strabo. Those people especially whose country grows no vines were taught by Dionysius to prepare this kind of beverage. Therefore, the English, Scots and Irish now use this drink, likewise the French and Germans, all of whom live near the Ocean in the northwest and can get wine only from abroad. But when the Germans make beer, they mix grain with the hop-plant, commonly known as hops, for this makes the drink more wholesome.

Dioscorides does not much approve of this beverage, however, 11 writing as follows in book 2: The drink named *zythos* is made from barley; it increases urination, agitates the kidneys and nerves, obstructs the membranes (especially those covering the brain), brings on flatulence, creates a corrupt humor and causes elephantiasis. Whoever bathes in this sort of liquor comes out nimble and ready for the task at hand. Dioscorides says this. But beer seems to have less of this effect on those who have used it since childhood.

Minerva discovered the olive tree at Athens, as Vergil writes: 12

Minerva found the olive.

This is how she did it. When Neptune and she were vying over the naming of Athens, according to Servius, the gods decided that the city should be called after the one who brought mortals the

Neptunus percusso littore equum animal bello aptum produxit. Minerva iacta hasta oleam creavit, quae melior iudicata fuit propterea quod est insigne pacis. At Diodorus in 6 dicit Minervam non creasse primum oleam, sed inter alias arbores natam monstrasse mortalibus quibus ignota esset. Etenim, uti nos infra aperte ostendemus, ante huius deae ortum erat haec arbor cum aliis sylvestribus immista; olei tamen usus, ut Diodorus ait, aberat cum esset ignota. Et eo pacto illam olei exprimendi modum comperisse ferunt.

13   At Cicero libro *De natura deorum* 3 Aristaeum Apollinis filium oleam invenisse tradit. Oleum vero quanquam ipse Diodorus, ut monstravimus, dicit Minervam reperisse, tamen libro 5 hoc Aristaeo assignat, sicut lac coagulare atque mel conficere, quod Iustinus in 13 etiam tradit, quamvis in 2, uti antea diximus, olei usum Athenienses invenisse prodat. Plinius vero in 7 scribit oleum et trapetes (hoc est, molam oleariam) Aristaeum Atheniensem item mellam invenisse. Oleam praeterea longo tempore Athenis tantum reperiri testatur Herodotus, qui libro 5 dicit Epidaurios, cum eis de agrorum sterilitate oraculum consulentibus Pythia iussisset ut Damiae et Auxesiae simulacra ex ligno oleae erigerent, quoniam ferebatur nusquam gentium nisi Athenis illa tempestate oleam esse, rogasse Athenienses ut sibi permitterent oleam incidere.

14   Quod aeque falsum esse ex Iosephi testimonio deprehenditur ac illud Minervam vel Aristaeum hanc arborem aut olei usum primo monstrasse, is enim in 1 *Antiquitatum* scribit Noe, cum iam recedentibus aquis arca in Armenia super verticem cuiusdam montis resedisset, emisisse columbam et eam mox oleae ramum ferentem ad illum redisse. Quo quidem tempore, ut palam est, nondum erant Athenae. Deinde in 3 eiusdem operis docet Mosen in sacrificiis oleo esse usum ad lumina servanda, post quem, autore Eusebio

better gift. Striking the shore, Neptune produced the horse, a beast fit for war. Minerva cast her spear and created the olive tree, judged the better gift because it is an emblem of peace. But Diodorus says in book [5] that Minerva was not the first to create the olive; rather she revealed it growing among other trees to mortals who were not aware of it. In fact, before the coming of this goddess the olive was mixed in with other forest growth, as we shall clearly prove below, but olive oil was not in use because the tree was unknown, as Diodorus says. Consequently, they claim that she learned how to press the oil.

But Cicero says in book 3 *On the Nature of the Gods* that Aristaeus, son of Apollo, discovered the olive-tree. And although we have shown how Diodorus says that Minerva learned about olive-oil, in book [4] he assigns it instead to Aristaeus, along with curdling milk and making honey—the same account given by Justinus in book 13, though in book 2 he declares that the Athenians discovered the use of oil, as we have already explained. Pliny writes in book 7 that Aristaeus the Athenian discovered oil, the oil-mill (a device for pressing the olive) and hydromel as well. Moreover, Herodotus testifies that for a long time the olive was known only at Athens. In book 5 he writes that when the Epidaurians consulted the oracle about their barren fields, the Pythoness commanded them to set up statues of olive-wood to Damia and Auxesia, and because they were told that none of the peoples of that time except the Athenians had the olive, they asked permission of the Athenians to cut down an olive-tree. 13

From the evidence in Josephus one sees that this tale is as false as the story that Minerva or Aristaeus first taught how to use this tree or its oil, for in book 1 of the *Antiquities* he writes that when the waters had receded and the ark came to rest atop a certain mountain in Armenia, Noah sent forth a dove, which soon returned to him bearing an olive-branch. At this time, Athens did not yet exist, as is well known. Later, in book 3 of the same work, 14

in 10 *De praeparatione evangelica*, Apollo Aristaei pater genitus est. Ex quo credere convenit Minervam et Aristaeum in Graecia duntaxat haec primo monstrasse.

15   In Italiam olea omnino tarde pervenit. Nam Theophrastus, teste Plinio in principio 15 libri, urbis Romae anno circiter CCCCXL negavit nisi intra XL millia passuum a mari nasci. Fenestella vero dicit hanc arborem omnino non fuisse in Italia, Hispania atque Africa Tarquinio Prisco regnante ab anno populi Romani CLXXIII.

16   Mel et lac coagulare Aristaeum omnium primum comperisse Diodorus et Plinius autores sunt, cum quibus consentit Iustinus in 13, licet libro 44 usum mellis colligendi Gargori regi Curetum attribuat, qui in Hispania saltus Cartesiorum incoluit. Sed hic, ut opinor, tantum in Hispania primus fortasse huius rei autor fuit. Verum haec Hebraeis potius assignaverim siquidem teste Iosepho et mortalium omnium primi pastores fuerunt, et apud eos multo ante Aristaeum mellis usus fuerat.

: IV :

A quibus quaedam peregrinae arbores in Italiam translatae.

1   Arbores tam magno sunt mortalibus usui ut sine quis vita degi non possit. Arbore enim, ut Plinius ait, sulcamus maria, terram vertimus, tecta aedificamus, simulacra deorum conficimus. Arbores praeterea communem animantibus victum suppeditant, quarum aliae peregrinae sunt de quibus hoc loco carptim ac breviter dicemus. Hae aliae alibi nascuntur quia non omnis terra, sicuti poeta inquit, omnia ferre potest.

he informs us that Moses used oil in his sacrifices as fuel for lamps, but Apollo, father of Aristaeus, was born after Moses, according to Eusebius in book 10 of the *Preparation for the Gospel*. Hence, it seems one should conclude that Minerva and Aristaeus first disclosed these things only in Greece.

The olive came quite slowly into Italy. Theophrastus, according 15 to Pliny in the beginning of book 15, said that around the year 440 AUC there were no olives growing more than forty miles from the sea. Fenestella says that there was no sign at all of this tree in Italy, Spain or Africa in the year 173 AUC, during the reign of Tarquinius Priscus.

Pliny and Diodorus maintain that Aristaeus was the first to 16 learn about honey and curdled milk, and Justinus agrees with them in book 13, yet in book 44 he attributes the practice of collecting honey to Gargor, king of the Curetes, who lived in the forest of the Cartessians in Spain. But I think it likely that he started this practice only in Spain. I would assign it instead to the Hebrews, since according to Josephus they were the first among mortals to become shepherds, and they had the use of honey long before Aristaeus.

: IV :

Who brought certain exotic trees into Italy.

Trees are so great a boon to mortals that life could not be lived 1 without them. We use the tree to plow the seas, turn the earth, build our houses and make statues of the gods, as Pliny says. Trees are also a common source of nourishment for living things, and some are exotic varieties that we shall discuss here separately and briefly. These different varieties grow in various places since not all lands, as the poet says, can support all kinds.

2   Ex quo multae in Italiam aliunde translatae sunt — sicut cerasus, quam Lucius Lucullus post victoriam Mithridaticam, teste Plinio libro 15, anno urbis DCLXXX primus vexit e Ponto. Testatur etiam divus Hieronymus ad Marcellam, sic lepidissime scribens: Accepimus et canistrum cerasis refertum talibus et tam virginali verecundia rubentibus ut ea nunc a Lucullo delata existimarem. Siquidem hoc genus pomi, Ponto et Armenia subiugatis, de Cerasunto primus Romam pertulit, unde et de patria arbor nomen accepit. At annis CXX post trans Oceanum in Britanniam usque pervenit.

3   Et zizipha et tuberes malorum genera; haec ex Africa, illa ex Syria Sextus Papinius novissimis divi Augusti temporibus primus attulit. Et armeniacus et persicus arbores quae ex nomine ipso peregrinae esse apparent; quis tamen eas transtulerit non facile dixerim. Multa etiam ficorum genera sunt quae ex aliis gentibus ad nos pervenerunt, incertis propemodum autoribus, testis Plinius.

4   Sed platanus in primis ex iis quae aliunde vectae sunt mirum in modum celebrata est, quae ut ad nos venerit aut quantum ei honoris accesserit Plinius in 12 docet, sic scribens: Sed quis non iure miretur arborem umbrae gratia tantum ex alieno petitam orbe? Platanus ea est. Haec per mare Ionium in Diomedis insulam eiusdem tumuli gratia primum invecta. Inde in Siciliam transgressa atque inter primas donata Italiae. Etiam ad Morinos usque pervecta, ad tributarium etiam pertinens solum, ut gentes vectigal et pro umbra pendant. Dionysius prior Siciliae tyrannus Rhegyum in urbem transtulit eas domus suae miraculum, et reliqua.

5   At nihil ad nostram laurum, quae nonnullis in locis aliquando in peregrinis arboribus fuit, dicente eodem Plinio: Notatum antiquis nullum genus lauri in Corsica fuisse, quod nunc satum et ibi

For this reason, many trees have been imported into Italy 2
from abroad—the cherry, for example, which Lucius Lucullus first
brought from Pontus after his victory over Mithridates in the year
680 AUC, according to Pliny in book 15. There is similar evidence
in a letter to Marcella from St. Jerome, where he writes these elegant lines: We have also received a basket full of cherries blushing
so red with virginal modesty that one would think Lucullus had
just carried them off. After conquering Pontus and Armenia, he
first brought this kind of fruit to Rome from Cerasus, the native
country from which the tree took its name. After a hundred and
twenty years had passed, it crossed the ocean as far as Britain.

Both the jujube and the azarole are varieties of tree-fruit. To- 3
ward the end of the reign of the divine Augustus, Sextus Papinius
first brought the former from Africa, the latter from Syria. From
the names of the Armenian apricot and Persian peach it is clear
that both are exotics, but who first imported them I cannot readily
say. Many varieties of fig have also come to us from other countries, though almost all their discoverers are unknown, according
to Pliny.

Of all the trees that have come from abroad, however, the fame 4
of the plane tree is especially outstanding. How it came to us and
how greatly it was prized Pliny teaches in book 12, writing this:
Who would not be amazed, and rightly so, that people have
searched foreign lands for a tree just because of its shade? This is
the plane tree. It was first carried across the Ionian sea to the island of Diomedes to shade his tomb. Then it crossed over into
Sicily and was among the first trees introduced to Italy. They
brought it as far as the land of the Morini, reaching to tributary
soil, so that the tribes would pay tribute even for their shade.
Dionysius I, tyrant of Sicily, introduced these trees to the city of
Rhegium as a curiosity for his house, and so on.

But the plane is nothing compared to our laurel, once consid- 5
ered an exotic in some places, as Pliny also says: The ancients

provenit et cetera. Haec inquam post hominum memoriam felicissima arbor est ad cuius comparationem platanus nihil, quippe non unam habet laurus dotem. Dicatur enim triumphis quando triumphantes ea coronantur. Valet adversus fulmina, quare ante limina excubat. Quapropter ferunt Tiberium Caesarem tonante coelo consuevisse laurea uti corona. Item exornat domos, et idcirco Caesarum pontificumque olim ianitrix erat. Quin et pacifera habetur quam praetendi inter armatos hostes quietis sit indicium. Romanis praecipue laetitiae victoriarumque nuntia. Addebatur lituis militumque lanceis ac imperatorum fasces decorabat. Abdicat insuper ignes crepitu et detestatione quadam. Et denique Apollinis est arbor.

6   Quas ob res tantum est huic arbori semper honoris habitum ut eam prophanis usibus pollui fas minime esset — vel quod fortasse unius arborum latina lingua nomen viris imponatur, et cuius folium vocetur laurea. Appellavi supra nostram laurum utpote quam nostrae Vergilianae familiae nomini sacram mei maiores una cum duobus lacertis insigne gentis ratione non inani habuere, id quod carmen illud indicat:

> Sum laurus virtutis honos pergrata triumphis,
>   Ianitrixque domus fulmina dira fugo.
> Hostibus immissa et pacem requiemque laborum,
>   Victori palmam laetitiamque fero.
> Phoebus amat laurum, et capitis nos illius instar
>   Formosam gerimus tempus in omne comam.
> Ecce — mea gemini ludunt sub fronde lacerti,
>   Qui mecum quare haec accipe signa colant.

knew that there was no species of laurel in Corsica, but now it has been planted there and prospers, and so on. I say that the laurel is the most fruitful tree known to man and that the plane is nothing compared to it because the laurel has more than one gift to give. In triumphs it is sacred because those holding triumph are crowned with it. Because the laurel has power against thunderbolts, it keeps watch over our thresholds. When heaven thundered, Tiberius Caesar used to wear a laurel crown, so they say. It also decorates our houses, and so it used to guard the door for Caesars and pontiffs. The laurel is even considered a peacemaker: to hold it out between two armed enemies is a sign of truce. For the Romans especially it was a messenger of joy and victory. They attached it to the staffs of magistrates and the lances of soldiers and decorated the fasces of generals with it. Moreover, it announces its dislike of fire by crackling out a kind of execration. Finally, it is Apollo's tree.

For these reasons, they always held this tree in such high honor 6 that defiling it with profane uses was never permitted — or perhaps it was because this was the only tree whose Latin name was applied to people, the one whose leaf is called laurel. I have called it our laurel above because my ancestors considered it sacred to the name of our family of Vergil. Together with two lizards, it was the family's device. The following poem shows that this was no thoughtless gesture:

> I am the laurel, beloved: a triumph for the best,
> Doorkeeper and bane of dreadful lightning.
> To enemies I bring peace and painless rest
> And I am the joyous crown of victory.
> Phoebus loves the laurel; we see it on his brow,
> And we too wear its leaves at every season.
> See — twin lizards play beneath my leafy bough.
> You ask, Why leaves with lizards? — And I answer:

Ver ago perpetuum, hi primo ver tempore monstrant;
  Unde tenet nomen Vergiliana domus,
Quae tam immota diu casuraque tempore nullo
  Stabit quam viridi fronde perennis ero.

7   Quid quod praeterea malorum pirorumque genera pene infinita quotidie atque huc atque illuc deferuntur, quarum nonnullae ab autoribus ut appia et pipina, quaedam a sapore ut quae ferunt melimela, aliae ab odore, aliae a colore nomina habent? De his satis superque: non est enim suscepti operis munus peregrinas arbores describere. Sed haec quando ad agriculturam attinent perstrinximus ut illi quos res rustica delectat plurimas arbores quae modo ubique gentium abundant aliunde originem habuisse intelligerent.

: V :

Quis primus animalibus rebusque aliis nomen imposuerit;
  et de primo immolandi instituto ac carnium esu usuque
    victus delicatioris; et more nominandi eum cui
      in convivio poculum tradatur; ac de usu venandi,
    piscandi et salis inventione; et quis apud Romanos
      aviaria ferarumque vivaria instituerit;
    aut quae animalia legionum insignia fuerint.

1   Quoniam rus diversi generis animalibus abundat quae veluti humanae vitae necessaria Deus finxit, consentaneum est ut summatim de iis aliquid dicatur. Animalibus itaque simul ac creata sunt, Adam, teste Iosepho in I *Antiquitatum* et Eusebio in II *De praeparatione evangelica*, nomina imposuit quibus etiam nunc vocantur. Imposuit et rebus aliis quibus iam tum uti coeperat quod a

I am Spring eternal, early Spring they cry;
And thence the house of Vergil takes its name.
That house will never long lie still nor die
So long as I shall grow eternal green.

And why every day do they carry hither and yon almost num- 7
berless varieties of apple, some of them named for their originators, like the appian and pippin, others named for their flavor, like
honey-apples, and others for their fragrance or color? But this is
enough — or perhaps too much — on this topic, for it is not the
purpose of the work we have undertaken to describe exotic trees.
Yet because they have to do with agriculture, we have mentioned
them so that those interested in country affairs might understand
that many trees now found in every land had their origins abroad.

: V :

*Who first gave a name to animals and other things; who first
established sacrifice, the eating of meat and the use of fine
foods; on the custom of naming the one to whom the cup is
passed at banquets; on the practice of hunting and fishing and
the discovery of salt; who began the keeping of aviaries and
game-preserves at Rome; and which animals were the
insignia of legions.*

Since the countryside abounds in a diversity of animals that God 1
put there as necessities of human life, it is fitting that we make a
brief statement about them. Just after the animals were created,
according to Josephus in book I of the *Antiquities* and Eusebius in
book II of the *Preparation for the Gospel*, Adam gave them the names
by which they are still known today. Doubtless one should count

vero non utique abhorrere existimandum est, nam multis rebus cum ipsi Adam tum eius filiis opus fuerat quae sine nomine internosci minime potuissent. Istuc autem facere, teste Cicerone in *Tusculanis*, summae sapientiae visum est Pythagorae.

2   At animalia secundum Plinium volumine 7 Hyperbius Martis filius occidere primus instituit, sicut Prometheus bovem. Quod magis Abel Adam filio tribuerim qui omnium primus, ut Iosephus est autor, primogenita suorum gregum Deo immolavit. Manavit postea iste immolandi mos tam ad Abel posteros Iudaeos quam ad alias quoque gentes, reique apud eas initium fecit suillum pecoris genus, si Varroni credimus, qui libro *De re rustica* 2 eius opinionis argumentum sumit ex eo quod initiis Cereris porci immolabantur, quod in foedere feriendo porcus occidebatur, quod in coniunctione nuptiali nova nupta et novus maritus primum porcum immolabant, quod denique prisci Latini et etiam Graeci in Italia idem factitabant. Et illi porci ad sacrificium electi eximii porci dicebantur quod ut maiores et optimi de grege eximerentur.

3   Ritus vero sacrificandi talis erat: Primum lotis manibus, hostias pura aqua purgabant, fruges capitibus earum inspergentes: deinde precabantur votaque nuncupabant, postea hostiarum tempora vectibus percutiebant, ac occidentes membratim divedebant. Ita primitias ex omnibus membris et exta collecta postquam farris involvissent farina proiiciebant diis in altaria focumve aut aras, hoc est vasa quae tripodes dicebantur. Atque postremo succendebant vina fundentes.

4   Huius moris meminit Vergilius cum diis marinis sacrificium fieret:

it likely that he also gave names to other things that he had already
begun to use at that time, for without those names neither Adam
nor his children could tell apart the many things they needed. According to Cicero in the *Tusculans*, Pythagoras reckoned it supreme
wisdom to do just the same thing.

Pliny says in book 7 that Hyperbius, son of Mars, first began 2
the killing of animals, just as Prometheus was the first to kill an
ox. I prefer to attribute this to Adam's son, Abel, who was the first
to offer the firstborn of his flocks to God, as Josephus tells us.
This practice of making sacrifice later came down both to Abel's
descendants, the Jews, and to other peoples as well. The first animals that they used for this purpose were swine, if we believe
Varro, who reaches this conclusion in book 2 *On Country Life* because pigs were sacrificed in the rites of Ceres; because a pig was
killed on striking a contract; because a new bride and groom sacrificed a pig at the beginning of their marriage; and finally because
the ancient Latins and the Greeks who lived in Italy used to do
the same thing. And those pigs selected for sacrifice were called
choice because they were chosen from the flock as the best and
largest.

The rite of sacrifice was as follows: After they washed their 3
hands, they cleansed the victims with pure water and sprinkled
meal over their heads; next they prayed and made vows; then they
clubbed the victims on the temple and when they had fallen divided them limb from limb. After collecting first-offerings from all
the limbs and major internal organs, they rolled them in spelt-
meal and offered them up to the gods on a high altar or pyre or
else in altar-vessels called tripods. Finally they poured wine on
them and set them afire.

Vergil mentions this practice when sacrifice is made to the sea- 4
gods:

Dii quibus imperium est pelagi, quorum aequora curro,
Vobis laetus ego hoc candentem in littore taurum
Constituam ante aras voti reus, extaque salsos
Porriciam in fluctus, et vina liquentia fundam.

Qui vero immolabant non deos modo voce precabantur sed etiam
aras manibus prehendebant. Idem:

Talibus orantem dictis arasque tenentem.

Quapropter Varro scribit aras primo ansas dictas quod a sacrifi-
cantibus tenerentur, quae deinde mutatione literarum arae vocatae
sunt. Et is hostiarum etiam humanarum diis immolandarum modus, quem Homerus in sua poesi posuit, et Romani quoque teste
Dionysio Halicarnasseo libro 7 usurparunt.

5   Carnes autem sub Saturno, hoc est, in aureo seculo cum omnia
humus funderet, nullum comedisse sed universos vixisse frugibus
et pomis quae sponte terra gigneret, divo Hieronymo *Adversus Iovinianum* testatur Dicaearchus in libris *Antiquitatum* et *Descriptione
Graeciae*. Et Asclepiades Cyprius aetate qua Pygmaleon in Oriente
regnavit scribit usum comedendarum carnium non fuisse. Cheremon Stoicus, de vita antiquorum Aegypti sacerdotum scribens,
narrat eos ex eo tempore quo coepissent divino cultui deservire
carnibus et vino abstinuisse. Ovum quoque pro carnibus vitavisse
et lac, eorum alterum carnes liquidas alterum sanguinem esse dicentes colore mutato. Brachmanae apud Indos, teste Eusebio libro
6 *De praeparatione evangelica*, nihil animatum edebant.

6   Iosephus libro 2 *De bello Iudaico* et in 13 et 18 *Antiquitatum*
treis describit sectas Iudaeorum, Pharisaeos, Sadducaeos, Essenos;
quorum novissimos fert ad coelum laudibus propterea quod ab

Gods, you sea-masters, as I race across
Your waves: With joyous spirit shall I pay
At your altar the bull all shining white
And keep my vow, throwing entrails
To the salty flood and pouring fluid wine.

And those who made offerings not only prayed aloud to the gods
but also gripped the altars with their hands, as the same poet
writes:

With such words he prayed, grasping the altar.

Varro writes that for this reason altars were originally called han-
dles because they were held by those making sacrifice, and they
came to be called altars later, owing to a shift of letters. They also
sacrificed human victims to the gods in this way, as Homer set it
down in his poem, and according to Dionysius of Halicarnassus in
book 7 the Romans followed the same practice.

According to St. Jerome *Against Jovinian* Dicaearchus testifies in   5
the *Description of Greece* and the *Antiquities* that no one ate meat in
Saturn's time—that golden age when everything poured from the
soil—but all lived on the grain and fruit that grew up naturally
from the earth. And Asclepiades of Cyprus writes that the practice of eating meat did not exist at the time when Pygmaleon ruled
in the East. Writing on the life of the ancient Egyptian priests,
Cheremon the Stoic says that they abstained from meat and wine
once they began to devote themselves to worshipping the gods.
They also avoided eggs and milk too as if they were meat, saying
that the one was liquid flesh and the other blood with its color
changed. The Brahmans in India would eat nothing living, according to Eusebius in book 6 of the *Preparation for the Gospel*.

In book 2 of the *Jewish War* and books 13 and 18 of the *Antiq-*   6
uities, Josephus describes three Jewish sects, Pharisees, Sadducees
and Essenes. The last of these he praises to the skies because

uxoribus et vino et—ut Hieronymo placet—carnibus semper abstinuerint. Nec etiam, sicut idem sentit, Hebraico populo statim
post peccatum Adam ut carne vesceretur a Deo concessum est,
hoc est, non ante tempora Noe.

7   In Creta, ut Euripides tradit, Iovis prophetae non solum carnibus non vescebantur sed ne coctis cibis quidem. Herodotus vero in
1 Babylonios piscibus olim tantum victitasse dicit. Xenocrates autem philosophus ex Triptolemi legibus apud Athenienses tria duntaxat praecepta in templo Cereris Eleusinae remansisse scribit: ho-
norandos parentes, venerandos deos, carnibus non vescendum.
Lacedaemoniorum etiam mensae summae frugalitatis erant. Multa
denique huiuscemodi continentiae exempla referre possem quae in
praesentia non invitus consulto omitto, nonnulla post ad haec ad-
diturus cum de modo Christianae abstinentiae tractabitur in libris
insequentibus.

8   Secundas mensas quae bellaria nuncupantur Iones primi omnium, teste Valerio Maximo, invenerunt. Iidem et unguenti et
coronarum in convivio dandarum consuetudinem, haud parva
luxuriae invitamenta, repererunt. Quamobrem Spartana civitas, ut
idem autor est, severissimis Lycurgi legibus obtemperans, aliquan-
diu civium suorum oculos a contemplanda Asia retraxit, ne illecebris eius capti ad delicatius vitae genus prolaberentur, utpote quae
audierat lautitiam inde etiam immodicos sumptus et omnia non
necessaria voluptatis genera fluxisse. Quae ea omnia ipsa tamen
Sparte non potuit ita abstinere quin postremo receperit, siquidem
apud Graecos passim convivia magnifice et splendide concelebra-
bantur quorum moris fuit nominare eum cui poculum tradituri
erant quo una biberent.

9   Mos iste hodie ubique prope gentium retinetur, sed certe quidem nescio quam salubriter—ne dicam quam prudenter—ut quis
edendo cogatur pro alterius arbitratu bibere. Nam idcirco cibum
potumque capimus ut corpus nutriatur, quare aeque debemus ci-

they always abstained from women and wine and—so Jerome believes—from meat. Jerome also thinks that God did not allow the Hebrew people to enjoy meat immediately after Adam's sin—not until Noah's time, that is.

In Crete, as Euripides reports, the prophets of Jupiter abstained 7 not only from meat but even from cooked foods. Herodotus says in book 1 that the Babylonians once lived only on fish. But Xenocrates the philosopher writes that in the temple of the Eleusinian Ceres there remained only three precepts of the laws that Triptolemus gave the Athenians: to honor one's parents; to worship the gods; and to eat no meat. The meals of the Lacedaemonians were also exceedingly spare. In sum, I could offer many examples of this sort of restraint which for now I deliberately omit, though later I will add some of them when treating the Christian practice of abstinence in the books that follow.

The Ionians first invented the afters called desserts, according 8 to Valerius Maximus. They also devised the custom of giving perfumes and wreaths at banquets, and these were no small inducements to luxury. For this reason, as the same author tells us, there was a time when the city of Sparta had its citizens avert their eyes from Asia, thus complying with the very strict laws of Lycurgus, meant to prevent their falling captive to its charms and sinking into a softer way of life, for Sparta had learned that high living, excessive spending and every needless kind of pleasure came from that quarter. But not even Sparta could abstain so strictly from all these things that she did not finally allow them, for everywhere in Greece they held splendid, showy banquets where it was the custom to name the one to whom they would pass the cup and drink with him.

People keep this custom almost everywhere today, but I certainly have doubts about its healthfulness—not to speak of its prudence—for who should be forced to drink at another's whim while eating? The reason we take food and drink is to nourish the

bum potione temperare atque fabricator murorum temperationem facit aquae, arenae et calcis; quae si nimis dura aut liquida sit ut tenacior non est ad consolidandum murum, sic cibus multo liquore in stomacho fluctuans minime alit. Fuit alius ipsorum Graecorum mos valde quidem honestus, ut in convivio virorum non accumberent mulieres, autor Marcus Tullius in *Tusculanis* et *In Verrem.*

10   Redeo rursus eodem. Unde postea ad Romanos hanc mali contagionem transisse verisimile est, apud quos in dies magis magisque latius serpere, nam tanta erat conviviorum luxuria ut facile una mensa patrimonium etsi amplum absumeretur, magnumque saepius republica detrimentum pateretur. Quare Cato verus in hac parte vates, teste Plutarcho, aiebat difficile esse eam rempublicam salvam fore ubi pisciculus pluris quam bos vaenit. Quod Iuvenalis *Satyra* II conquerens inquit:

> Multos porro vides quos saepe elusus ad ipsum
> Creditor introitum solet expectare macelli
> Et quibus in solo vivendi causa palato est.
> Egregius coenat meliusque miserrimus horum, [etc.]

Ex quo multae leges quas Cato cibarias vocat de coercendis sumptibus latae sunt.

11   Sed quid de Romanis loquor? Nonne illa Cleopatra luxuriosissima centies sestertium, ut testis est Plinius in 9 (hoc est, centies centenis sestertiis, quae faciunt CCL milia aureorum nostrorum), coenata est hausto unione pretiosissimo? At ut veterum mores omittamus, quae aetas unquam maiore aut cura aut luxu gulae indulsit quam nostra? Palati enim causa totum percurrimus aequor et, ut ait Hieronymus, propter brevem gulae voluptatem terram

body, so we should balance food with drink in the way that a builder of walls makes a balanced mixture of water, sand and lime. If this mixture is too stiff or too wet, it will not be firm enough to hold the wall together; likewise, food floating about in a stomach full of liquid will give very little nourishment. Truth to tell, these same Greeks had another custom which was quite virtuous: that women should not recline at table in men's banquets, according to Cicero in the *Tusculans* and *Against Verres*.

To get back to my subject, Greece was the likely source of con- 10 tagion from which this evil came later to Rome, where it spread more and more widely every day. Banquets became so extravagant that in just one month they gobbled up an ample inheritance, often causing the state great harm. On this topic, then, Cato was a true prophet, for he used to say that security would come hard to a state where a little fish sells for more than a cow, according to Plutarch. This is what Juvenal writes in the eleventh *Satire*, complaining that:

You see them all over, an outmaneuvered creditor
Always waiting at the market gate for them to enter,
They live only to please the tongue, and dine
Like lords, the wretches, the more they're on the skids.

Out of this came the many proposals that Cato calls sumptuary laws, whose aim was to control spending.

Why talk about the Romans? Did not Cleopatra, that most ex- 11 travagant woman, spend ten million sesterces (100 times 100,000 sesterces, which makes 250 of our gold pieces) on a banquet where a large and very costly pearl was drunk? But if I may leave aside the customs of the ancients, what age ever indulged the appetite more excessively and eagerly than our own? Truly, to please the palate we cross a whole ocean and, as Jerome says, we travel land and sea for the sake of a moment's pleasure in the mouth, giving a

lustramus et maria, et ut mulsum vinum pretiosusque cibus fauces nostras transeat totius vitae opera desudamus. Iuvenalis:

Interea gustus elementa per omnia quaerunt.

Verius vero igitur est quod Socrates dictabat: Multos propterea velle vivere ut essent et biberent, se autem bibere atque esse ut viveret. Possem in hoc loco multorum invitamentorum gulae inventores prodere, quos tamen malo in tenebris iacere quam eos nominando tot convitiis obnoxios reddere.

12   Usum venandi et piscandi quidam, teste Eusebio in 1 *De praeparatione evangelica*, apud Phoenices repertum volunt, veluti salem et eius usum Misor et Selech invenisse dicuntur. Romae pavonem Quintus Hortensius augurali coena primus posuit, autores Varro in 3 *De agricultura* et Plinius in 10 et Macrobius libro *Saturnalium* 3. Aviaria, hoc est loca in quibus domi aves educantur, primus, teste Plinio, instituit inclusis omnium generum avibus Marcus Laelius Strabo Brundusii equestris ordinis. Habuit etiam Romae Alexander imperator voluptatis gratia, autor Lampridius.

13   Ex quo coeptum est animalia carcere coerceri quibus natura coelum aut terram assignaverat, nam et leporaria, id est, vivaria ferarum muris undique septa, autore Plinio in 8, a Fulvio Hirpino primum condita sunt ut etiam hodie nonnulla in Italia extant. Divus enim Federicus dux Urbini duo equidem fecit in quibus omne ferarum genus inclusit ut quoties per negocia liceret animi causa se honestissimo huiusmodi venationis genere exercere posset. At alibi, et praesertim in Anglia, passim eiusmodi vivaria sunt, quae cum roboreis sudibus septa sint recte veteri vocabulo roboraria dici possunt. Et haec loca Angli in summis cum voluptatibus

lifetime's labor so that honeyed wine and costly food will pass our throats, as Juvenal writes:

They sample every substance to find a snack.

What Socrates used to say, then, is actually more to the point: That many wish to live for the sake of eating and drinking, but that he ate and drank in order to live. Here I might identify those who discovered many ways to stimulate the appetite, but I prefer to let them lie in the shadows rather than make them liable for all those banquets by naming them.

According to Eusebius in book 1 of the *Preparation for the Gospel*, 12 they say that the Phoenicians started the practice of hunting and fishing, just as Misor and Selech discovered salt and how to use it. In Rome Quintus Hortensius was the first to serve peacock at an augural feast, according to Varro in book 3 *On Farming*, Pliny in book 10 and Macrobius in book 3 of the *Saturnalia*. Marcus Laelius Strabo, a member of the knightly class of Brundisium, first established aviaries, places for rearing domestic birds, according to Pliny, and birds of all kinds were kept in them. The emperor Alexander also had birds at Rome for his amusement, says Lampridius.

Thus began the practice of caging the living things to which nature had given earth and sky. Warrens or game-preserves fenced in 13 with walls on all sides were first built by Fulvius Hirpinus, according to Pliny in book 8, and there are still some of them in Italy today. In fact, the divine Federico, Duke of Urbino, constructed two of them in which he kept game of every kind so that he could amuse himself with exercise in this most gentlemanly kind of hunting whenever he had the time. Elsewhere, especially in England, there are game-preserves of this sort all over the country, and since they are fenced in with strong wooden stakes, it is appropriate to call them by the old term, stockades. The English value these places highly and take the greatest pleasure in them, for they

tum opibus habent, quando nulla apud eos videtur magnifica villa quam vivarium ferarum cervorum et damarum non ornarit.

14   Non est insuper ab re demonstrare tantum honoris quibusdam accessisse animalibus ut legionum Romanarum insignia forent; erant enim signa lupi, minotauri, equi, apri et aquila, quam legionibus Gaius Marius in secundo consulatu suo proprie dicavit, autor Plinius libro 10 *Naturalis historiae*.

: VI :

Quis primus invenerit linum, retia, nendi texendique modum vel artem fulloniam et saponem; aut qui lanas infecerint aut repererint lanificii vestiumque variarum ac pellium usum, fusos, aulaea, sutoriam artem, sericum; et quando eius copia per Europam fieri coeperit ac bombycinam vestem atque purpuram; et quid ipsa sit purpura ac quanto in honore olim et pretio fuerit.

1   Mille lini usus sunt sed praesertim in velis faciundis, quod execratione dignum est ad perniciem hominum. Quod enim maius miraculum videri potest quam ut herba sit hoc linum quae eatenus Aegyptum, Syriam, Africam, Hispaniam, Galliam Italiae admoveat, ut multi parvo quidem temporis spatio ad ea ipsa loca levissimo etiam ventorum flatu perveniant? Audax itaque vita et scelerum plena, ut Plinius ait, aliquid serere voluit ut ventos procellasque reciperet, ita enim tam parvo semine nascitur quod orbem terrarum ultro citroque portat hominemque ipsum, perinde quasi parum fuisset in terra mori, cogit perire in aquis ubi insepultus a monstris marinis voratur. Propter quod Plinius ait haud se scire quae execratio satis esset contra inventorem.

regard no estate as grand unless it is equipped with a game preserve for stags and deer.

In addition, it is relevant to point out that some animals were   14
so much honored that they became the insignia of the Roman legions, whose standards were wolves, minotaurs, horses, boars and
the eagle. Gaius Marius presented the latter to the legions as their
own in his second consulate, according to Pliny in book 10 of the
Natural History.

: VI :

*Who first invented linen cloth, nets, the technique of spinning
and weaving, fulling and soap; who dyed wool or discovered
the use of woolworking, various garments, skins, spindles,
tapestries, the art of shoemaking and silk; when there came to
be a good supply of silk in Europe, and who invented silk
clothing and purple cloth; what the purple actually is, and
how greatly it was once esteemed and valued.*

Linen has a thousand uses but is especially good for making sails,   1
which is why it deserves to be cursed as a danger to mankind.
What could be more amazing? This linen, made from a plant,
brings distant Egypt, Syria, Africa, Spain and Gaul near to Italy,
enabling many to reach these places in a short space of time on
even the slightest puff of wind. Hence, his was a reckless life full
of iniquity who decided to sow a crop to catch wind and storm,
says Pliny, for what springs from such a little seed carries the globe
hither and yon, driving people to perish in the waters and find a
grave in the belly of a sea monster, as if dying on land were not
good enough. On account of this Pliny says it is hard to know
what would be curse enough for this inventor.

2   Sed ad rem veniamus. Linum Arachne virgo, quae Lydia fuit, omnium prima, teste Plinio libro 7, invenit, quanquam eius usum apud Hebraeorum antiquissimos multo ante fuisse comperimus. Haec lanificii peritissima Minervam in certamen provocavit, a qua in bestiolam quae araneola dicitur conversa est, autor Ovidius in 6 *Metamorphoseon*. Haec eadem retia invenit quae feris avibusque atque piscibus capiundis tenduntur. Nendi autem texendique artem Palladem instituisse nemo ambigit, quippe quae Minervae ars nominatur, quod innuere videtur Naso in 1 *De arte amandi* his versibus:

> Quid facis Aeacide? Non sunt tua munera lanae;
>> Ah, titulos alia Palladis arte pete.

Et Ausonius libro primo:

> Litia qui texunt et carmina, carmina Musis
>> Litia contribuunt, casta Minerva, tibi.

3   Plinius tamen in 7 dicit Aegyptios textilia comperisse, qui etiam plurimis litiis texere quae πολύμιτα vocant simul instituerunt, idem autor libro 8. Fulloniam artem Nicias Megarensis invenit, quam qui exercent fullones nominantur. Ii vestimenta curant poliuntque et ad id sapone utuntur, quem Plinius libro 28, capite 12, a Gallis inventum tradit. (Graece dicitur σμῆγμα quicquid purgat.) Idem libro 27 cum de osyris herbae foliis et semine tractat, smegmata, inquit, faciunt mulieribus ex his. Lanas infecere primum Sardibus Lydi, autor Plinius.

4   Usum vero lanificii Iustinus libro 2 Athenienses primos docuisse tradit, quod ego Minervae potius tribuerim siquidem illa erat antequam Athenae conditae forent, et quoniam lanificium callebat, credibile est eam primo lanificium monstrasse — praesertim Atheniensibus, apud quos castissime colebatur. Quapropter Iusti-

But on to my topic. Pliny says in book 7 that the Lydian 2
maiden Arachne first discovered linen, though we have uncovered
its use far earlier among the oldest Hebrews. A great artist in
woolworking, this girl dared Minerva to a contest, and the goddess
changed her into the little animal we call a spider, according to
Ovid in book 6 of the *Metamorphoses*. The same girl invented the
nets that are stretched to capture wild animals, birds and fish. No
one doubts that Pallas began the art of spinning and weaving,
however, for it is called the art of Minerva, as Ovid seems to hint
in these lines from book 1 of the *Art of Love*:

What's this, Achilles? Wool is none of your business.
Go seek your fame in another art of Pallas.

And Ausonius in book 1:

Weavers of threads and poems give poems to the Muses,
And threads to you, purest Minerva.

But in book 7 Pliny says that the Egyptians learned how to 3
make textiles, the very people who also began using a great many
threads to weave what they call *polymita*, as the same author notes
in book 8. Nicias of Megara discovered the art of fulling, and
those who practice it are called fullers. They finish garments and
smooth them, using for this work the soap that Pliny in book 28,
chapter 12, says that the Gauls invented. (In Greek something that
cleans is called *smēgma*.) Describing the leaves and seed of the
plant osyris in book 27, the same author says that they make soaps
(*smegmata*) for women out of them. Pliny also says that Lydians
from Sardis were the first to dye wool.

Justin claims in book 2 that the Athenians first taught the craft 4
of woolworking, but I would rather attribute it to Minerva if in
fact she lived before Athens was founded. Since she was clever at
woolworking, it is conceivable that she taught it first—especially
to the Athenians, who worshipped her with such devotion. This is

nus, ut puto, facile intelligit Athenienses lanificii usum primos post Minervam docuisse, veluti eos, autore Diodoro, primos secundum Cererem vel Siculos, frumentum monstrasse probavimus. Fusos in lanificio reperit Closter filius Arachnae, testis Plinius.

5   Illud quasi praeteriens non omittam, olim in plerisque Italiae locis lege pagana sancitum fuisse ut ne mulieres fusos per itinera ambulantes torquerent neve detectos ferrent quod id adversaretur omnium spei, praecipueque frugum. Hinc cognoscere licet quam vana fuerit veterum religio, hodie enim Italicae mulieres illud passim faciunt sine tamen alicuius rei maleficio.

6   Aulaea ornamenta quibus parietes et aulae teguntur primum, teste Servio super 3 *Georgicorum*, in aula Attali regis Asiae, unde nomen habent, inventa sunt. Postquam is populum Romanum fecit haeredem. Sutoriae artis inventionem Plinius nescio cui Boethio assignat, ego vero dixerim Hebraeos primos sutores fuisse quando satis constat Mosen calceatum extitisse; cui, velut in Exodo capite 3 patet, dictum a Domino fuerit: Solve calceamentum de pedibus tuis.

7   Vestium usum Palladem invenisse Diodorus libro 6 autor est, sed, ut ait Eusebius cum de rebus Phoenicum in primo *De evangelica praeparatione* scribit, Uso ex Saeculi genere ortus traditur primus corporibus tegmina ex pellibus ferinis confecisse. Quod ego illi apud Phoenices duntaxat tribuendum duco, quando Adam primus a Deo creatus pelliceam sibi vestem fecit, quod proculdubio vestes faciundi posteris exemplar extitit.

8   Praeterea, quoniam vestibus facta est mentio, videtur locus exigere ut singulorum vestimentorum inventores prodamus. Latus

why it was easy, I believe, for Justin to conclude that the Athenians were the first after Minerva to teach the art of woolworking just as they were the first to follow Ceres or the Sicilians in teaching about grain, as we have proven on the authority of Diodorus. Closter, Arachne's son, devised spindles for woolworking, according to Pliny.

One thing I will not omit as if it had escaped my notice: In 5 many parts of Italy it was once established in local law that women should not twirl their spindles while walking on the roads nor carry them uncovered because this would ruin everyone's hopes, especially where crops were concerned. Thus one sees how empty was the religion of the ancients since Italian women do this everywhere today and cause no harm at all.

The decorative tapestries that cover walls and palaces are called 6 *aulaea* because they were first invented for the hall of King Attalus of Asia, according to Servius on the third *Georgic*. Later he made the Roman people his heir. Pliny assigns the invention of the shoemaker's craft to an obscure Boeotian, though I would have said that the first shoemakers were the Hebrews since everyone knows that Moses wore shoes; the evidence is in chapter 3 of Exodus, where the Lord says to Moses: Loose the shoes from your feet.

Diodorus tells us in book [5] that Pallas first discovered the use 7 of clothing, but when Eusebius writes about the Phoenicians in the first book of the *Preparation for the Gospel*, he says that Uso, sprung from the line of Aeon, is said to have been the first to make coverings for the body from the skins of wild animals. Since Adam made himself a garment of skins after God had created him, I conclude that one should assign this discovery to Uso only as far as the Phoenicians are concerned, for later generations surely took their example from the garments that Adam made.

Since the topic of clothing has come up, this seems the right 8 place to record the inventor of each different garment. The *latus*

clavus primum repertus est ab incolis Balearium insularum; quo
Gaius Caesar, autore Tranquillo, ad manus fimbriato usus est, et a
latis clavis qui eius vestitus tunicae inserti erant nomen habet,
unde tunica lati clavi palmata a genere picturae dicta. Auri in-
texendi modum, uti Plinius in 33 et in 8 est testis, Attalus rex
Asiae invenit, unde attalicae vestes dictae. Acu facere excogitaverunt Phryges Idaei, ideoque phrygiones vocati sunt et vestes ipsae
phrygianae. Rectam tunicam Tanaquil prima contexuit.

9   Apud Graecos inventum est pallium sicut apud Hetruscos
praetexta, ita nuncupata quod eius circuitus et orae purpura prae-
textae essent. Et magistratuum vestitus erat. Contra toga alia pura
dicebatur, cui nihil purpurae foret praetextum; qua, teste Plinio in
8, tyrones ac novae nuptae induebantur. Item colores diversos intexere Babylonii coeperunt. Martialis:

Veste semiramia, quae variatur acu.

Undulatam vestem, quae toga regia dicebatur qua Servius Tullus
usus est, fecit Gaia Caecilia, quae eadem Tanaquil vocata est, autor
Plinius in octavo, et undulata dicta quod undis aspersa foret quae
fit ex pilis hircorum caprarumque. Hoc genus panni nos symballoton vulgo vocamus.

10   Dalmatica vestis longa non admodum lata a Dalmatis primum
confecta. Gabanium a Graecis inventum eiusdem fere formae ac
dalmatica est manicis eius longitudinem aequantibus, quo Itali
etiam nunc una cum Graecis utuntur. Eorundem Graecorum inventum fertur mantaele, quod est genus penulae, quam ipsi μαν-
δύαν vocant, nos vero mantaelum (at vulgo cappam), cuius nunc
ubique gentium usus est perquam celebris. Braccae Gallorum vestitus fluxus intonsusque ac varii coloris, unde pars Galliae frigidior

clavus, named after the broad stripes put on the garment called a tunic, was first devised by the natives of the Balearic islands. According to Suetonius, the one that Gaius Caesar wore had fringes reaching to the hands. A tunic with the broad stripe was called palmate from the type of design it bore. Attalic garments got their name because Attalus, King of Asia, discovered the technique of interweaving in gold, as Pliny tells us in books 33 and 8. Since Phrygians from Ida learned how to do needlework, one who worked in embroidery was called *phrygio* and the garments were called phrygian. Tanaquil was the first to weave a straight tunic.

The Greeks invented the cloak and the Etruscans the bordered 9 toga, so called because its edges were bordered all round with purple. This was the garment of magistrates. Another toga was called plain, however, because it had no purple border, and it was the clothing for recruits and new brides, according to Pliny in book 8. The Babylonians also began weaving various colors together, whence Martial writes:

A garment embroidered with the needle of Semiramis.

Gaia Caecilia, the same woman who was called Tanaquil, made the wavy garment called the royal toga that Servius Tullius wore, according to Pliny in book 8. The term *wavy* referred to the waves running through cloth made from the hair of male and female goats. In the vulgar tongue we call this kind of cloth *symballoton*.

The dalmatic, a long garment but not very wide, was first made 10 by the Dalmatians. The overcoat, an invention of the Greeks, has almost the same shape as a dalmatic with sleeves of the same length; Italians and Greeks wear them even now. They say that the Greeks also invented the hooded cloak that they call a *mandua*; it is the sort of coverall that we call a cape (or *cappa* in the vernacular), and it is now very commonly used by all peoples. Flowing, shaggy, varicolored trousers are worn by the Gauls, whence the colder part of their country is called Gaul-in-Trousers. It is well

Braccata appellata est. Sindonem ex lino amictum primum in urbe Sidone factam constat, qua corpus Servatoris nostri involutum Matthaeus tradit. Haec de vestimentis quorum autores produntur dicere habui.

11   Erant vestes aliae aliis peculiares, ut toga Romanis et Gallis — ex quo Gallia Cisalpina Togata nuncupata est. Togam autem ipsam Tertullianus libro *De pallio* scribit a Pelasgis inventam ad Lydos primum, a Lydis deinde ad Romanos delatam fuisse, apud quos diversa eius fuerunt genera.

12   Tunica interior vestis sine manicis senatoria, eadem nobis linea proxima carni est quam camisiam vocamus. Bulla aurea puerorum nobilium Romanorum erat, trabea triumphantium, lacerna ludorum spectantium. Militum vero paludamentum, chlamys (quae et Macedonum Graecorumque), abolla, laena et sagum (quod vulgo sayon vel cotta dicitur), a quo milites nostros sagatos appellamus. At stola matronarum erat ad pedes usque demissa, extremaque in parte instita fasciola exornata. Atque haec Romanorum aliorumque populorum vestimenta propria quae uno alterove tempore ab illis ipsis inventa dixerim.

13   Est et cilicium vestis genus confectum ex villis hircorum atque caprarum quod, teste Varrone, Cilicia, unde nomen habet, primum invenit, ut illud dense duplicatum adhiberetur ad sagittarum ictus excipiendos. In eo apud nos summa est sanctitatis tutela, quando viri sanctissimi ad domandum corpus proxime carnem utuntur. Pellium usus frigoris vitandi causa olim apud Britannos fuit, quemadmodum in nostra *Anglica historia* ostendimus.

14   Item apud Scythas, Ovidius *De tristibus* libro tertio inter quos exulavit:

known that the *sindon* or shroud, a linen covering, was first made in the city of Sidon, and Matthew reports that the body of our Savior was wrapped in a shroud. This is all I have to say about garments whose inventors are known.

There were others peculiar to other peoples as the toga was to   11
the Romans and Gauls, which is why Cisalpine Gaul was called Gaul-in-a-Toga. In his book *On the Cloak* Tertullian writes that the toga itself was invented by the Pelasgians and that it came first to the Lydians and then from the Lydians to the Romans, who had togas of various kinds.

The senatorial tunic was a sleeveless inner garment, the same as   12
the linen worn next to the skin that we call a shirt. The golden locket was for children of Roman nobles, the state-robe for those holding triumph, the mantle for spectators at the theater. Soldiers, however, wore the military cloak, cowl (which was also a garment of the Greeks and Macedonians), mantle, double cloak and cape (called *sayon* or *cotta* in the vernacular), which is why we call soldiers *sagati*. The stole that matrons wore came down to the feet, and its bottom hem had a decorated border. The garments described here as belonging to the Romans or other peoples were those they themselves invented at one time or another.

There is also a garment called a *cilicium* made from the hair of   13
male and female goats which, according to Varro, takes its name from Cilicia, where it was first invented; it was worn in double thickness to absorb the force of arrows. For us it is the great guardian of holiness, and the saintliest men wear it next to the skin in order to tame the body. In Britain they once used skins as protection against the cold, as we pointed out in our *English History*.

It was the same in Scythia, where Ovid lived in exile and wrote   14
in book 3 of the *Tristia:*

Pellibus et laxis arcent mala frigora braccis,
Oraque de toto corpore sola patent.

Apud veteres Romanos non fuisse testatur Tranquillus, scribens
Augustum solitum esse hyeme se quaternis tunicis munire adversus vim frigoris—quod utique non fecisset si pellibus longe mol-
lioribus uti mos fuisset. Postea Neronis temporibus ea mollitia ad
ipsos quoque Romanos irrepsit, quando Seneca in *Epistolis* frigoris
causa meminit de pelliculis vulpium et murium Ponticorum (quas
Itali zebellinos et alii, praesertim Angli, *sables* vocant) quae ut
quam aliae molliores ita preciosiores multo sunt.

15   Sed longum etsi nimis facimus, non praeteribo tamen sericum,
foeminarum virorumque luxuriae uberrimum alimentum. Hoc Seres, Scytharum populi, a quibus nomen habet primum invenerunt,
dicente Plinio in 6: primi sunt hominum qui noscantur Seres, la-
nicio sylvarum nobiles; perfusam aqua depectentes frondium cani-
ciem, unde geminus foeminis nostris labor redordiendi fila rur-
sumque texendi. Tam multiplici opere, tam longinquo orbe petitur
ut in publico matrona transluceat. Item Vergilius in 2 *Georgicorum:*

Velleraque ut foliis depectant tenuia Seres.

Ex his autem Vergilii verbis multi suspicantur huiusmodi vellera
non a vermibus, ut apud nos fiunt, confici, sed sua sponte in frondibus illarum arborum nasci. Cui opinioni Solinus etiam suffragari videtur cum scribat Seres aquarum aspergine inundatis frondibus vellera arborum adminiculo depectere, liquoris et lanuginis
teneram subtilitatem humore domantes. Verum Servius hoc non

With pelts and loose pants they shut out the evil chill;
Of the whole body only the face goes uncovered.

Suetonius testifies that this was not the case in ancient Rome, writing that Augustus used to fortify himself against the violence of the winter cold with four tunics — which surely he would not have done had it been normal to wear the far softer skins. Later, in Nero's time, this softness had overtaken the Romans too, for in his *Letters* Seneca mentions the use of pelts of fox and ermine against the cold. These rodents (which the Italians call *zebellini* and others, especially the English, sables) are much more valuable than others because of their greater softness.

Though we are making far too much of this subject, I will not fail to mention silk, a great incitement to luxury in women and men. A Scythian people, the Seres, first invented this and gave it its name, as Pliny says in book 6: The first humans known there are the Seres, famous for the fleecy stuff that comes from trees. They comb out the white, hairy material from the leaves after sprinkling it with water, making two jobs for our women, who must unravel the threads and reweave them. With labor so complex they seek this material from a world so distant so that a woman may be seen in public in a diaphanous gown. Vergil says something similar in the second *Georgic*:

How they comb fine fleece from leaves in far Cathay.

Many surmise from Vergil's words that this fleece does not come from worms, as ours does, but grows naturally in the foliage of their trees. Solinus also seems to support this view when he writes that the Seres use an instrument to comb the fleece of the trees from their drenched foliage after sprinkling them with water, controlling the frail delicacy of the down with the moisture of a liquid. Servius explains this neatly and elegantly in commenting on

minus scite quam eleganter declarat super 2 *Georgicorum* ubi Maro
ostendit apud alias quoque gentes lanigeras arbores nasci, dicens:

Quid nemora Aethiopum molli canentia lana?

Et cetera. Ait enim apud Indos et Seres sunt quidam in arboribus
vermes qui bombyces appellantur, qui aranearum more fila tenuis-
sima deducunt, unde est sericum.

16   Haec Servius, cui Plinius suppetias ferre videtur, cum in 11 de
bombyce coa loquitur, scribens: Et in Co insula nasci traduntur
cupressi, terebinthi, fraxini, quercus florem imbribus decussum
terrae halitu animante; fieri autem primo papiliones parvos nu-
dosque, mox frigorum impatientia villis inhorrescere, et adversus
hyemem tunicas sibi instaurare densas pedum asperitate radente
foliorum lanuginem in vellera. Hanc ab his quoque cogi subigique
unguium carminatione, mox trahi inter ramos tenuari ceu pectine,
et reliqua. Bombycinas igitur vestes a sericis non distinguunt, quas
in filum retorquere ac inde texere in Co insula Pamphila, Platis
filia, invenit, autor Aristoteles *De animalibus* et Plinius in 11.

17   At serici usus tarde omnino ad nos accessit, magnique fuit pre-
tii. Nam uti Vopiscus testatur, Aureliano principe, qui regnare
coepit anno circiter salutis humanae CCLXXIIII, serici libra auri
pondo, id est, libra vendebatur, quare is princeps modestissimus
nunquam holosericam vestem, quae tota ex serico intexta erat, in-
duere voluit, qua paulo ante primus Romanorum Antoninus Heliogabalus homo luxuriosissimus usus est, autor Lampridius, cum
id temporis tantum in usu esset vestis subserica, cuius stamen ex
serico foret, trama autem ex alia materia, cuiusmodi hodie pan-
num in primis conficiunt Flandri, quem *satin de Bruges* vulgo appellant.

the second *Georgic*, where Vergil shows that woolbearing trees also grow in other countries:

What of the soft wool from white Aethiopian groves?

And so on. Servius says that where the Indians and Seres live there are certain worms called silk-worms in the trees, and like spiders they spin very fine threads from which silk is made.

What Servius says seems to be born out by Pliny, writing about   16 the Coan silk-worm in book II: They say the worms are born on the island of Cos when a vapor from the ground breathes life into the blossoms of cypress, terebinth, ash and oak, after the rains have beaten them down. At first the moths are small and unclothed, but soon they bristle with hairs because they cannot stand the cold, and they make themselves heavy coats against the winter by using their rough feet to scrape the down from the leaves into fleece. They work and compact the down by carding it with their claws and then draw it between twigs and thin it as if by a comb, and so on. Thus, they do not distinguish garments of silk from those of bombazine, which the Coan islander Pamphila, daughter of Plates, discovered how to twist into thread and then to weave, according to Aristotle *On Animals* and Pliny in book II.

But the use of silk was quite slow to reach us, and it was very   17 costly. In the reign of the emperor Aurelian, which began around the year 274 AD, a pound of silk was worth its weight in gold. In other words, as Vopiscus testifies, it sold for a pound of gold, which is why that unassuming prince was never willing to put on the clothing called pure silk, woven entirely of silk and first worn at Rome, according to Lampridius, by Antoninus Heliogabalus, a very extravagant person who ruled shortly before Aurelian. The only sik clothing in use at that time was called part silk because its warp was silk but its woof of some other fabric. Today the Flemish specialize in making cloth of this kind, called Bruges satin in the vernacular.

18   Posthac, circiter annum salutis DLV, ingens serici copia per totam Europam fieri coepit cum per idem tempus duo monachi, velut Procopius autor Graecus tradit, vermiculorum semen (hoc est, ova) ex Serinda Indiae urbe ad Iustinianum imperatorem Constantinopolim attulerint. Fit autem ex puro serico panni in primis triplex genus: unum vulgo dicitur rasum quod in eo nullus utrinque sit pilus, apud alios vocatur setin; alterum damascum floribus intextum, quod Damasci in Syriae oppido primo confectum sit: tertium villutum, id est, villosum quod ex altera parte villos habet.

19   Purpura vero quo pacto et quando sit inventa est apud Pollucem libro *De verbis idoneis ad Commodum* 1, qui inquit: Tyrii ferunt captum amore Herculem cuiusdam Nymphae indigenae cui nomen Tyros, quem sequebatur canis, qui irreptantem scopulis purpuram conspicatus, peresa caruncula, sua sibi labra cruore puniceo infecit; cum igitur ad puellam adisset Hercules, delectata illa insueta tinctura affirmavit sibi cum illo posthac nihil fore nisi ad se vestem afferret etiam canis illius labris splendidiorem; quocirca Hercules, inventa animante collectoque sanguine, munus puellae detulit primus, ut Tyrii dictitant, puniceae infecturae autor.

20   Sunt autem purpurae, teste Plinio libro 9, capite 36, pisces ex concharum genere, quae septem ut plurimum vivunt annos, congregantur verno tempore, mutuoque attritu liquorem quendam veluti cerae emittunt, sed nobilem illum succum quo vestes tinguntur in mediis habent faucibus, quem cum vita evomunt, ideo vivae capiendae sunt. Hinc purpureus color qui nigrantis rosae splendore sublucet. Est eiusdem concharum generis sed non idem murex piscis, qui et conchylium dicitur, cuius cruore conficitur color etiam purpureus, quem ostrum appellant. Ex quo a bonis autori-

Later, around the year 555 AD, a huge quantity of silk began 18
to be produced throughout Europe, when, as the Greek author
Procopius reports, two monks brought the seed of the worms
(their eggs, that is) from the Indian city of Serinda to the Emperor Justinian in Constantinople. But cloth made of pure silk
comes in three notably important varieties: One is called *rased* in
the vernacular because it has no pile on either side, though some
call it satin; another, woven with a floral design, is called *damask*
because it was first made in the Syrian town of Damascus; a third
is called *velvet*, meaning downy, because it has a nap on the opposite side.

In chapter 1 of his book *On Proper Usage to Commodus*, Pollux 19
explains how and when cloth of purple was invented: The Tyrians
say that when Hercules had fallen in love with a certain nymph of
their region named Tyros, there was a dog following him about
who caught a glimpse of a purple fish creeping into the rocks and
took a bite of it, thus staining its lips with purplish dye. When
Hercules approached the girl, she insisted that she would have
nothing more to do with him unless he brought her a garment
even more brilliant than his dog's lips, whose unusual tint she
found so alluring. Hercules therefore searched out the animal, collected its blood, presented it to the girl and became (so the
Tyrians assert) the first to discover a purple dye-stuff.

The purple-fish, according to Pliny in book 9, chapter 36, is a 20
kind of bivalve, living no longer than seven years. In the spring-
time they school, and by rubbing together they emit a waxy sort of
fluid. But deep in the gullet they keep the famous liquid that dyes
clothes, and they vomit it out with their lives, which requires their
being taken alive. From them comes a purple color that gleams
faintly with the lustre of a dusky rose. The *murex*, also called
conchylium, is of the same group of bivalves but is not identical to
the purple-fish, and its blood, called *ostrum*, also makes a purple

bus eiuscemodi piscium—purpurae, muricis, conchylii—nomina pro ipso colore passim usurpantur.

21   Fuit Romae purpurae usus iam inde ab initio urbis conditae, distinguebatque ab equite curiam, id est, insigne erat Romanorum magistratuum quae idcirco quam plurimo vendebatur. Nam violaceae purpurae libra tempore Augusti Caesaris centum denariis vaenibat, hoc est, decem nostris coronatis aureis. Postea *dibapha tyria* (ita dicta quod bis tincta esset et apud Tyrios infectores optimos) in libras, ut inquit Plinius, non poterat emi mille denariis, id est, centum coronatis. Quapropter cum posteritas semper luxuriosa fuerit, mirum profecto est purpurae usum tam rarum vel potius nobis penitus esse ignotum.

: VII :

De origine architecturae.

1   Homines primum more ferarum in sylvis et speluncis nascebantur ciboque agresti vescendo ibi vitam agebant, postea reperto igne, ut Vitruvio *De architectura* placet, cognitaque eius commoditate ad teporem propter vim frigoris arcendam, propius accedentes in unum plures convenire coeperunt, et in eo congressu quicquid vellent iam tum facile tractare ut qui rationis participes erant. Alii ex fronde tecta facere; alii speluncas sub montibus fodere, uti Troglodytae et Libyae quidam populi, Hesperiis Aethiopibus vicini, teste Strabone in 17 *Geographiae*, factitabant; nonnulli hirundinum nidos imitantes ex luto et virgultis condere loca quae subirent. Et sic usu venit ut homines—quorum ad quidvis intenditur ingenium valet, novis inventionibus gloriantes et alii aliis deinde ostendentes—ae-

color. This is why good authors use the names of these fish — purple, *murex* and *conchylium* — without distinction for the same color.

They used purple at Rome from the founding of the city on- 21
ward, and it distinguished senator from knight; in other words, it
was the mark of a Roman magistrate, and as a result its price was
very high. In Augustus Caesar's day a pound of violet-purple sold
for a hundred denarii or ten of our gold crowns. At a later time a
pound of Tyrian *dibapha* (so called because it was twice-dipped
and because the best dyers were from Tyre) could not be bought
for a thousand denarii, says Pliny — a hundred crowns. Thus,
since later generations kept up their extravagance, it is truly amazing how rare (altogether unknown, really) the use of purple has
become for us.

: VII :

On the origin of architecture.

At first people were born in caves and forests like animals and 1
spent their lives there feeding on what grows wild, but later, as
Vitruvius *On Architecture* believes, they discovered fire. Once they
recognized that its warmth was good for keeping off the force of
cold, they moved closer to it and many gathered into a single
group, an assembly in which they easily managed whatever they
wished because they shared a plan. Some built canopies out of foliage. Some dug caves beneath the hills, like the Troglodytes and
certain Libyan peoples, who were neighbors of the western Ethiopians, according to Strabo in book 17 of the *Geography*. Others
imitated swallows' nests, using clay and wattles to make dwell-
ings that they could enter. Thus it happened that humans — who
bragged about their new inventions, who showed them off to one
another, whose talent was equal to its every aim — began con-

dificia informare, parietes furcis rectis et virgultis interpositis luto texere, luteas glebas arefacientes struere et ut imbres et aestus vitarent arundinibus vel fronde tegere, vel ex ulva palustri tuguria componere coeperint.

2   Quae aedificia Vitruvius testatur sua etiam aetate construxisse Galliam, Hispaniam, Lusitaniam, Aquitaniam, Phrygiam. At etiam Aegyptus posuerat, secundum Diodorum. Imo apud omnes fere gentes talia hodie visuntur—nec mirum, cum sint qui etiam nunc sine aedificiis sub dio vitam ducant, pars in curribus, ut Scythae prope omnes, pars in campis, ut Nomades et Saraceni in Africa, qui sylvestres nuncupantur.

3   Atque eo pacto rem paulatim ad artem—id est, architecturam—deductam ferunt quae aedificandi rationem docet quam, autore Diodoro in 6, Palladi assignant. Quod ego ex Iosephi testimonio, aut Cain Adam primi hominis filio aut Iobal ex Lamech genito potius attribuerim, quorum alter primus, sicut infra dicemus, oppidum alter tabernaculum condidit. Unde deinceps non modo casas sed domos ex lateritiis parietibus et lapide structas tum deorum templa quam ornatissima facere coeperunt. Sed iam ad aedificiorum diversi generis autores transeamus.

structing buildings, fabricating walls from forked uprights and wattles woven in clay, piling dried clods of clay on top of one another and covering them with reeds or foliage to shield them from rain and heat, or erecting huts of sedge from the swamp.

Vitruvius certifies that in his own day such buildings were still 2 constructed in Gaul, Spain, Lusitania, Aquitania and Phrygia. Even Egypt built them, according to Diodorus. Indeed, they are seen today in almost every country — and no wonder, for even now there are those who live their lives beneath the sky without buildings, some in wagons, like nearly all the Scythians, and others in the open plains, like the Nomads and the Saracens in Africa, who are called wild people.

They claim that in such a way this activity was gradually re- 3 duced to an art — namely, architecture — that teaches a method of building which, according to Diodorus in book [5], they assign to Pallas. But on the basis of Josephus' testimony, I would rather attribute it to Cain, the son of Adam, the first man, or to Jobal, whom Lamech begot. The former, as we shall explain below, was the first to build a town, and the latter first pitched a tent. Eventually they began building not mere huts but houses of brick walls and stone, and richly appointed temples for the gods came later. But now let us move on to those who invented buildings of various kinds.

: VIII :

*Qui primi luteas aut lateritias domos aedificaverint; et tegulas
et lapidicinas invenerint; et de prima columnarum origine;
et quando primum marmorum usus Romae in aedificiis.*

1 Domos luteas, teste Plinio libro 7, Doxius Celii filius primus aedificavit, sumpto ab hirundinum nidis exemplo. Lateritias uero,
hoc est, ex lateribus constructas, eodem autore Euryalus et Hyperbius fratres Athenis primum fecerunt. Earum structuras Diodorus
in 6 dicit Vestam Saturni ex Rhea filiam primam invenisse. Domos ipsas et agros, teste Laertio, Epimenides Cretensis primitus
expiasse dicitur. Tegulas quibus domus teguntur Cinyra, Agriopae
filius, in Cypro insula invenit. Lapidicinas, hoc est loca ubi lapides effodiuntur, Cadmus Thebis (aut sicut Theophrasto placet in
Phoenice), autor Plinius.

2 Verum ego huiusmodi rerum inventionem verius, ut opinor,
Cain aut Seth eius fratris filiis assignarim, quando ille, teste Iosepho in 1 *Antiquitatum,* mortalium omnium primus oppidum condidit — de quo infra mentionem planiorem faciam. Isti vero, ut in
primo huius operis volumine demonstravimus, columnas duas, id
est unam lateritiam alteram lapideam, ut in eis rerum coelestium
disciplinam inscriberent construxerunt, quam primam columnarum atque laterum originem esse dixerim. Quo apparet in ipso
fere mundi primordio domos aliaque aedificia ex diversis materiis
construendi usum fuisse. Non eo tamen inficias eos quos ex autoritate Plinii prodidimus uspiam deinceps haec primos docuisse.

3 De marmore restat dicere, cuius fodiendi causa — tantum enim
delitiarum olim mortalibus obrepsit — natura ipsa rerum pene acta
est in planum, montes ipsi caesi, promontoria mari aperta, viscera

: VIII :

Who first built houses of mud or brick; who invented roof-tiles and quarries; on the origin of columns; and when marble was first used for buildings in Rome.

According to Pliny in book 7, Doxius the son of Celius first built 1
mud houses, taking swallow's nests as his model. But the same author says that the brothers Euryalus and Hyperbius in Athens built the first houses that were latericious or made of brick. Diodorus claims in book 6 that Vesta, Saturn's daughter from Rhea, first discovered how to construct them. They say that Epimenides of Crete was the first who used a ritual to purify these houses and fields, according to Laertius. Cinyra, Agriopa's son, invented tiles for roofing houses on the island of Cyprus. Thebes (or Phoenicia, if we believe Theophrastus) was where Cadmus made the first quarry, which is a place for digging stones — as Pliny tells it.

But I think it more accurate to assign the invention of such 2
things to the sons of Cain or of Seth, his brother, for Cain — as I shall explain more clearly below — was the first of all mortals to build a town, according to Josephus in book 1 of the *Antiquities*. These people, as I pointed out in the first book of this work, erected two columns on which to inscribe their astronomical learning, one of brick, the other of stone, and I would call this the origin of columns and bricks. Hence it is obvious that various materials were in use for constructing houses and other buildings almost at the very beginning of the world. But I do not deny that those of whom I have written on Pliny's authority were the first to teach about these things in other places for later generations.

It remains to tell about marble. So great a taste for luxury once 3
beguiled mortals that they nearly leveled the world in digging it up, hewing away the hills, opening headlands to the sea, tearing

denique terrae in sexcentas partes dilacerata sunt. Unde, ut de caeteris sileam, ad Romanos tanta marmoris (cuius convehendi gratia
naves etiam fiebant) copia venit ut Marci Scauri aedilitate, autore
Plinio libro 36 *Naturalis historiae*, trecentae sexaginta columnae
marmoreae ad scenam theatri non diutius ludorum celebritate du-
raturi portatae sint. At Lucius Crassus orator primus peregrini
marmoris columnas habuit. Marcus vero Lepidus primus omnium limina ex Numidico marmore in domo posuit—magna
reprehensione—qui consul fuit anno urbis DCLXXVI. Crusta marmoris primus, teste Cornelio Nepote, totius domus parietes Mamurra eques Romanus operuit qui fuit praefectus fabrorum Gaii
Caesaris in Gallia. Marmore autem scalpendo primi omnium in-
claruerunt Dipoenus et Scylus, geniti in Creta insula prius quam
Cyrus in Persis regnare inciperet.

: IX :

Qui primi condiderint oppidum, muros, turres, tabernacula,
delubra; aut quis primus Deo omnipotenti templum posuerit;
et qui puteos foderint.

1   Mortales ab initio conditis per rura casis, ut dictum est, paulatim
    inter se coeundo e fera agrestique vita ad mansuetiores mores per-
    venerunt, tuncque primum vinculo quodam societatis simul viven-
    tes oppidum—hoc est, locum muris munitum—aedificarunt ut eo
    opes suas conferrent ubi nullum esset hostium periculum; qui inde
    cives a coeundo vocati sunt, et ipsum oppidum urbs quam colit ci-

even the bowels of the earth into a thousand pieces. To say nothing of other consequences, so great a quantity of marble (whose transportation also required the building of ships) came to Rome that when Marcus Scaurus was aedile, 360 marble columns were imported for the stage of a theater meant to stand no longer than it took to celebrate the games, according to Pliny in book 36 of the *Natural History*. But Lucius Crassus the orator was the first to own columns of foreign marble, while the first to put sills of Numidian marble in his house—and to be greatly criticized for it—was Marcus Lepidus, consul in 676 AUC. Mamurra, the Roman knight who was Gaius Caesar's chief of engineers in Gaul, first covered the walls of his whole house with marble veneer, according to Cornelius Nepos. The first famous sculptors in marble were Dipoenus and Scylus, born on the island of Crete before Cyrus began his reign in Persia.

: IX :

Who were the first people to found a town; to make walls, towers, tents and shrines; to erect a temple to God Almighty; and to dig wells.

After mortals had raised their huts throughout the countryside, as explained above, they gradually came together with one another and left their wild, brutish life for gentler ways. Living together, they formed the first bonds of society, and they built a town—a place fortified with walls, in other words—so that they might bring their possessions together where there was no danger from enemies. Hence they were called citizens because of their coming together. And the town inhabited by the community or union of citizens was called a city from the plow-beam, the curved part of

vitas, id est, civium coetus dicta ab urvo, parte aratri curva, quo illi antiqui homines ritu hetrusco sulcum ducebant intra quem oppidum posituri essent, ut illud fossa muroque munitum foret.

2   Hoc primus omnium, teste Plinio, Cecrops condidit, qui fuit, ut Iustinus ait in secundo, ante Deucalionis tempora, idque a se Cecropiam nominavit, quae deinde arx fuit Athenis. Aliqui Argos quod Pelasgicum, autore Strabone libro 8 *Geographiae*, Homerus vocat a Phoroneo rege ante conditum volunt, de quo Lucanus in sexto:

>   ubi nobile quondam,
> Nunc super Argos arant.

Fuit alterum Argos in Attica, aliud, ut Plinius in 4 est testis, in Achaia Hippium cognominatum. Quidam etiam Sicyonem prius constructam dicunt. Aegyptii vero multo ante apud se Diospolin, id est Iovis oppidum, aedificatam asserunt, quod fidem propius est cum ipsi omnino antiquissimi sint. De hoc oppido Strabo libro 17 meminit.

3   Muros Thrason fecit primus omnium. Turres, ut Aristoteles ait, Cyclopes invenerunt, ut Theophrastus Phoenices, quod Vergilius Palladi assignare videtur in *Bucolicis*:

>   Pallas quas condidit arces
> Ipsa colat.

Quae quidem omnia postea inventa puto, cum Cain Adam filius (qui, sicut palam est, in ipso propemodum orbis principio fuit, autore Iosepho in primo *Antiquitatum*), mortalium omnium primus urbem condiderit murisque muniverit, quam ab Enoch filio suo seniore Enochiam appellavit. Turrim vero quae prae altitudine vix oculis terminari poterat in eo loco quae deinceps Babylon vocata est, ut idem testatur, iuventus post diluvium Noe rursum vim aquarum formidans, id suadente Nemroth, primum construxit.

the plow used by the ancients in an Etruscan ritual for cutting the furrow within which to establish a town, in order to fortify it with a trench and a wall.

Cecrops, according to Pliny, founded a town before anyone else. 2 In book 2, Justin says that he lived before Deucalion's time. He named his town Cecropia after himself, and afterwards it became the stronghold of Athens. Others maintain that King Phoroneus had already founded the Argos that Homer calls Pelasgian, according to Strabo in book 8 of the *Geography*. Lucan describes it in book 6 as

Plowland now, but once famous.

There was a second Argos in Attica, and another called Hippium in Achaia, as Pliny attests in book 4. Some say that Sicyon also was constructed earlier. But the Egyptians claim that Diospolis, the town of Jupiter, was built in their land long before this, which is nearer the truth since they are certainly a very ancient people. Strabo mentions this town in book 17.

Thrason made the first walls. The Cyclopes invented towers, 3 says Aristotle, but Theophrastus claims it was the Phoenicians, and in the *Bucolics* Vergil seems to assign them to Pallas:

Let Pallas live in the strongholds she erected.

I believe these were all later inventions because Cain, Adam's son (who obviously lived very near the beginning of the world, according to Josephus in the first book of the *Antiquities*), was the first of all mortals to found a city and fortify it with walls, naming it Enochia after Enoch, his elder son. After Noah's flood the young people erected the first tower in the place later called Babylon because they feared the return of the mighty waters and Nemroth urged them to it, as Josephus testifies, and the tower was so tall that the eye could hardly take it in.

4   Quare Cecropiam, Argos, Sicyonem, Diospolin urbes una cum
turribus postea conditas fuisse iam meo iudicio liquido constat.
Tabernacula, teste Iosepho in primo *Antiquitatum*, Iobal, filius Lamech, fecit, quamvis Phoenices Saeculi nepotibus attribuant, autor Eusebius *De praeparatione evangelica*.

5   Delubra Epimenidem Cretensem primum aedificasse, autor est
Diogenes Laertius libro 1. At Vitruvius Pythium architectum primum omnium Priene aedem Minervae fecisse tradit. Herodotus
tamen libro 2 Aegyptios, ut nos in primo huius operis volumine
scripsimus, primos diis delubra statuisse prodidit. Romae, teste
Livio, Romulus templum locavit Iovi Feretrio, quod primum omnium more gentis sacratum fuit.

6   Deo autem omnipotenti Solomon rex Hebraeorum ab ortu
Adam primi hominis tribus millibus centum et duobus post annis
primus omnium, autore Iosepho libro 8 *Antiquitatum*, Hierosolymis templum condidit, quod David illius patrem extruere paran-
tem, Deus per Nathan prophetam ab opere propterea quod manus
hostium sanguine pollutas haberet revocavit, eique iussit ut id So-
lomoni filio condendum relinqueret. Quod quidem templum cum
miro opificum artificio tum ingenti auri copia quo ornatum erat
omnium profecto operum quae tunc in orbe terrarum extabant ce-
leberrimum fuit.

7   Secus tamen factitavit Alexander romanus imperator, vir in hac
parte haud mehercle contemnendus, qui teste Lampridio in templis nunquam praeter quatuor aut quinque argenti libras, auri ne
guttulam quidem aut bracteolam posuit, identidem versum Persii
repetens:

        In sacro quid facit aurum?

8   Puteos, autore Plinio in 7, Danaus ex Aegypto advectus in
Graeciam quae vocabatur Argos Dipsion fodit. Quod sane absurdum est, nam ut ab ovo (veluti dicitur) incipiam, constat primo

So now it seems perfectly clear to me that the cities of Cecro- 4
pia, Argos, Sicyon and Diospolis along with their towers were
later foundations. Jobal, the son of Lamech, made tents, according
to Josephus in the first book of the *Antiquities*, though the Phoenicians attribute them to the grandsons of Aeon, according to
Eusebius in the *Preparation for the Gospel*.

Diogenes Laertius writes in book 1 that Epimenides of Crete 5
was the first builder of shrines. But Vitruvius reports that the architect Pythius, who built a sanctuary for Minerva at Priene, was
first. Herodotus, however, recorded in book 2 that the Egyptians
were the first to set up shrines for the gods, as we noted in the first
book of this work. Romulus established a temple in Rome for Jupiter the Striker, says Livy, and it was the first one consecrated in
the manner of his people.

But Solomon, king of the Hebrews, built the first temple for 6
God Almighty in Jerusalem in the year 3102 after the creation of
Adam, the first man, according to Josephus in book 8 of the *Antiquities*. When Solomon's father David was preparing to construct it,
God spoke through the prophet Nathan and called him back from
the work because his hands were stained with the blood of his enemies, and God commanded him to leave the building of it to his
son. The skill of this temple's artisans was as wondrous as the
abundance of its gold furnishings was immense, and it was surely
the most celebrated of all the works then standing on earth.

The Roman emperor Alexander behaved differently, and I cer- 7
tainly think one should not dismiss what he did: According to
Lampridius, he never gave more than four or five pounds of silver
for his temples, and of gold not a thin leaf nor even a speck. He always used to repeat the line from Persius:

What good is gold in a temple?

Danaus dug wells after he traveled from Egypt to a place in 8
Greece called Thirsty Argos, writes Pliny in book 7. But this is

Abraham et Isaac, sicut patet in Genesis libro capite 26, ac deinde alios Hebraeos de Aegypto egressos duce Mose per solitudines multos fodisse puteos, quo tempore nondum Danaus erat, dicente Iosepho *Contra Appionem:* Iam palam vero est ex praedictis annis tempore computato quia hi qui vocabantur pastores — id est, nostri progenitores — ex Aegypto liberati ante tres et nonaginta atque trecentos annos hanc provinciam inhabitavere quam Danaus Argos accederet.

9   Sed nec Argis quidem Danaus puteos fodit, verum eius filiae. Poetae enim aiunt, ut testis est Strabo libro 8, Argos aquis carere, unde Homeri versus:

θεοὶ δ 'αὖ θέσαν "Αργος ἄνυδρον.
Dii posuere Argos lympharum protinus expers.

Sed non ipsam regionem, quae amnibus irrigua est, aquarum inopia laborare volunt, verum oppidum. Urbem vero illam, ut Strabo ait, in loco iacuisse arido ferunt in qua magna erat puteorum copia quos non Danaus, sicut Plinio placet, sed eius filiae fecerunt, testificante hoc carmine:

"Αργος ἄνυδρον ἐὸν Δανααὶ θέσαν "Αργος ἔνυδρον.
Argos aquis vacuum Danaae struxere redundans.

truly ridiculous, for if I may begin from the ground up, as they say, it is obvious from chapter 26 of the book of Genesis that Abraham and Isaac were the first, and other Hebrews later dug many wells in the wilderness when Moses led them on their march out of Egypt. At this time Danaus was not yet born, as Josephus says in *Against Apion*: Now when the chronology of these years has been reckoned, it is clear that those who were called shepherds — our ancestors, in other words — were freed from Egypt and settled in this territory 393 years before Danaus reached Argos.

And even at Argos it was not Danaus but his daughters who dug wells, for Strabo tells us in book 8 how the poets say that Argos has no water, as in Homer's line:

Theoi d'au thesan Argos anundron.
The gods made Argos utterly lacking water.

They do not mean that the region suffers from want of water, for its rivers make it swampy, only that the town is dry. As Strabo says, they claim that the city was located in an arid spot where a great many wells were made not by Danaus, as Pliny supposes, but by his daughters, on the evidence of this verse:

Argos anudron eon Danaai thesan Argos enundron.
The daughters of Danaus watered Argos the waterless.

: X :

De primis labyrinthorum pyramidumque autoribus et de
Mausoleo sepulchro; ac de vario apud gentes olim sepeliendi
usu; et unde apud Romanos mos cremandi cadavera
consecrandorumque imperatorum post mortem;
atque de origine funebris orationis.

1 Operaepretium est ut antequam hinc digrediamur labyrinthos dicamus, portentosissimum humani ingenii opus. In se enim continent mille itinerum ambages, occursus ac recursus inexplicabiles
crebris foribus inditis ad fallendum occursus redeundumque in errores eosdem. Quatuor fuisse commemorantur, primus in Aegypto. Quem alii regiam Mothaerudis principis fuisse existimant,
alii sepulchrum Meridis (quod etiam Diodorus sentit.) Plures alii
Solis honori extructum ferunt. Hunc Plinius libro 36 ait a Petesuco rege sive a Tithoe esse conditum. At Herodotus libro 2 commune Aegyptiorum regum opus appellat, seque illum vidisse
paulo supra stagnum Myrios, versus Crocodilorum urbem, conditum testatur. De quo Strabo etiam in 17 meminit.

2 Hinc sumpsisse Daedalum exemplar illius quem fecit in Creta
non est dubium, sed centesimam tantum eius portionem imita-
tum. Alter hic ab Aegyptio labyrinthus fuit, de quo intellexit
poeta in sexto *Aeneidos*, dicens:

Hic labor ille domus et inextricabilis error.

Et Ariadne apud Ovidium *Epistola* 10:

Cum tibi, ne victus tecto morerere recurvo,
Quae regerent passus pro duce fila dedi.

: X :

On the first builders of labyrinths and pyramids and on the
tomb of Mausolus; on various burial practices of ancient
peoples; on the sources of the Roman customs
of cremating corpses and deifying emperors after death;
and on the origin of the funeral oration.

Before we leave this subject it will be worthwhile to say something   1
about labyrinths, those most fantastic works of human ingenuity.
Inside them are a thousand twisting passages, impassable comings
and goings set with frequent doorways to deceive those who meet
them and lead them back to their wanderings. Four such labyrinths have been reported, the first one in Egypt. Some think it
was the palace of Prince Mothaerus, others the tomb of Meris (as
Diodorus also believes). Several others report that it was constructed in honor of the Sun. Pliny says in book 36 that King
Petesucus or Tithoes built it. But in book 2 Herodotus calls it the
collective work of the kings of Egypt, and he declares that he saw
it standing just beyond the swamp of Myrios, near the City of
Crocodiles. Strabo also mentions it in book 17.

This undoubtedly was the model for what Daedalus built in   2
Crete, though he reproduced only a hundredth of it. His labyrinth
was second after the one in Egypt, and it was his that the poet had
in mind in the sixth book of the *Aeneid*, writing:

And here the house of labor, an endless maze.

And in Ovid's tenth *Epistle*, Ariadne says:

When I gave you guiding threads to rule your steps
Lest in a crooked house prevailer perish.

Idem Naso in 8 *Metamorphoseon:*

> Daedalus ingenio fabrae celeberrimus artis,
> Ponit opus turbatque notas et lumina flexu,
> Ducit in errorem variarum ambage viarum.

Plinius quoque et Plutarchus in *Vita Thesei* et Strabo atque divus Hieronymus mentionem faciunt.

3   Tertius in Lemno fuit quem, eodem Plinio autore, fecere architecti Zmilus et Rholus et Theodorus indigena; cuius Plinii aetate, ut ipse est testis, reliquiae extabant. Quartus in Italia. Omnes lapide polito fornicibus tecti. Italicum Labyrinthum, sicut testatur Plinius, sibi fecit Porsena rex Hetruscorum sepulchri causa, de quo Varro: sepultus est Porsena sub urbe Clusio, in quo loco monimentum reliquit lapide quadrato, singula latera pedum lata tricenum, alta quinquagenum, inque basi quadrata intus labyrinthum inextricabilem, et cetera. De labyrinthis satis est dictum.

4   Sequuntur pyramides, quarum autores minime sunt sua laude fraudandi propter videlicet earum magnitudinem. Tam altae enim in Aegypto fuisse traduntur ut magna omnium admiratio fuerit qua ratione in tantam altitudinem subvecta forent caementa. Tres autem pyramides, autore Plinio, inter Memphim et Deltam fuisse constat, quarum unam ac reliquarum maximam (teste Diodoro libro 2) CCCLX hominum millia annis XX construxisse produntur. Quam, ut idem dicit, sibi fecit ut in ea sepeliretur, quando istae pyramides aliud nihil erant nisi sepulchra, Chemis rex—quem Herodotus Cheopem appellat. Post hunc regnum obtinuit, sicuti Diodorus ait, Cephus eius frater; quidam non fratrem sed filium nomine Chabreum regnum tenuisse asserunt, quod similius vero Diodorus autumat. At Herodotus non Chabreum, nisi codex mendosus est, sed Chephrenem, et non filium, verum fratrem illius qui primam condidit pyramidem vocat.

Again in book 8 of the *Metamorphoses* Ovid writes:

Famous Daedalus, skilled in the art of building,
Puts confusion in his work and winding ways,
False signs and passages constructed to trick the eye.

Pliny, Plutarch in his *Life of Theseus*, Strabo and St. Jerome also make note of it.

The third labyrinth was on Lemnos, again according to Pliny, 3 and the architects who built it were Zmilus, Rholus and Theodorus, a native of the place. The ruins of the labyrinth were standing there in Pliny's day, as he himself tells us. The fourth was in Italy. All were roofed with arches of smooth stone. The Etruscan king Porsenna built the Italian labyrinth as his tomb, so Pliny testifies, and Varro says that Porsenna was entombed near the city of Clusium, where he left a sepulcher of fitted stone thirty feet on a side, fifty feet high, with a square base containing an impassable labyrinth, and so on. Enough about labyrinths.

Next come pyramids, whose inventors are by no means to be 4 cheated of glory for works of such magnitude. They say that those in Egypt were so high that everyone was much amazed to see quarry-stones conveyed by some technique to so great a height. According to Pliny, it is well known that there were three pyramids between Memphis and the Delta. One of them was much larger than the others (says Diodorus in book [1]), and reportedly it was built over a period of twenty years by 360,000 men. King Chemis — whom Herodotus calls Cheops — made it for his burial, Diodorus adds, for these pyramids were nothing more than tombs. His brother Cephus gained the throne after him, says Diodorus, though some claim it was not his brother but his son Chabreus who held it, which Diodorus maintains is the likelier. Unless the text is defective, however, Herodotus calls him Chephren, not Chabreus, and he makes him the brother rather than the son of the man who built the first pyramid.

5   Conveniunt tamen ut hic, sive filius eius sive frater fuerit, alteram pyramidem aedificaverit, arte priori similem magnitudine quidem imparem. Et hae duae, autore Strabone, inter septem spectacula mundi numeratae sunt. Martialis:

Barbara pyramidum sileat miracula Memphis.

Hunc regem, ut Herodotus et Diodorus produnt, secutus est Mycerinus rex, prioris pyramidis autoris filius. Is tertiam pyramidem longe minorem paterna vicenis (velut testatur Herodotus in 2) pedibus ex omni parte reliquit.

6   Hanc quidam, teste Strabone, Rhodopae meretriculae ab amantibus positam volunt, narrantes huiusmodi fabulam. Cum ea aliquando lavaretur, aquila alterum calceum e manu ancillae rapuit et in gremium regis iura Memphi dantis dimisit. Rex demiratus perquiri mulierem iussit, quam in urbe Naucratitarum inventam uxorem duxit, et mortuae inde pyramidem construxit. Quod Herodotus prorsus falsum esse dicit cum Rhodope mulier longe post fuerit quam reges qui pyramides fecissent.

7   Isti igitur reges quos commemoravimus pyramidum autores traduntur, etsi Diodorus libro 2 et Plinius in 36 *Naturalis historiae* a quibus factae sint non satis constare dicunt, iustissimo casu obliteratis tantae vanitatis autoribus. Pyramides autem faciendi, teste Plinio, causa a quibusdam traditur ne plebs esset ociosa.

8   Quare Iosephus in 2 *Antiquitatum* dicit Aegyptios coegisse Hebraeos pyramides aedificare ut eos huiusmodi labore attererent, aut ne reges pecuniam successoribus aut aemulis insidiantibus relinquerent vel praeberent. Propter quod ipse Plinius haec opera regum pecuniae ociosam ac stultam ostentationem vocat.

All agree that the latter, whether son or brother, built the sec- 5
ond pyramid, which was as well made as the first but smaller in
size. Both were counted among the seven wonders of the world,
according to Strabo. And Martial writes:

Silence, Memphis, exotic pyramidic spectacle.

Herodotus and Diodorus relate that King Mycerinus, son of the
builder of the first pyramid, succeeded this last-mentioned king
and left a third pyramid which was more than twenty feet smaller
than his father's in every dimension (claims Herodotus in book 2).

According to Strabo, however, some suggest that it was put up 6
for the courtesan Rhodope by her lovers, and the story runs as follows. One day she was bathing and an eagle snatched one of her
sandals from her maid's hand and dropped it in the king's lap as
he was holding court in Memphis. Puzzled, the king ordered a
search for the woman, and when he found her in the city of
Naucratis, he married her, and later when she died he built a pyramid for her. Herodotus says this is totally false because Rhodope
was a woman who lived long after the kings who made the pyramids.

Thus, the builders of pyramids are said to be the kings whom 7
we have mentioned, though Diodorus in book [1] and Pliny in
book 36 of the *Natural History* say that those who made them have
not been clearly identified, an obscure fate well deserved by the authors of so much vanity. According to Pliny some hold that the
motive for building the pyramids was to keep the common people
busy.

Hence Josephus says in book 2 of the *Antiquities* that the Egyp- 8
tians forced the Hebrews to build the pyramids in order to grind
them down with such labor, unless it was to keep the money of
the kings from their successors or from conspiring rivals. Accordingly, Pliny himself calls these works an idle and senseless display
of royal wealth.

9   Verum ego hanc potius fuisse causam opinor: quod Aegyptii, ut ait Diodorus, domos nostras diversoria appellabant tanquam brevi tempore a nobis inhabitandas. Mortuorum vero sepulchra sempiternas domos quoniam apud inferos infinitum sit tempus. Idcirco domus aedificandae curam contemnebant, sepulchrorum magnificentiae, ut stultissime fit etiam apud nos hodie, summum studium operamque tantum impendentes. Quamvis nonnulli, teste Diodoro, Aegyptios huiusmodi sepulchrorum praecipuum studium ab Aethiopibus esse mutuatos asseverent. Nemo tamen rex ex iis qui eas pyramides condiderant in illis sepultus est, autore Diodoro in 1.

10 Mausoleum autem, id est, Mausoli regis Cariae monimentum, autore Strabone libro 14 *Geographiae*, Artemisia eius uxor extruxit, quod teste Plinio libro 36 inter septem miracula adnumeratum est. Martialis:

Aere nec vacuo pendentia Mausolea.

De quo etiam meminit Cicero, Lucanus, Gellius et Vitruvius.

11 Varius praeterea apud gentes olim usus sepeliendi cadavera fuit. Mortui enim Persarum non prius humabantur quam aut ab alite aut a cane traherentur. Massagetae et Derbicae miserrimos putabant qui aegrotatione morerentur; et parentes, cognatos, propinquos cum ad senectutem pervenissent iugulatos devorabant, rectius esse ducentes ut ipsi potius quam vermes comessent. Tibareni quos dilexissent senes suspendebant patibulis. Albani Caucasi montis accolae mortuorum curam habere aut meminisse nefas putabant, quibus cum etiam pecunias defodiebant.

12 Aegyptii statim mortuo homine ferro incurvo cerebrum per nares educebant, locum illum medicamentis explentes. Dehinc acutissimo lapide Aethiopico circa ilia conscindebant atque illac omnem alvum protrahebant, quam ubi repurgaverant, rursus odoribus contusis resarciebant, inde iterum consuebant ubi haec fecis-

But they had another motive, I believe. The Egyptians used to 9
call our homes roadhouses, so Diodorus says, as if we were to live
in them only briefly. But the tombs of the dead were eternal
homes since time in the underworld was unending. Therefore they
made light of any worries about building a home, expending maximum effort and energy only on the grandeur of their tombs, just
as stupidly as we do today. And yet according to Diodorus some
insist that the Egyptians borrowed their special fondness for such
tombs from the Ethiopians. But Diodorus writes in book 1 that
not one of those kings who built the pyramids was buried in
them.

The Mausoleum, the sepulcher of King Mausolus of Caria, was 10
built by his wife Artemisia, according to Strabo in book 14 of the
Geography, and Pliny says it is counted among the seven wonders.
Martial writes:

Nor the Mausoleum hanging in empty air.

Cicero, Lucan, Gellius and Vitruvius also mention it.

In the past, the method of burying corpses also varied from 11
people to people. No Persian dead were buried before being
dragged by a large bird or a dog. The Massagetes and Derbicae believed that people who were dying of disease were the most unfor-
tunate. When parents, relatives or neighbors reached old age, they
cut their throats and ate them, thinking it better that they dine on
them rather than the worms. The Tibareni hung the old folks
whom they loved best on gibbets. The Albanians dwelling near
Mt. Caucasus thought it a crime to be concerned about the dead
or to mention them, and they put money in the grave with them.

As soon as someone died, the Egyptians drew the brain out 12
through the nostrils with a curved iron tool and filled the space
with medicines. Then they used a sharp Ethiopian stone to make
a cut around the lower abdomen and remove all the intestines
from it, cleaning the area, refilling it with crushed spices and then

sent. Saliebant nitro abditum LXX dies; nam diutius salire non licebat. Quibus exactis, cadaver sindone involvebant gummi illinientes. Eo deinde recepto, propinqui ligneam hominis effigiem faciebant in qua inserebant mortuum, inclusumque ita reponebant. Et id, ut arbitror, ideo factitabant ut eo pacto condita cadavera diuturnius incorrupta servarentur, nam Aegyptii, teste Servio in tertium *Aeneidos*, secuti Stoicorum sententiam persuasum habebant tandiu animam durare quandiu duraret et corpus.

13   Aethiopes Macrobii, id est longaevi, in vitreis sepulchris mortuos condere. Scythae eos qui a demortuis amati fuissent vivos infodiebant cum ossibus mortuorum. Regem autem suum ubi mortuum ad eas gentes quibus imperasset circuntulissent, similiter humo tegebant, atque cum eo sepeliebant aliquam eius pallacam strangulatam, et eum qui vina miscuisset, aut qui praefuisset nunciis, necnon omnium rerum primitias. Nasamones sedentes mortuos humabant, observantes ut dum quis coepisset agere animam eum sedentem constituerent ne supinus spiritum efflaret. Hyrcani volucribus et canibus semivivos proiiciebant.

14   Thraces mortuos suos per lusum et laetitiam terrae demandare, praedicantes in qua tot malis liberati essent felicitate. Contra edito puero, propinqui eum ploratu prosequebantur, exponentes quascunque necesse foret illi quod vitam ingressus esset perpeti humanas calamitates—institutum mehercle inter tot vitae mala sapientiae plenum. Eorum autem optimates simul atque combusti essent sepeliebantur. Quidam Aethiopum demortuos in flumen proiiciebant, existimantes id optimum sepulchrum esse. Aut vitro circundatos domi servabant; aliqui fictilibus condebant atque infodiebant. Assyrii melle condebant ac cera oblinebant. Nabathaei cadavera pro stercore habebant regesque suos in sterquiliniis defo-

stitching up the site of the operation. Next they salted the body away in niter for seventy days, allowing no longer period of salting. When all this was finished, they wrapped the corpse in a shroud coated with gum. Finally, the relatives took the corpse and put it into a wooden effigy made to resemble the deceased, and they stored it away enclosed in this manner. In my opinion, they did this so that corpses thus interred would be preserved unspoiled for a longer time. For the Egyptians, according to Servius on the third book of the *Aeneid*, followed a Stoic teaching in believing that the soul would endure only as long as the body.

The Macrobian or long-lived Ethiopians buried their dead in 13 glass coffins. The Scythians buried alive those whom the deceased had loved along with the bones of the dead person. They carried their dead king around to the tribes whom he had ruled, and in the same way they strangled, covered with earth and buried with him one of his concubines — also the person who mixed his wines, the one in charge of his messengers, as well as first-fruits of all sorts. The Nasamones interred their dead sitting, and when they saw someone about to give up the ghost, they sat him up straight lest he breathe out his spirit lying on his back. The Hyrcanians threw people half-dead to the birds and dogs.

Proclaiming the bliss to which their dead had been delivered 14 from so many troubles, the Thracians committed them to the earth with joy and celebration. But when a child was born, the kin gathered round to lament, telling all the mortal woes he must suffer because he had begun to live — a very wise practice in so evil an existence, I daresay. Their noblemen were buried immediately after they were burned. Some of the Ethiopians threw their dead into the river, which they considered the best tomb of all. Others kept them at home encased in glass, or else stored them in clay containers and buried them. The Assyrians preserved them with honey and covered them in wax. The Nabataeans thought of corpses as dung and buried their kings in dung-pits. The Taxili

diebant. Taxili mortuos vulturibus non secus proiiciebant atque Caspii caeteris bestiis.

15   Quaedam Indicae foeminae cum viris cremari sibi felicissimum gloriosumque putabant. Bactriani canibus ad hoc ipsum nutritis obiicere senes. Quod, ut divus Hieronymus est testis, cum Alexandri praefectus Nicanor emendare voluisset, pene amisit provinciam.

16   Parthorum sepultura aut avium aut canum laniatus erat. Isse-donum Asiaticae Scythiae populorum mos erat parentum funera cantibus prosequi, et proximorum congregatis coetibus, cadavera ipsa dentibus laniare pecudumque carnibus mista comedere, ac ca-pitibus auro incinctis pro poculo uti, quae autore Plinio libro 4 ul-tima erant pietatis officia. Herodotus tamen in quarto dicit illos parentum capitibus non loco poculi sed pro simulacro usos esse, immolantes illis quotannis maiores hostias multis cum caerimo-niis. Hyperborei hoc sepulturae genus optimum arbitrabantur. Ut si quos satietas teneret vitae, epulati delibutique de rupe nota praecipitarent sese in mare profundum.

17   Romani, teste Plinio in 7, postquam longinquis bellis obrutos erui cognoverunt cadavera comburere coeperunt. Primus omnium in Cornelia domo Sylla dictator crematus est, veritus talionem, id est, timens ne suum corpus e sepulchro extraheretur, perinde ac ipse Marii cadaver eruisset. Hinc igitur apud Romanos cremando-rum cadaverum usus increbuit, sed hunc magis foris quam domi servatum esse duco, nec tamen semper combusta sunt.

18   Illud vel scire licet apud Romanos consuevisse filios et propin-quos mortuorum corpora in rogum iniicere, autor Cicero, qui libro *Tusculanorum* I ita de ea re scribit: Metellum multi filii, filiae, nepo-tes in rogum imposuerunt. Fuit et apud alios huiuscemodi mos

did the same by throwing their dead to vultures, the Caspians by leaving them for other beasts.

Certain women in India thought it glorious and very fortunate 15 to be cremated with their husbands. The Bactrians cast old people to dogs that they had bred for this work. St. Jerome tells us that when Alexander's governor Nicanor aimed to correct this practice, he nearly lost the province.

Burial for the Parthians was to be mangled by birds or dogs. It 16 was customary for the Issedonians, a people of Asian Scythia, to follow the funeral processions of their parents while singing. When great crowds of relatives had gathered, they tore the corpses to pieces with their teeth and ate them mixed with the flesh of animals, and then they wreathed their skulls with gold and used them as cups which, according to Pliny in book 4, was the final act of filial duty. But in book 4 Herodotus says that they made likenesses, not cups, from their parents' skulls, offering great and ceremonious sacrifice to them every year. The Hyperboreans thought that the best kind of burial was this: When people felt themselves tired of life, they should dine and anoint themselves and then go to a particular cliff and throw themselves into the depths of the sea.

The Romans began to burn their corpses after they learned 17 that soldiers buried during foreign wars were being exhumed, according to Pliny in book 7. The first of the Cornelian house to be cremated was the dictator Sulla, for he feared retaliation. He was afraid that his body would be removed from the tomb, in other words, exactly as he had exhumed the corpse of Marius. From that time, then, the practice of cremating corpses increased among the Romans, but it was used more often abroad than at home, I gather, and their bodies were not always burned.

Certainly one may learn from Cicero that sons and relatives put 18 the bodies of the dead on the funeral-pile in Rome. In book 1 of the *Tusculans* he writes about it as follows: Many sons, daughters

433

comburendi, Plinius enim testatur in 19 cum de lini generibus loquitur, scribens regum inde funebres tunicae corporis favillam ab reliquo separant cinere. Optimates etiam Thracum, ut diximus, comburebantur. Sed de hac re funerea plura alibi dicemus cum de anniversariis nostrorum exequiis disseretur.

19   Non est tamen silendum de more imperatorum consecrandorum, qui Romanis talis fuit. Sepulto corpore, imperatoris imaginem fingebant, eamque in regiae vestibulo supra lectum eburneum ponebant, ad aegroti speciem pallidam, quam circunstantibus utrinque senatu et matronis nobilioribus medici invisebant quotidie. Septimo autem post die ubi visus erat obiisse mortem, iuvenes utriusque ordinis lectum humeris in vetus forum primo dein in campum Martium perferebant. Ibique in tabernaculo ad exemplum turris structo ac aridis fomitibus oppleto locabant cum ingente aromatum acervo. Hic caerimoniis patrio more concelebratis, successor imperii facem tabernaculo admovebat, caeterisque ignem subiicientibus cuncta comburebantur. Mox e fastigio quodam aquila dimittebatur quae in coelum credebatur ipsam principis animam deferre. Ac iam ex illo una cum caeteris numinibus imperator colebatur. De hac re Herodianus statim in initio 4 libri latius meminit. Caeterum hanc consecrandi rationem posteritas sumpsisse videtur ex Caesaris dictatoris funere, cuius forma non multum ab ista fuit diversa.

20   Funebrem orationem de Bruti laudibus primus Valerius Publicola habuit, quae adeo grata iucundaque Romanis fuit ut ex eo consuetudo manserit ut qui strenue pugnando interiisset ab optimatibus laudaretur. Dicitur etiam funebribus Graecorum orationibus illa vetustior fuisse, nisi iam Solon (qui teste Gellio libro

and grandchildren laid Metellus on the funeral-pile. The same custom of burning also existed among other peoples, for when he talks about the varieties of linen in book 19, Pliny writes that the funeral tunics of kings separate the ash of the body from other cinders. Thracian noblemen were also burned, as we have explained. But we will have more to say elsewhere on this question of funerals when we discuss our annual days of remembrance for the dead.

We cannot fail to mention the custom of deifying emperors, such as it was among the Romans. After the body had been buried, they fashioned a likeness of the emperor, gave it the pallid look of the unwell and put it on an ivory couch in the entryway of the palace, where senators and ladies of society gathered round it and physicians made daily calls. On the seventh day after the death had become known, young men of both orders bore the couch on their shoulders, first to the Old Forum and then to the Campus Martius. There they placed it in a tent built like a tower which was full of dry kindling and heaped high with spices. After the ancient and customary ceremonies had been performed, the successor to empire put a torch to the tent, and the whole affair went up in a blaze as others in attendance added more fire. Then from a sort of gable they released an eagle which was believed to carry the soul of the prince to heaven. From that moment on they worshipped the emperor along with other divinities. Herodian treats this question more extensively just after the beginning of book 4. Otherwise it seems that later generations found their model of imperial deification in the funeral of the dictator Caesar, and its form was not much different from the above.

The first funeral oration was the one that Valerius Publicola gave in praise of Brutus. The Romans found the speech so pleasing and agreeable that it gave rise to the custom whereby the nobility eulogized a person who fell in hard fighting. They say that this practice was more ancient than the funeral orations of the

435

17 Tarquinio Prisco Romae regnante leges Atheniensibus dedit)
huius rei autor, ut Anaximenes orator dicit, antea fuerit, testis
Plutarchus in *Vita Valerii*. Apud Romanos deinde, autore eodem
Plutarcho in *Vita Camilli*, cum mulieres ornamenta aurea quibus
utebantur ad conficiendam pateram in Delphum mittendam con-
tribuerint, senatus decrevit ut quemadmodum pro viris ita etiam
pro foeminis in funere orationem haberi liceret. Hinc igitur demortuos laudandi mos fluxit quem nos hodie servamus.

21   Servamus autem in laudandis illis, si ne quid falsi dicere aude-
mus, qui dum vixere summopere curarunt ut ab omnibus bene au-
dirent — nam hoc unum in primis indicium virtutis et vitii in homine existit. Quippe natura quadam optimus quisque invigilat ut
de se reliqui mortales non malam imbibant opinionem, et post
mortem omni tempore bene loquantur, at ignavissimus non item.
Cuius sane rei coniectura Plato in *Epistola* 2 ad Dionysium tyrannum se duci affirmat ut credat esse aliquem sensum iis qui mortui
sunt rerum nostrarum.

: XI :

*Qui primi obeliscos fecerint aut Romam invexerint; et inibi
locus Plinii emaculatus; et de notis obeliscorum et quales essent
Aegyptiorum literae.*

1 Labyrinthos ac pyramides, regum opera omni admiratione digna,
superiore capite descripsimus eorum simul proditis autoribus. Sequuntur modo obelisci, quos reges iuxta certatim fecerunt. Sunt
autem obelisci trabes lapideae Solis numini sacratae, propter quod
ad radiorum similitudinem fiebant. Apud Aegyptios nomen ha-

Greeks, unless Solon (who gave the Athenians their laws while
Tarquinius Priscus reigned in Rome, according to Gellius in book
17) had already invented it, as Anaximenes the orator says according to Plutarch in his *Life of Valerius*. Plutarch also writes in the
Life of Camillus that when the women of Rome gave the golden
jewels they wore to make a bowl to be sent to Delphi, the Senate
decreed that funeral orations should be said for women just as for
men. Hence arose the custom of praising the deceased that we
keep today.

To tell the truth, we keep this custom for those who took the 21
greatest care to be in good repute with everyone while they lived —
for this one thing stands out as special evidence of virtue and vice
in people. Indeed, that person has the noblest character who
watches carefully to see that others conceive no bad opinion of
him and always speak well of him after his death, but a person of
mean spirit does not behave this way. Though admittedly he was
guessing about this problem, Plato in his second *Letter* to the tyrant Dionysius reasons to the belief that there is some awareness
of what we do in those who have died.

: XI :

*Who first built obelisks and brought them to Rome; a passage
of Pliny on this topic is emended; of the signs on obelisks and
what sort of letters the Egyptians used.*

In the last chapter we described labyrinths and pyramids, kingly 1
works deserving all our admiration, and we also reported on their
makers. Now come obelisks, which kings likewise outdid each
other to build. Obelisks were stone shafts consecrated to the Sun
god, which is why they were made to look like sun-beams. The

bent a radio, et plane talis est radii forma dum per fenestram intrat. Graeci a veru similitudine nuncupant, apud quos ὀβελὸς veru est. Obelisci primum in Aegypto, inde Romae plures erecti sunt.

2 Primus omnium, teste Plinio libro 36, hoc opus instituit Mitres, qui in Solis urbe regnavit, somnio iussus; hoc enim ipsum in eo inscriptum erat. Postea et alii Aegyptiorum reges in eadem urbe fecerunt. Sochis enim quatuor erexit, quadragenorum et octonum cubitorum longitudine. Rameses autem, is quo regnante Ilium captum est, 40 cubitorum; idem et alium posuit longitudine undecentenis pedibus, per latera cubitis quatuor. Erant et alii duo, unus a Myrne positus, alter a Phio. Haec ex Plinio volumine 36. Verum quidam codices non a Myrne sed a Smarre et non a Phio sed ab Eraphio habent, ut in alterutris mendum sit. Unum Alexandriae statuit LXXX cubitorum Ptolemaeus Philadelphus.

3 Phaeron etiam duos in aede Solis posuit, hanc ob causam: Ferunt enim hunc regem, teste Herodoto libro 2, facinus admisisse quod spiculum in medios fluminis vortices contorserit, et propter id evestigio amisso visu decennio caecum fuisse. Undecimo autem anno ab urbe Buci oraculum accepisse visum esse sibi rediturum si oculos abluisset lotio mulieris quae caeterorum virorum expers suo tantum viro contenta fuisset. Et ante omnia cum lotium uxoris tentasset ac nihil amplius cerneret, reliquarum deinde urinam expertum tandem vidisse. Ibique omnes mulieres quas fuisset expertus praeter eam — uxorem enim duxit — cuius lotio lotus visum recepisset concremasse. Atque ea calamitate liberatum, cum alia in aliis templis donaria posuisse omnia egregia ad diuturnitatem memoriae, tum maxime memorabilia ac spectaculo digna in templo

name in Egyptian comes from 'beam,' and its shape is plainly that of a beam coming in through a window. The Greeks called it *obelos*, their word for a spit, which it resembles. The first obelisks were in Egypt; several came from there to be erected in Rome.

The first to undertake such a work was Mitres who ruled in the 2 City of the Sun, according to Pliny in book 36. He was directed by a dream, for this was carved on the obelisk. Other Egyptian kings built obelisks later in the same city. Sochis put up four of them, each forty-eight cubits high. Ramesses, who was king when Troy was taken, set up a forty-cubit obelisk and another ninety-nine feet high and four cubits on a side. There were two others, one set up by Myrnes, the other by Phius. This comes from book 36 of Pliny. But some texts have 'by Smarre' not 'by Myrnes' and 'by Eraphius' not 'by Phius,' which in one case or the other is a mistake. Ptolemy Philadelphus put one in Alexandria that was eighty cubits high.

Phaeron also set up two of them in the Temple of the Sun, and 3 this was his motive: According to Herodotus in book 2, they say that this king committed the crime of hurling his javelin into the middle of the river's whirlpools, causing him to lose his sight on the spot and remain blind for ten years. But in the eleventh year he heard an oracle from the city of Bucus that his sight would be returned to him if he washed his eyes with the urine of a woman who was happy with her husband alone and had nothing to do with other men. The first thing he did was to try the urine of his wife, and when his vision failed to improve he then tested the urine of other women, until at last he could see. He then burned all the women whom he had tested except the one whose urine had restored his sight when he washed with it—and her he married. Freed of his ailment, he set up a pair of spit-shaped stones called *obeli* in the Temple of the Sun, each a hundred cubits high and eight on a side. These most memorable and noteworthy sights

Solis gemina saxa quos obelos vocant a figura veru centenum cubitorum longitudinis, octonum latitudinis.

4   Fuerunt et plures alii in ipsa Aegypto, quapropter Augustus Caesar, teste Ammiano, duos Romam ex Heliopoli urbe Aegyptia transportavit. Quorum unus, qui ut autor est Plinius excisus fuit a rege Semneserteo, in Circo Maximo. Alter, qui a Sesostride factus est, in Campo Martio positus fuit. Tertius in Vaticano erat, a Gaio principe invectus, qui etiam nunc eo loci stat. De quo Plinius libro 16, capite 40, cum de arborum magnitudine loquitur: Abies admirationis praecipuae visa est in navi quae ex Aegypto Gaii principis iussu obeliscum in Vaticano circo statutum adduxit. Hunc, ut idem in 36 testatur, fecerat Sesostridis filius, Nuncoreus. Et deinde subdit: Eiusdem remanet et alius centum cubitorum, quem post caecitatem visu reddito ex oraculo Soli sacravit. Haec Plinius.

5   Ex his verbis facile coniicere possumus Plinium intelligere de altero obelisco quem, ut supra ostendimus ex testimonio Herodoti, Phaeronem — non Nuncoreum, ut apud Plinium legitur — recepto oculorum visu Soli sacrasse constat. Ex quo extra omnem controversiam Plinii locus depravatus est, qui ut emaculetur loco Nuncoreus legendum esse duco Phaeron ne duo inter se gravissimi autores certare videantur, cum haud difficulter fieri potuit alterum ex iis quos Phaeron fecerit eundem esse quem Gaius Romam portarat.

6   Quod demiror Hermolaum Barbarum, virum utique sagacissimi ingenii, non animadvertisse, praesertim cum paulo superius admonuisset undecimo capite eiusdem trigesimisexti Plinii voluminis ubi Nuncoreus inscriptus est legendum esse Sesostridis, non Sesotidis. Qui, teste Herodoto, fuit huius Phaeronis pater de quo

were among other offerings in other temples, all of them magnificent monuments and enduring.

There were several other obelisks in Egypt. Augustus Caesar   4
transported two of them to Rome from the Egyptian city of
Heliopolis, according to Ammianus. One, which Pliny says King
Semneserteus carved, was set up in the Circus Maximus. The
other, which Sesostris built, stood in the Campus Martius. A
third, imported by the Emperor Gaius, was in the Vatican and
stands in the same spot even now. Pliny mentions it when dealing
with the size of trees in book 16, chapter 40: A particularly remarkable fir was seen in the ship carrying the obelisk from Egypt
that the Emperor Gaius ordered to be put in the Vatican Circus.
Nuncoreus, son of Sesostris, built this one, as Pliny again testifies
in book 36. He then adds that another obelisk of the same king
still stands. It was a hundred cubits high, and he dedicated it to
the Sun on the advice of an oracle when he recovered his sight after a period of blindness. This much from Pliny.

From these words we can easily infer that he has in mind   5
a different obelisk which, as shown above on the testimony of
Herodotus, is known to have been consecrated to the Sun by
Phaeron when he regained his vision — not by Nuncoreus, as one
reads in Pliny. Hence there can be no doubt that the passage in
Pliny is corrupt, and I conclude that it should be emended to read
'Phaeron' for 'Nuncoreus' in order to remove the appearance of
conflict between two of our weightiest authorities. For it could
well be that the obelisk which Gaius brought to Rome was another of those that Phaeron had built.

I am surprised that this was not noticed by Ermolao Barbaro,   6
an exceptionally keen-minded man to be sure, especially since he
had warned us to read 'Sesostridis' instead of 'Sesostidis' where
'Nuncoreus' appears a little earlier in the eleventh chapter of
the same thirty-sixth book of Pliny. According to Herodotus,
Sesostris was the father of the Phaeron that Pliny mentions in

Plinius libro 6, capite 29 meminit et Strabo libro 17 et Iosephus *Contra Appionem* volumine 2.

7 Non est etiam tacitum relinquendum obeliscos quamplurimum notis quibusdam, id est, varia animalium effigie insculptos fuisse quae vel regum gloriam vel eorum persoluta vota sequentibus aetatibus monstrarent, quae loco literarum erant, dicente Plinio libro 36: Etenim sculpturae illae effigiesque quas videmus Aegyptiae sunt literae. Et Cornelius Tacitus libro suarum *Historiarum* 14: Primi, inquit, Aegyptii per figuras animalium sensus mentis effingebant, et antiquissima monimenta memoriae humanae impressa saxis cernuntur. Strabo etiam libro 17 ait: In obeliscis quibusdam literae sunt quae regum illorum divitias ac potentiam declarant. Nam per speciem apis mella conficientis regem indicabant cui cum iucunditate moderante aculei inesse debent. Per accipitrem rem denotabant cito factam quoniam haec aliarum ferme omnium avis sit velocissima. Per instrumenta etiam quaedam membrave humana scribebant, quod Diodorus statim in principio 4 libri plane demonstrat.

: XII :

A quibus primo asylum constitutum fuerit et quo nos pacto
asylis utamur.

1 Postquam Hercules migravit e terris, nepotes eius, autore Servio in 8 *Aeneidos*, timentes insidias eorum quos avus afflixisset Athenis sibi primi omnium asylum, hoc est, templum misericordiae, collocarunt unde nullus per vim posset abduci. (Nam componitur ex α, quod est sine, et σύρω, traho.) Quod Statius affirmat in 12 *Thebaidos*, dicens:

book 6, chapter 29, Strabo in book 17 and Josephus in book 2 *Against Apion*.

Besides, we should not fail to note that obelisks were generally   7
engraved with certain signs — that is, with various images of animals that took the place of letters and showed to succeeding ages
the glory of kings or the vows they had fulfilled. The carvings and
images that we see are actually Egyptian letters, according to Pliny
in book 36. And Cornelius Tacitus in book 14 of his *Histories*
maintains that the Egyptians were the first to represent concepts
with shapes of animals and that the oldest records in human
memory are seen imprinted in their stones. Strabo also speaks of
this in book 17: On some obelisks are letters that declare the
wealth and power of their kings. A bee making honey indicated a
king, for example, because a king must use his stings and temper
them with kindliness. A hawk denoted something done quickly
because it is faster than almost any other bird. They also used certain instruments and human limbs in their writing, as Diodorus
clearly shows right at the start of book 4.

: XII :

Who first established an asylum and how we make use
of asylums.

After Hercules departed the earth, his descendants feared the   I
plots of those whom their ancestor had overthrown, according to
Servius on book 8 of the *Aeneid*, and so they set up the first asylum for themselves in Athens; it was a temple of mercy from
which no one could be taken by force. ('Asylum' is a compound of
the α-privative with *suro*, which means 'I drag.') Statius affirms
this in book 12 of the *Thebaid*, writing:

Fama est defessos acie post busta paterni
Numinis herculeos sedem fundasse nepotes;
Sic sacrasse loco commune animantibus aegris
Confugium.

Cuius Plutarchus etiam in *Vita Thesei* mentionem facit.

2   Verum ego hoc primum inventum Mosi verius, ni fallor, assignaverim qui, ut autor est Eusebius, longe ante Herculem fuit. Is
enim, teste Iosepho libro *Antiquitatum* 4, in tribus ex iis urbibus
quas ipse condiderat dum Hebraeum populum in patrium solum
reduceret asylum constituit, quod illis tantum profugio foret qui
minime scientes homicidium commisissent.

3   Secundum haec longo deinde tempore Romulus ut haberet ad-
venas plures cum quibus conderet Romam ad imitationem Atheniensis, ut Servius tradit, asylum, teste Livio in primo *Ab urbe
condita* et Dionysio libro 2, aperuit quo quisquis proficisceretur ab
omni noxa liberatus esset. Ovidius in 3 *Fastorum*:

Romulus ut saxo lucum circundedit alto,
    Quilibet huc, inquit, confuge; tutus eris.

Vergilius quoque in 8 ait:

Hinc lucum ingentem quem Romulus acer asylum
Rettulit.

4   Fuit et aliud asylum, autore Strabone in 8 *Geographiae*, non procul Troezene, in insula nomine Calauria, Neptuno dicatum. Tum
aliud quoque in Aegypto ad Canopicum Nili ostium Herculi
consecratum, de quo Herodotus libro 2 meminit: Erat, inquit, et
in eo litore quod nunc quoque est Herculis templum ad quod, si
quis cuiuscunque hominis servus confugiens capiat sacras notas,
sese Deo tradens, eum nefas est tangere. Quae sanctio ad meam

Their godlike father had his rites, the story goes,
And then the sons of Heracles, worn out by battle,
Set up a common shelter here for sorrowing souls.

Plutarch also makes note of it in his *Life of Theseus*.

But unless I am mistaken, it would be more accurate for me to 2
assign this invention to Moses who, as Eusebius tells us, lived long
before Hercules. For Moses established asylums in three of the cities that he founded while leading the Hebrew people back to their
native soil, according to Josephus in book 4 of the *Antiquities*, but
this was only to shelter those who had committed involuntary homicide.

A long time afterward, says Servius, Romulus imitated the 3
Athenians and opened an asylum to attract more foreigners while
he was founding Rome; everyone who came to it was freed from
all punishment, according to Livy in the first book *From the Foundation of the City* and Dionysius in book 2. In book 3 of the *Fasti*
Ovid writes:

Romulus girdled the grove with lofty stone.
Safety, he said, for all who shelter here.

In book 8 Vergil also writes:

A great grove that shrewd Romulus turned
Into the asylum.

There was also another asylum not far from Troezen on the is- 4
land named Calauria, according to Strabo in book 8 of the *Geography*, and it was dedicated to Neptune. Then in Egypt at the
Canopic mouth of the Nile there was another sacred to Hercules,
which Herodotus mentions in book 2: On that shore was a temple
of Hercules that still stands, and if anyone's slave flees there, re-
ceives its sacred signs and gives himself to the god, it is forbidden
to touch him. This ordinance has survived to my own day entirely

usque aetatem prorsus immota perseveravit. Fuit etiam in ipsa Aegypto, sicut commemorat Strabo libro 16 et ultimo *Geographiae*,
Osiris asylum et in Syria Apollinis.

5   Sunt hodie in orbe nostro Christiano, praesertim apud Anglos,
passim asyla, quae non modo insidias timentibus sed quibusvis
sontibus, etiam maiestatis reis patent, quod facit ut manifeste appareat nos id institutum non a Mose qui illis duntaxat qui nolen-
tes hominem occidissent asylum posuit, sed a Romulo esse mutuatos. Quae nempe res haud dubie in causa est cur bene multi a
maleficiis minus abstineant manus. Quid quod templa nostra
ubique gentium istiusmodi sceleratis hominibus instar asylorum
sunt et id contra quam Moses etiam constituerit? Qui in Exodo
capite 21 ita sanxit: Si quis per industriam occiderit proximum
suum et per insidias, ab altari meo avelles eum ut moriatur.

: XIII :

De origine theatri et in eo recitandi comoedias tragoediasque
modo; et qui primo Romae theatrum et amphitheatrum ac
circum construxerint; et quare amphitheatrum arena
spargeretur; et inibi de frequenti apud veteres lavandi usu
ac thermarum origine.

1   Theatri, quod hemicycli specie constructum erat, ἀπὸ τοῦ
θεάομαι quod est 'video' appellatum, latine dici spectaculum potest, consuetudo, teste Cassiodoro in *Epistolis*, a Graecis sumpta
est. Nam cum agrorum cultores feriatis diebus sacra diversis numinibus per lucos vicosque celebrarent, Athenienses primum hoc
in urbanum spectaculum transtulerunt, theatrum graeco vocabulo
appellantes quod in eo eminus astans turba conveniens sine aliquo
impedimento conspiceret.

unchanged. In the last book of his *Geography* Strabo mentions an asylum of Osiris also in Egypt, and in the sixteenth book an asylum of Apollo in Syria.

Asylums exist today throughout our Christian world, especially in England. They are open not only to those who fear plots but to any and all criminals, even those accused of treason, which makes it quite clear that we have borrowed this institution not from Moses, who established asylum only for involuntary homicides, but from Romulus. Doubtless this is the reason why so many refrain so little from wrongdoing. Why are our churches in every land used as asylums for wicked people of this sort when this is actually against what Moses decreed? In chapter 21 of Exodus he ordained: If anyone purposely and craftily kill his neighbor, you shall remove him from my altar and let him die.

: XIII :

On the origin of the theater and how comedies and tragedies were performed there; who built the first theater, amphitheater and circus at Rome; why the amphitheater was strewn with sand; and, in connection with these topics, on the frequent use of bathing by the ancients and the origin of warm baths.

The theater, built in the shape of a semi-circle, was named from the word *theaomai*, which means 'I see,' and in Latin it can be called a *spectaculum*. According to Cassiodorus in his *Letters*, its use came from the Greeks. While farmers in their festivals celebrated the rites of various divinities in grove and village, the Athenians first transformed this into an urban spectacle. They called it a theater in Greek because a crowd gathered there and stayed to watch without hindrance from a distance.

2   Apud quos, autore Eusebio in 2 *De evangelica praeparatione*, Dionysius primus theatrum fecit, propter quod, ut mea fert opinio, Servius ait theatrales ludos in honorem, duntaxat apud veteres, Liberi patris fieri consuevisse. Plutarchus similiter Athenis theatra fuisse in *Vita Thesei* aperte ostendit. Sane apud Alexandriam in Antirrhodo insula theatrum etiam fuisse, Strabo in 17 autor est.

3   Hunc morem Romani quoque ut pleraque alia in urbem construendi theatri transtulerunt, quod ita dispositum erat ut a fronte inter duo cornua scena esset, dicta ἀπὸ τῆς σκηνῆς, quod apud Graecos tabernaculum significat, ita appellatum a facienda umbra. Scena primo inventa est umbrae gratia, in qua ludi ab eo loco scenici nuncupati a principio facti sunt. Qui, teste Livio, anno urbis conditae cccxci, Gaio Sulpitio Petico, Gaio Licinio Stolone consulibus, pestilentiae sedandae causa instituti sunt. Porro cum vis morbi nec humanis consiliis nec ope divina levaretur, inter alias irae coelestis placationes eiusmodi ludos introducere placuit. Insanis certe hominum mentibus qui putarent Deum lascivis saltationibus sibi placatum iri!

4   Itaque ex Hetruria ludiones acciti qui — sine carmine ullo, sine imitandorum carminum actu — ad tibicinis modos saltantes haud indecoros motus dabant. Res nova sic bellicosum populum delectavit ut iuventus, inde iocularia simul inter se versibus inconditis fundentes, eos imitari coeperint. Haec ridicula carmina sine cantu iactitata Graece exodia appellabantur, sicut epodia quae cantabantur. Et quia *hister* thusco verbo ludius vocabatur, id nomen histrionibus est inditum. Post annos deinde centum et vigintiduos, qui fuit annus ab urbe condita dxiii, Livius Andronicus fabulam versibus intextam primus recitandam dedit. Ac ita ludus paulatim in artem versus est cum in scena comici tragicique et caeteri poetae

Dionysius first built a theater in Greece, according to Eusebius   2
in book 2 of the *Preparation for the Gospel*. In my view, this is why
Servius says that theatrical shows used to be put on in honor of
Father Liber, at least among the ancients. In his *Life of Theseus*,
Plutarch also shows clearly that there were theaters in Athens.
There was another near Alexandria, of course, on the island of
Antirrhodos, as Strabo says in book 17.

The Romans brought this custom of building theaters into   3
their city along with many others. The theater was arranged so
that in front between two wings there was a stage or scene, so
called from *skēnē*, which in Greek means 'tent' because a tent gives
shade. The stage was first invented for the sake of shade, and from
the beginning the plays put on there were called stage-plays after
their location. According to Livy, this first began in the year 391
AUC, when Gaius Sulpicius Peticus and Gaius Licinius Stolo were
consuls, and the reason was to halt a plague. Thereafter, when neither human plans nor divine assistance could allay the power of
disease, they saw fit to introduce such plays among other means of
quieting heaven's wrath. How mad are the notions of humans,
who think to appease God with wanton dances!

For this purpose they called in performers from Etruria who   4
made graceful movements and danced to the measures of the flute-
player — but with no singing, no acting-out of dramatic verse. The
novelty so delighted this warlike people that the young soon began
imitating them, telling jokes to one another in artless verse. These
funny poems without music were called exodes in Greek, like the
epodes that were sung. And because actors were known by the
Tuscan word *hister*, they gave them this name. One hundred and
twenty-two years later, in AUC 513, Livius Andronicus first produced a verse drama for recitation. Gradually the stage-play became an art as comic, tragic and other poets recited their poems
on stage in this way. Heralds, flute-players, singers accompanying

sua recitarent poemata. In ea etiam erant praecones, tibicines, citharoedi et huiusmodi qui vel in fine cuiusque actus canerent.

5   Hoc sane loco non abs re videtur esse aliquid dicere de modo in primis agendi comoedias tragoediasque. Nam cum Cicero libro 3 *De oratore* de Roscio, qui fuit homo Gallus et comoedus peritissimus ac eius praeceptor in pronunciationis gestuumque exercitatione, dixerit: Nunquam agit hunc versum Roscius eo gestu quo potest. Nonnulli suspicati sunt comicos et tragicos sua poemata recitare solitos et mimos, hoc est histriones, praesto fuisse qui personarum inductarum facta dictaque exprimendi causa eorum voces gestibus tantum persequerentur. Id quod alibi Cicero (in *Paradoxis*) falsum esse demonstrat, cum inquit: Histrio si paulo se moveat extra numerum aut si versus pronunciatus est syllaba una brevior aut longior, exibilatur et exploditur. Si igitur histrio gestu non item voce agebat, qui fieri potuit ut mutus in pronunciatione reprehenderetur?

6   Theatralis autem scena apud antiquissimos parietem non habebat sed frondibus tantum tegebatur. Postea tabulata coeperunt componere instar parietis et sic binis et saepe pluribus contignationibus constabat. Deinde erat proscenium, suggestum in quo ludi exercebantur. Vergilius:

Et veteres ineunt proscenia ludi.

In medio orchestra in qua senatorum sedibus erant loca designata unde omnium agentium gestus spectari possent. Dicta orchestra quod in ea saltationes fieri consueverunt, ὄρχησις enim graece saltatio dicitur. In cavea vero, quae pars media theatri erat, subsellia equitum erant in cuneos eodem modo divisa. In circuitu hemicycli erant gradus ita dispositi ut altiores in ambitu semper excrescerent. In his plebs promiscue sedebat.

7   Quibus non erat locus sedendi, ii stantes in cavea spectabant, nam senatus a populo secretus ludos spectare. Cuius rei, teste Li-

themselves on the lute and others who joined in the singing also appeared on stage, especially at the end of each act.

In this context, it seems appropriate to say something of how 5 comedies and tragedies were first performed. In book 3 *On the Orator*, Cicero speaks of Roscius, his teacher in the practice of delivery and gesture, who was a Gaul and an expert comedian: Never, he says, does Roscius deliver this line with his full force of gesture. From this some have inferred that comedians and tragedians used to recite their poems accompanied by mimes or actors who simply followed their words with gestures in order to express what was done and said by the characters portrayed. But elsewhere (in the *Paradoxes*) Cicero shows that this is false when he says: They hiss and hoot if an actor moves the least bit out of step or speaks a line with one syllable too long or too short. So if the actor was performing through gesture but not through language as well, how could they possibly criticize his speech when he was silent?

In the oldest times the stage of the theater had no wall and was 6 simply roofed over with foliage. Later they began to put planks together in the form of a wall so that the stage had two stories and often more. Then came the proscenium, the platform on which the plays were performed, as Vergil says:

And the old plays appear on the proscenium.

In the middle was the orchestra where senators had places reserved for seats from which they could watch the movements of all the players. It was called the orchestra because dances used to be performed there, since *orchēsis* means dancing in Greek. But in the *cavea* — the central part of the theater — the benches of the knights were divided into wedges in the same way. Around the semicircle were placed steps whose circumference increased as they rose. The common people sat there in no particular order.

Those with no place to sit stood in the *cavea* and watched, for 7 the Senate saw the plays apart from the people. Scipio Africanus

vio in quarto *De bello Macedonico* et Plutarcho, Scipio ille Africanus et Valerius Sempronius Longus consules primi autores fuerunt. Quod et vulgi animum avertit et favorem Scipionis magnopere quassavit. Valerius autem Maximus hoc ex sententia posterioris Africani actum esse narrat. Caveae theatri, nullis fornicibus obductae, velis tegi solebant, ex quo primus omnium Quintus Catulus, teste Plinio in 19, linteis theatro umbram fecit primusque byssina vela duxit.

8   In hanc sane formam theatrum Marcus Scaurus in sua aedilitate, non quidem perpetuo duraturum sed in triginta tantum dies scenicorum ludorum, principio enim ad tempus fiebant theatra, primus omnium Romae extruxit, dicente Plinio libro 36, capite 15. Hic fecit in aedilitate sua opus maximum omnium quae unquam fuere humana manu facta, non temporaria mora verum etiam aeternitatis destinatione, et reliqua.

9   Gaio autem Curio, qui bello civili in Caesarianis partibus obiit, in patris funere theatra duo e ligno construxit, quibus inter sese aversis ne invicem obstreperent scenae, et repente circumactis ac cornibus inter se coeuntibus faciebat amphitheatrum et gladiatorum spectacula edebat. Mansurum theatrum e quadrato lapide, ut ait Cornelius Tacitus, primus Romae construxit Pompeius Magnus, cuius exemplar ex eo quod Mitylene erat post devictum Mithridatem sumpsisse, testis est Plutarchus.

10   Amphitheatrum autem, qui locus erat spectaculorum gratia, forma rotunda, et veluti (ut supra ostendimus) ex duobus constans theatris, primus omnium, teste Cornelio de gestis Neronis, in Campo Martio posuit Gaius Iulius Caesar, quod paulo post, autore Tranquillo, Augustus mausoleum aedificaturus destruxit, qui et ipse amphitheatrum destinavit media urbe, quod a Vespasiano

himself and Valerius Sempronius Longus began this custom when they were consuls, according to Livy in his fourth book *On the Macedonian War* and Plutarch. But it offended the pride of the masses and greatly damaged Scipio's popularity. Valerius Maximus tells us that it was the decision of the younger Africanus, however. The *cavea*, having no arches above it, used to be covered with awnings. For this purpose Quintus Catulus first used linen to provide shade in the theater and introduced the first awnings made of flax, according to Pliny in book 19.

This was doubtless the form of Rome's first theater, built by   8
Marcus Scaurus when he was aedile. It was meant to last only for a thirty-day run of stage-plays, not to stand forever, since theaters were built temporarily at first, as Pliny says in book 36, chapter 15. As aedile, Scaurus produced the greatest of any works ever made by human hand, excelling not only those designed for some space of time but even those intended for eternity, and so on.

Gaius Curio, who fell in the Civil War on Caesar's side, built   9
two wooden theaters for his father's funeral. They were set back to back so that one performance would not drown out the other. They could be wheeled together quickly and their wings joined to form an amphitheater where Curio put on gladiatorial shows. Pompey the Great built the first permanent theater of hewn stone in Rome, as Cornelius Tacitus says. He took his model from the one he saw in Mitylene after conquering Mithridates, according to Plutarch.

The amphitheater, which was a place for public shows, was   10
round in shape, as if it were made from two theaters (see above). Tacitus writes in his account of Nero that Gaius Julius Caesar put up the first theater in the Campus Martius. But Augustus pulled it down shortly afterward to build a mausoleum, says Suetonius. Augustus himself intended to build an amphitheater in the middle of the city. Construction began under Vespasian, and it was

conditum fuit et a Tito consecratum, autor Suetonius in eorum *Vitis*.

11   Sed quoniam Domitianus (ut idem est testis) omnibus operibus quae post mortem illorum vel restituit vel perfecit suum duntaxat titulum addidit sine ulla pristini autoris memoria, hinc, ut opinor, illi de hoc amphitheatro Martialis statim in principio sui operis adulatur, dicens:

> Omnis Caesareo cedat labor amphitheatro,
>   Unum pro cunctis fama loquatur opus.

Augusto etiam Caesari Herodes Hierosolymis theatrum et amphitheatrum condidit, autor Iosephus in 15 *Antiquitatum*. In amphitheatro autem bestiarum et gladiatorum ludi celebrabantur. Nam permulti capite damnati aut in bellis capti illic cum feris pugnando mortem oppetere cogebantur. Quod epigrammaticus poeta affirmat, de delatoribus dicens:

> Nec cepit arena nocentes.

Seneca testatur duos qui ad id certamen destinati erant sibi prius mortem conscivisse.

12   Arena, ut hoc commodum moneamus, aliquando pro amphitheatro—id est, contentum pro continente—ab autoribus eleganter ponitur. Martialis rursus:

> Quicquid fama canit, donat arena tibi.

Et id quoniam amphitheatrum spargi arena solebat vel ne pugnantes foedarentur cruore occisorum vel ne cruor sparsus spectantibus esset horrori, propter quod iuvenum multitudo arenam vertendo cruorem obtegebat. At quidam aliam spargendae arenae causam commentati sunt, tradentes eam sterni ne gladiatores diffluerent.

dedicated by Titus, according to Suetonius in his *Lives* of these emperors.

But since Domitian — with no acknowledgment of the original builder — put his own name alone on all the works of these emperors that he completed or restored after their deaths (Suetonius is our witness again), it seems to me that Martial is flattering Domitian at the beginning of his book when he says of this amphitheater:

> Caesar's amphitheater beats them all;
> One job makes more news than all the rest.

Herod also built a theater and an amphitheater for Augustus Caesar in Jerusalem, according to Josephus in book 15 of the *Antiquities*. They put on shows with beasts and gladiators in the amphitheater. Many persons condemned to die or captured in war were made to meet death there in combat with wild animals. The epigrammatic poet affirms this, saying of informers that

> The sand can't hold all the guilty.

Seneca testifies that two who had been destined for this contest killed themselves beforehand.

Note here that in literary usage 'sand' sometimes stands for 'amphitheater' — the contained for the container — as again in Martial:

> Whatever tale they tell, the sand presents you.

They used to sprinkle the amphitheater with sand so that the blood of the slain would not defile the combatants or else to protect the audience from the horror of being sprinkled with blood, and a crowd of young men turned the sand to cover up the gore. But some have discussed another reason for sprinkling the sand, claiming that they scattered it about to prevent the gladiators from slipping apart.

11

12

13 Circo—de cuius forma libro superiore, capite 14, affatim diximus—regnante Tarquinio Prisco locus primum designatus est. Atque simul patribus equitibusque loca divisa unde spectarent ludentes. Certamen fuit equorum pugilumque qui ex Hetruria accersiti fuerant. Is Maximus Circus dictus est. Postea duo alii positi sunt, Flaminius et Neronis. In hoc obeliscus olim fuerat qui nunc Romae in Vaticano extat. In Circo item, teste Dionysio, athletae certabant qui aut pugnabant aut currebant vel luctabantur, quorum certamen tum primo Romanis spectaculo fuit cum Spurius Posthumius Albinus et Quintus Martius Philippus consules fuere, anno urbis conditae DLXVIII, autor Livius libro 9 decadis 4.

14 Sed horum operum magnificentiae iam iungatur thermarum luxuria, fuit enim mos priscorum quotidie lavari quod ea res (credo teste Celso) ad prosperam valet conservandam valetudinem. Ex quo usu venit ut civis quisque pro opibus privata haberet balnea, sed postea, crescente principum luxuria, publicae balneae haberi coepere. Quippe loca assignata erant quae aut aquis calentibus aut igne calefactis lavandi sudandive usum praeberent, quae graece thermas appellarunt.

15 Et cum alibi tum Romae—in modum provinciarum, ut ait Ammianus—videbantur extructae in quibus plebs etiam lavaretur. Fuitque adeo populare principibus id cum ea promiscue facere ut Commodum, Gordianum et Galienum iuniores alios ter, alios quinquies vel septies aestate, bis vero hyeme in die lavasse Capitolinus tradat, in thermisque coenitasse. Admittebantur et mulieres, idoneum voluptatis instrumentum. Thermae in primis celebres Romae fuere Agrippinae, Neronianae, Titi Vespasiani, Domitiani, Antonianae, Alexandrinae, Gordianae, Severianae, Diocletianae, Aurelianae, Constantinianae, Novatianae—hae magno sumptu aedificatae sunt, instar fere urbium. Erant in his areae amplissimae, erant porticus, in porticibus exedrae habentes sedes in quibus phi-

They first chose a site for the Circus—whose form we dis- 13
cussed sufficiently in chapter 14 of the previous book—during the
reign of Tarquinius Priscus. Places from which to watch the performers were assigned to senators and also to knights. There were
contests for horses and for boxers brought in from Etruria. This
Circus was called the Greatest. Two others, the Flaminian and
Nero's, were built later. In the latter was the obelisk that now
stands in the Vatican in Rome. Athletes competed in boxing, running and wrestling in the Circus, according to Dionysius. These
contests were first put on as a public show for the Romans when
Spurius Posthumius Albinus and Quintus Martius Philippus were
consuls, in 568 AUC, according to Livy in book 9 of the fourth
decade.

Related to the grandeur of these works is the extravagance of 14
warm baths, for the ancients were in the habit of bathing daily because (so I believe, following Celsus) it was a way to stay in good
health. From this custom it came about that all citizens who could
afford them had private baths, but later, as the extravagance of the
emperors mounted, they began to use public baths. These were located in places, called *thermae* in Greek, that offered the benefit of
washing or sweating in hot waters or in waters heated by fire.

They were seen to be constructed at Rome and elsewhere—to 15
the ends of the provinces, as Ammianus says—and even the common people bathed in them. Hence it became popular for the emperors to do this together with the people. Commodus, Gordian
and Gallienus bathed three or five or seven times a day in the
summer, twice a day in winter, when they were young, according
to Capitolinus, and they also dined in the baths. They admitted
women too, for easy access to pleasure. Rome's most famous
baths were those of Agrippa, Nero, Titus Vespasian, Domitian,
Antoninus, Alexander, Gordian, Severus, Diocletian, Aurelian,
Constantine and Novatian—built at great expense, almost like cities. They had great open spaces and galleries, and in the galleries

losophi, rhetores, reliquique quibus studia erant cordi sedebant disputantes. Erat et palaestra in qua se athletae exercebant. Erant praeterea multa intus loca ad fovendam luxuriam faberrime extructa. Adeo vesana dementia omnium voluptatum quaesisse tentamenta videntur Romani principes cum tanto impendio tam paucis profuturo.

: XIV :

Quis primus invenerit fabricam materiariam, et in ea serram, asciam, perpendiculum, terebram, glutinum, normam, libellam, tornum, clavem, circinum, securim, dolia et vasa viminea.

1   Fabricam materiariam, hoc est, lignariam Daedalus, ut Plinius libro 7 scribit, primus omnium invenit, et in ea serram, asciam, perpendiculum (id est instrumentum quo plumbo a filo et gnomone pendente rectio sive obliquitas operis perpenditur, hoc est, examinatur) et terebram et glutinum (quod Graeci *collam* nominant) quo ligna ferruminantur. Normam autem et libellam et tornum atque clavem Theodorus Samius reperit.

2   Ovidius tamen libro 8 *Metamorphoseon* dicit Perdicem Daedali ex sorore nepotem circinum (hoc est instrumentum quo circuli vertendo designantur) et serram invenisse. Traxerat enim in exemplum spinas in medio pisce notatas, de quo etiam in *Ibim* ait:

Ut cui causa necis serra reperta fuit.

At secundum Diodorum libro 5 Talus, non Perdix — adolescens filius sororis eiusdem Daedali qui ab eo erudiebatur — reperta serpentis maxilla parvulum cum secuisset lignum, imitatus postea

were halls furnished with seats where philosophers, rhetors and others devoted to study sat disputing. There was also a wrestling-hall where athletes practiced. Inside were many places constructed most cleverly to encourage licentiousness. Thus it seems that the Roman emperors tried in their mad frenzy to taste every pleasure, spending so much to benefit so few.

: XIV :

Who first invented carpentry, including the saw, the hatchet, the plumb-line, the drill, glue, the square, the level, the lathe, the lever, the compass, the axe and wickerwork pots and vessels.

Daedalus, as Pliny writes in book 7, first of all invented carpentry   1
or woodworking, including the saw, the hatchet, the plumb-line (which is a tool using a lead weight and pointer hung from a line to ponder or gauge whether a piece of work is square or slanted), the drill and glue (which the Greeks call *colla*) for cementing wood together. Theodorus of Samos discovered the square, the level, the lathe and the lever.

But Ovid says in book 8 of the *Metamorphoses* that Perdix, a   2
nephew of Daedalus on his sister's side, invented the compass (a tool for drawing circles by turning it around) as well as the saw. Noticing the spines on a fish's back, the boy found his model, which Ovid also mentions in the *Ibis*:

He devised the saw and died for it.

According to Diodorus in book 5, however, it was Talus and not Perdix who was the first to make a saw from iron. This young man — also a son of the sister of Daedalus and tutored by him —

dentium serpentis spissitudinem serram ferream primus omnium fecit. Reperit etiam tornum et rotam figuli, ut ante monstravimus. Ita cum pluribus rebus hominibus profuisset magna laude celebratus est. Hunc puerum Daedalus invidia motus, existimans turpe esse magistrum ab adolescente gloria vinci dolo interfecit.

3 At normam, cuius ratio ut longe alia sit ac communis normae, non modo in mensuris sed etiam in aedificiis utilis est. Inventum Pythagorae esse Vitruvius libro 9 dicit, eiusque formam valde artificiosam ponit. Securim Panthesilea Amazonum regina invenisse fertur.

4 Caeterum ego huius lignariae artis vel eiusdem instrumentorum, quamvis alia aliubi usurpentur, inventionem potius Hebraeis tribuerim, apud quos multo ante Daedalum optimi opifices fuerunt, praesertim in constructione tabernaculi quod Moses (qui etiam Daedalo, ut autor est Eusebius, antiquior fuit) Deo dicavit. Vel assignaverim Tyriis qui, teste Iosepho in 8 *Antiquitatum,* in ea arte Hebraeis longe excellentiores fuerunt, propter quod Solomon Deo templum conditurus ab rege Tyri per literas fabros lignarios, sicut idem Iosephus et Eusebius testimonio sunt, petiit.

5 Quo pacto autem ex gracilioribus lignis capacia et in ventrem tumentia vascula veluti sunt dolia fierent, Speusippus, autore Laertio, docuit. Vasa ex viminibus facta ut qualos, corbes et cetera, teste Servio in primum *Georgicorum,* Ceres omnium prima monstravit.

made his discovery when he found that a snake's jaw made a cut in a bit of wood, and then he imitated the closeness of the snake's teeth. He also discovered the lathe and the potter's wheel, as we have shown above. In this way he won great praise as humanity's benefactor in many things. Driven by envy, Daedalus treacherously killed the boy, thinking it disgraceful for a master to be vanquished in fame by a youth.

Note that the square — used not only in measuring but also in building — is much unlike an ordinary square in construction. Vitruvius says in book 9 that it was invented by Pythagoras, and he states that its shape is quite intricate. They say that Panthesilea, queen of the Amazons, invented the axe. 3

Although the art of woodworking and its tools were used in various places, I would still rather attribute their invention to the Hebrews, among whom were excellent craftsmen long before Daedalus, especially those who built the tabernacle that Moses consecrated to God. (Moses was more ancient than Daedalus, as Eusebius tells us.) Otherwise, I should assign this invention to the Tyrians who were far better at this art than the Hebrews, according to Josephus in book 8 of the *Antiquities*. This is why Solomon wrote the king of Tyre to ask for carpenters when he was about to build the temple for God, as Josephus and Eusebius also testify. 4

Speusippus taught how to use lighter woods for small, roomy containers widened in the waist like pots, according to Laertius. And in his commentary on the first *Georgic* Servius says that Ceres was the first to demonstrate the making of vessels such as hampers and baskets from wicker. 5

: XV :

Quis primus mari imperaverit et ut primo navigari coeptum
sit; et qui invenerint artem navigandi, navigia diversi generis,
remum, vela, anchoram, gubernaculum et pugnam navalem.

1 Quis non fatetur humanum genus merito suo insaniae audaciae-
que coargui cum sese intra suos fines minime sciat tutum conti-
nere? Nam quamvis Deus Optimus Maximus ei abunde consulue-
rit, sua tamen sponte in pericula ruit. Ille enim nobis terram veluti
solidum et ad nos sustentandum idoneum elementum dedit, at
nos coelum atque mare tentamus. Nonne Daedalus fabricatis alis
coelum ipsum adivit? Nonne modo, saeva pecuniae cupiditate ob-
caecati, tenui ligno freti mare non dico sulcamus sed propemodum
habitamus?

2 Quod Flaccus Horatius dolens in primo *Carminum* inquit:

Nequicquam Deus abscidit
    Prudens Oceano dissociabili
Terras, si tamen impiae
    Non tangenda rates transiliunt vada.
Audax omnia perpeti
    Gens humana, ruit per vetitum nefas.

Et in eum paulo superius qui hoc primum tentavit:

Illi robur et aes triplex
    Circa pectus erat, qui fragilem truci
Commisit pelago ratem
    Primus.

Et Propertius libro 3 de Peti naufragio dicit:

Ergo sollicitae tu causa pecunia vitae es,
    Per te immaturum mortis adimus iter.

: XV :

Who first ruled the sea and how sailing first began; who invented the art of sailing; on the different sorts of ships, the oar, sails, the anchor, the steering-oar and the naval battle.

Will anyone deny that mankind gets its just deserts when con-   1
victed of madness and recklessness for not knowing how to keep safe within its own borders? Although the good God Almighty cares abundantly for man, he rushes on his own into peril. God gave us the solid earth, an element well suited to sustain us, but we venture into sky and sea. Daedalus constructed his wings and approached heaven itself, did he not? Blinded as we are by a fierce lust for wealth, do we not plow the sea supported by a flimsy board? No, I should say we all but live there.

This is what Horace tells us, sadly, in the first book of *Odes*:   2

> Little good it did, though wise he is,
> That God made the disuniting sea cut into land
> If ships wickedly still skip across
> Waters meant to be left alone.
> Nothing is too much for rash humankind,
> Rushing past restraint of crime.

Just before this he writes of the person who first tried it:

> He had oak and triple bronze
> Around his heart who first risked
> A fragile craft on the savage sea.

And in book 3 Propertius tells about the shipwreck of Petus:

> Money—you're the reason for an anxious life,
> Starting us early on the path to death;

Tu vitiis hominum crudelia pabula praebes,
Semina curarum de capite orta tuo.

Et deinde subiungit:

Ite rates curvae, et leti quoque texite causas,
Ista per humanas mors venit acta manus.

Idem:

Natura insidians pontum substravit avaris.

Et reliqua. Quid denique, ut poeta ait, non mortalia pectora cogit auri sacra fames?

3   Itaque adeo ab initio mare a mortalibus frequentatum est ut deinceps, omissis ratibus quibus primum est navigatum, naves instar domorum aedificaverint quibus etiam nunc totum fere pelagus sternitur. Et ita navigandi arte comperta, maris imperium sibi pro se quisque vindicare ausus est in eoque non secus ac in terra bella gerere.

4   Sed iam ad rem veniamus. Minos, teste Strabone libro 10 *Geographiae*, mari primus imperavit. Quod Diodorus in 6 Neptuno assignat, qui primus navigandi artem invenit; ait enim: Neptunus, secundum Cretenses, primus navigandi arte inventa classem instituit eiusque praefectus est a Saturno factus, quapropter traditum est posteris Neptunum imperasse mari. Cretenses omnino iampridem, ut Strabo demonstrat, navigandi principatum tenuerunt. A quibus propter id fluxit proverbium, Cretensis nescit pelagus, in eum qui ea quae probe novit se ignorare dissimulat, ut in nostris *Adagiis* exposuimus.

5   Primum autem, autore Plinio in 7, inventis ratibus in Mari Rubro inter insulas ab Erythra rege navigari coeptum est. Quod etiam testatur Quintilianus in 10 dicens: Si nemo plus effecisset eo quod sequebatur, nihil in poetis supra Livium Andronicum, nihil

You feed our vices on a cruel ration,
The seeds of worry that you propagate.

Then he adds:

Go build the curved ships,
And weave the forces of death that move them,
The ruin made by human hands.

And again:

Nature, always plotting, fits the sea for greed.

And so on. Is there nowhere, the Poet asks, that the accursed craving for gold will not drive the human heart?

As a result, the sea was so crowded with people from early on 3 that they abandoned the rafts first used for sailing and finally built the ships resembling houses that now cover almost all the ocean. Having learned the art of sailing, each one boldly claimed rule of the sea for himself and waged war upon it as if it were land.

But now let us come to our topic. Minos first ruled the sea, ac- 4 cording to Strabo in book 10 of the *Geography*. But Diodorus in book [5] assigns this to Neptune, who first invented the art of sailing: According to the Cretans, says he, Saturn gave Neptune command of the fleet he first assembled after the art of sailing had been invented, and so it was handed down that Neptune ruled the sea. The Cretans were long the undisputed leaders in sailing, as Strabo shows. From them came the proverb — the Cretan knows nothing of the sea — used against a person who pretends not to know something of which he is well aware, as we have explained in our *Adages*.

But sailing first began with rafts invented by King Erythras for 5 the island traffic in the Red Sea, according to Pliny in book 7. Something Quintilian says in book 10 also bears this out: If no one accomplished more than his predecessor, we would have no

in historiis supra *Pontificum annales* haberemus; ratibus adhuc navigaremus, etc. Ipsas vero rates sunt qui non Erythram regem sed Mysios et Troianos priores invenisse in Hellesponto putent cum transirent adversus Thracas. Alii in Britannico oceano primo inventas produnt corio circunsutas.

6   Navem, sicut Plinius libro 7 scribit, primus in Graeciam ex Aegypto invexit Danaus, at alii, teste Eusebio in 1 *De evangelica praeparatione,* a Samothracis inventam dicunt aut, ut Clementi placet, ab Atlante. Alii vero, velut ostendimus, a Neptuno, alii a Minerva, autor Tertullianus libro *De militis corona.*

7   Verum ego hoc aliquanto verius, ut par est, Noe tribuendum iudico, qui ex testimonio Eusebii libro 10 *De praeparatione evangelica* perdiu ante Danaum et Neptunum fuit. Is enim vir sanctus et innocens, autore Iosepho in 1 *Antiquitatum,* cum a Deo diluvium ad perniciem humani generis futurum esse cognovisset, ut aquarum vim evaderet arcam sibi ligneam fabricatus est. Quae haud dubie nihil aliud fuit nisi navis, et condendorum diversi generis navigiorum primum ac unicum posteris exemplar. Berosus itidem Chaldaeus, ut Iosephus est testis, eam ipsam arcam navim appellat. Ac non iniuria igitur et navigandi et condendarum navium usum primum a Noe, ante quem quod memoriae proditum sit nemo mare tentaverat, fluxisse credere convenit, cum praesertim ab eodem Iosepho accipiamus illius nepotes, dum alii aliam orbis regionem ad habitandum peterent, multis navibus esse usos.

8   Tibullus autem hoc Tyriis assignat, *Elegia* 7 dicens,

Utque maris vastum prospectet turribus aequor,
     Prima ratem ventis credere docta Tyros.

poetry beyond Livius Andronicus, no history beyond the *Pontifical Annals*; we would still be sailing on rafts, and so on. There are those who think that these same rafts were invented earlier, however, not by King Erythras but in the Hellespont by the Mysians and Trojans when they crossed over against the Thracians. Others report that rafts made of hides sewn together were first invented in the Britannic Sea.

Danaus first introduced the ship to Greece from Egypt — as 6 Pliny writes in book 7 — though others say the Samothracians were the inventors, according to Eusebius in book 1 of the *Preparation for the Gospel*, or else Atlas, as Clement believes. Still others say it was Neptune, as we have shown, and others Minerva, according to Tertullian in his book *On the Soldier's Wreath*.

But I think it correct to be rather more accurate and attribute 7 this discovery to Noah, who lived a very long time before Danaus and Neptune, according to the testimony of Eusebius in book 10 of the *Preparation for the Gospel*. When this holy and blameless man saw that God would send a flood to destroy the human race, he fashioned an ark of wood for himself to escape the violence of the waters, according to Josephus in book 1 of the *Antiquities*. Obviously this was nothing other than a ship, posterity's first and only model for producing vessels of various kinds. Josephus testifies that Berosus the Chaldaean calls this same ark a ship. Therefore, people came rightly to believe that the practice of sailing and shipbuilding came first from Noah, before whom there is no record of anyone's attempting the sea, especially since we have it from the same Josephus that his descendants used many ships when they sought out various regions of the globe to inhabit.

Tibullus assigns this to the Tyrians, however, saying in *Elegy* 8 [1.]7:

From towers that look on ocean's endless flats
Tyre learned first to trust a ship to winds.

Ob hoc hercle, ut puto, quod Tyrii, teste Strabone libro 16, diu navigandi arte excelluerunt. Ex quo fit ut etiam qui post tempora Noe ad hanc usque aetatem huiusmodi artem exercuerunt nonnihil bene meriti sint.

9 Nam cum nulla fere ars intra initium suum steterit, multa idcirco cum navigiorum tum caeterarum rerum nauticarum genera reperta sunt, quae plurimum artem illustrarunt; quorum proinde autores commemorare haud omnino alienum instituto nostro ducimus. Longam itaque navem Iason primus aedificavit, qua apud Aegyptios, ut puto, Diodoro libro I teste, Sesostris rex Aegyptiorum primus omnium postea usus est. Biremem Erythraei fecerunt. Triremem Amoclem Corinthium invenisse prodit Thucydides, quadriremem Carthaginenses secundum Aristotelem. Quinqueremem instituit Nesichthon Salaminius, quod navigii genus, teste Polybio volumine I, Romani primi omnium in Italia in apparatu primi belli Punici aedificarunt. Sex ordinum Zenagoras Syracusanus; ab ea ad deciremem Nesigiton; ad XII ordines Alexander Magnus; ad XV Ptolemaeus Soter; ad XXX Demetrius Antigoni; ad XL Ptolemaeus Philadelphus; ad L Ptolemaeus Philopator, qui est Tryphon cognomimatus.

10 Onerariam navem Hippius Tyrius invenit. Lembum Cyrenenses; cymbam Phoenices; celecem Rhodii; cercirum Cyprii; lintres Germani circa Danubium habitantes; scaphas Illyrii, quae naviculae maiores sequuntur naves. Remum autem Copae invenerunt, latitudinem eius Plateae, vela Icarus. Diodorus tamen dicit Aeolum velis uti nautas primum docuisse. Malum, id est, arborem navis et antennam Daedalus; hippagines — hoc est, ut Festo placet, naves quibus equi vehuntur — Salaminii vel Athenienses.

11 Tectas longas Thasii; rostra addidit Piseus; Tyrrheni anchoram. Eupalamius eandem fecit bidentem. Quod inventum quidam, autore Strabone libro 7, Anacharsidi ascribunt qui invenit harpago-

His reason, surely, was that the Tyrians long excelled in the art of sailing, according to Strabo in book 16, which shows that some credit also goes to those who have practiced this art after Noah's time, up to our own day.

Since almost no art stays where it started, many kinds of ships 9 as well as other nautical gear were discovered, shedding much light on this art. Accordingly, we think that commemorating these inventors does not at all stray from our purpose. Jason first built a warship, which I believe Sesostris, king of Egypt, was the first to use after him, according to Diodorus in book 1. The Erythraeans made a war galley with oars in two tiers. Thucydides reports that Amocles of Corinth invented a galley with three tiers, and the Carthaginians used four, according to Aristotle. Nesichthon of Salamis launched a five, and the Romans first built such craft in Italy when preparing for the first Punic War, according to book 1 of Polybius. Xenagoras of Syracuse used six, whence Nesigiton increased it to ten; Alexander the Great to twelve; Ptolemy Soter to fifteen; Demetrius, son of Antigonus, to thirty; Ptolemy Philadelphus to forty; and Ptolemy Philopator, whose surname was Tryphon, went to fifty.

Hippius of Tyre invented the sailing merchant ship. Cyrenians 10 invented the light galley; Phoenicians the skiff; Rhodians the cutter; Cypriots the oared river transport. Germans living near the Danube built rowboats, and the Illyrians made dinghies, which are little boats used to follow after larger ships. But Copae invented the oar, Plateae its blade and Icarus sails. Yet Diodorus says that Aeolus first taught sailors the use of sails. Daedalus devised the mast or ship's tree and the yard. The Salaminians or the Athenians made cavalry ships, which were vessels for transporting horses, so Festus believes.

The Thasians invented decked warships. Piseus added beaked 11 prows and Tyrrhenians the anchor. Eupalamius made an anchor with two flukes, but, according to Strabo in book 7, some ascribe

nas, id est, telum in summitate aduncum quo navigia capiuntur, ab ἁρπάζειν, quod est rapere. Adminicula gubernandi Tiphys, sumpto a milvo ave exemplo. Haec enim avis, teste Plinio libro 10, videtur artem gubernandi docuisse caudae flexibus, in coelo monstrante natura quod esset opus in profundo. Classe vero primum depugnasse Minoem, autor est Plinius.

12   Haec de navigiis dicta satis sint, quae cum potissimum merces ultro citroque convehendi causa reperta sint, eis utique convenire visum est mercaturae inventores quamprimum subtexere.

: XVI :

Qui primi mercaturam invenerint, et de primis institoribus.

1 Mercatura haud equidem parvo mortalibus auxilio est quando in asportandis mercibus vitae humanae necessaria ubique locorum suppeditat; multarum quoque ac maximarum rerum usum experientiamque homines edocet; ad barbarorum insuper necessitudines regumque amicitias contrahendas plurimum valere censetur. Quapropter Plinius in 33 haud temere putat commercia victus gratia esse inventa, sed ibi, ut opinor, de rerum commerciis loquitur quae (ut ipse tradit) Troianis temporibus in permutandis rebus ad victum necessariis mortales inter se exercebant; propter quod cum illis tunc haud dubie multo praeclarius agebatur. Posthac autem reperto, sicut idem sentit, aureo numo, tanta hominibus lucri cupiditas incessit ut merces asportandi causa sese ad omnia pericula (vel, ut ita dicam, ad aleam) veluti etiam hodie fit exponerent.

this invention to Anacharsis, who invented grappling-hooks. Called *harpagones* from *harpazein*, to grasp, these are weapons with hooked tips used in capturing vessels. Following the example of the kite, Tiphys invented devices for steering. According to Pliny in book 10, this bird seems to have taught the art of steering by shifting its tail about — a natural demonstration on high of what was needed for the deep. Minos was the first to give battle with a fleet, according to Pliny.

Enough about ships. Since they are known to be the main 12 means of conveying goods hither and yon, it seems fitting to move immediately from them to the inventors of trade.

: XVI :

Who first invented trade, and on the first hucksters.

Trade is no small help to mortals, clearly. By transporting goods it 1 provides the necessities of human life everywhere, teaching people the use and handling of many things and of their abundance as well; it is also thought to be of great value in making connections with barbarians and alliances with kings. Hence, Pliny reasonably concludes in book 33 that commerce was invented for the sake of survival, but here, I imagine, Pliny is talking about the commerce in articles that people conducted among themselves in the days of Troy (as he himself says) by bartering things necessary for sustaining life. For this reason, no doubt, they handled these affairs in a much nobler way at that time. But when gold coinage was invented later, as the same author believes, so great a passion for gain came over mankind that in order to transport goods they exposed themselves to every risk (or to chance, as I would put it), just as it happens today.

471

2   Ex quo verissime Flaccus Horatius de his ait:

Impiger extremos mercator currit ad Indos
Per mare pauperiem fugiens, per saxa, per ignes.

De huiusmodi mercatura Cicero quoque in 1 *De officiis:* Mercatura autem, inquit, si tenuis est, sordida putanda est; sin magna et copiosa, multa undique apportans multisque sine vanitate impertiens, non est admodum vituperanda; atque etiam si satiata quaestu (vel contenta potius) ut saepe ex alto in portum, ex ipso portu se in agros possessionesque contulerit, videtur iure optimo posse laudari. Mercaturam etiam, teste Plutarcho, viri praeclarissimi exercuerunt—Thales, Solon, Hippocrates mathematicus et Plato.

3   Hanc, autore Plinio libro 7, Poeni invenerunt, verum Diodorus in 6 Mercurio assignat, id quod Galli quondam sibi persuasum habuere. Qui, ut Caesar ait, deum maxime Mercurium colebant cuius plurima erant apud eos simulacra. Hunc enim omnium inventorem artium ferebant, hunc viarum atque itinerum ducem, hunc ad quaestum pecuniae mercaturasque vim maximam habere arbitrabantur.

4   Sed Plinius sibi omnino repugnare videtur cum in eodem libro dicat emere ac vendere instituisse Liberum patrem, praesertim cum mercatura, quam ait Poenos invenisse, nil aliud sit nisi actus quidam emendi vendendique merces. Quare ita fortasse intelligendum est ut Poeni mercaturam a Libero patre institutam primi exercuerint.

5   Caeterum neque hoc primo Poenis aut Mercurio vel Libero patri assignandum ducimus quando ex testimonio Iosephi libro 1 *Antiquitatum* usum vendendi et emendi multo ante apud Hebraeos, hoc est, Noe temporibus fuisse constat.

Thus, what Horace says of them is quite true: 2

To the ends of the Indies the hard-driving tradesman runs
Through fire, sea and mountains, escaping poverty.

Cicero also writes about trade of this sort in book 1 *On Duties*: If trade is petty, he says, it is considered disreputable; but if it is great and plentiful, bringing in a multitude of goods from all over and sharing them honestly with many people, it is not greatly to be despised. Further, if trade is glutted (or better, contented) with profit and moves from port to farm and property, as it has often moved from sea to port, it seems actually to deserve all our praise. Even people of the greatest renown, according to Plutarch, have engaged in trade — Thales, Solon, Hippocrates the mathematician and Plato.

Pliny says in book 7 that the Phoenicians invented trade, but in   3 book [5] Diodorus assigns it to Mercury, a notion of which the Gauls were once convinced. The Gauls, as Caesar says, greatly honored the god Mercury and had many statues of him. They considered him the inventor of all the arts, their guide on trips and journeys, and they thought his influence on trade and financial gain was very great.

But Pliny seems to contradict himself completely when he   4 writes in the same book that Father Liber established buying and selling, especially since trade, which he says that the Phoenicians invented, is nothing but a particular transaction of buying and selling trade-goods. Perhaps we are to understand that the Phoenicians first engaged in trade after Father Liber established it.

All that aside, we conclude that this discovery should be as-   5 signed neither to the Phoenicians nor to Mercury nor to Father Liber since it is clear from the testimony of Josephus in book 1 of the *Antiquities* that the practice of buying and selling existed among the Hebrews much earlier, in Noah's time.

6   Institores vero primi, teste Herodoto in primo, Lydi fuerunt. Sunt autem institores non qui egregie mercaturam exercent sed qui a mercatoribus emunt ut deinde emptas merces minutatim vendant. De quibus Marcus Tullius libro *Officiorum* primo ita sentit: Sordidi etiam, inquit, putantur qui mercantur a mercatoribus quod statim vendant, nihil enim proficiunt nisi admodum mentiantur.

7   His item hodie vestium linteorumque venditores dare solent vestimenta circunferenda ac ipsi ab aliis opificibus mercari res minusculas ad vendendum, qui idcirco omnes urbis vicos rurique ex mercatu mercatum circuire parati sunt suas pariter merces ac amicorum vendendi causa. Unde vulgo circuitores vocamus, et institores teste Ulpiano dicuntur quod negotio gerendo instent. At Labeo iuris consultus muliones quoque, stabularios, tabernarumque praepositos loco institorum habet. Quanquam sunt institores iidem atque mercatores et negotiatores, sed ut isti honesti, sic illi sordidi habentur — quemadmodum Cicero, sicut supra dixi, eorum conditionem recte tenuerat.

: XVII :

Quis primus instituerit artem meretriciam et Bacchanalia sacra, ac qualis poena adulterii; aut invenerit tincturam capillorum vel usum tondendi, et quando primum tonsores Romae.

1   Venerem, quam ex spuma maris procreatam, princeps apud nos poetarum et Ovidius testimonio sunt, impudicam ad omnesque divulgatam libidines fuisse propalam est, quippe quae plures ex

The first hucksters, according to Herodotus in his first book, 6
were the Lydians. Hucksters are not those who carry on trade of
great prestige but those who buy trade-goods from merchants in
order to sell them by the piece. Cicero expresses his opinion of
them in the first book *On Duties:* They are also considered disreputable who buy things from merchants for direct resale, he says,
for they make their profit only by considerable deception.

In the same way, it is also customary today for vendors of cloth- 7
ing and fabrics to give garments to hucksters for distribution and
to buy small goods from other craftsmen in order to sell them,
thus equipping themselves to travel from market to market on the
highways of town and country so that they can sell their own
goods as well as those of their friends. Hence, we commonly call
them travelers, and according to Ulpian they are called hucksters
because they do their business by hawking goods insistently. But
Labeo the jurist also puts mule-drivers, hostlers and tavern-keepers in the same place with hucksters. Although hucksters are like
merchants and businessmen, the latter are thought to be respectable, the former disreputable—just as Cicero had correctly described their status, as I have explained above.

: XVII :

*Who first established the art of prostitution and Bacchanalian
rites, and what was the penalty for adultery; who invented
hair-dying or the practice of cutting hair, and when barbers
first came to Rome.*

Shameless Venus, born of the sea-foam, notoriously lowered her- 1
self to every passion, according to Ovid and our prince of poets,
for she gave birth to several children in adultery: From her famous

adulterio filios procreavit: Nam ex famoso Martis stupro genuit Harmoniam, de qua Plutarchus in *Vita Pelopidae* affatim meminit; ex Mercurio Hermaphroditum, ex Ioue Cupidinem, ex Anchisa Aeneam et ex Bute Erycem; quas ob res amorum gratiarumque, item pulchritudinis et deliciarum et voluptatum omnium, et libidinis atque coitus dea habita est.

2   Haec autem ne sola impudica virorumque appetens videretur, omnium prima, teste Lactantio libro I (ut est in *Historia* quam prisci *Sacram* appellabant), meretriciam artem instituit, autorque mulieribus in Cypro insula fuit uti vulgato corpore quaestum facerent. Ex quo apud Cyprios, teste Iustino libro 18, mos inolevit ut virgines ante nuptias statutas dotalem pecuniam quaesituras in quaestum ad littus maris mitterent, pro reliqua pudicitia libamenta Veneri soluturas. Harum ex numero LXXX admodum virgines rapi et in naves imponi iussit Elisa, cum illac transiret e Tyro fugiens, ut iuventus matrimonia et urbs sobolem haberet.

3   Apud Babylonios etiam consuetudo fuit ut, cum rem domesticam consumpsissent, unusquisque plebeius ob victus inopiam filias suas adigeret ad quaestum corpore faciundum. Item mulieres semel in vita omnibus indigenis communes erant. Sane ad templum Veneris sedebant nodis corollisque tempora revinctae, e quibus aliae ad diverticula quae aditum externis praebebant ad mulieres dum se conferebant, aliae regrediebantur. Etenim cum semel illic sederant, non prius domum redire fas erat quam hospitum aliquis pecuniam in sinum mulieris iecisset ac cum ea consuetudinem habuisset. Mulier acceptam pecuniam ad sacrum usum reservabat, hospes vero dans dicebat: Tanti ego tibi deam Mylittam imploro — ita Assyrii Venerem vocant. At pulchriores cito expediebantur, deformiores non item, quas saepe uno vel altero anno ex-

debauch with Mars she conceived Harmonia, of whom Plutarch has plenty to say in his *Life of Pelopidas*; from Mercury she begot Hermaphroditus, from Jupiter Cupid, from Anchises Aeneas, from Butes Eryx; and because of all this she was considered the goddess of love and charm, also of beauty and delight and every pleasure, and of passion and lovemaking.

But lest she alone seem to be a shameless, man-hungry female, she first of all established the art of prostitution, according to book 1 of Lactantius (who follows the *History* called *Sacred* by the ancients), and she showed women on the island of Cyprus how to make a living by offering their bodies to the public. This, according to Justinus in book 18, was the origin of the Cypriot custom of sending their unmarried maidens to seek dowry money by plying their trade on the seashore, making offerings to Venus in exchange for what remained of their chastity. When Dido passed by Cyprus while fleeing from Tyre, she ordered no less than eighty of these maidens to be seized and put aboard ship so that her young men would have marriages and her city children. 2

After they had exhausted their country's wealth, it was also the custom among the Babylonians for any commoner who lacked a livelihood to compel his daughters to make a living with their bodies. Also, once in their lifetimes women were the common property of all the populace. They sat near the temple of Venus with garlands tied about their heads, some of them moving into the passageways that gave outsiders access when going to the women, others moving out of them. Once a woman had taken her seat there, she was forbidden to return home until one of the strangers tossed money in her lap and had intercourse with her. The woman saved the money she received for some holy use, while the stranger in giving it said: So much I entreat you, goddess Mylitta—for this was the Assyrian name for Venus. The prettier women were quickly released, but not so the plain, who often had to wait a year 3

pectare oportebat. Ac talis erat lex honoris deae Veneri habendi gratia, autor Herodotus volumine 1.

4   Sed Bacchanalia sacra uberrimum apud cunctas ferme gentes libidinis seminarium fuere, quorum, ut idem testatur Herodotus, autor fuit Melampus, Amytheonis filius, primusque ad Graecos detulit ex Aegypto, ubi ea sacra fieri coepere. Foeminae enim statuas cubitales e nervis compactas, quibus ingens mentula in ventre extabat, per pagos praeeunte tibia circumferebant Bacchum canentes. Deinde in Parnaso monte Bacchanalia, quae Graecis Dionysia dicuntur, alternis annis acta sunt, magno cum hominum multo mero incalentium clamore tum tympanorum crepitu.

5   Haud ita multo post graecus quidam homo ignobilis eiusmodi sacrorum antistes in Hetruriam venit docuitque ritus. Ex Hetruria ea mali labes mox Romam penetravit, ubi mirandum in modum morbi contagione matronarum pudicitiam corrupit. Primo sacrarium foeminarum fuit, nec quisquam virorum admittebatur. Tres in anno statutos dies habebant quibus interdiu Bacchis initiarentur. Sacerdotes invicem matronae creabantur.

6   Cum demum Paculla Minia Campana facta est sacerdos, haec omnia tanquam deorum monitu immutavit. Sane viros et cum primis filios initiavit. Nocturnumque sacrum ex diurno, et pro tribus in anno diebus quinos in singulos menses dies initiorum sacros fecit. Tum promiscuo sacra viri foeminis permisti facere coeperunt ubi, cum per noctis licentiam quidvis scelerum unicuique edere liceret, nihil facinoris, nihil flagitii praetermittebatur. Siquidem eo loci stupra pariter atque caedes redundabant quando qui aut ad Venerem pigriores aut dedecoris minus patientes erant (nam postremo nemo maior viginti annis initiabatur) morte afficiebantur. Nec id multis cognitum, cum nulla vox queritantium prae ululatu tympanorum cymbalorumque strepitu exaudiri posset, et mortui ex conspectu illico in specus abderentur.

or two. Such was the law whose purpose was to preserve the honor of the goddess Venus, according to Herodotus in book I.

Among almost all peoples, however, the Bacchanalian rites were 4 the most fertile seedbed of passion. Their founder, as Herodotus again testifies, was Melampus, son of Amytheon, who first brought them to Greece from Egypt, where these rites originated. Singing of Bacchus and preceded through the villages by a flute, women carried figurines a cubit long joined together with strings, each with a huge phallus projecting from its middle. The Bacchanalia, which the Greeks call the Dionysia, later took place every other year on Mount Parnassus, as timbrels banged and shouts came loud from people heated up by much unmixed wine.

A certain obscure Greek who was a minister of these rites came 5 into Etruria not long after and taught the rites there, whence this evil blight soon penetrated Rome, where like an infectious disease it corrupted the chastity of married women with astonishing force. At first the rites were a sacred preserve of women, and no man was admitted. Three dates in the year were set aside on which they were initiated into the Bacchic mysteries by day. A succession of married women were created priests.

But then when Paculla Minia, a Campanian, was made a priest, 6 she changed all this as if the gods had told her to do so. She actually initiated men, her sons among the first of them. She moved the rite from day to night, and she reserved five days in each month instead of three in a year for initiations. Men then began to perform the rites in promiscuous combination with women, and since night's license permitted everyone his choice of crime, no disgrace, no outrage went uncommitted. Slaughter and debauchery so abounded that anyone slow to fornicate or intolerant of vice (eventually they initiated no one older than twenty) was murdered. Nor was this widely known, for no voice of complaint could be made out above the moaning and the banging of timbrels and cymbals, and the dead were immediately removed from sight into a cave.

7   Summa religionis erat inter eos viros velut mente captos corporis iactatione fanatica vaticinari, matronas Baccharum habitu crini-
bus passis cum facibus ardentibus discurrere. Et mactatos dici a
diis raptos. Verum ad extremum tantorum scelerum indicio ad
Spurium Posthumium Albinum et Quintum Martium Philippum
consules delato, religio pestifera extincta est, anno urbis conditae
DLXVIII.

8   Atqui non est quod plura veterum probra vitae repetamus cum
nos forsitan magis reprehendendi simus quando apud nos prae Veneris institutis parum Dei Optimi Maximi praecepta rite servantur. Moses enim mulierem adulteram cum adultero, ut in Levitico
capite 20 est, morte mactandam statuit. Apud Romanos et Graecos adulterium crimen etiam capitale fuit. Arabes qui Felicem Arabiam incolunt virum etiam adulterum capite mulctabant. Quin et
divus Clemens *Epistola* sua prima dicit secundum haeresim adulterium omnium gravissimum esse peccatum atque apud iustum iu-
dicem maiore poena lui.

9   Et tamen ioco habetur. Quid? Quod uxores et viri palam multis
adulteriis inquinati, eo quod aut ad nullam aut ad minorem poenam quam culpa sit vocantur nihil pensi habent sacrosanctum matrimonii foedus violare. Ita apud nos mansuetudo puniendi illece-
bra est peccandi.

10   Non sola igitur, ut ipsa cupiebat, Venus impudica est, nec tamen prima fuit. Siquidem satis constat iam inde ab initio ferme
orbis conditi fuisse mulieres quae vulgato corpore quaestum fecerint. Legimus enim in Geneseos libro Iudam Iacob filium eo rem
habuisse cum Thamar, nuru sua, quod suspicatus esset illam esse
meretricem—prout mulier talem se esse vestitu pariter atque arte
simularat.

11   At quanto Venere praestantior Lucretia fuit? Quae non pudicitiae omnibus pervulgandae sed constanter servandae unicum edi-

Their religion reached its apex when men made demented 7
prophecies and contorted their bodies in frenzy, while married
women dressed as Bacchae ran about with hair disheveled and
torches blazing. The people they killed were said to be taken
by the gods. In the end, when evidence of such great crimes
was brought before the consuls, Spurius Posthumius Albinus and
Quintus Martius Philippus, the pestilent religion was extin-
guished, in the year 568 AUC.

But it is not for us to recall more scandals from the lives of the 8
ancients since we may be more to blame who seldom pay due heed
to the commandments of Almighty God, as opposed to the precepts of Venus. Moses, as it is written in chapter 20 of Leviticus,
ordained that the adulterous woman along with the adulterer
should be punished with death. Adultery was a capital crime
among the Greeks and Romans. The Arabs who live in Arabia Felix also punish an adulterous man with death. Indeed, St. Clement
says in his first *Epistle* that adultery is the gravest sin of all after
heresy and that a just judge will see that it is punished with a se-
vere penalty.

And yet people make a joke of it. Why? Because wives and 9
husbands stained with many sins of adultery think nothing of violating the holy bond of matrimony if they are cited for no punishment or for a penalty less than the crime. Thus, our softness in
punishing entices to sin.

Just as she wished, then, Venus is not alone in her shameless- 10
ness, nor was she the first. For it is well agreed that almost from
the beginning of the world there were women who made a living
by offering their bodies to the public. We read in the book of
Genesis that Judah, son of Jacob, had relations with Tamar, his
daughter-in-law, because he thought she was a prostitute — as the
woman pretended in her dress and her conduct.

But how much more worthy than Venus was Lucretia? She 11
made no public offering of her chastity but preserved it steadfastly

dit exemplum sibi ipsi mortem consciscens. Haec tamen non facile multas sui similes habet adeo libido crevit, qua mehercule nihil in vita mortalium turpius foediusque esse potest, quando haec nobis cum belluis communis est, et hac una tantum humanae vitae internoscitur infirmitas. Quapropter Magnus Alexander, ut testis est Plutarchus, se duabus potissimum rebus mortalitatem intelligere aiebat, sopore ac coitu, quas sola naturae infirmitas pareret. Pythagoras vero, rogatus quando concumbendum esset, tunc inquit: Cum teipso infirmior fieri vis, autor Diogenes libro 8. Quod nos, etsi recte scimus, nihilominus tamen mulierum illecebris in libidinem trahimur, veluti canis, ut dicitur, ad vomitum suum revertitur. De his satis.

12   Tincturam capillorum, teste Clemente, Medea primum invenit. Usum autem tondendi ab Abantibus fluxisse ferunt. Ita enim huiusmodi populi cum natura bellicosi forent, expeditius cum hostibus cominus congrediebantur. Testatur utrunque Plutarchus in *Vita Thesei*, scribens: Vigebat etiam illis temporibus consuetudo ut qui ex ephebis excessissent delati in Delphos de comis Deo primitias darent. Accessit igitur in Delphos Theseus et anteriorem partem capitis arrasit. At Abantes primi hoc tondendi more usi sunt, quem quidem non ab Arabibus (ut quidam existimant) didicerunt nec Mysios imitati. Sed quod natura bellicosi essent et prope pugnandi ac praeter caeteros manus cum hostibus conserendi peritiam tenerent. Et post paulo infert: Ne igitur ullas hostibus ad capiendum ansas darent, tondebantur. Haec ille.

13   Ea etiam de re Magnus Alexander suis ducibus imperasse dicitur ut Macedonum barbas arraderent. Tonsores in Italiam ex Sicilia primum venere anno post conditam urbem CCCCLIIII, addu-

and set us a unique example in her suicide. Yet it will be hard to find many like her when lust has so much prospered. Nothing in human life can be filthier or more disgraceful than lust, God knows: it is what we have in common with animals, and just in this respect the weakness of human life is evident. Therefore, as Plutarch tells us, Alexander the Great used to say that he felt his mortality in two things especially, sleep and sex, caused only by the weakness of nature. Asked when one ought to lie with a woman, Pythagoras answered: When you wish to become weaker than you are, according to Diogenes in book 8. Though we know this well enough, women's wiles still draw us into lust, as a dog returns to its vomit, so the saying goes. Enough of this.

According to Clement, Medea first invented the dying of hair. 12 But they say that the practice of cutting hair came from the Abantes. Since people of their sort were by nature warlike, they found that this let them fight more freely in close combat with their enemies. In his *Life of Theseus*, Plutarch testifies on both points, writing: In those times flourished the custom whereby those who advanced from the ranks of the ephebes were brought to Delphi to offer the god the first cuttings of their hair. So Theseus came to Delphi and shaved the front part of his head. But the first to practice this custom of cutting the hair were the Abantes, copying it neither from the Arabs (as some suppose) nor from the Mysians. They did it because they were warlike by nature and exceptionally skilled at close-in fighting and hand-to-hand combat with their enemies. A little farther on he concludes: Thus, in order to avoid giving the enemy anything to catch hold of, they had their hair cut. So much from Plutarch.

They say that for the same reason Alexander the Great also or- 13 dered his commanders to shave the beards of the Macedonians. Barbers first came to Italy from Sicily in AUC 454 at the behest of Publius Ticinius Mena, says Varro, before which time the Italians

cente Publio Ticinio Mena, testis Varro; ante intonsi fuere. Primus omnium radi quotidie instituit Africanus. Sequens divus Augustus cultris iugiter usus, autor Plinius volumine 7 *Naturalis historiae.*

: XVIII :

Multa cum vetera tum nova inventa esse quorum
autores ignorentur.

1 Quanquam probe scimus quantum laudis praemiique debeatur illis qui olim aliquid suo ingenio vel ad usum vitae vel ad animum excolendum utile nihil non necessarium excogitarint; eoque huiuscemodi rerum autores hoc uno opere omnes complecti, ne quempiam sua laude fraudasse videremur, diligentius elaboravimus; attamen nobis per vetustatem — quae, ut Varro inquit, multa tollit, pauca non depravat — id praestare minus licuit quod multis utimur quae aut ad suos minime referuntur autores aut omnino ad nullos utpote qui non produntur. Quapropter, si scriptores quos sequeremur nullos plane habuimus, nemini sane mirum sit nos quaedam silentio praeterisse, quando illud admiratione dignius est ut plurima nova inventa sint quorum inventores non tradantur et ex iis quaedam nec scripta habeamus quo nomine vocari possint.

2 Nam quid iucundius reperiri potuit horologio, quo nobis etsi occultato sole per tintinabulum sua ut ita videtur sponte sonans horae nuntiantur? Aut quid gratius ipso tintinabulo, quod alii campanam, nonnulli nolam nuncupant, inveniri potuit? Quod licet recens inventum non sit, Mosis enim temporibus, teste Iosepho in 3 *Antiquitatum,* eius usus erat; de quo Martialis ait:

went unshaven. Africanus first of all took up shaving daily. Following him, the deified Augustus used his razors regularly, according to Pliny in book 7 of the *Natural History*.

: XVIII :

That there are many inventions, both old and new, whose authors are unknown.

Although we know full well how much glory and reward are due   1
those who by their own skill have at some time devised something
useful, something in no wise irrelevant to the conduct of life or to
the perfection of the spirit; though we have taken considerable
pains to include in this one book all discoverers of such things lest
we should seem to cheat anyone of his glory; yet because we use
many things that are not at all traceable to their authors or that
lack the expected tradition of authorship, the evidence of discovery allowed us has diminished through time which, as Varro says,
destroys many things and distorts others. Therefore, if we have no
sources at all that we may follow, no one should be surprised if we
have passed over certain things in silence, for the greater surprise
is that there are many new inventions whose inventors are unrecorded and from whom we have no writings to tell us what names
to give them.

What discovery could be more delightful than the clock, whose   2
bell seems to ring of its own accord and tell us the hours on a
cloudy day? What invention could be more pleasant than the bell
itself, which some call a *campana*, others a *nola*? This cannot be of
recent origin for it was used in the time of Moses, according to
Josephus in book 3 of his *Antiquities*. Martial also speaks of it:

Redde pilam, sonat aes thermarum, ludere pergis?
Virgine vis sola lotus abire domum?

Utriusque tamen pariter autor latet. Sed et aliud meo iudicio ad-
mirabilius fuit invenire pyxidem illam qua nautae admodum peritissime navigationem moderantur; quis tamen eam repererit omnino in aperto non est.

3   Adde praeterea illud tormentum aeneum quod bombardam
vocant, omni admiratione execrationeque dignum ad perniciem
hominum excogitatum. Quod haud adduci possum ut humanum
ingenium invenisse credam. Sed mehercule potius malum quempiam daemonem mortalibus monstrasse puto, ut inter se non
modo armis verum etiam fulminibus — est enim, ut alio loco diximus, quam simillimum fulmini — pugnarent.

4   Cuius autor Perilli exemplo, sicut opinor, monitus non temere
nomen suum occultavit ne in se, uti merebatur, primum huiusmodi tormentum experiri cogeretur. Perillus enim, teste Plinio libro 34, vir Atheniensis — ut Phalaridi Agrigentinorum tyranno
post hominum memoriam crudelissimo placeret — ex aere taurum
artificiosissimum fabricavit, cui ianuam in latere posuit ut cum
reus inclusus subiectis ignibus torqueretur mugitum non hominis
vocem videretur emittere. Pro quo opere cum a tyranno pretium
postulasset, in illo ipse includi omnium primus a Phalaride iussus
suppositis ignibus, artificii sui verum experimentum praebuit. De
quo Ovidius in 1 *De arte amandi* ita cecinit:

Et Phalaris tauro violenti membra Perilli
    Torruit; infelix imbuit autor opus.
Iustus uterque fuit: neque enim lex aequior ulla est
    Quam necis artifices arte perire sua.

486

The bronze rings through the baths and you're still playing?
Turn in your ball.
You'd like a solitary soak to see you off?

And yet the makers of both these discoveries are hidden from us. Still more wonderful, to my mind, was the invention of that little box that sailors use so skillfully to guide their sailing, but the identity of its inventor is completely unknown.

Consider also that bronze catapult called the cannon, devised 3 for the ruination of mankind and worthy of all amazement and execration. That this was a product of human ingenuity I can scarcely credit. I would far rather think some evil demon had shown it to mortals so that they could combat one another not just with arms but with thunderbolts as well—for it is very much like a thunderbolt, as I have said elsewhere.

I suppose that the cannon's inventor, warned by the example of 4 Perillus, wisely concealed his name so that he would not be the first obliged to experience this terrible instrument, as he deserved. According to Pliny in book 34, Perillus was an Athenian who, in order to please Phalaris—tyrant of Agrigentum and the cruelest man in human memory—fashioned from bronze a most ingenious bull. In its side he put a door so that a prisoner could be shut within and tortured with flames lit beneath it, and the bull would seem to emit a bellowing noise, not the voice of a man. When Perillus asked the tyrant for a reward for his work, Phalaris ordered that he be the first shut inside and put to the flames, thus giving Perillus a true test of his workmanship. In part 1 of the *Art of Love* Ovid sang this of him:

Phalaris racked the body of Perillus in his raging bull;
The unlucky maker was first to feel his handiwork.
Both were just: there is no law more equitable
Than that craftsmen in death should perish by their craft.

5   Est et illud novum inventum in quo uterque pes utrinque eius quiescit qui equo insidet, nam ut in marmoreis statuis Romae conspicitur antiqui non utebantur, nec quo nomine appelletur apud autores legitur. Vulgo *staffa* nominatur, quod in eo pedes commode stent. Sunt et huiusmodi plurima, sed illa in primis incitamenta gulae quae hodie tam diversi generis ex saccaro fiunt. Vel etiam pars maxima armaturae quae cum suis vocabulis haud apte explicari queant nihil est quod proferam.

6   Est vel novitium inventum illud laneum tegmen capitis quod biretrum vocant. Veteres enim omnino caput non velabant, sicuti testantur numismata, vel ipsae statuae quae, ut Romae vidimus, apertum caput habent — praesertim cum propalam sit nos patrio more eo fingi vestitu quo prorsus utimur. Sed hoc omnino Gaii Caesaris exemplo significantius comprobatur. Is enim, autore Tranquillo, cum calvitii deformitatem iniquissime ferret obtrectatorum saepe iocis propositam, deficientem capillum revocare a vertice consuevit ut illam obtegeret. Quod quidem quis non videt ab eo fieri subabsurdum fuisse si more patrio commodius decentiusque caput, hoc est, dehonestamentum illud calvitii obnubere potuisset? Ex quo apparet recens esse inventum hoc operimentum capitis quo nunc passim utimur; autor tamen ignoratur. Et sic huiusmodi sexcenta sunt, quorum iuxta autores non produntur.

7   Acutius est etiam invenisse et multo utilius qua ratione frumentum ad decurrentis aquae impetum molere possemus. Quamvis non utique recens sit, tamen apud idoneos autores suo nomine caret; vulgus *molendinum* vocat. Multa insuper novissimis temporibus instrumenta musica inventa sunt quorum autores iam in oblivionem venerunt. Ex quibus propter suavitatem concentus omni admiratione et laude digna sunt illa quae organa nuncupant, valde quidem ab illis dissimilia quae David Iudaeorum rex — ut in 1 huius operis volumine memoravimus — fecerat; quibus Levitae sa-

The device that holds the feet of a rider on either side of his   5
horse is another new invention; one can see from marble statues in
Rome that the ancients did not use it, and in their writings one
finds no word for it. They say *staffa* in the vulgar tongue because
the foot stands comfortably in it. There are many things like this,
especially those stimulants for the palate made of sugar in so many
ways today. Or again, the enormous field of armament, which
with its nomenclature can hardly be well explained — so there is
nothing that I will put forward.

Or take an invention newly imported, the woolen covering for   6
the head that they call a beret. The ancients did not clothe the
head at all, as shown by pieces of money or by those statues that
we see in Rome with heads uncovered — especially since we obviously imagine our ancestors wearing clothing in the way that we
still use it. The example of Julius Caesar confirms this much more
meaningfully. Since he could not bear the deforming baldness that
his detractors often made the butt of their jokes, he used to bring
the missing hair down from the crown of his head, according to
Suetonius. Who does not see that it would have been completely
silly for him to do so if ancestral custom had given him some easier and seemlier way to cover up his head — his disfiguring baldness, that is to say? Hence it is obvious that this covering of the
head that we now practice is a recent invention. Yet the inventor is
unknown. And there are hundreds of things like this whose authors have not been handed down.

More intelligent and also much more useful was the invention   7
of the method by which we can grind grain with the power of running water. Although not especially recent, it still lacks a name in
the better authors; the people say *molendinum*. Many musical instruments too have been invented in very recent times, and their
inventors have already passed into oblivion. Of these, those that
they call organs deserve the greatest admiration and praise because
of their sweet harmony. Though they are much unlike the organs

cros hymnos concinerent sicut nos his pariter canimus. Item alia id genus sunt, quae monochordia, clavicymbala varieque nominantur; eorum tamen aeque inventores magno quidem suae gloriae damno in nocte densissima delitescunt.

8   Non proditur itidem quis primus fecerit candelam ex sevo — rem etsi sordidam, attamen apprime utilem. Neque is qui primum aves ad venandum domuerit, quod similiter recens inventum est, nec memoriae proditum est quis annulos primo repererit, quibus apud Romanos, ut demonstravimus, magnus honos accessit.

9   Sed quid miramur eiusmodi rerum admodum tenuicularum inventores diuturnitatem temporis obliterasse cum imprimendarum literarum artis, nuper divino quodam ingenio excogitatae, ipse autor propemodum in tenebris iaceret? Nos tamen pro virili parte operam impendimus, quemadmodum alibi apposite ostendimus, ut ab omni oblivionis iniuria vindicaretur.

10   Est vel memoria nostra tegumentum crurum tam commodissime quam decentissime confectum, quod nos caligas dicimus, etsi caliga calceamenti genus fuerat apud veteres. Ast autor tam necessarii vestitus tamque honesti iamiam in occulto latet.

11   Extant plures praeterea artes quae intra suum initium tanquam humile cum minime steterint, deinde ab insequentibus auctae neutiquam ad suos priores autores sed ad eos a quibus incrementum acceperint perperam, ut in plerisque locis huius operis docuimus, referuntur. Quare proinde si vetera quaedam inventa aut nova minus attigimus, id profecto in causa fuit: quod maluerim paucis verbis certa tradere quam multis incerta persequi.

LIBRI III FINIS.

made by David, king of the Jews (as noted in book 1 of this work), we sing to their accompaniment just as the Levites sang their sacred hymns. There are other instruments of this kind, called monochords, clavichords and various other names, whose inventors also lie hidden in dimmest darkness, to the great detriment of their fame.

Likewise, there is no record of the person who first made a candle from tallow—an undistinguished achievement but a notably useful one. Nor do we know who first tamed birds for hunting, another recent invention, nor have we anything to mark the memory of the first maker of rings, to which the Romans attached great honor, as we have shown. 8

But why should we wonder that the passage of time has erased the renown of the inventors of such trifles when even the originator of the art of printing letters, a recent product of godlike genius, has been almost enshadowed? We, however, have done our part to rescue him from all the insults of oblivion, as explained in the appropriate place. 9

We also remember a leg-covering of the most comfortable and attractive design that we call *caligae*, though the ancients used this word for a sort of footwear. And yet the inventor of this necessary and handsome garment is already a secret to us. 10

There are several arts besides whose humble beginnings made them inconspicuous until they were developed by those who came later. We have frequently shown in this work that they were wrongly attributed to those who enhanced them, never to their original authors. Thus, if we have not mentioned certain inventions, new or old, this certainly was our reason: that I would rather pass on reliable information in few words than use many to pursue uncertainties. 11

END OF BOOK III.

Note on Chronology

꘏꘏꘏꘏

In his chapter on the origin of religion (*DIR* 1.5.2), Polydore makes the following chronological argument, one of many in *On Discovery*. He begins with Lactantius, who maintains that 'temples were first constructed and new ways of worshipping the gods began in Jupiter's time or a little before . . . But in order to establish its origin precisely,' he adds,

> let us put the beginning of this custom in the time of Belus, the father of Ninus, who first reigned over the Assyrians about 3180 years after the creation of the world. The Babylonians and Assyrians called this Belus their god and worshipped him. Those who maintain that the gods have been worshipped since the beginning are therefore mistaken.

Writing in the early fourth century and contending that pagan religion was not as old as had been thought, Lactantius referred to Theophilus (who in turn had cited Thallus) to show that Saturn was contemporary with a Belus worshipped by the Assyrians and Babylonians 322 years before the Trojan War, about eighteen centuries before his own day. But Polydore locates Belus more than five centuries earlier.

Theophilus was bishop of Antioch in the latter part of the second century. His only surviving work is the apologetic *Ad Autolycum*, written after 180 and containing a chronology of world history in its third book. Thallus of Samaria was one of the chronographers used by Theophilus and also by Eusebius, who is the main source for Polydore's temporal scheme of cultural history, by way of Jerome's translation of the second book of the *Chronicle* of Eusebius. Eusebius constructed parallel sequences of regnal dates for Assyrian, Hebrew, Greek and Egyptian history, thus enabling Christians to synchronize the sacred history recorded in the scriptures with secular events and figures known from Greek and Latin texts and tradition.

In the preface to the second book of the *Chronicle*, Eusebius establishes that Moses was a contemporary of Cecrops. But he begins his chronol-

493

ogy with the birth of Abraham, before whose time nothing was known about secular history:

> From year 80 of Moses and the departure of Israel from Egypt . . . back to the first year of Abraham you will find that 505 years passed, and you will reckon the same number from year 45 of Cecrops to Ninus and Semiramis, rulers of the Assyrians. In fact, Ninus, the son of Belus, was the first to rule all Asia, except for India. Hence it is obvious that Abraham was born in the age of Ninus . . . But your curiosity should not stop here. Carefully paging through sacred scripture, you will discover that there were 942 years from Abraham to the global deluge and from the deluge to Adam 2242 years, during which time one finds no history at all for the Greeks or barbarians or — to use the common term — the gentiles . . . If you calculate carefully, from the last year of Ninus to the capture of Troy you will find 834 years, . . . [and] we locate Abraham, Ninus, Semiramis, Europs and the Thebans of Egypt in one and the same era . . . Then we divide the years of the Hebrews into four periods, from Abraham to Moses, from Moses to the first building of the temple, from the first building of the temple to its second restoration, and from its restoration to the coming of Christ the Lord.

The *Chronicle* next explains that 505 years passed from Abraham to Moses; 478 from Moses to Solomon's temple; 512 from Solomon's temple to its restoration, in year 2 of Darius; 548 from Darius to Christ's public preaching, in year 15 of Tiberius; and 351 from Christ to the death of Valens. He then synchronizes these dates with key secular events (Ninus, Cecrops, the first Olympiad) and concludes that '2395 years make up this history.' Since Valens was killed at Adrianople in 378, almost forty years after Eusebius died, the last part of this reckoning belongs to Jerome, who in introducing his translation takes credit for some of the *Chronicle* after the fall of Troy and for all of it after year 20 of Constantine.

As Eusebius conceived of it, the possibility of history begins not with the creation of the world or of Adam but with Adam's expulsion from Paradise, the moment when human experience continuous with our own

began. In practice, however, Eusebius had to begin his chronology with Abraham because it was only by starting with this period that he could find any record of secular persons and events to be correlated with sacred history. This is why Eusebian chronology begins effectively with Abraham, 942 years after Noah's flood and 3184 years after Adam's expulsion, roughly in our year 2016 BCE. Accordingly, Moses was born in year 425 of Abraham (1592 BCE), spoke with God on Mt. Sinai in year 502 (1515 BCE), and died in year 545 (1472 BCE). Moreover, when Moses was 35, in year 460 of Abraham (1557 BCE), 'Cecrops ruled in Attica . . . , from which time to the Fall of Troy 375 years passed.' Troy fell in year 835 of Abraham (1182 BCE).

These and other key elements in the chronology that Polydore learned from Eusebius are summarized in the table below. The first column is the *annus mundi* in the Venice, 1483, text of the *Chronicle*, which does not give years of Abraham. This crudely printed incunabular book, needless to say, does not precisely match the chronology in the text established by Helm.

1483 Chronicle	Sacred History	Secular History	Year of Abraham	Year BCE/CE
	Adam's expulsion		−3184	5199
	Noah's flood		−942	2957
3184	Abraham born	Ninus year 43; 23 Europs; Dynasty 16	1	2016
3189		Zoroaster	7	2010
		Semiramis	11	2006
		Zeus and the Curetes; Knossos; Cybele	56	1961
	Abraham's Covenant		75	1942
3245	Jacob born	Inachus in Argos	160	1857
		Apis or Sarapis in Egypt	180	1837
3395		Phoroneus in Argos; first laws	210	1807

1483 Chronicle	Sacred History	Secular History	Year of Abraham	Year BCE/CE
		Ogygus founds Eleusis; Athena	237	1780
	Jacob and Laban		238	1779
3439		Ogygus' flood	260	1757
	Joseph governs Egypt		281	1736
		Apis founds Memphis	282	1735
		Spartus founds Sparta	300	1717
3516		Prometheus	332	1685
		Atlas and astrology	380	1637
3609	Moses born		425	1592
		Hercules (first report)	443	1574
3645	Moses: year 35	Cecrops in Attica	460	1557
		Triopas in Argos	464	1553
		Cecrops sacrifices to Zeus	471	1546
		Curetes dance at Knossos	474	1543
		Poseidon against Athena in Athens	483	1534
3674		Deucalion's flood; Phaeton's fire	491	1526
3691	Moses on Sinai		502	1515
		Corinth founded	503	1514
3688	Moses gives the Law		505	1512
		Court of the Areopagus founded	507	1510
		Dionysus and vines; not Semele's son	510	1507
		Danaus in Egypt	528	1489
		Erichthonius or Erechtheus in Athens	529	1488

496

1483 Chronicle	Sacred History	Secular History	Year of Abraham	Year BCE/CE
		Arcas, Pelasgians, Arcadia	534	1483
		Danaus in Argos	543	1474
3728	Moses dies; Joshua		545	1472
3744		Cadmus in Syria	563	1454
		Minos, Rhadamanthys and Sarpedon	572	1445
3769		Cadmus in Thebes	587	1430
3780		Linus, Zethus and Amphion	596	1421
		Dactyls of Ida discover iron	599	1418
		Demeter or Isis	603	1414
3797	Aod is judge	Triptolemus distributes grain	613	1404
		Pelops in Argos	619	1398
		Dionysus born to Semele	629	1388
		Perseus	633	1384
3830		Melampus	650	1367
		Apollo	665	1352
		Acrisius in Argos	673	1344
3869		Dionysus in India	687	1330
	Deborah		682	1325
		Cadmus sows humans	701	1316
		Midas in Phrygia (first report)	707	1310
3897		Dionysus dies	719	1298
	Gideon		731	1286
		Daedalus	735	1282
		Argonauts	747	1270
3934		Orpheus	752	1265

1483 Chronicle	Sacred History	Secular History	Year of Abraham	Year BCE/CE
		Thamyris	770	1247
3948	Abimelech	Hercules labors	772	1245
		Lapiths fight Centaurs	776	1241
3962		Priam in Troy	781	1236
		Theseus in Athens	782	1235
		Seven against Thebes	783	1234
		Theseus and the Minotaur	785	1232
	Jair	Theseus unites Athens	797	1220
3977		Minos makes laws	802	1215
		Hercules founds Olympic Games	805	1212
	Jephtha	Menelaus in Sparta	819	1198
4005		Agamemnon in Mycenae	818	1197
		Hercules dies	821	1196
	Esebon		825	1192
		Paris takes Helen	826	1191
	Labdon		832	1185
4019		Troy falls	835	1182
		Aeneas in Latium	838	1179
	Samson		840	1177
		Lydians rule the sea	842	1175
4024		Odysseus wanders	845	1172
		Homer (first report)	857	1160
	Heli		860	1157
4086	Samuel and Saul		901	1116
		Eurystheus in Sparta	913	1104
4124	David		940	1077
		Agis in Sparta	957	1060
		Pelasgians rule the sea	960	1057
		Carthage founded	978	1039
4165	Solomon		980	1037

1483 Chronicle	Sacred History	Secular History	Year of Abraham	Year BCE/CE
4168	Temple begun		984	1033
		Hesiod (first report)	1110	1017
	Solomon dies		1020	997
4181		Homer (last report)	1104	913
		Lycurgus	1134	883
		Lycurgus legislates	1198	819
		[Th]alcamenes in Sparta	1203	814
		Hesiod (last report)	1208	809
4382		Phidon invents weights and measures	1219	798
4425	Jotham in Judah	Olympiad I; Iphitus; Coroebus	1241	776
4429		Romulus and Remus born	1254	773
4443	Achaz in Judah	Ephors in Sparta	1259	758
		Romulus rules; asylum; Sabine women	1264	753
		Milesians found Naucratis in Egypt	1268	749
4456	Captivity: Sennacherib	Thales (first report)	1270	747
		Midas in Phrygia (second report)	1275	742
4472		Romulus: Senate, temples, walls	1289	728
		Numa Pompilius	1302	715
		Midas dies	1321	696
		Glaucus invents welding	1324	693
4528		Tullus Hostilius: fasces and purple	1343	674

1483 Chronicle	Sacred History	Secular History	Year of Abraham	Year BCE/CE
		Tullus conquers Alba, Veii, Fidena	1353	664
4538		Zaleucus' legislation	1354	663
		Cypselus in Corinth	1356	661
		Psammetichus in Egypt (first)	1358	659
		Phalaris in Acragas	1365	652
4559		Ancus Marcius	1375	642
		Thales (second report)	1377	640
		Periander in Corinth	1389	628
		Draco's legislation	1393	624
		Tarquinius Priscus	1398	619
4590	Captivity: Nabuchodonosor		1407	610
		Psammetichus in Egypt (second)	1408	609
		Tarquinius: ludi Romani, cloaca	1419	598
		Solon's legislation	1423	594
4611	Temple destroyed	Tragedy invented	1426	591
		Thales: eclipse predicted	1431	586
		Servius: census	1435	582
		Anaximander	1441	576
4641		Cyrus; Anaximines	1456	561
		Croesus in Lydia	1454	563
		Simonides	1458	559
		Xenophanes	1463	554
		Tarquinius Superbus	1469	548
4659		Pherecydes of Syros	1476	541
		Tarquin and Lucretia	1480	537
		Cambyses in Persia	1486	531
4679		Pythagoras	1487	530

1483 Chronicle	Sacred History	Secular History	Year of Abraham	Year BCE/CE
4690	Temple restored	Darius: year 2	1496	521
		Harmodius and Aristogiton	1497	520
		Rome: kings expelled	1505	512
		Rome: first consuls	1507	510
		Rome: first dictator	1515	502
4726		Democritus, Heraclitus, Anaxagoras	1516	501
		Aeschylus	1521	496
		Xerxes	1531	486
		Sophocles and Euripides	1548	469
4732		Herodotus	1549	468
		Socrates born	1551	466
	Esther (possibly)		1552	465
		Empedocles and Parmenides	1560	457
		Rome: decemvirs	1564	453
		Rome: Twelve Tables	1565	452
	Esdras		1570	447
4763		Phidias makes his Athena	1578	439
		Peloponnesian War	1585	432
4777		Plato born	1592	425
	Esther (probably)		1611	406
		Socrates dies	1618	399
		Aristotle studies with Plato	1650	367
4845		Alexander born	1662	355
		Plato dies	1672	345
	Manasses		1681	336

1483 Chronicle	Sacred History	Secular History	Year of Abraham	Year BCE/CE
		Alexander defeats Darius	1687	330
4875		Epicurus	1688	329
		Alexander dies	1692	325
4918	Septuagint	Ptolemy Philadelphus	1724	283
		Rome: silver coinage	1747	271
		Epicurus dies	1749	269
4937		Zeno of Citium dies	1753	264
		Ennius born	1778	240
		Plautus dies	1816	201
		Ennius dies	1849	168
4985	Judas Maccabeus		1856	161
		Terence dies	1859	158
		Varro born	1901	116
		Cicero born	1911	106
		Sulla in power	1937	80
		Pompey triumphs	1939	78
		Vergil born	1947	70
		Horace born	1952	65
5133	Jerusalem taken by Pompey		1954	63
		Caesar crosses the Rhine	1961	56
		Rome: Civil War	1968	50
5579		Death of Valens	2395	378

Note on the Text

꧁꧂

From its first publication in 1499 until the author's death in 1555, *De inventoribus rerum* appeared in thirty Latin editions, first catalogued by John Ferguson in 1892. The Latin text in this volume is based on a collation of the nine editions, listed below, that contain significant variants. Sigla assigned to these editions are as follows:

V *Polydori Vergilii Urbinatis de inventoribus rerum libri tres.* Venice: Christophorus de Pensis, 1499.

F *Polydori Vergilii Urbinatis adagiorum liber; eiusdem de inventoribus rerum libri octo; ex accurata autoris castigatione locupletationeque non vulgari adeo ut maxima fere pars primae ante hanc utriusque voluminis aeditioni accesserit.* Basel: Ioannes Frobenius, 1521.

f *Polydori Vergilii Urbinatis de rerum inventoribus libri octo per autorem summa cura recogniti et locupletati; dices supremam manum impositam.* Basel: Ioannes Frobenius, 1525.

B *Polydori Vergilii Urbinatis de rerum inventoribus libri octo per autorem tertio iam ac diligentius recogniti et locupletati, qua re ille contentus tum demum supremam manum imposuit; eiusdem in dominicam precem commentariolum.* Basel: Ioannes Bebelius, 1532.

b *Polydori Vergilii Urbinatis de rerum inventoribus libri octo per authorem quarto iam ac diligentius recogniti et locupletati quia longior in studiis labor, semper plus cumulet inventis licet; eiusdem in dominicam precem commentariolum.* Basel: Ioannes Bebelius, 1536.

I *Polydori Vergilii Urbinatis de rerum inventoribus libri octo; eiusdem in dominicam precem commentariolum; item dialogorum de prodigiis libri tres; omnia recens per autorem regustata atque non poenitenda accessione locupletata siquidem longior in studiis labor, semper plus cumulet inventis licet.* Basel: Michael Isingrinius, 1540.

i   *Polydori Vergilii Urbinatis de rerum inventoribus libri octo; eiusdem in dominicam precem commentariolum.* Basel: Michael Isingrinius, 1545.

j   *Polydori Vergilii Urbinatis de rerum inventoribus libri octo; eiusdem in dominicam precem commentariolum.* Basel: Michael Isingrinius, 1550.

A   *Polydori Vergilii Urbinatis de rerum inventoribus libri octo; eiusdem in dominicam precem commentariolum.* Basel: Iacobus Parcus for Michael Isingrinius, 1553–55.

Because the author was improving and enlarging his text until his death, the last edition published in his lifetime (**A**) has been chosen as the copy text. Variants in the other eight editions listed above have been noted, as indicated by the following symbols:

/   the reading to the left of the slash is the reading chosen; to the right of the slash are shown variants from the edition(s) indicated

t   all editions up to and including the one named in the siglum, in chronological order, contain the reading indicated

omt   all editions up to and including the one named in the siglum, in chronological order, omit the reading indicated

om   the editions named omit the material indicated

a :   the words following the colon are inserted, in the editions named, after the word following the *a*

c :   the words following the colon are inserted, in the editions named, before the word following the *c*

r   editions published after those named in the same note

e   editorial conjecture

;   within the same note, separates readings from different editions or groups of editions

,   within the same note, same as above; also separates different readings of the same word(s) in different editions or groups of editions

[ ]   imbeds a shorter variant within a longer

{ . . . }   marks a lacuna in the printed text of the edition indicated

Polydore's use of sources, including those that he cites directly, varies from exact quotation to loose paraphrase or summary, and in all cases the texts that he uses may differ from modern editions even when he intends to supply the exact words of his source. In the Latin text and in the English translation, his spelling of proper names has been preserved, but most primary references in the index use familiar versions of these names. Superscripts in the notes to the Latin text refer to paragraph numbers, and are used to indicate the end of a lacuna in cases where it extends over more than one paragraph.

For the publishing history of *De inventoribus*, see the Introduction to this volume and the notes to the three prefatory letters written by Polydore. The English translation in this volume is the first based on an edited Latin text. The version published by Thomas Langley in 1546 drastically abridges what Polydore wrote. The translation recently done by Weiss and Pérez is complete (though based on an edition without independent authority) and may be useful as an English guide to books IV–VIII, not included in this volume.

Editions of early printed books listed below have been used to find the basis of Polydore's Latin text when it differs from modern editions and to locate other information. However, an early edition listed here is not necessarily a text used by Polydore; on this point, see the explanatory notes.

Appian. *Petri Candidi in libros Appiani sophistae Alexandrini ad Nicolaum quintum summum pontificem praefatio incipit felicissime.* Venice, 1477.

Apuleius. *Lucii Apulei opera.* Venice, 1493.

Barbaro, Ermolao. *Hermolai Barbari Veneti P. Aquiliensis in castigationes Plinianas ad Alexandrum Sextum pontificem maximum praefatio.* Rome, 1493.

Beroaldo, Filippo. *Ecce lector humanissime: Philippi Beroaldi annotationes centum; eiusdem contra Servium grammaticum notationes; eiusdem Plinianae aliquot castigationes . . .* Brescia, 1496.

Celsus. *Cornelius Celsus.* Venice, 1497.

Cicero. *Ciceronis opera quae nobis benignioria fata reservarunt in quatuor volumina digesta impressimus* . . . Milan, 1498.

Diodorus Siculus. *Diodori Siculi historiarum priscarum a Poggio in latinum traducti liber primus incipit.* Venice, 1481.

Diogenes Laertius (colophon). *Impressum Venetiis per Nicolaum Ienson Gallicum, anno domini* MCCCCLXXV *die* XIIII *Augusti.*

Dionysius of Halicarnassus. *Dionysii Halicarnasei originum sive antiquitatum romanorum liber primus.* Reggio, 1498.

Durandus, Guilielmus. *Incipit rationale divinorum officiorum Guilhelmi Minatensis ecclesiae episcopi.* Strassburg, ca. 1478.

Eusebius (colophon). *Erhardus Ratdolt Augustensis . . . Eusebii libros chronicos ac reliquas in hoc volumine de temporibus additiones . . . impressit Venetiis . . . 1483 Idibus Septembris.*

—— *Eusebii Pamphilii de evangelica praeparatione opus a . . . Georgio Trapezuntio e greco in latinum versum Michael Manzolinus Parmensis . . . impressit . . . Tarvisii anno . . .* MCCCCLXXX *pridie Idu Ianuarias.*

Eutropius. *Incipit Eutropius historiographus et post eum Paulus Diaconus de historiis italicae provinciae ac Romanorum.* Rome, 1471.

ps.-Fenestella (Andrea Domenico Fiocchi). *Fenestella de magistratibus romanorum et primo de pane liceo incipit* . . . Milan, 1477.

'Festus'. *Sexti Pompeii Festi librorum undeviginti fragmenta.* Venice, 1513.

Giglio, Zachario. *In hoc volumine continentur hi libri: primus de origine et laudibus scientiarum; secundus liber contra antipodes; tertius liber de miseria hominis et contemptu mundi; quartus liber de generibus ventorum; quintus liber vita Caroli Magni.* Florence, 1496.

Gorgerio, Lodovico. *In Polydorum invectiva:* Vatican MS Urb. Lat. 1244, ff. 1–18.

Herodian. *Herodiani historiae de imperio post Marcum vel de suis temporibus e graeco summa fide et diligentia ac doctrina translatae a Politiano.* Bologna, 1493.

Herodotus. *Herodoti historici incipit Laurentii Vallae conversio de Greco in Latinum.* Rome, 1475.

Hyginus. *Caii Iulii Hygini Augusti liberti fabularum liber . . . eiusdem poeticon astronomicon libri quatuor* . . . Basel, 1535.

Josephus (colophon). *Impressum Venetiis per Ioannem Vercelensem anno salutis* MCCCCLXXXVI *die* XXIII *octubris*.

Justinus. *Justinus historicus*. Venice, 1497.

Lactantius. *Lactantii Firmiani de divinis institutionibus adversus gentes*. Venice, 1497.

Livy. *Titi Livii decades*. Venice, 1498.

Lucretius. *Titi Lucreti Cari poetae philosophici antiquissimi de rerum natura liber primus incipit foeliciter*. Venice, 1495.

Macrobius. *Somnium Scipionis ex Ciceronis libro de republica excerptum; Macrobii Aurelii Theodosii viri consularis et illustris conviviorum primi diei saturnaliorum liber primus*. Venice, 1492.

Pastrengo, Guglielmo da. *De originibus rerum libellus authore Gulielmo Pastregico Veronense*. Venice, 1547.

Perotti, Niccolò. *Cornucopiae emendatissimum miro ordine novissime insignitum in quo toto opere facilius omnia vocabula reperies quam in sola tabula aliorum antea impressorum prius invenire posses; cui etiam additae sunt duae cartae quae in aliis omnibus antea impressis per incuriam scriptorum omissae fuerant; tabulam operis adeo ordinatum et multitudine vocabulorum refertum accipies ut melior ipsa tibi et utilior futura sit quam prius ipsum totum opus foret*. Venice, 1496.

———— *In hoc volumine habentur haec: Cornucopiae, sive linguae Latinae commentarii diligentissime recogniti atque ex archetypo emendati . . . eodem modo et fabulae collectae sunt et instituta et inventores rerum et mores et proverbia et remedia*. Venice, 1513.

Pliny. *Caii Plinii Secundi naturae historiarum libri* XXXVII *e castigationibus Hermolai Barbari quam emendatissime editi*. Venice, 1497.

Plutarch. *Plutarchi vitae*. Venice, 1496.

Solinus. *Solinus de mirabilibus mundi*. Brescia, 1498.

Strabo. *Strabo de situ orbis*. 1494.

Suetonius. *Caii Suetonii Tranquilli de grammaticis et rhetoribus claris liber incipit*. Florence, 1478.

Thucydides. *Thucydidis historiarum peloponnensium liber primus*. 1485.

Tortelli, Giovanni. *Ioannis Tortelli Arretini commentariorum grammaticorum de orthographia dictionum e graecis tractarum proemium incipit ad sanctissimum patrem Nicolaum Quintum pontificem summum*. Venice, 1471.

———*Ioannes Tortelli Aretini orthographia*. Venice, 1495.

Vergil, Polydore. *Proverbiorum libellus*. Venice, 1498.

———*Polydori Vergilii Urbinatis adagiorum aeque humanorum ut sacrorum opus per autorem anno isto* MDL *rursus novissime iam ac diligentius recognitum et magnifice locupletatum; item divi Ioannis Chrysostomi de perfecto monacho maloque principe libellus eodem Polydoro interprete*. Basel, 1550.

———Polydori Vergilii Urbinatis Anglicae historiae libri vigintiseptem ab ipso autore iam recogniti adque amussim salva tamen historiae veritate expoliti. Basel, 1555.

Notes to the Text

ॐॐॐ

Title. Polydorus Vergilius Urbinas Ludovico Odaxio Patavino S.D. ijA
Ludovicum FfBbI

1. Ludovice FfBbIijA   in fabulis duntaxat fBbIijA   Sed illis fBbIijA
esse ducimus/est BbIijA   nequaquam/non item fBbIijA

2. sicut ijA   comprehendere fBbIijA   materiem ijA   Etenim ut
fBbIijA   mox/deinde ijA   quemadmodum/sicut FfBbI
quemadomum docuimus *om* ijA

3. ipsos philosophos A   sint/essent FfBbIijA   eos *om* A
delirationes ijA   *a* impendio: magis bIijA   Chimaeram monstrum
FfBbIijA   percunctati f

4. commenta FfBbIijA   ut apud . . . legimus ijA   cottidie Ff
ecquid turpius FfBbIijA   rivuols V

5. orsus partim ut/orsus quamverissime potui omnia tradidi quo ijA
laude . . . est/laude fraudaretur quoniam invenire primum ijA
praecipuumque FfBbIijA   *a* possit: artis alicuius BbIijA   fraudaretur,
vellent sciant Bb   fraudaretur . . . tradidi/quod sine artibus satis
constet nullam omnino vitam esse potuisse. Ex quo diligentius multo
officium feci et ijA   deberent Bb

6. *a* locis: id genus FfBbIijA   *a* subest: ob FfBbIijA   haesimus
fBbIijA

7. malevolentissimos bIijA   et Marcum . . . praestrinxit/fabulas sic
secutus ut minus veritatem invesigarit FfBbIijA   Verum illud fBbIijA
Ecquid enim FfBbIijA

8. nova inventa fBbIijA   calce tertii operis libri FfBbI   extremo tertio
operis libro ijA   mihi assumo FfBbIijA   Guidoni FfBbIijA
cucurrimus FfBbIijA   nostra vestigia sequi fBbIijA

9. tibi uni . . . debuerat[10] *om* FfBbIijA

509

10. in quo/in quibus, continetur FfBbIijA   *a* continentur: nemini
convenientius dicari posse vel debere iudicavi FfBbIijA   monimenta
FfBbIijA   Troade FfBbIijA   ad Ostia F   Ostium Tyberinum
navigarint fBbIijA   *a* insuper: sic fBbIijA   illustrissimo *om* fBbIijA
tamquam/ut FfBbIijA   in *om* FfBbIijA   studiis . . . fecerit/
peritissimus evaserit FfBbIijA   gradum tenes FfBbIijA

11. Nec . . . sis splendor *om* FfBbIijA   lus decertasse V

12. eiusmodi FfBbIijA   legerere f   Nam . . . putabo *om* fBbIijA
probabitur/probari intellexero tum F

13. Urbini . . . XCIX *om* V   MCCCCXC F

SECOND LETTER TO GIAN MATTEO VERGIL

1. apertaque ijA   quaerat/petat BbIijA

2. introduxissent bIijA

3. hortatu/rogatu ijA   exposui etsi BbIijA   Docuique/
Demonstravique bIijA

BOOK I

Book Title. a primus: incipit V

CHAPTER I

Title. unde . . . dictus/quod veri dei nullum est exordium *t* f
et . . . dictus *om* B

1. aerii . . . exercerent et/genii (sic enim latino sermone interpretantur)
V   aerei F   *a* quos: (teste Eusebio *De evangelica praeparatione*) F   sacri
autores *om* F   principes . . . exercerent et/principes divinae appellant
literae animadverterent nonnullis mortalibus qui aliqua illustri causa
perpetuitatem meruissent simulachra esse dicata illisque honorem a
cunctis haberi hanc nacti decipulam inceperunt per ea simulachra
divinationes exercere ac simul F   et *om* f   ac nunc/et nunc *t* f
configerent/subinde fingentes *t* f   tantum . . . effuderunt/varios
humanis pectoribus errores effuderint V   effundere F   offuderunt j

ut . . . partis *om*, hominumque, prorsum/adeo V   tempore *om* Ff
Nec . . . putabantur ita² *om* V   Nec . . . redeo² *omt* I

2. nomen (ut ait Lactantius) assumentes Ff   nam genios FfBbI/quod
genios *r*   De hoc . . . hi daemones *om* Ff   De hoc . . . delegatum *om*
BbI   corrumpebant/vitiabant, ac his/atque his Ff   quibus/quae, *a*
semper: in, addebant/temperabant F   sua appareret ignorantia F
alios sicut/alia ut V   Sic/Hinc nimirum factum est V   opinio . . .
crevit *om* V   uti/ceu F   prope *om* V

3. post/mox *t* I   quaerendae ac *omt* b   nascuntur *t* f   Cleantes *t* B
aera *t* F   Unde Vergilius *t* F   movetur *t* f   vocat/censuit *t* f   Zenon
V   octo esse deos, putavit/dicit *t* f   *a* putavit: Autores Cicero
Eusebius *de evangelica praeparatione* Laertius et Lactantius Firmianus *t* f

4. liqueat V   an aliqua/utrum aliqua *t* f   eliminaverunt *t* F   *a*
Theodorus: auctore Cicerone, existimarunt/dixerunt *t* f   Quare/Unde *t*
F   in fine primi libri *t* b   potuerit V/possit *r*   ut/uti *t* F   est sed/
erat sed V

5. *c* De: Unde *t* F   eatenus/hoc loco, quoad/donec *t* F   veniemus *t* b
gloriantur/ fabulantur *t* I   *a* Solem: videlicet, illum/hunc *t* f
Osiridem, Isidem *t* F   quod/Qui *t* f   suscepit *t* F

6. *a* Perseus: teste Cicerone *t* f   numerum, habuerint/consecraverint,
Isidem *t* F   Aphri *t* F   Persae Mithram *omt* F   Uranum V, Urnanum
F, Uranium *r*   Bellum V   post homines natos *omt* F   valde/magis *t* F
ac importunissimum *omt* F   fecerint/habebant *t* f, *om* BbI   *a* fecerint:
Ex Herodoto Diodoro Strabone Cicerone Plinio Eusebio et Lactantio *t*
F   sibique constituerint *omt* f   sibique/sibi BbI

7. Hinc/Unde *t* F   sentiebent B   *a* vanissimi: fuerint *t* f   fuerit/
extiterit *t* f

8. nequeunt/non valent *t* F   inaccessae *t* b   et *omt* b   neque . . . acie
omt f   Nanque/Nam *t* f   Id quod/Quod idem V   *a* andabatarum:
gladium *t* F   versantes/ventiliantes V, ventilantes F   commenti *t* F/
commentati *r*   Satius/Sanctius V   *a* docere: Tentabimus tamen (nam
ut aiunt dii facientes adiuvant) nullam dei esse originem ostendere veluti
qui nunquam esse coepit *t* F

9. itaque/enim V   qui teste . . . erit *omt* b   primo libro *Tusculanarum*
f   dicente . . . terram *omt* F   Et divus/Unde divus *t* F   vere nomen/
verae nomen *t* F   tametsi/etsi *t* f

10. nominavit *t* F   licet/etsi, non sit/non est *t* f   omnibus . . .
precibus/bene precamur *t* F   quando . . . cunctis *omt* B   ex verbo . . .
sive *om* bIi   θεάομαι/θεωῶ bIi   δέος/δέομαι, quod dicitur *om*,
timeo bIi

CHAPTER II

1. isdem V   movit/detinuit *t*   F   inchoare/auspicari *t* b   *a* igitur:
secundo *t* F   ad *om*, veritati *t* I   insinuero V

2. *a* sapientibus: autore Eusebio et Marco Tullio in primo de natura
deorum, aquam *t* F   superius monstravimus *t* F   scriptorum *t* f
tenebrosus *t* I   censuerunt/dixerunt *t* f   *a* Lucretius: ait *t* f   *a* dicit:
Autor Eusebius in primo et in septimo et in decimoquarto de
praeparatione evangelica *t* f   *a* autem: quemadmodum idem testis est *t* f
ex *omt* F   recipiunt *t* F   quas/quos fBb   Lucretius . . . quae *t* F, *omr*
a quatuor: videlicet *t* F   *a* orbis: Et reliqua *t* f

3. *a* De: vanis *t* f   sacris . . . literis/sanctae religionis continent literae *t*
F   ab initio/primitus *t* I   Moses . . . eo *omt* f   *Antiquitatum*
Iudaicarum/De antiquitatibus iudaeorum *t* f   Ioannes . . . Id *omt* f
scribens/inquiens *t* I   *a Timaeo:* teste Eusebio *t* f

4. Atque *om*, tale/hoc, fuit/est V   cum *om* b   intelligatur . . . sit *t* F,
intelligeretur . . . esset *r*

CHAPTER III

Title. an . . . divisione *om* V   an . . . necne *omt* j   ibidem/inibi F

1. origo/generatio *t* F   insempiterno in isto V

2. *a* homines: dixerunt *t* F   ortus/generationis, consecutos/sortitos *t* b
Quapropter/ Unde *t* F   principio/primordio orbis *t* F   generat, nutrit
t F   posteriori *t* F

3. cupido *t* I   paulo ante/recens *t* j   biennio post/post bimatum tempus *t* F   βεκὸς id est *omt* F   beccus *t* f   constat *t*   F   modo/
negotio *t* B

4. et eius/Cuius *t* F

5. Abderita *t* f   Zenon V; Citicus FfBbI   fingunt/fabulantur,
primitus *t* I

6. igitur V, *omr*   *a* veteri: legere *t* F   est/extat f   Quare/Unde *t* F
scienter/non indecenter *t* b

7. creatus/factus *t* f   ducta . . . Eva/accepta Eva coniuge *t* F   fuit
Idem Hieronymus/extitit Dicente Hieronymo *t* f   Ita/Unde *t* F
eminentissimus poeta cecinit *t* F

8. distinguit/distendit *t* b   sunt tot *t*   j   non . . . putavi/obiter
referre visum est *t* b   Nembroth enim filius Chan V   Nembroth enim
seu Nemroth utrumque scriptum reperitur filius Chan Ff
formidantes/ interminantis *t* f   revocare V   alibi apposite/suo loco *t* F
linguam divisit/discordiam immisit linguarum *t* B   intellectu *t* F,
intelligentia *r*   varietatis/diversitatis *t* F

9. At . . . oppleverint[12] *om* V   At . . . Iosephus[11] *om* Ff   quaerentes
om, utrum/an, an/vel Bb   Et libro . . . carmen *om* Bb   quando . . .
sciebant *om* Bb

10. facit/inducit BbI

11. *c* inde: qui Ff   discrimen/conversionem F   *a* discrimen: factam F,
factum f   et iis/et his F   occupaverint F   nominatae/nomen sortitae
FfBb   postea/postmodum FfBb   discreparent Ff, discreparint *r*
consentiant/adstipulentur FfBbI   id est/scilicet Ff

12. Eusebius . . . ille *om* FfB   deinde/subinde Ff

CHAPTER IV

Title. vario . . . usu/quod aliud aliae gentes habebant *t* F/ut aliud aliae
gentes haberent f   coibant *t* F   ac . . . nuptam *omt* B   ac . . . ritus *om*
V   ibidem/inibi F   divortii/ repudii *t* I

1. Moses tradit/sanctae literae tradunt *t* F   *Metamorphoseon* F,
Metamorphoseos r   idem *omt* b   Cicero inquit/Lactantius inquit *t* b
a Cicero: et post eum Lactantius I

2. conubii V, connubii *r*   postea subiiciam/postmodum referam *t* I
Adae *t* B   exemplar/effigiem *t* F   confictam/configuratam Atque
. . . origo *omt* V

3. tradidit/fabulata est *t* I   matrimonii foedus/matrimonium V

4. faciebant/inibant *t* I   porro *om* V   *a* Numidae: enim V   Scoti
Britanniae populi *t* j, Britanni A   lascive coire/lascivire *t* b   singulas/
unam, uxorem, *a* sed: ea *t* b   Caesare/ Eusebio *De evangelica
praeparatione* libro sexto *t* F   Ex iis/Ex his *t* F   capitis *t* I, capite *r*
alius/alieni V

5. *c* Hoc: Unde *t* F   memoria/relatu *t* b/memoratu I   sub/post,
continenter/iunctim *t* I   commenta *e*, machinata V, comminiscitur F,
meditata fBb, commentata *r*   ac statim ut/ex quo statim quod ab ea *t*
F   deinceps/subinde *t* f/deinde Bb   *a* deinceps: invicem *t* b   sororem
de stupro *t* f

6. et Assyrii *om* V   quod . . . servatur *om* V   dabant/tradebant *t* F
matrimonium/ uxores *t* F   Athenienses *t* f, *omr*   Augulas *t* f   moris/
mos V   post/mox *t* f   Adyrmachidae . . . nubebant[7] *omt* B

7. comprimeret/iniret bI   tertius *om* bI   *a* rex: eius nominis tertius
bI   Cristae *t* b   Essaei V   *a* Anthropophagi: Ex Herodoto Strabone
Diodoro Trogo Iosepho Salustio Divo Hieronymo Eusebio Aemilio
Probo Valerio Maximo et Solino *t* F

8. Sane . . . isti/Porro vide quam turpiter hi *t* F   laxabant *t* f
discimine b   edidisse/ perpetrasse *t* F   iis feliciores/his feliciores, *a*
teste: divo *t* F   foedus/sacramentum *t* F   primitus *t* I   turpiter
dehonestabant *t* F, turpi fiebant f   Id . . . revertamur[9] *om* V   inibique
Ff   quotus . . . revertamur[9]/ad quos usque necessitudine coniunctos
olim licuerit vel modo fas sit in ducendis uxoribus ascendere F

9. revertamur/repedemus F   fuisset/extitisset *t* F   divortium/
repudium *t* I   habuissent *t* F   quamobrem/cur V   Carvilius/
Servilius *t* B   anno . . . consulibus cum *omt* B   II Caio bI, Il Caio *r*

cum *om* bI   uxorem *t* I   causa divortium fecit/gratia repudiavit *t* f/
gratia repudiavit id est cum ea divortium fecit Sic boni latinitatis
autores ponunt quamvis iurisconsulti repudium inter nondum
coniunctos divortium vero coniunctorum esse velint BbI   Hinc . . .
commemorare[15] *om* V   Hinc . . . audivit *omt* B   postmodum b

10. decretis/institutis F   translatitium FfBbI   divortii autor fuit/de
ea re legem tulit FfBbI   ut extat . . . habui Sed[11] *om* FfBbI

11. divortii/repudiandi FfBbI   ab uxore discedere/repudiare FfBbI

12. quique/quive F   *a* unus: scilicet Ff   praeferebat F   tenebant F
Et . . . nutriret *om* FfB   id . . . capiebant *om* FfBb   consectura/
sectura FfBb   *a* foecunditas: Sed ad rem redeamus FfBbI

13. autem Thalasii F   per Thalasii F   *a* qui: graece Ff   autoribus Ff
a ferrent: Id F   Venetia/Cisalpina F   quod iis/quod his F   alio/suo
F   Ovidius/dicente Ovidio Ff   bibat/bibit *e*

14. vel quod . . . summa est *om* FfB   Catullus/Martialis F   Quod/
Qui F   tris FfBbIij/treis A   alterum/alium F

15. caeremoniis/solennitatibus FfBbI   Quo . . . capite 6 *om* Ff
domus . . . Item *om* Ff   commemorare/referre FfBb

CHAPTER V

Title. *a* vero: primiter *t* b

1. ad coelum *omt* F   ferre/iactare *t* F   ad adulationem/in adulationem
t F   Inde/mox *t* f   habere/impendere *t* F   coeperant V, inceperant F
ut . . . idolis *om* V

2. Quare/Unde *t* F   infra/inferius *t* F   Sed/Qui *t* B   faciamus . . .
nominatum/trecentis et viginti duobus annis ante [ante trecentos et
vigintiduos annos quam FfB] troianum bellum fuit [est FfB] quo etiam
tempore Bellus [Belus FfB] fuisse dicitur quem *t* B   *a* colebant: auctor
Theophilus in libro *De temporibus ad Autolicum* scripto *t* B

3. nisi/quam *t* I   iusta et debita obsequia praebeamus *t* F   veneremur
t B   sequamur *t* F   in ipso . . . coles *om* F   uti . . . coles *om* fBb
scribens/inquiens *t* I   hi dicti/ii dicti fBbI

4. deinde/subinde *t* **f**   fere ac *t* **F,** ac fere *r*   fierent/fiebant *t* **b**
permanserunt *t* **j,** permansuerunt **A**

5. nutrierant . . . rem/nutrierunt Unde *t* **F**   tradiderunt/fabulati sunt *t*
I

6. id genus *om* **V**   Numa *omt* **F**   fuit/extitit *t* **f**   cerimoniae **VbIij,**
caeremoniae *r*

7. Herodotus . . . Mosis *omt* **B**   Ac . . . origo/Sed haec omnia fatuae
ut ita dixerim impietatis plena erant *t* **f**

8. nos *om* **f**   Christiana praedicat et veneratur fides cuius *t* **F**   Cayn
V   Adae *t* **B**   detulit . . . solenne/tradidit Unde legitimum *t* **F**
gereret/capere posset *t* **F**   Iis/His, rem . . . facere/sacris operari *t* **F**
illud idem/sacrificium *t* **F**   *a* episcopos: divi Petri ministros cui
Christus salvator noster primo sacerdocium contulit *t* **F**   Sed . . .
tradetur *om* **V**

Chapter vi

Title. vel/aut *t* **B**   et . . . sono *omt* **B**   varietate *om* **bI**

1. res memoratu, has/de his *t* **I**   tractandum *t* **I**   cum . . . dignatur
omt **I**   cuius . . . dignatur *om* **ij**

2. Cicero . . . tertio/Lactantius *t* **I**   dedit *t* **I**   scribens/inquiens *t* **j**

3. Alii . . . autor est *t* **f,** Alii . . . volunt *omr,* idem . . . est *omr*   a Phoe-
nicia/e Phoenicia *t* **B**   octo/septem *t* **f**   ΑΒΓΔΕΖΙΚΛΜΝΟΠΡΣ
ΤΥΦ *omt* **f**   hoc est/videlicet *t* **f**

4. primitus Cadmum *t* **I**   *a* sed: secundo *t* **F**   Gephyraei **V,** Zephyrei
r   *a* sexto: dicens *t* **j**   hi sunt/ii sunt **V**   Quod autem omnino
Cadmus non primus, portaverit *t* **f**   longo post tempore/progressu
deinde temporis *t* **F**   *a* Diodorus: hoc **Ff**   ait/refert *t* **b**   demum/
postmodum *t* **b**   monumenta **V**   et eam/quam *t* **F**

5. cum inquit/inquiens *t* **j**   eo *omt* **f**   recentium/modernarum *t* **f**
Atqui Cicero . . . Item *omt* **f**   aiens/inquiens **BbI**   *a* Eusebius: tamen *t*
f   *a* Aristaeum: Sibyllam *t* **f**   ab iisque/ab hisque *t* **F**   exin/mox *t* **I**

6. ante Cadmum/maior natu quam Cadmus *t* **F**   *a* retulimus: videlicet
quod alii **V**   esse quando/volunt quando **V**   atque adeo . . . etc *omt* **B**

7. fuisse/extitisse *t* **F**   *Antiquitate* **f**   Adae *t* **B**   tractabitur/sermo fiet
V   subtilius *omt* **F**   iam tum/ iam tunc *t* **F**   advenisse **Ff**   Abrahae
assignat *t* **B**   antiquior est/maior natu fuit *t* **F**   praecesserunt *t* **F**

8. quae . . . fuerint etc *om* **V**

9. venerunt *t* **f**   Livius . . . literas *omt* **B**

10. ut superius *t* **F**   assignant/attribuunt *t* **F**   inquit/ait *t* **b**   fieri . . .
potest/ impossibile quippe est *t* **f**   Haec ille *omt* **F**

11. quod testatur . . . scribens/dicente Livio *t* **f**   Quapropter . . .
verbis¹² *omt* **B**   Phrygibus . . . conscripsisse *om* **bI**

12. 122 sicut/quemadmodum **bI**

CHAPTER VII

Title. et . . . valeat *omt* **B**   VIII **fB**

1. pluris . . . quia *omt* **b**, *a* reliquarum: artium *t* **b**   *a* dividitur: videlicet
t **f**   Cicero . . . sonus *omt* **f**

2. Eius/Cuius *t* **f**, autem *omt* **f**   apta aut inepta/utilia aut inutilia *t* **B**
a nam: teste Lactantio libro primo, pariter ac/et *t* **f**   ut ex . . . docet
omt **f**

3. *a* vim: idem testis est *t* **f**   est/esse dicitur *t* **f**   Inde/Mox *t* **b**
Mallotes *t* **b**, Malotes *r*

4. capescendas **V**   Fabius/Unde Fabius ait *t* **F**, dicente Fabio **f**

5. quamobrem/quod *t* **f**   quia/quod *t* **f**   disciplinis/facultatibus *t* **b**
sexcenti . . . existunt/milia errorum insurgunt *t* **F**   id quod . . .
didicerit *omt* **B**   illive **bIij**, illius **A**

6. *a* Theodotes: haec ex Tranquillo et Fabio Quintiliano *De*
institutionibus oratoriis t **F**

CHAPTER VIII

Title. et . . . emendatus *omt* **B**

1. in illam/circa illam *t* **F**   incubuerint/insudaverint *t* **F**   demonstrat/
docet *t* **b**   omnis **V**, omneis **F**

2. tunc que V, tunc quae F   *a* insaniunt: unde *t* F   *a* arte: inquit *t* F
Non fient f   unde/dicente etiam, Vergilio *t* f   nascentem *t* f,
crescentem *r*   *a* Quare: non ab re *t* I   *a* poetam: inquiens *t* I   nobis
carmen *t* I

3. Sed . . . videantur *omt* B   dicens/inquiens bI

4. vetustissima V   libro *omt* j   eos/Israhelitas *t* F   atque/quod V
quo . . . ageret/in laudem dei gratiarumque actionem *t* F   Idem
Iosephus/Dicente eodem Iosepho *t* f

5. Divus . . . decurrunt *omt* B

6. *a* quod: Lactantius testatur in primo et *t* I   testatur/dicens *t* j
Horpheus V   Andronychus V   *a* prodiderunt: anno fere
quadringentesimo decimo post Romam conditam V, post annum fere
quadringentesimum decimum quam Roma est condita FfB   qui fuit
. . . non item *omt* B   ratione/supputatione b, temporis inita a *om* b
Marcus *omt* j   undecimo . . . secundo/decimo *t* f   in ea re *t* F

CHAPTER IX

Title. *a* et: quod, esse/sunt *t* F

1. accusandus/accusatum iri *t* F   scripserim/rettulerim *t* b

2. *a* maximo: quippe *t* b   mundus/universum *t* F

3. inquiens *t* I   Atque *om* V; *a* metrum: igitur *t* f   memoravimus *t* b

4. primus/primitus *t* I   consueverunt *t* F   *a* affirmat: idem V

5. Horatius/dicente Horatio *t* f   emiserit *t* F, immiserit *r*
impraesentia VBbIij

CHAPTER X

1. factum/inchoatum, operam dabant/operabantur *t* F

2. uter/utris V   honestae Aeschylis . . . protulit Aeschylis V
Andronychus V   qua floruerunt *t* B   Accius *omt* B

3. urbe *t* b   inventus Attica A   κομαξεν V   lascive agere/
comessatum ire canentes *t* f   vel . . . cantus *omt* f   ᾠδής Bb, ᾠδη *r*

sicut inferius *t* F   *a* antiqua: videlicet *t* f   *a condita* et: Valerius
Maximus et *t* B   Andronychus V

4. peculiaris *t* j, pecularis A   Euripedes fB   Archilao f

CHAPTER XI

Title. novaeque comoediae *omt* B

1. Teste/Dicente *t* f

2. gesserant V   pro se quisque/unusquisque *t* f   inde/mox *t* f
caperet f

3. generaliter V   Cuius . . . concessam *omt* B   Caeclius b

4. *a* in primis: meo quidem iudicio *t* f   ferunt/facile dixerim *t* f

CHAPTER XII

Title. 1 Quis *t* I, Qui *r*   et . . . utilitate *omt* B   solutam/prosam *t* F
deque . . . regula *omt* j

1. caetera scripta *t* F   quod . . . vitae *omt* f   eos . . . profuderint/vita
egregie functos *t* I   adeunda/subeunda *t* F

2. nundus tertius V   scripserunt *t* f   aiens/inquiens *t* I   hoc *omt* f
potius/primitus *t* I   in actione positum/activum *t* b

3. probabile videtur/ut ita dicam minus ridiculum est *t* f   tradunt *t* b
solutam/prosam *t* F   nanque/nam *t* f   primiter *t* b   posterior Mose *t*
j   Ioathan/Achar *t* B   interfuerunt/fuerunt *t* F   DCC/DXX *t* f   circa *t*
F   *a Geographiae:* hoc *t* I, *omr*

4. floruerunt *t* b   *a* Livius: lactea Romani sermonis ubertas *t* I   A/At
t F   quos/quibus *t* F

5. De historiae . . . ornatum *omt* f   brevitae i

CHAPTER XIII

Title. et . . . contineatur *omt* B

1. viderent *t* j, viderint A

2. fuit/extitit *t* f   Horatius *omt* F   aliubi . . . aliubi *t* I

3. *a* Aristoteles: teste Laertio libro octavo *t* **f**   *a* Empedoclem: oratoriae *t* **I**   artis *omt* **b**   aspirarint/processerint *t* **F**   Thysias/Cthesias **f**

4. sed . . . continetur *omt* **f**   Et agendo . . . continetur *om* **B** interponendo/referendo **b**

5. vocent *t* **F**, vocant *r*   rhetoricem **V**

CHAPTER XIV

Title. et . . . labores *omt* **B**

1. Musice **V**   Horatio, *a arte*: dicente *t* **f**   *Aegloga* **f**   Orphi Calliopeia *t* **f**

2. Ioppas **f**   fuisse/extitisse *t* **f**   acthaeo **V**   *a* fertur: Flaccus *t* **j**

3. sentit/docet *t* **b**   qui inquit/inquiens *t* **j**   tinitu **V**   ordinem *t* **I**, ordinent *r*   ἁρμονίαν . . . appellamus *omt* **B**

4. postmodum *t* **b**   fuisse/extitisse *t* **f**   Tubal *t* **I**, Iubal *r*   praecessit *t* **f**   Haec . . . origo[6] *omt* **B**

5. statim/recens **bI**   sopitus dormitat/sopiri solet **b**   fatigationem **b** Sic canor remigem hortatur, laborem/arandum, *a* viamque: eundum **b**

6. interdum . . . murmurat *om* **b**

7. Caeterum/Caeteri **f**/Quod autem **V**   musice **V**, musicen **F**   *a* virorum: animos, effoeminantem *t* **F**   aestimaretur **V**   ait/refert *t* **b** *a* ait: quod quum, Themistocles, quod *om*, est habitus indoctior **V** explanavi/retulimus *t* **b**

8. ex . . . constet/quae circa artem musicam versantur *t* **F**   infra/mox *t* **f**   alterum/aliud *t* **F**   Ex . . . modis *omt* **f**

CHAPTER XV

Title. a instrumenta: musica *t* **I**   ac . . . organum *omt* **I**   usu tibiarum **V**

1. et postea/eo postea, regresso *t* **j**, esset *omt* **j**   easque/quas *t* **f**, Et *omt* **f**, hanc/quam, ille/ Mercurius *t* **f**   percussu *t* **j**   excitavisset ad similitudinem *t* **F**   *a* composuisse: fertur *t* **f**   post Orpheo/mox Orpheo, eam/quam *t* **f**

2. faciebant/componebant *t* f   *a* suavitatis: in modulando *t* F
superius *t* F

3. Marsyas *t* b   in Delo/Deli *t* F   Thamyra *t* F   Marsyas *t* I

4. iis ad/his in *t* F   *a* confecit: Unde *t* F   Appollini f

5. syringam V   fuit/extitit *t* f   Marsyas *t* I   Obloquitur *t* j,
Obliquitur A

6. *a* uti: in *t* b   memoravimus *t* b   aut . . . ambigitur *om* V   *a*
ambigitur: ita F   ad formam Δ/in formam deltae *t* F

7. teste/dicente *t* f   qui ait *omt* f

8. Hinc . . . dicetur *omt* I

9. Aphrycae V   Pysaeus F   interemptus fuisset *t* f   aethera/aequora
t f

10. quoniam is/quoniam hic *t* F   traherent *t* f   contumeliae causa/in
contumeliam *t* F   in auditu *t* f   Cirtaeum per c *t* f

11. quid multa cum *om*, inventor fuerit/faciendae exemplar *t* f   *a* dux:
primiter praebuisse fertur *t* f   qui est *t* f   *a* fistula: cantatoria *t* F
classicae *t* F, classici f   Asofra *t* f   aliubi *t* f

12. ponere/obiter referre *t* b   paratae/procinctae *t* b   inceptabant
FfBbI, incoeptabant *r*   ingressu *t* j, ingressi A   capescerent V
meminerunt *t* I   additis tympanis *om* fBb   Hunc . . . servat *omt* F

13. Halyates *t* F   fidicinas *t* F   pugnus B   Alexander Ff

CHAPTER XVI

Title. ac/aut *t* B

1. *a* vocat: id licet Lactantius falsum esse probet *t* f   sectae/dogmatis *t*
f   *a* teste: divo *t* F   Budda *t* b, Buddas *r*   Britannos et *om* I
Dryidas *t* F   Zamolxim *t* F

2. amplius mille/mille et amplius V   *a* annis: vel secundum Eusebium
circa septingentos annos V, vel secundum Eusebium paulo minus
septingentis FfB   Eusebius/Idem *t* B   demonstrat/edocet *t* b

3. Alterum quod/Unum quod *t* F   Tales V   instituit *t* j   valde
multum/quamplurimum *t* F   id est/videlicet *t* f

4. Cicerone *de Oratore*/Divo Hieronymo et Laertio   tris V, treis **Ff**
naturae . . . vocant/physicam ethicam et dialecticam *t* **f**   importavit/
invexit *t* **I**   Cicero/dicente Cicerone *t* **f**   *a* physicam: videlicet *t* **f**

5. diffinire V, et . . . facere *om*, earum/rerum V   docere/tractare *t* **j**
tantum *t* **f**   discimus/legimus V/dicimus F   vel . . . Teiove *omt* **B**

CHAPTER XVII

Title. primi/primitus *t* **b**   deprehenderint *t* **F**, *omr*   atque . . . sint *omt*
B   reppererint *t* **F**, *omr*

1. *c* Terra: Quoniam V   temperatione/bonitate *t* **b**   uberrimos *t* **F**
Iulio Firmico *t* **f**, ut . . . somniis *omt* **f**   subiecta/obnoxia *t* **b**
rationator **Iij**

2. Et hoc . . . existet *omt* **B**   igitur *om* V   in qua . . . conclusus est
omt **f**

3. Hanc/quam *t* **f**   a vero **B**   id *om* V   primum/primitus *t* **I**   inde/
mox *t* **b**

4. quapropter/unde *t* **F**   tradiderunt/fabulati sunt *t* **I**   bello, belli V
Et in . . . syderum *omt* **B**   ut alii volunt Assyrii reppererunt V
sextam *Eglogam* *t* **f**   Promotheum **f**

5. postmodum *t* **b**   Adae *t* **B**   primitus invenerunt *t* **I**   ne *om* V
reperissent/ab eis reperta fuerant *t* **F**   integra scripta *t* **f**   In his igitur *t*
F   in *om* **fBb**   ad . . . inscripserunt/ab se inventa fuerant circa
observationem syderum conscripserunt *t* **F**   pertinebant **f**   deinde/
subinde *t* **f**   Ac . . . initium *om* V   artis . . . excogitatae *omt* **f**

6. dicit/docet *t* **b**   approbat quod V   nocte *t* **F**

7. quia V, qui *r*   tempus *omt* **B**   Sphaerae/Spaerae V/Spaerae seu
sphaerae utroque enim modo scribitur **Ff**   Archimenides *t* **f**,
Archemides *r*   fuit/extitit *t* **f**   *c* quod: Id **F**   vel . . . Atlanti/in quo
sibi ipsi refragari videtur In secundo enim volumine capite octavo
Atlantem spaeram primum invenisse dicit *t* **f**

8. flaturi *t* **j**, staturi **A**

9. Ventos . . . regionum[11] *omt* B

11. est aliud, nisi/quam b**I**

CHAPTER XVIII

Title. primo *t* b   arithmetricam V

1. testantur *t* b   quotannis/singulis annis *t* F   caedem/necem *t* F
Pompei *t* B   *a* Strabo: in *t* F   discernebatur *t* F   metiri/mensurari *t*
F   *a* Strabo: in *t* B   *a* Herodotus: in *t* B   arithmetricam V   id . . .
scientiam *omt* F

2. *a* Iosephus: qui veri amantissimus est *t* f   mentionem/sermonem V
subiicit/infert *t* I   arithmetricam V   Abrahae B

3. Artem . . . dicitur *omt* I   teste . . . ita *omt* f   eodem *om* Bb**I**   *a* se:
perspectivam, *a* continet: et, quae/illa radiorum reflexiones atque
qualitates inquirit [inquitit F] haec vero *t* F   floruerunt *t* b   Tyberii V

CHAPTER XIX

Title. reppererit V, reperit *r*   et mensuras . . . modo *omt* B

1. reppererit V, reperit F, repererit *r*   arithmetricae V   procax V
apud Hierosolymos/ Hierosolymis *t* F   regnarunt *t* f   *a* libro 7:
Naturalis historiae gravis auctor *t* F   Phydoni *t* F   *a* libro 5: *Geographiae*,
Helidensem *t* F   *a* affirmat: de quo Gellius in secundo et Laertius
itidem in secundo mentionem faciunt *t* B

2. invenerint/reppererint *t* B   affirmat/refert *t* b   primo adinvenisse *t*
B   *a* Josephus: in *t* B   docet Cain *t* b   Adae *t* B   *a* haec: Hebraeis *t*
f   repertores Ff   dicunt V   *a* sculptorem: extitisse volunt *t* f   *a*
Mercurium: Diodorus et Laertius auctores *t* B   Livius . . . explicemus[4]
omt f

3. aut per/mox per b**I**

4. Bellum . . . placamen b**I**   CIDLMVX b**I**ij

CHAPTER XX

Title. et . . . usus *omt* B ac . . . usus *om* b**I**   XX/XIX V

1. praestoque *omt* I   inventores suos *t* j, inventionem suae artis A   et coelo dicavit *t* j, *om* A

2. primo Apollinis . . . filius *omt* I   qui . . . fertur *omt* b   ac purgationem alvi *om* I, invenisse fertur/invenit I

3. Atqui . . . vulnus⁵ *omt* B

5. Huius . . . vulnus *om* bI

6. medicina *omt* B   Coo Ff   *a* Nam: is V   ait/testis est *t* F scribere V   qui/unde *t* F   libro 26 V, libro 36 *r*   longe . . . memoriam *omt* F

7. *a* Romam: Cassius Hemina auctor est, ex/e *t* F   Paulo *omt* B quiritium *t* B, quiritum *r*   Is/Hic *t* F   inde/mox *t* f   facerent/ efficerent *t* b   sua medicina/arte medicinae *t* f   his/iis V

9. Atqui/Unde *t* F/Ergo f   aegrotos/languentes *t* b   alium noverit V Bastetani/ Lusitani *t* B   homines . . . spectat *omt* B   Ex quo Strabo/ dicente Strabone *t* f   Bastetani inquit *omt* B   Quanquam . . . occultis *omt* B

10. et *om*, in iis/inter quos fuere *t* b   Augusti Caesaris *t* b

CHAPTER XXI

Title. quae/quod *t* F/ut f   *a* remedia: quaedam *t* f   didicerunt *t* F

1. *a* quidam: ut *t* F   Alexander F   scribit/refert *t* b   comedebant *t* F reminiscebantur aut intelligebant *t* F   effodiebant *t* F   interibant *t* F

2. fuit/extitit *t* f   Phillyra *t* F   hulcera Bb   Ex quo/Unde *t* F tradiderit VBb, tradidit Ff   Samotracum V

3. primitus *t* b   inflicto/contracto *t* F   pertractaret *t* F   squalentia *t* b, squallentia *r*

4. At . . . revertor⁵ *omt* B   omnia medicamenta b   medicamentis purgat b

6. postea/mox *t* f   id quod Cornelius . . . sanescit *omt* f

7. fluiali V, fluviali FfBb   mittere/eximere V   phlebotomiam V nanque is/nanque hic *t* f   gravedinosus/obesus *t* b   factus *omt* F

clysteris usum/clyster facere *t* F/clysterium **fBbI**   *a* origano: haec ex
Plinio libro VIII *Naturalis historiae*

8. *a* autem: ut idem in XXV testis est *t* F   per idem temporis/eodem
tempore V   Pompei libertus *t* f   iussu . . . omnia/id sibi, Magno
Pompeio omni *t* F   potiti/potito mandante *t* F

<h2 style="text-align:center">CHAPTER XXII</h2>

Title. Quis *t* j, Qui A   primo *t* b   incantiones V   sedantur *t* F

1. libro *t* F   *a* quandoquidem: ut Plinius ait *t* F   in . . . *Epitomes*/in
liminari pagina sui *Epitomatis t* I   plus *om* V   fuerunt/extiterunt *t* B
cum . . . quarter millesimus *omt* B

2. tris V   eo usque/in tantum fastigii *t* F   invaluerit *t* I

3. *a* de Circe: maga *t* F   Circen socios **fBb**   Ulyxis V
quemadmodum/quod V   interemi f   fine V   nulla anie B

4. per *om*, peragraverit *t* F   infamem fuisse *t* f   quod . . . edocere *omt*
j   eventus/effectus *t* F   Ac . . . inventum *om* V   magiae/magicae
artis F

5. Hosthanem *t* b   *a* atque: idem docet *t* b   magicen *t* F
illustrantibus *t* I   circiter . . . annum/a trecentesimo urbis anno *t* f
longe . . . natos *omt* F   haud modestissimus/ut vere dixerim
insanissimus *t* f   Iochobel/Lotapea *t* f

6. Fuit . . . mater *omt* f   Caeterum . . . arbitror/Quod piaculum
iccirco ut arbitror ex eius ore *t* f   *a* Deus: Mosi *t* F   dedisse V,
dedisset F   Mosen/hunc, ipso/eo *t* F   demonstraret/doceret *t* b

7. Salomon *t* F   inquiens Vidi etenim *t* I   Solomone **fBbI**, Salomone
r   daemonium *t* f   Salomonis *t* F

8. et quibus . . . habebunt *omt* B   ut *om* **bI**   commemorare/referre *t* b
intelligant *t* F

<h2 style="text-align:center">CHAPTER XXIII</h2>

1. preces, *a* illis: ac *t* b   faciebant/offerebant, eorum/deorum *t* b, id
. . . natura *om*, generatione *t* b   usque eo/in tantum *t* F   profitebantur
t F   *a* fluxerunt: videlicet *t* f   pyromantia *om* f

2. *a* divinatio: quae fit *t* **f**   qua/quae, divinatur/ divinare consuevit *t* **f**
vis/potestas *t* **F**   Tanaquilla **f**   *a* Aeromantia: ea, per aerem/erat quae
in aere fieri solebat *t* **f**   utpote, cantumve *t* **b**   sicut ait Plinius/teste
Plinio *t* **f**   Hannibal *t* **F**

3. *a* Hydromantia: quae fit, *a* Varro: auctore Cicerone De *divinatione t* **f**
Geomantia *t* **j**, Geomantica **A**   *a* divinatio: est quae fit *t* **f**   *c* per: quae
t **f**   *a* inspectionem: divinat *t* **f**, *Satyra* sexta *omt* **f**   ridiculosa *t* **F**   ea/
haec *t* **f**   ab iis/ab his *t* **F**   dragmas *t* **f**   inquinantes/tabificantes *t* **b**
ac . . . audiant *om* **V**

<h2 style="text-align:center">CHAPTER XXIV</h2>

1. in iis/in his *t* **F**   humanaque fraude *omt* **f**

2. in iis/in his **F**

3. ut . . . praedicebant *omt* **f**   a quo/ab hoc igitur *t* **F**   vendicavit **V**

4. Amphiaraeo **V**   epar *t* **b**   Alexander **Ff**   fertur/haud dubie,
portendit *t* **f**

5. *a* consistit: Unde, *a* Vergilius: ait *t* **F**   *c* Haec: Et *t* **F**   tota aruspicia
FfBb

6. Amphiaraeus **Vf**

7. oscinae *t* **b**   Porro . . . vocamus *om* **V**

8. sapientissimus/lepidissimus **t** **F**   Is/Hic *t* **F**   bello/quadam
expeditione *t* **F**   iusserit *t* **F**, eatenus *omt* **F**   ageret/captaret *t* **f**   At
vate et *t* **F**   avis de sua ipsius salute **V**   potuisset/valuisset *t* **F**   ne **V**,
ut ne **F**, ut *r*

9. Quid . . . augur *om* **V**

10. Telmissinis **V**

11. tantum . . . ulla/ut Eusebius in IIII ait nulla, queunt **V**   ut etiam
. . . noceant *om* **V**   decimotertio *t* **f**   si adversa *t* **F**   si felicia *t* **f**
ademerit/defloraverit

12. *a* Praeterea: quia *t* **f**   ecquid/quid **V**   dicente Vergilio *t* **f**
fortisque **F**   Quapropter/Unde **F**   Quapropter . . . Finis *om* **V**
hariolis *t* **b**   *a* procul: a **F**

Ending. *a* Primi: De inventoribus rerum **FfB**

BOOK II

Book Title. II/secundus incipit **V**

CHAPTER I

Title. quis *t* **f**   primus *t* **f**, primitus **Bb**   dederit *t* **f**   et quae . . .
fuerit/et ut [quod **VF**] alii aliis leges constituerint [constituere **VF**] *t* **f**/
om **B**

1. deinde/subinde *t* **f**   *a* reliquis: voluminibus *t* **b**   primo *t* **F**   dicam/
disseram *t* **B**

2. *c* Ius: quoniam **V**   Crysippus diffinit **V**   sapientum *t* **j**

3. Nam/unde *t* **F**   a *omt* **B**

4. declarat/docet *t* **b**   recte summi **bI**

5. dicente Ovidio *t* **f**

6. Caeterum *om* **V**, primiter *t* **b**   edidit/condidit *t* **F**   Solon . . .
Aethiopes/Solon secundum Gelium libro X Aegyptiis (ut Lactantius
ait) quintus Mercurius (ut Diodorus) Aethiopes [+ tulerunt **F**] *t* **f**
Turiis Charundas *t* **F**/Tyriis Charandes *r*   ipsis . . . quartus/Cicero
Herodotus Strabo Plutarchus Iustinus et Laertius autores *t* **F**/*om* **fBbI**

7. muneris/numeris **f**   veri *omt* **F**

8. constitutum iri *t* **f**   deinde/mox, memoravimus *t* **b**   aetate supe-
rior/maior natu *t* **F**/antiquior **f**   dedit/contulit *t* **F**   Testis idem
Iosephus/Dicente eodem Iosepho *t* **f**   Locrensis **f**/Locrenus *r*   addit/
subdit *t* **b**   fertur primitus *t* **b**   Ac . . . haereditatem etc.[II] *om* **V**   *c*
iuris: extitit **Ff**   atque/ac **FfB**

9. Verum . . . haereditatem etc.[II] *om* **FfB**

12. extra/propter **V**   pontificium/divinum *t* **F**   memoriae nostrae **V**
Pinnius *om* **V**/Pinius **FfBb**   pontificii . . . atque/tum divini tum *t* **F**
a consultissimus: quorum nos etiam in hac parte et si longo intervallo in
praesenti [impraesenti **V**, inpraesenti **f**] vestigia sequimur *t* **f**

Chapter 11

Title. vel/aut *t* **B**   principio/primo *t* **b**   instituerint/condiderint *t* **F**
tyrannidemque/aut tyrranidem *t* **B**   Ariopagitarum **V**   magistratum/
consilium *t* **F**

1. proximo/infronte *t* **I**   demonstremus/edisseram *t* **f**   Platone . . .
regno/Strabone libro primo *Geographiae t* **f**   hoc est/id est **V**
optimatium *t* **f**   ac ob . . . videt *omt* **F**   proprium/suum *t* **F**   pro se
om **V**   Quare/Unde *t* **F**

2. ut qui/utpote qui *t* **b**   Caeterum . . . sacerdos *omt* **f**

3. aiens/inquiens *t* **I**   Mittra **V**   instituerunt/condiderunt, habuerunt
t **F**   quorum . . . Mosis *omt* **B**

4. *a* quo: uti *t* **f**   qui *omt* **f**   appellabantur *t* **f**   Et primus . . . ultimus
omt **B**   Eurystheus **b** 41 atque/unde *t* **F**

5. *a* Plinius: falso *t* **f**   hoc/id **V**   probat/docet *t* **b**   uti . . .
ostendimus *om* **V**   primitus *t* **I**

6. optimatium *t* **f**   si illud . . . natus est *omt* **B**   δυνασεία **bI**

7. fuisse/extitisse *t* **f**   *a* Sed: ut unius exemplo hoc falsum esse
probem, Nembroth *t* **f**   Ita . . . Iosephus/dicente Iosepho *t* **f**
Nembroth *t* **f**   primitus *t* **I**   Tyrannum . . . voluntas *om* **V**   vox/
appellatio *t* **b**   Hoc/Sic **F**   quando . . . metiuntur *omt* **I**

8. testificante *t* **f**   Hi . . . veneat *omt* **B**

9. fuisse/extitisse *t* **f**   et eius . . . emittebat *omt* **f**   tris **Bb**   viderit
BbI   multavit **BbI**

10. in servitutem datus/servitute affectus **BbIij**

11. Forma . . . emittebat *om* **B**

12. Ariopagitarum **V**   magistratum/consilium *t* **F**   Ariopagitis **V**
sit/est *t* **F**   Areopagus . . . pondararent *om* **V**   ἄρης/Ares **Ff**
scribit/refert **FfBb**   magistratus/ consilium **F**   institutum, Ii/Hi **F**
tantave **F**   pondararent/perpenderent **FfB**

Chapter iii

Title. De . . . civitatis/Quod [ut f] Romana civitas monarchiam
aristocratiam et democratiam habuit [habuerit f] *t* f   regiminis/
administrationis A   fierent/fiebant *t* F   atque/et *t* B   instituerit/
ordinaverit *t* F/egerit fBbI   et de . . . censu *omt* I   vel/aut *t* B   et ibidem . . . imponendi *omt* B

1. *a* sententiam: quod *t* F   immigravit/immigrarunt *t* F

2. nummum *t* F   ut/quam *t* I   longe minimi/humillimi *t* f

3. accidit/ingruit *t* F   delegebat *t* b   crescebat *t* F   cum ipsa/secum *t*
f   agebatur *t* F   Contra/E contrario *t* I   adeo . . . suo/pessum adeo
ire *t* I   nunquam . . . postea/nusquam eius status *t* I   poterat *t* F

4. Namque I/Unde *t* F   regiminis/dominationis A   Silvia V/Sylvia *r*
Exin/Mox *t* f   optimatium *t* F   duo/cum ij   testatur/docent *t* b   *a*
sunt: videlicet *t* f   Ii/Hi *t* f   notabatur/signabatur *t* B/signabantur b

5. Post annum/Anno V   vel . . . sunt/ut alii volunt VIII post actos V
esymnetae t F/ *elymnetae r*   In *om* V   mensibus V

6. Item . . . exemissent *omt* B   nisi/quam bI

7. Post annum/anno, altero V   officium . . . facientes *omt* F   *a*
officium: videlicet ex f, ex BbIij   ipsorum/suo, imprimis f   et . . . id/
eosque *t* F

8. Atratinus V/Atracinus *r*   Longus, Siculus *omt* B   plebei *t* b
conubia V   deinde/mox *t* b   anno . . . CCCLV *omt* B   Lateranus
omt B   anno . . . CCCLXXXIX *omt* B   anno . . . CCCXCIX *omt* B
libro F

9. postea/procedente tempore *t* F   inde/mox *t* b   regimen/potestate
gubernata est A   tum . . . tum *t* B   eius . . . facta est/sui interitus
ruina manavit *t* F

10. eborea *t* F   currules *t* b   Quare/Unde *t* F   Romae haberi/ut
Romae haberentur *t* I

11. Eiusmodi/Huiusmodi *t* F   capite 18/capite XIX *t* f

12. instituit/ordinavit *t* F/egit fBbI   rem veluti . . . census Romani[13]
omt I

13. Sed . . . grossos[16] *omt* **B**

17. Atque . . . licet *omt* **I**

Chapter IV

Title. quam/quod *t* **F**/ut **f**   varium/alii alium habebant *t* **F**/alii alium
habuerint **f**   qui invenerint/quis invenerit *t* **B**   vel/aut *t* **B**   atque . . .
aureum *omt* **B**

1. observatione/ordinatione *t* **F**

2. trecenis **V**   non ideo/ non id **V**

3. *a* ultimo: loco *t* **I**   cum inquit/inquiens *t* **I**   primitus etiam *t* **b**
instituerant/ ordinaverunt *t* **F**

4. varius *t* **F**   ratio/modus *t* **F**   demonstrare/referre *t* **b**
complebant/explicabant *t* **b**   *a* Macrobius: auctor integerrimae fidei *t* **F**

5. duodecim milia *t* **F**   *a* Censorinus: lepide *t* **b**

6. dicit/docet *t* **b**   constitutum/ordinatum *t* **F**   Romulus . . . est
nominatus *omt* **B**

7. iste annus *omt* **B**   inde/mox *t* **f**   postea/subinde *t* **f**/postmodum **Bb**
ex *omt* **b**   *a* habebant: Qui [sane annus **FfB**] cum non satis quoque
competeret *t* **B**   id est . . . distribuit[9] *omt* **B**

9. qui praerant **b**   Sic/Hinc *t* **B**   autore *omt* **b**   *a* Plinio: auctoribus *t*
b   *a* duos: videlicet *t* **f**

10. primi/primitus, constituerant/condiderunt *t* **b**   *a* videtur: Horum
autem apud Romanos nominum (variis enim apud gentes nominibus
nuncupantur) rationem Macrobius et Censorinus affatim docent *t* **B**
Atque annus . . . doceatur[14] *omt* **B**

11. medium mensis **bI**

12. antecedentis mensi **I**

13. *condita* in fine libri noni **b**

14. *a* excogitatus: sicut aiunt autores quos habeo **bI**   (ut fertur) *om* **bI**
vel . . . extat *om* **bI**   Quo/ac **bI**   quidem . . . quoque *om* **bI**   suo/tali
b   *c* dignum: optimo ac pio ingenio **bI**   est/sunt **b**

CHAPTER V

Title. primum *t* **b**; constituerit/ordinaverit *t* **F**

1. Aegyptiaca lingua *om* **V**   auctumnus **V**   eiusque rei/cuius ordinationis *t* **F**   Trimagistus **V**, Trimegistus **FfBbIi**

2. capite 76 **BbIijA**

3. Rhomae **F**   graecostasim **FfBbIijA**   Messala continente **V** Postea/Procedente tempore *t* **F**

4. reperit **FfBbIijA**   Utriusque . . . notandas *omt* **B**   *a deorum* 2: inquiens **bI**   inquit *om* **bI**   in fine secundi *Tusculanarum* libri **b**

5. quotidie/singulis fere diebus *t* **f**   de quibus/quae *t* **b** meminerimus/referemus *t* **b**

6. Illud . . . oporteat *om* **V**   medio noctis **FfBb**   notetur/signetur **FfBb**

CHAPTER VI

Title. ab initio/primitus *t* **b**   observabant *t* **F**, observarent **fBb**   ac . . . diviserint *om* **V**; divedebant **FfBb**

CHAPTER VII

Title. primi/primo *t* **f**/primum **Bb**   primiter inventus *t* **b**

1. copia/commoditate *t* **F**   capescendas **V**   gentium *omt* **f**   peccare . . . ducerem/ piaculum hercle me fecisse ducerem *t* **F**   hunc/hoc, laborem/munus *t* **f**   monumenta **V**   Quapropter/Unde *t* **F**   bene *om* **V**   eius/sui *t* **F**   simulachrum *t* **f**   monumenta **V**   esse opus *t* **b**

2. Atque ita/Unde *t* **F**   foras dandos *om*, curasse/publicasse *t* **f**

3. uti *t* **F**   milia *t* **f**

4. Theophrastus . . . ille *om* **V**

5. dicente Plinio, *t* **f**   ubi inquit *omt* **f**

6. scribens/inquiens *t* **I**

7. postea/mox *t* **f**   Guidus **V**   omnis . . . decus/lux doctrinarum fulgentissima, *a* ac: unicum *t* **j**

8. illud/hoc *t* F   cum hoc/huic *t* F   Ex quo/Unde *t* F

9. Itaque . . . dignitate/Quidam itaque Germanus nomine Petrus V
Iohannes Cuthembergus F   civibus/conterraneis *t* F   *a* quam: hodie
V   Magantiam V, Maguntiam F   minori *t* F   literarum *omt* j
Decimosexto . . . MCCCCLVIII/Mox V   homo *om* V   loquendi labore/
loqui, ac simul/vel potius V   *a* fuerit: Hoc enim palam est de
inventore vero non ita fidem nostram obstringimus V   Quae . . . vilior
om V   coepit/incepit F

CHAPTER VIII

Title. etiam per notas *om* V

1. monumenta V   inde/mox *t* I

2. adducit/inducit *t* F   *a* Alexander: uti testis est Gelius [Gellius **FfB**]
libro XVI [XVII B] *t* B   trecentis et amplius V   qui . . . consulibus
omt B

3. retinet/remansit V

4. iisque/hisque *t* F   monumenta V   emembrana **b**   Eleazarus *t* B
transmiserit *t* **b**

5. dumtaxa V   atque *omt* F

6. Usus . . . nuncupatas *om* V   *a* notas: alioqui **FfBb**   nisi/quam
FfBbI   50 videlicet *om* **Ff**

CHAPTER IX

1. qua . . . fuisse *omt* f   Ac ita videtur/Videtur enim *t* f

2. Adrianus F

CHAPTER X

Title. 1 et . . . praestet *omt* B   thesserae *t* B   de . . . modo/quod [ut f]
primo pugnis et calcibus dein fustibus pugnatum est *t* f

1. Quanquam . . . redeo *omt* B

2. Pallas fuit/Pallas extitit *t* f   repperit V   cunctos *t* F   fortiter/
decenter *t* **b**   Quamobrem/Ex quo, militaris ars V

3. Lucretius . . . fuerunt *om* V   Exin/Mox *t* b   testificante Herodoto *t* f   Libyae fluvio *om* V   scribens/inquiens *t* I   Aphros *t* F

4. thessaris *t* B   qui . . . credo *omt* B

CHAPTER XI

Title. De primo usu armorum, et qui primiter invenerint galeam, gladium, hastam, loricam, clypeos, ocreas, cristas, lanceas aetolas, iaculum cum amento, falcem, hastas velitares, pilum, securim, venabula, arcum, sagittas, et tormenta diversi generis, et artem ipsam machinamentorum, et de illo tormento aeneo quod bombarda vocatur *t* F

1. Ferunt/ Fabulae, *a* libro 6: tradunt *t* B   cui ob id/unde illi *t* F   principio/fronte *t* b

2. adinvenerunt *t* F   tradita *t* I   Mydias **BbIijA**   Praetus **FfB**   Acritus *t* F   bellantes *t* b   Aetolas *t* I   invenisse/reperisse *t* j   Claementem V   Fulgius F   imperator/consul **fBbIijA**   sagitandique F   fuisse/extitisse *t* f

3. Artabanus **IijA**   Mosem V   gloriosse V   apparauerit/fecit *t* f/ fecerit **BbI**   aliubi *t* I   ab initio/primitus *t* b   excogitari potest *t* F

4. Cretes *t* F   *Geographiae* illos/ *Gog.* eillos F   *a Georgicon:* inquiens *t* I   bellicarum machinarum/machinamentorum *t* b   incoharunt V   Machinam . . . fanum *omt* B   Aepeus *t* F   Vitruvio vero/Secundum vero Vitruvium V/Iuxta vero Vitruvium **FfB**   Carthaginenses/ Athenienses *t* f   Gadas V

5. omnia ad/omnia in *t* F   adinventa, et/sed *t* F   imprimis V   quo . . . excogitari *omt* F   inventorem/inventor (licet de eo nihil exploratum habeamus) V   fuisse . . . audiret *om* V   tradunt/ferunt Ff   Germanici sanguinis ignobilem alioqui Ff   cui . . . reperisse *om* Ff   ac inde/ac mox **BbI**   ad fossam/ circa fossam, *a* qui: teste Platina Ff   salutis humanae/a natali Salvatoris F

6. mortiferae/letiferae **FfBb**   eius/suum **FfBb**   dignus . . . ipse/ utinam V   scilicet/sane Ff   vice Salmonei/veluti Salmoneus *t* F   Salmoneus enim . . . detruditur *omt* b   adeo ut/adeo quod V, sit *om* V

a munitus: est V   Ex quo/Unde *t* F   iam . . . ut *om* V   ferme *omt* b
indecore/turpiter *t* b/in decore A   consistat . . . obtorpeat/dissidit V/
dissidat F   obtorpeat/marceat fBb   vocatur, id . . . βόμβος *omt* f

7. Et . . . inciperent *omt* B

8. extra . . . propositum/indecenter *t* b

CHAPTER XII

Title. primum *t* b   ungulos I   ungulas . . . ac *om* I   primum/
primitus *t* b

2. *a* qui: teste Servio   adinvenerunt *t* F   usum primiter *t* b   Lapitae *t*
F   Hos . . . ferunt *om* I   *a* hoc: obiter *t* b

3. *a* Bigas: quod V   iunxerit V   ut *om* V   semen/effectum *t* F   Is/
Hic *t* F   *a* curru: Unde *t* F   enim/quippe *t* I

4. At . . . ferunt *om* I

5. fabula . . . poetas/poetae fabulati sunt *t* I   semihomines et
semiequi/media parte homines media parte equi *t* F   hac/hec F   ex-
tra/citra *t* I   Aeuolo, superius *t* F   monstravimus *t* F   Diodorus/
Dicente Diodoro *t* f   postmodum *t* b   ex *om* V   ille *om* V

6. Et . . . trahunt *om* B

7. Sed/Mox *t* f   iam *omt* f   disseratur *t* f, disseremus Bb
dilaberentur V

CHAPTER XIII

Title. alios id genus *om* B   *a* ludos: Pythios Isthmios Nemeaeos
gimnicos funebres et *t* B   *a* aleae: et *t* B   thesserarum *t* B
furunculorum . . . talus *om* B

1. fuisse/extitisse *t* F   dedicati in Pelopis honorem *t* f   consecutum/
comparasse *t* F   Epaeis *t* F   Fuit is . . . filius *om* F   scribens/
inquiens *t* I   *a* Iphitus: Elaeus *t* F

2. Quapropter/Unde *t* f   Tigranes bIijA   sic ut . . . putant *om* B

3. Alteri/Secundi *t* F   Pythius dictus/cognomen Pythii adeptus,
Ovidius/dicente Ovidio *t* F

4. aliquandoque *t* f Isti/Hi *t* F in *om*, honore fBb in primis *omt* F
aiens/ inquiens *t* I

5. iis/his *t* F

6. interfecit *t* F

7. ex qua/de qua *t* F *a* loquitur: inquiens *t* I demonstrat Pyrrhicam
t f 81 ostendit/docet *t* b a Curet *t* f

8. *c* Tranquillus: Servius autem super V *Aeneidos* ait quod V autem
om V *a* autem: ut Servius ait super V *Aeneidos* F ludus ipse *t* F
Pyrrhicam *t* f Troia *t* F vocatur *t* F *a* et: quod, expresserit V
huius rei *t* F affirmaret V meminit/edocet *t* b habere/ sortitum
esse *t* b

9. Morae I

10. recreandi/relaxandi V Asiae *omt* B Quare/Unde *t* F Pithum
V fortase F Atqui . . . decet[17] *omt* B

11. monstraverim/docuerim b

13. unicum/singulum b

CHAPTER XIV

1. *a* proprium: ac suum *t* F nutrisset IijA esset/erat *t* F Silvanus *t*
F

2. Februarii *t* F ex . . . verberantes *t* B *a* Mulieres: vero *t* f dicente
Ovidio *t* f silvestria *t* F Testatur IijA hunc *om* V iis/his *t* F

3. Exin/Mox *t* f dicente Vergilio *t* F

4. *a* deinde: annuui *t* F Decembri *t* F inter se/invicem sibi *t* b
ξένος . . . appellatur, quod . . . referre *omt* f sacra/festa, primitus *t* b
dicit/docet *t* b suae/sui *t* b Epithomatis *t* F, Epitomatis fBb

5. paratur inquit/ita inquiens paratur *t* I voluptarem F Maximi V
commemorat/ memorat *t* b Nemesis . . . fortunae/fortunam *t* f
satiarent *t* f nudos, coeuntes *t* f dimicantes *omt* f profisciscentes f

6. alibi . . . fiebant *om* V libro . . . ultimo *om* FfB exponemus/
referemus FfBb et ludos . . . fiebant *om* FfB

CHAPTER XV

Title. primitus *t* **b**   de . . . genera/quod [ut **f**] alii alio modo foedus inibant [inirent **f**] *t* **f**

1. est Gelius **V**   Gelius enim **V**   Caeriti populo/Cereti *t* **F**

3. fuisse/extitisse *t* **f**   Iosepho/lectione Iosephi *t* **I**   memoria **A** foederis paciscendi/ ineundi foederis *t* **I**   cum sibi/dum sibi *t* **F** deserta loca/desertum, Exin/Mox *t* **b**

4. Foederum . . . constat *omt* **B**   multare **bI**   ii/hi **j**

5. alibi/aliubi *t* **f**   ici/iniri *t* **I**   demonstrat/docet *t* **b**   Si *om* **f**

6. agebant/componebant *t* **I**   pro hospite/hospitem, pro cive/civem *t* **F**

7. Sythae **V**   sanciebant/inibant *t* **I**   feriebant *t* **b**   cultelo **F** fecissent **ijA**   illi/hi *t* **F**

8. ferme . . . Item *om* **V**   Salustio **F**   permixtum **F**   conflabant/ componebant *t* **I**

9. faciebant/inibant *t* **I**   id *om* **V**   persequi/recensere *t* **f**   simulque . . . tempore *om* **V**

CHAPTER XVI

Title. *a* quo: primum *t* **F**   ac/et, liceret/licebat *t* **F**   et trophaei *omt* **I**

1. increbuit/inolevit *t* **j**   sui *Epitomatis t* **b**   Hastrubal, Hamilchari *t* **f**

3. mediocritatis/virilitatis *t*   **B**   eiusque . . . gratior *omt* **B**   Gelius **V** redimiti *t* **I**   *a* deinde: ad propriam *t*   **F**

4. Gelio **V**   *a* minusve: quam *t* **F**   exceptum/cautum *t* **F**

5. quatenus **V**   declarat/edocet *t* **b**

6. deinde/subinde *t* **b**   commodum/transeunter *t* **F**

7. Gelio, ovantis **V**   Tubettus *t* **F**

8. Fuit . . . viri[9] *omt* **I**

CHAPTER XVII

Title. primum *t* **b**   *a* invenerint: et flores miscere coeperint *t* **B** cocoronandi **V**   ac . . . ludos *omt* **I**

1. imposuit *t* F   edera f   seculis/aetatibus *t* b   plenissime *t* b
scribens/inquiens *t* I

2. mixtura *t* F   ut ait Plinius/dicente Plinio *t* f   capite II/capite X *t* f
meminit/ sermonem facit V   mixtura *t* F   versicolores *t* f

3. horret/silet *t* b

4. multiiugae *t* F   id est/videlicet *t* f   in *omt* b   primitus/ab initio
IijA   fuerat/erat *t* b

5. ante *t* F   *a* obsidebantur: Haec ex Gelio libro V suarum *Noctium t* F
a quam: ut idem ait *t* F   fuisset/fuerat *t* F   praebuit *t* b   exponit/
refert *t* b   Ex quo/Unde *t* F   Antonius FfBbIijA

6. cinamomo V   cynamomo Ff   interasili *t* B

8. At/Unde obiter *t* F   *a* illud: sceleratae V   reginae *omt* F
venenatis/veneno illitis [ilitis fBbI] *t* I   *c* Sane: ipsaque capiti imposita
t F   Sane/Mox *t* F   Ecquis/Quis V   coniecta/concerpta *t* F   corona
Antonio *omt* F   ilico fBb   occidit/expiravit *t* I   autore/nutore I

9. dixerim/maximis sponsionibus contenderem eminentissimum *t* I

10. Item . . . faciuntque[11] *omt* I

11. *c* Sed: Quod si plerique qui in eo loco vehementer haesitarunt
quandoque intellexissent non utique essent tot ambagibus usi *t* f

CHAPTER XVIII

1. assentiri/astipulari V/adstipulari FfBbI   id temporis/tunc *t* F   *a*
unguentum: basalmi *t* F   instituit/fecit *t* f   fuit . . . est/quadringentis
annis Troiae excidium antecessit V   CCCL/CCCC *t* B   myrrhae
electae *e*   cinamomi *t* F   coas *t* b   permixtis *t* F   fuisse/extitisse *t* f

2. scrinnium V   Lucium *omt* f   id est externa/sic enim appellaverunt
V

CHAPTER XIX

Title. primitus *t* F   fabriliaque instrumenta/forcipem marculum vectem
incudem aerariam ferrariamque fabricam ferri compactionem aeris atque
auri conflaturam *t* F   dein/mox *t* f

1. iam . . . invasit/caepit *t* F   propemodum *omt* I   Ovidius/dicente
Ovidio *t* f   Phaletii **BbIijA**   superiora *t* f   *a Geographiae:* non
indecenter *t* b

2. primus *omt* I   Occeani V   Mercurius . . . vel *omt* I   abundant *t* I

3. insulis . . . appellat/insula Cassitride *t* F   a quo/cui *t* I   discrepat/
non astipulatur *t* I   Calybas, Cyclopas *t* F   primi exercuerunt *t* F
Pannones *t* F   harpem *t* F

4. scribens/inquiens *t* I   fabricantur *t* F

5. ex lectione Iosephi *t* B   Quare/Unde *t* F

6. inde/mox *t* f   coeli . . . creatori *om* V   creatori/factori **FfBbI**
etiam *om* V

7. eis/sibi *t* F   ignaria **IijA**

CHAPTER XX

Title. nummus *t* F

1. penitus tolli/in totum abdicari *t* F   id quod/sicuti *t* F

2. quia/quatenus V/quatinus F   Adae *t* B   in *om,* cumulandis
pecuniis *t* b   utique/alioqui *t* b   nummum *t* F   praeteriiset V
Romanis *t* F, numo *omt* F   nummus *t* F   qui quod . . . dederat *om* V

3. At/Atqui, uti *t* F   in *omt* f, Aeginae *t* f   huiuscemodi *t* F   deinde/
mox *t* f   disentiunt V   menda, Phidonis *t* I   condita DLXXXV/
CCCCLXXXIIII *t* B   nummum *t* F

4. Macrobius/dicente Macrobio *t* f   redigisset V

5. Quapropter/Unde *t* F   assignati F   de illa prima aeris signatione *t*
j   principio/fronte *t* b   capite 3 *omt* f   dicit/docet *t* b   nummos *t* F
res se habeat *om* F   Sed . . . liquet *om* V   incoepisse F

6. *a* materiis: incertis tamen auctoribus *t* I   ab . . . *deorum* 3 *omt* I

CHAPTER XXI

Title. ac . . . usu *om* V   coronari/cingi A

1. cathena *t* f   Martialis/dicente Martiale *t* f   conubio V   renuntiasse
Vf   fecerat *t* I

538

3. et *omt* f   Ac/Et *t* f   Qui/Unde *t* F

4. in . . . vetustatem/Iosephus auctor antiquitatis integerrimae in
plerisque locis in libris quos *De antiquitatibus* Iudaeorum castigatissime
scripsit Plinium clausis (ut dicitur) oculis annulorum vetustatem
intuitum esse aperte demonstrat *t* f   Ibi . . . armillas *omt* f

5. Item Iosephus/Hic enim VF/Is enim f   constituit *t* F
ostendimus/ docuimus *t* b   fuit ante *om* V   CCL . . . annos/
quadringentis annis V/quadringentos annos FfB   quam . . .
Troianum/bellum Troianum praecessit V   aliisve *t* F   comissis *t* F
vitam F   hiacintinam V/hiacynthinam F   fecerat/fecit, superiori *t* F
Idem . . . lapillis *om* V   dicat/referat FfBb   sermo fiet/disseremus
FfB   *a* lapides: scilicet sardonycos seu F/scilicet f   onychinos F
smarados F   gemmarumque *om* V   credamus licet/credibile est *t* F/
credere licet fBb

6. *a* inquit: quod V   signacula/signaturas *t* F   omneis IijA
coronatur/ornatur A   *a* quidam: usque *t* f   pertinet/pergit *t* f
Deinde/Mox *t* b   nephas ijA   ponam/referam *t* I   id est . . . erant *t*
b   *a* tantum: Haec ex [eodem F] Plinio *t* F

CHAPTER XXII

1. scribit/docet *t*   b   Candebea *t* f   millium fBbIijA   voluntate V
littoris *t* j   littus *t* j   littoris VFIij

2. Belum amnem distare *t* F   annis b   est/sit, circumdatis, convehant
t F   mettalla V

3. Basilea *t* F   est/iacet *t* F   fabulae, tradunt V

4. Id *om* V   At . . . testatur *omt* B

5. *a* reperiatur: et *t* F   ab initio/primitus, quicquam dicere/quod
referam *t* b   nisi ubi/quam *t* I   inquiens *t* I

CHAPTER XXIII

Title. a simulacrorum: et statuarum *t* B   primo *t* b   et Graecos/et
quod Graeci *t* F/ac ut Graeci f   velabant *t* f   et de . . . coeperint *omt* j
item/et *t* j

1. essent/sunt *t* F   iccirco **VB**   *a* principio/profecto *t* f   post
homines natos *omt* F   visum sit/fieri potest **V**/fieri possit **Ff**   Quam
ob rem/Unde *t* F   *a* Moses: alioqui *t* **b**   inocens **V**   auctore **V**
modisque omnibus *om* **V**   Hierosolymae **fBb**   erigere *t* F

2. exceptum/cautum *t* F   colerentur/adorarentur *t* **b**   decreto/
instituto, Mosaicam doctrinam *t* F   aemulantis *t* F   *a* Strabone: in *t* F
Verum . . . ponemus *omt* f

3. auctores **V**   sotiorum **V**   amiserat *t* **I**   demortuorum/
defunctorum *t* **I**

4. Sane illi/Qui *t* F   erabundi **V**   venerint *t* F   sacra/festum *t* F
figuram/effigiem *t* **b**   fuit/invaluit *t* **I**

5. Aetiopes *t* F   cum inquit/inquiens *t* **I**   natum **b**

6. fictionem/fabricam **A**

7. Sic . . . prosequamur⁹ *omt* **b**

8. ipsemet **I**   initio ipsus **j**

9. Plinius **V**   Postea/Mox *t* f   et id . . . Quare *omt* **b**   *a*
Athenienses: enim *t* **b**   Armodio *t* f   se *omt* **IijA**

10. solidum **A**   Clabrio *t* F   ebore **VFbijA**, equore **I**

11. Illi . . . fecerunt *omt* **b**   *a* thus: adolere **Iij**   incendere/accendere **Iij**
Quem . . . fecerunt *om* **Iij**

12. ad coelum *omt* F   fert/effert *t* F

13. *a* hic: obiter *t* **b**   solenne/speciale *t* F   *a* reticulis: et dextrocheriis *t*
F   exculptum/semper, quod/nam *t* F   testatur/docet *t* **b**   diceretur/
dicuntur *t* F   gestitant *t* F/gestarent **fBb**   Quare/Unde *t* F

<h2 style="text-align:center">CHAPTER XXIV</h2>

Title. primum *t* **b**

1. ebore **VFbIijA**   varietate/diversitate *t* **b**   liniamentis *t* **I**

2. ante *om* **V**   milibus **V**/millia **fBbIijA**   se/ipsos **V**   *a* inventam:
prius **V**

3. Ac/At *t* **b**

4. Altera/Secunda *t* F   Phylocle *t* F   Thelephanes *t* F
auctor V   scribunt/referunt *t* b   munus/executio *t* B

5. Non . . . vitam *om* V   cive/conterraneo F   impraesentia **BbI**

<h2 style="text-align:center">CHAPTER XXV</h2>

Title. reppererit V

1. Chorebus *t* F   in duratum V

2. Rhoecum/Ideochum Rhetum *t* F   Eucirapum *t* F/Euchirapum **f**
iis/his *t* **f**   deinde/mox *t* b   figuram/imaginem *t* B   usque eo/
intantum *t* F

3. Scytha *t* F   Haec inquit/Inquiens haec *t* I   est/extat *t* **f**   otius *t* F
Hyperbios . . . invenit/ut alii volunt Hiperbeos Corinthius invenit V
Hiperbeos *t* F   Talaum **fBbIijA**   repperisse V

<h2 style="text-align:center">BOOK III</h2>

Book Title. *a* tertius: incipit V

<h2 style="text-align:center">CHAPTER I</h2>

Title. et . . . bonis *omt* B

1. nil dulcius *t* **f**   nil homine *t* b   De huius *t* F   dicemus/edisseram *t*
f   postquam/si prius tamen *t* F   demonstravero/docebimus *t* F/
docuerimus **fBb**   abundat/scatet *t* I

2. durata *e*/duratam *t* A   Ex quo/Unde *t* F   qui . . . dictator/cui in
agro aranti nuntiatum est eum dictatorem esse factum *t* F   Quare/Ex
quo *t* F

3. libro 17 A   inquit/refert *t* b   Et id . . . gignantur *omt* B

4. Philometer *t* I

5. Osiridem *t* F   *a* Tibullus: in primo *t* **f**

6. *a* Metamorphoseon: inquiens *t* I

7. Dicit/Docet *t* b   Adae *t* B   Atque . . . fuit *om* V   Quapropter
. . . non/Unde ut in confesso, memoravimus *t* b

Chapter ii

Title. primum *t* **b**

1. prohoemio **F**   dicente Vergilio *t* **f**   dicit/docet *t* **b**   adinvenisse *t* **F**
nascebatur *t* **f**   homines nascendi servandique et serendi usum *t* **f**
eidem/sibi, iis/his *t* **F**   oritur *t* **F**

2. cum . . . loquitur *omt* **F**   in Musitani terra Indiae **V**, in Musitani
sive Musicani utrumque scriptum reperio terra Indiae **F**   tritico
persimile *omt* **F**   priori *t* **F**   *a* assignat: inquiens *t* **I**

3. sui *t* **b**   *a* Aristotelis: auctore Laertio *t* **f**   consentit/adstipulatur *t* **I**
item *omt* **F**   *a* probe: ac significanter *t* **f**   *a* ipsi: mox *t* **f**

4. *a* ipse: enim *t* **F**

5. Pistores . . . revenio *omt* **b**   stercorandi *omt* **F**   Argeum *t* **F**

6. Plinius, teste/tradit quod bovem et **V**   *c* aratrum: bovem et **Ff**
tradunt *om* **V**   Super quem locum Servius *t* **f**   Ex quo/Unde *t* **F**
primo/primitus *t* **I**   Osiride *t* **F**

7. *a* Servius: Honoratus grammaticus *t* **f**   quia/nam *t* **F**

8. Verum omnia haec aut omnino fabulosa sunt aut, illi/hi **F**
memoravimus, vel/et *t* **b**   multis ante tempestatibus **V**   essent *t* **F**
ex lectione Iosephi in primo *Antiquitatum t* **f**   licet . . . enim/possumus
Sed magis *t* **F**   superiori *t* **F**   extra/citra *t* **I**   *a* ac: eas **V**   deinde/
subinde *t* **f**

9. grossiusculum *t* **b**   postea . . . Italia *omt* **I**

Title. primitus *t* **b**   et alias . . . docuerit *omt* **I**   *a* vini: et arborum
fructus, *a* miscuerit: et unde talis mos fluxerit *t* **f**   deque . . . modo *omt*
I   et qui . . . primi *om,* vel quis/aut quis *t* **f**   coagulaverit/coegerit **A**

1. animalibus *t* **F**   indumentum **A**   quas deinde/quae deinde *t* **I**
adinvenit *t* **f**   initio/ fronte *t* **b**   *a* tamen: quod **V**   haberent **V**

2. quis modo **V**   sexcentorumque/milleque *t* **F**   potum/poculum *t* **F**
dicemus/ docebimus *t* **b**   Quare/Unde *t* **F**   *a* quod: teste Valerio
Maximo *t* **j**, se *omt* **j**

3. Persae existimabant/Plato (uti testis est Macrobius libro *Saturnalium* 2) existimabat *t* f   et incitabulum *t* b   *a* flagraret: Quod etiam Persae sensisse videntur *t* f   Caeterum . . . procreantur *omt* f   unde . . . procreantur *om* **BbI**

4. idem aliubi *t* f   ac/et *t* F   dixerit V

5. Alii . . . Camilli[6] *om* V   in . . . *Elegiarum* 2 *om* F   apud *om* **Ff** Graeci vites oenas vocabant et oenos **Ff**   Plithinam F   primitus **FfBb**

6. Ad . . . Camilli *om* **FfB**

7. *evangelica praeparatione* V   Inserenti . . . intercluditur *omt* I

8. apud . . . egressus est/parum profecto fide digna sunt. Quapropter facile Lactantii sententiae inhaereo qui [quin F] in 2 suarum *Institutionum* (ut in nostris *Adagiis* itidem meminimus) scribit Noe quum extemplo eggressus foret *t* F   terrum F   *a* arguuntur: ait, *a* putant: Ille enim non modo Liberum sed etiam Saturnum atque Uranum multis antecessit aetatibus *t* F   id quod . . . tradit/idem etiam Iosephus in primo *Antiquitatum* et Hieronymus comprobant *t* F   Cauponam . . . fervet *om* B

9. *a* reddit: inquiens *t* I   vocare salvatorem *t* F   medicamentum . . . rex *om* I

10. primus fecit *t* f   zitum **VF**, zithum **fBb**   Olim . . . Strabo *om* B Dionysius/ipse *t* B   Quapropter . . . usi[II] *om* V   septemtrionalisve F Sed . . . usi[II] *om* **FfB**

11. Quanquam . . . usi *om* b

12. Atqui Diodorus *t* F   primitus *t* I   esset/erat *t* F   Etenim/Quippe *t* b

13. quod/cui, tradit/astipulatur *t* I   trapetas *t* F   hoc . . . oleariam *om* V   mellam *e*/mella *t* A   Olea, longo tempore/quod *t* F   reperiretur V, reperiretur hoc F

14. illud quod Minerva vel Aristaeus *t* f   monstraverint hic *t* F, monstraverit f   residisset *t* b   *evangelica praeparatione* V   Ex quo/ Unde *t* F

15. Aphrica *t* f   annis *t* F   CLXXXIII *t* B

16. coagulare *t* j, cogere A   consentit/congruit *t* F   Carchesiorum *t* F
Histania I   fuit/extitit *t* f   Hebraeis potius/primitus Hebraeis *t* b
fuerat/erat *t* F

CHAPTER IV

Title. *a* translatae: et quod aliae olio cottidie deportantur F, et ut aliae
alio cotidie deportentur f

1. exaedificamus *t* F   animalibus *t* F   dicemus/edisseram *t* f   quia
om, a non: enim V

2. canistrum cerasis *t* i, canistrum cerasiis *r*   At . . . pervenit *omt* B

3. zinzipha *t* B

4. imprimis V   ex iis/ex his *t* F   scribens/inquiens *t* I   et reliqua
. . . habent[7] *om* V

5. nullus genus F   post . . . memoriam *om,* felix F   coronantur
FfBbIij, coronati erant A   Quapropter/Unde F   pontificumve F

7. habent/sortiuntur FfBb   *a* satis: ac V   quos . . . delectat/qui
circam rem rusticam oblectantur VF   intelligant VF

CHAPTER V

Title. rebusque aliis *omt* I   *a* et de: ea occidere instituerit et VF
immolandi . . . ac *omt* f usuque . . . ac de/Et quod multi mortalium
carnibus olim abstinuerunt. Et qui fuerint auctores secundae mensae et
unguenti coronarumque in convivio dandarum et de primo VF/Et qui
fuerint auctores secundae mensae et unguenti coronarumque in convivio
dandarum et de primo f/et qui fuerint victus delicatioris autores et de
primo B   usuque . . . usu *om* bI   *a* venandi: et *t* B   *a* Romanos: primus pavonem in mensis vel *t* f   ferarumque vivaria *omt* I

1. rus/villa *t* F   summatim de iis/in transcursu de his *t* F   *a* iis: obiter
t b   Imposuit . . . At[2] *omt* I

2. animalia/Haec *t* I   Adae *t* B   tribuerem *t* F   immolavit/
sacrificavit *t* F   Manavit . . . usurparunt[4] *om* f   porcum immolabat
IijA

3. Ritus . . . usurparunt[4] *om* B

5. gignebat *t* F   *Adversus/Contra t* B   *a* Graeciae: Eantes etiam
Cizycenus *t* f   usum/ esum *t* b, comedendarum *omt* b   *a* Stoicus:
narrat V   scribens narrat *om*, eos/quod V   scribens/referens FfBb
a vino: se IijA   abstinuerint V   vitaverint V

6. tria V   sectas/dogmata, Saducaeos, Essaeos V   fert ad coelum/
miris effert *t* F   Adam . . . vesceretur/Adae esus carnium *t* B/esus
carnium b   concessus *t* b, hoc . . . Noe *omt* b

7. In . . . tradit/Euripides tradit quod in Creta V   sed ne/sed nec *t* F
dicit/docet *t* b   ex/de *t* F   Cereris *om* F   remansisse/residisse *t* b
impraesenti V, in praesenti F, impraesentia BbI   consulto/studio
brevitatis *t* b   post/mox Ff   nonnulla . . . insequentibus *om* V   libris
om F, sequentibus F   in libris insequentibus/in proximis libris fBb

8. invitamenta/irritamenta *t* b   Quamobrem/Propter quod V   Quae
ea . . . eodem[10] *omt* I

10. postea/mox *t* b   Quare/Unde VF   venit FfBbIijA

11. hoc . . . nostrorum *om* V   maiori *t* F   et . . . Hieronymus/dicente
divo Hieronymo *t* f   *a* desudamus: Item   essent/ederent *t* I   *a*
viveret: Auctor Macrobius in 2 *Saturnalium t* F   invitamentorum/
irritamentorum *t* b

12. Brumdusii V

13. in Italia *omt* f   quidem V   per . . . causa/ferebat animus *t* F   At
. . . ornarit *omt* f   cervorum et damarum *om* BbI

14. demonstrare/docere *t* b   Romanorum *t* b

CHAPTER VI

Title. primum *t* b   et saponem *omt* I   variarum *omt* j   ac pellium *omt*
I   sutoriam/ sutrinam *t* B   *a* artem: aut *t* F   et quando . . . coeperit
omt I   ac bombycinam/atque bombycinam V   atque purpuram *om* V
et quid . . . fuerit *omt* I

1. ad/in *t* F   perinde quasi/tamquam si *t* F   voretur fBbIijA   satis
esset/sufficeret *t* F

2. aranea **VF,** araneus **fBb**   avibusve *t* **F**   At titulos **ijA**

3. qui . . . libro 8 *omt* **I**   Nitias **VFI**   quam . . . ex his *omt* **I**

4. primos/primitus *t* **b**   docuisset **V**   tribuerem **VF**

5. Illud . . . maleficio *omt* **f**   quasi/obiter **Bb**   praeteriens *om* **Bb**
sancitum fuisse/ exceptum erat **Bb**

6. fecit/scripsit *t* **f**   Sutoriae . . . tuis *omt* **I**

7. ut ait *om* **V**   scribit/docet *t* **b**   *a* scribit: refert quod **V**   Seculi
FfB, Siculi *r*   creatus/factus teste Divo Hieronymo *t* **F**

8. *c* Praeterea: Sutrinam [Sutoriam **bI**] artem (ut testis est Plinius)
Boetius omnium primus invenit, *a* quoniam: de *t* **I**   Latus . . . quo/vi-
delicet quemadmodum teste Strabone libro 3 *Geographiae* laticlavum
primitus repertum *t* **F**/Laticlavum primitus repertum **fBbI**   et *om* **fBbI**
a latis . . . dicta *omt* **I**   Aurum intexere *t* **F**   modum *omt* **F**   attalicis
vestibus nomen est Et acu **V,** attalicis vestibus nomen Et acu **F**
vestes. . . . phrygianae *omt* **F**

9. Et apud *t* **F**   ita . . . multo sunt[14] *om* **V**   ita . . . induebantur *om*
FfBbI   Unde Martialis **F**   Undulatam . . . multo sunt[14] *om* **FfBbI**

10. frigidior *om* **ij**

11. Togam . . . genera *om* **ij**

15. longum . . . facimus/quum plurima sint vestimentorum genera,
quippe quorum nullus est modus, alii enim alia indies [singulos **fBbI**]
reperiunt atque usurpant, adeoque magna luxuriae vis irrepsit ut in his
[iis **BbI**] vana imprimis opum ostentatio appareat, suspendeo huiusmodi
(ut ita dixerim) deliramentorum haud gravate auctores requirere *t* **I**
petitus *t* **F**

16. in Coo **Ff**   hymbribus **V**   cogi/gigni *t* **f**   trahit **V**   sericeis *t* **f**
in Coo **Ff**   auctores *t* **b**

17. At . . . ignotum[21] *om* **V**   At . . . habet[18] *om* **FfBbI**

18. urbe/civitate **ij**   oppido/civitate **ij**

19. est apud/refertur **FfBb**   Tyro **FfBbI**   quem sequebatur/
sequebaturque eum **FfBbIij**   ut Syrii **fBbIijA**

20. Sunt . . . ignotum[21] *om* FfBbI

Chapter VII

1. *a* speluncis: et nemoribus *t* j   postea/mox *t* f   *a* tractare: incoeptantes *t* f   utpote qui *t* b   ex luto/de luto *t* F   usu . . . ut *om* V ad quidvis/ubi *t* b   deinde/subinde *t* f   aedificiorum effectus parietes *t* F   *a* texere: aut   coeperunt V

2. At etiam/Necnon *t* F   posuerat/fecerat t f   Imo . . . visuntur/ Hodie quoque in plerisque Italiae locis talia fiunt praesertim (ut ipsi conspeximus) in Gallia Cisalpina V   visuntur/ fiunt Ff   etiam/adhuc F   nec . . . nuncupantur *om* V   nunc *om* F

3. Atque/Et V   *a* ego: audacter ac libero (ut dicitur) pectore *t* f Adae *t* B   primitus *t* b   oppidum/civitatem V

Chapter VIII

Title. primum *t* b   *a* aedificaverint: vel earum structuras *t* B

1. *a* luteas: ut Gelio placet V   Doxius Gellii fBbIijA   furialos et V filiam primum j   Phoenicia fBbIijA

2. *a* opinor: primitus *t* f   assignarem, ille/hic *t* F   oppidum/civitatem, quo/qua *t* B   infra/mox *t* f   planiorem *omt* j   Isti/Illi, ut *t* F monstravimus *t* b   scriberent *t* b   atque laterum *omt* f   aliave *t* F usus V   uspiam deinceps/alicubi praecedente tempore *t* F

3. sexcentas/mille *t* F   trecenta F   non . . . duraturi/temporarii *t* b *a* Lepidus: Catulli in consulatu collega *t* F   DCLXXVI/sexcentesimo sexagesimo sexto *t* B   *a* inciperet: haec ex Plinio *t* F

Chapter IX

Title. Qui primitus *t* b   posuerit/fecerit *t* F

1. inde/mox *t* b   vocitati *t* I, urbs quam colit *omt* I   id . . . foret *omt* I curvatam i, curvata j

2. Argos erant F   id est/hoc est *t* f

3. *a* Phoenices: auctor Plinius in vii **V**   *a* Bucolicis: dicens *t* **I**   postea
inventa/prope fabulosa *t* **F**   Adae *t* **B**   palam est/in confesso est *t* **b**
urbem/ civitatem *t* **B**   Nembroth *t* **f**   primitus *t* **b**

4. urbes/civitates *t* **b**   postmodum *t* **b**   fecit/finxit *t* **b**

5. Prienne *t* **B**   Romae . . . fuit *omt* **B**

6. Salomon *t* **F**   *a* Hebraeorum: annis *t* **F**   Adae *t* **B**   post annis *omt*
F   Hierosolymae *t* **b**   struere *t* **F**   Natham **V**   propterea quod/
propter eius *t* **F**   haberet *om*, revocavit/amovit *t* **F**   iussit/mandavit *t* **f**
Salomoni *t* **F**   *a* tum: magis *t* **F**

7. In sacris *t* **F**

8. fodit/invenit *t* **b**   ut/ne, veluti/ut *t* **I**   primo . . . alios *omt* **I**   de
om, Aegyptum *t* **F**   solitudines/desertum *t* **b**

9. aiunt/fabulati sunt *t* **I**   Θεοì . . . ἄννδρον *omt* **B**   *a* oppidum: Ut
Homerus errorem creaverit illo versu { . . . }. Verbo enim illo { . . . }
non siticulosam Argolidem sed desiderabilem significari voluit **V**
fecerunt/invenerunt *t* **b**   Ἄργος . . . ἔννδρον *omt* **B**

CHAPTER X

Title. a autoribus: et quae esset eas construendi causa *t* **f**
consecrandorumque . . . mortem *om* **V**

1. digradiamur **V**   portentissimum *t* **F**   *a* Quatuor: hi *t* **F**
memorantur *t* **b**   principis *omt* **F**   *a* sentit: Sed Myridim non
Meridem uti Plinius vocat ut in alterutris per mutationem litterae
menda sit **V**   vidisse/aspexisse *t* **b**

2. *a* Hinc: utique *t* **B**   Alter/Secundus *t* **F**   morere **F**   regeret *t* **F**
lumina *e*/ limina *t* **A**

3. de quo Varrone *t* **f**

4. unam/primam *t* **F**   dicit/docet *t* **b**   ut *omt* **F**   ea sepeliretur/
sepulturam *t* **F**   nisi/quam **fBbI**   quando . . . sepulchra *omt* **F**
obtinuit/cepit *t* **F**   sed Chebrenem *t* **B**

5. alteram/secundam *t* **F**   Is/Hic *t* **F**

6. in Rhodopodis *t* F, Rhodopi fBb   *a* meretriculae: sepulturam,
positam/factam *t* F   Cum ea aliquando/Quod ea dum V   *a* dimisit:
Et quod V, Et F   mortuae inde/defunctae mox *t* I   Rhodopis *t* F
fecissent/reliquerunt *t* F

7. Isti/Huiusmodi *t* F   commemoravimus/rettulimus, *a* traduntur:
quod ego tamen pro certo affirmare non ausim, etsi/quando *t* F   in 36
V/in 26 *r*   *a* historiae: scriptores gravissimi *t* F

8. Quare/Unde *t* F   relinquerent vel *omt* b

9. Mortuorum/Defunctorum *t* I   *a* tempus: vocabant *t* F   *a*
contemnebant: circa, magnificentiam *t* f   iis/his, condiderunt *t* F

10. *a* uxor: sibi V   struxit *t* F   adnumeratum/computatum V
dicente Martiale *t* f   Mauseolea V   meminerunt *t* b

11. Derbices *t* F   moriebantur *t* F   ut a se potius quam a vermibus
comederentur, dilexerant *t* I

12. contusis reficiebant *t* b   inde/mox *t* f   fecerant *t* b   illinentes *t* F
a qua: mox *t* f   diutius *t* b

13. Aethiopes *om, a* longaevi: Indorum populi *t* B   demortuis/
defunctis *t* I   circuntulerant *t* I   atque/et *t* f   pallacam V, pallacum
FfBb, pellicum *r*   miscebat *t* b   praefuisset/erat a *t* F, praerat fBb

14. mortuos suos/defunctos *t* I   praedicantes/referentes *t* I   in qua
omt f   tot/quot *t* f, quod BbI   *a* liberati: in omni *t* I   ploratu/
comploratione *t* I   exponentes/ recensentes *t* f   essent/erant *t* I
oblivebant B   non secus *om,* atque/sicut *t* F   *a* Caspii: pariter *t* F

15. Bactri *t* F

16. Essedonum *t* B   congregatis/corrogatis *t* F   comedere ac/dapes
facere et *t* F   immolantes/agentes, multis cum *om,* cerimoniasque *t* f
praecipitem *t* F   sese/casum, *a* profundum: destinarent haec ex
Herodoto Diodoro Strabone Trogo Plinio Divo Hieronymo Eusebio
Solino et Valerio Maximo *t* F

17. ne *t* F, ut *r,* suum/eius *t* F   eruit *t* F   cremandi cadavera *t* b
increbruit V

18. Illud . . . imposuerunt *omt* I   scribens/inquiens *t* I   Sed . . . diversa¹⁹ *om* V

19. consecrandi F   mortem/diem F   ad exemplum/in formam F ingenti **FfB**   patrio/de F   nominibus F   meminit/refert **FfBb**

20. interiisset/obiisset *t* F   libro 17/libro 16 *t* f   ante, fuerit/exititit *t* F extiterit f   *a* quibus: circa corpus *t* F   habere **b**   demortuos/ defunctos *t* I

21. Servamus . . . nostrarum *omt* f

Chapter xi

Title. primum *t* **b**

1. superiori *t* F   inde/mox *t* I

2. eadem/supradicta V   Sothis *t* F   menda sit *t* I

3. *a* hanc: videlicet *t* f   fuisse/extitisse *t* F   tentasset ac/expertus quum V   *a* eam: in V   egregia . . . memoriae/memoratu digna *t* j

4. quapropter/unde *t* F   portavit *t* I   Senneserteo **B**   qui . . . stat *om*, dicente Plinio *t* f

5. testimonio/auctoritate *t* f   *a* Herodoti: nisi codex mendosus est *t* B Ex quo/Unde *t* F   extra/citra *t* I   qui ut/quare ut obiter Plinius *t* F, et ut obiter **fBb**   *a* videantur: praeterea, cum/quoniam *t* F fecit *t* f   portavit *t* F

6. utique/alioqui *t* **b**   praesentim V   *a* Strabo: in   libro 17 *t* F, libro 7 *r*

7. tacitum relinquendum/silentio praetereundum *t* **b**   monstrabant *t* F *Historiarum* 14 *t* F, *Historiarum* 13 *r*   libri plenissime edocet *t* **b**

Chapter xii

Title. et . . . utamur *omt* I

1. in/super *t* f   afflixerat *t* F   Cuius/De quo *t* F

2. primitus *t* I   15 ante Herculem/maior natu Hercule, Is/Hic *t* F iis/his *t* F   urbibus/civitatibus *t* B   dum/postquam *t* F   Hebraeum

populum/ Israhelitas V, Israelitas F   reduxerat V   illis/his, profugium
t F   commisissent/perpetrassent *t* b

3. Servivis V   aperuit/posuit V   Ovidius/dicente Ovidio *t* f

4. procul a Troezene civitate in *t* F   Nili hostium, *a* consecratum:
extitit *t* F   inquiens Erat *t* I   libro 16 *t* B, libro 17 *r*   Osiridis *t* F

5. Sunt . . . moriatur om V   bene, a *om* F   abstineant/temperent F
manus . . . moriatur *om* F   Quid . . . moriatur *om* f

CHAPTER XIII

Title. et . . . modo *omt* f   ac circum *omt* B   a construxerint: et de
utriusque forma, spargebatur *t* B   et inibi . . . origine *om* V

1. θεώμαι *t* j   urbanum *t* I, urbem *r*

2. *a* similiter: quod, fuisse/forent V   ostendit/docet *t* b   Sane/Unde,
Antirrodo *t* F

3. umbrationis *t* b   ludi . . . scena⁴ *omt* B   alia, placamina bI

4. inde/mox b   ludio bI   recitabant poemata *t* b   qui vel . . .
reprehenderetur⁵ *omt* f

5. cum inquit/inquiens BbI

6. instar/in modum V   suggestum/pulpitum   gestus/testus F
ορχησαι V, ὀρχῆσαι F   salto *t* F   vera F   In circumferentia *t* b

7. *a* linteis: in *t* F

8. duraturum, in *om* V   diebus, *a* ludorum: duraturum V   ad tem-
pus/temporaria *t* b

9. *a* duo: temporaria *t* b   *a* edebat: Haec ex Plinio *t* F   exempla A,
exemplar *r*   Mitylene *t* B, Mitylenae *r*

10. de/in *t* F

11. Hierosolymae fBb   capitis *t* F   dicens/inquiens *t* I   *c* Seneca:
Unde *t* F

12. commodum moneamus/transeunter doceam *t* F   rursus *om* V
a quidam: stulte quidem *t* B   commentati/augurati *t* F

13. Circo . . . profuturo¹⁵ *om* V   Circo . . . decadis 4 *om* FfB

14. magnificentiae/dignitati **FfB**   Ex quo/Unde **F**   haberent **FfBb**
postea/mox **Ff**

15. *a* Et: haec lavacra **FfBb**   extructa **FfBb**   Galienum **F**, Galenum *r*
Constantinae **FfB**   Erat . . . exercebant *om* **FfB**   extructa/erecta **F**

Chapter xiv

Title. terrebram **V**   *a* normam: fornicem *t* **B**   securim *omt* **B**

1. rectitudo *t* **b**   terrebram **V**   ferruminantur *t* **b**, coiunguntur
conglutinantur *r*   *a* autem: et fornicem et libellam *t* **B**, et libellam **bI**

2. dicit/docet *t* **b**   secundum *om* **V**   Talus *t* **F**, Talaus *r*   *a* Perdix:
nisi codex mendosus [sit **F**] est **V**   adulescente **F**

3. At . . . fertur *omt* **B**   *a* alia: quam **bI**, ac *om* **bI**   dicit/docet **b**
Panthesilea **j**, Pantesilea **bIiA**

4. in ea/in hac *t* **F**   Salomon *t* **F**   faberlignarios **V**

5. Speusippus **Vj**, Pseusippus *r*   ex/de, vimine *t* **F**   qualos *t* **b**, quallos
r   in/super *t* **f**

Chapter xv

1. suo *omt* **B**

2. primiter tentavit *t* **I**   Peti/Proeti *t* **F**   vitae es **VFfBbIj**, vitae aes *r*
leti . . . texite/laeti contexite *t* **F**

3. pro se quisque *omt* **F**   vendicare *t* **F**   ausi sunt *t* **b**

4. iampridem/prioribus annis *t* **F**   demonstrat/docet *t* **b**   A quibus
propter id/Unde ab eis *t* **F**   propter/ob **fBb**   Cretes *t* **F**
exposuimus/docuimus *t* **b**

5. Thracas *t* **F**, Thraces *r*   Alii . . . circunsutas *omt* **F**

6. alii *a* . . . *corona omt* **I**

7. perdiu ante *omt* **F**   Danaum . . . Is/et Danao et Neptuno longe
grandior natu fuit Hic *t* **F**   ad perniciem/in perniciem *t* **F**   itidiem *t* **F**
usus **V**   peterent/tenerent *t* **I**

8. vastum/fastum *t* **F**   hercle/videlicet *t* **f**   tempora Noe/Noe
dilivium *t* **b**   excreverunt **B**

9. idcirco/quippe V commemorare/recensere *t* f/referre **Bb**
instituto nostro *omt* **b** Longa *t* **F** navem . . . puto/navi Iason (ut
placet Philostephano) primus navigavit. Verum Aegesias hoc inventum
Parolo [Parrhalo **F**] attribuit Ctesias Samyrae Saphanus Semirami
Archimachus Aegaeoni At *t* **F** Diodoro/Diodorus, teste/ait quod **V**
Sesostris/Sesoosis, postea/longa navi [nave **F**] *t* **F** Sex/Sed **A**
ordinum . . . Syracusanus *om* **A** Zenazoras *t* **F** ab ea . . .
cognominatus/Et sic deinde progressae sunt usque ad L ordines *t* **F**
Philopater f

10. celocem, circerum *t* **A** lintres . . . naves *omt* **F**
a Icarus: haec ex Plinio *t* **F** Salamini *t* **F**

11. Eupalmius f ab { . . . } quod **V** *a* sumpto: ut arbitror *t* **F**
improfundo **V**

12. satis sint/sufficiant *t* **F** reperti **B**

CHAPTER XVI

Title. primum **VfBb,** Quis primum **F**

1. cum illis/secum *t* **F** Posthac/Mox *t* **b** cupido *t* **I**

2. impartiens **F** mathematicus *t* **F,** *omr*

3. id . . . arbitrabantur *omt* **b**

4. Quare/Unde *t* **F**

5. primo/primitus *t* **I**

6. fuerunt/extiterunt *t* f ut divisim deinde merces emptas vendant *t* j
libro/in primo *t* j primo . . . sentit/intellexit inquiens *t* **I**/intellexit **ij**
inquit *om* **I**

7. His . . . tenuerat *omt* j

CHAPTER XVII

Title. primum *t* **b** et . . . adulterii *omt* **I**

1. princeps/eminentissimus *t* **I** ad *om,* omnibusque prostitutam
libidinibus *t* **b** quas ob res/unde *t* **F**

2. appellant *t* **B** 19 in naves/navibus *t* **F**

3. Item . . . peccandi[9]/auctor Herodotus volumine primo. Sed quid de externis loquimur quum apud nos longe constantius accuratiusque Veneris instituta quam Dei optimi maximi praecepta serventur? Nunc enim in fertilissimo quaestu sunt adulteria. Nunc passim lupanaria patent. Nunc iuventus incestos amores (ut Flaccus ait) de tenero meditatur ungui. Nunc meretrices ditescunt utpote quae non amant sed spoliant amantes (uti urbanissimus poeta de tonstrice impudica muliere scribit). Dicit enim:

Sed ista tonstrix, Ammiane, non tondet.
Non tondet, inquam. Quid ergo facit? Radit.

Nunc ipsa Veneris ars sola viget. Nulla [Rara FfB] enim mulier [+ adeo FfB] casta est nisi quam nemo rogat [nisi . . . rogat/quin si rogetur FfB]. At nec ipsa quidem. Nam [At . . . Nam *om* FfB] (ut Ovidius docet) eius mens [+ non fiat quandoque F, fiat quandoque fB] adultera est [est *om* FfB]. Hinc divus [Ex quo fB] Hieronymus Contra Iovinianum verissime inquit: Nullam in pudicitia [impudicitia F] servari posse. Unde [Hieronymus . . . Unde *om* fB] Essaei [Esseni F] tertium [tertia fB] apud Iudaeos philosophorum genus [secta fB] viri sane prudentissimi [viri . . . prudentissimi *om* fB] auctore Iosepho in 2 *De bello iudaico* uxores non ducebant, nullam omnino mulierem uni viro fidem servare arbitrantes propter quod alienos duntaxat filios enutriebant. Cuius rei manifestissimum exemplum praebuit Phaeron Aegyptiorum rex qui vix unam castam mulierem in tota Aegypto repperit, cuius lotio lotus [lotus *om* FfB] (ut probe docuimus quum de obeliscis sermonem fecimus) visum recepit [Sermonem . . . recepit/ meminimus visum recuperandi gratia iuxta oraculum oculos lavaret FfB]. Quo fit ut qui uxorem pudicam habuerit [habet fB], id profecto [profecto *om* fB] veluti divinum munus deo acceptum referat, dicente Iuvenale Satyra VI:

Tarpeium limen adora
Pronus, et auratam Iunoni caede iuveneam,
Si tibi contigerit captis matrona pudici *t* B

5. invicem b/inter se IijA

7. mente capta **b**

8. cum adultero . . . est *om* **bI**   capite 20 ij/capite 10 **A**   morte mactandam/lapidibus caedendam **bI**   etiam *om* **bI**   multabant **bI**

10. nec . . . simulant *omt* **B**   facerent **bI**

11. fuit/extitit *t* **f**, omnibus *omt* **f**   pervulgandae/prostandae **VF**/ prostituendae **fBb**   edidit/praebuit *t* **F**   non . . . habet/sola pudica est **V**   adeo/intantum *t* **F**   internoscitur/ dignoscitur, Quapropter/Unde *t* **F**   ut/velut *t* **B**   potissime *t* **F**   sapore *t* **F**   *a* sopore: videlicet *t* **f**   recte/probe **VF**   *a* satis: ac superque **V**, ac super **F**

12. expeditis **F**   scribens/inquiens *t* **I**   capitis partem *t* **F**

CHAPTER XVIII

Title. c Multa: Quod *t* **F**, Ut **f**   esse/sunt *t* **F**/sint **f**   ignorantur *t* **F**

1. Quanquam/Quoniam *t* **F**   excogitaverint. Eo profecto huiuscemodi *t* **F**   elaboravimus . . . quae/operam enavavimus. Sed quum vetustas *t* **F**   elaboravimus **fBb**, elaboravi **IijA**   tollat, depravet *t* **F**   id . . . quod/ea propter *t* **F**   ex iis/ex his *t* **F**   scriptum *t* **I**   possent *t* **F**

2. inveneri **V**   potuit/valuit *t* **F**   usu erat **F**   loetus **V**, laetus **F**

3. ad perniciem/in perniciem *t* **F**   ut alio/ut suo *t* **F**   diximus/ docuimus *t* **b**   pugnare valerent *t* **F**

4. *a* ne: videlicet **f**   experiretur *t* **F**, cogeretur *omt* **F**   Acrigenti **V**, Agrigenti **F**   post . . . memoriam *omt* **F**   pretium/munus *t* **b**   quo *t* **j**/pro **A**

5. quod . . . stent *omt* **b**   irritamenta *t* **b**, invitamenta **I**   nihil . . . proferam/referre supersedeo *t* **F**

6. apertum/nudum *t* **f**   cum . . . utimur/cum id propalam sit quod ea fingimur effigie qua prorsum sumus *t* **F**   Is/Hic *t* **F**   propositam/ obnoxiam *t* **b**   obnubere/operire *t* **b**   nunc/modo *t* **B**   sexcenta/milia *t* **F**

7. possemus/possimus *t* **F**   id genus/quaedam **V**   eorum/horum **V**

8. Neque/sicut *t* **F**   monstravimus *t* **b**

9. eiusmodi/huiusmodi *t* F   tenuium *t* b   nuper/novissime V, novissimae F, noviter fBbIij   Nos/Quem *t* F   alibi . . . ut/suo loco ostendimus quantum per me fieri potuit *t* F   vindicare *t* F, vendicaretur ijA

10. Est . . . latet *omt* I

11. deinde/subinde *t* f   malui *t* b   a persequi: Age iam, per tot mortalium opera corporis commodum cum primis adferentia evagati, ad alia quae vitam tantum sapiunt spiritalem veniamus F   Libri III *om* V

Notes to the Translation

꽃꽃꽃

Abbreviated references to classical texts follow the formulae used for *The Oxford Classical Dictionary*, 3rd ed.(1996). When Polydore's citation of an ancient text differs in numbering from modern editions, his version is preserved in the Latin text but the modern numbering will appear in the translation within square brackets and in the source notes.

Other abbreviations are as follows:

AH   Polydore Vergil, *Anglica Historia, A.D. 1485–1537*, ed. and tr. D. Hay, Camden Series 74 (London: Royal Historical Society, 1950)

Helm   R. Helm, ed., *Eusebius Werke, Siebenter Band: Die Chronik des Hieronymus*, 'Die Griechischen Schriftsteller der ersten Jahrhunderte' (Berlin: Akademie-Verlag, 1956)

Keil   H. Keil, ed., *Grammatici latini*, 7 vols. (Leipzig: Teubner, 1857–1880)

PL   J.-P. Migne, *Patrologiae cursus completus, series latina*, 221 vols. (Paris: Migne, 1844–1891)

LETTER TO LODOVICO ODASSIO

1. Lodovico Odassio was tutor to Guidobaldo, the son of Federico da Montefeltro (DIR 2.7.7); he edited the first printed version (1489) of Nicolo Perotti's *Cornucopiae* (DIR 2.6.1), which Polydore edited again in 1496, probably taking from it the inspiration for his first two books, *Proverbiorum libellus* (1498; DIR 1.14.7) and *De inventoribus rerum*. For this letter and the two that follow, the copy-text is the first printing of each letter, not the version in the last lifetime edition (1553–5) of *De inventoribus*.

2. Pi. frg. 205. See DIR 1.1.5 on euhemerism.

3. Cic. *ND* 2.2.5; Hdt. 3.17–24. Herodotus explains that Cambyses II (*DIR* 2.18.2) mounted his expedition to Ethiopia partly in order to see the Table of the Sun, whose daily bounty of food may have been supplied by the citizens of the place or may have appeared spontaneously.

4. Cic. *ND* 2.2.5; Gel. 12.11.7.

7. Stat. *Theb.* 10.37; Gen. 3:19. The last tenth of book 7 of Pliny's *Natural History* (*DIR* 1.6.3) is a digest of lists of discoveries that accumulated from the fifth century BCE onward and eventually formed an ancient genre (heurematography) on this topic. The brief poem by Marcantonio Sabellico (1436–1508) was printed with *De inventoribus* in the Strasbourg editions of 1509 and later. See also *DIR* 1.18.3 for Zachario Giglio.

10. Hier. *Comm. Paralip.* (*PL* 29: 399). In book 3 of Vergil's poem, Aeneas tells Dido how he led his family and friends from Troy across the sea to Sicily. Aristotle tutored Alexander for about three years after he accepted Philip's invitation in 343 BCE. For Jerome, see *DIR* 1.1.9, 2.2.

11. Cic. *Arch.* 19.7. Since the basis of Polydore's comparison of Odassio to Homer was a text from Cicero's famous defence of another poet, Aulus Licinius Archias, the flattery was indeed thick, even though Cicero did not get the poem that he expected his client to write for him.

13. The first edition of *De inventoribus*, printed at Venice in 1499, gives no date for the letter to Odassio, but the date of the colophon of this edition is August 31, 1499; the correct date for the letter appears in the 1525 and later editions.

FIRST LETTER TO GIAN MATTEO VERGIL

1. Polydore wrote this letter to his brother primarily to introduce the five books added to *De inventoribus* and published in 1521, though in par. 10 he also mentions having revised the first three books. The letter was first printed in Johann Froben's 1521 edition, starting a series by Basel publishers that Polydore continued to revise (see par. 10) until 1553, two years before his death. In the 1521 edition, the letter appears at the front of the book, before the letter to Odassio, but in 1525 a shorter version (see below) appears between books 3 and 4.

2. Verg. *A* 1.94, 4.589, 12.155, *G* 2.399. See the letter to Odassio, par. 1.

3. Polydore's claim to have finished *De inventoribus* so quickly is more plausible in light of his earlier work on the 1496 revision of Perotti's *Cornucopiae* (*DIR* 2.6.1), which contains a great deal of material on inventions as well as proverbs, a feature particularly visible in the 1513 Aldine edition of Perotti's huge commentary on Martial, where one sub-index lists 115 *inventores* and another 58 *proverbia*. Polydore's assertion of priority on both topics became sensitive in the year he wrote this letter, when signs appeared of a dispute with Erasmus over proverbs or adages. Erasmus had published the first edition of his famous *Adagia* in 1500, never admitting (no doubt sincerely) that Polydore's *Proverbiorum libellus* had come out two years earlier. A lesser humanist, Lodovico Gorgerio, also complained that Polydore plagiarized him on proverbs. By 1521 the controversy peaked, with Erasmus maintaining that only his intervention persuaded Froben to publish Polydore's revision, the *Adagiorum liber* of that year, printed with the expanded *De inventoribus*, where the original letter to Gian Matteo Vergil first appears.

4. Polydore moved to England in 1502 as sub-collector of the papal tax called Peter's Pence. He began the *Anglica historia* around 1506 but published it only in 1534, enlarging and revising it for new editions of 1546 and 1555.

6. Cic. *Hort.* frg. 113 in Aug. *De trin.* 19.26. Cicero's lost *Hortensius* was the exhortation to philosophy that stimulated Augustine (*Conf.* 3.4.7) to turn away from his youthful life of dissipation.

7. This paragraph alone explains why Polydore decided to suppress this letter by shortening it, moving it and completely changing its content in the Basel editions of 1525 and later. Written in 1517, first printed in 1521 and drastically altered in 1525, this evolving letter reflects the religious turmoil in Polydore's Europe.

10. Polydore's description of his revisions of *De inventoribus* is accurate: almost all are meant either to add new material or to make small corrections; for a conspicuous exception, see *DIR* 3.17.3. Although a note before the colophon of the first edition complains emphatically about a printer's error that threw off the numbering of the last few chapters of book 1, the

next eleven editions repeat the mistake, first corrected in the 1521 expansion published by Froben. Thus, when Polydore says here that he 'reviewed the earlier edition,' he seems to have meant the text as he left it in 1499. The absence of significant variants in editions before 1521, as compared to many substantive changes through seven Basel editions after 1521 but before Polydore died in 1555, also suggests that Polydore left the book alone between 1499 and 1521, when his research was focused mainly on the *Anglica historia*. Then, sometime before 1517, his decision to add five books to *De inventoribus* created the occasion to revise the first three, a procedure also followed with the *Proverbs* and the *English History*. Although many early printed books carry misleading publisher's blurbs advertising authorial correction, it is worth noting that the Basel editions of 1525, 1532 and 1536 claim explicitly to be the second, third and fourth revisions by Polydore. The remaining lifetime editions with significant variants (1540, 1545, 1550, 1553–5) were also printed in Basel. For internal evidence of Polydore's involvement with later editions, see *DIR* 2.17.11, 3.16.5.

11. For the meaning of *lustrum*, see *DIR* 2.3.14.

SECOND LETTER TO GIAN MATTEO VERGIL

1. Matt. 5:17, Isa. 1:11–12. Although this letter carries the same date as the longer letter from Polydore to his brother, this shorter revision was written not in 1517 but after 1521, the year when the longer and original version was printed to introduce the last five books of the expanded *De inventoribus*. In 1525 and later Basel editions revised by Polydore, the shorter letter replaces the longer, whose inclusion in the 1528 edition of Stephanus indicates that Polydore did not authorize this Paris printing. Religious events after 1517 clearly made Polydore nervous about the last five books of *DIR*, which, in broad terms, historicize the development of Christian institutions. The risk created by comments like those in par. 7 of the longer letter was later realized in the Church's condemnation and expurgation of *De inventoribus* (*DIR* 1.17.1, 5; 3.12.5). Harder to explain than shortening the letter — given Polydore's insistence in the first three books on Jewish priority in discovery — is its attack on Jews for legalism and ritualism, a defensive Christian reflex stimulated, no doubt, by the

hazardous content of the last five books. The shorter letter reverses the stance of books 1–3, which is anti-pagan and pro-Jewish.

ON POLYDORE

The main achievements of the Swiss humanist and Hellenist Simon Grynaeus (1493–1541) were to discover the remains of the fifth decade of Livy in 1527 (*DIR* 1.6.9) and to produce the second edition of Plato in Greek in 1534. A friend of Budé, Erasmus and More, Grynaeus was also connected with the reformers Bucer, Oecolampadius and Zwingli. When he came to England in 1531 to hunt for manuscripts, Henry VIII consulted him on his marital problems. This poem first appeared with *De inventoribus* in the Basel edition of 1540. Thespiae was a town in Boeotia near Mt. Helicon, sacred to the Muses; Thespius, its founder, had fifty daughters, the Thespiades, whom he gave to Heracles, who swiftly fathered fifty sons by them. For the name Polydore, see *DIR* 2.20.1; Grynaeus alludes here to its etymology, 'much-giver.' Like his namesake, the hero described by Vergil (*A* 3.12–68) was sent abroad by a mighty ruler to carry gold (first letter to Gian Matteo Vergil, par. 4).

BOOK I

CHAPTER I

1. John 12:31, 14:30, 16:11; 2 Cor. 2:8; Eph. 3:10; Lact. *Inst.* 2.15; Eus. *PE* 4.5.1–4, 6.2–4, 8.4, 10.2–6, 23.2–4; 5.2.-3.1   2 Cor. 11:14   Matt. 14:22–33; Lact. *Inst.* 2.15. Eusebius of Caesarea (260–339 CE) in Palestine was an apologist, church historian, biblical scholar and ecclesiastical states-man. The *Ecclesiastical History* is his most influential work, but the *Chronicle* and the *Preparation for the Gospel* were more important for Polydore. His views on the primacy of the ancient Hebrews in discovery owe a great deal to the case made in these works for the antiquity of Jewish religion and its consequent superiority over Greek belief, of Moses over Plato. Polydore used the notoriously loose translation of the *Preparation* made by George of Trebizond in 1448 (ed. prin. 1470). On the *Chronicle*, see the Note on Chronology.

2. Lact. *Inst.* 2.15; Matt. 18: 10   Hier. *Comm. in Matt.* 3, ad 18:10 (PL 26:130)   Lact. *Inst.* 2.15   DIR 1.1.4, 5.8   Plin. *Nat.* 2.16. The *genius*, which may have referred originally to a birthday spirit like the *idios daimōn*, was the double of the male person, but especially of the *paterfamilias*, as the *iuno* was of the female, and the concept extended to places and buildings. Polydore refers here to the five books added in 1521 to *De inventoribus*.

3. Lact. *Inst.* pr., 1.5; Cic. ND 1.25–27, 32, 34, 36–37, 39; Verg. G 2.325–327; Diog. L. 1.27; 2.3, 6–8; 7.135–9; 9.51–2; 10.139; Eus. PE 1.8.1, 3; 7.12.1; 14.14.1, 3, 8–15.1, 16.6. Polydore uses two dozen Ciceronian texts, mainly the philosophical works written near the end of his life — *De natura deorum, De divinatione, Disputationes Tusculanae, De officiis* — but also the earlier *De oratore* and *De legibus*. But he often cites Cicero on religion by way of Lactantius (250–325 CE), whose literary talent earned him praise as 'the Christian Cicero.' The most important of his derivative works is the *Divine Institutes* (ed. prin. 1467) which defends Christian revelation by exposing the emptiness of pagan polytheism and philosophy. Polydore also cites two shorter works, *On God's Anger* and *On God's Workmanship*. Diogenes Laertius probably wrote his unreliable but very influential account of the lives and teachings of the Greek philosophers early in the third century CE. Polydore used the translation completed by Ambrogio Traversari in 1433 (ed. prin. c. 1472). Cleanthes of Assos, who headed the Stoic school in the middle of the third century BCE and wrote a book on Heraclitus, should not be grouped with Thales, Pythagoras and other pre-Socratic philosophers named in this passage. Ancient writers made Antisthenes the Athenian (445–360) head of the Cynic school; it is likelier that this follower of Socrates taught monotheism than the doctrine of creation that Lactantius also attributed to him. According to Cicero, Zeno of Citium (335–263), first head of the Stoa, taught that 'the law of nature is divine,' but Lactantius made the stronger claim that God is natural and divine law. Chrysippus of Soli, who (280–207) followed Cleanthes, made reason (*logos*) and fate (*heimarmenē*) prominent in his theology, but Cicero's Epicurean spokesperson criticizes him for an extravagant polytheism. Xenocrates of Chalcedon (396–314), who headed the Academy in the second half of the third century, produced a system-

atic theology that anticipated Neoplatonism. Cicero says that his eight gods were the five visible planets, the sphere of the fixed stars, the sun and the moon — the familiar ogdoad.

4. Lact. *De ira dei* 4, 9; Cic. *ND* 1.2, 29, 45, 63, 117   Lucr. 1.49   Verg. *Ecl.* 8.35   Cic. *ND* 1.121, 124; Lact. *De ira dei* 8. Atheism in the strict sense was rare in antiquity, but the term also applied to people who believed in the wrong (e.g., alien) gods or to those who criticized the gods or simply to one's enemies. Protagoras of Abdera (490–20 BCE) may have been only technically an agnostic in that he found the existence of the gods philosophically problematic, so the story of his having been banished for his beliefs may be compatible with Plato's account of his excellent reputation (*Men.* 91E). The alleged atheism of the lyric poet, Diagoras of Melos, who flourished in the late fifth century, rests on thinner evidence. The mathematician Theodorus of Cyrene (460–380) was a pupil of Protagoras, but the notorious atheist of the same name lived after 340. He was a pupil of Aristippus, founder of the Cyrenaic school of skeptical hedonism, and a teacher of Euhemerus. Epicurus (341–270) learned the atomism of Democritus, who probably died around 370, from Nausiphanes of Teos around 324. The Epicurean ideal of impassivity (*ataraxia*) required the gods to be indifferent to human affairs. The didactic Epicurean poem by Titus Lucretius Carus (94–55), *De rerum natura* (ed. prin. c. 1471), was little read after the ninth century CE until Poggio Bracciolini found a manuscript in 1417.

5. Cic. *ND* 1.25   Diod. S. 1.11.1; *DIR* 1.3.2; cf. Eus. *PE* 3.2.6; Hdt. 2.50–1 Lact. *Inst.* 1.13–14. The citation from Cicero is one of several texts that depict Anaximander of Miletus (d. 547 BCE) as believing in *apeiroi kosmoi* or innumerable worlds. In the first century, Diodorus Siculus wrote a world history in forty books, of which only fifteen survive intact. Polydore uses the translation done (badly) by Poggio by 1449, then revised by Pier Candido Decembrio (ed. prin. 1472). Diodorus traced the origins of religion to the awesome sight of the sun and moon, adding that the name of the solar Osiris meant 'many-eyed' while the lunar Isis meant 'old,' both of which could have been Egyptian etymologies. Lactantius also provides much information on pagan philosophy and religion, drawing on the *Euhemerus* or *Sacra historia* of Quintus Ennius (239–

169 BCE), who in turn had used the *Hiera anagraphē* of Euhemerus of Messene (340–280), a philosophical travel novel which claims that the gods are actually mortal rulers deified by grateful subjects. Here Lactantius cites Ennius for the union of Saturn and Ops which produced Jupiter, Juno, Neptune, Pluto and Glauca. According to Hesiod, however, there were six children of Kronos (Saturn) and Rhea (Ops): Zeus, Hera, Poseidon, Hades, Demeter and Hestia. Hestia normally corresponds to the Latin Vesta, but according to Ennius she is a sister of Ops, not a daughter. Glauca was the twin of Pluto and died young, according to Ennius, who does not mention Ceres (Demeter) in his genealogy. Cicero (*ND* 3.58) says that Glauce and Upis were the mother and father of the third Diana, but Oupis appears elsewhere as one of Diana's names, hence designating a female figure. The name Glauce is very common.

6. Cic. *ND* 1.38; Lact. *Inst.* 1.15; Str. 10.3.11, 12; 11.8.6, 14.16; 14.2.5; 15.3.13; Hdt. 1.60, 216; Diod. S. 1.28.1; Isid. *Orig.* 8.11.23; Hom. *Od.* 1.19–26 Plin. *Nat.* 2.16; Eus. *PE* 2.1.33–50. The Stoic Persaeus of Citium was active in the third century BCE. From the Sophist Prodicus of Ceos he learned that humans first worshipped food and other physical objects from which they derived benefit, later shifting their worship to those who discovered such things, as when Dionysus found the vine and Demeter grain. In the opening scene of the *Odyssey*, Poseidon has gone off to enjoy the sacrifices of the distant Ethiopians. Kings named Juba ruled in Numidia and Mauretania in the first century BCE. Juba II died around 23 CE. The 1497 Lactantius has *Macedones Gabyrum*, which is a corruption of *Cabirus* from *Kabeiroi* (Semitic *kabir*, lord), a group of fertility gods worshipped in the northern Aegean and western Asia. MSS of Lactantius read *Delos, Delphi* and *Delphos*, of which Delos is best because Apollo was native there but not in Delphi, but the 1497 text has *Delphos*. The Massagetes were a Scythian people located southeast of the Aral Sea. Berecynthia was part of Caria in southwest Asia Minor, and Strabo associates Rhea there with the Phrygian worship of Cybele. The cult of Anahita or Anaitis, originally a Persian fertility goddess, spread throughout southwest Asia, and in Greek religion she was associated with Artemis, Aphrodite and Athena. Diodorus says that Belus (Ba'al) was an

Egyptian who colonized Babylon and introduced religion there. Guarino Guarini began to translate the first ten (European) books of Strabo's *Geography*, a work of early imperial times, by 1453, and by 1458 he had gone on to finish all seventeen, showing no awareness of Gregorio Tifernate's version of the last seven on Africa and Asia. The version that Polydore follows (ed. prin. 1469) uses Guarino for books 1–10, Gregorio for books 11–17.

7. Hdt. 1.131. Polydore used the translation of Herodotus by Lorenzo Valla (ed. prin. 1474), begun in 1448 but left without its final touches when Valla died in 1457.

8. Cic. *ND* 1.60   Hier. *Adv. Helvid.* 5; *Adv. Jov.* 1.36 (*PL* 23:188C, 260A). The lyric poet Simonides of Ceos (556–468 BCE) visited Hieron I of Syracuse around 476. Since the helmet of an *andabata* was completely closed, a gladiator of this type fought blind.

9. Macr. *Comm.* 1.6.8; Isa. 43:10–11   Cic. *Tusc.* 1.23.54; Gen. 1:1   Hier. *Ep.* 15.4 (*PL* 22:356)   Verg. *A* 6.724–727   Ov. *Met.* 1.79. Cicero's *De re publica* in six books survives only in fragments, many of them undiscovered until the nineteenth century, but the conclusion of book six, the *Dream of Scipio*, was known to the middle ages because it had been preserved with the Neoplatonic commentary of Macrobius Ambrosius Theodosius, who wrote around the year 400 CE. Polydore also cites his *Saturnalia*, some of whose books are likewise fragmentary. It is a learned miscellany in dialogue-form on questions of time-keeping, costume, religion, law, humor and other topics, but most of all on the poet Vergil. Macrobius' works were first printed in 1472. Pope Damasus I (366–84) encouraged Jerome's career after 382, especially his revision of the Old Latin Bible.

Because ancient authors located most discoveries in early times and ascribed them to mythical persons, Ovid's poetry (43 BCE-17 CE) was of great value to Polydore—most of all the *Metamorphoses*, both for cosmogonical material and for unforgettable tales of mythic heroes and heroines. Among other poems by Ovid (ed. prin. 1471), Polydore most often cites the *Fasti*, which follows the months of the Roman religious calendar. He also uses the *Ars amatoria* and *Amores*, as well as the *Epistulae heroidum* or *Heroides*, the *Ibis* and the *Tristia*. Instructed by the Sibyl of Cumae,

Aeneas goes down to the underworld where he finds his father Anchises among the blessed and learns the cyclical movement of souls, beginning with the primal life-force that pervades the whole universe.

10. Lact. *Inst.* 1.5   Tortelli *Orth.* sig. i7v; Perotti *Corn.* fol.VIr   Ambros. *De fide* 1.1.7. The reference to Plato comes from Lactantius; cf. *DIR* 1.2.4 for a citation of Plato from Eusebius. Like these, most of Polydore's thirteen references to Plato are indirect. Ambrose (339–97 CE), Bishop of Milan, was one of the most learned of the Latin fathers. His *Five Books to the Emperor Gratian on Faith* (ed. prin. 1492), completed in 380, defend the Nicene dogma on Christ and the Holy Spirit against the Arians. Ninety-one letters (ed. prin. 1491) survive, seven addressed to an Irenaeus who was not Irenaeus of Lyon.

CHAPTER II

1. *DIR* 1.1.3.

2. Lact. *Inst.* 1.5; Cic. *ND* 1.25; Eus. *PE* 1.8.1, 14.14.1; *DIR* I.1.42–45   Eus. *PE* 14.14.4; Cic. *ND* 3.35; cf. *Fin.* 2.5.15; Hier. *Adv. Jov.* 1.1 (*PL* 23:211B-12A); Diog. L. 9.7–8   Serv. *Ecl.* 6.31; Eus. *PE* 1.8.10, 14.14.6; Lact. *Inst.* 2.13; Diog. L. 8.76   Lucr. 1.715   Eus. *PE* 1.8.11, 7.12.1, 14.14.3, 5; 15.33.5; Lact. *Inst.* 1.5; Cic. *ND* 1.113, 120; Serv. *Ecl.* 6.31; Lucr. 1.329–345, 2.112–141; Diog. L. 10.39–41   Verg. *Ecl.* 6.31–34. The main point of Jerome's polemic against Jovinian was the latter's denial that celibacy was preferable to virginity, but Jerome (347–420 CE) also assembled historical and ethnographic detail of interest to Polydore. Because the Pythagorean Hippasus of Metapontum (fifth century BCE) chose fire as a cosmological principle, he was confused with the enigmatic Heraclitus of Ephesus (fl. 500). Empedocles of Acragas (495–35) responded to Eleatic monism with a plurality of principles, the four divine roots or elements. Metrodorus of Chios (fourth century), a pupil of Democritus, was atomist in his matter-theory but thought of the whole universe as changeless in the Eleatic manner. In Vergil's sixth *Eclogue*, two shepherds force Silenus to sing about the origin of the world and its creatures; his cosmology has Lucretian ingredients.

3. Gen. 1–2:3; Jos. *AJ* 1.27–33   John 1:3   Lact. *Inst.* 2.9; *De ira dei* 11
Hier. *Dial. c. Pelag.* 1.1 (*PL* 23:499a)   Eus. *PE* 11. 29; Lact. *De ira dei* 11; cf.
Pl. *Ti.* 29E-47, 68E-69C. According to tradition, the author of the Pen-
tateuch was Moses. Modelled on the *Roman Antiquities* of Dionysius of
Halicarnassus, the *Jewish Antiquities* of Flavius Josephus (b. 37 CE) is an
apologetic history of the Jews in twenty books, beginning with the Biblical creation and ending with the start of the war whose story Josephus
told in *The Jewish War*. *Against Apion* defends the antiquity of Jewish culture against the pretensions of Greek critics. A Latin translation of all
three works (ed. prin. 1470) is usually attributed to Rufinus of Aquileia
(345–410). The citation of Plato is from Eusebius.

CHAPTER III

1. Diod. S. 1.6.3   Censor. *DN* 4.3–4. Pythagoreans, including Archytas
of Tarentum (fl. 400–350 BCE), taught that the world is eternal once it
came to be. Xenophanes of Colophon (sixth century), not Xenocrates of
Chalcedon, may have been the first to link Aristotle with a theory of cy-
clic disaster and recovery. The grammarian Censorinus wrote *De die natali*
(ed. prin. before 1497), a work on the divisions of time and the beginnings of humanity, in the early third century CE. Although Polydore mentions Aristotle fourteen times in the first three books of *De
inventoribus*, all citations but one (*DIR* 3.6.16) are indirect.

2. Diod. S. 1.6.3, 10.1–2.

3. Hdt. 2.2   Just. *Epit.* 2.1.5–21. Psammetichus was the name of three
kings of Egypt's XXVIth dynasty (672–525 BCE). Herodotus has in
mind the founder (664–10) and was probably right about *bekos* as the
Phrygian word for 'bread.' He traveled widely in the Black Sea region, so
that much of his description of Scythia was based on his own observation. Scythians, Ethiopians and other real or imagined peoples were
vilified or idealized by classical authors as exotic examples of primitive
life. Pompeius Trogus, working in the Augustan period, wrote *Historiae
Philippicae* in forty-four books which covered Near Eastern history from
legendary Babylon until 20 BCE. Marcus Junianus Justinus, perhaps in
the third century CE, epitomized (*ed. prin.* 1470) the lost history of

Trogus. Contrary to Justinus, Herodotus reports that the Scythians saw themselves as the most recent of all peoples.

4. Diod. S. 3.2.1. See the 1481 edition of the Poggio-Decembrio translation and *DIR* 1.1.5.

5. Censor. *DN* 4.6–10   Verg. *G* 1.61–63. Hesiod gives Prometheus a leading role in the beginnings of human culture, not in the origin of humankind itself, but Censorinus and other later authors credit the Titan with shaping humans out of mud. Moreover, he and his brother Epimetheus were the ancestors of humanity by way of their children, Deucalion and Pyrrha, who in Ovid and other later authors regenerate the human race after Zeus destroys it in a flood. They survive in an ark that Prometheus tells them to build; Hermes then directs them to throw stones over their heads so that the new generations will spring from them. Eusebius puts Deucalion's flood in year 491 of Abraham (1528 BCE), 451 years after Noah's flood; see the Note on Chronology.

6. Verg. *A* 1.65   Jos. *AJ* 1.34; Gen. 2:1–7   Ov. *Met.* 1.78–79   Hier. *Ep.* 69.6; *Dial. c. Pelag* 1.1 (*PL* 22:659; 23:499C)   Lact. *Inst.* 6.12, 7.4; *Op. dei* 1   Cic. *Leg.* 1.7.22; Lact. *Inst.* 2.12.

7. Hier. *Ep.* 13.13, 22.19; *Adv. Jov.* 1.16 (*PL* 30:173C; 22:406; 23:235A); *DIR* 1.4.2   Verg. *G* 1.133–134; Diod. S. 1.8.5–9   Verg. *G* 1.145–146. Vergil's claim that the development of culture was gradual (*paulatim*) and deliberate (*meditando*) had been made by others (Hippocrates, Protagoras) since the fifth century, but its fullest expression in a Greek text is the passage cited here from the first book of Diodorus Siculus.

8. *DIR* 1.3.6; Hor. *Ars* III   Jos. *AJ* 1.113–117   *DIR* 3.9.3. At Gen. 10:8, the Septuagint has *Nebrōd* for the Hebrew *Nimrod*; the Vulgate has *Memrod*. Josephus has *Nabrōdēs . . . huiōnos . . . Chamou*, but the Latin Josephus has *Nembroth filius Cham*.

9. Cic. *De Orat.* 3.12.44–45, 14.52; *Orat.* 51.173; *Tusc.* 1.16.37. Polydore mentions the 'Questione della Lingua,' the controversy that Dante opened with his *De vulgari eloquentia* (1305). The narrower issue of the relation between the vernacular and a plebeian Latin of classical times emerged in a debate between Leonardo Bruni and Flavio Biondo in 1435. Polydore sides with Biondo against Bruni. Laelia was Cicero's mother-in-

law. Discussing correct pronunciation, Cicero claimed that women preserved the pure Roman accent because they spoke with very few people. Gnaeus Naevius wrote epic poetry and drama in the third century BCE, but the comedies written by Plautus shortly before and after 200 are the first Latin texts that survive in complete form. Both died before Laelia could have been born.

10. Cic. *Brut.* 74.258–9. Titus Pomponius Atticus (110–32 BCE) was the close friend to whom Cicero addressed his *Letters to Atticus*. Titus Quinctius Flamininus and Quintus Caecilius Metellus Baliaricus were consuls in 123.

11. Jos. *AJ* 1.120–153. In the time of Josephus, Cilicia in southeast Asia Minor was no longer a distinct province of the Roman Empire, and Cappadocia to the north was also joined with Galatia. Paphlagonia on the south central coast of the Black Sea was part of the province of Pontus and Bithynia. The province of Lycia and Pamphylia was on the south central coast of Asia Minor. The Sabaeans lived on the southwest coast of Arabia.

12. Eus. *Chron.* (1483) sig. A8*v*. For the expanded version of Jerome's Latin adaptation of the *Chronicle* of Eusebius that Polydore used, see the appendix and *DIR* 1.1.1.

Chapter IV

1. Gen. 1–2; Cic. *ND* 2.61.154 Ov. *Met.* 1.76–78 Cic. *Leg.* 1.9.27, *ND* 2.60.151–162; Jos. *AJ* 1.102; Plin. *Nat.* 7.1; Lact. *Inst.* 2.1; *Op. dei* 8; cf. Ov. *Met.* 1.85–86.

2. *DIR* I. 3.7, 4.3 Jos. *AJ* 1.35–8 Hier. *Ep.* 22.19; *Adv. Jov.* 1.16 (*PL* 22:406; 23:235A). Although Jerome says that matrimony began after Adam and Eve broke God's commandments, Josephus implies that God instituted marriage before they sinned. Julia Eustochium was the daughter of Paula, one of the wealthy Roman widows for whom Jerome acted as spiritual adviser.

3. Just. *Epit.* 2.6.7. Where Polydore has *bifrons*, Justinus has *biformis*, closer to *diphuēs* (two-natured) as an epithet of Cecrops, who had a snake's lower body instead of legs; Justinus and others took this to refer

to androgyny and thus to the invention of marriage as a union of the sexes. Cecrops appears as an early member of the royal line of Athens, often linked with Erichthonius and also credited with other cultural inventions such as funerals and writing. In his *Chronicle* Eusebius made him a contemporary of Moses and thus a pivotal figure for synchronizing the regnal dates of the gentile nations with biblical chronology; see the Note on Chronology.

4. Sal. *Jug.* 80; Str. 7.3.9; 15.1.54, 62, 3.17; 17.3.19; Diod. S. 1.80.3; Solin. 30.2; Eus. *PE* 6.10.28; Hdt. 1.135, 4.172, 5.5–6; *DIR* 1.4.8   Hier. *Adv. Jov.* 2.7; *Ep.* 69.3 (*PL* 22:656–7; 23:296A); Str. 7.3.7, 9; Hdt. 4.104; Nep. *praef.* 4, *Cim.* 1.2; Pl. *R* 457D   Str. 11.8.6   Caes. *Gal.* 5.14; Eus. *PE* 6.10.28   Str. 16.4.25. The Numidians, Garamantes and Nasamones lived on the coast of North Africa. Thrace was at the north end of the Aegean. West of the mouth of the Danube lived the Scythian Agathyrsi. Parthia was east of Syria and Arabia, south of the Euphrates. The Taxili were a people of western India, east of Bactria. Strabo says that the Scyths share their wives and children 'in the Platonic manner' (*Platōnikōs*). Disagreeing with Herodotus (2.92), Diodorus claims that Egyptians were polygamous. Jerome mentions the *Attacoti*, a people of Ireland whose cannibalism he describes. Although Polydore refers to Julius Caesar frequently, he cites his works (ed. prin. 1469) only twice, here and at *DIR* 3.16.3.

5. Str. 16.4.25.

6. Str. 3.4.18, 16.1.20; Hier. *Adv. Jov.* 2.7 (*PL* 23:296A); Nep. *praef.* 4, *Cim.* 1.2; Str. 16.4.25   Hdt. 4.168, 172; cf. Mela 1.8.46. Cantabria was on the north central coast of the Iberian peninsula. Media was south and east of the Caspian, halfway to the Persian Gulf. The Magi were a priestly tribe of the Persians. *Augila* in Herodotus is a land to which the African Nasamones migrate in order to gather fruit from palm trees.

7. Hdt. 1.93   Str. 7.3.3; Jos. *AJ* 18.11, 21   Str. 11.8.6, 15.1.56; Hdt. 1.201, 203, 3.101, 4.172; Val. Max. 9.1. ext. 2. Although the notion of a right of the first night (*ius primae noctis*) appears in a thirteenth century text, Hector Boece first connected it with Malcolm III of Scotland (1058–93) in his *Scotorum historiae ab illius gentis origine* (1526), reporting that Malcolm

revoked the evil law enacted long before by a mythical King Evenus. Polydore added the story from Boece to his *English History* for the first printed edition of 1534 and to *DIR* in 1536. What the Greeks and Romans took to be outlandish sexual and marital practices — promiscuity, incest, sex in in public, various sexual positions — were favorite topics for ethnographic comment. *Ctistae* transliterates *ktistai*, founders or builders, but the word may actually correspond to a Thracian term **skistai*, meaning 'isolated' and referring to celibate hermits. Josephus writes that 'the Jews had three philosophies (*philosophiai*) right from the start of their ancestral ways, the Essenes (*Essēnōn*) and the Sadducees and the third group . . . called Pharisees.'

In editions after 1521, Polydore eliminated his reference here to eleven authors, some not previously mentioned. The influence of Sallust (86–34 BCE; ed. prin. 1470) on Renaissance historiography deepened after Valla's commentary became available. Marcus Valerius Probus (*DIR* 1.7.6) was a grammarian and textual critic of the first century CE; the name of the copyist Aemilius Probus attached itself to manuscripts of *De excellentibus ducibus exterarum gentium* (ed. prin. 1471) in the fourth or fifth century, but the true author of this work was the biographer, Cornelius Nepos (first century BCE), whose *Lives of Excellent Leaders* served as a model for Renaissance biography. The *Nine Books of Memorable Deeds and Sayings* (ed. prin. 1471 or before) was composed by Valerius Maximus, a contemporary of the emperor Tiberius. Drawn mainly from Livy and Cicero, the *Facta et dicta* is a compendium of anecdotes and aphorisms for moral edification and quick reference. Likewise, the *Collectanea rerum memorabilium* of Gaius Julius Solinus (third century CE; ed. prin. 1473) is a geographical digest that adds little to its sources, Pliny and Mela.

8. Hier. *Adv. Jov.* 1.3, 19–25; *Ep.* 22.19–21 (*PL* 22:405–9; 23:212B–14B, 237B–45A); *DIR* 1.4.4, 5.5.

9. Plu. *Comp. Thes. et Rom.* 6.3; Dion. H. 2.25.7; cf. Gel. 4.3; Val. Max. 2.1.4. Plutarch of Chaeronea (50–120 CE) wrote philosophical essays and rhetorical works in addition to the fifty *Lives* (ed. prin. 1470) that Polydore cites most frequently. Dionysius of Halicarnassus, a rhetorician and historian of the late first century BCE, wrote *Roman Antiquities* in twenty books, of which only the first ten survive intact, covering the

period down to the mid-fifth century. Lampo Birago made a Latin translation (ed. prin. 1480). Polydore's date of 231 BCE for the divorce of Spurius Carvilius Ruga agrees with Dionysius and Gellius, though Valerius Maximus gives a slightly earlier date. Moreover, the Twelve Tables recognized divorce in the fifth century, and a specific case is known from the late fourth century. The legal effect of Ruga's case was to permit divorce of a morally blameless wife but to require giving the wife her dowry. Polydore or his source confused Marcus Pomponius Matho with his father, Manlius, who was consul in 233; it is this confusion that makes 231 the second consulate of Marcus. Note the shift here and below from *repudium* in I and preceding editions to *divortium* thereafter. Polydore's explanation of the distinction in **BbI** (*repudium* for breaking an engagement, *divortium* for dissolving a marriage) seems to be based on *Dig.* 50.16.101,191, but usage was actually more complex in Roman law and language. In canon law, *divortium* was the normal term; *repudium* from Matt. 19 would indicate the husband's action against the wife without a court's judgment. As a canonist who took part in the proceedings for Henry VIII's divorce, Polydore would have been sensitive to the terminology and perhaps changed his language for this reason.

10. Deut. 24:1–4   Hier. *Comm. in Matt.* 3, ad 19:8–9 (*PL* 26:134D–5B) Jos. *AJ* 4.253.

11. Matt. 19:6–9   Jos. *AJ* 15.259; Deut. 24:1; *Dig.* 24.2.1–11, 50.16.91,101, 191. By implication divorce is a male prerogative in Deut. 24:1. Originally, when all Roman wives were in the husband's *manus* or power, the same was true in Rome, but by the late Republic few women entered *manus* through marriage and it became possible for wives to choose divorce.

12. Paul. *Fest.* p. 283L; Plu. *Quaest. rom.* 65 (279E–F)   Paul. *Fest.* p. 77L Val. Max. 2.1.1; Serv. *A* 4.45, 166; Cic. *Div.* 1.16.28. Sextus Pompeius Festus was a grammarian of the second century CE whose epitome of the *De significatu verborum* of Marcus Verrius Flaccus, a scholar of the Augustan period, was itself abbreviated by Paul the Deacon (Paulus Diaconus) in the eighth century. It was Paul's version (ed. prin. 1471), discovered by Poggio in the early fifteenth century and studied by Perotti and other humanists, that Polydore called 'Festus.' A different Festus was the historian of the fourth century who wrote a *Breviarium rerum gestarum populi*

Romani. At Roman weddings sacrifice was made to Ceres, who corresponds to Demeter, one of the six children of Kronos. After her brother Hades (Pluto) stole her daughter, Persephone, and took her to the underworld, Demeter's grief deprived the earth of its fertility, which she restores for that part of each year when Persephone returns to her. While Demeter mourned, her wanderings took her to many parts of the world, where she brought her gift of grain.

13. Plu. *Quaest. rom.* 31 (271F–2B); Paul. *Fest.* p. 479L; Serv. *A* 1.651; Plin. *Nat.* 8.194; cf. Plu. *Rom.* 15.2–4; *Pomp.* 4.4–5; Liv. 1.9.12   Plu. *Quaest. rom.* 1 (263D-E); Paul. *Fest.* p. 77L   *DIR* 5.7–8   Ov. *Fast.* 4.151–154; cf. Paul. *Fest.* p. 351L. The meaning and origin of the exclamation Talassio or Thalassio (cf. *thalamos*, bride-chamber) was much disputed by the ancients. Livy's story seems to have come from the annalists, while the antiquarians proposed such roots as *talaron* (wool) or *talla* (layer of an onion, cf. *humēn*).

14. Paul. *Fest.* p. 55L; Ov. *Fast.* 2.477; Plu. *Quaest. rom.* 87 (285B-D); *Rom.* 15.7   Hom. *Od.* 11.245; Catul. 2a.3; Paul. *Fest.* p. 55L; Var. *L* 5.114   Non. p. 531L. The *caelibaris hasta* was actually used to comb the hair. Several of Juno's festivals had to do with female fertility, others with political organization, including a possible bond between each *curia*, a division of the archaic Roman *tribus*, and Juno Curitis. Tyro is the first of fourteen famous women whom Odysseus meets in the underworld. Zeus destroyed her father, Salmoneus, with a thunderbolt, but she survived, having opposed her father's audacity, and fell in love with Enipeus, a river-god whose form Poseidon assumed. Catullus (ed. prin. 1472) alludes not to Tyro, however, but to the tale of Atalanta, Hippomenes and his golden apples. The language of Paul's epitome of Festus is clearer on *lana* (wool) as the antecedent of *illa*. Note also that Paul has *cingillo*, which is *cingulo* in Perotti's edition of 'Festus' published with the *Cornucopiae* (1513, col. 1143). The source of the passage on the three coins is not 'Festus' or Paul but Nonius Marcellus (ed. prin. 1470), who probably wrote his dictionary of early Latin, *De compendiosa doctrina*, in the early fourth century CE. Perotti also edited Nonius and published him in the *Cornucopiae*. Homer was available in Latin (ed. prin. 1474, 1497) and Greek (ed. prin. 1488) printed texts before the first edition of *De inventoribus*.

15. Boeth. *In Top. Cic. comm.* 2 (*PL* 64.1071); Tert.*Virg. vel.* 11.9; *Apol.* 6.5
Verg. *G* 1.31; Serv. *ad loc.*   Isid. *Orig.* 9.7.12; Perotti, *Corn.* fol. XXIXv
Plu. *Quaest. rom.* 29 (271D); *Rom.* 15.6. The commentary of Boethius
(480–524 CE; ed. prin. 1484) on Cicero's *Topica* grew out of his unfinished project of translating Aristotle and Plato. Tertullian (160–240)
wrote his major apologetic work, the *Apologeticus,* to protest the persecu-
tion of Christians. *De virginibus velandis* deals with Christian morals. At
the beginning of the *Georgics,* Vergil adresses Octavian, who had recently
won his great naval victory at Actium in 31 BCE. Octavian will become a
son-in-law of Tethys if he marries one of the Oceanides, the myriad
daughters of Tethys and Oceanus. The verb *emat* from *emere* refers to any
purchase, like the noun *emptio,* but in this context implies *coemptio,* which
was not really a purchase; it was the conveyance of a woman into the
power or *manus* of her husband.

<h2 style="text-align:center">CHAPTER V</h2>

1. Lact. *Inst.* 1.15; Cic. *ND* 3.19.50   *DIR* 1.1.2–3   Cypr. *Idol.* 1, 3 (*PL*
4.565–566, 569). Cicero attacks euhemerism as irreligious, but Lactantius
praises it for showing that the old gods were false. Cyprian of Carthage
(200–258 CE) may not have written *Quod idola dii non sint* (ed. prin.
1471), another euhemerist attack on paganism by a Christian.

2. Lact. *Inst.* 1.22–23, 2.11; *DIR* 1.5.5; Eus. *Chron.*, Helm, p. 20, 1483 ed.,
sig. b6v. Ouranos (Uranus) and Gaia (Tellus) were the parents of the
Titans, including Kronos (Saturn), the father of Zeus, who wanted
to swallow him along with his other children by Rhea. Hidden from
Kronos in a cave, the infant Zeus was fed by the daughters of Melisseus,
the Cretan king who founded religion, according to Lactantius. Arguing that pagan religion was not especially venerable, Lactantius cites
Theophilus to show that Saturn was actually contemporary with a Belus
worshipped by the Assyrians and Babylonians 322 years before the Trojan
War, about eighteen centuries before his own day. Belos appears in the
classical period as the son of Libya and Poseidon, the father of Danaus
and Aegyptus, and the grandfather of Arabus and Phoinix, eponyms that
bring to mind the Semitic deity called Ba'al or Bel. The only surviving
work of Theophilus, bishop of Antioch in the later second century, is the

apologetic *Ad Autolycum*, which contains a chronology of world history, but the first Latin translation by Conrad Clauser appeared only in 1546, and Polydore dropped his reference to Theophilus (by way of Lactantius) after 1532. Thallus of Samaria was one of the chronographers used by Theophilus and also by Eusebius, the main source of Polydore's temporal framework for world history (see the Note on Chronology). Eusebius locates Kronos around his year 685 of Abraham, closer to the key date of the Fall of Troy than Lactantius placed Saturn and Belus. In any case, by dating Saturn and Belus thirty-two centuries after the creation, Polydore, like Eusebius, was assuming that the world began about fifty-two centuries before Christ. Ninus was the eponymous ruler of Nineveh, known as the second husband of Shammuramat, famed in Greek legend as Semiramis but actually belonging to a later period, the ninth century BCE.

3. Lact. *De ira dei* 14; *Inst.* 4.28   Deut. 6:13; cf. 5:9   Cic. *ND* 2.28.72; Lact. *Inst.* 4.28.

4. Hdt. 2.4; Str. 17.1.29   Diod. S. 1.16.1, 45.1, 3.2.2–4; Hom. *Il.* 1.423–4. Diodorus has *Mēnan* (*Menan* in the Poggio-Decembrio translation), but Herodotus called him *Min*, and traditionally he was the first king of Egypt, Mnij. In the third century BCE, Manetho identified a *Mēnēs* with Narmer as founder of the First Dynasty, which is probably correct. However, Diodorus confuses Menas with other names — Moeris, Mendes, Marrus — which derive from one of the names of the great Middle Kingdom ruler, Ammenemes III (1842–1797 BCE). The Hermes whom he names as the inventor of worship is Thoth, a moon-god responsible for the lunar calendar and hence for the rhythms of religious life. Among the remote races whose idealized closeness to nature fascinated the ancients, the Ethiopians were famous as pious, upright and prosperous. Their faraway location made them handy for explaining the absence of a god, but the Homeric poems assign them no precise place, while Herodotus later speaks of two groups, one Indian, another African. On the oldest Greek poets, see *DIR* 1.6.5, 9.4.

5. Lact. *Inst.* 1.22.

6. Lact. *Inst.* 1.22   Cic. *ND* 2.27.67; Macr. *Sat.* 1.7, 19–24, 9.1–3   Serv. *A* 4.302   Diod. S. 3.65.5–6; Lact. *Inst.* 1.22   Eus. *PE* 10.4.4; *Chron.*, Helm, pp. 46–9 = 1483 ed., sig. d8r–e1r. Faunus or Silvanus, a Roman forest-god, came to be identified with Pan. According to Dionysius, he led the indigenous people who welcomed the Arcadians whom Evander led to Latium. But Ovid says that Janus, god of beginnings, was the first king of Latium. According to Macrobius, Janus already ruled in Italy before Saturn arrived to teach him agriculture. Having established the Saturnalia after the god vanished, Janus also started the first rites and temples. 715–673 BCE is the traditional reign of Rome's second king, Numa Pompilius, also honored as a founder of Roman religion. As distinct from state festivals, *orgia* were ecstatic mysteries or initiations, especially of Demeter and Bacchus (Father Liber), or worship and sacrifice in general, or even non-religious mysteries; *caerimonia* meant a sacred rite or the reverence expressed by it. For Eusebius, who wanted to prove Greek philosophy inferior to Biblical teachings or derived from them, the myth of Cadmus was particularly useful since this culture-hero and founder of Thebes in Boeotia was said to have come from Phoenicia. Only in the fifth century did Orpheus emerge with his full identity and the tale of his going down to Hades and dismemberment by Thracian women. The commentary by Servius on Vergil is a product of the late fourth or early fifth century CE. Although printed editions appeared in the 1470s, these were of a shorter recension not augmented until 1600 by Pierre Daniel. Even when Polydore does not cite Servius, he frequently depends on him.

7. Hdt. 2.50–53   Eus. *Chron.*, Helm, p. 12 = 1483 ed., sig. a4r; *PE* 2.3.11. Since Zeus was an Indo-European god, his entry into Greece in the early second millenium is broadly consistent with what Herodotus maintains about the Pelasgians. Otherwise the archaic Greek gods came from Asia rather than Egypt. Homer and Hesiod inherited the results of a process that preceded them by more than a millenium, organizing and enriching a theology that they did not invent. More a literary construct than a historical people, the Pelasgians were placed by Homer in various Aegean locations and came eventually to represent the original population of this area. Although they once occupied all of Greece, according to

Herodotus, he associates them mainly with Ionia and Attica, claiming that the Athenians first learned the Herm-cult from them but that they later adopted Egyptian names for the gods on the advice of the oracle of Dodona, whose origins were from Thebes in Egypt. The *Odyssey* mentions Dodona's oracular oak, thus supporting what Herodotus says about its antiquity. The dating of Cecrops as a contemporary of Moses was a pivotal issue for the chronology worked out by Eusebius (see Note on Chronology), who mentions Eëtion. One Eëtion was a son of Zeus and brother of Dardanus (the first ruler of Troy), perhaps the same as Iasion and therefore a lover of Demeter; another was Andromache's father.

8. Jos. *AJ* 1.54   Gen. 4: 26; Hier. *Adv. Jov.* 1.17 (*PL* 23:236A–B); Eus. *PE* 7.8.9   Jos. *AJ* 3.188–192, 20.225–226   *DIR* 4.1–2, 5–6. Gen 4:25 puts *Enos*, the son of Seth, in the time when 'people began to invoke the Lord by name'; in Hebrew his name is *Enosh*, in Greek *Enōs*, in Latin *Enos*; Josephus has *Anōs*, *Enos* in the Latin (1486). Eusebius explains that the pious Enos, whose name means 'true man,' was the first properly to be called human, unlike the earthbound and fallen Adam. Hebrew *Chanoch*, Greek *Enōch*, Latin *Henoch* is Enoch, the name of the son of Cain in Gen. 4:17–18 and of the father of Methuselah in Gen 5:21–4; cf. Heb. 11:5; Josephus has *Anōchos*, *Enoch* in the Latin. Nonetheless, Jerome writes that *Enoch . . . primus invocaverit Deum*. In Gen. 14:18–20, Melchizedek, king of Salem, is 'priest of God the most high,' and his priesthood was an important precedent in later tradition, both Jewish and Christian. For Aaron and the later Mosaic priesthood, see Exod. 28:1–5, 29:44, 39:1; Lev. 8:1–5, 36; Num. 3:5–10. Historically the distinctions among Aaronites, Zadokites and Levites and their attachments to Jerusalem and other cult-centers were complex and contentious.

CHAPTER VI

1. Cic. *Tusc.* 1.25.61–2.

2. Diod. S. 1.16.1   Cic. *ND* 3.22.56; Lact. *Inst.* 1.6   Diod. S. 1.69.5   Plin. *Nat.* 7.193   Diod. S. 3.4.1; *DIR* 3.11.7. The association of the herald-god Hermes (cf. *hermēneuō*, interpret or utter) with messages led naturally to a connection with writing. Hesiod says that he was the son of Zeus by Maia, a daughter of Atlas, which is the parentage of the third of

Cicero's five Mercuries. The Egyptian lunar god Thoth shared some features with Hermes; he was the scribe of the gods and hence the inventor of writing. His full Greek name was Hermes Trismegistus, and he came last of five on Cicero's list in a section of *De natura deorum* that distinguishes among gods called by the same names. See *DIR* 1.5.4 for an Egyptian called *Mennan*.

3. Plin. *Nat.* 7.192   Plin. *Nat.* Palmario ed. [1497], sig. iiv; Barbaro, *Cast.* sig. r8v. Because of the catalogue of inventors in its seventh book, the encyclopedic *Natural History* in thirty-seven books by Pliny the Elder (23–79 CE) is Polydore's single most important source. Although he expressed no coherent philosophy, Pliny punctuated his mammoth work with vivid moral sketches of contemporary decline from a simpler Roman past uncorrupted by alien or aristocratic luxury. Ermolao Barbaro (1454–93) made his greatest contribution to classical scholarship by interpreting and improving the text of the *Natural History*. His *Castigationes Plinianas ad Alexandrum Sextum pontificem maximum* were published in Rome in 1493. Barbaro's commentary used the earlier printed texts of Perotti (1473) and de Bussis (1472). G. B. Palmario later incorporated Barbaro's corrections into his 1497 edition of Pliny, as did several later editors. Pliny's early appearance in print and the wide incunabular diffusion of the *Natural History* stimulated scholarly inquiry, especially after Perotti attacked the de Bussis edition; the *Natural History* became a focus of controversy, which heated up when Niccolò Leoniceno and Pandolfo Collenucio quarreled about Pliny's medical and pharmacological terminology.

Of the several candidates for inventor of letters mentioned by Polydore, Simonides of Ceos was an Ionian lyric poet of the late sixth and early fifth centuries BCE, and Epicharmus was a comic poet of the fifth century, but Palamades, like Cadmus, is a mythic figure. Cadmus, brother of Europa and son either of Agenor or of Phoinix, is associated with Eastern locations — Sidon, Tyre and Phoenicia — and became the founder of Thebes. Palamades, son of Nauplius, was a descendant of Europa, a rival of Odysseus and a hero famous for cultural benefactions: letters, numbers, weights, measures, laws, games, military tactics, astronomical observations and others. The sixteen Roman letters that Polydore attributes to Cadmus correspond to those in the 1497 edition,

which reads ΘΥΦΧ for the first four added by Palamedes and ΖΗΨΩ for the second group from Simonides; Barbaro also supports these readings of the Palamades and Simonides groups. Pliny did not specify either the sixteen letters introduced by Cadmus or the eighteen mentioned by Aristotle; the latter were added by a corrector of a ninth century manuscript and adopted by pre-nineteenth century editors. The 1497 Pliny gives ΑΒΓΔΕΖΙΛΜΝΞΟΠΡΣΤΦΨ, which differs from Polydore in four places. Barbaro did not spell out the eighteen letters, but he ruled that the list should contain Ρ and end with Φ or Ψ rather than Χ. Since Barbaro specifically mentions Χ as belonging to Epicharmus and not to Aristotle's list, it is likelier that Polydore was working with an edition based on Barbaro, like the 1497, than with the *Castigationes* directly.

4. Diod. S. 3.67.1; 5.74.1   Hdt. 5.58   Diod. S. 5.74.1   Luc. 3.220–221   Diod. S. 5.56.5, 57.2–5. *De bello civili* (ed. prin. 1469) by Marcus Annaeus Lucanus (39–65 CE) is an unfinished epic poem in ten books about the Civil War in 49–8 BCE, centering on Caesar, Pompey and Cato Uticensis. Diodorus calls the fourth son of Helius *Actis*, which means sun-beam. The Poggio-Decembrio version of Diodorus gives both *Actinus* and *Actis*.

5. Jos. *Ap.* 1.11–12   Cic. *Brut.* 18.71; Hom. *Od.* 1.150, 325, 8.43, 13.27, 17.263, 22.330; cf *Il.* 1.603–4, 2.595, 3.54, 9.186   Eus. *PE* 10.11.27; *Chron.*, Helm, pp. 13, 63, 66, 71, 77   Diod. S. 3.3.1–4.1. Apion was an Alexandrian grammarian and lexicographer of the first century CE against whom Josephus launched this apologetic work in defense of the ancient heritage of Israel. The *Iliad* mentions (6.168–9) the 'scratching' (*grapsas*) of 'ruinous signs' (*sēmata lugra*) on a 'folded tablet' (*pinaki ptuktō*) to carry a message, a very broad description that could refer to cuneiform, Linear B or, in fact, a sign of any type. At 7.175–7, however, nine heroes simply 'make their mark' without writing in any way. Noting the disagreement among ancient authors on Homer's date, Eusebius gives year 851 of Abraham (1166 BCE) as the earliest and 1104 (913) as the latest. He mentions Linus, Zethus, Amphion, Musaeus, Orpheus, Minos, Perseus, Aesculapius, Castor, Pollux and Hercules as having lived as much as two centuries after Cecrops, close to his year 600 of Abraham or 240 years before the Fall of Troy and hence long before the poet of the Trojan War.

He dates the musical activity of Linus, Zethus and Amphion to year 596 of Abraham (1421), putting Orpheus much later in year 752 (1265). Like Orpheus, most of the singers in Polydore's list are mythical, but Epimenides of Crete (c. 500 BCE) may have written the epic and theogonic poetry attached to his name. Epic poetry under the name of Aristeas of Proconnesus was known in the sixth century. Demodocus, the most renowned of the professional bards named by Homer, appears first in book 8 of the *Odyssey*. Phemius sings for the suitors in books 1 and 17, and the Thracian Thamyris turns up in a digression in the *Iliad*'s Catalogue of Ships. Achilles sings as an amateur in book 9.

6. Eus. *PE* 8.1.1, 9.26.1, 10.5.1–2, 9.6–10; *Chron.*, Helm, pp. 13, 46b, 48–50b, 53b, 55–6b   Plin. *Nat.* 5.66, 7.192; Eus. *PE* 10.5.2; *DIR* 1.6.3.

7. Jos. *AJ* 1.69–71   *DIR* 1.17.5   Clem. Alex. *Strom.* 1.23.151–3. Eupolemus, who probably lived in Palestine in the second century BCE, wrote an apologetic history of the Jewish kings; its fragments survive in Eusebius and Clement of Alexandria. The dating established for Moses by Eusebius in the *Chronicle* and described in *PE* 10.9 was critical to Polydore's argument for the priority of the Jews in discovery. Moses was born in year 425 (1592 BCE) of Abraham and died in year 545 (1472), according to Eusebius, but Phoinix and Cadmus went from Thebes in Egypt to Syria in 563 (1454)—later than Moses, though only by two decades. After Septimius Severus (193–211 CE), the Roman province of Syria Palaestina, which included the ethnarchy of Judaea, was on the coast south of Tyre; most of Syria Phoenice was on the coast north of Tyre. Syria Coele (*koilos*, hollow) extended north beyond Antioch and inland to the Euphrates. Describing the secret astrological writings carved on stone, Josephus has *Seirida* or *Seiris* not *Suria*, but the Latin Josephus has *Syria*.

The pseudepigraphal *Book of Jubilees* (12.25–7) records the tradition, known to Byzantine scholars by the ninth century, that Abraham was the first to speak and write Hebrew after the Tower of Babel and the confusion of languages. Although reference by these scholars to Eupolemus indicates that Jewish historians of the Hellenistic period connected Abraham with the origins of writing, the more usual attribution was to Moses. Eusebius, who cites Eupolemus, does not mention Abraham.

Clement also uses Eupolemus, but his account of the transmission of writing from Moses to the Jews and thence to the Phoenicians and the Greeks is the third version of the story that he tells. In his first version, Moses is a Chaldaean born in Egypt of ancestors who had migrated from Babylon. The second variant in Clement, attributed to Philo's *Life of Moses*, suggests that in Egypt a royal child would have had occasion 'to learn the letters of the Assyrians from the Chaldaeans and the science of the heavens from the Egyptians.' Since Polydore knew Clement's *Stromata*, he could have seen Philo of Alexandria cited there to show not that Moses *taught* letters to the Jews but that he *learned* them from Chaldaeans, thus placing this discovery in the land of Abraham's birth, Ur of the Chaldees. Otherwise, I have not been able to find the attribution to Abraham — directly or indirectly — in any author called 'Philo.'

8. Eus. *PE* 10.5.4   Hier. *Praef. II Reg.* (*PL* 28:547B-50A). The Temple was rebuilt around 520 BCE in the reign of Darius I, when Zerubbabel was governor of Jerusalem. Ezra was probably commissioned by Artaxerxes II in 398 to undertake a religious reform, though the traditional dating is 458 under Artaxerxes I. The apocryphal *II Esdras* of the late first century CE attributes the writing of the scriptures in new characters to Ezra.

9. Plin. *Nat.* 7.193, 210; Solin. 2.7   Perotti, *Corn.* fol. CLIIIlv; Isid. *Orig.* 1.4.1; Tortelli, *Orth.* sig. q2v   Dion. H. 1.33.3–5   Liv. 1.7.8   Tac. *Ann.* 11.14.3. Augustus completed the temple (*aedes*) of the Palatine Apollo in 28 BCE. Part of its structure was a library for Latin and Greek books. The inscription recorded by Pliny reads *Nausikratēs anetheto tai Dios korai tan dekatan*, 'Nausicrates dedicated the tenth part to the daughter of Zeus.' Evander was the legendary leader of the second group of Arcadians — preceded by the Pelasgians and by an earlier expedition from Arcadia — who came to Italy from Greece; they were associated with the settlement of the Palatine, the Lupercalia and the cults of Hercules and Pan. The *Collectanea rerum memorabilium* (ed. prin. 1473) of Gaius Julius Solinus (fl. 200 CE) is mainly geographical. Titus Livius (59 BCE-17 CE) wrote an annalistic history of Rome in 142 books, *From the Foundation of the City* through 9 BCE, which quickly became authoritative for the history of the Roman Republic. We now have books 1–10 and 21–

45, of which Petrarch knew the first, third and fourth decades; the first printed edition, by Giovanni Andrea Bussi, appeared in 1469. Simon Grynaeus added the first half of the fifth decade in the Basel edition of 1531. Only the *Agricola* and *Germania* of Publius Cornelius Tacitus (56–118 CE) survive complete. Of the sixteen to eighteen books of the *Annales*, we now have only twelve, some in fragments, and little beyond the first four of the twelve to fourteen books of the *Historiae*. A large part of the *Dialogus de oratoribus* is also missing. The *Agricola*, the *Germania*, the *Dialogus*, Annals 11–16 and Histories 1–5 were printed as early as 1473–75, but the Corvey manuscript of Annals 1–6 became known only in 1508.

10. Plin. *Nat.* 7.193   DIR 1.6.7   Diod. S. 1.9.2. Epigenes of Byzantium, who wrote on Chaldaean astrology in the second century BCE, was Pliny's source by way of Varro. The disclaimer by Diodorus of *reliable* knowledge of the first kings who ruled before history was written has been traced to Ephorus of Cyme (405–330), whose reservations were even stronger but who still used traditional stories DIR 1.14.7.

11. Liv. 6.1.2, 9.36.3   Tac. *Ann.* 11.14.3   Cic. *ND* 3.15.42. Demaratus of Corinth, possibly a historical figure, was said to be the father of Tarquinius Priscus, traditionally the fifth king of Rome (616–578 BCE). Speaking of the late fourth century, Livy says something different from what Polydore claims: that Roman boys of that period learned Etruscan just as they learned Greek in Livy's day. What the Greeks called Phrygia was in central Asia Minor, comprising the provinces of Asia and Galatia under the Roman Empire. In another passage on homonymous gods, Cicero makes one of several figures called Hercules an Egyptian son of the Nile and also the inventor of Phrygian writing, though Diodorus Siculus (3.67.5) attributed a 'Phrygian poem' about Dionysus of Nysa to Thymoetes, a Trojan hero and a contemporary of Orpheus. Diodorus mentions this just after describing Hercules, Thamyras and Orpheus as pupils of Linus, who wrote about the adventures of Dionysus in 'Pelasgic letters' derived from Phoenician writing.

12. Prisc. *Inst.* 1.12, 16   Suet. *Cl.* 41.3; Tac. *Ann.* 11.13.2–14.3   Quint. *Inst.* 1.7.26   Prisc. *Inst.* 1.25   cf. Tortelli, *Orth.* sig. o3r; Perotti, *Corn.* fol. CLVr   Quint. *Inst.* 1.4.9   cf. Prisc. *Inst.* 1.15. An Etruscan alphabet of twenty-six signs derived from Greek letters appears from about 700

and was used as late as the first century CE, though Roman conquest of
the peninsula had long since made Latin dominant. The Roman alphabet
also came from the Greek, either directly or by way of the Etruscan
script; Latin inscriptions begin in the seventh or sixth century but remain scarce until the third. The twenty-three letters of Polydore's Roman
alphabet (F H K Q X Y Z plus the sixteen from Cadmus) are correct.
The *Institutiones grammaticae* was the principal work of Priscianus of
Caesarea, who wrote in the sixth century CE. The first printed edition of
Priscian's *Opera* appeared in 1470, the same year in which the rhetorician
Marcus Fabius Quintilianus (35–95) was first published. The subject of
his *Institutio oratoria* in twelve books is the orator's education, but it con-
tains much other material of literary and historical interest. For Poly-
dore's reference to German pronunciation, the 1546 English translation of
De inventoribus by John Langley makes a regional substitution: 'And even
so our English men use to speak in Essex, for they say Fineger for
Vineger, Feal for Veal, and contrariwise, a Vox for a Fox, vour for four.'

CHAPTER VII

1. Perotti, *Corn.* fol. CCXLVIIr; Tortelli, *Orth.* sig. m1r   Quint. *Inst.*
1.2.14, 4.1–7, 2.1.4, 14.3   Suet. *Gram.* 4   Quint. *Inst.* 1.4.2, 7.30–2   Cic.
De orat. 1.42.187. The *grammatistēs* taught elementary reading and writing,
beginning with the letters, *grammata*, of the alphabet, and went on to the
memorization and study of Homer and other poets. A *grammatikos* was
either an elementary teacher or a more advanced literary scholar, also
called a *kritikos*. A *litterator* was the equivalent of a *grammatistēs*, both
terms sometimes pejorative. *Litteratus* and *criticus* were more dignified titles for a man of letters or a scholar, but *grammaticus* was the usual term
for a serious student of language and literature, and the study itself was
litteratura. Gaius Suetonius Tranquillus (70–130 CE) is best known for
the twelve biographies of Roman emperors in his *De vita Caesarum* (ed.
prin. 1470), but he also wrote a *De viris illustribus* containing short biographical sketches of important scholars. One section of this work, for
the most part lost, was *De grammaticis et rhetoribus* (ed. prin. 1473).

2. Suet. *Gram.* 1–2; *Rhet.* 1   Lact. *Inst.* pr., 1.1, 3.13, 25   Cic. *De orat.*
3.11.40

3. Diog. L. 3.25, 10.2   Suet. *Gram. et rhet.* 2.1. Hermippus of Smyrna was a biographer of the third century CE. Diogenes (*DIR* 1.1.3) actually says that Epicurus 'started as a schoolmaster'—*grammatodidaskalon auton gegenēsthai: grammaticam vero illum docuisse primum* in Traversari's Latin. Crates of Mallos, a Stoic who taught grammar and rhetoric in Pergamum, visited Rome around 159 or 168 BCE. Quintus Ennius died in 169. These events occurred in the reigns of Eumenes II (197–160) and Attalus II (160–139) of Pergamum. The Second Punic War ended in 201; the Third began in 149.

4. Quint. *Inst.* 1.proem.5, 4.5.

5. Perotti, *Corn.* fol. CLIv; cf. Hor. *Ep.* 2.1.51; Quint. *Inst.* 2.1.4; Cic. *Fam.* 9.10.1; *DIR* I.7.6–9   cf. Cic. *Arch.* 10.26.

6. Macr. *Sat.* 5.18.9   Suet. *Gram.* 7   Gel. 4.9.1   Suet. *Gram.* 2, 14, 23, 24; Quint. *Inst.* 1.4.18. Aristotle's rhetoric and poetics are well known, but he also made contributions to grammar. Theodotes may be Theodectas of Phaselis (375–34 BCE), a poet, grammarian and rhetorician cited by Quintilian and Cicero. In the *Rhetoric* (1410^b1–3) Aristotle refers to a collection of *Theodectea*, probably rhetorical techniques. Another possibility is Theodotus of Chios or Rhodes, active in the first century. Aristarchus of Samothrace, head of the Library of Alexandria after 153, championed a rationalist grammar and helped lay the foundations of philological scholarship. Didymus studied Homer, the tragedians and other Greek writers in Alexandria in the first century. Marcus Terentius Varro (116–27) is said to have written dozens of works on many topics. Only *De re rustica* (ed. prin. 1472), six books of *De lingua latina* (ed. prin. 1471), and other fragments survive, but these contain the fullest account of grammar from the Republic. His contemporary, the Pythagorean astrologer Publius Nigidius Figulus, rivaled Varro for erudition. Antonius Gnipho (not Enipho) was a Gaul and a freedman who served the family of Julius Caesar early in the first century. When Cicero was already a famous orator, he came several times to hear Gnipho declaim. Starting as a slave, Quintus Remmius Palaemon (first century CE) became a pedagogue and a famous *grammaticus* who wrote the first comprehensive Latin grammar of whose contents anything is known. Valerius Probus worked

in the same period as an editor of Latin poets and dramatists and a teacher of grammar.

CHAPTER VIII

1. Str. 1.2.3. The polymath Eratosthenes of Cyrene (275–194 BCE), head of the Library of Alexandria after 246, had criticized Homer's knowledge of geography, but Strabo defends poetry as a source of instruction as well as pleasure.

2. Cic. *Div.* 1.37.80; Pl. *Phdr.* 245a   Hor. *Ars* 295–297, 408–409   Verg. *Ecl.* 7.25   Ov. *Ars* 3.549   Verg. *Ecl.* 5.45. Horace (65–8 BCE) was in print by 1471.

3. Cic. *Arch.* 8.18.

4. Eus. *PE* 11.5.7   Jos. *AJ* 2.346, 7.305. The Eusebian chronology puts the death of Moses three centuries before the first report of Homer in year 851 of Abraham (1166 BCE), half a century before Linus, Zethus and Amphion. Jews had written in Greek hexameters before the time of Josephus, in the earlier *Sibylline Oracles*, but Josephus wanted to claim the greatness of Homer for Moses. *Vates* means both prophet and poet, the latter regarded as divinely inspired; likewise, *carmen* means song or poem but also ritual chant.

5. Hier. *Praef. in II Chron. Eus.* 2 (= *Chron.* 1483, ed. sig. a2v; *PL* 27:36A-B; Helm, pp. 3–4).

6. Lact. *Inst.* 1.5–7; Hor. *Ars* 40   Porph. *ad Artem* 391–392   Cic. *Tusc.* 1.1.3–2.1; cf. *Brut.* 18.72; Quint. *Inst.* 10.2.7   Cic. *Sen.* 14.50; Liv. 29.11.10; cf. 7.2.8–13   Gel. 11.2.5–6; Cic. *Brut* 40.148; cf. *Tusc.* 1.1.3. Few oracular responses survive in verse from before 100 CE, more after Plutarch's essay 'On the Oracles at Delphi No Longer Given in Verse.' Pomponius Porphyrio probably wrote his commentaries (ed. prin. 1481) on Horace early in the third century CE. Ennius was born in 515 AUC (239 BCE), not 513. In modern editions, Cicero mentions Caius Claudius Centho, not his father Appius, as the colleague of Marcus Sempronius Tuditanus. Their consulship was actually in 240. Cicero also depicts Cato the Censor as remembering Andronicus in his old age while claiming that he had put on a play six years before Cato was born, in 240. For that year he

gives the consuls as Cento and Tuditanus, but he also represents Marcus
Cethegus as known in his old age to Cato. Livy, who makes Marcus
Cornelius Cethegus and Publius Sempronius Tuditanus consuls in 204,
dates the first performances with dramatic elements to 364. Following
this, Livy says that 'after some years' Andronicus 'first linked play-acting
with a story (*argumento fabulam serere*).' Andronicus may have come from
Tarentum to Rome, where he became a freedman and worked as *grammaticus*, playwright and actor. Accius (170–86), the tragedian and scholar,
may have caused the chronological confusion by putting Andronicus in
Rome after the taking of Tarentum in 209 rather than after its earlier
capture in 272. Another possibility is that neither event at Tarentum
caused his arrival and that his coming to Rome was closer to 240.

Aulus Gellius (b. 125 CE) wrote the scholarly miscellany called *Noctes
Atticae* (ed. prin. 1469) sometime before 165. He quoted Cato as saying
'Poeticae artis honos non erat,' but he had also cited Cicero on the fru-
gality of Lucius Licinius Crassus and Quintus Mucius Scaevola, who
were consuls in 95 BCE. Cicero, defending Latin as a medium for philosophy, maintains that Rome surpassed Greece in many spheres of wisdom
but admits that the Greeks excelled in learning and literature. 'It was late
when we knew or welcomed poets,' he writes, 'and there was no respect
(*honorem*) for the genre . . . [which] was held in low esteem (*honoris*).'

CHAPTER IX

2. Wisd. Sol. 11:21   Quint. *Inst.* 1.10.12; Diog. L. 8.33; cf. Arist. *Metaph.*
986[a]

3. Diod. S. 4.7, 5.74.1   *DIR* 1.8.4. About a third of the language of the
Hebrew Bible is poetry, but its structure has not yet been explained.

4. Serv. *De centum metris* 1.1; *DIR* 1.8.4   Plin. *Nat.* 7.205   Str. 9.3.5;
Cic. *Div.* 2.56.116. The oldest Greek verse is in hexameters, but Calli-
machus (third century BCE) and other later poets wrote hexameters that
differ slightly from Homer's epic or heroic meter. Heroic poetry is a
broader conception. Pyrrhus (319–272) ruled Epirus intermittently after
307. Cicero rejects the ascription by Ennius of a verse oracle about
Pyrrhus to the Delphic oracle.

5. Serv. *De centum metris* 1.1   Hor. *Ars* 77–79   Diod. S. 4.84.3. The first Greek lyric poet, Archilochus of Paros (680–640 BCE) wrote *iamboi*, but the iambic form is even older. The asclepiad can be found in Alcaeus (b. 625) but takes its name from Asclepiades of Samos (fl. 290), the major writer of epigrams in the early Alexandrian period. The elegiac couplet consists of a line of dactylic hexameter followed by a pentameter; the elegy, beginning in the seventh century, came to be associated with mourning, but its uses were much wider. In general, bucolic is a type of lyric poetry originating with Theocritus in the third century.

Chapter x

1. Euanthius *De fabula* 1.1–2   Hor. *Ars* 220; Diom. *Ars gram.* (Keil, I, p. 487.15–18); Don. *De com.* 5.7. Aelius Donatus, the grammarian, wrote commentaries on Vergil (mostly lost) and Terence in the middle of the fourth century CE. Euanthius, his contemporary, also commented on Terence and introduced his work with a general discussion of ancient drama; this material, called *De fabula*, is prefixed to modern editions of Donatus (ed. prin. 1472) and was Polydore's chief source (no doubt *via* Perotti) on tragedy and comedy. The citation of Varro comes indirectly from the *Ars grammatica* of Diomedes (ed. prin. 1475), written in the fourth or fifth century CE. As a god of vegetation and wine, Liber Pater was identified with the Greek Dionysus, honored at the City Dionysia, the Athenian festival at which tragedies were performed by the late sixth century BCE. The god's cult was also the occasion for the first dithyrambs, choral songs performed by a festive group (*kōmos*) costumed as satyrs; Aristotle located the origins of tragedy in such songs. *Tragos* means he-goat; *ōdē* means song; thus, *tragoedia* would mean goat-song.

2. Euanthius *De fabula* 1.2; cf. Diom. *Ars gram.* (Keil, I, p. 487.11–31)   Hor. *Ars* 275–9; cf. Don. *De com.* 5.9   Quint. *Inst.* 10.1.66–67   Don. *De com.* 5.4; Quint. *Inst.* 10.1.97–98; Perotti *Corn.* fol. LXXXVIIᵛ. The *Suda* claims that Thespis, often credited with the first prize for tragedy at the City Dionysia around 534 BCE, invented the mask; though its religious use was earlier, performers in the dithyramb were not masked. Thespis probably contributed to the drama but more likely in rural festivals than in Athens, where 501 is a better date than 534 for the first plays

at the City Dionysia. The first surviving depiction of a theatrical mask dates from 470 or after. The Greek for *faex* or dregs is *trux*, whose initial consonants are the same as *tragōdia*. Lucius Accius wrote plays in the second century, overlapping the earlier career of Marcus Pacuvius. Lucius Annaeus Seneca, the younger, who committed suicide in 65 CE, was primarily a philosopher, but he also wrote nine of the tragedies ascribed to him. Ovid's *Medea* has not survived despite its success in its own time.

3. Euanthius *De fabula* 1.3; Diom. *Ars gram.* (Keil, I, p. 488.6–7) Don. *De com.* 5.4; *DIR* I.11.19–25; Euanthius, *De fabula*, 1.5 Don. *De com.* 5.4; Liv. 7.2.8; Val. Max. 2.4.4. Polydore's etymology from *kōmos* and *ōdē* is correct, giving something like festival-song, where satyrs made fun of exaggerated sexuality. Evidence for comedy begins in the seventh century BCE, but at the City Dionysia only around 488. The earliest literary remains are mid-fifth century, the first complete text from 425—the *Acharnians* by Aristophanes, who put on his last plays shortly before he died in 386. Eupolis and Cratinus, both of the later fifth century, were also masters of the Attic Old Comedy. Cicero says that the play put on by Livius Andronicus at the Roman Games in 240 was a tragedy, but he also wrote comedies.

4. Diom. *Ars gram.* (Keil, I, p. 488.13–23); Ov. *Tr.* 2.381. Archelaus was king of Macedon from 413 to 399 BCE. Euripides went to Macedon after 408 and never returned to Athens; while there he wrote a play about an ancestor of the king.

CHAPTER XI

1. Perotti *Corn.* fol. CLVIII[v] Diog. L. 5.85 Gel. 2.18.6–7; cf. Apul. *Fl.* 20; Macr. *Sat.* 1.11.42 Diom. *Ars gram.* (Keil, I, p. 485) Quint. *Inst.* 10.1.93. Demetrius of Tarsus is an obscure entry in a list of figures of this name compiled by Diogenes. Menippus of Gadara (probably before 250 CE) expressed his Cynic philosophy humorously by mixing verse with prose, the form imitated by Varro in his *Saturarum Menippearum libri*, which survive in fragments. In the later second century, Gaius Lucilius developed the specifically Roman *satura* that Quintilian describes. Gellius refers to Varro and Menippus, as Polydore says, but Apuleius attributes *satira* to Xenocrates or, more likely, Crates of Thebes,

the Cynic philosopher and poet (368–288). Instead of Apuleius (b. 125 CE; ed. prin. 1469), Polydore probably meant to cite Macrobius, whose comments resemble what Gellius wrote. Since the *Florida* is an anthology, confusion with the learned miscellanies of Macrobius or Gellius might easily arise.

2. Euanthius *De fabula* 2.4–6.

3. Diom. *Ars gram.* (Keil, I, p. 489.5–6)   Gel. 13.23.16, 15.24   Quint. *Inst.* 10.1.100. Menander, Philemon and Diphilus were the major authors of New Comedy, beginning around 325 CE. While Aristophanes and other writers of Old Comedy had attacked prominent individuals savagely and by name, Middle Comedy became tamer, less political and more interested in the humor of everyday life, leading eventually to the stock characters and universal situations of New Comedy, which was thus adaptable for non-Athenian audiences. Gnaeus Naevius, who died around 200, preceded Titus Maccius Plautus (fl. 205–184), Caecilius Statius (d. 168) and Publius Terentius Afer (fl. 160). Gellius calls Licinius Imbrex *vetus comoediarum scriptor.*

4. Euanthius *De fabula* 2.5; Paul. *Fest.* pp. 306, 314L; cf. Diom. *Ars gram.* (Keil, I, p. 485)   Quint. *Inst.* 10.1.93–4. *Satura* comes from *satur,* meaning 'full' and applying to foods that were stuffed (sausage) or mixed (salad) with various ingredients. The genre included elements that explain the reference to *satyrus,* though this is incorrect as etymology. Ennius, who pioneered Latin satire, was followed by Lucilius, Quintus Horatius Flaccus (65–8 BCE) and Aulus Persius Flaccus (32–64 CE; ed. prin. c. 1470), and all were known to Quintilian, who died sometime after 95 CE. Decimus Iunius Iuvenalis (ed. prin. 1469), who began his public career as a poet around 100, is mentioned by Marcus Valerius Martialis (38–104) but was not widely appreciated before the fourth century.

CHAPTER XII

1. Cic. *De orat.* 2.9.36.

2. Plin. *Nat.* 7.205; Jos. *Ap.* 1.6–10, 13, 28–29; Eus. *PE* 10.7.9, 9.7–10, 11.4.4. The shadowy Cadmus of Miletus was probably a real and dis-

tinct figure, not the mythical founder of Thebes. Eusebius mentions the Theban culture-hero in the *Preparation* but also cites Josephus on the other Cadmus, whom Josephus connects with Acusilaus of Argos and locates before the Persian Wars. Strabo groups him with Pherecydes and Hecataeus as originators of 'structured prose.'

3. Plin. *Nat.* 7.205; Apul. *Fl.* 15   *DIR* 1.12.2   Eus. *PE* 10.12.29, 14.1–5; *Chron.* Helm, pp. 103, 111   Str. 1.2.6. If the Exodus had been in the thirteenth century BCE, Jotham would have ruled Judah about five hundred years after Moses. But Josephus suggests a sixteenth century date, putting roughly eight centuries between Moses and Jotham. In the *Chronicle* of Eusebius, 781 years — close to Polydore's 788 — separate the key synchronicities of Moses with Cecrops and of Jotham with the first Olympiad. Eusebius used the traditional date for the first Olympic victory, 776, which falls in the reign of Jeroboam II of Israel (786–46); Uzziah and Jotham were his contemporaries in Judah. In the *Preparation*, Eusebius puts the first Olympiad in the reign of Jotham's son and successor, Ahaz or Jehoahaz I (735–15), while the *Chronicle* confirms that 'the first Olympiad was in the time of Joatham, King of the Hebrews.' Reflecting this discrepancy, early editions of *DIR* through 1532 read *Achar* (Ahaz) for *Ioathan*.

The *Preparation* also places Pherecydes of Syros around the first Olympiad, but the *Chronicle* locates 'Ferecydes the famous historian' in Olympiad 59 (541), almost a century before a 'second Ferecydes' in Olympiad 81 (456). Pherecydes of Syros wrote treatises on myth and theogony in the middle of the sixth century, establishing the prose form called logography and leading eventually to history as such. With his contemporary, Anaximander, he seems indeed to have been one of the earliest prose writers, around the time of Cyrus (559–30). The later Pherecydes placed by Eusebius in the fifth century was an Athenian who also wrote about myth and genealogy and was sometimes confused with his namesake. Hecataeus of Miletus (fl. 500), whose influential *Journey Around the World* dealt with geography and ethnography, also wrote *Genealogies* in which he distinguished among mythic, genealogical and historical times. The same interests, along with ethnography and geography, can be found in Herodotus of Halicarnassus, whose *Histories* were known by 425.

4. Diog. L. 2.48; Quint. *Inst.* 10.1.75   Quint. *Inst.* 10.1.73–74, 101, 2.7; Perotti *Corn.* fol. CXCI^v. Antiquity thought of Xenophon (430–354 BCE) primarily as a military leader and a philosopher, but he wrote a wide variety of works on historical, technical and other topics. Theopompus of Chios (b. 378) wrote *Hellenica* to continue the history of Thucydides (455–400) as well as *Philippica* centered on the career of Philip of Macedon. In Greece, the structure of local history or horography was annalistic: annual lists of events keyed to the magistracies whose names identified the civil year. But the Greeks kept horography apart from history proper, the larger record of wars and other great public events involving all Hellas. Romans did not respect the distinction, however, and their history became essentially annalistic. Tradition dated the first *Annales* to the reign of Numa Pompilius (715–673). *Tabulae pontificum* were kept by 400, and Publius Mucius Scaevola published the *Annales maximi* around 120. Ennius wrote *Annales* in Latin verse, but prose histories of Rome appeared in Greek in the late third century, beginning with Quintus Fabius Pictor around 200. The sources of native historiography in Latin prose were the *Origines* of the elder Cato, begun in 168, and the annalistic works of Lucius Cassius Hemina (fl. 150). Gaius Sallustius Crispus (86–35) wrote annalistically in his lost *Histories*, but the surviving works (ed. prin. 1470) on the Catilinarian conspiracy and the Jugurthan War are monographic studies of Rome's moral decline.

5. Cic. *De orat.* 2.15.62–64.

CHAPTER XIII

1. Quint. *Inst.* 3.2.3.

2. Diod. S. 1.16.2; Hor. *Carm.* 1.10.1–3   Diod. S. 5.75.3.

3. Diog. L. 8.57; Quint. *Inst.* 3.1.8   Suet. *Rhet.* 1   Quint. *Inst.* 3.1.8, 10.1.76. Tradition makes Empedocles (492–432 BCE) the teacher of Gorgias (485–380), another native of Sicily and the most important source of Sophistic rhetoric. Corax and Tisias, also fifth century Sicilians, developed handbooks of technical rhetoric. Demosthenes lived in Athens from 384 to 322. The rhetoricians expelled from Rome by senatorial decree in 161 were probably individual teachers, but in 92 Lucius

Licinius Crassus, himself a great orator, was responsible for the censorial edict that ordered the closing of the Latin rhetoric school of Plotius Gallus.

4. Cic. De orat. 1.31.142; Quint. Inst. 3.5.2.

5. Perotti Corn. fol. CXCIII^v. Originally the rhētōr was a public speaker, later a teacher of techniques of speaking, but rhetor in Latin applied mainly to the professor rather than the practitioner, though it was also used pejoratively of someone trained in rhetoric. The orator was a spokesman, ambassador or public speaker, the office idealized in philosophical, political and literary terms by Cicero and Quintilian. Declamatio at first meant voice-training, but eventually the word came to be used for practice-speaking in general.

CHAPTER XIV

1. Quint. Inst. 1.10.9   Hor. Ars 391–393   Verg. Ecl. 4.55–57. Some sources say that Orpheus was the son of Apollo and Calliope, others say Oiagrus and Calliope. In one genealogy Linus is a son of Apollo by Aithousa or Psamathe and the great-grandfather of Orpheus. Another story tells that Apollo killed him for contesting his skill in music; still another says that Hercules, his student in music, killed Linus. Linos was also the name of a harvest song.

2. Verg. A 1.740–746; Quint. Inst. 1.10.10   Plin. Nat. 7.204; Serv. Ecl. 2.24; Verg. Ecl. 2.23–24   Hor. Ars 394–395   Stat. Theb. 1.9–10. The bard Iopas appears at the end of the first book of the Aeneid, singing at the feast that Dido gives for Aeneas. Antiope is the daughter of a Theban king, Nycteus, who wanted her killed for conceiving the twins Amphion and Zethus, fathered by Zeus. Dirke carried out the order by confining and abusing Antiope, whose sons were raised by a cattle-herder until they rescued their mother and punished Dirke. Some authorities say that Amphion first played the lyre, that his music made animals and even stones move, and that the walls of Thebes were assembled by his musical power. The mountain called Aracynthus was on the border between Boeotia and Attica or Acte. Publius Papinius Statius (45–96 CE) wrote two epic poems, the Thebaid and the unfinished Achilleid. The

Silvae are five books of shorter poems. These three works were printed with commentaries by Lactantius Placidus (5th–6th century) in 1483.

3. Eus. *PE* 2.2.8, 11; 10.12.17, 28   Solin. 11.6   Plb. 4.20.7   Diod. S. 1.16.1; Quint. *Inst.* 1.10.12. In the *Chronicle*, Eusebius says that Linus, Zethus and Amphion were famous musicians eleven years after Cadmus came to Thebes in year 587 of Abraham (1430 BCE), adding that Dionysus or Father Liber was the son of Semele, the daughter of Cadmus. He also notes that in the time of Perseus Dionysus was fighting in India, in year 687 of Abraham, 262 years after Moses was born. But the *Preparation* dates 'the apotheosis of Dionysus' more than six centuries after Moses, though again in the reign of Perseus. A *daktulos* is a finger, and the Dactyls (*DIR* 2.19.3) were smiths and magicians associated with Mt. Ida, Rhea and the birth of Zeus, like the Curetes (*kourētes*) or shield-dancers who protected the infant Zeus in his mountain cave. The innovative Greek *Histories* of Polybius (200–118 BCE) told the story of Rome's growth from the First Punic War through 146. Despite Perotti's translation (ed. prin. 1473) of the five surviving books and their keen intererest in method, Polydore, like most Renaissance historians, was less attracted by Polybius than by Livy.

4. Jos. *AJ* 1.64. According to Gen. 4:18–22, Methushael's son Lamech 'married two women, one named Adah, the other named Zillah. Adah gave birth to *Jabal* (*Yaval; Iōbēl*, LXX; *Iabel*, Vulg.), the ancestor of tent-dwellers who raise flocks and herds. His brother's name was *Jubal* (*Yuval; Ioubal*, LXX; *Jubal*, Vulg.); he was the ancestor of those who play the harp and pipe. Zillah, the other wife, bore *Tubal-cain* (*Tuval Qayin; Thōbel*, LXX; *Tubalcain*, Vulg.), the master of all coppersmiths and blacksmiths.' The version in Josephus is that 'Methusela's son Lamech had seventy-seven children by two wives, Sella and Ada. *Jobel* (*Iōbēlos; Iobal* in Latin), one of Ada's children, put up tents and led a shepherd's life, and *Jubal* (*Ioubalos; Tubal*), who had the same mother, trained himself in music and invented harps and citharas. But *Jubel* (*Ioubēlos; Tubalcain*), born of the other mother and surpassing all in strength, excelled in the pursuit of battle by which he procured for himself the pleasures of the body, and he was also the first to make bronze.' Confusion among Jubal, Tubalcain and Tubal as inventors of music was common in medieval sources.

5. Quint. *Inst.* 1.10.16; Verg. *Ecl.* 1.56   cf. Liv. 21.33.7, 44.5.1.

6. Plin. *Nat.* 10.81–82.

7. Diod. S. 1.81.7; Plb. 4.20.5; Quint. *Inst.* 1.10.13, 19, 20; Cic. *Tusc.* 1.2.4; *Adagia* (1550), p. 14. Ephorus of Cyme (*DIR* 1.6.10) wrote a universal history which, despite its censure by modern critics, deeply influenced Polybius and other authors. He also wrote a work *On discoveries*. Themistocles (524–459) led Athens against the Persians in 480, was ostracized around 470 and then appointed governor of Magnesia by Artaxerxes I. The *Salii* were a minor priesthood, a dozen young patricians who dressed like old-time soldiers and chanted an archaic song, the *Carmen Saliare*, as they danced through the city. For Polydore's *Proverbiorum libellus*, see his letter to Odassio, par. 1, and his first letter to Gian Matteo Vergil, par. 3.

8. Perotti *Corn.* fol. CLIIIIr   *DIR* 1.15   Cic. *De orat.* 1.42.187.

CHAPTER XV

1. Serv. G 4.463; Isid. *Orig.* 3.22.8; Perotti *Corn.* fol. LXXIIIr   Hor. *Carm.* 1.10.5–6   Diod. S. 1.16.1   Serv. A 4.242; Verg. A 4.242–243   Perotti *Corn.* fol. LXXIIIr; Tortelli, *Orth.* sig. o7r; Hyg. *Astr.* 2.7.1–3. Mercury equips himself with his wand (caduceus) and winged sandals of gold as Jupiter sends him to warn Aeneas that he is wasting his time with Dido in Carthage. The Homeric *Hymn to Hermes* and later sources tell the story of his use of the tortoise-shell to make a lyre, his theft of Apollo's cattle and his gift of the lyre to that god in recompense, who in turn gave him his magic wand. Normally the *lura* had seven or eight strings, but Diodorus obviously has three in mind.

2. *DIR* 1.14.1.

3. Plin. *Nat.* 7.204   Diod. S. 3.58.3; Eus. *PE* 10.6.4; 2.2.41; Plin. *Nat.* 7.204   [Plu.] *De mus.* 14   Plin. *Nat.* 7.204; Perotti *Corn.* fol. CLVr. According to modern editions, Pliny attributed the invention of the *monaulos* and the *fistula* to Pan, Mercury's son, but the 1497 edition supports Polydore. The woodwind called *aulos* (*tibia*) was a reed instrument, either single or double, whose body was a tube with holes for fingering, but one piper usually played two as a pair. The *tibia obliqua* may

have been fitted with a reed *slanted* at an angle. The *surinx (fistula)* was played by blowing into one end of a single tube with finger holes or across the ends of several tubes tied together. Lydian, Dorian, Phrygian and other ethnic names were given to different modes or scales which varied in interval and tonality. Terpander of Antissa became famous as a poet and musician in seventh century Sparta, notably for his invention of the cithara (lyre) with seven strings. Thamyras was blinded by the Muses for challenging their primacy in music, as Apollo punished Marsyas and Midas. The 1497 Pliny has *Dardanus* as the inventor of singing to the accompaniment of pipes, but later editors conjectured Ardalus from [Plu.] *De mus.* 5, where *Ardalos Troizēnios* teaches this art. Dardanus, ancestor of the Trojans, was associated with the Troad, not Troezen.

4. Plin. *Nat.* 7.204; Serv. *Ecl.* 2.31   Ov. *Met.* 1.689–712; Verg. *Ecl.* 2.32–33   [Plu.] *De mus.* 14. Corydon is the lovesick shepherd of Vergil's second *Eclogue*.

5. Plin. *Nat.* 29.6   Eus. *PE* 2.2.41   Plin. *Nat.* 7.204; Diod. S. 3.59.2   Hyg. *Fab.* 165   Plin. *Nat.* 7.204; Verg. *A* 6.646; Isid. *Orig.* 3.22.4. Herophilus of Chalcedon (330–260 BCE) laid the foundations of a scientific anatomy in Alexandria. His theory of pulse rhythm as a diagnostic indicator was related to the musical teaching of Aristoxenus of Tarentum. The poet Timotheus of Miletus (450–360) was a famous performer on the lyre. Diodorus actually writes that Cybele and Marsyas 'came upon Apollo when he had gained great acclaim for the lyre, which—they say—Hermes invented but Apollo first used correctly . . . and Apollo first played without accompaniment,' but Hermes had disappeared from the Latin Diodorus that Polydore used. Two mythological sources, the *Fabulae* (ed. prin. 1535) and *Astronomica* (ed. prin. 1475), are attributed to a Hyginus and may have been written in the second century CE. Polydore mentions Hyginus only once by name, on which occasion he (or his source) seems to be citing the as yet unprinted *Fabulae*.

6. *DIR* 1.14.4; Ps.-Hier. *Ep.* 23.5–6 (*PL* 30:214C–D).

7. Jos. *AJ* 7.305–306. The *kinura (canora)* and *nabla* also occur in the list of instruments in Psalm 150 as the *kinnor* and *nevel*, the 'psaltery and harp' of the Authorized Version.

8. August. *Enarr. in Ps.* 150.7   *DIR* 3.18.7. The term that Josephus uses, *organon (organum)*, can mean any instrument in general or a particular musical instrument. The water organ *(hudraulis)* of Ktesibios was described by Vitruvius (10.8). Pneumatic organs were used in Byzantium and introduced to the West by the eighth century. Polydore cites Augustine only twice, here and at *DIR* 2.2.12.

9. Clem. Al. *Strom.* 1.16.76.4; Solin. 56.   Plin. *Nat.* 7.201; Diod. S. 5.40.1   Verg. *A* 8.526. The Trogodytae (*Trōgodutai*) were a desert people of the northern Sudan and southern Egypt, whereas *Trōglodutai (trōglē,* 'hole') was used of various African and Asian groups thought to live in caves — whence 'Troglodyte.' Aristotle knew the Greek form (*sambukē*) of the Aramaic *sabbeka*, a four-stringed instrument shaped like a triangle. Titus Flavius Clemens (150–215 CE) was the second head of the Christian school of Alexandria. His *Stromateis* or *Scrapbooks* (ed. prin. 1551) is a miscellany on the relationship between Christian teaching and Greek thought, expressing a relatively positive evaluation of the latter. Modern editions of Pliny give 'Pisaeus, son of Tyrennus' from *Pisaeum Tyrreni*, but the 1497 text has *Piseum Tyrrhenum* or 'Piseus the Etruscan.' Pliny credited this otherwise unknown figure with the battle-axe, the trumpet, and the 'beak' used by one ship to ram another. The main use for brass musical instruments in antiquity was military.

10. Hor. *Ars* 401–403; Ps.-Acro ad loc.; Porphyrio ad loc.; Just. *Epit.* 3.5.3–14   Lact. Plac. *Comm. in Theb. Stat.* 4.224. Horace has *Tyrtaeus*, the Spartan war poet of the mid-seventh century BCE. Modern editions of Justinus also have *Tyrtaeus*, but the 1497 text has *Cyrteus* or *Cyrtheus*, the reading in earlier editions of *De inventoribus*. *Dircaeus* means Boeotian, the epithet Vergil gives to Amphion in *Ecl.* 2.24. The commentaries of Helenius Acro (c. 200 CE) on Terence and Horace are lost. The extant material (ed. prin. 1474) attached to his name in the Renaissance comes from many sources. Lactantius Placidus (ed. prin. c. 1476), to whom scholia on the *Thebais* of Statius are attributed, probably lived in the sixth century CE.

11. Jos. *AJ* 3.291. Josephus has *asōsra* for *chatsotsrah*, a straight, thin metal trumpet flared at the end.

12. Dion. H. 1.33.4 Gel. 1.11.1–5; Th. 5.70; Plb. 4.20.6; Plu. *Lyc.* 21.4; Quint. *Inst.* 1.10.14. Instead of *non voluptatis causa*, Lorenzo Valla's Latin Thucydides (ed. prin. 1483) has *non rei divinae gratia* for *ou tou theiou charin*. Gellius, whom Polydore follows here, has *non prorsus ex aliquo ritu religionum neque rei divinae gratia*.

13. Gel. 1.11.6–7; Hdt. 1.17 Plu. *Crass.* 23.7; Ps.-App. *Liber Parthicus*, tr. Candido, 1477, sig. h8 Verg. *A* 6.164–165. Alyattes (610–560 BCE), king of Lydia and father of Croesus, won some of his battles against the Ionian Greeks but did not capture Miletus. In the early second century BCE, Appian of Alexandria wrote a *History of Rome*, eleven of whose twenty-four books survive complete. The *Liber Parthicus*, recognized as inauthentic by the sixteenth century but treated in early editions as part of book eleven on Syria, is an early Byzantine addition that Polydore could have read in Pier Candido Decembrio's translation (ed. prin. 1477).

CHAPTER XVI

1. Cic. *Off.* 2.2.5; *Tusc.* 5.2.5; Lact. *Inst.* pr.; 1.1; 3.13, 25–8 Diog. L. 1.pr.1; Hier. *Adv. Jov.* 1.42 (*PL* 23:273A). The first mention of Magi as a Zoroastrian priestly tribe among the Medes appears in Herodotus (1.101, 181), who also identifies the Chaldaeans as priests of Bel in Babylon. Chaldaeans appear as a distinct ethnic group in ninth century Babylonia. The *gumnosophistai* are the famous naked philosophers of India, where the Buddha died in the early fifth century BCE. Caesar described the Druids of Gaul in the middle of the first century. Strabo (16.2.24) identifies Mochus (*Môchos*) as a philosopher from Sidon in Phoenicia who lived before the time of Troy. Diogenes writes *Môchon*, but *Ochus* occurs in Traversari's Latin. For Zalmoxis, Diogenes has *Zamolxin*, but Herodotus has *Salmoxis* for the god of the Getae. Atlas, the mountain-bearing Titan associated with the range of that name in northwest Africa, was credited with astronomical and other wisdom. The Egyptian god whom Herodotus calls Hephaestus (Vulcan) is Ptah, also a god of crafts; Cicero makes the second Vulcan a son of the Nile, called Opas by the Egyptians.

2. Eus. *PE* 9.1–3.3; 10.3.26, 9.11–28, 14.18–19; 11.6.1, 28.17–19; 13.12.1–4; *Chron.* Helm, pp. 88, 104 Lact. *Inst.* 3.2; Diog. L. 1.pr.12; Cic. *Tusc.*

5.3.8–9; Eus. *PE* 10.4.13; Perotti *Corn.* fol. CCLr; Tortelli *Orth.* sig. r8v. In the *Preparation*, Eusebius cites Porphyry's polemic *Against the Christians* on the relative chronology of Mosaic and Greek philosophy, concluding that 'Moses came 1500 years before the Greek philosophers' and specifically listing Pythagoras and Democritus. Eusebius does not mention Thales here, but in the *Chronicle* he names him before Pythagoras, placing Thales as early as the year 1270 of Abraham (747 BCE), Pythagoras in year 1487 (530) — 845 and 1062 years after the birth of Moses, respectively. This interval between Moses and Pythagoras (but not the chronology that Eusebius attributes to Porphyry) supports Polydore's claim that the Greek philosophers 'came more than a thousand years after Moses.' Editions before 1536 reduce the figure to about seven centuries, which is closer to the time between Moses and Thales in the *Chronicle*. In the 1483 *Chronicle*, for example, there are 728 *anni mundi* from Moses to Thales. Moses as philosopher was sometimes identified with Mochus or Musaeus.

3. Diog. L. 1.pr.13; Eus. *PE* 10.4.17; Tortelli *Orth.* sig. r8v. That Anaximander studied with Thales is chronologically possible but not evident before Theophrastus and the later doxographic tradition. The departure of Pythagoras from Samos to Croton in Italy was probably in reaction to the tyranny of Polycrates (535–22 BCE). Xenophanes of Colophon (570–470) also left Ionia for Italy and may have visited Elea but was probably not the founder of the Eleatic school, though the doxographers treat him as such. Instead of *Eleatica*, the 1480 Trapezuntius version of Eusebius also has *Cleatica*, but see below, paragraph 4, for Elea spelled correctly.

4. Cic. *De orat.* 1.15.68; Diog. L. 1.pr.18; Eus. *PE* 11.1.1, 2.1; Hier. *Ep.* 30.1; *Dial. c. Pelag.* 1.21 (*PL* 22:441, 23:514C) Eus. *PE* 11.1.1 Diog. L. 1.pr.18, 2.16 Cic. *Tusc.* 5.4.10 Diog. L. 1.pr.18, 8.57; Tortelli *Orth.* sig. r8v, z5v; Perotti *Corn.* fol. CCLr. The threefold division of philosophy into physics, ethics and dialectic can be found in Aristotle (*Top.* 105^{b}20) and has also been traced to Xenocrates of Chalcedon, third head of the Academy. It was probably Anaxagoras rather than Archelaus (later fifth century) who brought Ionian physics to Athens. Perhaps because he wished not to acknowledge the Sophists as philosophers, Aristotle (*Part. An.* 642^{a}28; *Meta.* 987^{b}1, 1078^{b}17) established the false view, stated most memorably

by Cicero, that Socrates was the first to turn from natural to moral philosophy. Plato (*Phaedo* 96A) describes the young Socrates as deeply interested in nature, which is consistent with the attack on him by Aristophanes in *The Clouds*. Diogenes claims that dialectic began with Zeno of Elea (not Zeno of Citium, the Stoic); he used arguments whose striking patterns (drawing two contradictory conclusions from the negative of the proposition to be proved) rather than any technical contributions to logic won him the reputation of having invented dialectic, which in some broad sense Socrates and the Sophists had used.

5. Diog. L. 3.48. Diogenes writes: 'they claim that the first to write dialogues *(dialogous . . . prōton grapsai)* was Zeno of Elea. But Aristotle in book 1 *On Poets* says that it was Alexamenus of Styra or Teos . . . Yet I believe that Plato, who perfected the genre, should rightly take first place for its invention *(heureseōs)* as well as its beauty.'

Chapter xvii

1. *Adagia* (1550), p. 85 Firm. Mat. 1.2.1, 3.7.7, 8.17.3, 19.3. The *Mathesis* (ed. prin. 1497) of Julius Firmicus Maternus (fl. 334 CE), who wrote under Stoic influence, is more revealing for its ethics than reliable for its technical astrology. Firmicus, who eventually became a Christian, also wrote a polemic against paganism, *Concerning the Error of Profane Religions*. The horoscopic material here — but not the comment on complexions — was one of the few passages omitted from books 1–3 of *De inventoribus* in the expurgated Roman edition of 1576 (*DIR*, second letter to Gian Matteo Vergil, 1.17.5, 3.12.5).

2. Hdt. 2.82 Diod. S. 2.31.1 Ov. *Ep.* 8.87–88. Egyptian belief in a system of lucky and unlucky days was based on climate, myth and the religious calendar, merging eventually with astrology. The assignment of gods to months as tutelary deities was also traditional. Babylonians used astronomical omens for political purposes early in the second millennium. In Ovid's *Heroides* 8, the jealous Hermione begs Orestes, who has already murdered his mother and her lover, to kill her husband.

3. Diod. S. 1.16.1, 81.4; 5.56.4–57.4; Clem. Al. *Strom.* 1.16.74.2 Jos. *AJ* 1.154–157, 167–168; *Ap.* 1.14. 21–4. Among the many discoveries of the

Egyptian Thoth were mathematics and the calendar, thus providing an easy link to astronomy. Pherecydes, Pythagoras and Thales were all credited with knowledge of the heavens and of Eastern wisdom.

4. Plin. *Nat.* 7.203   Verg. *A* 6.796–797   Plin. *Nat.* 5.67, 6.121, 7.203; Serv. *Ecl.* 6.31. 33–37. Since Atlas is the father of the Pleiades and Hyades, his association with astronomy is natural. In the *Preparation* (9.17.8), Eusebius accommodates the Greek claim for Atlas with Hebrew tradition by arguing that Atlas and Enoch were the same, and the *Chronicle* puts him in year 380 of Abraham (1637 BCE). Pliny is describing a temple of Ba'al in Babylon, distantly linked with the Belos who was born to Poseidon and Libya and fathered Aegyptus, Danaus and Damno.

5. Jos. *AJ* 1.69–71. The third son of Adam and Eve was Seth, from whose son Enos came the part of the human race that did not come from Lamech, offspring of the cursed Cain and father of Noah. The last sentence of this paragraph is omitted in the Roman edition of 1576.

6. Plin. *Nat.* 2.43, 53   Plu. *Nic.* 23. Gaius Sulpicius Gallus was a soldier, politician and astronomer; he wrote about eclipses, including the lunar eclipse of 168, before the battle of Pydna. Endymion is a mythical character, though Pliny writes that he was 'the first human' to observe lunar phenomena. A son of Zeus, his father let him choose the manner of his death — eternal sleep — a choice somehow related to Selene's love for him. Selene appears in Homer as the moon. Anaxagoras, prosecuted for impiety in the middle of the fifth century BCE, had a more sophisticated view of astronomy than the earlier pre-Socratics — so much so that Pliny (2.149) and Diogenes (2.10) credit him with the impossible feat of predicting the meteorite that fell on Aegospotami in 467. Nicias was a general responsible for the defeat of Athens by Syracuse in 413, preceded by an eclipse of the moon, famously recounted in Thucydides 7.

7. Diog. L. 8.14, 9.23   Cic. *Tusc.* 1.25.63; Diog. L. 1.pr.3; Plin. *Nat.* 2.31, 7.203. Diogenes knew that the first recognition of the identity of morning and evening stars was attributed both to Pythagoras and to Parmenides. He also says that Anaximander made a *sphaira*, more likely a star-map than a celestial globe, but it is unlikely that the primitive pre-Socratic cosmology would have motivated either effort. The *sphaira*

of Archimedes (287–11) may have been a physical model, an armillary sphere or orrery, as described in his lost work *On Sphere-Making*.

8. Plin. *Nat.* 3.94, 7.203; Str. 1.8–9, 6.2.10. Describing the volcanic Aeolian islands northeast of Sicily with their strong winds and tell-tale smoke and fire, Strabo comments that 'the Poet's tale that seems to be quite fabulous is actually the truth wrapped in a riddle—that Aeolus controlled the winds.' He mentions the same story in the defense of Homer that introduces his *Geography*.

9. Plin. *Nat.* 2.119; Vitr. 1.6.4–5; Gel. 2.22.3–4; Perotti *Corn.* fol. CIIv. Andronicus Cyrrhestes took his name from *Kurrhos* or *Kurrhēstikē*; in Syria, but he built his wind-tower in Athens in the first century BCE. Vitruvius, author of *De architectura* (ed. prin. 1483–90), wrote late in the Republic or early in the Principate; his work was known to Petrarch before Poggio's discovery of a manuscript at St. Gall in 1416.

10. Gel. 2.22.9–15; Perotti *Corn.* fols. CIIv–CIIIr.

11. Gel. 2.22.19–29; Plin. *Nat.* 2.120–1.

12. Plin. *Nat.* 7.209.

CHAPTER XVIII

1. Diod. S. 1.34–6; Hdt. 2.13–14, 19; Plin. *Nat.* 5.58; Str. 17.1.3   Str. 17.1.3; Hdt. 2.109; Diod. S. 1.81.2. Claudius reigned from 41 to 54 CE. Pompey lost to Caesar at Pharsalus on June 6, 48 BCE, and was murdered in Egypt on September 28 of the same year. Strabo puts the highest rise at fourteen cubits, the lowest at eight. Herodotus gives figures in roughly the same range for the height required for adequate irrigation. The association between the heliacal rising of Sirius and the annual flooding of the Nile seems to have stimulated astronomy and the astronomical (decan) calendar more than geometry in Egypt, though astronomy also remained crude until the Hellenistic period. The Greeks, impressed by the antiquity of Egyptian culture, generally overestimated their sophistication in geometry, astronomy and other sciences. The geometry of the Egyptians, who developed a good approximation for π, was better than their arithmetic. The early development of mathematics was most advanced in Babylonia.

· NOTES TO THE TRANSLATION ·

2. Jos. *AJ* 1.105–106, 167–168. Josephus has 'God granted them longer life both because of their goodness (*aretēn*) and because of the usefulness (*euchrēstian*) of the things they discovered—astronomy and geometry,' and the Latin Josephus rendered this *propter virtutes et gloriosas utilitates quas iugiter perscrutabantur id est astrologiam et geometriam*. Polydore made the phrase more obscure by omitting *et . . . utilitates*.

3. Cic. *ND* 3.88; *De orat.* 1.42.187   Lilius *Orig.* sig. b8*v*. Tiberius ruled from 14 to 37 CE; Trajan from 98 to 117; and Antoninus Pius from 138 to 161. Claudius Ptolemaeus (fl. 127–148), in addition to his astronomical, astrological and mathematical works, wrote a *Geography*. This passage on ancient geometry shows the influence of a work by Zachario Giglio (Lilius) da Vicenza *De origine et laudibus scientiarum*, which appeared in 1496 before the first edition of *De inventoribus*.

CHAPTER XIX

1. Eutropius *Hist.* [1471], fol. 10r   Diod. S. 5.75.2   Plin. *Nat.* 7.198   Str. 8.3.33; Diog. L. 2.105; Gel. 2.18.1–5. The *Breviarium ab urbe condita*, written in the later fourth century CE by Eutropius, secretary to the emperor Valens, is an epitome of Roman history from the kings to the accession of Valens (364 CE). Paul the Deacon amplified Eutropius and continued the story down to Justinian (527–65). The first printed text (1471) differs substantially from modern editions because it contains material from medieval sources. Since natives of Sidon in Phoenicia were famous as traders, it was natural to attribute weights and measures to them. But *Sidonius* is probably a mistake by a continuator of Eutropius for *Phidon* or *Fidon* of Argos, who appears in the *Chronicle* of Eusebius as the inventor of weights and measures in the year 1219 of Abraham. In this period, to which Eusebius assigns Jeroboam in Israel and Azarias in Judah, he also places Procas of Alba, who became king in year 1197 of Abraham (820 BCE). Jeroboam I actually ruled from 924 to 903, Asa from 905 to 874. Livy (1.3.3–9) writes that Ascanius, the son of Aeneas, founded Alba Longa and that Proca was the twelfth to succeed him. Strabo also has *Pheidōna . . . Argeion, dekaton . . . apo Tēmenou*, which in the 1494 Latin version became *Phedon origine decimus a Temeno*. This Pheidon, who invaded *Eleia*, ruled Argos in the early seventh century.

602

Stories about his work with measures and coinage (Hdt. 6.127) led to confusion with Phaedon of *Elis*, the slave who founded the philosophical school of that city in the early fifth century and gave his name to one of Plato's dialogues. The 1497 Pliny and modern editions have *Phidon Argivus*; Diogenes has *Phaidōn Eleios*. The Gellius mentioned here, one of Pliny's sources, is Gnaeus Gellius, the annalist of the second century, not Aulus Gellius (*DIR* 1.8.6), who describes Phaedon of Elis as a slave and a follower of Socrates.

2. Diog. L. 8.14; Jos. *AJ* 1.61   Diog. L. 8.11–12, 47; Diod. S. 1.98.2; Serv. *A* 4.577; Gel. 1.9.6   Liv. 7.3.3–9. Diogenes claims that Pythagoras 'brought geometry to completion, while Moiris first discovered the beginnings of its elements, . . . [and] Pythagoras applied himself mainly to its arithmetical side,' noting that another Pythagoras, 'a sculptor from Rhegium . . . was the first who tried for proportion (*rhuthmou*, cf. *numerus*) and symmetry.' Like the philosopher, the sculptor (490–450 BCE) came from Samos, but he moved to Rhegium in Italy.

3. Paul. *Fest.* p. 49L; Perotti, *Corn.* fol. LXVIIr; *DIR* 2.4.8. The Roman census was to be taken every five years, when a ceremony of purification or *lustrum* marked the end of the period. *Lustrum* was also the term of the censor's office as well as any five-year period and, confusingly, the four-year interval between two Olympiads. The *Fasti consulares*, or list of consuls whose names designated years, was probably drawn up around 300 CE; the list began in 509, when the Capitoline temple of Jupiter Optimus Maximus was dedicated. The temple contained *cellae* for Juno and Minerva as well as Jupiter, these three constituting the Capitoline triad. The plague-year in question was 363, when the dictator was Lucius Manlius Imperiosus and his master of the horse was Lucius Pinarius. The dictator was appointed in emergencies, and when the emergency was a plague, the dictator's purpose in driving in the nail was to ward off evil through ritual, whereas the *praetor maximus* drove the annual nail on September 13 to mark the calendar. In the Etruscan city of Volsinii, the rite of driving the nail took place in the temple of the goddess Nortia, whom Roman authors identified with Fortuna and Nemesis.

4. Although Gerbert made some use the Indian or Arabic notation by the late tenth century, it was the *Algorithmus* or *Book of Restoration and*

Equalization by al-Khwarizmi (ninth century) that effectively introduced the new numerals to the West by way of the *Algorismus* of John of Holywood and other thirteenth century works. By Polydore's time, the new numerals had won acceptance through commercial transactions, but not without resistance and suspicion, even in the sixteenth century.

CHAPTER XX

1. Plin. *Nat.* 29.2–3.

2. Diod. S. 1.16.1, 5.74.5; Clem. Al. *Strom.* 1.16; Plin. *Nat.* 7.196 Ov. *Met.* 1.521–522; *Ep.* 5.151–2; cf. *Ars*, 2.239–40, *Rem. am.* 75–9, *Ep. ex Ponto* 2.9.43–4 Macr. *Sat.* 1.17.14; Clem. Al. *Strom.* 1.16; Cic. *ND* 3.22.57. Among the discoveries of the Egyptian Hermes, Diodorus lists 'the proper conformation of the body,' which becomes explicitly medical in the Latin translation: *numerorumque et ad corpora curanda medicinae artis.* Apollo sometimes destroys (*apollumi*) through disease, as when he shoots plague-arrows in the first book of the *Iliad*, but Macrobius notes another etymology from *apelaunō* (drive out). The god made the laurel (*daphnē*) his sacred plant when Zeus changed the maiden huntress Daphne into a laurel bush to save her from the god's pursuit. The nymph Oenone killed herself when she tried too late to save Paris, who had spurned her, from the wound of a poisoned arrow. The words that Polydore quotes, however, do not appear in the fifth of the *Heroides*, where Ovid records Oenone's complaint. For similar phrases, see the passages cited from Ovid's other poems. The archaic Asclepius was a hero rather than a god, his usual parents Apollo and Coronis; he learned his craft not from Apollo, however, but from Chiron the centaur. When Zeus killed Asclepius with a thunderbolt for trying to cure death, Apollo in revenge slew the Cyclops, and his punishment was to serve the mortal Admetus. The growth of the Asclepius cult in the fifth century and later invited the multiplication of divinities and genealogies reflected in Cicero's account.

3–5. *DIR* 1.13.1; Quint. *Inst.* 3.2.3 Cels. proem. 9, 30–35 Cic. *ND* 3.22.57 Diod. S. 5.74–5–6. Probably when Tiberius was emperor, Aulus Cornelius Celsus compiled an encyclopedic work titled *Artes* of which the sections surviving (ed. prin. 1478) deal with medicine and suggest that Celsus was a physician.

6. Plin. *Nat.* 26.10; 29.2, 4; Str. 8.6.15. Hippocrates of Cos, a contemporary of Socrates and the Sophists, probably did not write any of the fifty-odd treatises of the Hippocratic Corpus, which may derive from a medical school library and vary widely in date and content. By the fifth century there were physicians on Cos who regarded themselves as descendants of Asclepius. The distinctive feature of his rite was incubation, a dream in which the god revealed the course of treatment to the patient. Inscriptions as well as literary records preserve accounts of healing dreams. In 291 Asclepius came to Rome as Aesculapius.

7. Plin. *Nat.* 29.12–14. Allegedly the first Greek physician to come to Rome, Archagathus arrived in 219 BCE during the first consulate of Lucius Aemilius Paullus. The other consul in 219 was Marcus Livius Salinator. In a later generation Marcus Porcius Cato Censorius (234–149) was the great spokesman for anti-Greek nativism. Lucius Cassius Hemina, Pliny's source for Archagathus, was an annalist of the second century.

8. Plin. *Nat.* 29.11, 18.

9. Hdt. 1.197, 2.84; Str. 3.3.7, 16.1.20. Although this chapter on medicine is one of the few in *De inventoribus* that does not attribute the discovery of its subject to the Hebrews, Polydore praises the wisdom of eastern medicine from Babylon after repeating criticism of Greco-Roman medicine by Cato and Pliny. Strabo locates Bastetania on the southeast coast of the Iberian peninsula.

10. Plin. *Nat.* 29.6–7; Tortelli *Orth.* sig. n5r. The 1497 Pliny has *cassios carpitanos aruncios albucios rubrios*, implying five individuals, not the two suggested by the punctuation in all editions of *De inventoribus*. Antonius Musa, despite his name a Greek freedman, cured Augustus in 23 BCE. Galen of Pergamum (129–200 CE) came to Rome in 162, a year after the death of Antoninus Pius, and became court physician to Marcus Aurelius. Avicenna lived much later, from 980 to 1037.

CHAPTER XXI

1. Plin. *Nat.* 10.40, 25.14   Hdt. 3.100; Ps.-App. *Liber Parthicus*, tr. Decembrio, 1477, sig. i8v; cf. Plu. *Ant.* 45.5–6. After these references to In-

dia and Parthia, Polydore concentrates on Greco-Roman pharmacy. As
in the previous chapter on medicine, he makes no claim for Jewish discoveries in this field. The ethnographer and historian Xanthus of Lydia
lived in the fifth century BCE. The identity of the plant *balis* is unknown.
The Parthian expedition was part of the effort by Marcus Antonius (83–
31) and Cleopatra VII (69–30) to establish supremacy in the East, but
Antony's forces were defeated in 36.

2. Plin. *Nat.* 7.196, 25.16; Diod. S. 5.74.5–6   Ov. *Met.* 1.522, 2.629–645;
Diod. S. 5.74.6; Cic. *ND* 3.22.57; Eus. *PE* 1.10.14. As hybrids of human
and horse, Centaurs are wilder than men, yet capable of teaching them;
Chiron instructs Asclepius, Jason and Achilles. The 'soothing medicines'
(*ēpia pharmaka*) used by Machaon in the *Iliad* were shown to his father,
Asclepius, by Chiron. In the *Preparation*, Eusebius quotes from Philo of
Byblos (70–160 CE), who in turn cites Sanchuniathon on the cosmogony
of the Phoenicians, including an extensive passage on inventors. Among
them are *Misōr kai Sudek (Misora et Selech)*, who discovered salt. Misor was
the father of Taautos (Thoth or Hermes Trismegistus, Cicero's fifth
Mercury) and Sudek of the 'Dioskouroi or Kabeiroi or Korubantes or
Samothrakes . . . from whom were born others who discovered botanical
medicines, remedies for animal bites and incantations.' The island of
Samothrace was home to the Cabiri, whose cult was widespread in the
north Aegean and who were associated elsewhere with the Dioscuri
(Castor and Pollux), divine sons of Zeus. Sanchuniathon's *Phoenician His-
tory* may reflect genuine traditions in a fictional setting before the Fall of
Troy.

3. Plin. *Nat.* 25.33, 66; Ov. *Fast.* 5.397–398, 413–414. The bachelor's but-
ton, *Centaurea cyanus*, is the most familiar species of the large genus
Centaurea. Two Centaurs especially, Chiron and Pholus, are less savage
than the others, and in the Greek myths both die in the aftermath of
Hercules' hunt for the Erymanthian boar. Crazed by wine—a product of
human culture—at the victory feast, the Centaurs start a brawl, causing
Hercules to strike Chiron accidentally with an arrow coated with the
Hydra's venom. Ovid changed this story in the source that Polydore
used, the *Fasti*, where Hercules visits Chiron while Achilles is in his care,
dying when an arrow falls on his foot after he touches the hero's weapons

in admiration. The Centaur tries to treat himself with healing plants, but the Hydra's blood is too toxic.

4. Cels. 5 proem. Asclepiades of Prusias, a Greek medical writer of the first century BCE who came to Rome, was an atomist and a forerunner of the methodist sect; he depended more on regimen than drugs.

5. Plin. Nat. 25.26, 30, 42. Yarrow or *Achillea millefolium* is one of the best known species of the genus *Achillea*. It was sometimes called *panacea* or *panaces*, as were centaury and other medicinal plants, especially *Opopanax chironium*, known as woundwort in English. Panacea was a daughter of Asclepius. Pliny tried to find the botanical identity of the plant that Homer calls *mōlu*, a word from the 'language of the gods'; he identifies it as a nightshade. The god called *Sol* in Latin could be either a native Roman deity (*Sol Indiges*) or a Latinized Helios, identified with Apollo in Euripides and later authors, or—after Pliny's time—the Eastern *Sol Invictus*. Helios, born of the Titans, is a distinct god in Homer and Hesiod, where he emerges from Oceanus every morning. Making him Ocean's son rationalizes the genealogy, and his role in Pliny as an inventor may reflect euhemerism. Modern editions read *ex metallis*, but the 1497 Pliny has *ex melle*, which Polydore follows here even though *DIR* 2.19.2 treats Sol as a discoverer of precious metals.

6. Plin. Nat. 7.197   Plin. Nat. 8.97–8, 25.89; Cic. ND 2.50.126   Cels. De med. 6.6.39   Plin. Nat. 8.98. Aristotle (*HA* 612^{a}2–5) reported that goats use dittany (*Origanum dictamnus* or *Dictamnus creticus*) because it has the power to extract weapons. *Phalangium* might indicate any of a number of poisonous spiders, perhaps of the genus *Latrodectus*. Celandine or *Chelidonium majus* is also called swallowwort. *Cunila* may be a plant of the mint family, *Lamiaceae*.

7. Plin. Nat. 8.96–8, 10.62; Isid. Orig. 12.3.3, 7.33. Rue is the evergreen shrub, *Ruta graveolens*; perennial marjoram is *Origanum onites*. In the 1497 Pliny and in modern editions, the weasel hunts mice rather than snakes.

8. Plin. Nat. 25.4–7, 12; Tortelli Orth. sig. N5v. Cato the Censor composed *De agri cultura* or *De re rustica* (ed. prin. 1472) around 160 BCE. In addition to the medical sections of this work, he also wrote a *De medicina* which has not survived. Pompeius Lenaeus continued teaching in Rome

after Pompey's death in 48. Mithridates VI of Pontus (120–63), whom Pompey defeated in 66, was reputedly forced to ask one of his soldiers to kill him when he found that experiments with poisonous drugs had made him immune to them. Pedanius Dioscorides of Anazarbus was a Cilician physician who wrote his *Materia medica* (ed. prin. 1478) during the reigns of Claudius (41–54 CE) and Nero (54–68).

Chapter XXII

1. Plin. *Nat.* 30.2–3   Just. *Epit.* 1.1.9; Eus. *PE* 10.9.10; *Chron.* Helm, pp. 17–20, 1480 ed., sig. b6r; cf. Plin. *Nat.* 30.3–4. Zoroaster was a religious teacher in ancient Persia, not a king of Bactria. His dates are controversial among modern authorities, who put him between 650 and 1400 BCE. Pliny proposes a date 6000 years before Plato, 5000 years before the Trojan War. Eusebius calls Zoroaster 'a famous magus and king of the Bactrians' and makes him a contemporary of Ninus and Abraham, 828 years before the Fall of Troy and and thirty-two centuries after the creation. In the Eusebian chronology, Troy fell in the year 4019 after Adam, which is the year 835 of Abraham.

2. Lact. *Inst.* 2.14–16; Eus. *PE* 5.1–14; Plin. *Nat.* 30.1–2; *DIR* 1.22.1. Neither the 1497 Pliny nor modern editions are as hard on magic as Polydore is here.

3. Verg. *Ecl.* 8.69, 70, 71, 99; Perotti *Corn.* fol. CXCIII; Tortelli *Orth.* sig. o8*v*   Ov. *Am.* 3.7.31–32   Luc. 6.457–458. Damon is one of two shepherds in Vergil's eighth *Eclogue*; his companion Alphesiboeus wants to trap Daphnis with magic spells. In this context, Circe's *carmina* are charms as well as poems, spells with the power to turn humans into animals, to make a snake swell and explode and to perform the most notorious act of Thessalian magic — drawing down the moon. A magician gives Alphesiboeus plants from the venomous lands of the Black Sea, drugs to make him a werewolf and enable him to spirit crops from one farmer's field to another's. Twelfth and thirteenth century scribes who wrote a group of manuscripts of Ovid's *Amores* but did not know its title called it *Ovidius sine titulo* or *Ovidii liber de sine titulo*.

4. Luc. 6.434–830; Apul. *Met.* 1.2,5; 2.1; Plin. *Nat.* 30.6–7   Plin. *Nat.* 30.12, 28.17–18; cf. 28.59–60   Verg. *A* 7.1–10; Perotti *Corn.* fol. CCXXXIIv. *De magia* usually indicates the *Apologia*, also called *Pro se de magia liber*, but this work never mentions Thessaly, the witch-ridden land described by Apuleius (*DIR* 1.11.1) in the *Metamorphoses* and by Lucan in *De bello civili*. This is Polydore's second uncertain or confused reference to Apuleius (*DIR* 1.11.1, 23.3). The passages of the Twelve Tables to which Pliny refers in book 30 are cited in book 28. Apuleius refers to the same ancient laws in the *Apology* (47). In the *Odyssey* Circe's island is *Aiaiē*, originally regarded as far to the east but later thought to be in the west, where the descendants of Odysseus and Circe ruled the Tyrrhenians or Etruscans, thus justifying such names as Circeii, the modern Capo Circeo north of Naples.

5. Plin. *Nat.* 30.8–11. Diogenes Laertius (9.34) records the story that Xerxes provided Magi as tutors for Democritus of Abdera, and Pliny mentions a Magus called Osthanes, who accompanied Xerxes when he invaded Greece, as the author of the first surviving work about magic. An Egyptian of the third century BCE named Bolus who wrote on magical drugs is sometimes called Bolus Democritus because he was confused with the fifth-century philosopher. Like Pythagoras, Plato and Empedocles, also renowned for magical wisdom, Democritus was thought to have learned from the sages of the East. 300 AUC (454) falls within the early lifetimes of Hippocrates and Democritus. Modern texts of Pliny have *Mose et Ianne et Lotape* or *Iotape*; the latter is *iota pe*, a transliteration of ιπ, the first two letters (reversed) of πιπι, which is in turn a Greek permutation of the Hebrew יהוה, the Tetragrammaton or unutterable name of God. The Egyptian wizard Iannes appears in 2 Tim. 3:8 and in the pseudepigraphal *Iannes and Iambres*. The 1497 Pliny and *DIR* editions before 1532 have *Mose etiamnum et Lotapea* (glossed as *Iochapela, Iochabela, Iotopata*), thus swallowing up Pharaoh's magician in the minims of the adverb *etiamnum*. In the *Castigationes*, Barbaro conjectured *Iochabela* (cf. LXX Exod. 6:20 *Iōchabed*) from Josephus, who has *Iōchabelē* (*Johuel*) ˙ for the mother of Moses.

6. Jos. *AJ* 2.217, 280, 284–7; 8.155–9; Eus. *PE* 9.27.27.

7. Jos. *AJ* 8.45–7. Titus Flavius Vespasianus ruled from 69 to 79 CE.

8. Mark 16:15–18. Polydore omits the reference to snake-handling in the Vulgate Mark and in the Greek.

CHAPTER XXIII

1. Diog. L. 1.pr.6; Cic. *Div.* 1.23.46; Tortelli *Orth. sig.* O8*v*–P1*r*; Perotti *Corn.* fols. CXCIIv–CXCIIIr   Serv. *A* 3.359; Isid. *Orig.* 8.9.13; cf. August. *DCD* 7.35. Servius and Isidore have the same list of four — pyromancy, aeromancy, hydromancy, geomancy — from Varro's lost *Rerum divinarum libri XVI*. Necromancy and chiromancy, missing from Varro's list, were added in the middle ages.

2. Luc. 6.434–840   Liv. 1.39.1–4; Dion. H. 4.2.4   Plin. *Nat.* 2.147; Liv. 21.62.6. When Tarquinius Priscus was murdered, his wife Tanaquil secured the throne for Servius Tullius (578–35), her son-in-law, who had been a slave before she saw that the prodigy of his flaming head revealed a royal future for him. Livy reports the prodigy in Picenum in 218, the year when Hannibal crossed the Alps and defeated the Scipios, beginning the Second Punic War (218–201). Intending the conquest of Parthia, Marcus Licinius Crassus died at Carrhae in Mesopotamia in 53. After his father was defeated at Pharsalus in 48 BCE, Sextus Pompey campaigned against Caesar and then joined Antony against Octavian. He was killed in Miletus in 35.

3. Apul. *Apol.* 42; cf. Cic. *Div.* 1.32.68–9   Juv. 6.583–584   Cic. *Div.* 1.58.132. Despite the citation of Cicero in editions through 1525, the story about hydromancy (including the reference to Varro) comes from Apuleius (*DIR* 1.11.1, 22.4), though modern editions of the *Apology* as well as the 1493 text have 160 verses in the prediction. Rome waged three wars between 88 and 66 BCE against Mithridates VI of Pontus. For Juvenal, see *DIR* 1.11.4.

CHAPTER XXIV

1–2. Cic. *Div.* 1.3, 11–12, 34, 72, 79, 95–7; Lact. *Inst.* 2.115–17. Stoic theism, determinism and materialism enabled Cicero to give a rational account of the traditional evidence for divination. The categories *natural* and *artificial* distinguish an innate or divinely inspired gift for seeing the

future from learning to do so by using various techniques. From the conception of a prophetic soul inspired by divine ecstasy, it was a short step to the view of Lactantius that demons who invade human bodies are the authors of false divination. And yet Lactantius respected the Sibyls as righteous pagan prophets. Erythrae, on the cost of Ionia, was home to one of the ten Sibyls named by Varro; she was thought to prophesy through her own power. The oracle of Hammon or Zeus-Ammon (Amun of Thebes in Egypt) was at the Libyan oasis of Siwa. *Auguria* was a Roman technique based on *auspicium*, the observation of birds and other natural phenomena as signs of the disposition of the gods. Strictly understood, auspices affected only the timing of an action, while augury extended to other matters.

3. Cic. *Div.* 1.3, 36; 2.50; Perotti *Corn.* fols. Vr, LVIIIr. The *ars haruspicina* or *aruspicina* was an Etruscan technique of divination from lightning (*fulgur*), prodigies (*ostenta*) and the liver and other internal organs (*exta*) of animals. Polydore found his (incorrect) etymology in Perotti. Cicero tells the story of Tages to emphasize the absurdity of traditional belief in divination. This half-divine 'aged child' had a major role in Etruscan myth and religion, which was a revelation based on divinatory books.

4. Plin. *Nat.* 7.203, 11.186; Cic. *Div.* 1.72, 119; 2.28–29, 42, 49, 109; App. *BC* 2.116; Plu. *Caes.* 61.4, 63.4 Hdt. 7.57; Cic. *Div.* 1.93. Amphiaraus of Argos was a great seer and one of the seven heroes who marched against Thebes. Delphus was the eponymous hero of a famous oracular site. Appian and Cicero are unclear about the timing of this prediction before Caesar's assassination on March 15, 44 BCE, but Plutarch, who mentions the ox without a heart, refers to Caesar's sitting on the chair and wearing a triumphal robe on the previous February 15, the day of the Lupercalia when Antony offered him a crown. Xerxes invaded Europe in 480.

5. Verg. *Ecl.* 1.17; Perotti *Corn.* fol. CCXXXVIIr Cic. *Div.* 2.49; Perotti *Corn.* fol. LVIIIr. Meliboeus, the goatherd in Vergil's first *Eclogue*, regrets not having noticed the portent which warned him that trouble would strike his flock.

6. Cic. *Div.* 1.33–4, 87–8; Paul. *Fest.* p. 2L; Plin. *Nat.* 7.203; Perotti, *Corn.* fol. LVIII. Polydore's etymology of *auspicium* is correct, but the derivation of *augurium* is dubious. Tiresias, having lost his sight by offending a goddess, gained the gift of prophecy — especially the ability to read omens from birds. Car and his brothers, Lydus and Mysus, were eponymous ancestors of the Lydians, Mysians and Carians. Mopsus and Calchas were famous in Greek myth as diviners.

7. Gel. 7.6.3; Serv. *A* 3.361, 6.15; Clem. Al. *Strom.* 1.16.74.4; Var. *L* 6.76; Cic. *Div.* 1.27–28, 2.72; Paul. *Fest.* p. 215L; Plin. *Nat.* 10.49; Perotti *Corn.* fols. XLVIIr, CLV. *Praepes* suggests swift, direct flight and thus a favorable omen. The suffix *-cen* in *oscen* comes from *canere*, to sing. *Tripudium* refers to a ritual dance or the falling of grain in the omen. *Solistimus* is the superlative of the Oscan *sollus*, complete.

8. Jos. *Ap.* 1.201–204. Josephus refers to the ethnographer Hecataeus of Abdera (360–290 BCE). When Artaxerxes II sent the scribe Ezra to Jerusalem to restore the Jewish law around 398, one of his associates was Meshullam (*Mosollamos*), but the name in Josephus probably belongs to another person. Josephus has *kakodaimones*, which means nothing stronger than 'poor devils,' but the Latin Josephus also has *mali daemonii*.

9. Cic. *Div.* 1.95   Liv. 1.6.4, 18.6–10; 10.6–9; Dion. H. 2.6; Ps.-Fenestella (1477) sig. a5; Cic. *Leg.* 2.12.31; Plu. *Quaest. Rom.* 99 (287D-E). Livy's story of the victory of Romulus over Remus begins with a contest of augury. When Numa was offered the throne, he asked for confirmation by augury. Livy also reports later events when the right to hold office as augur was a crucial element of the struggle between plebeians and patricians. Fenestella was an author of the Augustan period whose work survives only in fragments, indicating strength in legal, institutional and cultural history, but not political narrative. An epitome survived into the fourth century CE, but only citations by other authors preserved it afterward. When Polydore cites Fenestella, he is either referring to a source (such as Pliny) that names him or using the pseudonymous compilation by Andrea Domenico Fiocchi (c. 1400–1452), *De magistratibus sacerdotisque Romanorum libellus* (ed. prin. 1477). Fiocchi himself seems not to have been responsible for the misattribution to Fenestella, identified as author of *De magistratibus* by Polydore and many other readers through the early

seventeenth century. Some later editions carry a warning about the false ascription.

10. Cic. *Div.* 2.41.85–6; Suet. *Tib.* 14.3   Plin. *Nat.* 7.203; Just. *Epit.* 36.2.8; Jos. *AJ* 2.10–17; Clem. Al. *Strom.* 1.16.74. Cicero calls Numerius Suffustius *honestum . . . et nobilem*; Praeneste was a major Latin city. An amphictiony was a federation of Greek communities who joined to maintain a religious site and its cult. A figure called Amphictyon appears as king of Athens after Cecrops and Cranaos. A son of Deucalion who founded the Delphic amphictiony is also named Amphictyon.

11. Eus. *PE* 4.2–3   Gel. 14.1.36. The rhetor and philosopher Favorinus of Arles was active in the second century CE; Gellius was his pupil.

12. Verg. *A* 10.501   Lev. 19:26, 31; Exod. 20:2–6; Matt. 19:17; *DIR* 4.14, 5.8. As Turnus kills Pallas and rages boastfully over him, these words warn that he will regret this victory.

BOOK II

CHAPTER I

2. Paul. *Dig.* 1.1.11. pr. 1   Cic. *Leg.* 3.1.3   Marc. *Dig.* 1.3.2. pr. 5–9. Book I of the *Digest*, part of the *Corpus iuris civilis* compiled under Justinian (527–65 CE), opens with texts from Ulpian (d. 223), Marcian, Paul (both early third century) and other classical jurists illustrating various applications of the basic term *ius*. The reference to the book *On Law* by the Stoic Chrysippus (280–207 BCE) is from Marcian in the *Digest*. Cicero's unfinished work *On the Laws* transmitted the Stoic concept of natural law.

3. Ulp. *Dig.* 1.1.1.2.4–4.1   Cic. *Leg.* 1.6.18–19, 7.22–3   Ulp. *Dig.* 1.1.1.4.1–2   Pompon. *Dig.* 1.2.1. pr. 1–12.7. The Roman *ius civile*, both traditional and statutory, applied to Roman citizens. It included *leges* or statutes enacted by three legislative assemblies — the *comitia centuriata*, the *comitia tributa* and the *concilium plebis*, whose resolutions, *plebis scita*, were eventually regarded as *leges*. Particularly important was the *lex* of the Twelve Tables, compiled according to tradition by the Decemvirs and approved in 450 BCE. The Senate did not make law; but when the Republican assemblies withered away in the Empire, its recommendations

(consulta) acquired the force of law. Higher magistrates issued *edicta*. As chief magistrate the emperor in time became the only legislator. The *decreta* or decrees of the emperor were his decisions as judge.

4. Cic. *Leg.* 2.4.8, 10, 5.13.

5. Ov. *Met.* 5.343   Diod. S. 5.5.2   Hdt. 6.16   Verg. A 4.57–8. *Legifer* translates *thesmophoros*, an epithet of Demeter. The important festival of the Thesmophoria honored Demeter as goddess of agriculture. The term *thesmos* is generally interpreted as the 'law and order' that Demeter brings.

6. Plin. *Nat.* 7.191   Aug. *DCD* 18.3; Cic. *Leg.* 1.22.57; *ND* 3.23.57; Diod. S. 1.94.1, 3.3; Dion. H. 1.33.4, 2.61.2; Diog. L. 8.3; Eus. *Chron.*, Helm, pp. 13, 29, 47, 49; Gel. 11.18.1–5; Hdt. 1.29, 65–6; Isid. *Orig.* 5.1.1–2; Just. *Epit.* 2.7.3–9, 3.2.7; 20.4.4; Lact. *Inst.* 1.6; Lact. Plac. ad Stat. *Theb.* 1.541–3, 4.589; Plu. *Thes.* 16.4, *Rom.* 22.3, *Sol.* 17.1–2; Str. 12.2.9; Val. Max. 6.5. ext. 4. Rhadamanthus judges the dead in the Underworld. Phoroneus was the primal human in the mythology of Argos. Eusebius dates him in year 210 of Abraham (1807 BCE), long before Rhadamanthus, Minos and the myth of Eleusis. The latter all came after the death of Moses, according to Eusebius, but Phoroneus preceded the birth of the Hebrew lawgiver by more than two centuries. The first human lawgiver among the Egyptians, according to Diodorus, was King Mneues (*Mneuēn, Minam,* another variant of Menes) who got his laws from Thoth. Noting claims of divine origin for their laws by Menes and others, Diodorus puts Moses in the same euhemerist context. He depicts the Arcadians as civilizers who introduced religious rites, letters, music and laws. Cicero explains that they called the fourth Apollo 'Nomion' because they believed him to be their lawgiver, but the epithet probably means 'herdsman.' The traditional date of Draco's legislation is 621 BCE, but Lycurgus was said to have established the Spartan constitution even earlier, bringing his laws from Crete. Solon reformed the Athenian laws around 594. Although Valerius Maximus associates Charondas with Thurii on the mainland of Italy, he was actually the lawgiver of Catania in Sicily, probably in the sixth century.

8. Jos. *AJ* 3.88–101, 317–22   Eus. *PE* 10.9.8–10   Jos. *Ap.* 2.154–5; cf.
Diod. S. 1.94.1–2   Jos. *Ap.* 2.279–80   Eus. *PE* 10.9.8–10; *Chron.* (Helm,
pp. 13, 49). Locri was a Dorian colony in southern Italy, where Zaleucus
was honored as author of the first Greek law code after its foundation in
the early seventh century. Although Homer never uses *nomos*, the term
specified by Josephus, he has other words *(themis, dikē)* for related concepts. Eusebius connects Demeter (Ceres) with various early figures and
events from Greek mythology, but he does not describe her as a lawgiver.
Her date is the year 603 of Abraham (1414 BCE), 58 years after the death
of Moses; Triptolemus distributed the grain given by Demeter ten years
later. Polydore does not seem to have noticed that if Phoroneus was a
lawgiver, as Eusebius acknowledged, Moses had competition for priority
in this important field.

9. Rom 4:15.

10. Ambr. *Ep.* 73.2–11 *(PL* 16: 1305–8)   John 1:29.

12. *DIR* 2.1.3.

Chapter II

1. Str. 1.1.18; Pl. *Plt.* 291C-292A   *SHA Aurel.* 26.43.2. Historical persons
called Flavius Vopiscus lived in the reign of Diocletian (293–305 CE),
and the name is one of six known as the *Scriptores Historiae Augustae.* This
is a series of imperial biographies (ed. prin. 1475) long thought to have
been written under Diocletian and Constantine (305–37) and covering
the period from Hadrian (117–38) through Numerianus (283–4). But
many modern scholars have attributed the work to a single author of the
late fourth century or after.

2. Plin. *Nat.* 7.199   Hdt. 2.147   Hdt. 2.4; Diod. S. 1.45.1   Pl. *Plt.* 290
D–E

3. Plin. *Nat.* 7.191   Diod. S. 4.4.4   Plin. *Nat.* 7.200   Eus. *Chron.*,
Helm, pp. 9–10. Tales of the triumph of Bacchus in Asia may have
encouraged his connection with sumptuous trappings of royalty. The
phrase 'have too much wine' *(pleonazontos oinou)* in Diodorus might be
Latinized as *vinum sumente* from *sumere,* but Polydore has *vino fumante*
from *fumo;* Poggio's version is *ex potu bibentis.*

4. Just. *Epit.* 1.1.1   Nep. *Ag.* 21.1   Eus. *Chron.*, Helm, pp. 66–83; cf. Hdt. 7.204   Just. *Epit.* 1.1.4–8; Eus. *PE* 10.9.10. Eurystheus was the mythical king of Argos who assigned Hercules his twelve labors. Eurysthenes was one of the Heraclids who reconquered the Peloponnese, gaining the rule of Sparta. The other names, which come from Eusebius, correspond to the first eight Agiads, the senior ruling house of Sparta, traditionally 930–700 BCE (1104–814 according to Eusebius). Historical records of the Agiad house begin around 530.

5. Plin. *Nat.* 7.200   Jos. *AJ* 1.120–53, 20.234; *DIR* 1.3.11–12.

6. Eus. *Chron.*, Helm, pp. 16–20. Eusebius correlates the regnal dates of Assyrian, Hebrew, Greek and Egyptian rulers, beginning with Ninus, Abraham and Europs in the year 2016 before Christ, at which time 'the 16th Dynasty (*potestas; dynastia*) was in Egypt . . . when the Thebans ruled for a hundred and ninety years.'

7. Plin. *Nat.* 7.200   Jos. *AJ* 1.135   Just. *Epit.* 12.15.8–10; Tortelli, *Orth. sig.* y8v   Verg. *A* 7.266; cf. Isid.*Orig.* 9.3.19; Tortelli, *Orth. sig.* y8v   Isid. *Orig.* 9.3.20; Tortelli, *Orth. sig.* y8v. In modern editions of Pliny, Theseus is the rightful monarch after whose time the Athenians devised a democratic constitution, not a tyrant who came before Phalaris, but Polydore followed the 1497 edition. Theseus is in the royal Attic line of Erichthonius, Erectheus, Cecrops and Pandion, though sometimes his father is Poseidon. His succession to the throne is legitimate but tragic, following the suicide of his father. Archilochus, who first used the word *turannis* in the seventh century BCE, may have been recording an increase of one-person rule. Later historiography often (but not always) treated tyrants as bad rulers, whether autocrats or usurpers or both. Phalaris, an icon of cruelty, was tyrant of Acragas in the second quarter of the sixth century. Infamous for torturing his enemies by roasting them in a brazen bull, he was the first tyrant in Sicily but not in the larger Greek world. Cypselus (657–27) and Periander (627–587) in Corinth, for example, and Pittacus in Mitylene (c. 650–570) came earlier. Justin has harsh things to say about tyrants, but his remark on the *vir fortis* is about Alexander. In the line cited from the *Aeneid*, *tyrannus* is not pejorative.

8. Plin. *Nat.* 7.200   Macr. *Sat.* 1.11.34   Isid. *Orig.* 5.27.32, 9.4.43   Gel. 6.4.4–5. Pliny may be thinking of the Greek practice—best known from Sparta—of subjugating helots not through one person's ownership of another but through the compulsion of an ethnic or political group. Cleomenes III of Sparta (235–22 BCE) was forced to flee to Egypt after he had sold freedom to six thousand helots. Slaves sold wearing garlands (*coronati*) were certified as captured in war, but those sold wearing caps (*pilleati*) carried no guarantee.

9. Jos. *Ap.* 2.133, 215   Gen. 9: 20–7; Jos. *AJ* 1.140–2.

10. cf. *Adagia* (1550), pp. 188–9.

11. Paul. *Fest.* p. 149L.

12. Plu. *Sol.* 19; Plin. *Nat.* 7.200; August. *DCD* 18.10; cf. Tortelli, *Orth. sig. fir*; Lucian, *Hermot.* 64; *Dom.* 18   Plin. *Nat.* 7.202; Serv. *A* 2.81, 7.637; Perotti, *Corn.* fol. LXVIIIv. The mythical origin of a court on the Areopagus or hill of Ares was in a conflict between Poseidon and Ares when Cecrops was king of Athens. A court of twelve gods found Ares not guilty of murdering Poseidon's son. This was the story told by Euripides and others through Augustine. According to Plutarch, however, and contrary to Polydore, the tradition that Solon founded the Council of the Areopagus was proved wrong. Evidence for Draco's earlier laws (traditionally 621 BCE) indicates trials for homicide on the Areopagus before his time. All three of the great tragedians wrote plays about Palamedes, noting his many discoveries in writing, laws, numbers, weights and measures, astronomy, games, tactics, signal-fires, and the ordering and feeding of armies. Pliny says that he invented military organization, signalling, sentries and passwords (*tesserae*), as well as weights and measures and part of the alphabet. The military *tessera* was a physical object, a tablet marked with a sign and passed among the troops. The same word was used for a six-sided die. A *tesserula* was a small die but also a voting-ticket. A *suffragium*, however, was not a physical ballot but a vote in the sense of an action or an expression of will.

Chapter III

1. Plin. *Nat.* 14.5 cf. Liv. 1.pr.11–12; Verg. *A* 3.57. Pliny introduces what might have seemed a morally neutral topic—trees that grow in different countries—with a long prologue on political expansion, economic growth and cultural decline. Polydore links this diatribe with Vergil's famous words about the curse of greed and with Livy's comment on Rome's moral decline.

2. Plu. *Lyc.* 9.2.

3. Val. Max. 4.4.11 Plin. *Nat.* 14.5. In 509 BCE, according to tradition, Publius Valerius Poplicola became one of the first consuls. Lucius Aemilius Paullus won the victory that ended the third Macedonian war in 168. In the early third century, Gaius Luscinus Fabricius had many victories, especially in the war with Pyrrhus. His contemporary, Manius Curius Dentatus, ended the Samnite war in 290. Publius Cornelius Scipio Africanus Major, the greatest of a great family, defeated Hannibal at Zama in 202. Such heroes became models of Republican virtue, though Marcus Aemilius Scaurus (d. 89) won his power and wealth by dubious means.

4. Flor. *Epit.* 1.1; Liv. 1.60.3, 2.1–2; Dion. H. 4.76.1–2, 5.1.1–2; Cic. *Leg.* 3.3.8; *DIR* 2.13.2. The traditional date for Rome's foundation is 753 BCE, and her first king, Romulus (753–717), is an eponymous hero. His mother is Rhea Silvia, a Vestal Virgin who claimed that Mars had raped her. Lucius Tarquinius Superbus (534–509), last of the kings, lost his throne and Lucius Junius Brutus and Lucius Tarquinius Collatinus became the first consuls in 509 after the despised Tarquin's nephew had caused the suicide of Lucretia, the wife of Collatinus, by raping her. This is roughly Livy's story. But the two and a half centuries between Romulus and Tarquin is too long for seven kings. Cicero derives *consul* from *consulere*, but Dionysius suggests 'counsellors (*sumboulous*) or commissioners (*proboulous*) since the Romans say *consilia* for *sumboulas*.' The author of the *Epitome bellorum omnium annorum DCC* (ed. prin. 1471) was probably named Lucius Annaeus Florus and wrote after 138 CE. Summarizing Livy and other sources, he praised the growth of Roman military power from the beginnings through Augustus.

5. Liv. 2.18.1–5; Ps.-Fenestella [1477] sig. d; Dion. H. 5.73.3, 74.4; Just. *Epit.* 19.1.7. Tarquinius Superbus had extended Roman power throughout Latium by cementing alliances with such figures as Octavius Mamilius of Tusculum. When Tarquin lost the throne, Mamilius joined him with the towns of the Latin League, which the Romans defeated around 496 BCE. Titus Larcius Flavus had become consul a few years earlier and had also been the first dictator. Dionysius compares the term *dictator* with *aisumnētēs*, a legal, elective, non-hereditary tyranny. On the annual dictators at Alba Longa, he cites Gaius Licinius Macer, an annalist of the early first century.

6. Plb. 3.87.8; Plu. *Fab.* 9.2   Plu. *Marc.* 24.7   Liv. 4.31.1–5, 8.23.14–16. Plutarch's explanation is either that the consul declares (*legei; dicit*) who is dictator or that the dictator declares law on his own. When Rome's three wars with Etruscan Veii reached a crisis in 426 BCE, a dictator had to be named irregularly by a consular tribune, Aulus Cornelius Cossus, rather than a consul. A century later, during the Samnite Wars, when the augurs challenged another choice of dictator as ritually flawed, the tribunes claimed that no error in the auspices could have been detected 'since the consul had risen at night (*consul oriens de nocte*) and named the dictator in silence.' Although Polydore has the dictator named 'at nightfall' (*oriente nocte*), *oriens* in modern texts of Livy modifies *consul*.

7. Liv. 3.31–33.1–2, 36.1–7, 44.1–2, 54.6–55.1; Ps.-Fenestella [1477] sig. e2r. The story is that after the plebeians demanded published laws, the first college of Decemvirs was appointed in 451 BCE and completed ten of the Twelve Tables. A second college, including plebeians, added the final two in 450 but abused their power. When their leader, Appius Claudius Crassus, tried to rape Verginia, her father killed her. The outraged plebeians seceded, and the Decemvirs were forced from office. Laws enacted in 449 ensured plebeian rights, making this year pivotal in Rome's political development and justifying a stronger verdict than Polydore's bland remark that 'the state returned to its earlier form of rule' once the Decemvirs were expelled.

8. Liv. 4.1.1–3, 7.1; 5.12.9–10; 6.42.9; 7.17.6; Dion. H. 6.89.1–2; 11.61.3–62.1; Plu. *Cam.* 1.1–2, 39.1–2, 42.1–7. Military tribunes with consular authority were first appointed in 445 BCE (309 AUC). Gaius Canuleius

was tribune of the *plebs* in that year, giving his name to the law that enabled plebeians to marry patricians and raise their social status. Plebeians then became military tribune in 400 (354), consul in 366 (388), and dictator in 356 (398). Although Polydore sees this as movement toward democracy, few plebeians profited from the changes.

9. App. *BC* 1.11.98–9. Gaius Marius (157–86 BCE) was a brilliant soldier of equestrian background who was elected consul seven times, thus straining the Republican constitution. His patrician rival, Lucius Cornelius Sulla (138–78), won his first consulate in 88, but a setback provoked him to lead his own troops against Rome. He was named dictator in 81, having invaded Italy in 83. Sulla subdued his enemies ruthlessly, using the notorious proscription lists and remaining dictator until 79. Gaius Julius Caesar (100–44) became consul in 59 and dictator for life in 44, the year of his assassination. His adopted son Octavian became consul in 43. His third consulship began in 31 and continued until 23. In 27 he came to be called Augustus. He refused the dictatorship in 22, by which time other imperial assets had made the title redundant.

10. Dion. H. 3.61–2; Flor. *Epit.* 1.5.5–6, 8.5; Str. 5.2.2; Macr. *Sat.* 1.6.7. *Lictores* carrying *fasces* or rods bundled around an axe attended officials to show their power of physical and capital punishment. These and other symbols of authority—the ivory folding-chair, the toga with purple stripes, and so on—belonged originally to the kings and later to civil and military authorities. Ancient sources trace them to the Etruscans. Livy makes Romulus the first Roman king to use them, but Macrobius opts for Tullus (not Tullius) Hostilius, Strabo for Tarquinius Priscus and Dionysius likewise for the elder Tarquin or Romulus.

11. Liv. 1.8.3; Dion. H. 3.61.2, 2.29.1; Perotti, *Corn.* fol. LXXIIr; Plin. *Nat.* 16.74–5.

12. Liv. 1.42.5–43.7. Tradition remembers Rome's earliest political organization as based on three tribes each divided into ten *curiae*, in which membership came from birth. Servius Tullius replaced this aristocratic constitution by creating new tribes based on residence and by establishing a census to organize the population according to wealth. He may have wanted a heavy infantry force (like the Greek hoplites) with more

expensive arms and armor. In political terms, this would have amounted to expanding the male citizenry. The five-class system, however, is not the original Servian model but the product of a longer evolution. The censors assigned each citizen to a century every fifth year or so, thus making up the classes to keep pace with the growth of population. Long before Livy described them, however, the centuries had become political rather than military, as power shifted toward age and wealth, reversing the populist Servian plan.

13. Plin. *Nat.* 33.43; Suet. *Aug.* 41   Eutr. 1.7; cf. *Hist.* [1471], fol. 10r. A reformer of the time of Servius could have used the bronze *as* as a measure of weight and value, but not as a coin. The *aes* became a round coin only in the late fourth century. Silver coins appeared soon afterward and gold by the time of the First Punic War, when the first *denarius* was also minted, worth ten (later sixteen) *asses*. A *sestertius* was one fourth of a silver *denarius*, but a *sestertium* was a thousand times more valuable.

14. Liv. 1.43.13–44.2, 4.8.2, 7; Dion. H. 4.22.1–2; Var. *L* 6.2.11; cf. Serv. *A* 1.283; Censor. *DN* 18.12–13. Livy credits Servius Tullius with the sacrifice of a pig, a sheep and a bull to mark the end of the first census. Three bulls (*tauris tribus*) is a mistake from *suovetaurilibus*, a word that stumped more than one scribe copying Livy. As the need for a census became regular, it would have been natural to preserve the lustration as a way of marking off one period of time from the next. In 443 BCE, two censors were first appointed to do this job. The census period marked by the lustration was called a *lustrum*, but its duration varied. The power of the censors was political classification, eventually encompassing a wide moral jurisdiction. In the larger sense *vectigalia* were state revenues, in a narrower sense indirect taxes paid by citizens in Italy. The direct tax called *tributum* was paid by Romans until 167. The censors managed both taxes.

15. *DIR* 2.13.2   Exod. 30: 12–14.

16. Jos. *AJ* 3.194   cf. Tortelli, *Orth.* sig. y5r   Matt. 20: 2, 22:19–20. The Hebrew word *sheqel* originally meant 'weight' but later referred to a coin. Coins with the name of the Persian province Yehud (Judaea) survive from the fourth century. Despite their traditional association with Solon, the first Athenian coins are dated in the middle of the sixth century, sev-

eral decades after Solon was archon. In both texts cited here, the Vulgate Matthew uses the transliterated *dēnarios* for the silver coin worth a day's wage. The drachma was basically a measure of weight, roughly four to six grams. The groat (*grossus*) was an English silver coin of the later medieval period.

17. Liv. 1.33.8   Eutr. *Hist.* [1471], fol. 12v; Eus. *Chron.*, Helm, p. 103; Isid. *Orig.* 5.27.23   Hdt. 3.123–4; Jos. *AJ* 2.73, 11.17, 103   Jos. *AJ* 1.113–14. The Sabine Ancus Marcius (641–17 BCE) was remembered favorably for a number of building projects, including the city jail, used only for temporary confinement. Eusebius attributes chains and other penal technology to Tarquin the Proud in 547.

Chapter IV

2. Hdt. 2.4; Clem. Al. *Strom.* 1.16.2   Diod. S. 1.50.2; Hdt. 2.15. The Egyptian civil year was adopted early in the third milennium, probably after its Sumerian counterpart. It was primarily a sequence of 365 days and only secondarily a division into three seasons and twelve thirty-day months with five extra days each year. Because the civil year was six hours shorter than the lunisolar religious year and because there was no intercalation, the civil year fell one day behind every four years, but it was a simple system and set the standard for Hellenistic astronomy. The Greeks used a lunisolar year with intercalation when the authorities deemed it necessary — every other year according to Herodotus. When Diodorus attributes a solar calendar to the *Thēbaioi*, he probably means all Egyptians. Herodotus wrote that Egypt used to be called Thebes (*hai Thēbai*), which was the Greek name both for a city in Boeotia and for the city that the Egyptians called Waset (now Luxor).

3. Serv. *A* 5.49   *DIR* 2.4.9,14   Diog. L. 1.27   Jos. *AJ* 1.80–1, 88, 90, 107; 3.182. Eudoxus of Cnidus wrote his *Phainomena* in the fourth century BCE, aiding the development of an exact astronomical calendar. Two centuries later, Hipparchus commented on the *Phainomena* and achieved remarkably precise measurements. Prediction of solstices and equinoxes was possible in the time of Thales. Little is known of Hebrew time-keeping before the Babylonian conquest. After 586 the Babylonian lunisolar

calendar of twelve months with intercalations was used, often disagreeing with local time in Jerusalem.

4. Plu. *Num.* 18.6; Macr. *Sat.* 1.12.2; Censor. *DN* 19.7   Solin. 1.34; Censor. *DN* 19.4   Macr. *Sat.* 1.12.2; Hdt. 2.15. The comments of Solinus and Censorinus probably reflect a primitive seasonal calendar in Egypt, where the civil calendar was very early but not fixed since it co-existed with a different lunar year.

5. Serv. *A* 1.269, 3.284; Cic. *ND* 2.51–2, *Hort.* fr. 35 [Müller] Jos. *AJ* 1.106   Censor. *DN* 18. Censorinus attributed a Great Year of 59 years to the Pythagorean Philolaus. Hipparchus gave a Great Year of 304 years. These were mathematical devices for matching solar and lunar cycles, not the measures of physical phenomena that Polydore describes from Cicero and Servius. The Greeks alternated 'full' months of thirty days with 'hollow' months of twenty-nine, six of each making a total of 354, without intercalations.

6. Macr. *Sat.* 1.12.2–3, 8, 16; Plu. *Num.* 19.1–6   Ov. *Fast.* 5.73, 78   Macr. *Sat.* 1.12, 3, 16, 34–6. The name of our last month, December, which means 'tenth,' shows that the primitive Roman year was agricultural, counting only divisions of that part of the year when farmers were active. Polydore compressed two lines from different stanzas of book 5 of Ovid's *Fasti*.

7. Macr. *Sat.* 1.7.19–20, 12.39–13.3; Eutr. 1.3; *Hist.* [1471] fol. 9^r. 715–673 BCE is the traditional reign of Numa Pompilius, but the twelve-month pseudo-solar calendar is often attributed to the Decemvirs of the mid-fifth century.

8. Plu. *Num.* 19.8; Perotti, *Corn.* fol. IX^r, CXCI^r; Macr. *Sat.* 1.13.3–7; Verg. *Ecl.* 8.75. Before the Julian reform, there were two years of 355 days in every four-year cycle (355, 378, 355, 377) with a month of 27 or 28 days intercalated every other year.

9. Macr. *Sat.* 1.13.8, 16–19, 14.1, 6–7; Perotti, *Corn.* fol. XII^r, CXCI^r; Censor. *DN* 20.8–9   Suet. *Jul.* 40.1–2; App. *BC* 2.21.154; Plin. *Nat.* 18.211   Macr. *Sat.* 1.14.6; Perotti, *Corn.* CXCI^v . To bring the seasons into phase with his new year, Caesar added ninety days to 46 BCE. Next, starting with January of 45, he attached a total of ten additional days to the ends

of various months, extending the year to 365 days. In order to come closer to the true solar year, he also added a quarter-day per year by inserting a day every fourth year after February 23, whose Latin name was *ante diem VI Kalendas Martias*, so the new day that was counted twice became *bisextum* or 'the second sixth.'

10. Cic. *ND* 2.26.69   Diod. S. 1.50.2; *DIR* 2.4.2. *Mensis* is probably not related to *metior* but to the Greek *mēn* and similar lunar words.

11. Macr. *Sat.* 1.15.9–14, 17; Serv. *A* 8.654. *Idus* is related to the Oscan *eiduis*, but its further etymology is unknown.

12. Perotti, *Corn.* fol. CXCII[r]. December 30 was *ante diem III Kal. Jan.* because the Romans counted inclusively from December 30 through 31 to January 1. Again inclusively, the Nones was always the ninth day before the Ides, the official day of the full moon, which was the thirteenth day of all months except March, May, July and October, when it was the fifteenth day. Usually the fifth day of the month, the Nones in these four came seventh. Thus, in Polydore's reckoning, eight months have 'four Nones' made up of the fifth day plus the three days preceding it (the next before them is the Kalends), while four months have 'six Nones,' including the seventh day and the five preceding it. All months have 'eight Ides' — the thirteenth and the seven days preceding it (the next before them being the Nones) or the fifteenth and the seven days preceding it. Strictly speaking, however, only three days in each month have the names Kalends, Nones and Ides, all others being designated by reference to these named days

13. Liv. 9.45.1, 46.1, 5; Macr. *Sat.* 1.15.9. In 304 BCE (450 AUC), when Publius Sempronius Sophus and Publius Sulpicius Saverrio were consuls, the conservative enemies of Appius Claudius the Censor were horrified when his secretary, Gnaeus Flavius, son of a freedman, won curule office. Flavius is credited with a law that divulged legal information previously held by the pontiffs and with a published court calendar.

14. Durandus, *Rationale* (c. 1478), fol 195[v]. The Western Church eventually agreed to celebrate Easter on the Sunday after the first full moon on or after March 21. To find the date, clerics used the Metonic cycle of nineteen Julian years, which related the lunar to the solar year. Given the

convention of a full moon on January 1 of the year 1 CE, if this and the following eighteen years are numbered from one to nineteen, other full moons can be predicted by knowing the corresponding number, called the Golden Number, of any year in another cycle. This system was in use by the sixth century. Guilielmus Durandus attributes the discovery of the Golden Number to Julius Caesar in his *Rationale officiorum divinorum*.

CHAPTER V

1. Macr. *Sat.* 1.21.13   Perotti, *Corn.* fol. CCXXX^r. The ancients divided the daytime between sunrise and sunset as well as the night between sunset and sunrise into twelve segments so that hours varied by season and place. Hellenistic astronomers used an Egyptian day of twenty-four equal hours of sixty minutes each, following Babylonian sexagesimal usage.

2. Plin. *Nat.* 2.182, 187. A gnomon is the pointer on a sundial, at its simplest a straight stick throwing a shadow. Pliny says that Anaximenes invented *gnomonice*, which he calls a theory (*ratio*) of shadows.

3. Plin. *Nat.* 7.212, 214–15. Rome's first Senate House was at the base of the Capitoline and north of the Comitium, where the original Rostra was a speaker's platform. After the victory of Gaius Maenius at Antium in 338 BCE, the prows or beaks (*rostra*) of captured ships were used to decorate a platform in the Forum proper. Pliny's descriptions of the Graecostasis do not fit the earlier sites of the Rostra. Varro locates this place where ambassadors waited to be received by the Senate near the original Rostra. *Columna aerea* is a misreading for *Maenia*, the column erected to commemorate the victory of Maenius. Just north is the site of the Carcer or jail. Manius Valerius Maximus Messala was consul in 263 when he won his Sicilian victories. 595 AUC is 159, when Scipio Nasica Corculum was censor.

4. Vitr. 9.8.5–15   Cic. *ND* 2.34.87, *Tusc.* 2.27.67. The simplest waterclock was the clepsydra, a vessel with a small opening to allow water to escape over a fixed time. Ktesibios (fl. 270 BCE) used a valve-and-float system to keep a constant flow out of one clepsydra into another whose

volume was divided and marked. Cicero alludes to the use of the water-clock to time practice in rhetorical declamation.

5. *DIR* 3.18. The first clear evidence for mechanical clocks in Europe comes from the early fourteenth century, though these instruments had precursors. The earliest clocks were large, public devices; domestic clocks and watches were in use by the fifteenth century. Europeans knew the mariner's compass by the twelfth century, the Chinese even earlier.

CHAPTER VI

1. Plin. *Nat.* 2.188; *DIR* 2.4.2, 5.1; Diod. S. 1.50.2, cf. 5.57; Plu. *Quaest. Rom.* 84 (284C); Mart. 4.8.1–6; Gel. 3.2.4–7; Macr. *Sat.* 1.3.4. The Roman civil day, observed as a unit of the calendar, ran from midnight to midnight, but the day in Martial's poem is the natural day starting at dawn. The ninth or dinner hour was about 2:00 PM. Gellius cites Varro's *De rebus humanis* on various systems of time-keeping. Marcus Valerius Martialis issued his first epigrams in 80 CE; in 84 he published the *Xenia* and *Apophoreta*, connected with the Saturnalia; and he wrote his last poems just before he died in 104. Little known in the middle ages, his poetry regained its fame after Boccaccio found a manuscript around 1361. The first printed text appeared after 1469, and Perotti's edition came out anonymously in 1473, by which time Domizio Calderini (1446–78) had already been lecturing on the poet. Perotti ridiculed Calderini's errors, and Calderini replied with a commentary (1473), launching a controversy that outlived both antagonists. Perotti had finished an early version of his own commentary, the gargantuan *Cornucopiae*, by 1473, but it was not printed until 1489 and then covered only a little of Martial's poetry. So comprehensive was Perotti's lexical work that it inspired the *Dictionarium* of Ambrogio Calepino, which in turn foreshadowed Estienne's *Thesaurus* and other such monumental reference works, not to speak of Polydore and *De inventoribus*, on which see the letter to Odassio (par. 1) and the first letter to Gian Matteo Vergil (par. 3).

2. *DIR* 2.5.6   Veg. 3.8   Ps.-Hier. *Brev. in Ps.* ad 89:4 (*PL* 26:1093a; cf.*CCSL* 78:120). Between 383 and 450 CE, Flavius Vegetius Renatus wrote an *Epitome rei militaris* (ed. prin. c. 1473) on military and naval science.

CHAPTER VII

1. Hier. *Ep.* 34.1 (*PL* 22:448) [Plu.] *Ap. Spart.* 215A; cf. *Ages.* 2.2. In his *Life* of Agesilaus II of Sparta (445–359), Plutarch says that 'we have no likeness of him because he did not want one, . . . but they say he was small and not much to look at.' The *Spartan Sayings*, a collection attributed to Plutarch, provide more uplifting material. Marcella was one of the aristocratic Roman women whom Jerome advised (*DIR* 1.4.2). His letter to her praises the martyr Pamphilus for collecting a library of scriptural studies in Caesarea, building on Origen's work.

2. Diog. L. 2.11 Gel. 7.17.1 Jos. *Ap.* 1.6–9, 21, 28–9. What Diogenes writes (*prōtos . . . biblion exedōke suggraphēs*) might mean either that Anaxagoras was the 'first to publish a book with diagrams' or that he was 'the first to bring out a book written by himself.' If Anaxagoras began to philosophize after 480 BCE, so late a date for the first book would have seemed wrong even to Diogenes, who seems to attribute literary activity earlier to Anaximenes (2.2.3). Pisistratus was tyrant of Athens from 560 to 527, when the city emerged as a hub of cultural activity. Tradition traces the first written texts of Homer to this period.

3. Gel. 7.17.1–3. When Xerxes forced the evacuation of Athens in 480 BCE and burned the Acropolis, there was probably no 'great store of books' there in the sense of a public library. Such institutions were first established by Hellenistic rulers, who took Aristotle's collection as their inspiration. Seleucus I Nicator established his dynasty in 312 and helped start this type of cultural patronange. His contemporary, Ptolemy I Soter, founded the great Library of Alexandria, which at its peak held almost half a million books. When Julius Caesar entered the city after the battle of Pharsalus, he set fire to Ptolemy's anchored fleet. Flames spread to warehouses that contained books, but—contrary to what Gellius claims—there was no burning of the Library, which seems to have been spared any direct assault until the late third century CE.

4. Str. 13.1.54. Erastus and Coriscus were Platonic philosophers who lived in Skepsis, whose king assigned them the town of Assos, where after 347 BCE Aristotle and Xenocrates joined them, so that as a boy

Neleus (340–260), the son of Coriscus, could have met Aristotle (384–22) as well as Theophrastus (372–286), his successor.

5–6. Plin. *Nat.* 35.9–10; cf. 7.115, 13.70. Pliny repeats Varro's story that parchment was invented at Pergamon when Ptolemy V Epiphanes (210–180 BCE) forbade the export of papyrus in order to prevent the success of the library that Eumenes II (197–58) had founded. Parchment was in use before this time, however, and never displaced papyrus in antiquity. Gaius Asinius Pollio (76 BCE–4 CE) used the spoils from a military victory in 39 to found the first public library in Rome.

7. Federico da Montefeltro (1422–82), a great friend of learning and the arts, opened the library of the ducal palace in Urbino to scholars who sought his patronage and motivated him to expand his famous collection of manuscript books. Guidobaldo, his son and successor, was the last of the line to rule.

9. In the two decades before 1450, while Gutenberg was working in Strasbourg and Mainz, others also contributed to the development of movable type: Johann Fust and Peter Schoeffer, Gutenberg's associates; Procopius Waldfogel in Avignon; and, perhaps, a Laurentius Janszoon or Coster in Amsterdam. Note that Polydore did not name Gutenberg until the 1521 edition. The Mainz Psalter, the first dated book, appeared in 1457, but other works, including the 42-line Bible, are known to have been printed at Mainz shortly after 1450. Conrad Sweynheim and Arnold Pannartz, having left Germany for Italy around 1464, printed the first book there in Subiaco or in Rome, and printers were active by 1469 in Venice, where Nicolaus Jenson worked.

CHAPTER VIII

1. Plin. *Nat.* 13.68–71; Verg. *A* 6.74. Aeneas asks Apollo to speak to him directly and not entrust his oracles to leaves (like those of the Sibylline books) that may scatter in the wind. When Homer tells the story of Bellerophon and Proteus, he mentions a folding tablet marked with signs. Although papyrus was used in Egypt long before Alexander, the Ptolemaic kings made it a product for export at the time that Polydore suggests. The oldest surviving Greek papyri date from the mid-fourth

century BCE. Paper was known in China in the second century CE, but it came to Western Europe only in the twelfth century. Thus, the Latin *charta* as used in this chapter by ancient writers really means papyrus.

2. Plin. *Nat.* 13.84–5; Gel. 17.21.31; Liv. 8.23.17–24–1, 40.29.2–5; Lact. *Inst.* 1.22; Plu. *Num.* 22.2, 7–8. Gaius Poetelius Libo Visolus and Lucius Papirius Cursor were consuls in 326 BCE (428 AUC), but Alexandria was founded in 331. For Cassius Hemina see *DIR* 1.12.4.

3. Perotti, *Corn.* fol. CXXVI^v; Plin. *Nat.* 13.70; Isid. *Orig.* 6.11.1; *DIR* 2.7.5.

4. *DIR* 1.12.45 Jos. *AJ* 12.90 Hdt. 5.58. Although the 'Letter of Aristeas,' the basis of the account in Josephus, is a pseudepigraphical creation of the second century BCE, an official Greek translation of the Torah in Alexandria during the reign of Ptolemy II Philadelphus (285–46) is possible. Parchment had probably become the required material for Torah scrolls by this time, and such scrolls were in use much earlier.

5. Plin. *Nat.* 13.74–6.

6. Euseb. *Chron.*, Helm, p. 168 Gel. 17.9.21 Suet. *Jul.* 56.6. The writing system ascribed to Marcus Tullius Tiro, freed by Cicero in 53 BCE, was a shorthand rather than a cipher, but medieval elaborations of the *notae* would have masked their efficiency for Polydore. Gellius tells the story of the Persian Histaeus, who tattooed a message on the shaved head of a slave and then waited for the hair to grow in before sending the slave to his correspondent.

CHAPTER IX

1. Plin. *Nat.* 7.88–9; Quint. *Inst.* 11.2.1, 11–16, 30; Cic. *De orat.* 2.86.352–4. Although Simonides of Ceos enjoyed the support of Scopas in Thessaly, the patron rudely turned on the poet when he included conventional praise of Castor and Pollux in his verse. The appearance of the two unnamed youths who saved Simonides is a typical epiphany of the Dioscuri.

2. Plin. *Nat.* 7.88, 91; Solin. 1.108–9; *SHA Hadr* 20.11. Cyrus the Great (d. 530 BCE) had a famous memory for names, which some attributed to his use of drugs. The Thessalian orator Cineas served as ambassador for

Pyrrhus of Epirus (319–272) when he defeated Roman forces around 279. The ruthless brilliance of Mithridates VI of Pontus made him legendary among the peoples whom he briefly unified. Great linguistic gifts would have been almost as useful to him as his immunity to poison, described in *DIR* 1.21.8. Seven of the *Lives* in the *Historia Augusta* are ascribed to Aelius Spartianus; Hadrian ruled from 117 to 138 CE.

CHAPTER X

1. Cic. *Marc.* 2.6–7.

2. *DIR* 2.10.3; Cic. *ND* 3.21.53, 23.59; Stat. *Theb.* 7.72–3 Diod. S. 5.74.4; Mart. *Spect.* 6.1 Jos. *AJ* 1.64. Like Pallas Athena, the Roman Minerva was a warrior, but she was not identified with Bellona, whom Cicero does not mention. Josephus has Jubel (*Ioubēlos*), not Tubalcain; see *DIR* 1.14.4.

3. Don. Ter. *Hec.* 33 Lucr. 5.1283 Hdt. 4.180 Diod. S. 1.24.3 Plin. *Nat.* 7.200. Herodotus (2.43) says that Hercules was an ancient Egyptian god whose name the Greeks used for a later hero, and Diodorus claims that Alcaeus took the name of the older god, proof of whose antiquity is that in his time humans wearing animal-skins were still fighting with sticks and stones.

4. Plin. *Nat.* 5.67, 7.202. Sinon pretends to desert to the Trojan side in order to persuade them to accept the fateful Horse; Vergil reports that a Greek ship signalled him, but others say that he lit a fire to signal the Greeks. The modern text of Pliny has 'watch-towers' (*specularum*), but the 1497 edition has *specularem significationem*, from *speculum* (mirror). Pliny attributes the *artes bellicae* along with the alphabet, astronomy and navigation to the *Phoenices* and makes *Phoenice* a part of Syria, but Polydore may have been thinking of the distinction between *Phoenicus* and *Poenicus* or *Punicus*.

CHAPTER XI

1. Diod. S. 5.74.4 Verg. *A* 1.1d–1. The words *at nunc horrentia Martis* stand at the end of one of the anonymous verse arguments which during

the middle ages often appeared before each book of the *Aeneid*; they were sometimes attributed to Ovid in the manuscript tradition.

2. Plin. *Nat.* 7.200–1; Hdt. 4.180; Clem. Al. *Strom.* 1.16.75.5; Val. Max. 2.3.3; cf. Liv. 26.4.4–8; Diod. S. 5.74.5. The words used here could apply to arms of many different sizes, shapes and purposes as they changed with place and time in the military experience of Greece, Rome and their many allies and enemies. Following Valla's Herodotus and other sources, Polydore renders some of them generically, though his Latin terms also reflect differences in Roman armament. Quintus Fulvius Flaccus carried out the siege of Capua in 211 during the Second Punic War. Midias, Mydias or Meidias of Messene is unknown beyond this mention in Pliny. Acrisius quarreled with his brother Proetus in the womb and was accidentally killed by his grandson, Perseus, who married Andromeda, the mother of Perses. A Chalcon but no Chalcus appears in the myths involving Athamas, a son of Aeolus, from whom the eponymous Aetolus is descended by way of Calyce, his daughter, and Endymion, her son. Tyrrhenus, the eponymous Tuscan hero, appears once in the *Aeneid* (11.612), and Pliny twice calls him the father of Pisaeus, otherwise unknown, but possibly related to the Italian Pisae in Etruria. The Thracian Penthesileia was daughter of Ares and Queen of the Amazons. The Scythians and hence their ancestor Scythes were famous as mounted bowmen.

The telegraphic entries in Pliny's catalogue of discoveries have caused modern editors to differ in punctuation and thus in deciding which inventor belongs with which invention. Polydore follows the the 1497 edition, producing the attributions in the following table, as compared with the Loeb and Budé texts.

	Polydore	Loeb	Budé
Spartans	galea, gladius, hasta	same	same
Midias	lorica	same	same
Proetus & Acrisius	clypeus	same	same
Chalcus	clypeus	same	same
Carians	ocreae et cristae	same	same
Aetolians	lancea	same	same

Aetolus	iaculum cum ammento	same	same
Tyrrhenus	hasta velitaris et pilum	same	hasta velitaris
Penthesilea	securis	same	pilum
Pisaeus	venabulum	venabulum et scorpio	securis
Scythes	arcus et sagitta	same	same
Perses	sagittae	same	same
Cretans	scorpio	catapulta	venabulum et scorpio
Syrians	catapulta	*	catapulta
Syrophoenicians	*	ballista et funda	*
Phoenicians	ballista et funda	*	ballista et funda
Pisaeus	aenea tuba	same	same

3. Eus. *PE* 9.27.4   Jos. *AJ* 2.238–53. Artapanus (second century BCE) was an Egyptian Jewish historian whose fragments are preserved by Eusebius.

4. Plin. *Nat.* 7.201   Veg. 1.16; Str. 3.5.1; Verg. G 1.309   Plu. *Marc.* 14.5   Vitr. 10.2.11   Plin. *Nat.* 7.201–2;Vitr. 10.13.1. Dionysius I of Syracuse used a kind of crossbow in 399 BCE, and catapults with ropes under tension were soon able to launch stone shot as well as arrows or bolts as far as 300 meters. The *catapulta* and the smaller *scorpio* shot iron bolts, but the *ballista* threw large stones a third of a mile. The Balearic islands (Maiorca and Minorca) were Carthaginian before the end of the third century; Gades (Cadiz), originally a Phoenician colony, around 500 BCE. Bringing down deer with a sling is one of the attractions of the winter hunting-season in the first *Georgic*. Archytas of Tarentum and Eudoxus of Cnidus, his pupil, were outstanding mathematicians of the fourth century BCE. The 'art of instruments *(technē organikē)*' that Plutarch mentions was probably not military engineering but applied mathematics. Disdain for application could have distanced it from geometry, however, making it 'one of the military *(stratiōtidōn)* arts.' Ctesiphon was a city in Mesopotamia, confused here with Chersiphron of Knossos, an architect mentioned several times by Vitruvius and by Pliny (36.95–7) in connection with Diana's temple in Ephesus. The ram *(krios, aries)* used to batter down defenses was in use by the mid-fifth century BCE, when the

military engineer, Artemon of Clazomenae, worked for Pericles. *Testudo* could refer either to a protective military formation of interlocking shields or to a mobile siege-engine protected by wicker-work and hide. Modern editions of Pliny have *Epius*, who built the Trojan horse with Athena's help.

5. The ignoble German (contrast the knightly Gutenberg, *DIR* 2.7.9) in Polydore's story could have been one of the Germans present at the siege of Cividale in 1331, where history records the first military use of cannon in Europe. In Polydore's day, the effectiveness of artillery in battle was still erratic, despite continued improvement of the technology. Chioggia, one of three breaks in the barrier islands between Venice and the Adriatic, was the focus of Venice's Fourth Genoese War (1378–80), which ended when the Genoese surrended their galleys on June 22, 1380. Often called the War of Chioggia, this conflict was the first in which the Venetians mounted cannon on their warships. The fire was inaccurate but harmful enough to kill Piero Doria, the Genoese commander.

6. Verg. *A* 6.585–94; Serv. ad loc.; cf. Diod. S. 4.68–1–2; Tortelli, *Orth. sig.* n3*v*, u7*v*. See *DIR* 1.4.14 for the audacious Salmoneus.

7. Pers. 5.13. 'Arquebus' means 'hook-gun' (M. Germ. *hakebusse*), perhaps referring to the hook by which the weapon was attached to other apparatus. Polydore's etymology was popular in his day, however. For Persius, see *DIR* 1.11.4.

CHAPTER XII

1. Plin. *Nat.* 7.202; Hor. *Carm.* 4.11.26–8; Tortelli, *Orth. sig*, f8*v*; Perotti, *Corn.* fols. CLXXI*ᵛ*, CCXXXII*ʳ*; cf. Hes. *Th.* 319–25   Diod. S. 5.69.4   Luc. 6.396–8   Verg. *G* 1.12–14. Pegasus springs from the body of Medusa, with whom Poseidon had mated, after Perseus beheads her, and Bellerophon rides the winged horse to kill the Chimaera. Some stories make this hero Poseidon's son and tell how Pegasus threw him when he tried to ride up to Olympus.

2. Plin. *Nat.* 7.202; Verg. *G* 3.115–17; Serv. *G* 3.115   Catul. 17.26   App. *Pun.* 10.71. Lucan says that Neptune (Poseidon) produced the first horse in Thessaly, where a district called Pelethronium gave its name to the

eponymous hero who was king of the Lapiths. *Stratum*, the word that Pliny uses, and Polydore's *ephippium*, may both refer to a horse-blanket or saddle-cloth rather than a saddle, which the Romans did not use until the early empire. Iron (but not nailed) horse-shoes, mentioned by Catullus, were not common until the late empire.

3. Plin. *Nat.* 7.202   Ov. *Met.* 2.552–64; Verg. G 3.113–14; Serv. G 3.113; Plin. *Nat.* 7.202; Eus. *Chron.*, Helm, pp. 45–6. Chariots were used in Greece by Greek-speakers by the early sixteenth century BCE, but in Homer they seem to be mainly for transport rather than combat. Cornelius Nepos, whom Polydore usually calls Probus, does not deal with Phrygian chariots. Eusebius makes Erichthonius the third king of Athens after Cecrops, at the time when Danaus ruled Argos, about three centuries before the Fall of Troy. He was born of the earth from the seed of Hephaistos, spilled on the ground in a failed rape of Athena. Cecrops, who was half-snake, had three daughters, assigned by Athena to guard the infant, whom she put in a basket with two snakes for protection.

4. Cic. *ND* 3.23.59   Plin. *Nat.* 7.199, 202. Although Hesiod (*Th.* 346–61) names forty-one daughters of Oceanus and Tethys, Coryphe is not among them. *Athēna hippia*, also called Coria, needed no mother since she sprang from Zeus's head, armed and accompanied by a horse, though in one story she is the daughter of Poseidon and Coryphe. Polydore gives no special attention to the wheel as such, which appeared after the middle of the fourth millenium in the form of the potter's wheel and probably around the same time in wheeled vehicles.

5. Serv. G 3.115   Lact. *Inst.* 1.11, 7.22   *DIR* 1.17.8   Diod. S. 4.70.1. Servius rejects the story that the Centaurs got their name *apo tou kentan tous taurous*, 'from goading the cattle.' When a king of Thessaly sent his workers to round up strays and the Centaurs were seen riding fast or their mounts bent to drink at a stream, the workers called them cattle-goaders.

7. Cic. *Off.* 1.29.104.

CHAPTER XIII

1. Serv. *A* 10.179; G 3.19; cf. Eus. *PE* 2.6.10   Diod. S. 4.14.1–2, 53.4–6; Plin. *Nat.* 7.205; Plu. *Thes.* 25.5   Eus. *PE* 10.14.5   Diod. S. 5.64.6; Str. 8.3.30   Str. 8.3.30, 33   Perotti, *Corn.* fol. CLXVII^r; cf. Vell. 1.8.1; Paus. 5.4.5; Eus. *Chron.* 2 (Helm, p. 86)   Solin. 1.28. The four great *agōnes* involving contestants and visitors from all over the Greek world were the Olympic, Pythian, Nemean and Isthmian. Archaeological evidence is compatible with the traditional date of 776 for the first games in Olympia. The tomb of Pelops there commemorated his victory in a chariot-race that had killed all previous contestants. When Augeas refused payment to Heracles for cleaning his stables, the hero acted to recover the cattle owed to him and in the process killed two sons of Poseidon by ambushing them on their way to the Isthmian games and next killed Augeas and his sons. He then founded the Olympic games and set up the altar for Pelops. In another story, the person killed by Heracles in similar circumstances is Iphitus, whom Eusebius credits with the first Olympic contest 406 years after the Fall of Troy and 776 years before Christ, 'after which time one takes Greek historical chronology to be true.' The people of Elis, however, traced the first shrine at Olympia to an earlier Heracles, one of the five Dactyls of Ida (*DIR* 1.14.3). The later Heracles was a successor and an eventual holder of the games, which ceased until Iphitus reorganized them and named Coroebus as his first victor. Eusebius has *Koroibos Eleios*, but the Trapezuntius translation has *Argivus Corylus*.

2. Hdt. 8.26   Perotti, *Corn.* fol. CLXVII^r   Mart. 1.15.3. The name in Herodotus of the son of Artabanus is *Tritantaichmēs*, *Tritantechines* in Valla's Latin, not, as in editions after 1532, Tigranes, a leader of the Medes. Mardonius, given command of the Persian forces in Ionia in 492, died at Plataea in 479.

3. Ov. *Met.* 1.445–51; Serv. *A* 3.73; Tortelli, *Orth.* sig. s5r

4. Plu. *Thes.* 25.5–6; Ov. *Fast.* 6.547; Tortelli, *Orth.* sig. r1v; Serv. *A* 5.241; G 1.437; cf. Paus. 1.44   Ov. *Met.* 4.512–42   Plu. *Thes.* 25.5. Portunus was a Roman god of ports associated with Melicertes of Corinth (near Isthmia), who became Palaemon after his mother drowned him. The bandit Sinis is a son of Poseidon killed by Theseus, who also

claimed the games as Athenian property. Sciron is another of the brigands killed by Theseus.

5. Str. 8.6.22   Solin. 7.14; Hdt. 1.20, 5.92. Olympiad 49 is 584–1 BCE. Cypselus (657–27) preceded Periander (627–587), who was tyrant of Corinth just before this period when the games in Isthmia became Panhellenic, though the original shrine goes back to 1050.

6. Str. 8.6.19; Plb. 2.70.4; Serv. G 3.19   Vergil's only use of the word *Nemea* is at A 8.295, where modern editions have *prodigia et vastum Nemeae sub rupe leonem.*

7. Plin. *Nat.* 7.204   Solin. 11.5   Str. 10.3.8, 4.16   Dion. H. 7.72.7–9   Plin. *Nat.* 7.204. Like the Curetes (*DIR* 1.14.3), Athena performed a martial dance when she emerged fully armed from Zeus's head, and her performance was commemorated by the *purrhichē* at the Panathenaia. Although Pyrrhus (or Pyrrhicus) is not a prominent name in Greek mythology, some thought it belonged to the son of Achilles, Neoptolemus. In any case, the ritual dance required an eponymous inventor. Strabo writes that armed dancing was a requirement for the Cretan youth and that it was taught there 'first by the Curetes, later also by Pyrrhicus (*Purrhichon*).'

8. Serv. *A* 5.602   Apul. *Met.* 10.31   Verg. *A* 5.602; Paul. *Fest.* 504L; Suet. *Jul.* 39.2; cf *Aug.* 43.2, *Cl.* 21.3; Tac. *Ann.* 11.11; Hyg. *Fab.* 273.19. Servius cites a lost work by Suetonius on Greek games, in which he described the *purrhichē.* The *Troia,* probably from Etruscan *truia* and not from the name of the city, was a mock-battle on horseback fought by boys.

9. Plin. *Nat.* 7.205   Diod. S. 1.16.1   Hor. *Carm.* 1.10.1–4. The best known stories about Lycaon of Arcadia involve his daughter Callisto, changed to a bear by Artemis. In other narratives, Lycaon himself becomes a wolf (*lukos*) after serving Zeus a human meal. The Lycaian games were celebrated on Mt. Lycaion in Arcadia, where Zeus had a shrine. The funeral games for Jason were organized by his son, Acastus.

10. Hdt. 1.94   Plin. *Nat.* 7.205   Hdt. 1.94. The 1497 Pliny has *Hercules olympiae athleticam; Pythus pilam lusoriam; Gyges Lydius picturam in Aegypto.* Modern texts divide this passage differently, making Pythus responsible

for *athletica*, Gyges of Lydia (680–45 BCE) for ball-games, which does not contradict Herodotus.

11. Although board-games are very old, the evidence for games closer to chess than to checkers or backgammon and begins around 600 CE in India, whence early forms of chess spread through Persia and the Moslem world to Western Europe by the twelfth century. Polydore's description resembles the account in *De ludo scachorum* by Jacobus de Cessolis, a Dominican of the thirteenth century. Xerxes might be a Sassanian Artaxerxes or the figure called Sassa (cf. Shah) in Arabic legends about the origin of chess. In the Eusebian chronology the date assigned to the Xerxes of the Persian Wars is 4728 (486 BCE), while 3635 is in the time of Moses and Cecrops.

12. Perotti, *Corn.* fol. LXVIII; Mart. 14.17; cf. Isid. *Orig.* 18.63; Poll. 10.99–103; Arist. *HA* 499[b].

13. Perotti, *Corn.* fol. LXVIII; Pers. 3.48–50.

14. Plaut. *Cur.* 354–9. Polydore has compressed parts of several lines from Plautus (ed. prin. 1472) here.

15. Perotti, *Corn.* fol. LXVIII; cf. Poll. 10.101.

16. Suet. *Aug.* 71–4.

17. Non. 550L.

CHAPTER XIV

1. Dion. H. 1.31.1, 4; 32.1–5; 80.1–4; Serv. *A* 8.343; Plu. *Rom.* 21.4, 8–10; *Caes.* 61.1–3; Liv. 1.5.1–2; Ps.-Fenestella [1477], sigs. a1r–a2v; Tortelli, *Orth.* sig. o5v. Evander settled near a hill by the Tiber and worshiped the Arcadian Pan at a place called the Lykaion (*lukos*, wolf) or Lupercal, according to Livy and Dionysius.. In a cave called by that name at the base of the Palatine, a she-wolf (*lupa*) nursed Romulus and Remus. The Romans sacrificed goats and a dog on February 15 and used their blood to mark two young priests called *Luperci*, who then ran about nearly naked and struck people with strips of goat-skin. The verb *luo* means to atone. Faunus was a wild woodland god called Inuus (*ineo*, copulate)

from his promiscuous behavior but sometimes identified with Silvanus, a better behaved forest god.

2. Plu. *Quaest. Rom.* 68 (280B-C); Paul. *Fest.* pp. 49/56–7 Juv. 2.142 Ov. *Fast.* 2.279–88   Verg. *A* 8.663; Serv. ad loc.; Liv. 1.5.1–2; Dion. H. 1.31.1, 4; 32.1–5; 80.1; Ps.-Fenestella [1477], sigs. a1r–a2v   Just. *Epit.* 43.1.7   App. *BC* 2.109.

3. Serv. *G* 3.18; Perotti, *Corn.* fol. CCXLI[v]   Liv. 1.35.8, 8.20.1   Verg. *A* 5.109. Polydore's etymology is from *circum enses* (around the swords). Since the main purpose of a *circus* was to race chariots, its form was two level, parallel tracks separated by a long, narrow *spina* (spine) with *metae* (cones) for turning-posts at either end. Tradition dates the earliest such structure, the Circus Maximus, to the time of the kings, but renovations and enlargements continued until the massive projects of Trajan and Constantine. *Ludi circenses* eventually included horse-racing, plays, gladiatorial fights, athletic contests, animal-hunts, triumphal parades and other spectacles.

4. Perotti, *Corn.* fols. XI[r], LI[r], CLIX[v], CCXLI[v]   Mart. 13.1.4   Macr. *Sat.* 1.7.23–4, 28, 36–7   Just. *Epit.* 43.1.3–4. The Saturnalia was a feast of several days beginning on December 17 that featured gift-giving and social inversion. On Saturn, Janus and the Pelasgians, see *DIR* 1.5.2, 6–7.

5. Cypr. *Ep.* 1.7 [*PL* 4: 204]   *SHA Max.* 8.5–7 66–8. The Romans had learned about gladiators at funeral games from the Etruscans by the early third century BCE. Offering opportunities for patronage and display, they sometimes involved thousands of combatants by the early empire. See *DIR* 1.5.1 on Cyprian of Carthage.

6. Cic. *Off.* 1.29.103–4   *DIR* 4.14.

CHAPTER XV

1. Plin. *Nat.* 7.202   Gel. 1.25.1–8, 15–16   Liv. 1.15.5, 7.20.8. This Lycaon (not the Arcadian founder of the Lycian games; *DIR* 2.13.9) is a son of Priam captured by Achilles, sold, ransomed and then finally killed by the relentless hero after an escape. The traditional date for the conquest of Veii by Romulus was in the middle of the eighth century BCE; the war ended with a truce of a hundred years, the same period granted in 353 to

Caere. The Samnite general Gavius Pontius defeated a Roman army in 321. Claudius Quadrigarius, whom Gellius cites along with Varro here, was an annalist of the late Republican period.

2. Plin. *Nat.* 7.202; Diod. S. 5.75.1.

3. Jos. *AJ* 1.299–300; 4.76, 86; 5.49–61; Eus. *PE* 10.9.9; *Chron.*, Helm, pp. 9–12, 30. Eusebius dates Jacob's contract with Laban in year 238 of Abraham (1779 BCE), almost two centuries before the birth of Moses, and Joshua's succession after the death of Moses in year 545 (1472).

4. Liv. 34.57.7–9. Menippus, representing Antiochus III, stated this theory of treaties in 193 BCE when his master was threatened in Asia unless he respected Rome's authority in Europe.

5. Liv. 1.24.3–9;   Plb. 3.25.6–9. In Latium the *fetiales* were priests who declared war and made treaties. In Rome they were a college of twenty, responsible for the ritual described here.

6. Hdt. 3.8.

7. Hdt. 4.70, cf. 1.74, 3.8. Herodotus notes this and other examples of the common practice of the blood-oath among barbarians, whose use of human blood contrasts with the Greek use of animal blood for this purpose.

8. Sal. *Cat.* 22.1–2   Hdt. 3.13, 4.201. When the Persians were unable to tunnel beneath the lines of the Barcaei, they covered a trench and then invited the enemy to parley on the spot. Swearing to keep their bargain with the Barcaei as long as the ground stood firm, the Persians had devised a tactic that technically kept their word. For Sallust, see *DIR* 1.12.4.

CHAPTER XVI

1. Diod. S. 3.65.4–8; 4.3.1; Plin. *Nat.* 7.191; Solin. 52.5   Just. *Epit.* 19.1.6–7. Justin says that Hasdrubal and Hamilcar, sons of the patriarch Mago, conducted military campaigns toward the end of the sixth century.

2. Dion. H. 2.34.2, 4; Plu. *Rom.* 16.2–8; Val. Max. 3.2.3; Liv. 1.10.1–8 Eutr. 1.6; *Hist.* [1471], fol. 12r. Livy, Dionysius and Plutarch are in broad agreement that Romulus dedicated armor to Jupiter Feretrius on the Capitoline, thereby founding Rome's first temple, but Plutarch disagrees

with Dionysius on the four-horse chariot, a sensitive point because the team that stood atop Jupiter's temple on the Capitoline implied a claim to divinity.

3. Dion. H. 2.34.3   Liv. 5.23.4–6; Plu. *Cam.* 7.1–2. Plutarch says that either Tarquinius Priscus or Publicola was the first to use the gilded chariot and white horses. The dictator Marcus Furius Camillus won his triumph in 396 BCE.

4. Plu. *Marc.* 22.7–9   Paul. *Fest.* p. 213   Gel. 5.6.20–21   Val. Max. 2.8.1. The standard for earning a triumph was to have killed five thousand enemies in one battle. In use by the early Republic and continuing through the early Empire, the ovation might be awarded if the victory was less glorious militarily, but more often the reasons were political. A crown of myrtle rather than laurel was one of several indications that an ovation was less important. *Ovatio* is the noun corresponding to *ovare*, to rejoice, cf. *euazō*, to cry *eua*, Thus, the etymology from Festus is better than *ovis* (sheep) from Plutarch.

5. Liv. 31.20.1–3, 6. Lucius Cornelius Lentulus conducted his campaigns in Spain from 206 to 201 BCE.

6. Plin. *Nat.* 15.125–6; Plu. *Marc.* 22.2, 9–10; Gel. 5.6.27.

7. Publius Postumius Tubertus was consul in 505 and 503 BCE. The Masurius Sabinus whom Gellius cites was an important jurist of the early principate.

8. Cic. *Inv.* 2.23.69–70. The word *tropaeum* (*tropaion*) comes from *tropē* or turning, originally honoring a god called *tropaios* as the giver of victory who turns the enemy away. Trophies were erected permanently by the fourth century. In 371 the Thebans won a surprising victory over the indomitable Spartans at Leuctra.

9. Verg. *A* 11.5–9; cf. Tortelli, *Orth.* sig. z3r   *DIR* 2.17. Mezentius is the cruel Etruscan king of Caere. After his ally Turnus kills Pallas, a favorite of Aeneas, Aeneas kills Mezentius and uses his armor to erect a trophy.

1. Plin. *Nat.* 16.9   Eus. *PE* 10.9.9, 12.13; *Chron.*, Helm, pp. 13, 48, 52; Jos. *AJ* 3.172, 8.93. According to Eusebius, Dionysus or Liber Pater was born to Semele, the daughter of Cadmus, in year 629 of Abraham, 84 years after Moses died—not quite the 'many centuries' claimed by Polydore. But Eusebius also mentions an earlier Dionysus who discovered vines in the year 510 of Abraham, while Moses was still alive.

2–3. Plin. *Nat.* 21.4–6, 35.125. In the fourth century BCE, Pausias of Sicyon painted in encaustic and became famous for his depictions of flowers. Marcus Licinius Crassus (d. 53) was a general and political leader of the late Republican period. The cognomen Dives (Rich) had been in his family for generations.

4–5. Gel. 5.6.1–5, 8–9, 11–12, 16–21; Plin. *Nat.* 16.7–14, 22.6–8; Plu. *Cor.* 3.3–6   *SHA Ant. Pius* 9.10. During the Republic the Romans gave military decorations according to the heroism of the soldier honored, but in the Empire it was mainly rank and class that mattered. As Pliny says, the highest honor was the grass wreath earned for relieving a siege or saving a whole army. The Greeks also used wreaths for various religious, ceremonial and honorific purposes, most notably for victors in athletic games. The life of Antoninus Pius (138–161 CE) appears in the *Historia Augusta*, ascribed to Iulius Capitolinus.

6. Val. Max. 2.6.5   Plin. *Nat.* 12.94, 18.6, 22.6. Pericles reached the peak of his power and popularity around 440 BCE. Pliny says that the first to wear the wheat crown were Romulus and the other original members of the Arval Brethren, a priesthood of early Rome. Vespasian, whom Pliny advised, began the Templum Pacis after taking Jerusalem in 71 and rebuilt the Temple of the Capitoline Jupiter around the same time.

7. Perotti, *Corn.* fol. CCXXXIIII^r *DIR* 3.5.8.

8. Plin. *Nat.* 21.12; Perotti, *Corn.* fol. CCXXXIIII^r. Antony was defeated at Actium in 31 BCE, escaping with Cleopatra and then ending his own life when Octavian took Alexandria.

9. Plu. *Pel.* 30.6–7   Verg. *A* 1.724, 7.147. Pelopidas (410–364 BCE), a Theban military and political leader, led an embassy to Artaxerxes II of Persia in 367.

10. Cic. *Tusc.* 1.35.86; *Att.* 8.16.1 [166]   Cic. *Leg.* 2.25.63   Liv. 10.47.3, 25.12.15. Cicero maintains that Pompey would have been spared the catastrophes of his last two years had he died in Naples in 50 BCE. Livy says that decorated soldiers wore their military crowns at the Roman Games for the first time in 292.

11. The story about St. Paul's, added in the 1545 edition, indicates Polydore's personal involvement in changing and expanding the first three books of *De inventoribus* at least until this state of the text, produced in Basel, where no one would have thought to insert an anecdote about life in London. Moreover, Polydore added whole chapters to the last five books through the 1553–5 edition, which also shows evidence of authorial change in books 1–3 (*DIR* 3.16.7).

Chapter XVIII

1. Plin. *Nat.* 13.2; Jos. *AJ* 2.118, 3.197; Eus. *Chron.*, Helm, pp. 27, 43. Jacob was born in year 160 of Abraham, 675 years before the Fall of Troy, according to Eusebius. Moses gave the Law in year 505 of Abraham, 330 years before Troy fell. The Latin Josephus has *myrrham electam siclos quingenta* for *smurnēs epilektou siklous pentakosious*, and for *ein*, representing *hin*, a measure of liquid volume, it has *bin*. The *chous* was about three quarts.

2. Plin. *Nat.* 13.3; Solin. 46.1   Hdt. 3.20–22   Plin. *Nat.* 13.24. Cambyses II succeeded his father, Cyrus the Great of Persia, in 530 BCE and ruled until 522. Alexander defeated Darius III at Issus in 33. Antiochus III lost decisively to Lucius Cornelius Scipio Asiagenes in 189 (AUC 565). Statutes meant to control dress, meals, entertainment and other forms of display and consumption — *leges sumptuariae* — are known from 161 and 143, the last of these being a *lex Licinia sumptuaria*. But Publius Licinius Crassus, who passed a sumptuary law, was censor with Lucius Julius Caesar in 89, exactly a century after Scipio defeated Antiochus the Great, by which time the Seleucid dynasty was in contention among lesser figures called Antiochus.

CHAPTER XIX

1. Ov. *Met.* 1.138–42; cf. Plin. *Nat.* 33.1–3   Str. 3.2.9   Diog. L. 6.51. Echoing Ovid's criticisms of the Age of Iron, Pliny opens book 33 on metals and minerals with another of his sermons on cultural decline, the moral ruin caused by wanton pillaging of the earth and driven by greed, pleasure, warfare and medicine. Mining and metallurgy were both prehistoric, and trade in metals—first copper, then iron after the thirteenth century BCE—was an important cause of exploration and colonization throughout the Mediterranean area. The Latin Strabo has *Phalerii* (*Phalēreōs*), meaning Demetrius of Phaleron, who ruled in Athens after 318 and became librarian in Alexandria after he lost power in 307. The doxographer Diogenes Laertius cites the Cynic philosopher Diogenes (400–325).

2. Plin. *Nat.* 7.197   Hdt. 7.112; cf. Clem Strom. 16.75.8–9. Clement connects Cadmus with Mt. Pangaeus in Thrace, whose mines Herodotus describes, but Plutarch (*De Is. et Os.* 23) considers Panchaia a euhemerist concoction, while Diodorus (5.46.4) provides a long account of this marvelous island and its mineral riches. Polydore's *Eaclis* and *Ceacus* also appear in the 1497 Pliny, but in modern editions both become *Aeacus*, son of Zeus and Aegina. The island of Aegina was an early producer of coins, and Aeacus was a judge or doorkeeper in the underworld. Of the several figures called Thoas, Pliny's is the only man on Lemnos (geologically active and therefore a site for metals) who survives the slaughter of all males there by the island's women, before the visit of Jason and the Argonauts. In *DIR* 1.21.5, Polydore follows the 1497 Pliny in attributing medicines *ex melle* (not *ex metallis*) to Sol, though he lists him here with other discovers of metals.

3. Plin. *Nat.* 4.119; 7.195, 197; 34.94–109; Str. 2.5.15, 30   Solin. 11.15   Clem. Al. *Strom.* 1.16.75.4   Plin. *Nat.* 7.197–8   Clem. Al. *Strom.* 1.16.76.2   Plin. *Nat.* 7.197   Str. 14.2.7   Hdt. 1.25   Plin. *Nat.* 7.197. The many names in Polydore's account of bronze technology reflect competition for the few metallurgical innovations before iron came into use. Copper was a major commodity in the economy of Cyprus (*kuprinos*, made of copper). Of the several places called Chalcis (*chalkos*, copper), the most important was the capital of Euboea. Tin (*kassiteros, plumbum al-*

bum) and lead (*molubdos, plumbum*) were not always clearly distinguished in antiquity, even though tin was needed to make bronze. The islands that Strabo calls *Kattiterides* are probably the Scillies, though he locates them by reference both to the Iberian peninsula and to Britain. Paphos on Cyprus was an iron-age foundation variously attributed to Aphrodite, Agapenor or Cinyras. Renowned for wealth and skill in metals, Cinyras gave intricately wrought armor to Agamemnon. If his mother was Argiope (*Agriopa*), his father could have been Agenor, making him a sibling of Cadmus. Since Hyginus (*Fab.* 274.6) identifies 'the Phrygian king Midas' as the discoverer of lead and tin, Pliny or his source probably had in mind this semi-legendary ruler of Phrygia rather than Midacritus.

Although many authorities say that the Dactyls (*DIR* 1.14.3) discovered iron, there is disagreement on the location — Crete or Phrygia — of the Mt. Ida that gave them their name. Identified with the Curetes and the Telchines of Rhodes, another group of magical smiths and divine armorers, the Dactyls include Kelmis (*kelomai*, command), Damnameneus (*damnamenē*, magic spell), Akmon (*akmōn*, anvil) and sometimes Delas (*dēloō*, make known, or *dēleomai*, make mischief). Explaining that 'Kelmis and Damnameneus, the Daktyls of Ida (*Idaiōn*), first discovered iron on Cyprus,' Clement does not claim that they were Jews (*DIR* 2.19.5). The *Ioudaiōn* more familiar to Christian readers, however, was an easy mistake for *Idaiōn*. Clement adds that 'another Idaian, Delas, found how to smelt bronze, though Hesiod says he was a Scythian,' evidently drawing on the same Peripatetic catalog of inventors that lies behind Pliny's citation of Aristotle and Theophrastus for Delas the Phrygian and Scythes the Lydian. Clement also writes that 'the Noropes (*nōrops*, flashing), a people of Paeonia, were the first to work with copper and purify iron,' thus locating these achievements in Macedonia rather than Pannonia. As their name suggests, the Chalybes of Pontus (*chalups*, steel) were also famous as iron-workers, but not for bronze as Pliny indicates. The Glaucus mentioned by Herodotus worked for Alyattes of Lydia (610–560 BCE). He made an iron stand that Herodotus describes as *kollēton*, 'closely joined,' usually translated as 'welded'; Valla's translation is *compactionem ferri*.

4. Diod. S. 5.64.5, 74.2. *Berekunthon* in Diodorus suggests Phrygia as the home of the Dactyls.

5. Jos. *AJ* 1.64; Clem. Al. *Strom.* 1.16.75.4. For Jubel (*Ioubēlos*) in Josephus, see *DIR* 1.14.4. The Latin Josephus has *Tubalcain*. The citation of Hesiod comes from Clement.

6. Diod. S. 1.13.3   Vitr. 2.1.1   Diod. S. 5.64.5   Plin. *Nat.* 7.198. Hephaestus resembles the Egyptian Ptah in being a craftsman, but neither was normally credited with discovering fire, the famous gift of Prometheus. *Purōdēs* means fiery and *silex* means flint, but the flinty Cilix, son of Agenor and brother of Phoenix and Cadmus, is the eponymous hero of Cilicia in Asia Minor.

7. Plin. *Nat.* 16.207–8.

8. Str. 7.3.9   Clem. Al. *Strom.* 1.16.74.2. Anacharsis, a Scythian prince, is supposed to have visited Athens toward the end of the sixth century BCE. As an ideal type of the wise and noble savage, he was credited with various inventions, but his criticisms of technology — seafaring especially — were also legendary.

CHAPTER XX

1. Verg. *A* 3.57   Hier. *Adv. Jov.* 2.9 [*PL* 23:298C]; Diog. L. 6.87–8, 93   Hom. *Il.* 7.467–75, 23.740–52, *Od.* 1.184, 430–1. The curse of gold would have been meaningful to Polydore from Vergil's story of one of his several namesakes, the Polydorus whom Priam sent carrying gold to the Thracian king Polymnestor in case war took all his other sons. Polymnestor killed Polydorus for the gold, inciting his mother Hekabe to revenge. The name of Crates the Cynic (365–285 BCE), a disciple of Diogenes, was a byword for philosophical poverty. Although barter is the usual type of trade in Homer, his poems also imply a transition to the exchange of conventionally valued objects used as currency.

2. Jos. *AJ* 1.53–4, 60–2, 66   Plin. *Nat.* 33.8, 42–7   Hdt. 1.94. The first coins of electrum, an alloy of gold with silver, were made around 600 BCE in Western Anatolia where Lydia bordered Greek territory. Croesus of Lydia (560–46) was sometimes credited with this invention. Pliny has *proximum* rather than *pessimum*, making coinage not the *worst* scandal on

record but next after the wearing of extravagant gold jewelry. He also says that the first gold coin was struck at Rome in 218 BCE (modern authorities say 216), rather than Polydore's date of 106 (647 AUC). Suetonius (*Nero* 35) uses *ducatus* as an abstract noun for 'leadership,' long before the reign of Justin II (565–78 CE). As the name of a coin, ducat came much later, in the twelfth century.

3. Str. 8.3.33, 6.16 DIR 2.20.2 Plin. *Nat.* 33.44–6 Liv. 4.60.6
Eutr. *Hist.* [1471] fol. 19^r. Although Polydore distinguishes Phaedon from Phidon, both of Strabo's references as well as those of Herodotus (6.127) and Pliny (7.198) are to Pheidon, king of Argos in the seventh century, too soon for the invention of coinage, but he was also tyrant of Aegina, a city which did in fact issue coins at an early date, though still more than a century later. The first Roman silver coin, carrying an image of Mars, a horse and the word *Romano*, dates to 310, probably from a Campanian mint. A bronze coin showing Apollo and the word *Rōmaiōn* had already been made at Naples a few years earlier. For a Roman mint, Pliny's later date of 269 (485 AUC) for silver coins may be correct. This is close to 271 in ps.-Eutropius, although the sixth year of the First Punic War was 258. *Quadrigati* and *bigati* appeared later.

4. Macr. *Sat.* 1.7.21–2 Ov. *Fast.* 1.229–30, 239–40. Bronze *asses* with the double head of Janus on one side and a ship's prow on the other survive from the last quarter of the third century BCE. On Saturn and Janus, see *DIR* 1.5.6.

5. Plin. *Nat.* 33.43, 45 Plin. *Nat.* 18.11–12 Macr. *Sat.* 1.7.19–24, 9.1–18
Eutr. *Hist.* [1471] fol. 9^r. Although a *libra* was a balance and an *as* was a bar of copper or bronze, both *as* and *libra* can also mean 'pound' as a measure of weight The *as* was established at about twelve ounces by the early third century BCE, but less uniform bars of cast bronze (*aes*) were used as money much earlier. Bronze ingots survive from the sixth century, the period traditionally assigned to Servius. Crude designs like the *pecus* (sheep or cattle; cf. *pecunia*) described by Pliny are known. Pliny cites the *History* of Sicily by Timaeus of Tauromenium (350–260), and he connects the *aes* showing Janus and a ship's prow with the First Punic War (264–241).

6. Plin. *Nat.* 33.130 Cic. *ND* 3.2.57. Bronze was the usual material for Greek and Roman mirrors, examples of which survive from around 1200 BCE, but iron, silver and glass mirrors have also been recovered, and frames were made from other materials. The Roman sculptor Pasiteles of the first century is here confused with the great Athenian sculptor Praxiteles of the fourth century. The first Aesculapius, according to Cicero, invented the surgical probe *(specillum)* rather than the mirror *(speculum)* and also taught how to bandage wounds.

CHAPTER XXI

1. Perotti, *Corn.* fol. CLXXIIII^v; Mart. *Sp.* 7.1–2; Serv. *Ecl.* 6.42; cf. Hyg. *Astr.* 2.15. Athenaeus (15.16) writes that Zeus had Prometheus wear a garland to remind him of his punishment, but Hyginus says it was a ring.

2–3. Plin. *Nat.* 33.8, 11–12; 37.2; App. *Pun.* 493. The finger-ring was known to the Mycenaeans, and Sappho, Herodotus and Aristophanes use *daktulios*, which does not appear in Homer—nor does *sphragis*. *Od.* 8.443–8 mentions the use of tying *(desmon)* that Pliny contrasts here with signet-rings. In Homer's famous passage about the 'folded tablet' *(Il.* 6.168–9) there is no device for tying, however, though writing tablets known to Pliny were held together by rings or thongs. Appian writes that 'the military tribunes wore gold, those of lower rank iron,' but Pliny connects the iron ring with betrothal.

4. Gen. 38:18; Jos. *AJ* 1.249, 8.47, 11.269–70, 19.185, 20.32. The Vulgate has *annulum*, the Septuagint *daktulion*, but *chotamcha* in Gen 38:18 seems to refer to a seal strung on a cord.

5. Jos. *AJ* 3.162, 164, 170; cf. Exod. 28:6 Eus. *Chron.*, Helm, pp. 42, 60–1; *DIR* 1.5.2, 6.7; 4.5 Jos. *AJ* 3.140, 165–6. Since Troy fell in year 835 of Abraham, according to the *Chronicle* of Eusebius, the time that Polydore mentions was around year 485. Where Polydore follows the Latin Josephus with *annulus*, the Greek is *krikos*, which means a ring that joins one thing to another, rather than *daktulios*, the finger-ring. For *shoham* in Exod. 28:9, which might mean any number of gemstones, Josephus has

647

sardonyx, a stone that varied from the onyx only in color; LXX has *smaragdos*; the Latin Josephus *sardonici lapides*.

6. Macr. *Sat.* 7.13.8, 12–13   Plin. *Nat.* 33.22, 29.

CHAPTER XXII

1. Plin. *Nat.* 36.190–1. Pliny's story is not altogether incredible. Natron is a naturally occurring form of sodium carbonate which, with quartz sand and calcium carbonate, can be used to make glass. The glazing of clay and other substances was known in Egypt from pre-dynastic times and reached Crete in the second millennium. In the same era Egyptian artisans began to make whole objects of glass, although glass-blowing was not invented until the first century BCE—probably in Syria, the region described here by Pliny.

2. Jos. *BJ* 2.189–91.

3. Diod. S. 5.23.1–4; Plin. *Nat.* 37.30–51. Both amber and the alloy of gold with silver are called *electrum (ēlektron)*. The only source of amber for the ancients was the Baltic. Phaethon's grieving sisters turn into weeping poplars.

4. Plin. *Nat.* 33.113   Vitr. 7.8.1   Plin. *Nat.* 33.111–12; 37.18, 21. *Minium* is vermilion, a pigment made from cinnabar or mercuric sulfide. Pliny dates the discovery of cinnabar to 349 AUC (405 BCE), making this the Callias who died in 370. Tradition says that Camillus became dictator for the first time in 396. *Murrina* was made of flourite or agate. Pompey celebrated his triumph for defeating the pirates in 61.

5. Plin. *Nat.* 37.23–6   Solin. 15.31   Diod. S. 2.52.2.

CHAPTER XXIII

1. Lact. *Inst.* 2.2   Jos. *Ap.* 1.199, 2.12, 73–8; *AJ* 17.151–63, 18.261–309. When Caligula ordered his statue set up in the Temple in 39 CE, the Jews complained and Publius Petronius advised against enforcing the emperor's command. News of Caligula's death reached Petronius ahead of the imperial suggestion that he take his own life. Marcus Julius Agrippa, Tetrarch of Galilee and other territories, also warned against this provocation when he visited Rome in 40.

2. Eus. *PE* 6.10.12   Clem. Al. *Strom.* 1.15.71.1   Plu. *Num.* 8.12–14
Hdt. 1.131; Str. 15.3.13   *DIR* 2.23.7–8.

3. Macr. *Sat.* 1.11.47–8. A site of legendary events and religious power,
the ancient wooden pile-bridge or Pons Sublicius probably stood below
the Insula Tiberina. Livy attributes it to Ancus Marcius, traditionally a
king of the late seventh century. For Hercules see *DIR* 3.2.5; Epicadus is
not identified.

4. Dion. H. 1.19, 34, 39–42; Macr. Sat. 1.7.27–32, 11.1; Perotti, *Corn.* fol.
CLIX^v. Dionysius calls the lake *Kotulia* and says that the Pelasgians saw
'a little island whirling about *(peridinoumenēn)* in it.' Editors of Macrobius
read *enatam, enantem, nantem* or *natam.* Macrobius and Dionysius give
different versions of the oracle. Macrobius has *kai kephalas Haidē kai tō
patri pempete phōta,* but for *Hades* Dionysius has *Kronos (Kronidē).* The
Greek pun on *phōta* (light/man) is lost by the Latin *lumen.*

5. Diod. S. 3.3.4   Lact. Inst. 2.11.

6. Eus. *PE* 3.8.1, 10.11.16–20, 12.22; *Chron.* (Helm, pp. 31, 40–1); Jos. *AJ*
1.310. Eusebius mentions Prometheus more than seventy years after the
flood but still before Moses, while noting that some authorities put him
in the time of Cecrops and Moses.

7. Gen. 18:20–1   Exod. 7:4   Ps. 17:1, 51:11   Isa. 6:1.

8. Mark 12:30.

9. Plin. *Nat.* 34.15, 17; Sal. *Jug.* 4.5–6. Spurius Cassius Vecellinus is supposed to have been executed in 485 BCE. The cult of Ceres was associated with the *plebs,* and Spurius Cassius was remembered as a popular
leader. Varro says that the early Romans did not use statues in their worship, but archaelogical evidence contradicts this claim. Portrait statues
appeared in Rome as early as the fifth century. The Republican custom
of displaying masks *(imagines)* of the family dead continued into the Empire and influenced the remarkably realistic style of Roman portraiture.
Aristogiton and Harmodius were executed after their failed attempt to
kill the tyrant Hippias in 514. Antenor set up their bronze statues after
Hippias was expelled in 510. Pliny's mention of the monument has to do
with sculpture depicting human rather than divine subjects.

10. Plin. *Nat.* 33.82–3, 151   Val. Max. 2.5.1   Perotti, *Corn.* fol. XXXVI^r. The Sicilian sophist Gorgias of Leontini (483–380 BCE) was born after olympiad 70 (500–497), so the right time for his statue is probably olympiad 90 — LXXXX in some editions of Pliny instead of LXX, the reading in the 1497 text. The worship of the Persian goddess Anahita spread widely after Artaxerxes II (404–358) put her statues in cities that he controlled. Pharnaces I of Pontus ruled from 189 to 154. Pompey's triumph in 61 followed a number of successes, including his installation of Pharnaces II as a client-king. In 190 the father of Manius Acilius Glabrio celebrated a triumph after defeating Antiochus III. The son honored his father with the first *gilt* statue in Italy. Equestrian statues had been known since the fourth century.

11. Plin. *Nat.* 34.18   Cic. *Off.* 3.20.80   Plin. *Nat.* 12.51–4, 13.2. Polydore takes this story to be about the famous Gaius Marius, but Cicero, having just criticized Marius for his ambition, is speaking here of Marcus Marius Gratidianus, who was literally idolized by the plebeians in 85 CE after he falsely took sole credit for a scheme to stabilize the currency.

12. Plin. *Nat.* 34.49–93   Quint. *Inst.* 12.10.8–9. The best known works of Phidias, the Athenian sculptor of the fifth century BCE who executed Pericles' plan to rebuild Athens, were ivory and gold statues of Athena in the Parthenon and Zeus in Olympia, as well as the design of the external Parthenon sculptures.

13. SHA *Tyr. Trig.* 14   Suet. *Aug.* 50. This part of the *Augustan History* is traditionally attributed to Trebellius Pollio, not Julius Capitolinus.

CHAPTER XXIV

1–2. Plin. *Nat.* 7.205; 35.2, 15–16, 58, 152; *DIR* 2.23. Most of this chapter is another confused reading of Pliny's invention catalogue. Although the 1497 Pliny makes Pythius the inventor of ball-games, Gyges of painting in Egypt and Pyrrhus of painting in Greece, modern editors link the Pythian god (Apollo) with athletic contests, Gyges with ball-playing, painting with the Egyptians, and Greek painting with Polygnotus or Euchir. Editors since the sixteenth century have read *Euchir* (Gk. *eucheir*, handy), but *Pyrrhus* appears in the 1497 text. Pliny and Pausanias (6.4.4)

both mention a potter named Euchir. Although Pliny rejects the Egyptian claim to have invented painting six thousand years before the Greeks, the first painter he names is an Egyptian called Philocles. Polygnotos of Thasos (fifth century BCE) painted Homeric subjects. Gyges ruled Lydia a century earlier.

3. Quint. *Inst.* 10.2.7. In this remarkable passage, Quintilian argues that the perfect orator must innovate and, more generally, that growth (*crescere*) is necessary in the arts and technology. Although things had to be invented when there were no models to copy, imitation is not enough. Poetry, history, navigation and painting would have stood still if people had been afraid to try new things.

4. Plin. *Nat.* 35.15–16, 58–60; Quint. *Inst.* 12.10.3–6. Strabo (8.3.12) and Athenaeus (8.346B–C) also mention the painter Cleanthes. Apollodorus (fifth century BCE) invented *skiagraphia*, a technique of shading. Two Aglaophons painted in fifth century Athens, one the father of Polygnotus, the other his son. *Ardices* and *Cleophantus* in the 1497 Pliny become *Aridices* and *Ecphantus* in modern texts, though most manuscripts have *elephantus*.

5. Polydore was older than Raphael Sanzio of Urbino (1483–1520) by ten years or more. When he moved to Perugia to work with Perugino after 1494, the painter was still a boy, and by the time of his early employment with Pinturicchio in Siena, Polydore had already left Italy for England. Since Raphael's greatest fame came from his Roman commissions after 1508, it is not surprising that Polydore did not mention him in the first version of *De inventoribus*.

Chapter xxv

1–2. Plin. *Nat.* 7.198, 35.151–3. For *Chorebus* in the 1497 Pliny, modern editions have *Coroebus* (*Koroibos*), although Wilamowitz conjectured the craft-eponym Ceramus (*keramos*, clay). *Dibutades* should be *Butades*, but Polydore follows the 1497 text, which also has *Euchirapum et Eugrammum*, merging Euchir with Diopus, the second potter mentioned in modern editions. *Eugrammos* is another name in the spirit of *Eucheir* (DIR 2.24.1–2). When Lucius Mummius sacked Corinth in 146, he removed great

quantities of art to Italy. For Demaratus and Tarquin, see *DIR* 1.6.11. Theodoros of Samos (sixth century BCE), whose colleague or relative was Rhoecus, won renown for sculpture, architecture and other arts. Lysistratus of Sicyon was less famous than Lysippus, his brother. Both worked in the fourth century and made bronzes, for which Lysistratus used wax and plaster casts.

3. Str. 7.3.9; Hom. *Il.* 18.600; Plin. *Nat.* 7.198, 35.154; Diog. L. 1.105; Diod. S. 4.76.5. The potter's wheel was in use before 3000 BCE, though improvements continued through Roman times. In the Greek world it became common by the early second millennium. Homer mentions a potter *(kerameus, figulus)* spinning a wheel *(trochos, rota)* in his depiction of the shield of Achilles. For Anacharsis, see *DIR* 2.19.68; for Ephorus, *DIR* 1.6.10, 1.14.7. Hyperbius is unidentified. Diodorus has *Talōs* for the figure whom Sophocles called Perdix. Daedalus killed him in a jealous rage because of his clever inventions. Pliny says that Damophilus and Gorgasus decorated the Temple of Ceres, which Spurius Cassius dedicated in 493. Modern editions have *Damophilus et Gorgasus*, the 1497 Pliny *Dimophilus*, who may or may not be Damophilus of Himera, a fifth-century painter.

BOOK III

CHAPTER I

1. Cic. *Off.* 1.42.151.

2. Col. 1. Pr. 17　Cato *Agr.* 1.4　Cic. *Sen.* 16.56. Tradition locates the famous call to duty and quick return to the farm of the patrician hero, Lucius Quinctius Cincinnatus, in 439 or 458 BCE. A *viator* was a minor official, like a bailiff, who summoned higher officials and also performed arrests. Manius Curius Dentatus (d. 270) was another icon of Republican virtue, idolized by Marcus Porcius Cato Censorius (234–149), whose *De agri cultura* (ed. prin. 1472) is the only one of his many works that survives complete. The most extensive Latin treatment of agriculture (ed. prin. 1472) was written by Lucius Iunius Moderatus Columella (fl. 50 CE).

3. Plin. *Nat.* 18.11　Cic. *S. Rosc.* 27.75.

4. Plin. *Nat.* 18.22   Cic. *Sen.* 17.59. Hieron II of Syracuse (271–16 BCE) supplied Rome with grain during the First Punic War and developed a tax for agricultural products. Attalus III Philometor of Pergamum (170–33), a student of botany and pharmacology, becomes two kings in Polydore's text. Archelaus of Cappadocia ruled for more than five decades after Antony appointed him in 36. Cicero cites a story from the *Oeconomicus* of Xenophon (430–354) about a visit of Lysander (d. 395) to the younger Cyrus (d. 401) when the prince proudly showed his Spartan ally a park where he had planted trees himself.

5. Diod. S. 1.13.5–14.1, 25.1   Tib. 1.7.29–32   Just. *Epit.* 2.6.12   Ov. *Fast.* 4.559–60   *DIR* 3.2.4. After Osiris ended cannibalism, Isis discovered grain growing wild and then Osiris learned to cultivate it and led humans from their savage ways. The correspondences Osiris/Dionysus/Bacchus and Isis/Demeter/Ceres were obvious inferences from similar stories of Egyptian and Greek gods, in which vegetation and agriculture inspire tales of death and rebirth. Albius Tibullus (d. 19 BCE) wrote two of the three books (ed. prin. c. 1472) of elegies and love poems collected in the *Corpus Tibullianum*.

6. Cic. *ND* 2.26.67   Verg. G 1.147–8   Ov. *Met.* 5.341–2. Cicero compares the shift from *Geres* to *Ceres* to the change from *Gē mētēr* to *Dēmētēr* or Earth Mother to Demeter; Diodorus Siculus (1.12.4) suggests something similar. For Ceres and Demeter see *DIR* 1.4.12.

7. Jos. *AJ* 1.53, 62.

CHAPTER II

1. Plin. *Nat.* 16.1   Ov. *Met.* 1.103–6   Verg. G 1.147–50   Plin. *Nat.* 7.191 Diod. S. 5.2.4–5, 68.1. Ovid's picture is of a happy Golden Age, but Virgil describes the hard life that people lived after Saturn's easy reign, when Jupiter's harsher rule made them needy and gave rise to various inventions. Although Ceres (Demeter, Isis) was widely praised as inventor of agriculture, various places (including Sicily) claimed that the goddess had honored them with her discovery. Hence, Polydore's *Attica, Italia et Sicilia*, as in the 1497 Pliny, masks conflicting claims made more visible in modern editions that read *Attica ut alii in Sicilia*. Dodona's oracular oak was as-

sociated with the acorns that fed primitive people. *Arbutus unedo* is a Mediterranean shrub called the strawberry tree.

2. Str. 15.1.22　Diod. S. 1.13.5, 14.1; cf. 1.25.1　Ov. *Met.* 5.342.

3. Just. *Epit.* 2.6.5, 12–13　Diod. S. 5.68.2　Diog. L. 5.17　Diod. S. 5.4.4. As usual, Polydore cites Aristotle indirectly, here from Diogenes Laertius. For Triptolemus, see *DIR* 3.2.6, 8.

4. Macr. *Sat.* 1.7.21, 25; Eutr. *Hist.* [1471] fol. 9ʳ. Macrobius credits Saturn with teaching Janus the 'knowledge of the land,' including grafting, arboriculture and fertilizing.

5. Serv. *A* 1.179, 9.4, 10.76; Plin. *Nat.* 18.107–8; Non. p. 222L; Tortelli, *Orth.* sig. i2r; cf. Perotti, *Corn.* fol. CXXVIᵛ　Plin. *Nat.* 17.50. Small stone devices for crushing and grinding grain were in use from prehistoric times. Improvements in size and efficiency began by the fifth century BCE; rotary mills were a Roman innovation of the third century; and Vitruvius knew the water mill in the first century. 580 AUC is 174 BCE. Perseus, who ruled Macedonia from 179 to 168 BCE, went to war with Rome in 171. Picumnus (woodpecker, *picus*) and Pilumnus (pestle, *pilum*) are associated with both Mars and Saturn and are defenders of the newborn and their mothers. Circe turned Picus, the son of Stercutus (dung; *stercus*), into a woodpecker. Pliny alludes to *Od.* 24.219–31, where Odysseus finds Laertes digging in the ground and wearing a 'befouled' (*rhupoōnta*) tunic. The stables of Augeas were full of manure from the huge herds given him by Helios. Heracles, one of whose labors was to clean the stables, came to Italy (as Hercules) in the time of Evander (*DIR* 1.5.6, 6.9) to complete other tasks—capturing the herd of the monster Geryon and killing the giant Cacus (*DIR* 2.23.3–4).

6. Diod. S. 3.64.1, 4.4.1–2　Plin. *Nat.* 7.199　Verg. *G* 1.19; Serv. ad loc.; cf. Tib. 1.7.29–32　Just. *Epit.* 44.4.11　*DIR* 3.1.5. *Briges* in the 1497 Pliny should be *Buzyges* (*Bouzugēs*, ox-yoker), also the name of an Athenian priesthood. The boy mentioned by Vergil is Triptolemus, sometimes called one of the people of Eleusis, sometimes identified with Demophoon, a human infant adopted there by Demeter and made immortal. Like Demeter, he was credited with agriculture and law. Justin tells the story of Habis as a king and culture-hero of primeval Spain.

7. Verg. G 1.147–8; Serv. G ad loc.

8. Eus. *PE* 9.23, 10.8.4, 9.9, 12.23; *Chron.* (Helm), 12–13, 48–9, 62; Lact. *Inst.* 1.18 Jos. *AJ* 1.54, 2.95 *DIR* 3.1.7 Quint. *Inst.* 10.2.8. Eusebius says in the *Chronicle* that Janus, Saturn, Picus and Faunus ruled Latium for a century and a half after Troy fell, which puts Saturn around year 690 of Abraham at the earliest, but Joseph was in Egypt more than four centuries before. Demetra (Ceres or Isis) and Triptolemus come a little earlier in his chronology, between years 603 and 613 of Abraham (*DIR* 2.1.8), but still long after Joseph managed Pharaoh's grain. Dionysus was born in year 629.

9. Plin. *Nat.* 18.108.

CHAPTER III

1. Cic. *Div.* 1.1 Plin. *Nat.* 7.1.

2. *DIR* 3.3.8 Hier. *Ep.* 22.8 (*PL* 22:399) Val. Max. 2.1.5. For Eustochium and Jerome, see above *DIR* 1.4.2.

3. Plin. *Nat.* 14.58 Macr. *Sat.* 2.8.4; Gel. 15.2.3–8 Str. 15.3.20 Pl. *Lg.* 637D, 666A–C, 671B, 673E–74C; Macr. *Sat.* 2.8.5–7; cf. Eus. *PE* 12.25.

4. Diod. S. 3.63.1–4, 73.5–6, 5.2.4 Verg. G 2.2. Lenaeus refers to the *lēnos* or vat for pressed wine but also to the Lenaea, a festival of Dionysus, who is the god of wine in many sources, but not in Homer; his domain is a larger sphere of natural force. Euripides saw the god's religion as a conquering missionary cult, coming to Greece by way of triumphs in Asia. Later writers conflated these Asian exploits with Alexander the Great's victories as far east as India. Vergil does not explicitly mention Bacchus in connection with fruit-trees, as Polydore suggests.

5. Mart. Cap. 2.158 Serv. *A* 8.319, G 1.19, 2.389; Eutr. *Hist.* [1471], fol. 9ʳ Tortelli, *Orth.* sig. n7v Prop. 2.33.29 Ath. 1.34ᵃ, 2.35ᵃ⁻ᵇ. *The Marriage of Philology and Mercury* (ed. prin. 1499) by Martianus Capella is an encyclopedic work of the late fifth century CE. Homer's Ithacan Icarius is not the figure of that name in a later story of the Attic hero who welcomes the wine-god and his gift, only to be killed by peasants who think that the wine is killing them. Sextus Propertius (ed. prin. 1472) wrote four books of love poems in the later first century BCE. Athenaeus of

Naucratis wrote his *Deipnosophistae* (ed. prin. 1514), a learned miscellany in the form of a symposium, shortly after 192 CE.

6. Plu. *Cam.* 15–16. The story of Arruns and Lucumo is meant to explain an invasion of Rome by the Gauls in the early fourth century BCE. The names are Etruscan, the latter meaning 'king.' Arruns invites the invasion to take revenge on Lucumo, who stole his wife.

7. Eus. *PE* 1.10.7 Plin. *Nat.* 7.199 Macr. *Sat.* 1.7.25 Col. 5.11.1. Describing the Phoenician cosmogony (*DIR* 1.21.2), Eusebius says that Aeon (*Saeculum*) and Protogonos were mortals born of Kolpia, a wind, and a woman named Baau, and that Aeon discovered the food that comes from trees. Eumolpus, son of Poseidon and rival of Erechtheus, was an Eleusinian and a founder of the famous mysteries or else an ancestor of that Eumolpus. Macrobius has *omnium cuiuscemodi fertilium tribuunt disciplinas* with no mention of trees.

8. Jos. *AJ* 1.140–1; Lact. *Inst.* 2.14; Hier. *Ep.* 22.8, 69.9 (*PL* 22:399, 663) Hdt. 1.94; *DIR* 2.13.10. Herodotus says that the Lydians were the first tavern-keepers (*kapēloi*), but *kapēlos* like *caupo* can also mean any minor retailer; Valla has *caupones institoresque*.

9. Plin. *Nat.* 7.199, 30.145 Diod. S. 4.3.4. For *Sitheni* in the 1497 Pliny, modern texts read *Sileni*. The *Silenoi* were companions of Dionysus, so this paternity for Staphylus (*staphulē*, bunch of grapes) is natural enough. Polydore follows Poggio's Latin where Diodorus writes: 'When they serve wine unmixed, the words they add are for the Good Spirit (*agathou daimonos*), but when they serve it mixed with water . . . they call upon Zeus the Savior (*Dios sōtēros*).'

10. Tortelli, *Orth. sig.* k7v; cf. Plin. *Nat.* 7.191 Eus. *PE* 2.2.4; Diod. S. 4.2.5 Hdt. 2.77; Str. 17.2.5. The Egyptians made beer from barley, wheat and dates but used no hops. Pliny (22.164) mentions *zythum* in Egypt and *cervesia* in Gaul as drinks made from grain, but he does not connect beer with Liber Pater, who gets credit for wine-making in the catalog of inventions.

11. Dsc. 2.109. For Dioscorides see *DIR* 1.21.8.

12. Verg. G 1.18–19 Serv. G 1.12 Diod. S. 5.73.7 *DIR* 3.3.14. Ovid's version, reflecting the account in Herodotus, makes the gods judges of a

contest between Athena (Minerva) and Poseidon (Neptune) for the lordship of Athens. After Poseidon produces a spring by striking a rock with his trident, Minerva makes an olive-tree rise from the earth with her spear. The Roman Minerva was even more a goddess of handicrafts than her Greek counterpart.

13. Cic. *ND* 3.18.45   Diod. S. 4.81.2; Just. *Epit.* 2.6.5, 13.7.10.   Plin. *Nat.* 7.199   Hdt. 5.82. Vergil treats Aristaeus both as a god (G 1.14) and as a mortal (G 4.281–558), in the latter case as having learned to produce bees from the corpses of cattle. Hydromel (*mella*) is a mixture of honey (*mel*) and water. The names of Damia (*damos*, land) and Auxesia (*auxēsis*, growth) declare their role as fertility deities. The Epidaurians promised annual offerings to Athena and Erechtheus in return for the olive-wood.

14. Jos. *AJ* 1.90–2, 3.199; Eus. *PE* 10.9.9–10; *Chron.*, Helm, pp. 13, 51; Cic. *ND* 3.18.45. Cicero says that Aristaeus is the son of Apollo, and Eusebius, having put Tantalus and Tityos around the year of Abraham 660, writes that 'in the time . . . when Tantalus and Tityos lived, Apollo was born.'

15. Plin. *Nat.* 15.1. Traditional dates for Tarquinius Priscus are 616–579. 173 AUC is 581 BCE; 440 AUC is 314 BCE.

16. Diod. S 4.81.2; Plin. *Nat.* 7.199; Just. *Epit.* 13.7.10, 44.4.1   Jos. *AJ* 1.53–4, 2.118; *Ap.* 1.91. For *Cartesiorum* Justinus has *Tartessiorum* from Tartessus (perhaps the Tarshish of the Bible) in southern Spain, but some of the manuscripts have *Carcertiorum*. See *DIR* 3.2.6 for Habis, like his grandfather Gargor, a primordial hero of Spain.

Chapter IV

1. Plin. *Nat.* 12.5   Verg. *Ecl.* 8.63. Vergil asks the help of the Muses in telling what Alphesiboeus replied to Damon, 'since not everyone can do everything.'

2. Plin. *Nat.* 15.102; Hier. *Ep.* 31.3 (*PL* 22:445). Cerasus was on the Black Sea in Pontus Galaticus. In 74 BCE (680 AUC), Lucius Licinius Lucullus drove Mithridates VI from Pontus to Armenia, where he defeated Tigranes II in 69. Lucullus, who died insane in 56, was notorious

for his luxurious life. Jerome writes to Eustochium, not Marcella; see *DIR* 1.4.2.

3. Plin. *Nat.* 12.14; 15.47, 68–83; 16.103. Pliny uses *pomum* and *malum*, both often translated as apple, to cover a wider range of fruit—including even figs—than the English word suggests. A *malum Persicum* was a peach, for example. In the same way, although *prunum* meant 'plum,' a *prunum Armeniacum* was probably an apricot. *Zizuphum* transliterates *zizuphon*, the jujube, and *tuber* is the azarole, an Asian crab-apple. Sextus Papinius Allenius was consul in 37 CE, twenty-three years after Augustus died.

4. Plin. *Nat.* 12.6–7. The Diomedeae are islands in the Adriatic off the coast of Apulia. After the fall of Troy, the hero Diomedes went to this part of Italy. The Belgian Morini lived in what is now the Pas de Calais.

5–6. Plin. *Nat.* 15.127, 132–8; Perotti, *Corn.* fol. CLXXXV^v. *Ver* means spring.

7. Plin. *Nat.* 15.49–52. Pliny says that the *appiana*, based on a graft from a quince, was bred by one of the Appius Claudii, but he does not mention *pipina*, which as the name of a fruit is medieval.

CHAPTER V

1. Jos. *AJ* 1.35; Eus. *PE* 11.6.8   Cic. *Tusc.* 1.25.62. According to Josephus (both Greek and Latin), God gave the animals their names, but Eusebius follows the Biblical version in which God 'brought them to Adam to see what he would call them.' The high esteem that Pythagoras had for the person who first named things occurs in a passage of the *Tusculans* in praise of discovery, supporting Cicero's contention that the human soul must be divine and hence immortal because it invents. The great inventors devised not only names but society, language, astronomy, music, philosophy and other things indispensable to human life. 'Great were they all, and also those who came before them and discovered (*invenerunt*) crops, clothing, housing, a life based on order (*vitae cultum*) and protection against wild beasts, those who tamed and improved us through our progress (*mansuefacti et exculti . . . defluximus*) from crafts that are necessary to those that are more refined. . . . And what is discovery (*inventio*)?

Surely one can conceive of nothing greater than this, not even in God. . . . Homer gave human features to the gods, but I would rather give the divine to us. And what is divine? To thrive, understand, discover *(invenire)* and remember. Thus, I conclude that the soul is divine.'

2. Plin. *Nat.* 7.209 Jos. *AJ* 1.54 Var. *R* 2.4.9–10 Paul. *Fest.* p. 72L; Perotti, *Corn.* fol. CCXI^v. Hyperbius is a son of Aegyptus, but Mars has no son of this name—one reason why some modern editors of Pliny have condemned a passage retained here in the 1497 text.

3. cf. Dion. H. 7.72.15.

4. Verg. *A* 4.219, 5.235–8; Serv. *A* 4.219; Perotti, *Corn.* fol. V^r Hom. *Il.* 23.171–6; cf. Dion. H. 7.72.15–18; Eus. *PE* 4.16.13–18. Achilles kills twelve Trojans along with dogs and horses for the funeral of Patroclus, the only such case of human sacrifice in Homer—in contrast to its frequency elsewhere in Greek mythology.

5. Hier. *Adv. Jov.* 2.13–14 (*PL* 23: 302B-3C) Eus. *PE* 6.10.14. Arguing for asceticism, Jerome cites the polymath Dicaearchus of Messana (fl. 320 BCE), Chaeremon (fl. 50 CE), an expert on Egypt, and Asclepiades, perhaps an authority on Cyprus. Pygmalion is a legendary king of Cyprus or of Tyre.

6. Jos. *BJ* 2.119–33; *AJ* 13.171–2, 18.11–22; Hier. *Adv. Jov.* 1.18, 2.14–15 (*PL* 23:236B-37C, 303B-6C).

7. Hier. *Adv Jov.* 2.14 (*MPL* 23: 304A) Hdt. 1.200 Hier. *Adv. Jov.* 2.13–14 (*PL* 23:302C-4A) *DIR* 6.3, 4–6. For Xenocrates, see *DIR* 1.1.3.

8. Val. Max. 2.6.1; Gel. 13.11.6–7; Macr. *Sat.* 2.8.3; Perotti, *Corn.* fol. CLVIII^r Cic. *Tusc.* 1.40.96, cf. 5.41.118. Gellius and Macrobius note that the Latin *bellaria* corresponds to *pemmata* (pastry) or *tragēmata* (dessert) in Greek.

9. Cic. *Ver.* 2.1.26.66. For the reference to the Tusculans, see *DIR* 3.5.8.

10. Macr. *Sat.* 3.17.4 Plu. *Cat. Maj.* 8.2 Juv. 11.9–12 Macr. *Sat.* 3.17.1, 13. Beginning in 182 BCE, Marcus Porcius Cato led a contentious effort to reverse what he saw as the decay of Rome's moral standards. He described *leges sumptuariae* (*sumptus*, spending) as *cibariae*—literally, having

to do with food, suggesting that their effect was not just moral restraint but also the rationing of resources.

11. Plin. *Nat.* 9.119–21; Macr. *Sat.* 3.17.14–17   Hier. *Adv. Jov.* 2.8 (*PL* 23: 297C)   Juv. 11.14   Macr. *Sat.* 2.8.16.

12. Eus. *PE* 1.10.11, 13   Var. *R* 3.6.6; Plin. *Nat.* 10.45; Macr. *Sat.* 3.13.1 Plin. *Nat.* 10.141   *SHA Alex. Sev.* 41.6–7. For Misor and Suduk (or Selech), see *DIR* 1.21.2. Polydore follows the Latin Eusebius of Trapezuntius. Quintus Hortensius Horatius (114–49 BCE) was a famous orator and a notorious gourmand. The 1497 Pliny has *Laelius* for *Laenius* in modern editions.

13. Plin. *Nat.* 8.211, 10.141; Macr. *Sat.* 3.13.14–15; Var. *R* 3.3, 12; Gel. 2.20.4; Perotti, *Corn.* CVII^v. Macrobius criticizes the use of *leporaria* to confine hares *(lepus)* and fatten them for the table; he and Gellius both cite Varro. *Hirpinus* should be *Lippinus*. For Federico see *DIR* 2.7.7.

14. Plin. *Nat.* 10.16. Marius (*DIR* 2.3.9) was consul for the second time in 104 CE, when he gave every legion an eagle. First made of silver and then gold by Pompey's day, the *aquila* was much venerated and closely identified with the welfare of the legion.

CHAPTER VI

1. Plin. *Nat.* 19.2–6. Linen was used in the Greek world by the late second millenium, much earlier in Egypt. Before discussing horticulture, Pliny first describes flax and other valuable plants found in the wild. Since sails were made of linen, the subject gives him the opportunity to denounce navigation as another destructive discovery. He alludes to an unnamed author of this catastrophe—probably Icarus, renowned for recklessness.

2. Plin. *Nat.* 7.196, Lev. 13: 47–59; Ov. *Met.* 6.1–145   Verg. *A* 8.409; Serv. ad loc.; Ov. *Met.* 4.33, *Am.* 1.691–2   Auson. 27.1–2. Arachne (spider-web), a great artist from Lydia, rashly challenged Athena to a contest at the loom and even more recklessly wove salacious stories about the gods into her fabric. The insulted goddess beat her to death and changed her into a spider. Decimus Magnus Ausonius wrote his poems (ed. prin. 1472) in the later fourth century CE.

3. Plin. *Nat.* 7.196, 8.196, 27.III, 28.191; *Dig.* 33.7.12.6; Perotti, *Corn.* fol. CCXII^v. *Polumitos*, literally *many-threaded*, is sometimes translated as damask, which can refer to several kinds of fabric — in this case a rich material using different types of thread in the woof. For fabrics made of wool, the fleece was dyed before spinning into yarn. After the yarn had been woven into fabric, fulling cleaned the unfinished cloth of grease and dirt, thereby shrinking it and changing its texture. The *fullo* also laundered finished clothing.

4. Just. *Epit.* 2.6.5, 9; Diod. S. 1.13.5, 14.1; 5.2.4–5, 4.4, 68.1–2; *DIR* 3.2. Plin. *Nat.* 7.196. Closter's name means spindle.

5. Plin. *Nat.* 28.28.

6. Serv. G 3.25; A 1.697; cf. Plin. *Nat.* 8.196   Plin. *Nat.* 7.196   Exod. 3:5. Attalus III of Pergamum (see *DIR* 3.1.4) bequeathed his kingdom to Rome in 133 BCE. In the 1497 Pliny, the inventor of shoemaking is simply *Boetius*, further identified as *Tychius* (*teuchein*, to make) by later editors. Homer (*Il.* 7.219–23) names him as a leather-cutter from Boeotia, and Ovid (*Fast.* 3.823–4) connects him with shoe-making.

7. Diod. S. 5.73.8   Eus. *PE* 1.10.10   Gen. 3:21; Hier. *Ep.* 51.5 (*PL* 22:522). Summarizing the Phoenician cosmogony (*DIR* 1.21.2, 3.3.7), Eusebius writes: 'From the race of Time (*Aiōnos*) and First-begotten (*Prōtogonou*) were born mortal children in turn . . . From them was born Samemroumos, they say, also the Supercelestial (*Hupsouranios*) and Ousoos (*Ousōos*) . . . who first invented a covering for the body from the skins of animals.' The Latin Eusebius omits the names of the brothers of Ousoos or *Uso*. Jerome's *Letter 51* translates a Greek letter written in 394 CE by Epiphanius, Bishop of Salamis. Attacking Origenism, Epiphanius criticizes the allegorical interpretation of the tunics of skins that God made for the fallen Adam and Eve before expelling them from Paradise.

8. Str. 3.5.1; Suet. *Jul.* 45.3; Paul. *Fest.* pp. 228–9L; cf. Mart. 7.2.8; Liv. 10.7.9   Plin. *Nat.* 8.194–7, 33.63. Those who first wore tunics with broad stripes were the Phoenician conquerers of the Balearics, according to Strabo, but Polydore seems to have thought that it was the natives. The straight (*recta*) tunic worn by brides and boys nearing puberty was made on a special loom. Tanaquil was the wife of Tarquinius Priscus,

(perhaps) the mother of Tarquinius Superbus and the protector of Servius Tullius.

9. Plin. *Nat.* 8.194, 9.136; Mart. 8.28.17–18; Non. 189.24; Isid. *Orig.* 19.24.1–2, 17; Perotti, *Corn.* fols. XXVIᵛ, LXIIIIᵛ–LXVᵛ. Both the Greek *pallium* and the Roman *tunica* were smaller garments worn by folding a square or rectangle of fabric in two and then belting it, while the toga was a larger semi-circle of wool with more complex folds. Magistrates and young boys of good family wore the toga bordered (*praetexta*) with a broad purple stripe, unlike the unbordered *toga virilis* or *pura* worn by other adult males. The wavy (*undulata*) robe of Servius Tullius might have been either pleated or else full and billowy. *Symballoton* from *sumballō* (join together) might mean twisted or braided.

10. Isid. *Orig.* 19.22.9, 29; 24.7; 26.6; 31.3; cf. *SHA Comm.* 8.8, *Pert.* 8.2; Plaut. *Capt.* 520; Serv. G 4.376; *SHA Hadr.* 3.5; LXX Jdg. 3:16; Perotti, *Corn.* fol. LIIʳ   Plin. *Nat.* 3.31; Mela 2.74; Perotti, *Corn.* fol. CCLXXIXᵛ   Matt 27:59; Perotti, *Corn.* fol. LXVIᵛ; cf. Mart. 4.19.12. The dalmatic was a type of tunic that eventually became a prestige garment. *Gabanium* (Italian *gabbano*) is not a classical term, and *mandua* was a foreign import into Greek. Romans did not wear *bracae*. *Sindōn* referred generally to cloth of high quality, usually linen, but Matthew means a shroud made of such material. The name of the Phoenician city is unrelated.

11. Plin. *Nat.* 3.112; Verg. *A* 1.282; Perotti, *Corn.* fol. CCLXXIIIIʳ   Tert. *Pall.* 1.

12. Var. *L* 5.133, 7.37, 9.47.79; *Men.* 223; Paul. *Fest.* pp. 104, 406–7L; Quint. *Inst.* 11.3.137–9; Isid. *Orig.* 19.22.6–8, 29; 24.13; 25.3; Perotti, *Corn.* fols. LXIIIIʳ, LXVI   Plin. *Nat.* 33.10, cf. 8.195, 18.225; Verg. *A* 5.250; Serv. *A* 4.262, 5.421, 11.334; Mart. 6.11.8, 14.137; Suet. *Aug.* 40.5, *Cl.* 6.1   Non. pp. 538–9, 553–4; Isid. *Orig.* 19.24.13; Perotti, *Corn.* fol. LXVI   Hor. *S* 1.2.29, 94; Ov. *Am.* 1.32; Val. Max. 6.1.pr; *Dig.* 34.2.23.

13. Var. *R* 2.11.11–12; Veg. 4.6   Hier. *Ep.* 60.8, 71.7, 77.4 (*PL* 22:594, 672, 693)

14. Ov. *Tr.* 3.10.19–20, 5.8.49–50   Suet. *Aug.* 82   Sen. *Ep.* 90.16; cf. Plin. *Nat.* 8.132, 10.200. In 8 CE, Augustus ordered Ovid's exile to the Black Sea, where he wrote his *Tristia* and *Epistulae ex Ponto*, portraying

himself as surrounded by barbarians. Trousers, depicted in his verse and in pictorial remains, made good clothing on horseback in cold weather, but the Greeks and Romans found this Scythian dress exotic. The lines cited by Polydore conflate different sections of the *Tristia*. After the tragedies (*DIR* 1.10.2), the best known works of the younger Seneca are his *Moral Letters* (ed. prin. 1475).

15. Plin. *Nat.* 6.54 Verg. G 2.121 Solin. 50.2 Verg. G 2.120; Serv. ad loc. Historical evidence of contact with the Chinese begins in the first century CE. Ancient Western sources attribute the making of silk (*sericum*) to silk-people (*Seres*) through whose territory it might have passed or to whom its manufacture had spread — India, for example. Byzantine authorities acquired the eggs of the Chinese silk moth from smugglers by the middle of the sixth century, but remains of silk fabric survive from Athens as early as the fifth century BCE. The silk moth of Cos known to Aristotle and Pliny was probably *Pachypasa otus*, one of many insects that spin silk, but the fine silk made in China came from the *Bombyx mori* larva fed on mulberry leaves. Vergil's Ethiopian wool, however, is cotton, cultivated in India since the second millenium, imported to Mesopotamia and known to Herodotus.

16. Plin. *Nat.* 11.76–7; Arist. *HA* 551^{b}16. Bombazine is a blend of silk and wool. This reference to the *History of Animals* (ed. prin. 1476) is Polydore's only direct citation of Aristotle.

17. SHA *Aurel.* 45.4–5, *Heliogab.* 26.1; Isid. *Orig.* 19.22.14 Marcus Aurelius Antoninus Elagabalus, named after a Syrian sun-god, was probably still in his teens when he was murdered after a reign of four years in 222 CE. Aurelian (215–75) won decisively in the West (Châlons) in 274, having been proclaimed emperor by his soldiers in 270.

18. Procop. *Bel.* 8.17.1–7. Procopius (fl. 550 CE), a court official under Justinian, gave a positive account of the emperor in his *History of the Wars of Justinian* (ed. prin. 1470) but told a much darker story in his *Secret History*.

19. Poll. 1.45–7. As the title given by Polydore indicates, Julius Pollux wrote his Greek dictionary or thesaurus (*Onomasticon*; ed. prin. 1502) in the last quarter of the second century CE.

20. Plin. *Nat.* 9.80, 125–30; Vitr. 7.13; Perotti, *Corn.* fol. LXXVIII[r].

21. Plin. *Nat.* 9.127, 136–7.

Chapter VII

1. Vitr. 2.1.1–5; Str. 17.3.7.

2. Vitr. 2.1.4–5; Diod. S. 1.43.4   Str. 7.3.7, 17.3.7.

3. Vitr. 2.1.6–7   Diod. S. 5.73.8   Jos. *AJ* 1.60, 62, 64; *DIR* 3.9.3. Josephus writes that the tent-maker was Ada's son Jobel (*Iōbēlos*); see *DIR* 1.14.4.

Chapter VIII

1. Plin. *Nat.* 7.194–5   Diod. S. 5.68.1   Diog. L. 1.112. Modern editions of Pliny have Toxius, son of Caelus, but Polydore follows the 1497 text with *Doxius Celii filius*. Pliny cites the annalist Gnaeus Gellius for his material. Epimenides of Crete was a semi-legendary shaman of the seventh century BCE.

2. Jos. *AJ* 1.60, 62, 70–1   *DIR* 1.17.5; 3.9.3.

3. Plin. *Nat.* 36.1–3, 5, 7, 9, 48–9, 133–14. Pliny argues that nature made the mountains to contain the forces of the elements and to separate the nations, but man rashly destroys nature's works to suit his whims. Marcus Aemilius Scaurus was aedile in 58. Marcus Aemilius Lepidus was consul with Quintus Lutatius Catulus in 78. Crassus (*DIR* 1.8.6) was Cicero's model of the ideal orator. Mamurra was with Caesar in Spain and Gaul after 61; Pliny cites Cornelius Nepos (*DIR* 1.4.7) for this information about him.

Chapter IX

1. *DIR* 3.7.1; Perotti, *Corn.* fol. XXXIX[v]–XL[r]; Macr. *Comm.* 1.8.1 (Cic. *Rep.* 6.13); Var. *L* 5.143; Paul. *Fest.* p. 375M; *Dig.* 50.16.239.6–7; Isid. *Orig.* 9.4.2; 15.2.1, 3–8.

2. Plin. *Nat.* 4.17, 7.194; Just. *Epit.* 2.6.7; Str. 6.3.9, 8.6.5, 17.1.46; cf. Hom. *Il.* 2.681; Luc. 6.355–6. Athens was called *hē Kekropia* after its founding king; the Acropolis was the Cecropian rock. Some stories say

that Deucalion fled there during a great flood in the reign of Cranaos, who followed Cecrops, but others mention a later Cecrops. From the point of view of Argos, however, the first human (or Argive) was Phoroneus, father of Niobe, who mated with Zeus to beget Argos and Pelasgos. Complicating matters further, the Argos in the northeastern Peloponnesus was only one of several cities of that name. The *Argos hippion* in Strabo is Arpi (Argyrippa) in Italy, but Pliny's *Argos Hippium* is the Peloponnesian city. Sicyon west of Corinth was already famous in the archaic period. Diospolis was another name for the Egyptian Thebes, much declined from its ancient greatness when Strabo saw it.

3. Plin. *Nat.* 7.195; Verg. *Ecl.* 2.61–2 Jos. *AJ* 1.62, 113–16. Thrason is unidentified. The Cyclopes are the mythical builders associated with the lion-gate at Mycenae and the walls of Tiryns. In modern editions of Pliny, Theophrastus attributes towers to the *Tirynthii*, but the 1497 text has *Phoenice*, perhaps reflecting confusion between *Turos* in Phoenicia and the Argive *Tiruns*, famous for Cyclopean structures. According to Gen. 4:16, Cain 'settled in the land of Nod (*beeretz-Nod*) to the east of Eden,' which in Josephus becomes 'a place called Naid (*Naida*).' Cain then built a city and named it Anocha (*Enoicha*) after his son Chanoch (*Enoch* or *Henoch*). Vergil's lovesick shepherd, Corydon, declares himself at home in the countryside, not in Athena's city.

4. Jos. *AJ* 1.64; Eus. *PE* 1.10.10. Eusebius has 'huts (*kalubas*) from reeds, rushes and papyrus,' which become *tabernacula* in Latin. On Jobel, see *DIR* 1.14.4 and on Aeon 1.21.2 and 3.3.7.

5. Diog. L. 1.112 Vitr. 1.1.12 Hdt. 2.4; *DIR* 1.5.4; Liv. 1.10.5–7. The earliest surviving Egyptian temples are Middle Kingdom, though simpler shrines are in evidence from earlier periods. Nothing Egyptian of this kind came before the Mesopotamian buildings dedicated to the gods. See *DIR* 2.16.2 on Romulus and Jupiter Feretrius.

6. Jos. *AJ* 7.91–3, 8.62, 69.

7. *SHA Sev.* 44.9; cf. Pers. 2.69.

8. Plin. *Nat.* 7.195 Hor. *S* 1.3.6 Gen 26: 15, 18; Exod. 15: 27; 17: 1–7; Num. 20: 17; 21: 16–17; Deut. 6: 11; Jos. *Ap.* 1.103. Danaus, son of Belos and grandson of Libya, was born in Egypt, where Io, Libya's grand-

mother, had been driven by Hera's usual jealousy. His fifty daughters, the Danaides, when pursued by the fifty sons of his brother, Aegyptus, fled to Argos, where they sought the protection of Pelasgos and discovered springs. After killing the Aegypti on their wedding night, the Danaides were condemned to carry water in leaky jars to Hades.

9. Str. 8.6.7–8; cf. Hes. frg. 24. When Agamemnon refers to Argos as 'very dry' (*poludipsion*) at *Il.* 4.171, the reference is to the whole Peloponnesus, not to the city. Neither *enudros* (well-watered) nor *anudros* (unwatered) occurs in Homer, but a line attributed to Hesiod contains both words:

> *Argos anudron eon Danaos poiēsen enudron.*
> Danaus gave water to waterless Argos.

This is close to the line that Strabo cites in arguing that neither Argos nor the Peloponnesus could be described as dry:

> *Argos anudron eon Danaai thesan Argos enudron.*
> The daughters of Danaus watered Argos the waterless.

Strabo applies this line not to Argos but to Lerna, slightly to the south, where despite the soggy terrain the Danaides had to dig wells. Earlier he had condemned another phrase—*Argos anudron*—as counterfeit, explaining that it contradicted the physical facts and then citing another (unattributed) line to prove his case:

> *Theoi d'au thesan Argos enudron.*
> The gods made Argos well supplied with water.

In this last line, however, Polydore reads *anudron*. Moreover, the 1499 *De inventoribus* (leaving blanks for the Greek to be written in) adds Strabo's conjecture that Homer had used *poludipsion* as a synonym for *polupothēton*, meaning 'much-desired.'

CHAPTER X

1. Plin. *Nat.* 36.84–5; Diod. S. 1.51.5, 61, 66.3; Hdt. 2.148, cf. 2.13; Str. 17.1.37–8. Herodotus tells the story of the XXVIth or Saite Dynasty, but no ruler of this period built the Labyrinth of Hawara in the Fayyum

south of Memphis. This huge structure, 800 by 1000 feet in size, was the creation of Ammenemes III (1842–1797 BCE) of the XIIth Dynasty. He also left two pyramids, one of them next to the mortuary temple that Herodotus and others called the Egyptian Labyrinth and attributed to the Dodecarchs of Dynasty XXVI — though Diodorus says that Mendes or Marrus (M[e]ridim and Maronem in the Latin version) built it. Compounding the confusion was that Moirios was a name both of Ammenemes and of the large lake that filled part of the Fayyum depression when Herodotus saw it. Diodorus uses Moiris as the name of a lake and of a king who built a lake. Motherudis, Meridis, Petesuco, and Tithoe in the 1497 Pliny are Moteris, Moeris, Petesuchis and Tithoes in modern editions.

2. Plin. Nat. 36.85–6   Verg. A 6.27   Ov. Ep. 10.71–2, Met. 8.159–61
Plin. Nat. 36.85–6; Plu. Thes. 15–22; Str. 10.4.8; Hier. Comm. in Ezek. 14 ad 45:1–9 (PL 25: 447D-48D). Of the monumental palaces on Crete built in the second millennium, the one at Knossos is often linked with the labyrinth made by Daedalus for Minos to imprison the Minotaur. Having landed at Cumae, Aeneas and his crew gaze at an image of the labyrinth that Daedalus carved for the gates of the temple of Trivia. Ariadne, daughter of Minos, complains that Theseus, whom she guided through the labyrinth, has abandoned her.

3. Plin. Nat. 36.86, 90–1. Zmilus et Rholus et Theodorus in the 1497 Pliny are Zmilis (Smilis), Rhoecus and Theodorus in modern texts. Pliny's Lemnian labyrinth is probably a mistake (cf. 36.83) for the shrine of Hera built on Samos by the architect, sculptor and inventor Theodorus (fl. 535 BCE; DIR 2.25.2) on construction begun by Rhoecus. After Tarquin was expelled in 509, Lars Porsenna, the king of Clusium, came to his aid against Rome, but Horatius Cocles stopped him at the Sublician bridge, according to Livy's famous story, though Pliny (34.139) seems to have known a version less flattering to Rome.

4. Perotti, Corn. sig. Iᵛ; Plin. Nat. 36.75–6, 78, 81; Diod. S. 1.63.2–64.6; Hdt. 2.124, 127. During Dynasty III (2700–2625 BCE), Djoser built the first step-pyramid. The first great pyramid at Giza, whose base is 230.3 meters, was Khufu's, called Cheops by Herodotus, Chemmis by Diodorus. He was the second ruler of Dynasty IV (2625–2510), suc-

ceeded first by a son named Djedefre or Ra'djedef, then by Khafre (*Chephrēn, Chebrenes, Cephus*), another son by a different mother. At 215.3 meters, the base of Khafre's pyramid is slightly smaller than his father's.

5. Str. 17.1.33; Mart. *Sp.* 1.1; Hdt. 2.129, 134; Diod. S. 1.64.6–9. Menkaure (*Mukerinos, Mycerinus*) succeeded his father Khafre and built the smallest of the three Giza pyramids, with a base of 104.6 meters. From Djoser to Khendjer of Dynasty XIII (c. 1750), rulers of the Old and Middle Kingdoms built about three dozen pyramids now known.

6. Str. 17.1.33 Hdt. 2.134. The legend of Rhodopis (rosy-faced), elaborated in the Ptolemaic period, began with a woman called Nitocris who became powerful at the end of Dynasty VI (2460–2200), but a Rhodopis of Naucratis appears in the fragments of Sappho.

7. Plin. *Nat.* 36.75, 79; Diod. S. 1.64.13.

8. Jos. *AJ* 2.203 Plin. *Nat.* 36.75.

9. Diod. S. 1.51.2, 64.4; 3.3.4. Polydore follows Poggio's Latin, where Diodorus may be rendering either a specific Egyptian term or a broader concept such as *house of eternity* (*aidious oikous*).

10. Str. 14.2.16; Plin. *Nat.* 36.30 Mart. *Sp.* 1.5 Cic. *Tusc.* 3.31.75; Luc. 8.697; Gel. 10.18; Vitr. 2.8.10–11. Mausolus, satrap of Caria under Persian authority from 377 to 353 BCE, ruled with his sister and wife, Artemisia, over a wide territory reaching from Rhodes and Crete to his new capital at Halicarnassus, where after 367 he built his tomb. Work continued after 351 when Artemisia died—her husband's partner in this grandiose project but not its sole author, despite the romantic tale. Its monumental size, unusual form and magnificent decoration won the Mausoleum fame as one of the Seven Wonders of the ancient world.

11. Hdt. 1.140; Hier. *Adv. Jov.* 2.7 (PL 23:296A); Eus. *PE* 1.4.7; Str. 11.4.8. Strabo's Albania was between modern Georgia and the Caspian Sea. The Caucasus mountains, home of the Derbicae, run between the Black Sea and the Caspian. The Tibareni were from Asia Minor near the Black Sea.

12. Hdt. 2.86; cf. Diod. S. 1.91; Serv. *A* 3.68. The Egyptian technique of mummification, described in detail by Herodotus and Diodorus, had de-

veloped by the early New Kingdom (1552–1069 BCE) and reached its peak soon thereafter. The Ethiopian stone may have been obsidian, and the embalming fluid was based on natron, a mixture of sodium compounds found naturally in Wadi Natrun near the Delta. The period of soaking in natron was probably not as long as 70 days.

13. Hdt. 3.24; 4.71, 190; Str. 17.2.3; Diod. S. 2.15.1; Hier. Adv. Jov. 2.7 (PL 23:296B); Eus. PE 1.4.6–7. Herodotus writes that the body lies in a 'hollow pillar made of transparent stone' (stēlēn ex huelou pepoiēmenēn koilēn; Valla has sepulchra . . . e vitro constructo). Strabo uses the same word (hualon), which Plato first used for glass, whereas Herodotus and other earlier writers meant some kind of transparent mineral, such as alabaster. Nonetheless, Diodorus cites Ctesias of Cnidos, author of a Persika in the fifth century BCE, as having criticized Herodotus for claiming that glass (huelon; vitro in Poggio's Latin) was actually poured over the embalmed corpse. Archaeology confirms much of what Polydore learned from Herodotus about Scythian burial customs—transporting the king's embalmed body and burying him in a mound with grave goods, horses and strangled, mutilated companions. Hyrcania was south of the Caspian Sea.

14. Hdt. 1.140, 198; 5.4, 8; Str. 15.1.62, 16.4.26, 17.2.3; Diod. S. 3.9.3; Hier. Adv. Jov. 2.7 (PL 23:296B). Petra, south of the Dead Sea, was the center of Nabataean territory.

15. Str. 15.1.62, 3.20; Val. Max. 2.6.14; Hier. Adv. Jov. 2.7 (PL 23:296B); Just. Epit. 41.3; Eus. PE 1.4.8; Hdt. 1.140. There were two commanders named Nicanor during Alexander's campaigns in Asia. One was the son of Alexander's eventual enemy, Parmenio; the other was the adopted son of Aristotle.

16. Solin. 15.13; Mela 2.1.9; Plin. Nat. 4.88–9; Hdt. 4.26. Herodotus locates the Issedones far to the northwest of the Caspian Sea. That Scythian peoples scalped and beheaded their enemies to make drinking bowls from their skulls is borne out by the archaeological evidence. They also buried their dead with ornate head-coverings of gold. Pliny does not tell the cup story found in Mela and other sources, but he does have the Hyperboreans jumping from cliffs.

17. Plin. *Nat.* 7.187; Cic. *Leg.* 2.22.56–23.58; Val. Max. 9.2.1; Luc. 1.580; Plu. *Sull.* 38; App. *BC* 1.105–6. From the earliest times, the Romans practiced both cremation and inhumation, but cremation dominated by the first century BCE until the upper classes reverted to inhumation in the second century CE to imitate the Greeks. When Sulla was named dictator in 82 BCE, he violated the grave of Marius, who had died in 86.

18. Cic. *Tusc.* 1.35.85   Plin. *Nat.* 19.19   *DIR* 3.10.14, 6.9–1. The plebeian Quintus Caecilus Metellus Macedonicus (d. 115 BCE) had four sons who, like him, rose to the consulate, as well as three daughters who married into the nobility, thus establishing a dynasty. As censor, Metellus gave a famous speech on the value of marriage and children, and Cicero cites his fortunate family situation as evidence against fearing death.

19. Hdn. 4.2.2–11; Suet. *Jul.* 84. Herodian wrote his *History of the Empire after Marcus* (ed. prin. 1493) in the third century CE.

20. Plu. *Publ.* 9.10–11; *Cam.* 8.3–4; Gel. 17.21.4. Solon was archon in 594/3 BCE. The traditional dates of Tarquinius Priscus are 616–578.

21. Pl. *Ep.* 2 (311 B–D).

CHAPTER XI

1–2. Plin. *Nat.* 36.64–70; Isid. *Orig.* 1.21.3–4, 18.31; Tortelli, *Orth. sig.* q3r, Perotti, *Corn.* fol. II^r; Barbaro, *Castigationes*, III, 1159 (Pozzi). Old Kingdom builders erected single obelisks in temple precincts sacred to the sun, and pairs of obelisks stood before New Kingdom temples to represent the sun and moon. Some were more than a hundred feet high. Important surviving obelisks are associated with Sesostris I (1962–28 BCE), Aazehre (c. 1540), Hatshepsut (1478–58), Tuthmosis III (1479–25) and other rulers. Of the eleven pharaohs named Ramesses who ruled in Dynasties XIX and XX (1295–1069), the best known is Ramesses II (1279–12). Eusebius (*Chron.* [Helm], pp. 45, 53) locates an Egyptian Remesses in year 534 of Abraham, a Ramses in 695, but the Fall of Troy comes much later in his chronology, in 835 (1182 BCE). Ptolemy II Philadelphus took the throne in 282 and ruled until 246. *Mitres, Sochis, Ramises, Smarre* and *Eraphio* in the 1497 Pliny are Mesphres, Sesothes, Rhamses, Zmarres and Phius in modern editions.

3. Hdt. 2.111. Herodotus makes Phaeron (*Pherōs*, a transliteration of the Egyptian title that means 'great house') the successor of Sesostris, the Greek name for three rulers of Dynasty XII (1991–1785 BCE), the last of whom provided the basis of later legends about the figure called Sesostris (Senwosret). The Septuagint and New Testament use *Pharaō*, Josephus usually writes *Pharaōthēs* (*Pharo* in the Latin version) and the Vulgate *Pharao*.

4. Marcellin. 17.4.2   Plin. *Nat.* 36.71, 74; 16.201. Augustus brought two obelisks to Rome in 10 BCE. One of them, made in Dynasty XIX by Sethos I and his son, Ramesses II, stood in the Circus Maximus as a memorial to Rome's conquest of Egypt. Psammetichus II (595–89) had put up the other obelisk, which Augustus used for the gnomon of an enormous sundial in the Campus Martius. Pliny reversed the makers of the two monoliths, of which the younger was rediscovered in 1512 and eventually found its way to the Piazza di Montecitorio. The older one, found in 1587, now stands in the Piazza del Popolo. The obelisk now in St. Peter's Square is the only one to have stood since antiquity, though not in exactly the same place. It came to Rome from Heliopolis in the reign of Caligula, who wanted it for the Circus planned by him and built by Nero. *Semneserteo, Sesostride*, and *Sesostridis filius Nuncoreus* in the 1497 Pliny are Psemetnepserphreus, Sesothis, and Nencoreus, son of Sesosis, in modern texts.

6. Barbaro, *Castigationes*, III, 1160 (Pozzi); Hdt. 2.111; Plin. *Nat.* 6.165; Str. 17.1.5, 25; Jos. *Ap.* 2.132. Pliny, Herodotus, Strabo and Josephus (Greek and Latin) all have Sesostris.

7. Plin. *Nat.* 36.64   Tac. *Ann.* 11.14   Str. 17.1.46   Marcellin. 17.4.11   Diod. S. 3.4.2–4.

<h2 style="text-align:center">CHAPTER XII</h2>

1. Serv. *A* 2.761, 8.342; Tortelli, *Orth. sig.* f3ν   Stat. *Theb.* 12.497–8, 503–4; Plu. *Thes.* 22.6–7.

2. Eus. *PE* 10.9.9, 11.28–9, 12.18 *Chron.*, Helm, pp. 40 43, 49, 51, 56–62; Jos. *AJ* 4.172. Although Eusebius first mentions Hercules in year 443 of Abraham and hence during the lifetime of Moses, he places most of the

labors more than three centuries later in year 772 (1245 BCE) and dates the hero's death to year 821 (1196), just before the Fall of Troy.

3. Verg. *A* 8.342–3; Serv. ad loc.; Liv. 1.8.5; Dion. H. 2.15.4; Ov. *Fast.* 3.431–2. The Capitoline hill has two peaks, and the low place between them seems to have been the site of the asylum attributed to Romulus, which may have been enclosed in the early principate.

4. Str. 8.6.14 Hdt. 2.113 Str. 16.2.6, 17.1.23. Herodotus describes the asylum near Canopus in describing the abduction of Helen. Driven to Egypt by unfavorable winds, Paris was deserted by his companions, who then sought asylum in a temple of Hercules—whom the Greeks identified with Chonsu, Shu or some other Egyptian god.

5. Exod. 21: 14. See *DIR*, second letter to Gian Matteo Vergil, 1.17.1, 5.

CHAPTER XIII

1. Perotti, *Corn.* fol. XXIVᵛ; Tortelli, *Orth.* sig. y3r; Cassiod. *Var.* 4.51.5; cf. Isid. *Orig.* 15.2.34. Magnus Aurelius Cassiodorus Senator (490–585 CE), who held high office under Theodoric and other kings and popes, helped connect the new Christian culture with its Greco-Roman past; the *Variae* (ed. prin. 1533) is a collection of his official papers.

2. Eus. *PE* 2.2.11; Serv. G 2.381 Plu. *Thes.* 16.3; Str. 17.1.9. Both Eusebius and the Latin of Trapezuntius can be read as saying either that Dionysus 'introduced theater' or that he 'invented the theater.'

3. Prisc. *Inst.* 1.51; Isid. *Orig.* 18.43; Perotti, *Corn.* fol. XXIVᵛ; Tortelli, *Orth.* sig. u8v; Liv. 7.2.1–3. The Greek word for shade is *skia.* Gaius Sulpicius Peticus and Gaius Licinius Stolo were consuls in 364 BCE (390 AUC). Livy says that the Romans resorted to these *ludi scaenici* only when another apotropaic device failed to end the plague that struck at that time.

4. Liv. 7.2.3–11; Perotti, *Corn.* fol. CXCVIʳ, CCXXIII. 513 AUC is 241 BCE. Before Livius Andronicus introduced plays with plots around this time (*DIR* 1.8.6), salacious, mocking verses (*Fescennini*) heard at weddings and harvest-time or improvised farces (*Atellanae*) affected the development of the *fabulae palliatae* known later from Plautus and Terence and based on Attic New Comedy. Fescennine verses took their name either

from *fascinum* (evil eye, penis) or from an Etruscan town. Atellan farces, named for a town in Campania where Oscan was spoken, used stock characters or masks in the manner of the *commedia dell'arte*. When professionals took over the job of acting, says Livy, the young kept up the joking verses as their own, and these became the *exodia* (*ex-odos*, exit; cf. *epōdos*, refrain) or skits presented after a longer drama.

5. Cic. *De orat.* 3.26.102, *Parad.* 3.26; Perotti, *Corn.* fols. LXVʳ, CXCVIʳ; Tortelli, *Orth.* sig. n3r. In the *Paradoxes of the Stoics*, Cicero makes rhetorical use of technical philosophical problems. In this case the paradox is 'that all wrongs are equal and likewise all rights,' which rules out the possibility of being wrong *by a little* and leads to the analogy with an actor whose timing is *slightly* off. Quintus Roscius Gallus (d. 62 BCE), the greatest Roman actor of his age, was a friend of Cicero, who defended him in his *Pro Roscio comoedo*.

6. Perotti, *Corn.* fols. XXIVᵛ–XXVʳ; Tortelli, *Orth.* sigs. q6v, y3r; Serv. *A* 1.164; Verg. *G* 2.381; cf. Isid. *Orig.* 18.44; Vitr. 5.6.2. References by Plautus indicate that the audience was seated when his plays were first put on at the end of the third century BCE.

7. Liv. 34.44.5, 54.4–8; Plu. *Flam.* 19.8; Val. Max. 2.4.3, cf. 4.5.1; Plin. *Nat.* 19.23. Livy says that senators were first assigned special places apart from the people in 194 BCE, when the consuls were Publius Cornelius Scipio Africanus (the elder) and Tiberius Sempronius Longus. Valerius Maximus mistakenly attributes this unpopular action to Publius Cornelius Scipio Aemelianus Africanus, grandson of the elder Scipio. The *equites* got their special places (or had them restored) in 67 through a law proposed by the tribune Lucius Roscius Otho, whom Cicero had to defend from popular attack four years later. Quintus Lutatius Catulus (d. 61) oversaw the renovation of the Capitoline Temple and in 69 celebrated the conclusion of the work with games.

8–10. Perotti, *Corn.* fols. XXIVᵛ–XXVʳ; Tortelli, *Orth.* sig. y3r; Plin. *Nat.* 36.5, 114–17; Tac. *Ann.* 3.4.1, 13.31.1, 14.20.2; Plu. *Pomp.* 42.4, 52.4; Suet. *Jul.* 44, *Aug.* 29, 100–1, *Ves.* 9, *Tit.* 7; Dio Cass. 43.49.2; cf. Str. 5.3.8. On the Aemelius Scauri, father and son, see *DIR* 2.3.3, 3.8.3; Polydore has in mind the younger, who was aedile in 58 BCE. Gaius

Scribonius Curio's father, an opponent of Caesar, died in 53, only a few years before his son. Meanwhile, in 55 Pompey had started his permanent theater of stone in the Campus Martius, before Julius Caesar planned what later became the Theater of Marcellus, dedicated by Augustus in 13. In the previous decade, the same emperor had put up his Mausoleum (also in the Campus Martius), where he buried Marcellus in 23. The Flavian Amphitheater dedicated by Vespasian in 79 CE (and again by Titus in 80) became known as the Colosseum in the middle ages. Neither Tacitus nor Suetonius says exactly what Polydore reports here.

11. Suet. *Dom.* 5; Mart. *Sp.* 1.7–8, 4.3; Jos. *AJ* 15.268, 273–4; Sen. *Ep.* 26–7. Domitian added some finishing touches to the Flavian Amphiteater after Vespasian and Titus had done most of the original construction. It became the prime location for gladiatorial fights, which had begun at Rome in the third century BCE and became large, public spectacles by the end of the Republic. Herod the Great, appointed King of Judaea in 39, did most of his building toward the middle of his reign; he died in 4 BCE.

12. Mart. *Sp.* 5.4; Perotti, *Corn.* fol. CXXXVIII^v; cf. Juv. 4.100; Suet. *Tib.* 72.2

13. Liv. 1.35.8–9, 39.22.2; *DIR* 2.14.3; Perotti, *Corn.* fol. CCXLI^v; Dion. H. 7.73.3. Archaelogical evidence from the sixth century BCE supports an Etruscan origin for games involving horses and boxers such as Livy ascribes to Tarquin, but the assignment of seats to senators and *equites* came much later, in the second and first centuries. Although documents refer to a Circus Maximus as of the late fourth century, what now survives is imperial construction. Caius Flaminius Nepos built the Flaminian Circus in 282. Spurius Postumius Albinus and Quintus Marcius Philippus were consuls in 186. Caligula planned the Circus of Gaius and Nero and raised the Vatican obelisk on the site (*DIR* 3.11.4).

14. Perotti, *Corn.* fol. LX^r; Tortelli, *Orth.* sig. y5r; Suet. *Gram.* 23; Sen. *Ep.* 86.12; cf. Cels. 2.17.2–10; Var. *L* 9.41.68. Greeks began to build baths in the fourth century BCE. Those in Sicily and southern Italy provided early models for the Romans, who made them a normal feature of their

towns by the first century or before. Marcus Vipsanius Agrippa (62–12), a politician close to Augustus, began the first great public *thermae* in Rome in 25, requiring a new aqueduct, the Aqua Virgo, finished in 19. The term *thermae*, however, was first applied to the next of the great bathing establishments, finished by Nero in 62 CE, though the scale and magnificence of Agrippa's undertaking ensured that the emperors who emulated it would be targets for Pliny and other critics of luxury.

15. Perotti, *Corn.* fol. LX^r; Tortelli, *Orth.*, sig y5r; *Var. L* 9.41.68; Plin. *Nat.* 33.153; 36.121, 189; Suet. *Aug.* 94.4, *Nero* 31.2, *Tit.* 7.3; Tac. *Ann.* 14.97; Marcellin. 16.10.14; *SHA Gord.* 6.6, 32.7; *Comm.* 11.5; *Gall.* 17.4; *Heliogab.* 17.8, 31.7; *Sev.* 25.3–8; *M. Ant.* 9.4–10; *Tyr. Trig.* 21.7; Vitr. 5.11.2, 7.9; Clem. Al. *Paed.* 3.5. Nero's *Thermae* contained their own gymnasium and other splendid amenities. Those of Titus, opening in 80 CE, added more open space outside. Trajan built the greatest of the baths after 104, though Polydore does not mention it. The site of the *Thermae Novatianae* shows that a bath had been built there under Antoninus Pius (138–61). The *Thermae Antonianae* or Baths of Caracalla were dedicated in 216, though Septimius Severus (193–211) may have begun them, but he also built his own *Thermae Severianae* and *Thermae Septimianae*. When Alexander Severus renewed Nero's baths in 227, they became the *Thermae Alexandrinae*. He and his predecessor Elagabalus (218–22) also extended the Baths of Caracalla; this may be what Polydore means by *Thermae Aurelianae* since *Aurelius* was the *nomen* of both these emperors. In 306 Diocletian dedicated his *Thermae*, renowned for their enormous size but actually covering about the same area as the *Thermae Antonianae*. The last of these gargantuan projects in Rome began in the reign of Constantine (272/3–337). The *Thermae Domitii* were private, built for Nero's father, Gnaeus Domitius Ahenobarbus, but the *Thermae Gordiani* of Gordian III (238–44) were never built.

CHAPTER XIV

1. Plin. *Nat.* 7.198; Perotti, *Corn.* fol. LXIX^v. For Theodorus of Samos, see *DIR* 2.25.2, 3.10.3.

2. Ov. *Met.* 8.236–49; *Ib.* 498   Diod. S. 4.76.4–6; *DIR* 2.25.3.

3. Vitr. 9 pr. 6   Plin. *Nat.* 7.201; Perotti, *Corn.* fol. LXIX^r.

4. Eus. *Chron.*, Helm, pp. 55, 59; Jos. *AJ* 8.50–1. In the *Chronicle* Eusebius puts Daedalus in the year of Abraham 735 (1282 BCE), almost two centuries after Moses died.

5. Diog. L. 4.3; Serv. G 1.165. Speusippus (407–339), Plato's nephew, followed him as head of the Academy in 347. Diogenes says that he was 'first discovered how to make little carrying baskets (*phormia . . . euogka*) out of sticks (*phruganōn*).'

CHAPTER XV

2. Hor. *Carm.* 1.3.9–12, 21–6   Prop. 3.7.1–4, 29–30, 38   Verg. *A* 3.56–7.

3. Plin. *Nat.* 7.206.

4. Str. 10.4.8, 17; Diod. S. 5.69.4; *Adagia* (1550), p. 15. Long before Strabo's time, as his source Ephorus explained, the Cretans had lost the original habits that made their mastery of the sea proverbial. The proverb that he cites — *Ho Krēs agnoei tēn thalattan* — was already known in the seventh century.

5. Plin. *Nat.* 7.206; Quint. *Inst.* 10.2.7; *DIR* 3.15.4. Rafts made of logs tied together or buoyed by inflated animal skins were the earliest water-transportation in the Tigris-Euphrates area. Long before Caesar (*B. Civ.* 1.54) saw them in Britain, Herodotus (1.194) described coracles or round boats made by stretching hides over a frame; a clay model of the fourth millennium BCE depicts a Mesopotamian vessel of this shape. More effective boats of sewn planks probably evolved from the dugout canoes used almost everywhere by Stone Age people. The Egyptians sewed bundles of reeds together into boat-shaped rafts after the middle of the fourth millennium and made similar boats of planks early in the third millennium. By the same time, small ships driven by oar and sail explored the Mediterranean, the Persian Gulf and beyond. Like Troy, Mysia was in northwest Asia Minor; to reach Thrace in the far north of the Aegean would require crossing the Hellespont.

6. Plin. *Nat.* 7.206; Eus. *PE* 1.10.14; Clem. Al. *Strom.* 1.16.75.3; Tert. *Cor.* 8. On the Samothracians, see *DIR* 1.21.2.

7. Eus. *PE* 10.11.21, 13.11; *Chron.* (Helm, pp. 42, 45); Jos. *AJ* 1.75–9, 93–5, 120. In the *Chronicle* Eusebius first mentions Poseidon in the year 483 of Abraham and puts Danaus about forty years later, fifteen centuries after Noah. Around 290 BCE Berosus of Babylon wrote a Greek history of his country. According to Josephus, he says of the ark that there is 'still some of the ship in Armenia.'

8. Tib. 1.7.19–20; Str. 16.2.23.

9. Plin. *Nat.* 7.207–8; Diod. S. 1.55.2; Plb. 1.20.9; Perotti, *Corn.* fol. CLXXII. Diodorus (like editions of *De inventoribus* through 1521) has Sesoosis for the figure usually called Sesostris and treated in Greco-Roman texts as the greatest king of Egypt, a composite legend confused with Ramesses II (1279–12) but now linked mainly with Senwosret or Sesostris I (1962–28). Water-craft had been used for military purposes much earlier in Egypt, perhaps even in the pre-dynastic period, and there were sea-going vessels as early as Dynasty V (2510–2460), warships by the time of Ramesses III (1186–54). The first images of galleys from the Greek world come from the third millennium BCE. Similar pictures of long, straight, narrow ships of war appear through the archaic period. Homer's swift and hollow ships were deckless galleys of this type rowed by twenty to fifty oarsmen, guided by a single steering-oar and assisted by one sail. The rowers sat one to an oar in straight lines on each side, making the fifty-oared pentekonter very long—about 125 feet. To increase the oars without making the length even more unwieldy, a partial deck was used as an additional rowing platform by the eighth century. With rowers seated at two levels, the pentekonter could be shorter at 65 feet, the normal fighting ship mentioned by Herodotus and Thucydides. Heavier merchant-ships made more space for cargo in slower, rounded hulls.

By the fifth century the standard warship was the *triērēs* (*triremis*) or three-fitted sailing galley, which Thucydides (1.13.2) connects with the Corinthian Ameinocles in the eighth century. The trireme remained important through the fourth century CE, but the Hellenistic period also saw four-fitted (*tetērēs*, *quadriremis*), five-fitted (*pentērēs*, *quinqueremis*) and still larger vessels up to forty-fitted (*tessarakontērēs*). Most of the 170 rowers in a trireme, probably introduced in the seventh century BCE, sat

above one another in three staggered banks arranged in 27 groups on each side. The deck above became a complete cover in the fifth century.

Conflict among Alexander's successors led to a naval arms-race after 323. Anxious to overcome the advantage gained by Ptolemy I Soter (367–282), who had inherited most of Alexander's ships, Antigonus I Monophthalmos (382–301) added seven-fitted craft by 315, and his son Demetrius I Poliorcetes (336–283) moved up to a sixteen by 288. Ptolemy II Philadelphus (308–246) answered with twenties and thirties, but Ptolemy IV Philopator (244–205) topped them all with a forty late in the third century—though it was meant for display rather than combat. (The voluptuary Ptolemy VIII, not Philopator, was called *Truphōn*). After Actium in 31, however, the Romans went back to smaller, six-fitted warships. Superimposed seating for rowers working one to an oar, the pattern developed originally for the trireme, could work for Roman ships in this range, but not for the earlier Hellenistic dreadnoughts, equipped as boarding platforms for marines and sometimes armed with catapults. By putting as many as eight rowers to an oar (the physical limit), Demetrius could have manned his sixteen with two or three banks of oarsmen. But the 4,000 oarsmen of Philopator's gargantuan forty would have needed two hulls—a huge 420 foot catamaran—with 1,000 rowers stationed in banks of three on each of their sides.

For the naval inventions in this part of his discovery-catalogue, Pliny cites his sources, mostly unknown to Polydore, who omits most of them in editions after 1521. Thus, where Pliny has *quadriremem Aristoteles Carthaginienses, quinqueremem Mnesigiton Salaminios, sex ordinum Xenagoras Syracusios*, the Carthaginians, Salaminians and Syracusans are the inventors, while the authorities cited are Aristotle, Mnesigiton and Xenagoras. Like the 1497 text, however, Polydore has *Nesichthon* for *Mnesigiton* and makes him a Salaminian shipwright rather than an otherwise unknown scholar. Xenagoras (Zenagoras) likewise becomes a Syracusan who built ships rather than a chronographer and geographer of the second century BCE. Where Pliny cites Mnesigiton a second time on Alexander the Great's *decemremis*, Polydore takes Nesigiton to be the inventor and transfers Alexander to the ship with *XII ordines*. This moves the rest of the series up, requiring fifty rather than forty sets of rowers for Ptolemy

Philopator's ship, the last mentioned by Pliny in this part of his list of sea-faring discoveries. Polydore agrees with the 1497 edition in all these particulars, except that he writes *Zenagoras* instead of *Zenazoras*.

10. Diod. S. 5.7.7; Plin. *Nat.* 7.208–9; Paul. *Fest.* p. 89. In modern editions of Pliny the otherwise unknown Hippius becomes Hippus (horse; *hippios* is an epithet of Poseidon). The names given here to boats and ships built for special purposes remain imprecise in the absence of physical evidence. Most are Latinized Greek words. Copae and Plataea, the latter famous for the great victory over the Persians in 479 BCE, were inland cities of Boeotia, both listed by Homer (*Il.* 2. 502–4) with the Boeotian contingent of ships sent to Troy. Strabo, describing changes in this marshy region, suggests that the names recalled risks of flood that no longer existed in his time: *platē*, oar-blade; and *kōpē*, oar-handle. The doomed attempt of Icarus to escape on wings made by Daedalus was known by the sixth or fifth century BCE, though not in full detail until Strabo and Diodorus. A rationalized version appeared in fourth century mythography, claiming that the escape was by ship and that the great artisan or his son, who drowned in the attempt, invented such implements as sails out of necessity. In book 5, as Polydore notes, Diodorus writes that Aeolus made the first sails, but he also reports (4.77) the rationalizing story of of Icarus. Modern editions of Pliny connect Samians rather than Salaminians with cavalry ships, and Polydore omits Pliny's reference here to Pericles, who expanded Athenian sea-power. The 1497 text has *Salaminii* and mentions Pericles. The island of Salamis off the coast of Attica was the site of the great Persian naval defeat of 480 BCE; another Salamis was a city on Cyprus.

11. Plin. *Nat.* 7.209, 10.28; Str. 7.3.9; Perotti, *Corn.* fol. CLXXII. Thasos in the north Aegean was exploited for its timber, mines and wine. Diodorus (4.76.1) identifies Eupalamus (good-hand) as the grandfather of Daedalus and the son of Erechtheus. Modern editions of Pliny, having previously named Piseus as the son of Tyrrenus and the inventor of the beaked prow, make Eupalamus the inventor of the anchor, but Polydore and the 1497 edition treat Piseus and the Tyrrheni as separate inventors. Attributing the simple anchor to the Tyrrhenians, both then move the two-fluked anchor to *Eupalamius*, though Pliny, like Strabo, actually links

the *amphibolon agkuran* with Anacharsis. Tiphys was helmsman on the voyage of the Argonauts.

CHAPTER XVI

1. Plin. *Nat.* 33.6–7, 48. Bronze Age peoples of the eastern Mediterranean conducted long-distance trade in metals, and Greek pottery of the eighth century has been found at various places in the Middle East, before the invention of coinage. Cattle are the basis of exchange for Homer, but trade of any kind, as distinct from the exchange of gifts or the capture of booty, was not an honorable calling.

2. Hor. *Ep.* 1.1.45–6   Cic. *Off.* 1.42.151   Plu. *Sol.* 2. This grudging concession to large traders whose wealth eventually buys them into the landed class occurs at the end of an analysis of *decorum*, where Cicero has already explained that the small merchant's retail transactions must always be dishonest to turn a profit, as below in par. 6. The mathematician and astronomer Hippocrates of Chios, active at the end of the fifth century BCE, was a forerunner of Euclid in organizing the principles of geometry.

3. Plin. *Nat.* 7.199; Diod. S. 5.75.2; Caes. *Gal.* 6.17.1.

4. Plin. *Nat.* 7.191, 199; Perotti, *Corn.* fol. XLIII^r. Although the 1497 edition, like Polydore, reads *emere ac vendere instituit Liber Pater*, modern editors insert *Mercurius*, *vindemiare* between *vendere* and *instituit*, thus linking Mercury with the commerce (*merx*) traditionally attributed to him and shifting Father Liber to 'making the vintage.' To resolve the contradiction in Pliny's later assignment of *mercatura* to the Phoenicians, one suggestion is that the word refers specifically to maritime trade.

5. Jos. *AJ* 1.81.

6. Hdt. 1.94; Cic. *Off.* 1.42.150. See *DIR* 2.20.2 on the Lydians and early coinage and 3.3.8 on Lydian tavern-keepers.

7. *Dig.* 14.3.4–7; Perotti, *Corn.* fol XXXVIII^v. Marcus Antistius Labeo was a jurist of the early principate. Despite its roots in Perotti and in legal texts well known to Polydore, this passage, which reads as a first-person observation, does not appear until the last lifetime edition (1553–5),

indicating Polydore's hand in revising *De inventoribus* at this date; see *DIR* 2.17.11.

CHAPTER XVII

1. Cic. *ND* 3.23.59, *Red. sen.* 5.11; Ov. *Met.* 4.285–388, 538; *Fast.* 4.62; *Ars* 3.85–6; Verg. *A* 1.617–18, 663–5, 5.24; Serv. *A.* 1.574; Diod. S. 4.83.1; Plu. *Pel.* 19.2; Lact. *Inst.* 1.17.

2. Lact. *Inst.* 1.17   Just. *Epit.* 18.5.4–5. On Lactantius and the *Sacred History* of Euhemerus, see *DIR* 1.1.5.

3. Hdt. 1.196, 199. After the first sentence from Herodotus through par. 9, editions up to and including the 1532 have the text translated below, which in later editions is replaced rather than expanded, contrary to Polydore's normal practice, as indicated in his first letter to Gian Matteo Vergil, par. 10. The later editions, in other words, add the second passage from Herodotus, the material on the Bacchanalia and the exhortation to punish adultery by death, but they subtract what follows, perhaps because of the obscene material from Martial (2.17) and the generally coarse language: 'But why go on talking about these exotic problems when at home we keep the customs of Venus more fully and faithfully by far than the commandments of almighty God? For adultery is now a most productive business. Now the whorehouses are open everywhere. Now from a tender age—as Horace says—youth has its mind on sinful love. Now the prostitutes grow rich as they plunder their lovers rather than loving them—as that most urbane of poets tells us of the shameless woman barber. For he writes:

> You get no shave from this barber, Ammianus, no shave,
> I tell you. What does she give you, then? A skinning.

Now only that art of Venus thrives. No woman stays chaste unless no one asks her for it—not on her own, certainly. For her mind is adulterous, as Ovid explains, whence St. Jerome speaks the perfect truth in his work *Against Jovinian*: None can be kept in chastity. Thus the Essenes, the third sect of philosophers among the Jews, were men who showed great prudence in taking no wives, according to Josephus in book 2 of the *Jewish War*, since they thought that no woman could ever stay faithful to

one man, and because of this they raised only the children of strangers. Of this fact King Phaeron of Egypt offered the plainest proof possible when in all Egypt he could find scarcely one chaste woman to get back his sight by washing with her urine, as we carefully explained when dealing with obelisks. Hence, anyone who has a chaste wife certainly regards it as a divine gift received from God, as Juvenal says in the sixth *Satire*:

> Prostrate yourself at the Tarpeian slab
> And kill a young gilded one for Juno
> If you chance to find a chaste woman.'

4. Hdt. 2.47–9; Macr. *Sat.* 1.18.3–5. Dionysus here represents Osiris. The Egyptians worshipped him and other gods with huge *phalloi*, as Herodotus describes; other details such as the puppets and the music are plausible in an Egyptian context. Melampus of Pylos appears in the *Odyssey* as a seer who knew the language of animals.

5–7. Liv. 39.8–18; Tortelli, *Orth. sig.* F7r. The celebration of the Bacchic mysteries was forbidden in Rome when Spurius Postumius Albinus and Quintus Marcius Philippus were consuls in 186 BCE, but the cult had been active throughout Italy for some years, coming probably from the Greek south. Livy's sensational description, abbreviated by Polydore, reflects senatorial panic. Although they exaggerated the depravity of the Bacchantes for political effect, the authorities were right to fear the cult as a threat to the social order maintained by state religion. In modern texts of Livy, the Campanian woman is Annia Paculla; Livy calls the *Graeculus* who started the whole thing *sacrificulus et vates*, 'a ritualist and fortune-teller.'

8–9. Lev. 20:10; Plu. *Sol.* 23.1; Dion. H. 2.25.6–7; *Dig.* 48.5; Str. 16.4.25; cf. Ps.-Clement, *Ep. ad Jacobum* 7.4 [*Die Pseudoklementinen*, in *Griechischen christlichen Schriftsteller der ersten Jahrhunderte* (Berlin: Akademie-Verlag, 1953), 11]. For another change in Polydore's text that may have been influenced by Henry VIII's marital problems, see *DIR* 1.4.9.

10. Gen. 38:13–26.

11. Liv. 1.57–60; Dion. H. 4.64.4–67.2; Val. Max. 6.1.1; Perotti, *Corn.* fol. CCXCVI^v Plu. *Alex.* 22.3; Diog. L. 8.9. Although Livy shaped his

narrative to give it the feel of drama, the story of Lucretia and the Tarquins goes back to the earliest sources and may be historical at its core.

12. Clem. Al. *Strom.* 1.16.76.1; Plu. *Thes.* 5.1–2, 4.

13. Plin. *Nat.* 7.211. 454 AUC is 300 BCE. Publius Cornelius Scipio Aemilianus Africanus (184–29) was the second Africanus, so identified in the 1497 edition and in modern texts of Pliny that break the sentence between *sequens* and *Augustus*.

CHAPTER XVIII

1. Var. *L* 5.5.

2. Tortelli, *Orth.* sig. n3v; Jos. *AJ* 3.160, 184; Mart. 14.163. For the clock and compass see *DIR* 2.5.5.

3. *DIR* 2.11.5–6.

4. Plin. *Nat.* 34.89; Perotti, *Corn.* fol. CXCVI^v; Ov. *Ars* 1.653–6. For Phalaris see *DIR* 2.2.7.

5. Tortelli, *Orth.* sig. n3v–n4r. Stirrups came into use in the early middle ages after European contact in the fifth century CE with the Central Asians who had used them earlier.

6. Suet. *Jul.* 45.2.

7. Tortelli, *Orth.* sig. n3v–n4r. The Romans had watermills by the first century BCE. For the musical organ see *DIR* 1.15.8. The clavichord became an important instrument in Polydore's time.

8. Tortelli, *Orth.* sigs. i3r, n4r ; *DIR* 2.20. The Romans made candles (*candelae*) from tallow.

9. *DIR* 2.7.8–9.

Bibliography

ॐ࿐ॐ

Adler, William. *Time Immemorial: Archaic History and Its Sources in Christian Chronography from Julius Africanus to George Syncellus.* Washington, D.C.: Dumbarton Oaks Research Library, 1989.

Bickerman, E. J. *Chronology of the Ancient World,* 2nd ed. Ithaca, N.Y.: Cornell University Press, 1980.

Clough, Cecil H. 'Federigo da Montefeltro's Patronage of the Arts, 1468–1482,' *Journal of the Warburg and Courtauld Institutes,* 36 (1973), 129–44.

Cole, Thomas. *Democritus and the Sources of Greek Anthropology.* Monograph Series, American Philological Association, no. 25. Athens, Ga.: Scholar's Press, 1990.

Copenhaver, Brian P. 'The Historiography of Discovery in the Renaissance: The Sources and Composition of Polydore Vergil's *De inventoribus rerum,* I-III,' *Journal of the Warburg and Courtauld Institutes,* 41 (1978), 192–214.

—— 'Polidoro Virgilio of Urbino,' in *Contemporaries of Erasmus: A Biographical Register of the Renaissance and Reformation,* ed. Peter G. Bietenholz and Thomas B. Deutscher. Toronto: University of Toronto Press, 1987), III, 397–99.

Dodds, E. R. *The Ancient Concept of Progress and Other Essays on Greek Literature and Belief.* Oxford: Clarendon Press, 1973.

Edelstein, Ludwig. *The Idea of Progress in Classical Antiquity.* Baltimore: Johns Hopkins University Press, 1967.

Ferguson, John. 'A Bibliography of the Work of Polydore Vergil *De inventoribus rerum,*' typescript edited by John F. Fulton and Charlotte F. Peters. New Haven, Conn., 1945.

Gantz, Timothy. *Early Greek Myth: A Guide to Literary and Artistic Sources.* Baltimore: Johns Hopkins University Press, 1967.

Hay, Denys. *Polydore Vergil: Renaissance Historian and Man of Letters.* Oxford: Clarendon Press, 1952.

Hay, Denys, ed. and trans. *The Anglica historia of Polydore Vergil, A.D. 1485–1537.* Camden Series, 74. London: Royal Historical Society, 1950.

Hodgen, Margaret T. 'Ethnology in 1500: Polydore Vergil's Collection of Customs,' *Isis*, 57 (1966), 315–28.

Keller, Alex. 'A Renaissance Humanist Looks at "New" Inventions: The Article "Horologium" in Giovanni Tortelli's *De Orthographia*,' *Technology and Culture*, 11 (1970), 345–65.

Kleingünther, Adolf. *Protos Heuretes: Untersuchungen zur Geschichte einer Fragestellung.* Philologus, Supplementband 26, Heft 1. Leipzig: Dieterich, 1933.

Kopke, Ernst, ed. *Iacobus de Cessolis, [De ludo scachorum].* Mittheilungen aus den Handschriften der Ritter-Akademie zu Brandenburg A.H., 2. Brandenburg: A. D. Havel, 1879.

Lovejoy, Arthur O., and George Boas. *Primitivism and Related Ideas in Antiquity.* Baltimore: Johns Hopkins University Press, 1935.

Mosshammer, Alden A. *The Chronicle of Eusebius and the Greek Chronographic Tradition.* Lewisburg, Pa.: Bucknell University Press, n.d.

Pline l'Ancien. *Histoire naturelle, Livre VII*, ed. and trans. Robert Schilling. Paris: Les Belles Lettres, 1977.

Ruggeri, Romano. *Un amico di Erasmo: Polidoro Virgili.* Urbino, 1992.

Sirinelli, Jean. *Les Vues historiques d'Eusèbe de Césarée durant la période préniceéne.* Dakar: Université de Dakar, 1961.

Thraede, Klaus. 'Erfinder II (geistesgeschichtlich),' *Reallexikon für Antike und Christentum*, Band 5, 1962, cols. 1191–1278.

——— 'Das Lob des Erfinders: Bemerkungen zur Analyse der Heuremata-Kataloge,' *Rheinisches Museum zur Vorgeschichte*, 105 (1961), 158–86.

Uxkull-Gyllenbrand, Woldemar. *Griechische Kultur-Entstehungslehren.* Berlin: Leonhard Simion, 1924.

Weiss, Beno, and Louis C. Pérez. *Beginnings and Discoveries: Polydore Vergil's De inventoribus rerum: An Unabridged Translation and Edition with Introduction, Notes and Glossary.* Biblioteca humanistica et reformatorica, 56. Nieuwkoop: De Graaf, 1997.

Index

❦❦❦

References are to book, chapter, and paragraph numbers. Most references to proper nouns use familiar spellings, with differences from Polydore's usage indicated in parentheses. Many Roman names are entered by the *nomen* or family name, as in Tullius Cicero, Marcus. L1, L2, L3 and L4 refer to the three prefatory letters and the poem by Grynaeus. The letter *t* refers to Polydore's chapter titles.

Cornelius Scipio Africanus Major,
Publius, 2.3.3; 2.17.5; 2.23.9;
3.13.7
Cornelius Scipio Asiagenes,
Lucius, 2.18.2
Cornelius Scipio Nasica
Corculum, Publius, 2.5.3
Cornelius Sulla, Lucius, 2.3.9;
3.10.17
Cornelius Tacitus, 1.6.9,11–12;
3.11.7; 3.13.9–10
Coroebus (ceramics) 2.25.1
Coroebus (Olympic Games),
2.13.1
Coronis, 1.20.2
Corsica, 3.4.5
Corybantes, 1.21.2
Corydon, 1.15.4; 3.9.3
Corylus of Argos, 2.13.1
Coryphe, 2.12.4
Cos, 3.6.15–16
cotton, 3.6.15
Cotulia, Lake, 2.23.4
Cranaos, 1.24.11; 3.9.2
Crates of Mallos, 1.7.3
Crates of Thebes, 1.11.1; 2.20.1
Cratinus, 1.10.3
Crete, 1.1.6; 1.14.3; 1.15.13; 1.19.1;
2.1.6; 2.11.2,4; 2.13.7; 2.19.3;
2.22.1; 3.5.7; 3.8.1,3; 3.10,2,10;
3.15.4
Crocodilopolis, 3.10.1
Croesus of Lydia, 1.15.13; 2.20.2
Ctesias of Cnidos, 3.10.13
Ctesibius. *See* Ktesibios
Ctesiphon. *See* Chersiphron
ctistae, 1.4.7

culture, 1.3.5; 1.21.3; 2.3.1; 2.8.1;
2.10.2; 2.19.1
Cumae, 3.10.2
Cupid, 3.17.1
Curetes (*Kourêtes*), 1.14.3; 2.13.7;
2.19.3; 3.3.15
Curius Dentatus, Manius, 2.3.3;
3.1.2
Cybele, 1.1.6; 1.15.5
Cyclopes, 1.20.2; 2.19.3; 3.9.3
Cynics, 1.1.3; 1.11.1
Cyprian of Carthage, 1.5.1; 2.14.5
Cyprus, 2.19.3; 2.22.5; 3.5.5; 3.8.1;
3.15.10; 3.17.2
Cypselus of Corinth, 2.2.7;
2.13.5
Cyrenaics, 1.1.4
Cyrene, 3.15.10
Cyrus the Great, 1.12.3; 2.9.2;
2.18.2; 3.8.3
Cyrus the Younger, 3.1.4

Dactyls of Ida, 1.14.3; 2.13.1;
2.19.3–4,6
Daedalus, 2.24.2; 2.25.3; 3.10.2;
3.14.1–2,4; 3.15.1,10
Dalmatia, 3.6.10
Damascus, 3.6.18
Damasus I, 1.1.9
Damia, 3.3.13
Damnameneus, 2.19.3
Damon, 1.1.4; 1.21.3; 3.4.1
Damophilus, 2.25.3
Danaus, 1.5.2; 2.12.3; 3.9.8–9;
3.15.6–7
dance, 2.12.7; 2.13.t,7; 3.13.3–4
Daniel, Pierre, 1.5.6

Malcolm III of Scotland, 1.4.7
Maletus (Maleus), 1.15.10
Mamercus Aemilius, 2.3.6
Mamurra, 3.8.3
Man-eaters, 1.4.6–7
Manetho, 1.5.4
Manlius Imperiosus, Lucius,
 1.19.3
marble, 2.23.10; 3.8.t,3
Marcella, 2.7.1; 3.4.2
Marcian, 2.1.1
Marcius Philippus, Quintus,
 3.13.13; 3.17.7
Marcus Aurelius (emperor),
 1.20.10
Mardonius, 2.13.2
Marius Gratidanus, Marcus,
 2.23.11
Marius, Gaius, 2.3.9; 2.23.11;
 3.5.14; 3.10.17
Mark, 1.21.8; 2.23.8
marriage, L2.7; 1.3.7; 1.4; 2.3.8;
 2.21.2–3; 3.3.2; 3.5.2; 3.6.8–9;
 3.10.18; 3.13.4; 3.17.2
Marrus, 3.10.1
Mars, 1.15.13; 2.2.12; 2.3.4; 2.4.6;
 2.10.2; 2.11.2; 2.20.3; 3.2.5;
 3.5.2; 3.17.1
Marsyas, 1.15.3,5
Martial. See Valerius Martialis,
 Marcus
Martianus Capella, 3.3.5
Martius Rutilius, Gaius, 2.3.8
masks, 1.10.2; 2.23.4,9
Massagetes, 1.1.6; 1.4.4,7; 3.10.11
Masurius Sabinus, 2.16.7
mathematics, 1.16.4; 2.11.4

Matthew, 1.1.1–2; 1.4.9,11; 2.3.16;
 3.6.10
Mauretania, 1.1.6
Mausoleum of Augustus, 3.13.10
Mausolus of Caria, 3.10.t,10
meat, 3.5.5–7
Medea, 3.17.12
Media, 1.3.11; 1.4.6; 1.16.1
medicine, 1.20; 1.22.1–2,5;
 2.19.1–2
Medusa, 2.12.1
Melampus of Pylos, 3.17.4
Melchizedek, 1.5.8
Meliboeus, 1.24.5
Melicertes (Melicerta) of Corinth,
 2.13.4
Melissa, 1.5.5
Melisseus (Melissus), 1.5.2,5
Memnon, 2.22.2
memory, 2.9; 2.23.9
Memphis, 3.10.1,4–5
Menander, 1.11.3
Mendes, 3.10.1
Menes, 1.5.4; 2.1.6; 2.2.2
Menippus (Seleucid), 2.15.4
Menippus of Gadara, 1.11.1
Menkaure (Mycerinus), 3.10.5
Mennas, 1.5.4
Menon, 1.6.2
Mercury, L1.6; 1.5.4; 1.6.2; 1.9.5;
 1.13.2; 1.14.3; 1.15.1–3; 1.17.3;
 1.19.1–2; 1.20.2; 1.21.5; 1.23.3;
 2.1.6; 2.13.9; 2.15.2; 2.19.2;
 3.16.3–5; 3.17.1
mercury (quicksilver), 2.19.2
Mesopotamia, 2.23.6; 3.6.15; 3.9.5;
 3.15.5

Publication of this volume has been made possible by

The Myron and Sheila Gilmore Publication Fund at I Tatti
The Robert Lehman Endowment Fund
The Jean-François Malle Scholarly Programs and Publications Fund
The Andrew W. Mellon Scholarly Publications Fund
The Craig and Barbara Smyth Fund
for Scholarly Programs and Publications
The Lila Wallace–Reader's Digest Endowment Fund
The Malcolm Wiener Fund for Scholarly Programs and Publications